THE MOVIE LIST BOOK

HUNDREDS OF FUN AND FASCINATING LISTS OF FILMS BY THEIR SETTINGS AND MAJOR THEMES

About the Authors

Richard B. Armstrong has been a dedicated film buff ever since he saw *The Adventures of Robin Hood* at the age of seven. He has written film articles for various periodicals, spending seven years as the film critic for the *News-Enterprise* in Elizabethtown, Kentucky. He has also reviewed film reference books for *Film Quarterly* and *Filmfax*. Rick holds a doctorate degree in education from Indiana University and works for the Department of Defense.

Mary Willems Armstrong maintains dual careers as a film researcher and speech-language pathologist. She has written freelance film reviews and hosted her own radio program, *Mary's Movie Minute*. She also acted in *Beyond Our Control*, an award-winning youth television series which originated in South Bend, Indiana. In 1982, Mary, Rick, and other Kentucky film fans founded the Electric Bijou Film Society, a nonprofit film-showing organization.

THE MOVIE LIST BOOK

HUNDREDS OF FUN AND FASCINATING LISTS OF FILMS BY THEIR SETTINGS AND MAJOR THEMES

Richard B. Armstrong and
Mary Willems Armstrong

BETTERWAY BOOKS
CINCINNATI, OH

The Movie List Book. Copyright © 1994 by Richard B. Armstrong and Mary Willems Armstrong. Printed and bound in the United States of America. All rights reserved. No part of this book may be reproduced in any form or by any electronic or mechanical means including information storage and retrieval systems without permission in writing from the publisher, except by a reviewer, who may quote brief passages in a review. Published by Betterway Books, an imprint of F&W Publications, Inc., 1507 Dana Avenue, Cincinnati, Ohio 45207. 1-800-289-0963. Second edition. First edition published by McFarland & Company, Inc. Published by special arrangement with McFarland & Company, Inc., Publishers, Jefferson, North Carolina.

98 97 96 95 94   5 4 3 2 1

Library of Congress Cataloging-in-Publication Data

Armstrong, Richard B.
    The movie list book / Richard B. Armstrong and Mary Willems Armstrong. —
2nd ed.
        p.   cm.
    ISBN 1-55870-353-5
    1. Motion pictures — Plots, themes, etc. I. Armstrong, Mary Willems. II. Title.
PN1997.8.A76   1994
791.43'75 — dc20   93-48874
                                                                              CIP

Cover and interior design by Clare Finney

To those film characters (heroes and villains)
who deserved a film series, but never got one:

Beauregard Bottomley & Burnbridge (Dirty) Waters

Hawkins (aka Giacomo)

Inspector Cockrill

Klaatu and Gort

Dr. Julian Karswell

Waldo Lydecker

Laura Partridge

Captain Geoffrey Thorpe

Susan Vance & David Huxley

Matty Walker

Key to Dedication

Beauregard Bottomley & Burnbridge (Dirty) Waters	Ronald Coleman and Vincent Price in *Champagne for Caesar* (1950)
Hawkins (aka Giacomo)	Danny Kaye in *The Court Jester* (1956)
Inspector Cockrill	Alastair Sim in *Green for Danger* (1946)
Klaatu and Gort	Michael Rennie and Robot in *The Day the Earth Stood Still* (1951)
Dr. Julian Karswell	Niall MacGinnis in *Curse of the Demon* (aka *Night of the Demon*) (1958)
Waldo Lydecker	Clifton Webb in *Laura* (1944)
Laura Partridge	Judy Holliday in *The Solid Gold Cadillac* (1956)
Captain Geoffrey Thorpe	Errol Flynn in *The Sea Hawk* (1940)
Susan Vance and David Huxley	Katharine Hepburn and Cary Grant in *Bringing Up Baby* (1938)
Matty Walker	Kathleen Turner in *Body Heat* (1981)

Table of Contents

Throughout the work are "see" references not reflected in this table of contents: for instance, "Secret Service Series, *see* Bancroft, Brass."

THE MOVIE LIST BOOK

HUNDREDS OF FUN AND FASCINATING LISTS OF
FILMS BY THEIR SETTINGS AND MAJOR THEMES

Introduction

This second edition of *The Movie List Book* continues our neverending task of categorizing movies by topics. Whereas many film books tell you about a specific film, *The Movie List Book* tells you about a specific topic and then provides a list of the movies that fall under that topic. Therefore, you won't find a capsule review of the 1984 science fiction film *C.H.U.D.* But you will find *C.H.U.D.* mentioned under the entries **Acronyms in Title**, **Cannibalism** and **Sewers**. After all, the title is an acronym (standing for Cannibalistic Humanoid Underground Dwellers), the main characters ate people for dinner, and they resided in sewers.

We have defined over 550 categories, ranging from film themes and series to settings, occupations, animals and happenstances. Each entry consists of two parts: (1) a narrative description that defines the category and (2) a representative list of films in chronological order.

Typically, the narratives present a historic overview of the entry or subcategorize films within the entry. For example, the **Television** entry traces its treatment in films from the early 1930s to the present. The **Gangsters (Real-Life)** entry discusses how various individuals have been treated in the movies. At the conclusion of the narrative portion of some entries are "see also" references to other entries. For example, the **Abominable Snowman** entry refers readers to the **Bigfoot** entry. We figure that if you're interested in one type of large, hairy beast, you might want some information on similar creatures.

In addition to the "see also" references, the abbreviations *q.v.* or *qq.v.* may appear in parentheses following one or more subjects mentioned in an entry's narrative. A *q.v.* indicates that the subject in question appears as a separate entry elsewhere in the book. A *qq.v.* following a group of subjects indicates that they all appear as separate entries. For example, the **Plants** entry notes that the Mummy (q.v.) was revived with tana leaves in some films. The (*q.v.*) informs readers that there is a separate entry for **The Mummy**.

The films within each entry are listed chronologically, their dates indicating when the films were released theatrically or broadcast in their country of origin. Made-for-television movies are denoted with the abbreviation TVM. If a film played theatrically after its broadcast premiere, we still annotate it as a TV-movie. The first title is the film's most widely known U.S. title. Alternative titles, including the original foreign title if part of a series, are shown in parentheses. The size of the film lists varies from three to seventy titles depending on the scope of the entry (i.e., many films have taken place on **Trains**; few movies have featured **Gorgons**).

We have refrained from listing credits and plot summaries for each title. Most of the listed films can be found readily in mainstream reference works like Leonard Maltin's *TV Movies, Halliwell's Film Guide* and *The Motion Picture Guide*. More obscure films are likely to be found in periodicals such as *Variety* or cult movie volumes such as *The Psychotronic Encyclopedia of Film*.

We have tried to compile an exhaustive list of film series and, in the process, have included information on well-documented characters such as Sherlock Holmes and Tarzan. We have done this for two reasons. First, new movies are continually being made about these popular characters (e.g., 1992's *Sherlock Holmes in Caracas*). Secondly, we felt this book should be a one-stop reference on film series, at least for some users. A film buff trying to find out the name of Denny Miller's only Tarzan film (it was the 1959 version of *Tarzan, the Ape Man*) will find this a handy volume. A Burroughs scholar seeking more explicit details would be advised to seek a reference work devoted exclusively to the King of the Jungle. We formed some general ground rules to limit the scope of the book to a manageable size:

1. Most of the films listed are English-language pictures released during the sound era. Occasionally, we have included silent or foreign films to give the reader a historical or international perspective on the category. For example, no write-up of **Hood, Robin** would be complete without mentioning Douglas Fairbanks, Sr.'s 1922 version.

2. A notable exception to the above rule is the inclusion of popular foreign film series. For example, the Mexican wrestler Santo appeared in a film series spanning three decades, and many of these pictures have eventually shown up on American television. The Tora-san films are virtually unknown in the United States, but they comprise the longest-running film series in the world. We have listed foreign series films under their most common English-language titles, although the original foreign titles are shown as well.

3. We defined a series as three or more movies linked by a recurring theme or characters. Thus, we did not include the films of Abbott and Costello, the Marx Brothers or Laurel and Hardy. Their movies can be found in biographical film reference books. For the same reason, we left out Roy Rogers and Gene Autry — although they do play the same character (themselves) in most of their movies. B-Western fans can rest assured, however, that their favorite genre is well represented by the *Durango Kid*, the *Range Busters*, *Red Ryder* and others.

4. We have included many lengthy lists, but the sheer size of others mandated their exclusion. For example, a narrative overview and a representative sampling of Civil War or World War II movies would require a write-up far beyond the scope of this book. On the other hand, there are relatively few films about the Korean War and Vietnam. Hence, we have included entries on them. We expect that our decisions on what to include and exclude will spark some debate. Constructive criticism is most welcomed.

5. We included TV-movies only if they were shown originally in no more than two parts or were subsequently edited into a single film. Therefore, miniseries such as "The Thornbirds" and "Wild Palms" were excluded. The theatrical movie

The Quatermass Conclusion, which was culled from the British miniseries "Quatermass," was included.

6. Our cutoff point was movies released or broadcast through December 1993.

We have been delighted with the first edition's enthusiastic reception by readers and critics. We continue to receive many suggestions for new entries and titles. To that end, we have added over one hundred new entries and many new titles to the lists. To our entries on film series, we've added the obvious (the **Alien** movies), the obscure (**Black Cobra**), and the offbeat (**A Chinese Ghost Story**). Other new categories range from **Backwoods Feuds** to **Jewel Thieves** to **Zoos**. We work hard to double-check our entries, but mistakes can still find their way into a volume of this size. We have corrected all known errata from the first edition.

It would be difficult to acknowledge everyone who added a film or two, but there are some who made significant contributions. In compiling our original lists, we viewed several rare films at the Wisconsin Center for Film Research in Madison. Its staff was always courteous and helpful. Film buff Terry Brown of Bloomington, Indiana, made some useful recommendations for the second edition. We'd like to thank those people in the publishing business who believed in *The Movie List Book*, especially Robert Franklin, Rhonda Herman and our new friend Bill Brohaugh. We would also like to express our gratitude to Terri Boemker and the rest of the editorial staff at F&W Publications, who worked diligently on the second edition. Our parents—Oran and Jean Armstrong and Edward and Jean Willems—provided encouragement, support and, of course, love. Finally, we'd like to offer thanks to other family members and friends who have listened to a lot of movie talk over the years.

We heartily encourage reader correspondence, whether it be corrections, recommended additions, or comments over exclusions of favorite movies. Please address your letters to us in care of the publisher.

Mary Willems Armstrong
Richard B. Armstrong

The Abominable Snowman

Also known as the Yeti, the Abominable Snowman is a hairy, manlike creature reportedly inhabiting the Himalayas. His movie appearances have been almost as scarce as Yeti photographs. His film debut was probably 1954's *Snow Creature*, a *King Kong*-inspired cheapie in which a Yeti is captured and brought back to Los Angeles (where he escapes, of course). *Man Beast* (1955) kept the action in the Himalayas but didn't live up to its outrageous ad campaign: "See women stalked and captured for breeding by Yeti monsters!" A friendly snowman turned up unexpectedly at the earth's core in the 1993 TV-movie *Journey to the Center of the Earth*. However, the only semi-intelligent film on the subject was *The Abominable Snowman of the Himalayas*, scripted by science fiction/fantasy writer Nigel Kneale. See also **Bigfoot**.

Snow Creature (1954)
Half-Human (1955)
Man Beast (1955)
The Abominable Snowman of the
  Himilayas (1957)
The Seven Faces of Dr. Lao (1964)
The Werewolf and the Yeti (aka Night
  of the Howling Beast) (1976)
Snowbeast (1977 TVM)
Yeti (1977)
Journey to the Center of the Earth (1993
  TVM)

Acronyms in Title

The nondescriptive nature of acronyms has made them unpopular title choices, especially among theater owners. They have been the ones forced to field complaints from irritated patrons, such as the ones distraught to discover that Sylvester Stallone's *F.I.S.T.* was *not* a boxing film, but the story of a truckers' union. Still, that has not deterred the occasional use of acronym titles. Studios concerned about pronounceable titles have shown a preference for acronyms that also spelled words, such as *D.A.R.Y.L.* and *M*A*S*H*. In addition to film titles, acronyms have been used extensively in screenplays. For example, in *Our Man Flint* and *In Like Flint*, secret agent Derek Flint (James Coburn) worked for Z.O.W.I.E. — Zonal Organization on World Intelligence Espionage. On TV and in the movies, Robert Vaughn and David McCallum worked for U.N.C.L.E., which stood for United Network Command for Law and Enforcement.

The Bride Came C.O.D. (1941) CASH ON DELIVERY
O.S.S. (1946) OFFICE OF STRATEGIC SERVICES
D.O.A. (1950) DEAD ON ARRIVAL
The D.I. (1957) DRILL INSTRUCTOR
A Matter of WHO (aka *A Matter of Who*) (1961) WORLD HEALTH
  ORGANIZATION
The V.I.P.s (1963) VERY IMPORTANT PERSONS
The T.A.M.I. Show (1964) TEENAGE AWARDS MUSIC INTERNATIONAL
Agent for H.A.R.M. (1966) HUMAN AETIOLOGICAL RELATIONS MACHINE
U.M.C. (aka *Operation Heartbeat*) (1969 TVM) UNIVERSITY MEDICAL CENTER
M*A*S*H (1970) MOBILE ARMY SURGICAL HOSPITAL
R.P.M. (1970) REVOLUTIONS PER MINUTE
F.T.A. (1972) FREE (OR F--K) THE ARMY
Z.P.G. (1972) ZERO POPULATION GROWTH
F.I.S.T. (1978) FEDERATION OF INTERSTATE TRUCKERS

C.H.O.M.P.S. (1979) CANINE HOME PROTECTION SYSTEM

H.E.A.L.T.H. (1979) HAPPINESS, ENERGY AND LONGEVITY THROUGH HEALTH

H.O.T.S. (1979) HELP OUT THE SEALS

S*H*E (1980 TVM) SECURITY HAZARDS EXPERT

S.O.B. (1981) STANDARD OPERATING BULLSHIT

T.A.G.: The Assassination Game (1982)

Angel of H.E.A.T. (1982) HARMONY'S ELITE ATTACK TEAM

M.A.D.D.: Mothers Against Drunk Driving (1983 TVM)

C.H.U.D. (1984) CANNIBALISTIC HUMANOID UNDERGROUND DWELLERS

R.S.V.P. (1984) REPONDEZ S'IL VOUS PLAIT

D.A.R.Y.L. (1985) DATA ANALYZING ROBOT YOUTH LIFEFORM

C.A.T. Squad (1986 TVM) COUNTER ASSAULT TACTICAL SQUAD

R.O.T.O.R. (1988) ROBOTIC OFFICER OF TACTICAL OPERATIONS RESEARCH

B.O.R.N. (1989) BODY ORGAN REPLACEMENT NETWORK

Navy SEALS (1990) SEA AIR LAND

Robo-C.H.I.C. (1990) COMPUTERIZED HUMANOID INTELLIGENCE CLONE

Ad Lines (Selected)

As a general rule, bad movies have the best ad lines — which makes a lot of sense when you think about it. After all, if the movie stinks, then there must be something else — like a catchy advertising phrase — to lure unsuspecting patrons into the theater. That's why some of the most memorable (and tasteless) ad lines come from bottom-of-the-barrel horror flicks like *The Driller Killer* ("Several pints of blood will spill when teenage girls confront his drill"). Of course, a clever phrase can still accompany a big-budgeted science fiction film (*Alien*: "In space, no one can hear you scream") or a cult classic (*I Walked With a Zombie*: "She's alive . . . yet dead! She's dead . . . yet alive!"). Some of the cinema's more memorable ad lines:

> "Out of the dark fantastic madness of his science . . . He created them! Pig-Men . . . Wolf-Women . . . Thoughtful Human Apes — and His Masterpiece . . . The Panther Woman . . . Throbbing to the hot flush of new found love!" *Island of Lost Souls* (1933)

> "Jungle love tease! Bob Preston tears the heart out of Preston Foster by making jungle love to exciting Dorothy Lamour under that burning Burma moon!" *Moon Over Burma* (1940)

> "Bing Bong! Bing Bong! With song and sarong they hit the gong!" *The Road to Singapore* (1940)

> "Kiss me and I'll claw you to death." *The Cat People* (1942)

> "How'd you like to tussle with Russell?" *The Outlaw* (1943)

> "Body of a boy! Mind of a monster! Soul of an unearthly thing!" *I Was a Teenage Frankenstein* (1957)

> "It crawls! It creeps!" *The Blob* (1958)

> "You'll be sick, sick, sick — from laughing!" *A Bucket of Blood* (1959)

> "Beware the beat of cloth-wrapped feet!" *The Mummy* (1959)

> "Just ring for doom service!" *Horror Hotel* (aka *City of the Dead*) (1960)

"Beware the eyes that paralyze." *Children of the Damned* (1964)

"They're young . . . they're in love . . . and they kill people." *Bonnie and Clyde* (1967)

"The story of a homosexual who married a nymphomaniac." *The Music Lovers* (1971)

"You have nothing to lose but your mind." *Asylum* (1972)

"To avoid fainting, keep repeating: It's only a movie . . . it's only a movie . . ." *The Last House on the Left* (1972)

"They'll love the very lives out of your body!" *Invasion of the Bee Girls* (1973)

"The only thing more terrifying than the last twelve minutes of this film are the first 80." *Suspiria* (1976)

"Just when you thought it was safe to go back into the water." *Jaws 2* (1978)

"Roses are red. Violets are blue. '*My Bloody Valentine*' is absolute grue." *My Bloody Valentine* (1981)

"The story of a man who wanted to keep the world safe for democracy—and meet girls." *Stripes* (1981)

"Herbert West has a very good head on his shoulders—and another one in his desk." *Re-Animator* (1985)

"So young! So bad! So what?" *Reform School Girls* (1986)

"Like father, like son, like hell." *At Close Range* (1986)

"Sleep all day, party all night. It's fun to be a vampire." *The Lost Boys* (1987)

"There are no limits." *Hellraiser* (1987)

"A comedy about sex, murder, and seafood." *A Fish Called Wanda* (1988)

Addresses in Title

Street addresses have been used infrequently for movie titles, probably since they don't provide much in the way of description. Still, Gary Cooper played a nagging husband who found solace with younger woman Suzy Parker at *Ten North Frederick* (1958). A murder occurred at *10 Rillington Place* (1971), a fact-based account of the Christie-Evans case, which ended capital punishment in Britain. On the lighter side, Anthony Hopkins and Anne Bancroft formed a lasting friendship through exchanging letters mailed to *84 Charing Cross Road* (the address of Hopkins's bookstore).

Forty-Second Street (1933)
15 Malden Lane (1936)
52nd Street (1937)
13 Rue Madeleine (1946)
Green Dolphin Street (1947)
Dulcimer Street (aka *London Belongs to Me*) (1948)
711 Ocean Drive (1950)
Sunset Boulevard (1950)
99 River Street (1953)
Ten North Frederick (1958)
13 West Street (1962)

Madison Avenue (1962)
10 Rillington Place (1971)
11 Harrowhouse (aka *Anything for Love*) (1974)
Hester Street (1975)
Hanover Street (1979)
Cannery Row (1982)
Half Moon Street (1986)
84 Charing Cross Road (1987)
102 Boulevard Haussman (1990)
29th Street (1991)

Airplanes

Airplanes have provided the setting or functioned as the focal point for dozens of movies. Early efforts typically revolved around the adventures of World War I dogfight pilots or pioneer air mail carriers. William Wellman's *Wings* (1927), the first film to win a Best Picture Oscar, established the standard for combat flying sequences and sealed Gary Cooper's stardom. Howard Hughes's *Hell's Angels* (1930) also featured magnificent dogfight footage but is best remembered for launching Jean Harlow's career (her famous line: "Do you mind if I slip into something more comfortable?"). Despite their now-dated techniques, these World War I aerial actioners, along with both versions of *The Dawn Patrol*, still surpass similar films made in the 1960s and 1970s (e.g., *The Blue Max, Aces High, Von Richthofen and Brown*). The plight of air mail flyers proved an equally popular subject in the 1930s, with such memorable efforts as *Air Mail, Ceiling Zero*, and *Only Angels Have Wings* (the latter two directed by Howard Hawks). Airplanes played a strictly supporting role in most World War II pictures, although Hawks's *Air Force* and (much later) *Battle of Britain* gave them proper recognition. Interest in aviation had hit a low ceiling when, in 1954, Wellman's *The High and the Mighty* transplanted *Grand Hotel* drama into the clouds and added a generous dose of in-flight disaster. This successful formula was not fully exploited until sixteen years later, when Ross Hunter mounted an expensive adaptation of Arthur Hailey's best-seller *Airport* (q.v.). This time, a mass of second-class imitators flooded the screens, including three *Airport* sequels and eventually the highly successful spoof *Airplane!* (1980). Undoubtedly, the most bizarre airplane disaster film was the 1972 TV-movie *The Horror at 37,000 Feet*, in which a sacrificial druid stone unleashed evil spirits on screeching passengers. Films about real-life aviators have been scarce, consisting primarily of *The Spirit of St. Louis* (Charles Lindbergh), *The Winds of Kitty Hawk* (the Wright Brothers), *Amelia Earhart, Flight for Freedom* (Earhart again), *The Right Stuff* (Chuck Yeager), *Pancho Barnes* and *The Wings of Eagles* (Frank "Spig" Wead). Jet pilots can also lay claim to being ignored in favor of fictional dogfight specialists. Howard Hughes's *Jet Pilot* sat on the shelf for seven years before its 1957 release. Clint Eastwood's high-tech *Firefox* fared better, but it took 1986's *Top Gun* to give the jet pilot his proper recognition. However, Tom Cruise's cocky hero ("I feel the need—the need for speed!") was a far cry from the serious aviators portrayed in the films of Hawks, Hughes and Wellman. While the jets in these latter films looked impressive, none of them compared favorably with the Batplane from 1989's *Batman* in terms of sheer aesthetic design. But, alas, the Batplane proved to be just a pretty package when the Joker shot it down with his long-barreled handgun. Plane crashes have provided the premise for several memorable yarns, most notably *Lost Horizon, Back From Eternity, Fate Is the Hunter, Alive* and *The Flight of the Phoenix*. In the latter film, James Stewart and his fellow crash survivors escaped from the desert by building a miniplane from the wreckage. On a lighter note, *Flying Down to Rio* deserves an honorable mention for its delirious dance number featuring chorines high-stepping on top of an airplane's wings. See also **Airport; Helicopters; Iron Eagle**.

Wings (1927)
Hell's Angels (1930)

The Dawn Patrol (aka *Flight Commander*) (1930)

Air Mail (1932)
Christopher Strong (1933)
Flying Down to Rio (1933)
Central Airport (1933)
Ceiling Zero (1935)
Wings in the Dark (1935)
China Clipper (1936)
Non-Stop New York (1937)
Lost Horizon (1937)
Sky Giant (1938)
The Dawn Patrol (1938)
Men With Wings (1938)
Only Angels Have Wings (1939)
Flight Angels (1940)
Dive Bomber (1941)
Spitfire (aka First of the Few) (1942)
Flight for Freedom (1943)
Air Force (1943)
Gallant Journey (1946)
Broken Journey (1948)
Chain Lightning (1950)
Breaking the Sound Barrier (aka The
    Sound Barrier) (1952)
The High and the Mighty (1954)
Escapade (1955)
Back From Eternity (1956)
Zero Hour (1957)
Bombers B-52 (1957)
The Spirit of St. Louis (1957)
The Wings of Eagles (1957)
Jet Pilot (1957)
Wings of Chance (1961)
Fate Is the Hunter (1964)
Those Magnificent Men in Their
    Flying Machines (1965)
The Doomsday Flight (1966 TVM)
The Flight of the Phoenix (1966)
The Blue Max (1966)
Battle of Britain (1969)
Airport (1970)

Von Richthofen and Brown (aka The
    Red Baron) (1970)
Terror in the Sky (1971 TVM)
Wild in the Sky (aka Black Jack) (1971)
Only One More Day Left Before
    Tomorrow (aka How to Steal an
    Airplane) (1971 TVM)
Skyjacked (aka Sky Terror) (1972)
The Horror at 37,000 Feet (1972 TVM)
Ace Eli and Rodger of the Skies (1973)
The Great Waldo Pepper (1975)
Amelia Earhart (1976 TVM)
Aces High (1977)
Flight to Holocaust (1977 TVM)
Crash (1978 TVM)
The Winds of Kitty Hawk (1978 TVM)
Cloud Dancer (1980)
Airplane! (1980)
Firefox (1982)
Airplane 2: The Sequel (1982)
The Right Stuff (1983)
Tail of the Tiger (1984)
The Aviator (1985)
International Airport (1985 TVM)
Top Gun (1986)
Iron Eagle (1986)
Pancho Barnes (1988 TVM)
Batman (1989)
Party Plane (1989)
Slipstream (1989)
Die Hard 2 (aka Die Harder) (1990)
Miracle Landing (1990 TVM)
Crash: The Mystery of Flight 1501
    (1990 TVM)
The Tragedy of Flight 103: The Inside
    Story (1990 TVM)
Hot Shots! (1991)
Into the Sun (1992)
Passenger 57 (1992)
Alive (1993)

Airport

Ross Hunter's glossy adaptation of Arthur Hailey's best-seller has a lot to answer for, although it was little more than a slight variation of William Wellman's *The High and the Mighty* (1954). In addition to begetting three progressively inane sequels, *Airport* refined the all-stars-in-peril formula that kicked off the disaster movie craze (q.v.) of the 1970s. On its own terms, *Airport* was a slick entertainment package that afforded Helen Hayes another opportunity to win an Oscar. Burt Lancaster, as the dependable chief of airport operations, headed a cast that also included Dean Martin as a pilot, Jacqueline Bisset as a stewardess (and Dean's mistress), Van Heflin as a bomber, and sturdy George Kennedy as Burt's right-hand man. Kennedy was the only one who returned for *Airport 1975*, a silly sequel requiring stewardess Karen Black to take over the jet's controls after a midair collision. Charlton Heston gave her support from the sidelines (in a Burt Lancaster-type role), while the all-star passenger list included Helen Reddy as a singing nun (q.v.) and Linda Blair as a sick kid. *Airport '77* sent a jet crashing into the ocean, while *The Concorde: Airport '79* featured typically nice Robert Wagner as a ruthless tycoon out to destroy the jet. George Kennedy stood around in these films as well, just to lend some consistency to the proceedings and remind audiences that it was an *Airport* picture. Oddly, the films never spawned a TV series, perhaps because the ill-fated 1970-71 *San Francisco International Airport* had already beaten the producers to the punch. See also **Airplanes; Disaster Movies.**

Airport (1970)
Airport 1975 (1974)
Airport '77 (1977)

The Concorde: Airport '79 (aka *Airport '79*) (1979)

Alcoholism

The plight of the problem drinker has been glossed over by most major Hollywood pictures. Even Billy Wilder's landmark portrait of an alcoholic, 1945's *The Lost Weekend*, ended on an upbeat note with Ray Milland's "hero" indicating that he's on the road to recovery. Still, Wilder's film broke new ground with its straightforward treatment — Milland begging for drinks, stealing a woman's purse, experiencing D.T.s, etc. The female side of alcoholism followed three years later, with Susan Hayward giving a mannered performance in *Smash-up, the Story of a Woman*. Bing Crosby, playing against type, gave one of the best performances of his career as a singer battling the bottle in the film version of Clifford Odets's *The Country Girl* (1954). Once again, though, an optimistic ending blunted the film's impact, with Grace Kelly passing up caring William Holden to stay with unreliable husband Crosby. Blake Edwards's *The Days of Wine and Roses* (1962) injected a jolt of realism into its depressing story of married alcoholics. After introducing wife Lee Remick to the "pleasures" of drinking, Jack Lemmon becomes a reformed drinker by joining Alcoholics Anonymous. His wife lacks his strength, however, and her alcoholism keeps them apart. The drawing power of the stars made the film a hit, but few producers were interested in duplicating its downbeat ending. Subsequently, movies about alcoholism moved to television where they flourished during the 1970s and 1980s. Veteran TV nice guys Dick Van Dyke, David Janssen and Andy Griffith played self-destructive drunks in *The Morning After* (1974), *A Sensitive, Passionate Man* (1977), and *Under the Influence* (1986), respectively. Linda Blair, who battled a demon in *The Exorcist*, fought her own alcoholic demons in 1975's then-topical *Sarah T. — Portrait of a Teenage Alcoholic*. James Woods played the cofounder of Alcoholics Anonymous in the fact-based TV biography *My Name Is Bill W.* (1989). Dozens of movies, not principally about alcoholism, have featured main characters inflicted with the disease. Some of the most memorable performances have come from Albert Finney in *Under the Volcano* (1984), Dudley Moore in *Arthur* (1981), and Errol Flynn as John Barrymore in *Too Much, Too Soon* (1958).

The Lost Weekend (1945)
Smash-up, the Story of a Woman (aka *A Woman Destroyed*) (1948)
Come Fill the Cup (1951)
Something to Live For (1952)
The Country Girl (1954)
I'll Cry Tomorrow (1955)
The Bottom of the Bottle (1956)
The Voice in the Mirror (1958)
The Days of Wine and Roses (1962)
The Fire Within (1963)
The Late Liz (1971)
The Morning After (1974 TVM)
Sarah T. — Portrait of a Teenage Alcoholic (1975 TVM)

A Sensitive, Passionate Man (1977 TVM)
A Cry for Love (1980 TVM)
The Boy Who Drank Too Much (1980 TVM)
Special Treatment (1980)
Life of the Party: The Story of Beatrice (1982 TVM)
Under the Influence (1986 TVM)
Shattered Spirits (1987 TVM)
The Betty Ford Story (1987 TVM)
My Name Is Bill W. (1989 TVM)
Torch Song (1993 TVM)

Aldrich, Henry

"Wimmen—they bore me!" proclaimed the ad to *Henry Aldrich Gets Glamour*, thus separating Henry from rival film teen and renowned girl chaser, Andy Hardy (q.v.). Yet, for the most part, the Henry Aldrich series was Paramount's B-movie answer to MGM's more successful Andy Hardy films. Ezra Stone originated the character in Clifford Goldsmith's 1937 Broadway play *What a Life*. It spawned a popular radio program (also with Stone) and a big-screen version, adapted by Billy Wilder and Charles Brackett and starring veteran child actor Jackie Cooper as Henry. Two years later, Cooper and costar Eddie Bracken (as pal Dizzy) returned to their roles in *Life With Henry* ("You'll get a bang out of Henry and his gang!"). But Paramount sought a fresh face for its third installment and introduced Jimmy Lydon as Henry in 1941's *Henry Aldrich for President*. Lydon, who had made an impact two years earlier in *Tom Brown's Schooldays*, was the ideal choice for the bumbling, likable Henry. He made nine films, supported by Charles Smith as Dizzy, John Litel as his stern father, and Olive Blakeney as his mother. Like the Hardy films, the series ended shortly after World War II. However, in 1949, original author Goldsmith revived his characters in the half-hour TV series *The Aldrich Family*. It ran for four years and starred five different actors as Henry.

What a Life (1939)
Life With Henry (1941)
Henry Aldrich for President (1941)
Henry and Dizzy (1942)
Henry Aldrich, Editor (1943)
Henry Aldrich Gets Glamour (1943)

Henry Aldrich Haunts a House (1943)
Henry Aldrich Swings It (1943)
Henry Aldrich, Boy Scout (1944)
Henry Aldrich's Little Secret (1944)
Henry Aldrich Plays Cupid (1944)

Alien

The three *Alien* films provided hard evidence that stylish thrills can make big audiences overlook repetitive, mundane plotting borrowed from a forgotten 1958 sci-fi feature. That film was the low-budget *It! The Terror From Beyond Space*, a tidy programmer about a Martian monster that stowed away on a U.S. spaceship and proceeded to dispose of the crew members one by one. Screenwriter Dan O'Bannon served up the same storyline, albeit with a pleasant twist, in 1979's *Alien*. The film's popular success, though, can be attributed to Sigourney Weaver's likable heroine Ripley, director Ridley Scott's old-fashioned dark corridor chills, and the sharp special effects (especially H.R. Giger's terrifying creature). The 1986 sequel was a vast improvement, primarily due to director James Cameron's instinctive feel for the genre (he was coming off 1984's smash *The Terminator*). *Aliens* takes place fifty-seven years after *Alien* and finds Ripley, the original's lone human survivor, in hibernation. It's not long, though, before she returns to the planet where the creature was found—and discovers that it was not an only child! Ripley also finds a little girl and gets to display her maternal instincts in a terrific showdown with the "mother of all aliens." It's the highlight of the series and would have made a fitting conclusion. Unfortunately, Weaver returned for the depressing coda *Alien³*, which begins and ends with the deaths of the series' most endearing characters. Ripley spends almost the entire film on a prison planet where the disbelieving inmates are being devoured in Agatha Christie-like fashion. Director David Fincher, a music video veteran, created a grimy, murky atmosphere but displayed no gifts for storytelling or chill-creating. The downbeat climax put an end to the series. It would have been the last chapter anyway, on the basis of its disappointing box office returns. Weaver played Ripley in all three films, with Lance Henriksen as the Bishop androids in the last two installments.

Alien (1979) *Alien³* (1992)
Aliens (1986)

The Alilenas (The Peanuts Sisters)

These twin six-inch princesses hailed from Infant Island, home of the giant caterpillar Mothra (q.v.). They had the power to summon Mothra, which unfortunately required them to talk (which they did in unison—a very irritating habit). Stars Emi and Yumi Ito recorded songs in Japan as The Peanuts Sisters. See also **Mothra**.

Mothra (1962)
Godzilla vs. the Thing (aka *Godzilla vs. Mothra*) (1964)
Ghidrah, the Three-Headed Monster (1965)
Godzilla vs. the Sea Monster (aka *Ebriah, Terror of the Deep*) (1966)

Alligators and Crocodiles

These much-maligned reptiles made their mark in horror films but are more fondly remembered for their dancing and comedic talents. Dancing gators performed a ballet parody in the "Dance of the Hours" sequence from Disney's *Fantasia*. A pet alligator played cupid for a young British couple in the 1955 romantic comedy *An Alligator Named Daisy*. Daisy proved to be a gifted comic, especially in the scene where she was discovered in an upright piano. Prior to writing and directing intellectual fare like *Matewan* and *Eight Men Out*, John Sayles penned 1980's *Alligator*, a campy horror picture about a giant alligator running amok in Chicago's sewers. Between *The Texas Chainsaw Massacre* and

Poltergeist, director Tobe Hooper made *Eaten Alive*, a barely released film about a Louisiana hotel owner who feeds unwelcome guests to his pet crocodile. Stephen McNally really kept alligators in the moat of *The Black Castle*, while Whit Bissell was dead serious when he threatened to throw victims to the alligators in *I Was a Teenage Frankenstein*. Richard Crane slowly turned into an alligator in 1959's *The Alligator People*, a sobering little horror picture with a most sympathetic monster. *Crocodile Dundee* is the most famous "croc" hunter of recent years, while Tarzan (q.v.) surely holds the record for most crocodile wrestling matches. James Bond (Roger Moore) disguised himself as a crocodile to infiltrate a secret hideout in 1983's *Octopussy*.

Fantasia (1940)
The Black Castle (1952)
Peter Pan (1953)
An Alligator Named Daisy (1955)
I Was a Teenage Frankenstein (1957)
Naked Earth (1958)
The Alligator People (1959)
The Three Worlds of Gulliver (1960)
The Happiest Millionaire (1967)
Live and Let Die (1973)
Eaten Alive (aka *Starlight Slaughter*; *Death Trap*; *Horror Hotel Massacre*; *Legend of the Bayou*) (1976)

The Rescuers (1977)
Crocodile (1979)
Alligator (1980)
The Great Alligator (1980)
Octopussy (1983)
Romancing the Stone (1984)
Crocodile Dundee (1986)
Lady in White (1988)
All Dogs Go to Heaven (1989)

American Film Theatre Presentations

Producer Ely Landau created the American Film Theatre (AFT) in 1972 as a vehicle for preserving quality plays on film while concurrently introducing these notable works to large audiences. His project attracted a number of outstanding performers, such as Fredric March (*The Iceman Cometh*), Alan Bates (*Butley*), Katharine Hepburn (*A Delicate Balance*), and Maximilian Schell (Oscar nominated for *The Man in the Glass Booth*). Although Laurence Olivier's *Three Sisters* was released as part of the series in 1974, it was actually made independently and released in Britain in 1970. The AFT films were originally distributed to movie theaters on a subscription basis. Despite critical acclaim, the series folded in 1975. Today, the AFT concept is kept alive by PBS's *American Playhouse*, which distributes literary films selectively before broadcasting them on television.

Three Sisters (1970)
The Iceman Cometh (1973)
The Homecoming (1973)
A Delicate Balance (1973)
Rhinoceros (1974)

Butley (1974)
Luther (1974)
Lost in the Stars (1974)
The Man in the Glass Booth (1975)

American Ninja Series

Title tells all in this Cannon Films' action series about a U.S. soldier schooled in ninja-style martial arts. Michael Dudikoff played quiet-but-lethal Joe Armstrong in the first two films. Karate expert David Bradley, portraying a different character, took over in 1989's *American Ninja 3: Blood Hunt*. Both Dudikoff and Bradley appeared in the fourth entry, which found Dudikoff coming out of "retirement" to rescue captive Bradley. Steve James appeared as the hero's two-fisted sidekick in the first three movies.

American Ninja (1985)

American Ninja 2: The Confrontation (1987)

American Ninja 3: Blood Hunt (1989)

American Ninja 4: The Annihilation (1991)

Amityville

In 1979, American International Pictures turned Jay Anson's allegedly nonfiction best-seller about a haunted house, The *Amityville Horror*, into its biggest hit. It was a sorry excuse for a horror picture, despite the presence of the once-reliable Rod Steiger as a troubled priest. The 1982 sequel, *Amityville: The Possession*, turned out to be a prequel—but no one really cared either way. The third installment, *Amityville 3-D* (1983), made no attempt to connect itself with the first two films. Its box office failure (despite the added allure of 3-D) apparently signaled the end of a theatrical series. The series moved briefly to television, with the 1989 Patty Duke-Jane Wyatt movie *Amityville: The Evil Escapes*, before finding its niche with additional direct-to-videotape entries. See also **House Series.**

The Amityville Horror (1979)

Amityville: The Possession (1982)

Amityville 3-D (aka *Amityville: The Demon*) (1983)

Amityville: The Evil Escapes (1989 TVM)

The Amityville Curse (1990)

Amityville 1992: It's About Time (1992)

Amityville: A New Generation (1993)

Amnesia

A plot device staple, despite its unlikely real-life occurrence, amnesia has shown no favoritism toward any particular genre nor sex. Screen legend Greta Garbo made it fashionable for women to forget their identities in 1932's *As You Desire Me*, thus inspiring other actresses to ponder "Who am I?" A sample roster spans five decades and includes Jennifer Jones (*Love Letters*), Ava Gardner (*Singapore*), Karen Valentine (*Jane Doe*), and Lindsay Wagner (*Stranger in My Bed*). Males have proven to be equally forgetful, especially William Powell and Gregory Peck, both of whom suffered two bouts of amnesia (Powell in *I Love You Again* and *Crossroads*, Peck in *Spellbound* and *Mirage*). Greer Garson, who dealt with Ronald Colman's loss of memory in *Random Harvest* (1942), experienced it herself earlier in *Remember?* (1939). In an unusual plot twist, she and Robert Taylor played a bickering couple who take a potion that causes amnesia and then wind up falling in love again. Amnesia has also separated lovers in high-class soap operas such as *Random Harvest*, *Love Letters* and *Singapore*. It's hard to remember many amnesiac comedies, although *Desperately Seeking Susan* and *The Road to Hong Kong* spring to mind with little difficulty. The most interesting amnesiac plots have appeared in mysteries and espionage thrillers. Gregory Peck played the new head of an asylum who turns out to be an impostor with amnesia in Hitchcock's *Spellbound* (1945). Warner Baxter's *The Crime Doctor* (q.v.) was a sleuthing psychologist, who had been a master criminal before being reformed by amnesia. Unethical psychiatrist Tony Perkins tried to manipulate amnesiac killer Charles Bronson into murdering his wife's lover in the 1971 thriller *Someone Behind the Door*. James Garner, unable to remember his name, saw a Budweiser truck and an airplane and decided to call himself *Mister Buddwing* (1966). It was certainly one of the more commercial films of its time.

As You Desire Me (1932)
Remember? (1939)
Missing Ten Days (aka *Spy in the Pantry*; *Ten Days in Paris*) (1939)
I Love You Again (1940)
Crossroads (1942)
Dr. Gillespie's New Assistant (1942)
Street of Chance (1942)
Random Harvest (1942)
The Crime Doctor (1943)
Two O'Clock Courage (1945)
Identity Unknown (1945)
Love Letters (1945)
Spellbound (1945)
The Unknown (1946)
Somewhere in the Night (1946)
While I Live (aka *The Dream of Olwen*) (1947)
Singapore (1947)
High Wall (1947)
Lost Honeymoon (1947)
Girl in the Painting (aka *Portrait From Life*) (1948)
Shadow on the Wall (1950)
The Woman With No Name (1950)
A Tale of Five Women (aka *A Tale of Five Cities*) (1951)
Home at Seven (aka *Murder on Monday*) (1952)
The Unholy Four (aka *A Stranger Came Home*) (1953)
Man in the Dark (1953)
The Long Wait (1954)
The Constant Husband (1955)
Istanbul (1957)

Forger of London (1961)
Sundays and Cybele (1962)
The Road to Hong Kong (1962)
The Double (1963)
Hysteria (1964)
Mirage (1965)
The Third Day (1965)
Mister Buddwing (1966)
Project X (1968)
Jigsaw (1968)
Run a Crooked Mile (1969)
Someone Behind the Door (1971)
Richie Brockelman: The Missing 24 Hours (1976 TVM)
Beyond the Door 2 (aka *Shock*) (1979)
The Return of the Soldier (1981)
Jane Doe (1983 TVM)
Blackout (1985 TVM)
Desperately Seeking Susan (1985)
Stranger in My Bed (1986 TVM)
Lilac Dream (1987)
The Stranger (1987)
Overboard (1987)
Murder by Night (1989 TVM)
The Lady Forgets (1989 TVM)
Moving Target (1990)
Memories of Murder (1990 TVM)
Total Recall (1990)
Finding the Way Home (1991 TVM)
Regarding Henry (1991)
Shattered (1991)
A Stranger in the Family (1991 TVM)
With a Vengeance (1992 TVM)
The Disappearance of Nora (1993 TVM)

Amusement Parks, *see* Fairs and Carnivals

Androids and Cyborgs

Much to the dismay of science fiction purists, the cinema has often confused androids and cyborgs. The term "android" refers either to an artificial man made of organic substance or, in a looser sense, to a humanlike robot. The most famous artificial man, Mary Shelley's Frankenstein Monster (q.v.), is seldom described as an android, though he certainly fits the first definition. On a larger scale, Vincent Price tried to create a race of "synthetic men" and move them into government positions in 1970's *Scream and Scream Again*. However, artificial humans such as these remain rare, with most movie androids hailing from the humanlike robot school. In Fritz Lang's highly influential *Metropolis* (1925), a mad scientist kidnapped a peace-minded tunnel worker and replaced her with a trouble-making robot look-alike. Androids ran amok in a fantasy resort in Michael Crichton's *Westworld* (1973) and its semi-sequel *Futureworld* (1976). Men replaced their female companions with more easily controlled androids in *The Stepford Wives* (q.v.) (1975) and *Cherry 2000* (1988), although the hero of the latter film ultimately chose Melanie Griffith over his robot lover. Some androids, such as the "replicants" in *Blade Runner* (1982), gradually became so humanlike as to question their own identities. Androids far outnumber their relatives, the cyborgs. The term "cyborg," a contraction of "cybernetic organism," describes a hybrid between man and machine. Television's *The Six Million Dollar Man* and *The Bionic Woman* brought fame to cyborgs. Indeed, the pilot movie for *The Six Million Dollar Man* (q.v.) (1973) was originally called *Cyborg*. Technically, former Jedi knight Darth Vader had become a cyborg by the time Luke Skywalker encountered him for the first time in *Star Wars* (1977). Likewise, the Tin Man was one when he and Dorothy met in *The Wizard of Oz* (1939). In futuristic Detroit, a cop left for dead was transformed into the cyborgic crimefighter *Robocop*, one of the most popular movie heroes of 1987. See also **Computers; Robots; Six Million Dollar Man; The Stepford Wives.**

Metropolis (1925)
The Wizard of Oz (1939)
The Perfect Woman (1949)
Creation of the Humanoids (1962)
Dr. Goldfoot and the Bikini Machine (1965)
The Human Duplicators (1965)
Cyborg 2087 (1966)
Scream and Scream Again (1970)
The Six Million Dollar Man (1973 TVM)
Westworld (1973)
The Questor Tapes (1974 TVM)
The Stepford Wives (1975)
Futureworld (1976)
Future Cop (1976 TVM)
The Cops and Robin (1978 TVM)
Alien (1979)
Galaxina (1980)
Android (1982)
Blade Runner (1982)
Prototype (1983 TVM)
The Terminator (1984)
D.A.R.Y.L. (1985)

J.O.E. and the Colonel (1985 TVM)
Condor (1986)
The Vindicator (aka *Frankenstein '88*) (1986)
Deadly Friend (1986)
Eliminators (1986)
Robocop (1987)
Making Mr. Right (1987)
Not Quite Human (1987 TVM)
Cherry 2000 (1988)
Cyborg (1989)
Slipstream (1989)
Robocop 2 (1990)
Class of 1999 (1990)
Hardware (1990)
Robo-C.H.I.C. (1990)
Syngenor (1990)
Edward Scissorhands (1990)
Steel and Lace (1991)
Eve of Destruction (1991)
Terminator 2: Judgment Day (1991)
Bill and Ted's Bogus Journey (1991)
Toys (1993)
Nemesis (1993)

Angel Series

"High school honor student by day, hooker by night!" proclaimed the ad line to 1984's *Angel*. It's a concise plot summary, actually, except that fifteen-year-old Angel (Donna Wilkes) was "rescued" from a life of prostitution by caring cop Cliff Gorman. Viewers lured by the exploitative advertising campaign were probably disappointed by the film's tame content. Nevertheless, this B-picture generated some unexpected box office noise, and New World Pictures rushed out a sequel. Busy B-film actress Betsy Russell took over the title role for 1985's *Avenging Angel*, which found our heroine studying for a legal career. However, when her cop friend is murdered, she cuts her academic endeavors short, reverts to her tough girl persona, and hits the streets again to exact vengeance. For a couple years, it appeared as though Angel had fired her last bullet. Then, in 1988, *Angel III: The Final Chapter* reached the screen with Mitzi Kapture headlining as the third Angel in three films. This installment sent Angel, now an undercover cop, on a mission to rescue her kidnapped sister. Rory Calhoun and Susan Tyrell had supporting roles in the first two films but did not appear in the last series entry.

Angel (1984)

Avenging Angel (1985)

Angel III: The Final Chapter (1988)

Angels

One rather expects to find angels in heavenly fantasies like *Green Pastures* (1936), *Stairway to Heaven* (1946) and *Made in Heaven* (1987). However, earthbound angels outnumber their celestial counterparts on film. They have also made a more lasting impression, perhaps because they appear in smaller numbers, one or two to a film, allowing them to become more personable (and in some cases, more mortal-like). Guardian angels are the most common variety and have been sent to Earth to rescue misguided mortals from suicide, ambition and lousy baseball playing. Henry Travers played Clarence, an angel trying to earn his wings, in Frank Capra's annual Christmas favorite *It's a Wonderful Life* (1946). He dissuades a distraught family man (James Stewart) from ending his life by showing him how he has affected the lives of others. Cloris Leachman replaced Travers as the angel in the sticky-sweet 1977 TV-movie remake *It Happened One Christmas*, while Robert Carradine took his turn in the 1990 TV-movie sequel *Clarence*. Another holiday feature, 1985's *One Magic Christmas*, cast Harry Dean Stanton as an unlikely-looking angel who comes to the aid of a confused woman (Mary Steenburgen) who has lost the Christmas spirit. Cary Grant made a charming angel in *The Bishop's Wife* (1947), helping clergyman David Niven realize that his desire to build a cathedral had begun to cut him off from his family and his own love of God. Grant's angel also found himself in the precarious position of falling in love with Niven's wife (Loretta Young). Other angel-mortal love affairs occurred in the Jeanette MacDonald-Nelson Eddy musical *I Married an Angel* (1942) and the ridiculous comedy *Date With an Angel* (1987). Baseball collided with heavenly forces in *Angels in the Outfield* (1952), in which an angel guides the woebegone Pittsburgh Pirates (not the yet-unformed California Angels) to a winning season. The spirit of baseball great Shoeless Joe Jackson returned to earth to play on farmer Kevin Costner's baseball diamond in 1989's *Field of Dreams*. The roll call of performers who have played angels is an impressive one: Edmund Gwenn in

Between Two Worlds and *For Heaven's Sake*, James Mason in *Forever Darling* and *Heaven Can Wait*, Claude Rains in *Here Comes Mr. Jordan*, Sidney Poitier in *The Angel Levine*, and Clifton Webb in *For Heaven's Sake*. See also **Heaven.**

Green Pastures (1936)
Here Comes Mr. Jordan (1941)
I Married an Angel (1942)
Cabin in the Sky (1943)
Between Two Worlds (1944)
The Horn Blows at Midnight (1945)
That's the Spirit (1945)
It's a Wonderful Life (1946)
Stairway to Heaven (aka *A Matter of Life and Death*) (1946)
The Bishop's Wife (1947)
Heaven Only Knows (aka *Montana Mike*) (1947)
For Heaven's Sake (1950)
Angels in the Outfield (aka *Angels and the Pirates*) (1952)
The Angel Who Pawned Her Harp (1954)
Forever Darling (1956)
Barbarella (1967)
The Angel Levine (1970)
It Happened One Christmas (1977 TVM)

Heaven Can Wait (1978)
Human Feelings (1978 TVM)
Fear No Evil (1981)
The Kid With the Broken Halo (1982 TVM)
Two of a Kind (1983)
It Came Upon a Midnight Clear (1984 TVM)
The Heavenly Kid (1985)
One Magic Christmas (1985)
Date With an Angel (1987)
Made in Heaven (1987)
Wings of Desire (1988)
Field of Dreams (1989)
Always (1989)
Soultaker (1990)
Clarence (1990 TVM)
Earth Angel (1991 TVM)
Defending Your Life (1991)
Hi Honey, I'm Dead (1991 TVM)
Far Away, So Close! (1993)
Heart and Souls (1993)

Animated Movies (Feature-Length)

Not only was Walt Disney the father of feature-length animated films, but his studio completely dominated the field for nearly three decades. The Disney artists produced thirteen movies during that span, beginning with 1937's landmark motion picture *Snow White and the Seven Dwarfs*. For the most part, Disney had little competition, chiefly due to the high costs associated with animation. Nevertheless, Max Fleischer, creator of Betty Boop and Popeye, mounted some rival productions in the early forties. His *Gulliver's Travels* and *Hoppity Goes to Town* earned good reviews for their artwork, but critics complained about weak storytelling. Husband-and-wife team John Halas and Joy Batchelor produced an ambitious adaptation of George Orwell's *Animal Farm* in 1954. It was oriented toward a more sophisticated adult audience — but did not find one. The UPA studio, home of Mr. Magoo, tried unsuccessfully to duplicate the Disney magic with 1959's *1001 Arabian Nights* and 1963's *Gay Purr-ee*, a musical tale about Parisian cats. The latter film signaled the end of an era, as even the Disney product began to exhibit a lowering of standards. Rising costs and Walt Disney's death (in 1966) undoubtedly contributed to the decline. However, in 1972, a thirty-two-year-old animator named Ralph Bakshi revived the feature-length cartoon in grand fashion, with his stylish, controversial X-rated film *Fritz the Cat*. Although Bakshi's subsequent movies made little money, they acquired a strong cult following, principally among college-aged viewers raised on Disney cartoons. Sadly, soaring costs prevented Bakshi from completing his *Lord of the Rings* films. His 1978 adaptation ended abruptly, promising a sequel that was never made. Meanwhile, internal problems at the Disney studio resulted in scarce output during the 1970s. Several Disney animators, led by Don Bluth, quit and formed their own studio. Bluth's first independent feature *The Secret of NIMH* (1982) was a colorful, heartwarming return to the Disney formula. It led to a revival of quality feature-length cartoons in the 1980s, culminating with the simultaneous 1988 releases of Disney's *Oliver and Company* and Bluth's *The Land Before Time*. There were even novel experiments like *Starchaser: The Legend of Orin* (1985), the only feature-length 3-D cartoon. However, the genre became glutted with lower quality cartoon features based on best-selling toys such as the *Care Bears* (q.v.), the *Pound Puppies*, *Rainbow Brite* and *My Little Pony*. These films, like their Saturday morning counterparts, strove to sell as much as entertain. Thankfully, these commercial-generated features fizzled under the weight of Disney's animated blockbuster musicals *The Little Mermaid* (1989), *Beauty and the Beast* (1991) and *Aladdin* (1992) — which dominated toy store shelves as well as the box office. Fifty-four years after *Snow White and the Seven Dwarfs*, *Beauty and the Beast* became the first animated feature to be nominated for a Best Picture Academy Award. See also **The Care Bears; Cartoon/Live Action Features; Peanuts.**

Snow White and the Seven Dwarfs (1937)

Gulliver's Travels (1939)

Pinocchio (1939)

Fantasia (1940)

Dumbo (1941)

Hoppity Goes to Town (aka *Mr. Bugs Goes to Town*) (1941)

Bambi (1943)

Make Mine Music (1946)

Cinderella (1950)

Alice in Wonderland (1952)

Peter Pan (1952)

Animal Farm (1954)

Lady and the Tramp (1956)

Sleeping Beauty (1959)

1001 Arabian Nights (1959)

One Hundred and One Dalmations (1961)

Alakazam the Great (1961)

The Sword in the Stone (1963)

Gay Purr-ee (1963)

Pinocchio in Outer Space (1964)

Hey There, It's Yogi Bear (1964)

A Man Called Flintstone (1966)

Gulliver's Travels Beyond the Moon (1966)

The Jungle Book (1967)

A Boy Named Charlie Brown (1969)

The Phantom Tollbooth (1969)

The Aristocats (1970)

shinebone alley (1971)

The Point (1971 TVM)

Fritz the Cat (1972)

Snoopy, Come Home (1972)

Robin Hood (1973)

Fantastic Planet (1973)

Journey Back to Oz (1974)

The Nine Lives of Fritz the Cat (1975)

Hugo, the Hippo (1975)

The Rescuers (1976)

Wizards (1977)

The Hobbit (1977 TVM)

Raggedy Ann and Andy (1977)

Watership Down (1978)

The Lord of the Rings (1978)

Animalympics (1979)

Grendel, Grendel, Grendel (1980)

American Pop (1981)

The Fox and the Hound (1981)

Heavy Metal (1981)

Hey, Good Lookin' (1982)

Heidi's Song (1982)

The Secret of NIMH (1982)

The Plague Dogs (1982)
The Last Unicorn (1982)
Fire and Ice (1983)
Twice Upon a Time (1983)
Rock & Rule (1983)
Lensman (1984)
The Smurfs and the Magic Flute (1984)
The Black Cauldron (1985)
The Cosmic Eye (1985)
The Care Bears Movie (1985)
Here Comes the Littles (1985)
Starchaser: The Legend of Orin (1985)
Rainbow Brite and the Star Stealers (1985)
The Great Mouse Detective (aka The Adventures of the Great Mouse Detective) (1986)
Heathcliff: The Movie (1986)
My Little Pony (1986)
GoBots: Battle of the Rock Lords (1986)
An American Tail (1986)
The Chipmunk Adventure (1987)
The Brave Little Toaster (1987)
Pinocchio and the Emperor of the Night (1987)
Pound Puppies and the Legend of Big Paw (1988)
Oliver and Company (1988)
The Land Before Time (1988)
Light Years (1988)
All Dogs Go to Heaven (1989)

The Little Mermaid (1989)
Daffy Duck's Quackbusters (1989)
Jetsons: The Movie (1990)
Duck Tales: The Movie — Treasure of the Lost Lamp (1990)
The Rescuers Down Under (1990)
The Nutcracker Prince (1990)
Happily Ever After (1990)
Rock-a-Doodle (1991)
The Magic Riddle (1991)
Beauty and the Beast (1991)
Rover Dangerfield (1991)
An American Tale: Fievel Goes West (1991)
The Tune (1992)
FernGully . . . The Last Rainforest (aka FernGully) (1992)
Bebe's Kids (1992)
Little Nemo: Adventures in Slumberland (1992)
Freddie as F.R.O.7 (1992)
Vampire Hunter D (1992)
Tom and Jerry: The Movie (1992)
Aladdin (1992)
The Princess and the Goblin (aka A Hercegnö és a Kobold) (1992)
Jonny's Golden Quest (1993 TVM)
Once Upon a Forest (1993)
We're Back! (aka We're Back! A Dinosaur's Story) (1993)

Anthologies

Also called "episode films," anthology movies contain two or more separate stories, typically linked by a framing device. The format descended from D.W. Griffith's *Intolerance* (1918), which interwove four stories set in different time periods. One of the first American films to separate its "internal plots" was 1932's *If I Had a Million*. Richard Bennett played a millionaire who gave fortunes to people (e.g., Charles Laughton, Gary Cooper, W.C. Fields) randomly selected from the phone book. In the early 1940s, French immigrant Julien Duvivier directed two highly acclaimed anthology films, *Tales of Manhattan* and *Flesh and Fantasy*. The former film used a dress tailcoat to link five stories, while Robert Benchley tied the stories together in the latter film. Curiously, the three-part *Flesh and Fantasy* originally included a fourth tale, which was expanded by Reginald LeBorg into 1944's *Destiny*. Britain's initial foray in anthology films resulted in the classic 1945 chiller *Dead of Night*. Ironically, this film is best remembered for its frame, as opposed to the stories. It opens with an architect who visits a country manor and engages in a conversation about dreams with its inhabitants. After the last dream is told and a shocking murder takes place, the architect wakes up—for he has been dreaming all along. That morning, he drives to a client's estate in the country and arrives at the same manor. The recurring, and endless, nightmare has begun again. In the wake of *Dead of Night*, British studios produced three highly successful adaptations of Somerset Maugham short stories: *Quartet*, *Trio* and *Encore*. These inspired a 1952 U.S. author anthology, *O. Henry's Full House*, featuring John Steinbeck as narrator. Budget-conscious director Roger Corman reacquainted the anthology format with horror tales in his 1962 Edgar Allan Poe collection *Tales of Terror*. Amicus, a small British studio, followed Corman's example with 1964's *Dr. Terror's House of Horrors* and subsequently specialized in producing anthology horror films. It made seven additional anthology movies between 1968's *Torture Garden* and 1974's *From Beyond the Grave*. Throughout the 1960s, episodic films enjoyed great popularity in France and Italy, with distinguished filmmakers such as François Truffaut and Federico Fellini contributing segments to international efforts like *Love at Twenty* and *Spirits of the Dead*. In the 1970s, attempts to adapt the anthology format to U.S. made-for-TV movies met with modest success. Television viewers seemed to prefer the interlocking-story format made popular by the *Love Boat* and *Fantasy Island* TV series.

If I Had a Million (1932)
Tales of Manhattan (1942)
Flesh and Fantasy (1943)
Dead of Night (1945)
On Our Merry Way (1948)
Bond Street (1948)
Quartet (1948)
Trio (1950)
Actors and Sin (1952)
Encore (1952)
O. Henry's Full House (1952)
Tonight at 8:30 (aka *Meet Me Tonight*) (1952)
It's a Big Country (1952)
The Story of Three Loves (1953)
Love in the City (1953)
Daughters of Destiny (aka *Love, Soldiers and Women*) (1953)
Letters From My Windmill (1954)
Three Cases of Murder (1954)
Invitation to the Dance (1957)
Of Life and Love (1957)
Rising of the Moon (1957)
Love and the Frenchwoman (1961)
The Devil and the Ten Commandments (1962)
Tales of Terror (1962)
Seven Capital Sins (1962)

Yesterday, Today, and Tomorrow (1963)
Twice Told Tales (1963)
Dr. Terror's House of Horrors (aka *The Bloodsuckers*) (1964)
Black Sabbath (1964)
Kwaidan (1964)
Bambole! (1965)
Let's Talk About Women (1965)
Woman Times Seven (1967)
The Oldest Profession (1967)
The Torture Garden (1968)
Spirits of the Dead (1968)
The Illustrated Man (1969)
Night Gallery (1969 TVM)
The House That Dripped Blood (1970)
The Decameron (1970)
Triple Play (1971 TVM)
Asylum (aka *House of Crazies*) (1972)
Tales From the Crypt (1972)
Tales That Witness Madness (1973)
Vault of Horror (aka *Tales From the Crypt 2*) (1973)
From Beyond the Grave (aka *Creatures From Beyond the Grave*) (1974)
Immoral Tales (1974)
Trilogy of Terror (1975 TVM)
How Funny Can Sex Be? (1976)

The Uncanny (1977)
Roseland (1977)
Movie Movie (1978)
Tigers in Lipstick (aka Wild Beds)
   (1979)
Sunday Lovers (1980)
Creepshow (1982)
Nightmares (1983)
Twilight Zone: The Movie (1983)
Jealousy (1984 TVM)
Cat's Eye (1985)
Creepshow 2 (1987)
New York Stories (1989)
After Midnight (1989)

Two Evil Eyes (aka Due Occhi
   Diabolic) (1990)
Tales From the Darkside: The Movie
   (1990)
Grim Prairie Tales (1990)
Women and Men: Stories of Seduction
   (1990 TVM)
Campfire Tales (1991)
Seduction: Three Tales From the Inner
   Sanctum (1992 TVM)
Hotel Room (1993 TVM)
Two Mikes Don't Make a Wright
   (1993)
Bedevil (1993)

Apartments

The narrow confines of apartment living have created stress-inducing problems for many tenants, while implicating others romantically. In Roman Polanski's *Repulsion* (1965), a sexually repressed girl (Catherine Deneuve) spends a weekend alone in her sister's London flat and winds up murdering the lecherous landlord with a dinner knife. Polanski himself played an apartment dweller who became obsessed with his pad's former occupant in 1976's *The Tenant*. The Kowalskis' claustrophobic apartment served to feed the sexual tensions in Elia Kazan's 1951 adaptation of *A Streetcar Named Desire*. Supernatural creatures have displayed a special fondness for apartment living in films like *The Sentinel* (1977), *Poltergeist III* and *Demons 2* (both 1988). Even the Devil showed up, amid a building full of satanic tenants, in *Rosemary's Baby* (1968). A temporary housing shortage forced Jean Arthur to share her small Washington, D.C., apartment with Joel McCrea and Charles Coburn in the 1943 comedy *The More the Merrier*. Naturally, she and Joel discovered true love. The same plot, with a different setting (Tokyo), surfaced in 1966 as *Walk, Don't Run*. Apartments have also been the site for illicit love affairs. Fred MacMurray paid Shirley MacLaine's rent for *The Apartment* (1960), while Jason Robards visited Jane Fonda on *Any Wednesday* (1966) at his company-paid flat. The close proximity to his neighbors inspired James Stewart to engage in some hazardous window-peeping in Hitchcock's *Rear Window* (1954). Other nosy apartment neighbors proved meddlesome in *Terraces* (1977) and *Through Naked Eyes* (1983). In the 1943 comedy *Johnny Doesn't Live Here Anymore*, Simone Simon discovered that keys to her apartment were distributed freely during the war. *The Key* (1958) was an emotional drama about a woman (Sophia Loren) who passes the key to her apartment to a series of fighting naval officers. In *The Night We Never Met* (1993), complications naturally ensued when three people time-shared the same apartment on different days of the week.

Bachelor Apartment (1931)
The More the Merrier (1943)
Johnny Doesn't Live Here Anymore
   (aka And So They Were Married)
   (1944)

There Is a Family (1944)
Apartment for Peggy (1948)
A Kiss in the Dark (1949)
A Streetcar Named Desire (1951)
Love Nest (1951)

Rear Window (1954)
The Key (1958)
The Apartment (1960)
Why Bother to Knock? (aka Don't
   Bother to Knock) (1961)
The Notorious Landlady (1962)
Boys' Night Out (1962)
Repulsion (1965)
That Funny Feeling (1965)
Any Wednesday (1966)
Barefoot in the Park (1967)
The Penthouse (1967)
Rosemary's Baby (1968)
The Odd Couple (1968)
The Landlord (1970)
Strangers in 7A (1972 TVM)
Nightmare (1974 TVM)
They Came From Within (aka Shivers;
   The Parasite Murders; Frissons)
   (1975)

The Tenant (1976)
Terraces (1977 TVM)
The Sentinel (1977)
Through Naked Eyes (1983 TVM)
The Guardian (1984 TVM)
The Family (1987)
Demons 2 (1988)
Poltergeist III (1988)
Apartment Zero (1989)
Pacific Heights (1990)
The Super (1991)
World Apartment Horror (1991)
Single White Female (1992)
Through the Eyes of a Killer (1992
   TVM)
The Night We Never Met (1993)
Sliver (1993)

Apes and Monkeys

Ape and monkey performers have earned a notorious reputation for stealing scenes from their human costars. The chimpanzee Bonzo had little trouble upstaging future president Ronald Reagan in *Bedtime for Bonzo*. Clyde, a mugging orangutan, showed far more facial expression than iron-jawed Clint Eastwood in *Every Which Way But Loose*. King Kong towered over Fay Wray and Robert Armstrong in terms of on-screen impact as well as sheer size in his 1933 film debut. Although Kong reigns as the cinema's biggest ape in terms of popularity, his physical dimensions have been equaled by *Mighty Joe Young* (1949), *Konga* (1961), *Goliathon* (1977) and, to a lesser extent, *Son of Kong* (1933). There have been no oversized monkeys, although an equally unusual winged species abducted Dorothy and took her to the Wicked Witch's castle in *The Wizard of Oz* (1939). Ordinary apes have proven to be meddlesome as well, especially in horror/mystery fare such as *Murders in the Rue Morgue* (1932), *The Ape* (1940), and *Gorilla at Large* (1954). Typically, though, a villainous human lurks behind the ape's ghastly deeds—and in some cases, the true murderer turns out to be a man in an ape suit. David Warner longed to be a gorilla—and carry off his estranged wife—in the 1966 satire *Morgan!* Mad scientist Dr. Moreau (Charles Laughton) transformed apes into men with dubious results ("Are we not men?") in 1933's *Island of Lost Souls*. John Carradine turned a female ape into pretty Acquanetta in the *Captive Wild Woman* series, while Bela Lugosi injected himself with an ape-transforming serum in 1943's *The Ape Man*. Apes and humans became intellectual and sociological equals in *The Planet of the Apes* films (q.v.). For most of that series, the simian society was the dominant one, although it experienced internal conflicts between its chimpanzee scientists, orangutan politicians, and gorilla military leaders. The right to teach the theory that man evolved from apes was hotly debated in *Inherit the Wind* (1960), based on the famous Scopes Monkey Trial. A mysterious monolith brought intelligence to earthly apes in the dramatic opening of Stanley Kubrick's *2001: A Space Odyssey* (1968). Finally, Marlene Dietrich, in one of her most memorable scenes, sang "Hot Voodoo" while wearing a gorilla suit in 1932's *Blonde Venus*. See also **Dupree, Paula (The Ape Woman); King Kong; Planet of the Apes.**

Murders in the Rue Morgue (1932)
The Monster Walks (1932)
Island of Lost Souls (1933)
King Kong (1933)
The Wizard of Oz (1939)
The Ape (1940)
The Ape Man (aka *Lock Your Doors*) (1943)
Captive Wild Woman (1943)
Nabonga (aka *Gorilla*) (1944)
Mighty Joe Young (1949)
Bedtime for Bonzo (1951)
Road to Bali (1952)
Bonzo Goes to College (1952)
Monkey Business (1952)
Phantom of the Rue Morgue (1954)
Gorilla at Large (1954)
The Bride and the Beast (aka *Queen of the Gorillas*) (1958)
Alakazam the Great (1960)
Konga (1961)
The Monkey's Uncle (1965)
Morgan! (aka *Morgan — A Suitable Case for Treatment*) (1966)
Monkey, Go Home (1967)
2001: A Space Odyssey (1968)
Planet of the Apes (1968)

The Barefoot Executive (1970)
A Cold Night's Death (1973)
A.P.E. (1976)
Goliathon (1977)
Every Which Way But Loose (1978)
The Mafu Cage (aka *My Sister, My Love*) (1978)
Bye Bye Monkey (1978)
The Wild and the Free (1980)
The Ivory Ape (1980 TVM)
Any Which Way You Can (1980)
The Incredible Shrinking Woman (1981)
Going Ape! (1981)
Greystoke: The Legend of Tarzan, Lord of the Apes (1984)
In the Shadow of Kilimanjaro (1986)
Link (1986)
Project X (1987)
Gorillas in the Mist (1988)
Monkey Shines: An Experiment in Terror (1988)
Animal Behavior (1989)
The Fifth Monkey (1990)
Shakma (1990)
The Entertainers (1991 TVM)

Apu Trilogy

Satyajit Ray's simple, powerful films about the son of a Brahmin priest brought international attention to Indian cinema in the 1950s. Ray adapted the first film, 1956's *Pather Panchali*, from Bibhuti Bannerji's acclaimed novel. He bought the book's rights for a modest $1300, but encountered financial problems early in the production. He pawned his wife's jewelry (a last resort in Indian families) before eventually securing backing from the West Bengal government. The film's story dealt with life in a small village as seen through the eyes of Apu, a young boy. He watches his sister die, his father leave to find work, and finally his family forced to move from their home. This visually stunning, emotional drama soon attracted the attention of international critics. It was voted a special award at the 1956 Cannes Film Festival and was subsequently honored by festivals in Berlin, Tokyo and Denmark. Ray returned to Apu as both a young boy and an adolescent in 1957's *Aparajito*. In 1959's *Apur Sansar*, Apu marries and becomes isolated from village life by his own education.

Pather Panchali (aka *Father Panchali; Song of the Road*) (1956)
Aparajito (aka *The Unvanquished*) (1957)
Apur Sansar (aka *The World of Apu*) (1959)

Arthur, King, and the Knights of the Round Table

The legendary sixth-century British king, oddly ignored during Hollywood's swashbuckling days, has gradually evolved into one of the cinema's most durable mythic heroes. He was strictly a supporting character in both sound versions of Mark Twain's *A Connecticut Yankee in King Arthur's Court*. British comedian Arthur Askey dreamed he was a knight of the Round Table in 1942's *King Arthur Was a Gentleman*. Then in 1953, MGM followed its blockbuster *Ivanhoe* with the gloss-dripping Arthurian spectacle *Knights of the Round Table*. Mel Ferrer made a noble Arthur, with Ava Gardner (beautiful, but not quite right) as Guinevere and dashing Robert Taylor (a bit old, actually) as Lancelot. Despite its dramatic shortcomings, it remained the most complete recounting of the Arthurian epic for almost three decades. The next version of the legend came from an unlikely source, action star Cornel Wilde. He produced, directed and starred in *The Sword of Lancelot*, a straightforward, well-done drama focusing on the romance between Lancelot (Wilde) and Guinevere (Jean Wallace). Brian Aherne made a low-key Arthur. Novelist T.H. White's *The Once and Future King* provided the basis for Disney's animated feature *The Sword in the Stone* (1963) and the Broadway musical/film *Camelot* (1967). The former was a bland tale of Arthur's youth, while the latter benefited from star turns by Richard Harris and Vanessa Redgrave as Arthur and Guinevere. In the 1970s, French directors Robert Bresson and Eric Rohmer contributed the atmospheric, sometimes esoteric, knightly tales *Lancelot of the Lake* and *Perceval*, respectively. The Monty Python troupe spoofed Arthurian films hilariously in their finest feature, 1975's *Monty Python and the Holy Grail*. Disney added an unnecessary remake of *A Connecticut Yankee* in 1979, dubiously titled *Unidentified Flying Oddball*. Two years later, director John Boorman brought atmosphere, mystery and sexuality to his epic *Excalibur*. Based on Malory's *Le Morte d'Arthur*, Boorman's picture gave equal time to Merlin (played by Nicol Williamson) while telling Arthur's (Nigel Terry) tale in depth. Malcolm McDowell made a passable Arthur in the otherwise dreadful 1985 TV-movie *Arthur the King*, which costarred Dyan Cannon as a contemporary lass who falls through a hole in Stonehenge and winds up in Camelot. George Romero's heavy-handed 1981 parable *Knightriders* told the Camelot story in a contemporary setting with Ed Harris as the leader of a troupe of jousting motorcycle riders.

A Connecticut Yankee (1931)
King Arthur Was a Gentleman (1942)
A Connecticut Yankee in King Arthur's Court (1949)
Knights of the Round Table (1953)
The Black Knight (1954)
The Sword of Lancelot (aka *Lancelot and Guinevere*) (1963)

The Sword in the Stone (1963)
Siege of the Saxons (1964)
Camelot (1967)
Gawain and the Green Knight (1973)
Lancelot of the Lake (aka *Lancelot du Lac; Le Graal; The Grail*) (1974)
Monty Python and the Holy Grail (1975)

Perceval (aka Perceval le Gallois)
(1978)
Unidentified Flying Oddball (aka A
Spaceman in King Arthur's Court)
(1979)
Excalibur (1981)

Knightriders (1981)
The Sword of the Valiant (1982)
Arthur the King (1985 TVM)
Army of Darkness (aka Army of
Darkness: Evil Dead 3) (1993)

Artists, *see* Painters

Assumed Identity

The plot device where one person assumes another's identity has evolved into one of the cinema's most reliable conventions. Frequently, it is paired with related plotlines, such as amnesia, disguises and look-alikes (qq.v.). For example, amnesiac Gregory Peck assumed the identity of asylum director Dr. Edwardes in Hitchcock's *Spellbound*. In *The Great Impostor* (1961), Tony Curtis played real-life master of disguises Ferdinand Demara who assumed the identities of a prison warden, a naval doctor, a school teacher and others. Ronald Colman played a dashing gent who substitutes for his look-alike, the king of Ruritania, in an effort to thwart a usurper in 1937's *The Prisoner of Zenda*. Despite the utilities of these plotline pairings, some of the more intriguing films about assumed identities involve neither amnesia, disguises nor look-alikes. In 1975's *The Passenger*, Jack Nicholson played a man so unhappy with his own life that he assumed the identity of a dead man he knew nothing about. In *The Inspector General* (1949), Danny Kaye was *mistaken* for the title character, but he readily *assumed* the role once he realized the power it possessed. Gerard Depardieu was executed for assuming another man's identity in *The Return of Martin Guerre* (1982), even though everyone seemed to prefer him to the real Martin Guerre. Richard Gere experienced a similar fate in the 1993 Americanized version *Sommersby*. Poor Janet Leigh woke up from her wedding night with a stranger in her bed claiming to be her husband in the appropriately titled *Honeymoon With a Stranger* (1969). Still, that's not as bad as Gloria Talbott, who actually married an alien who had assumed her fiancé's identity in *I Married a Monster From Outer Space* (1958). See also **Amnesia; Disguises; Look-Alikes.**

The Masquerader (1933)
Maniac (1934)
The Great Impersonation (1935)
The Prisoner of Zenda (1937)
The Great Impersonation (1942)
The Imposter (aka Strange Confession)
(1944)
Spellbound (1945)
Detour (1945)
Hollow Triumph (aka The Scar) (1948)
The Inspector General (1949)
No Man of Her Own (1949)
The House on Telegraph Hill (1951)
Scarlet Angel (1952)

I Married a Monster From Outer Space
(1958)
Libel (1959)
The Great Impostor (1961)
Honeymoon With a Stranger (1969
TVM)
The Passenger (1975)
Kagemusha (aka Kagemusha, the
Shadow Warrior) (1980)
The Ninth Configuration (aka
Twinkle, Twinkle Killer Kane)
(1980)
The Return of Martin Guerre (1982)
I Married a Shadow (1982)

The Imposter (1984 TVM)
Critical Condition (1987)
Caroline? (1990 TVM)
Paper Mask (1990)
Taking Care of Business (1990)
The Stranger Within (1990 TVM)

The Couch Trip (1990)
Shattered (1991)
True Identity (1991)
White Sands (1992)
Sommersby (1993)
Dave (1993)

Asylums

The line between sanity and madness has frequently been portrayed as a thin one in films with an asylum setting. A common plot device has a sane person feigning insanity in order to be committed to an asylum. Journalist Peter Breck pulled the trick to win a Pulitzer Prize in Samuel Fuller's *Shock Corridor* (1963). He lost his mind as a result. The following year's *Shock Treatment* found Stuart Whitman as an actor who entered an asylum to discover where Roddy McDowell hid a fortune. However, the most famous picture along these lines was the 1975 multiple-Oscar winner *One Flew Over the Cuckoo's Nest*. Jack Nicholson's Randle Patrick McMurphy faked temporary insanity because he preferred a mental institution over hard labor at a prison. He discovered that the patients were saner — in their own way — than the medical staff. Alan Bates made a similar observation in 1966's *King of Hearts*, in which a group of inmates escaped into an evacuated town during World War I. Bates learned that these charming lunatics may be "touched," but at least they were not fighting a war to destroy each other. Another oft-filmed plot — sane people who are revealed to be mad — has been featured prominently in *The Cabinet of Dr. Caligari* and *The Ninth Configuration*. A highly influential expressionistic film, *Caligari* (1919) is ultimately the vision of a lunatic, for in its famous closing scene, the narrator is revealed to be a patient recounting the story to the head of an asylum. William Peter Blatty's *The Ninth Configuration* (1980) takes a similar theme one step further; the asylum director (Stacy Keach) turns out to be a mad impostor. Other movies that take place principally within the confines of an asylum include *Bedlam*, *The Snake Pit* and *Marat/Sade*. Escaped inmates are played for laughs in *Road Show* and horror in *Alone in the Dark*. *Frances*, the true story of actress Frances Farmer, and the James Stewart comedy *Harvey* have memorable closing scenes in mental institutions.

The Cabinet of Dr. Caligari (1919)
Road Show (1941)
Spellbound (1945)
Bedlam (1946)
The Snake Pit (1948)
Behind Locked Doors (1948)
Harvey (1950)
Blood of the Vampire (1958)
The Hideout (1961)
The Cabinet of Dr. Caligari (1962)
Shock Corridor (1963)
Shock Treatment (1964)
Signpost to Murder (1965)

King of Hearts (1966)
Marat/Sade (1967)
The Big Cube (1969)
The Night Visitor (1970)
Asylum (aka House of Crazies) (1972)
Don't Look in the Basement (1973)
Frankenstein and the Monster From Hell (1973)
One Flew Over the Cuckoo's Nest (1975)
High Anxiety (1977)
Down the Ancient Stairs (1977)
The Other Side of Hell (1978 TVM)
Dracula (1979)

The Ninth Configuration (aka
  Twinkle, Twinkle Killer Kane)
  (1980)
Alone in the Dark (1982)
Frances (1982)
Hellhole (1985)

The Dream Team (1989)
Crazy People (1990)
Committed (1990)
Disturbed (1991)
Against Her Will: An Incident in
  Baltimore (1992 TVM)

Atomic Bombs

The atomic bomb has been the subject of earnest fact-based dramas, escapist science fiction, chilling thrillers and one wild satire. The fact-based films began with 1947's *The Beginning or the End*, a stilted but historically interesting, government-approved story of the Manhattan Project. The personal drama behind the bombing of Hiroshima was better explored in 1952's *Above and Beyond* and in the 1980 TV-movie *Enola Gay: The Men, the Mission, the Atomic Bomb*. PBS's American Playhouse produced 1986's *Desert Bloom*, a perceptive family drama set in Nevada during the 1950s atomic bomb tests. Another American Playhouse production, *Testament* (1983), featured a powerful performance by Jane Alexander as a mother coping with her family's survival in the aftermath of an atomic explosion. It easily eclipsed the similar, heavily hyped 1983 TV-film *The Day After*. Both films owe a minor debt to Ray Milland's 1962 B-movie *Panic in the Year Zero*, a taut tale of a family's struggle to survive in a postatomic world, and a major debt to Peter Watkins's bleak *The War Game* (1967). Using a pseudo-documentary approach, Watkins showed what an atomic bomb would do to London. It's a brutal, frightening picture — so scary that its sponsor, the British Broadcasting Company, refused to air it on television. Today, it's shown frequently in conjunction with antinuclear protests. On a more positive note, scientists have used atomic devices for worthy purposes, such as destroying city-crunching monsters like 1953's *The Beast From 20,000 Fathoms*. Ironically, as in *The Beast*, many of these creatures were also created by atomic bomb testing. Mutant humans worshipped an atomic bomb in *Beneath the Planet of the Apes* (1970) (see **Planet of the Apes**). It was detonated in the film's climax and destroyed the world. At the conclusion of 1964's *Fail Safe*, President Henry Fonda ordered the atomic destruction of New York City (where his family lived) to avoid a nuclear confrontation with the Soviet Union. Other thrillers pale in comparison, although *The Bedford Incident* (1965) served as a potent reminder of just how easily an atomic war can be initiated. Industrious teenagers almost caused nuclear war in *WarGames* (1983) and *The Manhattan Project* (1986). In the latter film, a high school student built an atomic bomb to prove a point — a sobering premise despite an insufficient amount of credibility. The only film to effectively poke fun at atomic bombs and the threat of nuclear war remains Stanley Kubrick's *Dr. Strangelove, or How I Learned to Stop Worrying and Love the Bomb* (1964). Kubrick's black comedy closed with a classic image: Slim Pickens riding a falling bomb bronco-style to the closing strains of "We'll Meet Again." See also **End of the World/Post-Apocalypse**.

The Beginning or the End (1947)
Children of Hiroshima (1952)
Above and Beyond (1952)
The Beast From 20,000 Fathoms
  (1953)

The 49th Man (1953)
Port of Hell (1954)
Hiroshima, Mon Amour (1960)
The Flight That Disappeared (1961)
Panic in the Year Zero (1962)

Dr. Strangelove, or How I Learned to Stop
    Worrying and Love the Bomb (1964)
Fail Safe (1964)
The Bedford Incident (1965)
Finders Keepers (1966)
The War Game (1967)
The Day the Fish Came Out (1967)
Beneath the Planet of the Apes (1970)
Enola Gay: The Men, the Mission, the
    Atomic Bomb (1980 TVM)

The Atomic Cafe (1982)
Testament (1983)
The Day After (1983 TVM)
WarGames (1983)
One Night Stand (1984)
Desert Bloom (1986)
The Manhattan Project (1986)
Day One (1989 TVM)
Fat Man and Little Boy (1989)

Ator

Shortly after achieving (very) minor celebrity status playing *Tarzan, the Ape Man* (1981) opposite Bo Derek, hunky Miles O'Keeffe landed in this brief Italian sword-and-sorcery (q.v.) series. Aside from poor dubbing and O'Keeffe's inept thesping, these films are notable for their atrocious special effects (e.g., the hilarious giant spider slain by Ator in the original). Incredibly, Sean Connery played O'Keeffe's father in the non-Atorian *Sword of the Valiant* (1982). Meanwhile, Ator's son (Eric Allen Kramer) hit the quest trail to free Margaret Lenzey in 1990's *Quest for the Mighty Sword*, a direct-to-videotape release in the United States. See also **Sword and Sorcery.**

Ator, the Fighting Eagle (1983)
Blademaster (aka Ator, the Invincible)
    (1984)

Iron Warrior (1987)
Quest for the Mighty Sword (1990)

Auto Racing

The high-velocity thrills of auto racing date back to Howard Hawks's 1932 speedway drama *The Crowd Roars* with James Cagney as a cocky driver. Yet, despite other vintage efforts like *Speed* (1936), *Indianapolis Speedway* (a 1939 remake of *The Crowd Roars*) and *The Big Wheel* (1949), auto racing was virtually ignored by filmmakers until the late 1950s. The sport's grass-roots popularity grew rapidly in the early 1960s and so did the number of big-screen racing dramas. Some pictures catered to Southern stock car fans (e.g., 1960's *Thunder in Carolina*), while others offered European locales and sleek formula cars (e.g., 1963's *The Young Racers*). The common denominator in all these films was an inexpensive look supplemented by plenty of stock footage. Then, in 1966, director John Frankenheimer shifted racing films into high gear with his visually spectacular (but emotionally shallow) epic *Grand Prix*. With its trendy split-screen effects and international cast, *Grand Prix* made it fashionable for big stars to get behind the wheel. Paul Newman and Robert Wagner played pit stop rivals in 1969's *Winning*, and Steve McQueen took to the track in 1971's *Le Mans*. Other movies substituted real-life stories for big-name stars. Stock car legend Richard Petty played himself in 1972's *Smash-Up Alley*. Jeff Bridges portrayed Junior Jackson in *The Last American Hero* (1973), while his brother Beau played another race car driver in *Heart Like a Wheel* (1983), the biography of drag-racing champion Shirley "Cha Cha" Muldowney (Bonnie Bedelia). Beau was also in *Greased Lightning* (1977), the story of Wendell Scott (Richard Pryor), professional racing's first black driver. Of course, not all auto racing films have taken place at racetracks. Cross-country races have made popular film subjects ever since two genteel couples raced their antique roadsters across the English countryside in 1953's *Genevieve*. Blake Edwards's 1965 comedy *The Great Race* added a bevy of stars to the cross-country racing plot—a formula that's been duplicated in numerous films such as *Those Daring Young Men in Their Jaunty Jalopies* (1969), *Cannonball Run* (1981) and *Speed Zone* (1989). College campus cult movie *Death Race 2000* (1975) featured a cross-country race in which drivers earned points for running down pedestrians. See also **Automobiles** (for nonracing films); **Herbie, the Love Bug.**

The Crowd Roars (1932)
Racing Youth (1932)
Speed (1936)
Indianapolis Speedway (1939)
The Big Wheel (1949)
To Please a Lady (1950)
Genevieve (1953)
Race for Life (1954)
Johnny Dark (1954)
The Racers (aka *Such Men Are Dangerous*) (1955)
Checkpoint (1956)
The Killing (1956)
The Devil's Hairpin (1957)
Speed Crazy (1959)
Thunder in Carolina (1960)
The Green Helmet (1961)
The Young Racers (1963)
The Killers (1964)
The Lively Set (1964)
Viva Las Vegas (aka *Love in Las Vegas*) (1964)
The Great Race (1965)
Red Line 7000 (1965)
Fireball 500 (1966)
Grand Prix (1966)
Spinout (aka *California Holiday*) (1966)
A Man and a Woman (1966)
Thunder Alley (1967)
Fireball Jungle (1968)
Track of Thunder (1968)
Speed Lovers (1968)
Speedway (1968)
The Wild Racers (1968)
Drive Hard, Drive Fast (1969 TVM)

Those Daring Young Men in Their Jaunty Jalopies (aka *Monte Carlo or Bust*) (1969)
The Love Bug (1969)
Pit Stop (1969)
Winning (1969)
The Challengers (1969 TVM)
Le Mans (1971)
Corky (aka *Lookin' Good*) (1971)
Smash-Up Alley (aka *43: The Petty Story*) (1972)
Baffled (1972 TVM)
The Last American Hero (aka *Hard Driver*) (1973)
Death Race 2000 (1975)
Win, Place or Steal (1975)
Cannonball (aka *Carquake*) (1976)
The Gumball Rally (1976)
Bobby Deerfield (1977)
Checkered Flag or Crash (1977)
Greased Lightning (1977)
Bob Johnson and His Fantastic Speed Circus (1978 TVM)
The Betsy (aka *Harold Robbins' The Betsy*) (1978)
Cannonball Run (1981)
Safari 3000 (1982)
Six Pack (1982)
Heart Like a Wheel (1983)
Stroker Ace (1983)
Cannonball Run II (1984)
Born to Race (1988)
Speed Zone (1989)
Days of Thunder (1990)
Checkered Flag (1990)

Autobiographical Films

Many people have played themselves on film, but few have played themselves in film biographies. The reasons are obvious: the scarcity of motion picture biographies of *living* persons; the fact that "real" people do not necessarily make believable actors; and the image problem—that of having a big ego—created by portraying oneself in a favorable light. Sports players dominated early film autobiographies, tracing the careers of boxer Joe Louis (*Spirit of Youth*), baseball legend Jackie Robinson (*The Jackie Robinson Story*), track star Bob Mathias (*The Bob Mathias Story*), and football players Tom Harmon (*Harmon of Michigan*) and Elroy "Crazylegs" Hirsch (*Crazylegs*). None of these one-time actors went on to pursue an acting career (though Harmon's son Mark eventually did). Boxing great Muhammad Ali once said: "When you're as great as I am, it's hard to be humble." So naturally, he played himself in the modestly titled biopic *The Greatest* (1977). Actresses Ann Jillian, Sophia Loren, Shirley MacLaine, Patty Duke and Suzanne Somers all played themselves in made-for-TV biographies. MacLaine's film was adapted from her best-selling autobiography *Out on a Limb*. Ray Charles also appeared as himself in 1964's *Ballad in Blue*. To date, the best autobiographical film remains 1955's *To Hell and Back*, in which Audie Murphy traced his own rise from farm boy to the nation's most decorated soldier in World War II to movie star. Although not autobiographical, Will Rogers, Jr. played his father in *The Will Rogers Story* (1952) and Marie Osmond played her mother in *Side by Side: The True Story of the Osmond Family* (1982). In the following list, the subject's name is included in parentheses unless specified in the title. See also **Film Star Biographies.**

Spirit of Youth (1937) (Joe Louis)

Harmon of Michigan (1941) (Tom Harmon)

The Fabulous Dorseys (1947)

The Jackie Robinson Story (1950)

Crazylegs (1953) (Elroy Hirsch)

The Bob Mathias Story (1954)

To Hell and Back (1955) (Audie Murphy)

Rock Around the World (aka *The Tommy Steele Story*) (1957)

Ballad in Blue (aka *Blues for Lovers*) (1964) (Ray Charles)

Smash-Up Alley (aka *43: The Petty Story*) (1972) (Richard Petty)

The Greatest (1977) (Muhammad Ali)

Sophia Loren: Her Own Story (1980 TVM)

Victims for Victims—The Theresa Saldana Story (1984 TVM)

Out on a Limb (1987 TVM) (Shirley MacLaine)

The Ann Jillian Story (1988 TVM)

Call Me Anna (1990 TVM) (Patty Duke)

Keeping Secrets (1991 TVM) (Suzanne Somers)

Miss America: Behind the Crown (1992 TVM) (Carolyn Sapp)

Automobiles

While a number of auto-oriented movies revolve around auto racing (q.v.), they represent but one model in an eclectic line of car pictures. More imaginative auto movies have featured flying vehicles, gimmicky cars, living vehicles and high-speed car chases. Airborne autos appeared in the children's fantasies *The Absent-Minded Professor* (1961) and *Chitty Chitty Bang Bang* (1968). The latter film was adapted from a book by Ian Fleming, whose secret agent James Bond encountered an AMC Matador-turned-airplane(!) in *The Man With the Golden Gun* (1974). Bond movies are well-known for Q's gimmick-laden cars, the most memorable being the Aston-Martin in *Goldfinger* (1964). It boasted radar, machine guns, a smokescreen device, and an ejector seat that shot unwanted passengers out the roof. Its nearest competitor, gimmick-wise, was the Batmobile from 1989's *Batman*. In addition to an impressive battery of Bat-weapons, the Batmobile could be maneuvered at high speed by remote control and cover itself with protective armor in a matter of seconds. The next step up from remote-controlled vehicles are living ones. Alas, most self-functioning vehicles have exhibited a bad streak. *Christine*, a bright-red 1958 Plymouth, mowed down quite a few teens after deciding she had been insulted. *The Car* (1977) proved to be equally troublesome, as did other independent-minded vehicles in *Killdozer* (1974), *The Hearse* (1980), *Nightmares* (1983), *Maximum Overdrive* (1986) and *The Wraith* (1986). There have been friendly autos, though, such as Herbie the Love Bug (q.v.), a romance-minded Volkswagen Beetle that starred in four Disney movies. On television, Ann Sothern was reincarnated as a 1928 Porter in the 1965-66 sitcom *My Mother the Car*. In Steven Spielberg's 1971 TV-movie *Duel*, the director showed only fleeting shots of the driver of the truck dead-set on running Dennis Weaver off the road. Another 1971 picture, *Vanishing Point*, starred Barry Newman as an obsessed driver who turns a wager (Denver to San Francisco in fifteen hours) into a high-speed death drive. Consisting mostly of highway car chase footage, *Vanishing Point* attracted an enthusiastic youth audience and set the pattern for similar low-budget outings like *Dirty Mary, Crazy Larry* (1974), *Eat My Dust!* (1976), and *Grand Theft Auto* (1977). However, the most spectacular car chases of the 1970s and 1980s consisted of single extended sequences in cop thrillers, a practice perfected in the classic high-speed pursuit through San Francisco in 1967's *Bullitt*. Some films integrated the chase into the plot (e.g., *The French Connection*), while others hyped the chase scene as the main selling point (e.g., *The Seven-Ups*). Elaborate chase scenes faded in the 1980s, though William Friedkin staged a nail-grinding drive down a wrong-way street in 1985's *To Live and Die in L.A.* The 1988 Dirty Harry picture *The Dead Pool* spoofed the *Bullitt* chase with a scene of Harry being pursued through San Francisco by a remote-controlled toy roadster carrying a bomb. Of related interest, *Free for All*, *The Formula* and *The Water Engine* dealt with the invention of more cost-efficient gasoline. The cars in 1975's *Idaho Transfer* used people for fuel. See also **Auto Racing; Herbie, the Love Bug.**

Excuse My Dust (1951)	*Two-Lane Blacktop* (1971)
Jalopy (1953)	*Killdozer* (1974 TVM)
Inside Detroit (1955)	*Dirty Mary, Crazy Larry* (1974)
Young and Wild (1958)	*Cars That Eat People* (aka *The Cars*
The Absent-Minded Professor (1961)	*That Ate Paris*) (1974)
The Yellow Rolls Royce (1964)	*Gone in 60 Seconds* (1974)
Goldfinger (1964)	*The Man With the Golden Gun* (1974)
Chitty Chitty Bang Bang (1968)	*Idaho Transfer* (1975)
Traffic (aka *Trafic*) (1970)	*Eat My Dust!* (1976)
Duel (1971)	*Car Wash* (1976)
Vanishing Point (1971)	*The Car* (1977)

Double Nickels (1977)
Grand Theft Auto (1977)
Corvette Summer (1978)
Zero to Sixty (1978)
The Charge of the Model Ts (1979)
The Hearse (1980)
Used Cars (1980)
The Last Chase (1981)
Christine (1983)
Nightmares (1983)
Repo Man (1984)
Back to the Future (1985)
Car Trouble (1985)
Maximum Overdrive (1986)

Black Moon Rising (1986)
Gung Ho (1986)
The Wraith (1986)
Ford: The Man and the Machine (1987 TVM)
Tucker: The Man and the Dream (1988)
Dangerous Curves (1988)
Batman (1989)
Coupe De Ville (1990)
The Ambulance (1990)
Wheels of Terror (1990 TVM)
Drive Like Lightning (1992 TVM)

Babies

Infants have often exhibited a total disregard for adults, dropping in on unlikely fathers and unwed mothers at the most inconvenient times. *The Three Godfathers*, the story of three tough bandits who "adopt" an orphaned baby, has been filmed at least seven times as: *Bronco Billy and the Baby* (1909), *Three Godfathers* (1916), *Marked Men* (1920), *Hell's Heroes* (1929), *Three Godfathers* (1936), *Three Godfathers* (1948) and *The Godchild* (1974 TVM). John Ford's 1948 version remains the most popular, with John Wayne, Pedro Armendariz and Harry Carey, Jr. as the improbable parents. *The Baby and the Battleship* (1956) updated the premise and increased the number of dads, but still derived its humor out of showing macho males struggling helplessly to care for a little one. The same sturdy plot surfaced again in the 1985 French comedy *Three Men and a Cradle* and its 1987 American remake *Three Men and a Baby*. However, the most unlikely fathers were the dads-to-be in *Night of the Blood Beast* (1958) and *Rabbit Test* (1978) — two bizarre films about pregnant men. Unexpected infants provided the source of obvious misunderstandings for bachelorettes Ginger Rogers and Debbie Reynolds in the comedy *Bachelor Mother* (1939) and its remake *Bundle of Joy* (1956). Betty Hutton forgot who got her pregnant in Preston Sturges's *Miracle of Morgan's Creek* (1944), but her troubles ended when she gave birth to sextuplets. Tragically, no one believed the young mothers-to-be who claimed to have been blessed with immaculate conceptions in *Agnes of God* and *Hail Mary* (both 1985). A psychotic woman conceived (sans husband) "children of rage" in David Cronenberg's complex chiller *The Brood* (1979). Undesirable babies surprised their mothers in *Rosemary's Baby* (1968), *It's Alive* (1974), *The Stranger Within* (1974), *The Devil Within Her* (1975) and, most disturbingly, David Lynch's *Eraserhead* (1977). *Bobbikins* (1960), a baby who could talk like an adult, was surely a shock to his parents, too. Finally, some movies have dealt with societies that outlawed the birth of babies, as in 1971's *Zero Population Growth* and its TV-movie equivalent *The Last Child* (1971). See also **Babysitters; Child Custody Disputes; Having Babies Series; It's Alive; Governesses and Nannies; Surrogate Motherhood.**

Bronco Billy and the Baby (1909)
Three Godfathers (1916)

Marked Men (1920)
The Kid (1921)

Hell's Heroes (1929)
A Bedtime Story (1933)
Three Godfathers (aka Miracle in the Sand) (1936)
Bachelor Mother (1939)
East Side of Heaven (1939)
Little Accident (1939)
Miracle on Main Street (1939)
Miracle of Morgan's Creek (1944)
Three Godfathers (1948)
Father's Little Dividend (1951)
The Little Kidnappers (aka The Kidnappers) (1953)
The Baby and the Battleship (1956)
Bundle of Joy (1956)
Night of the Blood Beast (aka Creature From Galaxy 27) (1958)
Rock-a-Bye Baby (1958)
Unwed Mother (1958)
Bobbikins (1960)
A Global Affair (1964)
Rosemary's Baby (1968)
Zero Population Growth (aka ZPG) (1971)
The Last Child (1971 TVM)
A Brand New Life (1973 TVM)

The Godchild (1974 TVM)
It's Alive (1974)
The Stranger Within (1974 TVM)
Unwed Father (1974 TVM)
The Devil Within Her (aka I Don't Want to Be Born) (1975)
Having Babies (1976 TVM)
Eraserhead (1977)
Rabbit Test (1978)
The Brood (1979)
Possession (1981)
He's Not Your Son (1984 TVM)
Agnes of God (1985)
Hail Mary (1985)
Three Men and a Cradle (1985)
Raising Arizona (1987)
Baby Boom (1987)
Three Men and a Baby (1987)
Look Who's Talking (1989)
The Guardian (1990)
Look Who's Talking Too (1990)
Switched at Birth (1991 TVM)
Baby Snatcher (1992 TVM)
Born Too Soon (1993 TVM)
The Baby of Mâcon (1993)

Babysitters

Stalked by psychos and harassed by bratty children, it was inevitable that a babysitter or two would turn out bad. It finally happened in the 1980 TV-movie *The Babysitter*, with practically perfect sitter Stephanie Zimbalist first seducing her employer (much to the chagrin of his wife), then taking over the family and plotting murder. Diane Franklin was equally menacing in 1983's *Summer Girl*. However, nasty babysitters have been the exception, of course. More typically, they have been portrayed as helpless victims in low-grade horror fare like *Fright, Trick or Treats* and *Halloween* (though Jamie Lee Curtis managed to defend herself reasonably well). The favorite plot of babysitter comedies has been entrusting the child care to hapless males. Actually, Clifton Webb's Mr. Belvedere (q.v.) turned out to be a very capable babysitter in 1948's *Sitting Pretty*. However, Jerry Lewis played a stereotypically inept male babysitter in *Rock-a-bye Baby*, but then triplets could tax even a veteran sitter. Overall, though, the perils of babysitting were best explored in the hectic 1987 comedy *Adventures in Babysitting*. Teen sitter Elisabeth Shue and her charges somehow transformed a dull night of TV watching into a wild series of connected adventures through the streets of Chicago. Fortunately, they still made it back home before the parents' return, but only by a matter of seconds. Marilyn Monroe made the least likely of all babysitters, portraying a mentally disturbed one contemplating suicide in 1952's *Don't Bother to*

Knock. See also **Babies** (for films like *Three Men and a Baby*); **Belvedere, Mr.** **(Lynn); Governesses and Nannies.**

Sitting Pretty (1948)	*Trick or Treats* (1982)
Don't Bother to Knock (1952)	*Summer Girl* (1983 TVM)
Rock-a-Bye Baby (1958)	*First Affair* (1983 TVM)
The Babysitter (1969)	*Rita, Sue and Bob, Too* (1986)
Fright (1971)	*Adventures in Babysitting* (1987)
The Babysitter (aka *Wanted:*	*Uncle Buck* (1989)
Babysitter) (1975)	*Don't Tell Mom the Babysitter's Dead*
Halloween (1978)	(1991)
When a Stranger Calls (1979)	*The Sitter* (1991 TVM)
The Babysitter (1980 TVM)	

Back to the Future

Robert Zemeckis was a University of Southern California film student when he met wunderkind director Steven Spielberg during the 1973 filming of *Sugarland Express*. Spielberg went on to play a crucial role in Zemeckis's Hollywood career, acting as executive producer of his first film (1978's *I Wanna Hold Your Hand*) and directing the Zemeckis-Bob Gale script *1941* (1979). Yet, despite Spielberg's support, Zemeckis found few studios interested in a time travel comedy he cowrote with Gale in 1980. Then Zemeckis hit the big time with 1984's lighthearted adventure *Romancing the Stone*. With a big hit to his credit, his script for *Back to the Future* became a hot property. Eric Stoltz, best known for his acclaimed performance as Rocky Dennis in 1985's *Mask*, was cast in the lead role of Marty McFly. However, after five weeks of filming, Zemeckis decided that Stoltz was not right for the part. He replaced Stoltz with Michael J. Fox, who was still filming his TV series *Family Ties*. Despite some mixed reviews (which some critics will probably now deny), 1985's *Back to the Future* went on to become a monster hit and transform Fox from a TV personality to a film star. The film's plot sent teenager Marty back in time (via a modified DeLorean sports car) to 1955. He encounters his parents as high schoolers and, in something of an Oedipal twist, has to fend off the advances of his mother. Marty's presence in the past gradually threatens his existence in the future, for if his mother doesn't marry his father, the McFly family will cease to exist. Fox, in a very appealing performance, received excellent support from Christopher Lloyd as Dr. Emmett Brown and from Lea Thompson and Crispin Glover as Marty's parents. The 1989 sequel, *Back to the Future II*, confused most viewers with a complex plot sending Marty and Doc to various points in time. The series' third installment, *Back to the Future III*, was filmed concurrently and released less than six months later. It found Marty and Doc in the Old West, with Mary Steenburgen on hand as a love interest for Doc Brown. An animated *Back to the Future* TV series ran briefly on Saturday mornings. See also **Time Travel.**

Back to the Future (1985)	*Back to the Future III* (1990)
Back to the Future II (1989)	

Backwoods Feuds

The bitter, deadly feud between the Hatfields and the McCoys served as the basis for two films: 1949's *Roseanna McCoy* with Joan Evans in the title role and the 1975

TV-movie *The Hatfields and the McCoys*, with Karen Lamm as Rose Ann McCoy. Dramatically, however, both these films probably owed more to *Romeo and Juliet* than to the real-life feuding families. The fictitious *Trail of the Lonesome Pine* (1936) earned a place in cinema history as the first outdoor movie shot completely in Technicolor. It may also be the best feudin' film, with memorable performances by Fred MacMurray and Henry Fonda. Other serious films about backwoods feuds include *Lolly Madonna XXX* (1973) and the subdued Kurt Russell-Kelly McGillis vehicle *Winter People* (1989). Feuds have provided a rich source of gags for many comedians, such as Buster Keaton (*Our Hospitality*), Abbott and Costello (*Comin' Round the Mountain*), the Bowery Boys (*Feudin' Fools*), and Donald O'Connor (*Feudin', Fussin' and A-Fightin'*). The latter film also featured Marjorie Main and Percy Kilbride, though not officially as Ma and Pa Kettle (q.v.).

Our Hospitality (1923)
Kentucky Kernels (1934)
In Old Kentucky (1935)
Trail of the Lonesome Pine (1936)
Kentucky Moonshine (1938)
Feudin', Fussin' and A-Fightin' (1948)
Roseanna McCoy (1949)

Comin' Round the Mountain (1951)
Feudin' Fools (1952)
Lolly Madonna XXX (aka *The Lolly Madonna War*) (1973)
The Hatfields and the McCoys (1975 TVM)
Winter People (1989)

The Bad News Bears

The combination of Walter Matthau as a beer-guzzling coach and Tatum O'Neal as a foul-mouthed, female pitcher turned this little league baseball comedy into a surprise 1976 hit. Neither star appeared in the 1977 follow-up *The Bad News Bears in Breaking Training*, which weighed down the comedy with a large dose of sentiment. William Devane played the team's new coach. But he too was nowhere to be found in 1978's *The Bad News Bears Go to Japan*, a weak outing that ended the series. Young Jackie Earle Haley was the only Bear to star in all three films. A half-hour CBS TV series aired briefly during 1979. See also **Baseball**.

The Bad News Bears (1976)
The Bad News Bears in Breaking Training (1977)
The Bad News Bears Go to Japan (1978)

Baines, Scattergood

Guy Kibbee starred as Clarence Budington Kelland's genial country philosopher in this RKO series. Actually, the films were produced by little Pyramid Pictures Corporation, which convinced RKO that a six-film series based on the popular radio program was bound to be profitable. It wasn't — the public never warmed up to Scattergood, not even when RKO tried to hide the fact that a movie was part of the series (the studio changed the title of *Scattergood Swings It* to *Cinderella Swings It*). Nevertheless, the storekeeper of Coldriver stayed busy for three years, helping horseback orphans (*Scattergood Rides High*) and would-be recording stars (*Cinderella Swings It*).

Scattergood Baines (1941)
Scattergood Meets Broadway (1941)
Scattergood Pulls the Strings (1941)
Scattergood Rides High (1942)

Scattergood Survives a Murder (1942)
Cinderella Swings It (aka *Scattergood Swings It*) (1943)

Ballet/Ballerinas

The challenge of integrating a dynamic theatrical art form into the confines of cinema has proven to be a difficult task. Consequently, it has been undertaken almost exclusively by filmmakers/ballet lovers, whose artistic successes have been mixed equally with unmitigated failures. British filmmakers Michael Powell and Emeric Pressburger produced two outstanding ballet films, with Powell also contributing a third, less memorable solo effort. The first Powell-Pressburger ballet film was 1948's *The Red Shoes*, which starred real-life ballerina Moira Shearer as a young dancer driven to her death by her inability to choose between ballet and a "normal" life. The highlight of this dazzling, colorful film is a fourteen-minute ballet of Hans Christian Andersen's fairy tale "The Red Shoes," brilliantly danced and photographed against stylized sets. The elaborate sets returned in 1951's *Tales of Hoffman*, a fusion of drama, singing and ballet based on Offenbach's opera and featuring ballerina Shearer again. Powell turned to ballet once more, sans Pressburger, in 1959's all-but-forgotten *Honeymoon*, which featured excerpts from the Spanish ballets "Los Amantes de Teruel" and "El Amor Brujo." The most interesting pre-*Red Shoes* ballet picture was *The Specter of the Rose* (1946), an offbeat drama about a young dancer who is slowly losing his mind. It featured a rare screen appearance by drama teacher Michael Chekhov and the potent presence of Dame Judith Anderson. Gene Kelly, after choreographing a modern ballet for a set-piece in *An American in Paris* (1951), incorporated ballet into his all-dance 1957 picture *Invitation to the Dance*. Shot in 1952, this three-part anthology boasted energetic dancing and clever direction (including a combination of live action and cartoon), but it crashed at the box office and almost ended Kelly's career. In contrast, Herbert Ross's *The Turning Point* (1977) was a solid popular and critical favorite. Shirley MacLaine and Anne Bancroft had the starring roles as a pair of former ballerinas, but Mikhail Baryshnikov stole the film every time he took to the dance floor. Ballets filmed in their entirety have been rare, but have nevertheless been captured in *Peter Rabbit and the Tales of Beatrix Potter* (1971), *Nutcracker* (1982) and *Nutcracker: The Motion Picture* (1986). Numerous films, not expressly about ballet, have featured ballerinas as principal characters. The roll call of actresses who have played ballerinas is a varied one: Greta Garbo (*Grand Hotel*); Maureen O'Hara (*Dance, Girl, Dance*); Vivien Leigh (*Waterloo Bridge*); Loretta Young (*The Men in Her Life*); Margaret O'Brien (*The Unfinished Dance*); Janet Leigh (*The Red Danube*); Gene Tierney (*Never Let Me Go*); and Leslie Caron (*Gaby*). Ballet segments have highlighted many mainstream musicals, though the sequences in *An American in Paris* and *On Your Toes* stand out.

Grand Hotel (1932)	*The Red Shoes* (1948)
On Your Toes (1939)	*The Red Danube* (1949)
Dance, Girl, Dance (1940)	*Illicit Interlude* (aka *Summer Play*;
Waterloo Bridge (1940)	*Summer Interlude*) (1950)
The Men in Her Life (1941)	*An American in Paris* (1951)
The Dancing Masters (1943)	*Tales of Hoffman* (1951)
The Specter of the Rose (1946)	*Limelight* (1952)
Carnival (1946)	*Never Let Me Go* (1953)
The Unfinished Dance (1947)	*Dance Little Lady* (1955)
The Imperfect Lady (1947)	*Gaby* (1956)

Meet Me in Las Vegas (aka *Viva Las Vegas*) (1956)
Invitation to the Dance (1957)
Angel in a Taxi (1959)
Honeymoon (1959)
Vampire and the Ballerina (1962)
Peter Rabbit and the Tales of Beatrix Potter (aka *The Tales of Beatrix Potter*) (1971)
The Turning Point (1977)
Slow Dancing in the Big City (1978)

Nutcracker (1982)
The Cowboy and the Ballerina (1984 TVM)
Nutcracker: The Motion Picture (1986)
Dancers (1987)
Dancing for Mr. B: Six Balanchine Ballerinas (1989)
Brain Donors (1992)
George Balanchine's The Nutcracker (1993)

Balloons, Hot Air

Phileas Fogg may be the world's most famous balloonist, but *Around the World in Eighty Days* is but one of several balloon movies (indeed, Phileas's balloon flight is relatively short). Red Buttons and Barbara Eden spent *Five Weeks in a Balloon* in Irwin Allen's 1962 adaptation of Jules Verne's adventure tale. Civil War prisoners escaped via a hot air balloon and blew off course onto a *Mysterious Island* (1961) in another Verne-inspired epic. Toto's mad dash from the Wizard's hot air balloon kept Dorothy from returning home in a conventional fashion in *The Wizard of Oz* (1939). Good thing she kept those ruby slippers. Katharine Hepburn helped two children launch a balloon—and nearly land on an orchestra conductor—in *Olly, Olly, Oxen Free* (1978), while a boy and his grandfather made a transcontinental flight in the 1981 TV-movie *Charlie and the Great Balloon Chase*. James Bond (Roger Moore) made an unexpected arrival via hot air balloon in *Octopussy* (1983). Jessica Lange took a pleasure ride with Joan Cusack in 1990's *Men Don't Leave*. Baron von Munchausen can be credited for creating the most inventive hot air balloon—one made of ladies' bloomers—in 1989's *The Adventures of Baron Munchausen*. See also **Dirigibles**.

Queen of the Jungle (1935)
Penrod's Double Trouble (1938)
The Wizard of Oz (1939)
Around the World in Eighty Days (1956)
Flight of the Lost Balloon (1961)
Mysterious Island (1961)
Five Weeks in a Balloon (1962)
Those Magnificent Men in Their Flying Machines (1965)
The Great Race (1965)
Chitty Chitty Bang Bang (1968)
Charlie Bubbles (1968)

Olly, Olly, Oxen Free (aka *The Great Balloon Adventure*) (1978)
Charlie and the Great Balloon Chase (1981 TVM)
Night Crossing (1981)
The Flight of the Eagle (1982)
Octopussy (1983)
Cloud Waltzing (1987 TVM)
The Adventures of Baron Munchausen (1989)
It Nearly Wasn't Christmas (1989 TVM)
Men Don't Leave (1990)

Bancroft, Brass

A promising young star named Ronald Reagan played secret service agent Brass Bancroft in a series of four Warner Bros. programmers, beginning with 1939's *Secret Service of the Air*. The films were inspired by the memoirs of William H.

Moran, a former secret service chief. Reagan's heroics, though, were strictly Saturday afternoon kid's stuff. Brass fought smugglers, counterfeiters, and experimental death rays in his brief career. In real life, Reagan fought Warner Bros. to shelve his second Bancroft film, *Code of the Secret Service*, because he felt it was unfit for release. Director Bryan Foy backed Reagan, and Warner Bros. compromised (slightly) by not releasing the film in Los Angeles. Eddie Foy, Jr., the director's brother, played Brass's sidekick Gabby Watters.

Secret Service of the Air (1939)	*Smashing the Money Ring* (1939)
Code of the Secret Service (1939)	*Murder in the Air* (1940)

Barbers/Hairdressers

On those rare occasions when hairdressers are featured characters in a film, their profession rarely receives much exposure. Murder witness Kim Basinger could have easily been mistaken for a model instead of a hairdresser in *Nadine* (1987). Likewise, the fact that Frances McDormand's character was a beautician in *Mississippi Burning* (1988) had little bearing on the plot. Still, hairdressers have made a major impact in a handful of films. Warren Beatty played an amorous one in his 1975 hit *Shampoo*, and Julie Walters received an Oscar nomination for portraying an uneducated hairdresser seeking to better herself intellectually in 1983's *Educating Rita*. *Sweeney Todd, the Demon Barber of Fleet Street* (1936) was about a barber who killed his customers and turned them into "meat pies." Composer Stephen Sondheim transformed the same story into the Broadway musical smash *Sweeney Todd*.

Smart Money (1931)	*Educating Rita* (1983)
Diplomaniacs (1933)	*Old Enough* (1984)
Sweeney Todd, the Demon Barber of Fleet Street (1936)	*Nadine* (1987)
Keep Fit (1937)	*Conspiracy of Love* (1987 TVM)
The Great Dictator (1940)	*Mississippi Burning* (1988)
Abbott and Costello in Hollywood (aka *Bud Abbott and Lou Costello in Hollywood*) (1945)	*Getting It Right* (1989)
	Steel Magnolias (1989)
	Earth Girls Are Easy (1989)
Monsieur Beaucaire (1946)	*Skin Deep* (1989)
Wait 'Til the Sun Shines, Nellie (1952)	*Highway 61* (1991)
The Adventures of Hajji Baba (1954)	*Stan and George's New Life* (1991)
Staircase (1969)	*Victor's Big Score* (1992)
Five on the Back Hand Side (1973)	*The Crying Game* (1992)
Shampoo (1975)	*Who's the Man?* (1993)
Outrageous! (1977)	*Poetic Justice* (1993)

Barton, Dick

Barton, a British Dick Tracy (q.v.), evolved from a popular 1948 radio series. Don Stannard played him in three low-budget movies. The series concluded following the actor's death in 1949.

Dick Barton, Detective (aka *Dick Barton, Special Agent*) (1949)	*Dick Barton Strikes Back* (1949)
	Dick Barton at Bay (1950)

Baseball

Football may have been played in more movies, but no sport surpasses baseball in providing subjects for inspirational film biographies. Lou Gehrig, Babe Ruth, Dizzy Dean, Grover Cleveland Alexander, Jackie Robinson, Jimmy Piersall, Ron LeFlore, Roy Campanella and Monty Stratton have all had their stories brought to the screen — often with conviction, almost always with sentiment. Baseball fantasies have proven to be popular, too. In *It Happens Every Spring* (1949), college professor Ray Milland became a star pitcher for St. Louis when he accidentally invented a chemical that repelled wood (i.e., baseball bats). The Devil and an angel turned last-place teams into winners in, respectively, *Damn Yankees* (1958) and *Angels in the Outfield* (1951). In 1989's *Field of Dreams*, Kevin Costner built a baseball diamond in lieu of planting crops, so the legendary Shoeless Joe Jackson and other heavenly ball players would have a place to play their beloved game. Most filmmakers have preferred to gloss over the game's darker days, although John Sayles's *Eight Men Out* (1988) presented a factual account of the 1919 "Black Sox" scandal. Corruption was also an issue in 1984's *The Natural*, an unusual morality tale of a highly gifted player (Robert Redford) confronted by temptation and evil. Baseball comedies have ranged from the hilarious to the ridiculous, with some of the more successful ones incorporating unusual angles. *Rhubarb* (1951) was about a baseball team owned by a cat. *The Bad News Bears* (1976) were a team of foul-mouthed little leaguers transformed into winners by a beer-guzzling coach Walter Matthau. Abbott and Costello recreated their famous vaudeville baseball routine "Who's on First?" in 1945's *The Naughty Nineties*. Films about female baseball/softball players include *Aunt Mary* (1979), *Squeeze Play* (1980), and the 1992 fact-based hit *A League of Their Own*. See also **The Bad News Bears.**

> *Elmer the Great* (1933)
> *Death on the Diamond* (1934)
> *Alibi Ike* (1935)
> *The Pride of the Yankees* (1942)
> *The Naughty Nineties* (1945)
> *The Babe Ruth Story* (1948)
> *It Happens Every Spring* (1949)
> *The Kid From Cleveland* (1949)
> *The Stratton Story* (1949)
> *Take Me Out to the Ball Game* (1949)
> *Kill the Umpire* (1950)
> *The Jackie Robinson Story* (1950)
> *Angels in the Outfield* (1951)
> *Rhubarb* (1951)
> *The Winning Team* (1952)
> *The Pride of St. Louis* (1952)
> *The Kid From Left Field* (1953)
> *The Big Leaguer* (1953)
> *Roogie's Bump!* (1954)
> *The Great American Pastime* (1956)
> *Fear Strikes Out* (1957)
> *Damn Yankees* (1958)

> *Moochie of the Little League* (1959)
> *Safe at Home!* (1962)
> *Bang the Drum Slowly* (1973)
> *It's Good to Be Alive* (1974 TVM)
> *The Bad News Bears* (1976)
> *The Bingo Long Travelling All-Stars and Motor Kings* (1976)
> *Murder at the World Series* (1978 TVM)
> *One in a Million: The Ron LeFlore Story* (1978 TVM)
> *Here Come the Tigers* (aka *Manny's Orphans*) (1978)
> *A Love Affair: The Eleanor and Lou Gehrig Story* (1978 TVM)
> *Aunt Mary* (1979 TVM)
> *The Kid From Left Field* (1979 TVM)
> *Squeeze Play* (1980)
> *The Comeback Kid* (1980 TVM)
> *Don't Look Back: The Story of Leroy "Satchel" Paige* (1981 TVM)
> *Chasing Dreams* (1982)

Million Dollar Infield (1982 TVM)
Tiger Town (1983 TVM)
Blue Skies Again (1983)
The Natural (1984)
Brewster's Millions (1985)
The Slugger's Wife (1985)
A Winner Never Quits (1986 TVM)
Long Gone (1987 TVM)
Bull Durham (1988)
Eight Men Out (1988)
Stealing Home (1988)
Trading Hearts (1988)
Major League (1989)

Field of Dreams (1989)
Night Game (1989)
The Court-Martial of Jackie Robinson
    (1990 TVM)
Blood Games (1991)
Pastime (aka One Cup of Coffee)
    (1991) (about the minor leagues)
Talent for the Game (1991)
A League of Their Own (1992)
Mr. Baseball (1992)
The Sandlot (1993)
Rookie of the Year (1993)

Basket Case

Frank Henenlotter's original *Basket Case* (1982) mixed gore and black comedy with enough wit to earn a cult reputation among midnight movie fans and mainstream film critics. The plot centered on Duane and Belial Bradley, Siamese twins severed at birth by quack doctors who tossed the hideously deformed Belial into the garbage. Belial survives and is eventually reunited with Duane (Kevin Van Hentenryck), with whom he has formed a telepathic bond. With Belial in a wicker basket, Duane heads to New York City to take revenge on the unsuspecting doctors. Belial, despite being a homicidal monster, earns viewer sympathy for most of the film (until he kills Duane's girlfriend in a tasteless scene). Shot over three years, *Basket Case*'s reputation can be attributed chiefly to Henenlotter's quirky humor and offbeat supporting characters. These same qualities were present, but to lesser effect, in Henenlotter's long-awaited sequel, 1990's *Basket Case 2*. It found Duane (Van Hentenryck again) and Belial taking refuge in the Staten Island home of Granny Ruth (jazz singer Annie Ross), who provides sanctuary to a variety of freaks. Duane and Belial fall in love with Siamese twins Susan and Eve, but a nosy reporter interrupts their bliss and Susan winds up dead. In *Basket Case 3: The Progeny* (1992), Eve becomes pregnant and has a "litter" of little mutant babies. The children are kidnapped by some nasty Southern deputies, who naturally receive their comeuppance in gruesome fashion. The two sequels borrowed their basic premise from Tod Browning's 1932 classic *Freaks*: "Normal" people were portrayed as cruel and thoughtless, while the "freaks" were presented as caring individuals who simply wanted to be left alone. Unfortunately, neither *Basket Case* sequel matched the first film's inventiveness. Henenlotter fared much better with his gory Frankenstein (q.v.) satire *Frankenhooker* (1990). See also **Twins**.

Basket Case (1982)   Basket Case 3: The Progeny (1992)
Basket Case 2 (1990)

Basketball

While other sports films, particularly those involving baseball and football, have devoted extensive footage to real-life personalities, basketball movies have emphasized fiction over fact. Naturally, there have been a few exceptions. *The Harlem*

Globetrotters (1951) and *Go, Man, Go* (1954) employed realistic settings, even though they took dramatic license with their plots. *Hoosiers* (1986) was a fact-based story about a small-town Indiana high school team that staged an amazing series of upsets en route to a state title. However, most basketball movies have opted for make-believe tales that climax in dramatic, last-minute "buzzer shots," as in 1977's *One on One*. For a change of pace, *The Absent-Minded Professor* and *Teen Wolf* featured some rather bizarre basketball games. In the former film, professor Fred MacMurray ironed "flubber" onto the shoes of his college's team, allowing the players to bounce higher than the backboard. In *Teen Wolf*, mediocre player Michael J. Fox suddenly transformed into a basketball phenomenon after becoming a werewolf. Anthony Perkins (*Tall Story*) and Robby Benson (*One on One*) played more conventional star players. Inspirational coaches have been played by Robert Mitchum (*That Championship Season*), Bruce Dern (*Drive, He Said*), Gabe Kaplan (*Fast Break*), and Cathy Lee Crosby (*Coach*). And real-life players have appeared in *Cornbread, Earl and Me* (Jamaal Wilkes), *The Fish That Saved Pittsburgh* (Kareem Abdul Jabbar, Meadowlark Lemon, Julius Erving), and *Amazing Grace and Chuck* (Alex English).

Here Come the Coeds (1945)	*Inside Moves* (1980)
The Harlem Globetrotters (1951)	*The Harlem Globetrotters on Gilligan's*
Go, Man, Go (1954)	*Island* (1981 TVM)
Tall Story (1960)	*That Championship Season* (1982)
The Absent-Minded Professor (1961)	*Teen Wolf* (1985)
Drive, He Said (1971)	*Porky's Revenge* (1985)
Shirts/Skins (1973 TVM)	*Hoosiers* (1986)
Maurie (aka *Big Mo*) (1973 TVM)	*Amazing Grace and Chuck* (1987)
Mixed Company (1974)	*Laker Girls* (1990 TVM)
Cornbread, Earl and Me (1975)	*The Pistol* (aka *The Pistol: Birth of a*
One on One (1977)	*Legend*) (1990)
The Greatest Thing That Almost	*Heaven Is a Playground* (1991)
Happened (1977 TVM)	*One Special Victory* (1991 TVM)
Coach (1978)	*Final Shot: The Hank Gathers Story*
Fast Break (1979)	(1992 TVM)
The Fish That Saved Pittsburgh (1979)	

Beach Party Series

1959's *Gidget* (q.v.) and 1960's *Where the Boys Are* may have been the first mainstream pictures to put teens on the beach, but AIP's *Beach Party* (1963) was the one that spawned six sequels, accounted for countless clones, and made teen stars of Frankie Avalon and Annette Funicello. The formula was simple: Start with swimsuit-clad teens, add a way-out motorcycle gang, some cameos by aging stars (e.g., Buster Keaton, Boris Karloff), and plenty of surf music (provided by the likes of Dick Dale and the Del-Tones, the Hondells, and Little Stevie Wonder). In addition to Frankie and Annette, the regulars included Harvey (*Stalag 17*) Lembeck as bike gang leader Eric Von Zipper and Jody McCrea (Joel's son) as Bonehead. Tommy Kirk and one-time *Gidget* Deborah Walley took over for Frankie and Annette in the final series entry, 1966's *The Ghost in the Invisible Bikini*. Annette played the female lead in the first six films, while Frankie headlined four films and made cameo appearances in two others. The Frankie substitutes were Tommy Kirk (a Martian teen in 1964's *Pajama Party*) and Dwayne Hickman (1965's *How to Stuff a Wild Bikini*). *Beach Blanket Bingo* is considered the best of the Beach Party pictures and still shows up on TV regularly. In 1987, Frankie and Annette tried to spoof their old images in *Back to the Beach*, a nostalgic but generally overdone effort. See also **Gidget**.

Beach Party (1963)	*How to Stuff a Wild Bikini* (1965)
Muscle Beach Party (1964)	*The Ghost in the Invisible Bikini*
Bikini Beach (1964)	(1966)
Pajama Party (1964)	*Back to the Beach* (1987)
Beach Blanket Bingo (1965)	

The AIP Beach Party series also fostered rival mid-1960s sand-and-surf pictures, such as:

Ride the Wild Surf (1964)	*The Girls on the Beach* (1965)
For Those Who Think Young (1964)	*Beach Ball* (1965)
The Horror of Party Beach (aka	*Seaside Swingers* (1965)
Invasion of the Zombies) (1964)	*It's a Bikini World* (1967)
Surf Party (1964)	

Bears

Someone at Walt Disney Productions must have had a soft spot for bears, for the company produced four pictures about the furry forest denizens between 1947 and 1974. The first two were animated bears, Brer Bear in *The Song of the South* (1947) and Baloo in *The Jungle Book* (1967). As voiced by Phil Harris, Baloo has the distinction of being the only bear to sing an Oscar-nominated song—"Bare Necessities." The real-life Disney bears proved to be considerably less talented, and as a consequence, *King of the Grizzlies* (1970) and *The Bears and I* (1974) were also less entertaining. *Gentle Giant* (1967), a juvenile tale about a boy with a pet 650-pound black bear, could have passed for a Disney production. Its modest box office success led to a 1967-69 TV series starring Clint Howard (Ron's brother) and Dennis Weaver. Clint Walker encountered a less sociable bear in the climax of *Night of the Grizzly* (1966), while another wild bear mauled Richard Harris and left him for dead in *Man in the Wilderness* (1971). Christopher George had the worst luck with bears, battling an 18-foot, 2000-pounder in the 1976 *Jaws* rip-off *Grizzly* and then running into another one in the following year's *Day of the Animals* (actually, this latter bear was nice enough to dispose of troublemaker Leslie Nielsen). The mutant, pollution-made monster in John Frankenheimer's *Prophecy* (1979) looked like a conglomeration of several animals, but it was probably more bear than anything else. In the offbeat 1961 fantasy *The Two Little Bears*, Eddie Albert discovered that his two little children could turn into bear cubs at night. Director-actor Jean Renoir dressed as a bear to attend a climactic country manor costume party in his classic social satire *The Rules of the Game* (1939). Natassja Kinski sported a bear costume as well in John Irving's *The Hotel New Hampshire* (1984). In the 1978 TV-movie *B.J. and the Bear*, the "Bear" turned out to be a chimpanzee. Apparently, that was supposed to be funny.

Song of the South (1947)	*Hey There, It's Yogi Bear* (1964)
The Two Little Bears (1961)	*Night of the Grizzly* (1966)

The Jungle Book (1967)
Gentle Giant (1967)
King of the Grizzlies (1970)
Man in the Wilderness (1971)
The Bears and I (1974)
Grizzly (aka Killer Grizzly) (1976)

The Life and Times of Grizzly Adams
  (1976)
Day of the Animals (1977)
Prophecy (1979)
The Bear (1989)

Beauty Contests

Behind-the-scene exposés of the beauty pageant business, complete with bickering contestants and deceitful judges, have been the subject of *Contest Girl* (1964), *The Great American Beauty Contest* (1973), *Smile* (1975) and *Miss All-American Beauty* (1982). Ironically, while these films sought to criticize beauty contests, they are best remembered for the exposure they provided attractive young actresses such as Diane Lane, Farrah Fawcett, Melanie Griffith and Annette O'Toole. The lighthearted side of beauty contests was on display in 1950's *Peggy*, the story of a Rose Bowl queen, and 1951's *Lady Godiva Rides Again*, which introduced Joan Collins as a young contestant. A nonexistent woman won a beauty contest when Dick Powell submitted a composite photograph in the 1935 comedy *Page Miss Glory*. Carolyn Sapp played herself in 1992's *Miss America: Behind the Crown*, which focused on her relationship with an abusive boyfriend. *The Queen* was a well-received 1968 documentary about a beauty pageant for transvestites.

Case of the Lucky Legs (1935)
Page Miss Glory (1935)
Waikiki Wedding (1937)
The Crystal Ball (1943)
The Duchess of Idaho (1950)
Peggy (1950)
Lady Godiva Rides Again (1951)
Hear Me Good (1957)
Contest Girl (aka The Beauty Jungle)
  (1964)

The Queen (1968)
The Great American Beauty Contest
  (1973 TVM)
Smile (1975)
The Night They Took Miss Beautiful
  (1977 TVM)
Miss All-American Beauty (1982 TVM)
Miss Firecracker (1989)
Miss America: Behind the Crown
  (1992 TVM)

The Becker Family, *see* Children of the Bride

Belvedere, Mr. (Lynn)

Clifton Webb created the pompous, but likable, genius Lynn Belvedere in 1948's *Sitting Pretty*, in which Robert Young and Maureen O'Hara hired the fifty-nine-year-old as a babysitter (q.v.). The film inspired two sequels, sending Belvedere back to college and then to stir things up at a home for the elderly. Webb played a similar character in 1953's *Mister Scoutmaster*.

Sitting Pretty (1948)
Mr. Belvedere Goes to College (1949)

Mr. Belvedere Rings the Bell (1951)

Benji

What do a man-eating shark and a playful pooch have in common? Both were the subject of major hit films in 1975. While *Jaws* garnered waves of free publicity,

Benji, a 1974 release, built its family-oriented following on word-of-mouth. No one expected Joe Camp's Texas-shot, canine kiddie feature to snowball into a box office heavyweight. The familiar story thrust a stray little dog into a kidnap plot involving two youngsters. *Benji*, as played by a canine actor named Higgins, exuded plenty of charm, and the low-camera angles playfully conveyed a dog's point-of-view. The 1977 follow-up, *For the Love of Benji*, found the little pooch in Athens, with enemy spies seeking a valuable formula stamped on his paw. This sequel failed to duplicate the success of its predecessor, causing Camp to make a major miscalculation with his third Benji film. *Oh, Heavenly Dog!* starred Chevy Chase as a murder victim who returns to Earth as a dog to find his killer (a plot reversal of 1951's superior *You Never Can Tell*). Chevy as Benji (he voiced the dog's thoughts) lacked the charm of Benji as himself. Furthermore, the film's romance elements seemed aimed at adults. After a seven-year hiatus, Camp returned to his original formula with *Benji: The Hunted*, a children's film in which our canine hero "adopts" two orphaned cougar cubs. See also **Dogs**.

Benji (1974)	*Oh, Heavenly Dog!* (1980)
For the Love of Benji (1977)	*Benji: The Hunted* (1987)

Bermuda Triangle

In the mid-1970s, Charles Berlitz published two books about this site of several inexplicable disappearances in the Atlantic Ocean. A brief flurry of movie activity followed, beginning with 1974's made-for-TV feature *Satan's Triangle* and the pseudodocumentary *The Devil's Triangle*. Similar subpar films came in quick succession. Berlitz went on to write about Atlantis, Noah's Ark, and how to speak Italian, French and German.

The Devil's Triangle (1974)	*Mysteries From Beyond the Bermuda*
Satan's Triangle (1974 TVM)	*Triangle* (1977)
Beyond the Bermuda Triangle (1975 TVM)	*The Bermuda Triangle* (1978)
	The Bermuda Depths (1978 TVM)

A Better Tomorrow

This violent gangster series smashed box office records in its native Hong Kong and also scored well in many other Southeast Asian markets. American critics have praised the films, comparing them to the tough, fast-paced Warner Bros. gangster pictures of the 1930s. Produced and cowritten by Tsui Hark, 1986's *A Better Tomorrow* focused primarily on an explosive contemporary gangster named Cheung Chi-Keung (or Mark in subtitled prints). The role made a star of actor Chow Yun Fat but also created a dilemma for writer Hark, who killed off the lead character in the film's climax. Using a plot device familiar to American TV soap fans, Hark brought back Chow Yun Fat as Mark's revenge-minded twin brother Ken in *A Better Tomorrow II* (1988). However, Chow Yun Fat was back as Mark for *A Better Tomorrow III* (1989), a prequel (q.v.) set in Saigon in 1974. The plot centered on Mark's efforts to secure exit visas for relatives. When a North Vietnamese soldier double-crossed him, Mark rectified the situation in a bloody shoot-out. Although the *Better Tomorrow* films received very limited showings in the United States, their subject matter would make them ideal candidates for English-language remakes.

A Better Tomorrow (1986)	*A Better Tomorrow III* (aka *Love and*
A Better Tomorrow II (1988)	*Death in Saigon*) (1989)

Bicycles

Vittorio De Sica's touching 1949 Italian classic *The Bicycle Thief* chronicled a poor man's desperate search for the stolen bicycle on which his family's livelihood depended. *Breaking Away* (1979) and *American Flyers* (1985), both written by cycling enthusiast Steve Tesich, dealt with amateur riders and their infatuation with bike racing. Stockbroker Kevin Bacon dropped out of the rat race and became a bicycle messenger in *Quicksilver* (1986). Many movies have featured bicycles in memorable scenes, including *E.T.*, *Butch Cassidy and the Sundance Kid*, and *The Wizard of Oz* (Toto jumping off the back of Miss Gulch's two-wheeler).

Six Day Bike Rider (1934)	*Breaking Away* (1979)
A Boy, a Girl, and a Bike (1947)	*BMX Bandits* (1983)
The Bicycle Thief (1949)	*American Flyers* (1985)
Isn't Life Wonderful? (1952)	*Pee Wee's Big Adventure* (1985)
Smiley (1957)	*Quicksilver* (1986)
And Soon the Darkness (1970)	*Rad* (1986)
The Gang That Couldn't Shoot	
Straight (1971)	

Big Town Series

A CBS radio program provided the inspiration for this short-lived Paramount film series about crusading newspaper editor Steve Wilson (Philip Reed). Hillary Brooke played police reporter Lorelei Kilbourne, Wilson's spunky sidekick.

Big Town (aka *Guilty Assignment*) (1947)
Big Town After Dark (aka *Underworld After Dark*) (1947)
I Cover Big Town (aka *I Cover the Underworld*) (1947)
Big Town Scandal (1948)

Bigamy

It is amazing that so few filmmakers have explored the dramatic possibilities inherent in a serious film about bigamy. It's as if a discouraging cloud of "uncomfortableness" hung over the subject matter. Interestingly, a woman (Ida Lupino) directed one of the first serious films about a bigamous husband, 1953's appropriately titled *The Bigamist*. Although it failed to probe deeply into its protagonist's motivations, it was superior to 1988's *Double Standard* and 1993's *The Man With Three Wives*, two pointless TV-movies "inspired by true-life cases." The cinema's inability to deal seriously with bigamy has resulted in a plethora of multiple-marriage comedies. William Bendix, an unlikely candidate for bigamy, traveled up and down New York state visiting his two wives in *Don Juan Quilligan* (1945). Alec Guinness played a ferryboat captain with a wife in every port (well, two ports to be exact) in 1953's hilarious *Captain's Paradise*. Other male bigamists have included Rex Harrison (*The Constant Husband*), Clifton Webb (*The Remarkable Mr. Pennypacker*), and Dudley Moore (*Micki and Maude*). Female bigamists have been rare in the movies, perhaps reflecting a male chauvinistic attitude among filmmakers. Karen Valentine played a stewardess with multiple families in *Coffee,*

Tea, or Me (1972). Dyan Cannon's fashion design business allowed her to keep a husband on each coast in *Having It All* (1982). Sally Field lived with two husbands in *Kiss Me Goodbye* (1982), but one of them was a ghost (thus, according to the law, she was not a bigamist). Jean Seberg had two husbands in the gold rush musical *Paint Your Wagon* (1969), but that's only because Lee Marvin and Clint Eastwood bought her wifely services jointly at an auction. The movie bigamist with the most spouses was the one found dead on the floor of a hotel room in the beginning of *15 Wives* (1934). Needless to say, there was no shortage of murder suspects.

15 Wives (1934)
Don Juan Quilligan (1945)
Monsieur Verdoux (1947)
Captain's Paradise (1953)
The Bigamist (1953)
The Constant Husband (1955)
Autumn Leaves (1956)
The Remarkable Mr. Pennypacker (1959)
Two Wives at One Wedding (1960)
Decline and Fall of a Bird Watcher (aka *Decline and Fall*) (1968)
Paint Your Wagon (1969)

Coffee, Tea, or Me (1972 TVM)
Handle With Care (aka *Citizen's Band*) (1977)
Child Bride of Short Creek (1981 TVM)
Having It All (1982 TVM)
Micki and Maude (1984)
Double Standard (1988 TVM)
Near Misses (1990)
Deceived (1991)
The Man With Three Wives (1993 TVM)

Bigfoot

The Abominable Snowman's North American cousin has been the subject of several bottom-of-the-barrel features, such as *Bigfoot* (1969), *Curse of Bigfoot* (1972) and *Sasquatch* (1978). He was portrayed as a lovable big guy in 1987's *Harry and the Hendersons* and in the same year's made-for-TV feature *Bigfoot*. The pseudo-documentary *The Legend of Boggy Creek* (1973) traced the exploits of a Bigfoot-like creature who roamed around Fouke, Arkansas. John Frankenheimer's *Prophecy* (1979) was about a Bigfoot relative, a gangling mutant monster created by chemical pollution. See also **The Abominable Snowman; Boggy Creek.**

Bigfoot (aka *Big Foot*) (1969)
Curse of Bigfoot (1972)
Shriek of the Mutilated (1974)
The Mysterious Monsters (1976)
Creature From Black Lake (1976)

Sasquatch (1978)
Harry and the Hendersons (aka *Bigfoot and the Hendersons*) (1987)
Bigfoot (1987 TVM)

Billy Jack

Tom Laughlin's peace-loving, half-breed, former Green Beret first appeared in the 1967 biker film *Born Losers*, in which he protected the innocent, defied ineffective small-town police, and beat up bad guys. He did basically the same things in Laughlin's 1971 follow-up *Billy Jack*, but this time moviegoers identified with his loner hero and made the picture a low-budget smash. The movie's simplistic politics and thematic inconsistencies (Billy Jack preaches peace, but doesn't hesitate to use violence when necessary) dated it almost immediately. Laughlin's overblown 1974 sequel *The Trial of Billy Jack* focused on government corruption, as did *Billy Jack Goes to Washington* (1977). Allegedly, the latter was a remake of Frank Capra's classic *Mr. Smith Goes to Washington*. Neither of the last two films came close to duplicating *Billy Jack*'s success, so the series was mercifully allowed to die. Laughlin and wife/costar Delores Taylor produced, directed and wrote most of the series (often using the pseudonym T.C. Frank).

Born Losers (1967)	*The Trial of Billy Jack* (1974)
Billy Jack (1971)	*Billy Jack Goes to Washington* (1977)

Billy the Kid/Billy Carson

This low-budget PRC series had little to do with the real Billy the Kid. Its initial entry, 1940's *Billy the Kid Outlawed* presented Billy as a wronged hero, a victim of small-town corruption. He even went on to become a lawman in the next film, *Billy the Kid in Texas*. Veteran screen cowboy Bob Steele, one of the Three Mesquiteers (q.v.) in the 1930s, played Billy in the first six films. Steele left after 1941's *Billy the Kid in Santa Fe*, though he continued to appear in Westerns and eventually wound up as Trooper Duffy on TV's *F Troop* (1965-67). Serial star Buster ("Flash Gordon") Crabbe replaced Steele in 1941's *Billy the Kid Wanted* and remained for the rest of the series. Al St. John played Billy's grizzly sidekick Fuzzy Q. Jones, who was at least as popular as Billy (one film was even titled *Fuzzy Settles Down*). Sam Newfield directed all the films using various pseudonyms (e.g., Sherman Scott, Peter Stewart). Newfield's real name was Neufeld and his brother, Sigmund, was the head of PRC. Newfield shot the *Billy the Kid* films in two or three days, using the same footage for chases and gunfights repeatedly. In the late 1940s, after the series ended, Eagle Lion reedited (and drastically cut) some of the films and released them with different titles. Thus, the sixty-five-minute *Western Cyclone* became the thirty-nine-minute *Frontier Fighters*. See also **Outlaws (Real-Life Western)**.

Billy the Kid Outlawed (1940)	*Western Cyclone* (aka *Frontier Fighters*) (1943)
Billy the Kid in Texas (1940)	
Billy the Kid's Gun Justice (1940)	*The Renegade* (1943)
Billy the Kid's Range War (1941)	*Devil Riders* (1943)
Billy the Kid's Fighting Pals (1941)	*Frontier Outlaws* (1944)
Billy the Kid in Santa Fe (1941)	*Thundering Gunslingers* (1944)
Billy the Kid Wanted (1941)	*Valley of Vengeance* (1944)
Billy the Kid's Roundup (1941)	*The Drifter* (1944)
Bill the Kid Trapped (1942)	*Fuzzy Settles Down* (1944)
Billy the Kid's Smoking Guns (1942)	*Blazing Frontier* (1944)
Law and Order (aka *Billy the Kid's Law and Order*) (1942)	*Rustler's Hideout* (1944)
Sheriff of Sage Valley (aka *Billy the Kid, Sheriff of Sage Valley*) (1942)	*Wild Horse Phantom* (1944)
	Oath of Vengeance (1944)
	Lightning Raiders (1945)
The Mysterious Rider (aka *Panhandle Trail*) (1942)	*His Brother's Ghost* (1945)
	Shadows of Death (1945)
The Kid Rides Again (1943)	*Gangster's Den* (1945)
Fugitive of the Plains (aka *Raiders of Red Rock*) (1943)	*Stagecoach Outlaws* (1945)
	Border Badmen (1945)
Cattle Stampede (1943)	*Fighting Bill Carson* (1945)

Prairie Rustlers (1945)
Gentlemen With Guns (1946)
Terrors on Horseback (1946)
Ghost of Hidden Valley (1946)

Prairie Badmen (1946)
Overland Riders (1946)
Outlaw of the Plains (1946)

Birds

The mere word has a Hitchcockian ring to it now. But long before Hitch turned them into formidable little killers in 1963, birds were making their cinematic presence known. In Britain, a pair of rare birds disrupted a quiet hamlet in the quaint comedy *Tawny Pipit* (1944). Scottish islanders created some rare birds with a little paint in 1957's *Mad Little Island*, reasoning that such a discovery would block the construction of a government missile base. The establishment of bird sanctuaries provided the background for another British picture *Conflict of Wings* (1953) and an American romantic comedy *Something for the Birds* (1952). Shirley Temple went looking for the blue bird of happiness in the colorful 1940 fantasy *The Blue Bird*, her consolation prize for not being loaned to MGM for *The Wizard of Oz*. A toucan spread a "happiness virus" throughout New York City in George (*Miracle on 34th Street*) Seaton's *What's So Bad About Feeling Good?* (1968). In contrast, giant birds of the horrific variety flew across the screen in the Japanese import *Rodan* (1956) and the inept, U.S.-lensed *The Giant Claw* (1957). A contemporary witch brought a threatening stone eagle to life and sent it on a murderous mission in the 1962 supernatural gem *Burn, Witch, Burn*. Norman Bates (Anthony Perkins) stuffed birds for a hobby in Hitchcock's *Psycho* (1960), a film overloaded with bird symbolism: Its first murder victim, Marion *Crane*, was first glimpsed in *Phoenix*, Arizona. Hitch's next picture was, naturally, *The Birds* (1963), a vague but exciting thriller adapted from Daphne du Maurier's short story. There was nothing horrific or fantastic about 1962's *Birdman of Alcatraz*, an engrossing biography of convict-turned-bird-expert Robert Stroud (Burt Lancaster). However, cruel sorcerer Boris Karloff turned Peter Lorre into a black bird in 1963's amusing *The Raven*. Akim Tamiroff transformed himself into a ridiculous-looking bird/man in *The Vulture* (1967), while fetching Michelle Pfeiffer spent half her days as a hawk in the 1985 sword-and-sorcery fantasy *Ladyhawke*. Roddy McDowell believed himself to be an extinct bird in human form in the oddball satire *Lord Love a Duck* (1966). Army hospital schizophrenic Matthew Modine wanted to become a bird in *Birdy* (1984), while comic book writer Michael Crawford took flight—albeit briefly—as his own creation *Condorman* (1981). Audrey Hepburn played Rima the Bird Girl in the 1959 adaptation of W.H. Hudson's *Green Mansions*. Hunky warrior Marc Singer communicated with birds (and other animals) in 1982's *The Beastmaster*, yet another sword-and-sorcery picture. A frigid woman could make love only to a man in a bird suit in Roger Vadim's bizarre 1980 film *Night Games*. Finally, Larry Cohen's *Q—The Winged Serpent* (1982) flew and lived in a nest but turned out to be an Aztec god and not a bird at all.

The Blue Bird (1940)
Tawny Pipit (1944)
Champagne for Caesar (1950)

Something for the Birds (1952)
Conflict of Wings (aka *Fuss Over Feathers*) (1953)

Rodan (1956)
Mad Little Island (aka Rockets Galore!) (1957)
The Giant Claw (1957)
Green Mansions (1959)
Psycho (1960)
Burn, Witch, Burn (aka Night of the Eagle) (1962)
Birdman of Alcatraz (1962)
The Birds (1963)
The Raven (1963)
Those Calloways (1965)
Lord Love a Duck (1966)
The Vulture (1967)
What's So Bad About Feeling Good? (1968)
Harpy (1970 TVM)
Jonathan Livingston Seagull (1973)
The Blue Bird (1976)
Night Games (1980)
Condorman (1981)
Clash of the Titans (1981)
The Beastmaster (1982)
Birdy (1984)
Ladyhawke (1985)
Beaks: The Movie (1987)
Where Pigeons Go to Die (1990 TVM)

Black Cobra

With solid hits like *Black Caesar* and *Hell Up in Harlem* (both 1973), Fred "The Hammer" Williamson ranked as one of the biggest action stars of the blaxploitation films (q.v.). Yet, by the middle of the next decade, the forty-eight-year-old Williamson's audience had defected to newer action heroes such as Chuck Norris, Sylvester Stallone and Arnold Schwarzenegger. Unwanted in his homeland, Williamson headed overseas to make movies, as had Eastwood and Bronson before him. Unfortunately, Williamson's foreign stint did little for his career—the *Black Cobra* movies were released directly to videotape in the United States. Lensed in Italy, though set in the United States, 1986's *Black Cobra* cast Williamson as a big city detective with a penchant for violence named Robert Malone. The title appears to be an attempt to capitalize on Sylvester Stallone's *Cobra*, which was released the same year. *Black Cobra 2* (1989) improved on the original by sending detective Malone on an INTERPOL exchange program to Manila (shades of *Coogan's Bluff*). Once settled in the Philippines, he teamed up with Nicholas Hammond (Spider-Man in the short-lived TV series) to find Hammond's kidnapped daughter. In the following year's *Black Cobra III: The Manila Connection*, INTERPOL called in Malone when terrorists stole an arsenal of high-tech weapons. The *Black Cobra* films were indistinguishable from any of the other low-budget, foreign-set action film series of the 1980s (e.g., *Bloodfist*, *Eye of the Eagle*, and *No Retreat, No Surrender*).

Black Cobra (1986)
Black Cobra 2 (1989)
Black Cobra III: The Manila Connection (1990)

Blackie, Boston

Jack Boyle's thief-turned-detective has enjoyed a steady screen career, beginning with 1919's *Boston Blackie's Little Pal*. Bert Lytell, Lionel Barrymore and William Russell played Blackie in silent films. However, Chester Morris kicked off the "official" series with 1941's *Meet Boston Blackie*. Morris made an agreeable hero, always willing to bend the law to crack a case, and the series concluded a profitable run in 1949. Just two years later, Blackie turned up on TV, with Kent Taylor replacing Morris. The *Boston Blackie* TV series ran for fifty-eight episodes from

1951-53. Morris starred in all of the following film entries.

Meet Boston Blackie (1941)
Confessions of Boston Blackie (1941)
Alias Boston Blackie (1942)
Boston Blackie Goes to Hollywood (1942)
After Midnight With Boston Blackie (1943)
The Chance of a Lifetime (1943)
One Mysterious Night (1944)

Boston Blackie Booked on Suspicion (1945)
Boston Blackie's Rendezvous (1945)
A Close Call for Boston Blackie (1946)
The Phantom Thief (1946)
Boston Blackie and the Law (1947)
Trapped by Boston Blackie (1948)
Boston Blackie's Chinese Venture (1949)

Blackouts

Films revolving around power blackouts include *The Night the City Screamed* (1980), *Where Were You When the Lights Went Out?* (1968) and *Blackout* (1978). The latter two films were inspired by real-life power failures in New York City. The Doris Day vehicle *Where Were You* played the massive 1965 blackout for forced laughs, while *Blackout* went for thrills in its tale of apartment tenants victimized by a gang during the 1977 power failure. In other films: A blackout allowed inmates to escape from an asylum in *Alone in the Dark*; Gregory Peck lost his memory during a blackout in *Mirage*; and the entire world suffered a temporary blackout so Michael Rennie could make a point in *The Day the Earth Stood Still*.

The Day the Earth Stood Still (1951)
Mirage (1964)
Where Were You When the Lights Went Out? (1968)

Blackout (1978)
The Night the City Screamed (1980 TVM)
Alone in the Dark (1982)

Blane, Torchy

Short story writer Frederick Nebel's ace reporter Torchy Blane had a knack for getting involved with murder cases, which she did in nine B-movies churned out by Warner Bros. during 1937-39. Glenda Farrell played Torchy in all but two films, getting support from Barton MacLane as her charmless boyfriend, police detective Steve McBride (Steve to Torchy: "You're going to settle down and marry me before I throw you in jail"). The two non-Farrell films starred Lola Lane (*Torchy Blane in Panama*) and twenty-five-year-old Jane Wyman (*Torchy Plays With Dynamite*). The series is badly dated, and Steve's thoughtless attitude toward Torchy's career, especially in the Farrell films, is almost offensive. Still, the Torchy series contained a few offbeat touches, such as the appropriately titled Jerome Kern tune "Why Do I Have to Sing a Torch Song?" in *Smart Blonde* and the absence of a Chinatown setting in *Torchy Blane in Chinatown*.

Smart Blonde (1937)
Fly-Away Baby (1937)
The Adventurous Blonde (1937)
Blondes at Work (1938)
Torchy Blane in Panama (1938)

Torchy Gets Her Man (1938)
Torchy Blane in Chinatown (1939)
Torchy Runs for Mayor (1939)
Torchy Plays With Dynamite (1939)

Blaxploitation Films

The term *blaxploitation* was coined in the early 1970s to describe a rash of low-budget, action pictures that featured mostly black performers and typically played in black neighborhood theaters. Many critics considered these movies offensive, charging that they portrayed blacks as stereotyped private eyes, drug kingpins and prostitutes. While that may be true, these films nevertheless kept some talented performers employed (e.g., Richard Pryor in *The Mack*, Godfrey Cambridge in *Cotton Comes to Harlem*). A handful of action stars emerged, such as Tamara Dobson (as Cleopatra Jones), karate champion Jim Kelly, and Richard Roundtree (Shaft). However, their fame was fleeting, and by 1975, they were relegated to supporting roles in more mainstream films. A few blaxploitation films, such as *Shaft* and *Blacula*, broke the typical mold, gained wider distribution, and evolved into sizable hits. In 1983, *One Down, Two to Go* attempted to revive the genre. Yet, despite a formidable cast headed by Jim Brown, it flopped miserably. In 1989, Keenen Ivory Wayans, who would later create TV's *In Living Color*, produced a blaxploitation parody called *I'm Gonna Git You Sucka* starring the likes of Eve Plumb (*The Brady Bunch*) and Clarence Williams III (*The Mod Squad*). See also **Coffin Ed Johnson and Grave Digger Jones; Shaft; Superfly.**

Cotton Comes to Harlem (1970)	*Abby* (1974)
Shaft (1971)	*Black Eye* (1974)
Come Black, Charleston Blue (1972)	*Black Gunn* (1974)
Cool Breeze (1972)	*Blacula* (1974)
Top of the Heap (1972)	*Foxy Brown* (1974)
Melinda (1972)	*Hangup* (aka *Superdude*) (1974)
Hammer (1972)	*Three the Hard Way* (1974)
Hit Man (1972)	*Truck Turner* (1974)
Slaughter (1972)	*Blackenstein* (1975)
Shaft's Big Score (1972)	*Bucktown* (1975)
Superfly (Ron O'Neal) (1972)	*The Black Gestapo* (1975)
Black Caesar (1973)	*Cleopatra Jones and the Casino of Gold*
Cleopatra Jones (1973)	(1975)
Coffy (ad line: "Coffy . . . she'll cream	*Dr. Black and Mr. Hyde* (aka *The*
you!") (1973)	*Watts Monster; Dr. Black and Mr.*
Detroit 9000 (1973)	*White*) (1975)
Ganja and Hess (1973)	*Friday Foster* (1975)
Hell Up in Harlem (1973)	*Black Belt Jones* (1976)
The Mack (1973)	*Black Fist* (aka *The Black*
Scream, Blacula, Scream (1973)	*Streetfighter*) (1976)
Shaft in Africa (1973)	*Hot Potato* (1976)
Slaughter's Big Rip-Off (1973)	*The Big Score* (1983)
Superfly TNT (1973)	*One Down, Two to Go* (1983)

The Blind Dead

A gory Spanish import, the Blind Dead series based its premise on legendary thirteenth-century Templarios Knights who were blinded and then executed for their ritualistic killings of young women. In 1972's *The Blind Dead*, they were resurrected (as rotting, hooded ghouls) and promptly set about in search of more nubile females. The film proved immensely popular in Europe and earned a small cult following in the United States, chiefly due to its Bava-style atmosphere. Director Armando De Ossorio directed three additional, similarly plotted installments.

The Blind Dead (aka *Tombs of the Blind Dead; La Noche del Terror Ciego*) (1972)
Return of the Blind Dead (aka *El Ataque de los Muertos sin Ojos*) (1973)
Horror of the Zombies (aka *El Buque Maldito*) (1974)
Night of the Seagulls (aka *La Noche de las Gaviotas*) (1975)

Blindness

Although films dealing exclusively with blindness can be narrowed to a select few, there have been a disproportionate number of films featuring blind characters in critical roles. Edward Arnold played a blind detective in *Eyes in the Night* (1942) and *The Hidden Eye* (1945), while sleuths-by-chance have included writer Van Johnson in *23 Paces to Baker Street* (1956), reporter Karl Malden in *The Cat O'Nine Tails* (1971), and insurance investigator James Franciscus in *Longstreet* (1970). Blind people have been portrayed as musicians of startling talent in *The Enchanted Cottage* (1945), *Night Song* (1947), *Goha* (1957), *Blues for Lovers* (1964) and *If You Could See What I Hear* (1982). The latter two films were partially biographical, with Ray Charles playing himself in *Blues* and Marc Singer as composer Tom Sullivan in *If You Could See. Seven in Darkness* (1969) was a tense tale about a plane that crashed en route to a convention for the blind, thus stranding its seven sightless passengers in the wilderness. An alien-directed "meteorite shower" blinded most of the Earth's population in the opening frames of John Wyndham's *Day of the Triffids* (1963). As for serious films about persons adjusting to the sudden loss of their sight, few movies can match the emotional impact of *Bright Victory* (1951). Arthur Kennedy earned an Oscar nomination for his wrenching portrait of a blind ex-soldier who no longer knows his place in society. A Labrador retriever seeing-eye dog provided Elizabeth Montgomery with the needed support in the superior TV-movie *Second Sight: A Love Story* (1984). A blind couple desperately fought to adopt a child in the fact-based 1987 TV-movie *Eye on the Sparrow*. Along more traditional lines, a playboy responsible for a woman's blindness became a surgeon so he could cure her in both versions of Lloyd C. Douglas's tearjerker *Magnificent Obsession*. Al Pacino won a Best Actor Oscar for his portrayal of a blind retired army colonel in 1992's *Scent of a Woman*.

Orphans of the Storm (1922)	*The Enchanted Cottage* (1945)
Thunder Below (1932)	*Pride of the Marines* (aka *Forever in*
Wings in the Dark (1935)	*Love*) (1945)
Magnificent Obsession (1935)	*The Hidden Eye* (1945)
Bride of Frankenstein (1935)	*Night Song* (1947)
The Dark Angel (1935)	*Bright Victory* (aka *Lights Out*) (1951)
The Human Monster (aka *Dark Eyes*	*Journey Into Light* (1951)
of London) (1939)	*On Dangerous Ground* (1951)
The Light That Failed (1939)	*The Green Scarf* (1954)
The Four Feathers (1939)	*Magnificent Obsession* (1954)
Eyes in the Night (1942)	*23 Paces to Baker Street* (1956)
Mr. Skeffington (1944)	*Goha* (1957)

Witness in the Dark (1959)
Faces in the Dark (1960)
The Miracle Worker (1962)
Day of the Triffids (1963)
Blues for Lovers (aka Ballad in Blue) (1964)
A Patch of Blue (1965)
Cauldron of Blood (aka Blind Man's Bluff) (1967)
Wait Until Dark (1967)
Seven in Darkness (1969 TVM)
How Awful About Allan (1970 TVM)
Longstreet (1970 TVM)
The Cat O'Nine Tails (1971)
See No Evil (aka Blind Terror) (1971)
In Broad Daylight (1971 TVM)
Butterflies Are Free (1972)
Journey From Darkness (1975 TVM)

Love's Dark Side (1978 TVM)
Blind Rage (1978)
Ice Castles (1979)
The Miracle Worker (1979 TVM)
To Race the Wind (1980 TVM)
If You Could See What I Hear (1982)
Second Sight: A Love Story (1984 TVM)
Eye on the Sparrow (1987 TVM)
See No Evil, Hear No Evil (1989)
Blind Witness (1989 TVM)
Blind Fear (1989)
Blind Fury (1989)
Wild Hearts Can't Be Broken (1991)
Afraid of the Dark (1991)
Jennifer 8 (1992)
Scent of a Woman (1992)
Blindsided (1993 TVM)

Blondie

Probably more so than any other film series, *Blondie* established the format and style of the television sitcom — thirteen years before *I Love Lucy*. Penny Singleton and Arthur Lake starred as Chic Young's comic strip couple Blondie and Dagwood Bumstead in an amazing twenty-eight films spanning twelve years. Their supporting cast remained intact for most of the series, too, with Larry Simms as Baby Dumpling, Jonathan Hale as Mr. Dithers, and Marjorie Kent as Cookie. In 1950, long after most film series had expired, *Blondie* came to an end. Arthur Lake continued as Dagwood (with Pamela Britton as Blondie) in a short-lived 1957 television series. Meanwhile, Penny Singleton provided the voice for Jane during the original 1962-63 run of the TV cartoon series *The Jetsons*. She later became a union activist and then returned to Broadway in the 1970s in *No, No, Nanette*. In 1968, Patricia Harty and Will Hutchins revived the Blondie and Dagwood characters for another TV series. It lasted but a half-season. Ironically, the film series that inspired the TV sitcom genre never made it as a successful sitcom itself. See also **Comic Strip Characters.**

Blondie (1938)
Blondie Brings Up Baby (1939)
Blondie Meets the Boss (1939)
Blondie Takes a Vacation (1939)
Blondie Has Servant Trouble (1940)
Blondie on a Budget (1940)
Blondie Plays Cupid (1940)
Blondie Goes Latin (1941)
Blondie in Society (1941)
Blondie's Blessed Event (1942)
Blondie for Victory (1942)
Blondie Goes to College (1942)

Footlight Glamour (1943)
It's a Great Life (1943)
Leave It to Blondie (1945)
Blondie Knows Best (1946)
Blondie's Lucky Day (1946)
Life With Blondie (1946)
Blondie's Anniversary (1947)
Blondie's Big Moment (1947)
Blondie's Holiday (1947)
Blondie in the Dough (1947)
Blondie's Reward (1948)
Blondie's Big Deal (1949)

Blondie Hits the Jackpot (1949)   *Beware of Blondie* (1950)
Blondie's Secret (1949)   *Blondie's Hero* (1950)

Bloodfist

Real-life World Karate Association champion Don "The Dragon" Wilson took a shot at "kung fu" stardom in this low-budget action series. Yet, despite his fancy footwork, Wilson has thus far failed to duplicate the mainstream successes of recent genre stars Jean-Claude Van Damme, Sho Kosugi and Michael Dudikoff (see **American Ninja Series**). In 1989's *Bloodfist*, Wilson's character Jake trekked off to Manila when his brother was murdered following a kickboxing match. Wilson returned as Jake in the following year's sequel, *Bloodfist II*, which borrowed much of its plot from Bruce Lee's 1973's genre classic *Enter the Dragon*. It sent Jake back to Manila after he accidentally killed a man in a kickboxing bout. After some close encounters in the city, Jake found himself on an island fortress ruled by a villain named Su. The third film in the series dispensed with Jake altogether—Wilson played another character named Jimmy Boland who found himself fighting behind prison bars. That premise worked for Van Damme in *Death Warrant* (1990), so there's hope for Wilson yet. For other martial arts series, see **American Ninja Series, Kickboxer** and **No Retreat, No Surrender.**

Bloodfist (1989)   *Bloodfist III: Forced to Fight* (1991)
Bloodfist II (1990)   *Bloodfist IV: Die Trying* (1992)

The Blue Demon

This masked Mexican wrestler, known in his homeland as El Demonio Azul, briefly challenged fellow-wrestler Santo (q.v.) for the mid-1960s monster-destroyer crown. Santo proved to be the people's favorite, however, and the Blue Demon eventually joined forces with him to create a potent tag team to battle vampires, werewolves, witches and other evil creatures in a series of lively but ludicrous films. See also **Santo; Neutron** (yet another Mexican monster wrestler); **Wrestling.**

The Blue Demon (aka *El Demonio Azul*) (1964)
Blue Demon Against the Satanical Power (aka *Blue Demon Contra el Poder Satanicon*) (1964)
The Shadow of the Bat (aka *La Sombra del Murcielago*) (1966)
Blue Demon vs. the Infernal Brains (1968)
Santo Against Blue Demon in Atlantis (aka *Santo Contra Blue Demon en la Atlantida*) (1968)
The World of the Dead (aka *El Mundo de los Muertos*) (1969) (also with Santo)
Blue Demon and the Seductresses (1969)
Santo and Blue Demon vs. the Monsters (aka *Santo y Blue Demon Contra los Monstrous*) (1971)
Santo and Blue Demon vs. Dracula and the Wolfman (aka *Santo y Blue Demon Contra Dracula y el Hombre Lobo*) (1972)

Boarding Schools

Boarding schools have provided atmospheric settings for a wide variety of films—sentimental tales of dedicated teachers, satanic thrillers, mischievous comedies and student revolutions. Jean Vigo's 1933 surrealistic classic *Zero for Conduct* blended revolution with comedy in the story of mistreated students who rebel against a regimented boarding school run by a midget principal. British director Lindsay Anderson expanded on the same premise in his 1968 film *If . . .* (q.v.), in which defiant Malcolm McDowell and fellow students gun down the school's faculty on Speech Day (or is this massacre merely imagined by McDowell's character?). The girls known as *The Belles of St. Trinian's* (q.v.) (1954) were rebellious, too, but never mounted a revolt since they pretty much ran the school anyway. Convent and church-run schools have been especially prone to attracting mischief-making students, as evidenced by *The Trouble With Angels* (1966) and *Goodbye, Children* (1988). Dedicated teachers molded mischievous youths into mature students of life in *Goodbye, Mr. Chips* (1939 and 1969) and *Dead Poets Society* (1989). In contrast, schoolmaster David Hemming's students threatened to murder him — like they did his predecessor — in *Unman, Wittering and Zigo* (1981). Clint Eastwood found himself in a worse situation as a virile male hiding out in a girls' school populated by lonely, jealous females in 1971's *The Beguiled*. Pamela Franklin entered a girl's boarding school to investigate her sister's suicide in the 1973 TV-movie *Satan's School for Girls*. Despite its title, it turned out to be a nicer place than the demonic school run by a witches coven in Dario Argento's stylish *Suspiria* (1976). Many films such as *Jane Eyre* (1944) and *Oliver Twist* (1948) have been partially set in boarding schools. See also **Military Academies; St. Trinian's.**

Maedchun in Uniform (1931)
Zero for Conduct (aka *Zero de Conduite*) (1933)
Girls' Dormitory (1936)
Housemaster (1938)
Goodbye, Mr. Chips (1939)
Tom Brown's School Days (aka *Adventures at Rugby*) (1940)
The Happy Years (1950)
The Browning Version (1951)
Tom Brown's Schooldays (1951)
Her Twelve Men (1954)
The Belles of St. Trinian's (1954)
Les Diaboliques (aka *Diabolique*; *The Fiends*) (1955)
Tea and Sympathy (1956)
The Ladies' Man (1961)
13 Frightened Girls (1963)
The Trouble With Angels (1966)

If . . . (1968)
Goodbye, Mr. Chips (1969)
The House That Screamed (aka *The Boarding School*) (1969)
Walk a Crooked Path (1969)
The Beguiled (1971)
Child's Play (1972)
Satan's School for Girls (1973 TVM)
Our Time (aka *Death of Her Innocence*) (1974)
Suspiria (1976)
Boarding School (aka *The Passion Flower Hotel*) (1977)
Unman, Wittering and Zigo (1981)
Deadly Lessons (1983 TVM)
Goodbye, Children (aka *Au Revoir, Les Enfants*) (1988)
Dead Poets Society (1989)

Body Switching

The most overworked premise of 1988 was this one: A young person's soul magically changes places with an older person's, so that the youngster acts like an adult and the adult behaves like a kid. Actually, the plotline dates back to Peter Ustinov's then-original 1947 fantasy *Vice Versa*, in which a magic stone caused stockbroker Roger Livesey and school-aged son Anthony Newley to temporarily switch bodies. Disney updated the plot and changed the gender for 1977's *Freaky Friday*. It starred Barbara Harris and Jodie Foster as the mother and daughter making the switch for a day. A trio of mediocre 1988 releases revived the plotline (although in *18 Again*, George Burns played a body-switching grandfather). The best of the three was *Vice Versa*, a semiamusing, one-joke affair benefiting from funny performances by Judge Reinhold and Fred Savage. Unfortunately, it was released late in the cycle and faded quickly at the box office. Even fewer people saw the 1989 body-switching comedy *Dream a Little Dream*, despite a potentially interesting cast headed by Jason Robards. Of course, not all films have involved a transfer between parent and child. Actually, the first body-switching comedy, 1940's *Turnabout*, had a more risqué premise, with husband and wife Adolphe Menjou and Carole Landis switching bodies (courtesy of a magic Buddha). The film, based on a story by *Topper*-author Thorne Smith, served as the basis for a very short-lived 1979 sitcom. The 1986 Disney TV-movie *Hero in the Family* altered the body-switching premise slightly, with an astronaut finding himself in a chimpanzee's body. Dr. Frankenstein (Peter Cushing) transferred a dying man's soul into the body of his lover in 1967's *Frankenstein Created Woman*. Technically, that's not body switching since both souls resided in one body, but it's certainly close. See also **Brain Transplants**.

Turnabout (1940)	*Vice Versa* (1988)
Vice Versa (1947)	*Like Father, Like Son* (1988)
Freaky Friday (1977)	*Dream a Little Dream* (1989)
Hero in the Family (1986 TVM)	*Prelude to a Kiss* (1992)
18 Again (1988)	

Bodybuilding

This minigenre's sole superstar, Arnold Schwarzenegger, has appeared in only two films about bodybuilding. He played a supporting role in 1976's *Stay Hungry*, a Jeff Bridges-Sally Field vehicle about a rich young man who becomes infatuated with the flavorful characters he meets at a second-rate gym. Arnold's first starring role was in the following year's *Pumping Iron*, a popular documentary about bodybuilding competitions that also featured Lou (*The Incredible Hulk*) Ferrigno. A sequel of sorts, 1985's *Pumping Iron II: The Women*, promoted Rachel McLish as the superstar of female bodybuilders. She had already made a brief appearance in the 1984 TV-movie *Getting Physical*, in which Alexandra Paul becomes obsessed with pumping iron after being mugged. Like Schwarzenegger, McLish has gradually transitioned into mainstream action films like 1992's *Aces: Iron Eagle III*. Another real-life bodybuilder, the late Jayne Mansfield's husband Mickey Hargitay, appeared as himself in 1988's *Mr. Universe*. On a lesser note, Harry Grant—holder of the Mr. Southern California and Mr. Los Angeles titles—directed and starred in *Flex 90*. Finally, Bill Travers played the movies' most charming bodybuilder: the scrawny Scottish lad who sends off for a weightlifting program and becomes an Olympic hammer thrower in *Wee Geordie*.

Wee Geordie (aka *Geordie*) (1956)	*Pumping Iron* (1977)
Muscle Beach Party (1964)	*The Hustler of Muscle Beach* (1980
Stay Hungry (1976)	TVM)

The Rainbow Serpent (1983)	*Echo Park* (1986)
Getting Physical (1984 TVM)	*Mr. Universe* (1988)
Pumping Iron II: The Women (1985)	*Flex 90* (1990)

Boggy Creek

A "docudrama" about a Bigfoot-type beast glimpsed roaming around Fouke, Arkansas, 1972's *The Legend of Boggy Creek* piqued enough interest to earn a tidy profit for exploitation producer Charles B. Pierce. Sadly, Pierce's extensive use of "reenactments" has become increasingly popular in television news programs. *Return to Boggy Creek* (1977) was not a sequel, but rather a children's film about a friendly monster helping out some lost kids. It costarred Dawn Wells, better known as Mary Ann on *Gilligan's Island*. In 1985, Pierce returned to Boggy Creek by casting himself as an anthropology professor in *The Barbaric Beast of Boggy Creek*. See also **Bigfoot**.

The Legend of Boggy Creek (1972)	*The Barbaric Beast of Boggy Creek,*
Return to Boggy Creek (1977)	*Part II* (aka *Boggy Creek II*) (1985)

Bomba, the Jungle Boy

After playing Boy for eight years, Johnny Sheffield must have expected to find meatier parts following his farewell Tarzan picture, 1947's *Tarzan and the Huntress*. But no one seemed interested in a sixteen-year-old star so strongly identified with one role. Then, Monogram producer Walter Mirisch came up with a foolproof series for Sheffield and signed the teen to play Bomba, a junior Tarzan created by Roy Rockwood in the 1920s. *Bomba, the Jungle Boy* (1949) was a low-budget, backlot adventure that relied heavily on stock footage (from a 1930 documentary called *Africa Speaks*). The subsequent Bomba films were pretty routine, though journeyman director Ford Beebe managed to make them tolerable. The series ended in 1955, the twenty-four-year-old Sheffield having outgrown the "jungle boy" look.

Bomba, the Jungle Boy (1949)	*African Treasure* (1952)
Bomba on Panther Island (1949)	*Bomba and the Jungle Girl* (1952)
The Lost Volcano (1950)	*Safari Drums* (1953)
Bomba and the Hidden City (1950)	*The Golden Idol* (1954)
Bomba and the Elephant Stampede	*Killer Leopard* (1954)
(aka *Elephant Stampede*) (1951)	*Lord of the Jungle* (1955)
The Lion Hunters (1951)	

Bond, James

Ian Fleming's super secret agent celebrated twenty-five years of silver screen success in 1987. Sean Connery debuted as Bond in 1962's *Dr. No* and today — three Bonds and over a dozen movies later — 007 is still going in the person of Timothy Dalton. Interestingly, Connery was not Fleming's first choice for Bond. The author envisioned an actor closer to Cary Grant. And technically, the first Bond was played by American Barry Nelson in an adaptation of *Casino Royale* that appeared on the TV anthology series *Climax* in the late 1950s. The Bond movies, with the lead actor in parentheses, are listed below in chronological order. *Casino Royale* (1967), a spoof starring David Niven as an elder Bond, is not included since it was not part of the Cubby Broccoli-produced series. *Never Say Never Again* (1983), which was also not part of the "official" series, is included because it starred Connery. As Bond trivia buffs know, *Never* is actually a remake of *Thunderball* and was made only after a long legal dispute.

Dr. No (1962) (Sean Connery)

From Russia With Love (1963) (Connery)

Goldfinger (1964) (Connery)

Thunderball (1965) (Connery)

You Only Live Twice (1967) (Connery)

On Her Majesty's Secret Service (1969) (George Lazenby)

Diamonds Are Forever (1971) (Connery)

Live and Let Die (1973) (Roger Moore)

The Man With the Golden Gun (1974) (Moore)

The Spy Who Loved Me (1977) (Moore)

Moonraker (1979) (Moore)

For Your Eyes Only (1981) (Moore)

Octopussy (1983) (Moore)

Never Say Never Again (1983) (Connery)

A View to a Kill (1985) (Moore)

The Living Daylights (1987) (Timothy Dalton)

Licence to Kill (1989) (Dalton)

Bond Heroines

The ladies who play opposite 007 are famous not only for their beauty but also for their outrageous names. Who can forget such memorable monikers as Pussy Galore, Tiffany Case and Holly Goodhead? Even more interesting, though, is the fascinating trivia surrounding the actresses. For instance, prior to portraying Ms. Galore in 1964's *Goldfinger*, Honor Blackman played Patrick MacNee's sleuthing partner on the TV series *The Avengers*. Her popular *Avengers* replacement was Diana Riggs, who went on to play Tracy (aka Mrs. Bond) in 1969's *On Her Majesty's Secret Service*. Maud Adams is the only actress to play in two Bond flicks — she was a supporting villain-turned-good in *The Man With the Golden Gun*, then graduated to the title role in *Octopussy*. Claudine Auger and Kim Basinger played the same character; Claudia played Domino in *Thunderball* and Kim was Domino in *Never Say Never Again*. The Bond movies, the leading ladies and the characters (in italics) are as follows:

Dr. No — Ursula Andress — *Honeychile Rider*

From Russia With Love — Daniella Bianchi — *Tatiana Romanova*

Goldfinger — Honor Blackman — *Pussy Galore*

Thunderball — Claudine Auger — *Domino Vitali*

You Only Live Twice — Mie Hama — *Kissy Suzuki*

On Her Majesty's Secret Service — Diana Rigg — *Teresa (Tracy), the Countess di Vicenzo*

Diamonds Are Forever — Jill St. John — *Tiffany Case*

Live and Let Die — Jane Seymour — *Solitaire*

The Man With the Golden Gun — Britt Ekland — *Mary Goodnight*

The Spy Who Loved Me — Barbara Bach — *Major Anya Amasova*

Moonraker — Lois Chiles — *Holly Goodhead*

For Your Eyes Only — Carole Bouquet — *Melina Havelock*

Octopussy — Maud Adams — *Octopussy*

Never Say Never Again — Kim Basinger — *Domino*

A View to a Kill — Tanya Roberts — *Stacey Sutton*
The Living Daylights — Maryam D'Abo — *Kara Milovy*
Licence to Kill — Carey Lowell — *Pam Bouvier*

Bounty Hunters

What do disenchanted lawmen do when the system won't let them get their man? They become bounty hunters, of course. Thus, Rutger Hauer played an ex-government agent turned modern-day, high-tech bounty hunter in 1987's *Wanted: Dead or Alive*. Interestingly, Rutger's character was supposed to be the grandson of Josh Randall, the Western bounty hunter made famous by Steve McQueen in the 1958-61 TV series *Wanted: Dead or Alive*. McQueen played real-life bounty man Pappy Thorson on the big screen in 1980's *The Hunter*. It was his last film. Robert DeNiro and Clint Eastwood played skip tracers, contemporary bounty hunters specializing in bail jumpers, in the lighthearted adventures *Midnight Run* (1988) and *Pink Cadillac* (1989). Westerns typically portray bounty hunters in a negative light. *The Reward* (1965), for example, concerned a group of greedy bounty men who kill each other for a larger share of the reward money. Kenny Rogers played a kinder, more gentle bounty hunter in the Western telefilm *Rio Diablo*. And Sybil Danning proved that women could do the job just as well as men in 1989's *L.A. Bounty*.

The Naked Spur (1953)	*Rivkin: Bounty Hunter* (1981 TVM)
The Bounty Hunter (1954)	*Critters* (1986)
The Bounty Killer (1965)	*Wanted: Dead or Alive* (1987)
The Reward (1965)	*The Blue Iguana* (1988)
The Shooting (1966)	*Midnight Run* (1988)
Any Gun Can Play (aka *For a Few*	*Pink Cadillac* (1989)
Bullets More) (1967)	*The Bounty Hunter* (1989)
The Bounty Man (1972 TVM)	*L.A. Bounty* (1989)
Joe Kidd (1972)	*Grim Prairie Tales* (1990)
Santee (1972)	*Into the Badlands* (1991 TVM)
Manhunter (1974 TVM)	*Rio Diablo* (1993 TVM)
Truck Turner (1974)	*It's Nothing Personal* (1993 TVM)
The Hunter (1980)	

The Bowery Boys

The chronology of this popular, low-budget juvenile series spans three decades, from the Dead End Kids in the 1930s to the Little Tough Guys and the East Side Kids in the 1940s to (finally) the Bowery Boys in the 1950s. It all began with 1937's *The Dead End*, an adaptation of the sober 1935 Broadway play about New York slum life. That film introduced teen performers Leo Gorcey and Huntz Hall, an odd couple who would eventually form the comedy core of all these movies. At Warner Bros., the Dead End Kids appeared with major stars such as James Cagney (1938's *Angels With Dirty Faces*) and John Garfield (1939's *They Made Me a Criminal*). These efforts, though, did not constitute a series since they featured the Kids in changing roles. Some of the Kids (e.g., Billy Halop, Huntz Hall) defected to Universal in 1938 and made *Little Tough Guy*, a *Dead End* imitation with a downbeat ending (Halop goes to reform school). Additional Little Tough Guy movies followed, although the cast and characters again changed on a regular basis. Jackie Cooper even cropped up as the lead Little Tough Guy in 1938's *Newsboy's Home*. In the early 1940s, enterprising producer Sam Katzman brought some of the boys, including Gorcey and Halop, to Monogram Pictures and re-dubbed them the East Side Kids. Under Katzman's guidance, the series gradually shifted from juvenile drama to broad comedy. Gorcey and Hall also emerged as the principal stars. With their agent Jan Grippo, they revamped the series in 1946 and launched the Bowery Boys pictures for Monogram. As Terence Alyosius Mahoney (Slip) and Horace Debussey Jones (Sach), Gorcey and Hall mugged their way through forty-eight Bowery Boy comedies. The humor frequently centered around hapless Sach acquiring some strange power. A throat operation turned him into a great singer in *Blues Busters*. A punch in the nose gave him telepathic powers in *Private Eyes*. He also became clairvoyant (*Master Minds*), acquired great physical strength (*No Holds Barred*), and learned how to smell diamonds (*Jungle Gents*). In the end, though, he always returned to normal, inspiring Slip to slap him with his hat. Other Bowery Boys who appeared with some regularity were Whitey (Billy Benedict), Chuck (Gorcey's brother David), Gabe (Gabriel Dell), and Bobby (Bobby Jordan). The Boys hung out at Louie's Sweet Shop, which was run by Louie Dumbrowsky (Gorcey's father Bernard), who was always sorry for listening to Slip and company. Bernard Gorcey died in 1955, after completing *Dig That Uranium*. His father's death and his own alcoholism caused Leo Gorcey to leave the series after 1956's *Crashing Las Vegas*. Stanley Clements (Gloria Grahame's ex-husband) took over as Duke, the gang's new leader, in the series' final seven films. Huntz Hall continued to appear in movies in supporting roles. He and Gorcey had a cameo together in the dismal 1970 satire *The Phynx*.

The East Side Kids

East Side Kids (1941)
Boys of the City (1941)
That Gang of Mine (1941)
Pride of the Bowery (1941)
Flying Wild (1941)
Bowery Blitzkreig (1941)
Spooks Run Wild (1941)
Mr. Wise Guy (1942)
Let's Get Tough (1942)
Smart Alecks (1942)
'Neath Brooklyn Bridge (1942)

Kid Dynamite (1943)
Clancy Street Boys (1943)
Ghosts on the Loose (1943)
Mr. Muggs Steps Out (1943)
Million Dollar Kid (1944)
Follow the Leader (1944)
Block Busters (1944)
Bowery Champs (1944)
Docks of New York (1945)
Mr. Muggs Rides Again (1945)
Come Out Fighting (1945)

The Bowery Boys

In Fast Company (1946)
Mr. Hex (1946)
Spook Busters (1946)
Bowery Bombshell (1946)
Live Wires (1946)
Hard-Boiled Mahoney (1947)
News Hounds (1947)
Bowery Buckeroos (1947)

Angels' Alley (1947)
Trouble Makers (1948)
Smuggler's Cove (1948)
Jinx Money (1948)
Angels in Disguise (1949)
Hold That Baby! (1949)
Fighting Fools (1949)
Master Minds (1949)

Blonde Dynamite (1950)
Blues Busters (1950)
Lucky Losers (1950)
Triple Trouble (1950)
Ghost Chasers (1951)
Crazy Over Horses (1951)
Let's Go Navy (1951)
Bowery Battalion (1951)
Hold That Line (1952)
Feudin' Fools (1952)
Here Come the Marines (1952)
No Holds Barred (1952)
Clipped Wings (1953)
Jalopy (1953)
Loose in London (1953)
Private Eyes (1953)
Paris Playboys (1954)

Jungle Gents (1954)
The Bowery Boys Meet the Monsters
(1954)
Bowery to Bagdad (1955)
High Society (1955)
Spy Chasers (1955)
Jail Busters (1955)
Dig That Uranium (1956)
Crashing Las Vegas (1956)
Fighting Trouble (1956) (first with
Clements)
Hot Shots (1956)
Hold That Hypnotist (1957)
Spook Chasers (1957)
Looking for Danger (1957)
Up in Smoke (1958)
In the Money (1958)

Boxing

Filmmakers have long been fascinated by the sweaty, brutal world of boxing, making it by far the most popular sport in movies. Film biographies have chronicled the careers of John L. Sullivan (*The Great John L.*), Jim Corbett (*Gentleman Jim*), Jack Johnson (*The Great White Hope*), Joe Louis (*The Joe Louis Story*), Rocky Graziano (*Somebody Up There Likes Me*), Jake La Motta (*Raging Bull*), Muhammad Ali (*The Greatest*), Jack Dempsey (*Dempsey*), Rocky Marciano (*Marciano*), and Boom Boom Mancini (*Heart of a Champion: The Ray Mancini Story*). Fictitious prizefighters have fared even better, with Rocky Balboa (q.v.), Joe Palooka and Too Sweet (see **Penitentiary Series**) earning their own film series. Some movie boxers have hailed from other, more unusual professions. John Derek was a young minister who entered the ring to earn money for his congregation in *The Leather Saint* (1956). William Holden played a young man forced to choose between prizefighting and a promising career as a violinist in *Golden Boy* (1939). Almost every male comedy star has included a boxing routine in one of his movies. Danny Kaye made an unlikely boxer in *The Kid From Brooklyn* (1946), but he looked pretty good compared to Donald O'Connor in *Francis in the Navy* (1955), a hypnotized Jimmie Walker in *Let's Do It Again* (1975), Don Knotts in *The Prize Fighter* (1979), and Lou Costello in *Abbott and Costello Meet the Invisible Man* (1951). In the latter film, Costello's boxing prowess was aided considerably — and hilariously — by the presence of an invisible boxing chum. Serious fight films have tended to focus on the corruption within the sport. These include some of the genre's finest films: *The Champ* (1931), *Battling Bellhop* (aka *Kid Galahad*) (1937), *Body and Soul* (1941), *Champion* (1949), *The Set-Up* (1949), and Rod Serling's *Requiem for a Heavyweight* (1962). *The Set-Up* has the added distinction of taking place in real time, as indicated by the clocks shown at the beginning and end of the film. Barefisted fighters have been limited to backroom brawls, though Charles Bronson brought one to life memorably in *Hard Times* (1975) and Clint Eastwood had one of his biggest box office successes as slugger Philo Beddoe in *Every Which Way*

But Loose (1978). The most bizarre boxer has to be the spunky kangaroo in *Matilda* (1978), though Elvis Presley rates a close second for his pugilist performance in *Kid Galahad* (1962). See also **Rocky; Penitentiary Series; Wrestling.**

Battling Butler (1926)
Iron Man (1931)
The Champ (1931)
Winner Take All (1932)
The Prizefighter and the Lady (aka *Every Woman's Man)* (1933) (with real-life boxers Jack Dempsey and Max Baer)
King for a Night (1933)
The Life of Jimmy Dolan (aka *The Kid's Last Fight*) (1933)
Cain and Mabel (1936)
Battling Bellhop (aka *Kid Galahad*) (1937)
When's Your Birthday? (1937)
Ex-Champ (1939)
Golden Boy (1939)
Invitation to Happiness (1939)
They Made Me a Criminal (1939)
Kid Nightingale (1939)
City for Conquest (1940)
Body and Soul (1941)
Here Comes Mr. Jordan (1941)
Knockout (1941)
Ringside Maisie (1941)
Gentleman Jim (1942)
The Great John L. (aka *A Man Called Sullivan*) (1945)
The Kid From Brooklyn (1946)
Leather Gloves (1948)
Whiplash (1948)
The Big Punch (1948)
Champion (1949)
The Set-Up (1949)
The Golden Gloves Story (1950)
Right Cross (1950)
Abbott and Costello Meet the Invisible Man (1951)
The Fighter (1951)
Iron Man (1951)
Flesh and Fury (1952)
The Ring (1952)
The Joe Louis Story (1953)
Champ for a Day (1953)

Tennessee Champ (1954)
Francis in the Navy (1955)
The Leather Saint (1956)
The Harder They Fall (1956)
Somebody Up There Likes Me (1956)
World in My Corner (1956)
Kid Galahad (1962)
Requiem for a Heavyweight (1962)
Confessions of Tom Harris (aka *Childish Things*) (1967)
The Legendary Champions (1968)
AKA Cassius Clay (1970)
The Great White Hope (1970)
Ripped Off (aka *The Boxer*) (1971)
Jack Johnson (1971)
Fat City (1972)
The All-American Boy (1973)
Hard Times (1975)
Let's Do It Again (1975)
Rocky (1976)
The Greatest (1977)
Every Which Way But Loose (1978)
Penitentiary (1978)
Ring of Passion (1978 TVM)
Matilda (1978)
Movie Movie (the "Dynamite Hands" segment) (1978)
The Main Event (1979)
Marciano (1979 TVM)
The Champ (1979)
The Prize Fighter (1979)
Any Which Way You Can (1980)
Raging Bull (1980)
Body and Soul (1981)
Honeyboy (1982 TVM)
Edith and Marcel (1983)
The Fighter (1983 TVM)
The Last Fight (1983)
Dempsey (1983 TVM)
Heart of a Champion: The Ray Mancini Story (1985 TVM)
Streets of Gold (1986)
Heart (1987)
Spike of Bensonhurst (1988)

Split Decisions (1988)
Champions Forever (1989)
Blonde Fist (1991)
Gladiator (1992)

Far and Away (1992)
Diggstown (1992)
Night and the City (1992)
Percy and Thunder (1993 TVM)

Boy Scouts

Comedy and sentimentality have dominated movies about Boy Scouts. Clifton Webb played a grouchy kid-hater who wound up leading a scout troop—and liking it—in the 1953 comedy *Mister Scoutmaster*. In 1949's *The Great Lover*, scout leader Bob Hope had his hands full aboard a ship filled with his rowdy troupe, a murderer, and luscious Rhonda Fleming. On the sentimental side, Fred MacMurray portrayed a man who devoted his life to his boys in the sticky-sweet Disney picture *Follow Me, Boys!* (1966). *The Wrong Guys* was a 1988 comedy about a Cub Scout reunion, while the 1989 Shelley Long vehicle *Troop Beverly Hills* gave equal time to some *girl* scouts. In the prologue to *Indiana Jones and the Last Crusade* (1989), young Indiana Jones (River Phoenix) showed up in a scout's uniform. Robert DeNiro portrayed a scoutmaster with a drill sergeant attitude in 1993's *This Boy's Life*. There were no scoutmasters nor den mothers in 1991's *The Last Boy Scout*— only Bruce Willis as a rumpled private detective.

Henry Aldrich, Boy Scout (1944)
The Great Lover (1949)
Mister Scoutmaster (1953)
Follow Me, Boys! (1966)
Scout's Honor (1980 TVM)
The Wrong Guys (1988)

Troop Beverly Hills (1989)
Indiana Jones and the Last Crusade
    (1989)
Edge of Honor (1991)
This Boy's Life (1993)

Brain Transplants

Mad scientists have been obsessed with transplanting brains since the days of silent films. Almost all Frankenstein films (q.v.), beginning with Edison's 1910 version, have dealt with brain transplanting of some fashion. In James Whales's 1931 *Frankenstein*, the doctor's assistant Fritz stole a criminal's brain from a medical lab, thus explaining the Monster's homicidal tendencies. Yet, the basic Frankenstein operation—the implant of a spare brain into a nonliving body—is but one kind of brain transplant. More interesting films have involved the transplant of a brain from one living creature to another. *On Time* (1924) was a strange little adventure film with a subplot about some thugs trying to replace the hero's brain with a gorilla's. The reversal of that plot describes 1941's *The Monster and the Girl*, in which the implanted brain of a killer transformed an ape into the "Mangle Murderer." Similarly, John Carradine's brain wound up in the skull of a missing link in 1944's *Return of the Ape Man*. In contrast to such silliness, the 1986 TV-movie *Who Is Julia?* was a serious affair about a brain-dead mother (Mare Winningham) who receives new gray cells courtesy of a recently deceased model. Surprisingly, Terence Fisher's *Frankenstein Must Be Destroyed* (1969) dispensed with the required gruesome monster and opted for a straightforward brain transplant plot. In this ironic tale, Frankenstein (Peter Cushing) "cures" a brain-damaged fellow scientist by transplanting the man's brain into a new body. However, the scientist's gratefulness turns to bitter hate when his wife spurns his new appearance—the face of a stranger. In 1969's *Change of Mind*, a dying white district attorney awakes one day to find his brain in the body of a black man—but, after the initial shock, it all ends happily. The funny side of brain switching has been explored by Abbott and Costello (*A&C Meet Frankenstein*), the Bowery Boys (*Spook Busters*), and Steve Martin (*The Man With Two Brains*). Martin's delightful 1983 film cast him as a brain surgeon in love with a bodyless brain (although he eventually finds a happy home for it). Although it did not involve brain transplanting, *Hauser's Memory* (1970) deserves special mention for its plot about a man who injected himself with another's brain fluid to learn a valuable secret. See also **Body Switching.**

On Time (1924)	*The Revenge of Frankenstein* (1958)
Frankenstein (1931)	*The Head* (1959)
The Man Who Lived Again (aka *The Man Who Changed His Mind*) (1936)	*Monstrosity* (aka *The Atomic Brain*) (1964)
The Ghost of Frankenstein (1940)	*Frankenstein Must Be Destroyed* (1969)
Black Friday (1940)	*Change of Mind* (1969)
The Monster and the Girl (1941)	*Brainwaves* (1982)
Return of the Ape Man (1944)	*The Man With Two Brains* (1983)
Spook Busters (1946)	*Who Is Julia?* (1986 TVM)
Abbott and Costello Meet Frankenstein (1948)	

Brainwashing

By strict definition, brainwashing is the process by which a person is forcibly induced to forsake political, religious or social beliefs in favor of contrasting views. *Ticket to Heaven* (1981) and *Split Image* (1982) both explored how susceptible youths were brainwashed by religious cults and then rescued and "deprogrammed." A loathsome punk named Alex (Malcolm McDowell) was brainwashed by Liberals with the "Ludovico technique" in Stanley Kubrick's cult fantasy *A Clockwork Orange* (1971). Fact-based *Patty Hearst* (1988) detailed how the famous heiress was kidnapped and subsequently brainwashed into joining her terrorist captors. The Australian horror picture *Thirst* (1979) offered an intriguing twist, whereby a secret society tried to brainwash a young woman into becoming a vampire. Other movies have altered the definition of brainwashing to include plots in which a person is controlled subconsciously (usually by hypnosis) and forced to perform uncharacteristic acts. A Robert Frost poem, delivered over the telephone, triggered nice folks into becoming autonomous saboteurs in the thriller *Telefon*. The spy hero of *The Ipcress File* (Michael Caine) used self-induced pain as a defense against high-tech brainwashing techniques. However, the most famous film of this type remains John Frankenheimer's controversial classic *The Manchurian Candidate* (1962). Laurence Harvey starred as a patriotic soldier turned into a time-delayed assassin—controlled by his own mother (Angela Lansbury). The only brainwashing comedy of note is *Simon*, a decidedly offbeat tale in which a psychology professor (Alan Arkin) was brainwashed into thinking he was an alien from another world. See also **Hypnotists.**

1984 (1956)
Brainwashed (1961)
The Manchurian Candidate (1962)
Thirty-Six Hours (1964)
The Ipcress File (1965)
On Her Majesty's Secret Service (1969)
A Clockwork Orange (1971)
Hunter (1972 TVM)
Telefon (1977)
Thirst (1979)

Simon (1980)
Ticket to Heaven (1981)
Split Image (1982)
Circle of Power (aka *Mystique*;
   Brainwash; *The Naked Weekend*)
   (1983)
1984 (1984)
Patty Hearst (1988)
Total Recall (1990)

Bullfights, *see* Matadors/Bullfights

Buddy Action Films

The "buddy action film" requires careful definition. These pictures have existed for years but were not accorded their own genre until the late 1980s. The prototypical buddy film pairs up two individuals of the same sex—but opposite personalities—and throws them into a situation requiring them to work together. Of course, this formula can be traced back to much earlier films, such as 1958's *The Defiant Ones*. Sidney Poitier and Tony Curtis played two convicts, one black and one white, connected only by a pair of handcuffs and their mutual desire for freedom. In the end, they gained respect for each other—and that's the classical ending for all buddy films. Actually, the buddies do not always have to be the same sex. However, when one's a woman and one's a man, they typically fall in love and the film becomes a romantic adventure. For example, *The Thirty Steps* (1935) was a romantic adventure because the relationship between fugitives Robert Donat and Madeleine Carroll eventually blossomed into romance. That's significantly different from the mutual admiration that developed between detectives Clint Eastwood and Tyne Daly in 1976's *The Enforcer* (one of the few male/female buddy films). The label "buddy picture" may have been first used to describe 1982's *48 HRS*, the Eddie Murphy-Nick Nolte vehicle whose financial success guaranteed plenty of Hollywood knockoffs. By the end of the decade, moviegoers had encountered a variety of odd couples: black family man/cop Danny Glover and white out-of-control cop Mel Gibson in *Lethal Weapon* (q.v.); Chicago cop James Belushi and Russian cop Arnold Schwarzenegger in *Red Heat*; alien cop Kyle MacLachlan and Earthling cop Michael Nouri in *The Hidden*; slob cop Kurt Russell and neat cop Sylvester Stallone in *Tango & Cash*; and, for a change of pace, down-on-his-luck private eye Bruce Willis and former football quarterback Damon Wayans in *The Last Boy Scout*. Although Susan Sarandon and Geena Davis were friends at the start of *Thelma and Louise* (and hence did not experience the mandatory initial conflict), some critics labeled it a female buddy picture. The genre, and *Lethal Weapon* in particular, was spoofed unevenly in 1993's *National Lampoon's Loaded Weapon 1*. See also **Lethal Weapon**.

48 HRS (1982)
Renegades (1986)
Lethal Weapon (1987)
The Hidden (1987)

Collision Course (1987)
Red Heat (1988)
Midnight Run (1988)
Tango & Cash (1989)

The Rookie (1990)	*The Last Boy Scout* (1991)
Another 48 HRS (1990)	*National Lampoon's Loaded Weapon 1*
Pure Luck (1991)	(1993)

Buried Alive

A plot staple in most film adaptations of Edgar Allan Poe, the "buried alive" premise has been best used as a subplot. Nevertheless, it has been the focus of a few movies. In 1958's *Macabre*, a doctor frantically searched for his little girl, whom some fiend had buried alive. Producer/director William Castle hyped it by offering viewers fright insurance. In 1972's *The Screaming Woman*, no one believed recently released asylum resident Olivia de Havilland when she told them she heard a voice in the ground—but there was someone down there, all right. Kidnappers buried their victim in a tiny underground compartment in *The Longest Night* (1972), a film that should have conveyed a more claustrophobic feeling.

Isle of the Dead (1945)	*The Oblong Box* (1969)
Macabre (1958)	*The Screaming Woman* (1972 TVM)
The House of Usher (aka *The Fall of*	*The Longest Night* (1972 TVM)
the House of Usher) (1960)	*Buried Alive* (1990 TVM)
The Premature Burial (1962)	*83 Hours 'Til Dawn* (1990 TVM)

Buses

The Big Bus (1976) may be the only film that takes place almost exclusively on a bus. A disaster-movie spoof, it starred Joseph Bologna, Lynn Redgrave and Ruth Gordon as some of the passengers aboard the world's first nuclear-powered bus during its maiden journey from New York to Denver. In 1980's *Detour to Terror*, O.J. Simpson played a driver whose tour bus is hijacked en route to Las Vegas by a group of terrorists. Carl Betz and family set out aboard a restored bus to rediscover the U.S. in the 1971 TV-movie *In Search of America*. Despite their blue-collar reputation, buses have boasted their share of pulchritudinous passengers. Joan Collins and Jayne Mansfield took a ride on *The Wayward Bus*, adapted from a John Steinbeck story, while *Bus Stop* featured Marilyn Monroe as a rodeo champ's reluctant girlfriend. Alfred Hitchcock considered the bus explosion in *Sabotage* one of his greatest mistakes, since it cruelly killed the heroine's innocent younger brother. The issue of forced busing to schools was examined in the 1980 TV-movie *All God's Children*. Karl Malden portrayed a heroic bus driver in the fact-based 1993 TV-movie *They've Taken Our Children: The Chowchilla Kidnapping*. On the lighter side, a ghost drove a bus through the air in *High Spirits* (1988), and John Candy led fellow bus passengers in singing TV songs (much to Steve Martin's dismay) in 1987's *Planes, Trains and Automobiles*.

Friday the Thirteenth (1933)	*The Wayward Bus* (1957)
Sabotage (aka *A Woman Alone*) (1936)	*Where Angels Go . . . Trouble Follows*
Pardon My Sarong (1942)	(1968)
Dead of Night (1945)	*In Search of America* (1971 TVM)
Mexican Bus Ride (aka *Ascent to*	*The Magic Carpet* (1971 TVM)
Heaven; *Subida Al Cielo*) (1951)	*On the Buses* (1971)
The Runaway Bus (1954)	*The Laughing Policeman* (1974)
Bus Stop (1956)	*The Big Bus* (1976)

The Gauntlet (1977)
Long Journey Back (1978 TVM)
Lady on the Bus (1978)
Detour to Terror (1980 TVM)
All God's Children (1980 TVM)
Planes, Trains and Automobiles (1987)

High Spirits (1988)
Wheels of Terror (1990 TVM)
Love Field (1992)
They've Taken Our Children: The Chowchilla Kidnapping (1993 TVM)
Heart and Souls (1993)

Butchers

Thanks to Ernest Borgnine, butchers have avoided cinematic stereotyping as psychotic killers who chop more than meat with their sharp instruments. Borgnine earned a well-deserved Best Actor Oscar for his realistic portrayal of a lonely, likable butcher in 1955's *Marty*. George Dzundza also played a sympathetic butcher — one befuddled by his bride's clairvoyance — in *The Butcher's Wife* (1991). Other butchers, though, have displayed murderous tendencies. In 1989's *Out Cold*, butcher John Lithgow mistakenly believed he had killed his partner when he found a body in the freezer. Claude Chabrol's psychological thriller *Le Boucher* (1969) mixed murder and love in an unusual tale of a lonely, murderous butcher who found romance with a quiet schoolteacher. Victor Buono, in a role he'd like to forget, played a more conventional butcher-killer in 1972's Italian-lensed *The Mad Butcher*. The murderer in the 1981 Australian thriller *Road Games* may have been a butcher, but it's hard to say. Rory Calhoun turned people into sausage in 1980's *Motel Hell*, but he was not a butcher by profession. Likewise, the deranged family in *The Texas Chainsaw Massacre* films (q.v.) consisted of former slaughterhouse employees — so technically they were not butchers. On the lighter side, TV's *The Brady Bunch* (1969-74) featured Sam the butcher as Alice the housekeeper's boyfriend.

Marty (1955)
Le Boucher (aka *The Butcher*) (1969)
The Mad Butcher (aka *Meat Is Meat*; *Strangler of Vienna*) (1972)
The Homecoming (1973)
Road Games (1981)

The Cold Room (aka *The Prisoner*) (1984 TVM)
Out Cold (1989)
The Butcher's Wife (1991)
So I Married an Axe Murderer (1993)
Household Saints (1993)

Butlers

Stereotypically stuffy and very British, butlers have been cast as supporting characters for the most part. Even then, they have managed to upstage the principal stars, as exemplified by John Gielgud's scene-stealing performance in *Arthur* (1981). Arthur Treacher practically made a career of playing butlers, his most famous portrayal being that of P.G. Wodehouse's perfect butler Jeeves in 1936's *Thank You, Jeeves* and its 1937 follow-up *Step Lively, Jeeves*. Irrepressible Eric Blore made a very funny, very cynical valet to Fred Astaire in *Top Hat* (1935) and subsequently specialized in butler roles, too. Although butler leads have been rare, Charles Laughton and William Powell played them in two comedy classics. In 1935's *Ruggles of Red Gap*, Western millionaire Charlie Ruggles won British butler Laughton in a poker game. The cultured butler's clash with American customs provided much of the comedy. But his eventual understanding of American freedom gave the film a surprisingly patriotic ending. Bob Hope reprised the role in the loose 1950 remake *Fancy Pants*. William Powell played a millionaire mistaken by Carole Lombard for a bum in *My Man Godfrey* (1936). She undertook it as a personal project to transform him into a proper butler. It was also remade in 1957 with David Niven and June Allyson. Niven, who had played opposite Treacher in the first Jeeves film, played a butler again in Disney's *Candleshoe* (1977). Other memorable butlers have been played by Dan Duryea, Ralph Richardson and Dirk Bogarde. Duryea's butler pretended to be the master of the house while his employer was on vacation in the 1946 comedy *White Tie and Tails*. In *The Fallen Idol* (1948), a young boy idolized the family butler (Richardson) until murderous suspicions took their toll on the friendship. Bogarde played the screen's creepiest valet in Joseph Losey's *The Servant*, a character study in which a butler becomes master of his employer. On television, the future stars of *Dallas* and *Knots Landing*, Larry Hagman and Donna Mills, played an average American couple masquerading as a butler and cook for millionaire David Wayne in the 1971-72 sitcom *The Good Life*. See also **Chauffeurs; Maids and Housekeepers**.

Get Off My Foot (1935)
She Married Her Boss (1935)
If You Could Only Cook (1935)
Ruggles of Red Gap (1935)
My Man Godfrey (1936)
Thank You, Jeeves (1936)
Step Lively, Jeeves (1937)
The Baroness and the Butler (1938)
Her Man Gilbey (aka *English Without Tears*) (1944)
Nothing But Trouble (1944)
White Tie and Tails (1946)
The Fallen Idol (1948)
Fancy Pants (1950)

My Man Godfrey (1957)
Light Fingers (1957)
The Admirable Crichton (aka *Paradise Lagoon*) (1957)
The Servant (1963)
The Adventures of Bullwhip Griffin (1967)
Fitzwilly (aka *Fitzwilly Strikes Back*) (1967)
Blue Blood (1973)
Candleshoe (1977)
Arthur (1981)
Clue (1985)
Remains of the Day (1993)

La Cage aux Folles

The 1978 film version of Jean Poiret's French stage farce racked up an impressive $8 million in North America, making it the continent's all-time top-grossing foreign language film at the time. Ugo Tognozzi and Michel Serrault played the gay couple who try to "clean up their act" when Tognozzi's son brings his fiancée and her family over to dinner. Tognozzi and Serrault teamed up again for two mild sequels, neither of which approached the original's raging success. However, *La Cage aux Folles* was adapted into a smash Broadway musical headlining Gene Barry.

La Cage aux Folles (1978)
La Cage aux Folles II (1980)
La Cage aux Folles III: The Wedding (1985)

Camels

Although steadily employed in desert epics, camels have failed to land many starring roles. Indeed, the looney Western comedy *Hawmps!* (1976) and its offbeat inspiration, 1954's *Southwest Passage*, may be the only pictures expressly about camels. *Passage* was a 3-D Western that had Rod Cameron experimenting with using camels to transport settlers across the desert. Interestingly, the Indians refrained from attacking the wagon train because they feared the strange-looking camels. Unfortunately, a camel died and the Indians got wise. The less-serious *Hawmps!* headlined James Hampton (Dobbs on TV's *F Troop*) as a cavalry officer trying to convince the army to use camels instead of horses. In yet another Western, Disney's *One Little Indian* (1973), James Garner played a cavalryman trudging through the desert with an Indian boy and a trusty camel. Despite its promising title, 1967's *Follow That Camel* was nothing more than a *Carry On* (q.v.) spoof of *Beau Geste*. Two scene-stealing talking camels added some dry commentary to Hope and Crosby's wacky *Road to Morocco* (1942). Another talking camel had a cameo in Yvonne de Carlo's *Slave Girl*, while a blind camel had the best scene in the Dustin Hoffman-Warren Beatty flop *Ishtar* (1987). There was nary a camel in the 1931 Charlie Chan mystery *The Black Camel*, the title being derived from Charlie's line: "Death is the black camel that kneels unbidden at every gate."

Road to Morocco (1942)

Slave Girl (1947)

Southwest Passage (aka *Camels West*) (1954)

Follow That Camel (aka *Carry On Follow That Camel*) (1967)

One Little Indian (1973)

Hawmps! (1976)

Ishtar (1987)

Cannibalism

Cannibalism, prior to the gore-explicit 1970s, was restricted mostly to jungle adventure films such as *Cannibal Attack* (1954). A pleasantly gruesome exception was the 1936 film version of the old school melodrama *Sweeney Todd, the Demon Barber of Fleet Street*. Tod Slaughter, a noted British ham, portrayed the title character, who not only cut hair but also cut up his customers and sold them in meat pies. The story also served as the basis for 1970's *Bloodthirsty Butchers* and Stephen Sondheim's hit Broadway musical *Sweeney Todd*. By the mid-1960s, cannibalism had crept into exploitative, drive-in horror films. Often, the cannibalism was somewhat muted by the inclusion of fantastic elements. A man was barbecued and eaten in *Two Thousand Maniacs* (1964), but the "cannibals" turned out to be ghosts. The flesh-eaters in George Romero's cult classic *Night of the Living Dead* (1968) were ghouls (q.v.), not normal humans. However, the demented family members in 1964's *Spider Baby* were physically normal. Their cannibalistic tendencies were a result of inbreeding. Three cannibal films were released in 1972. Both *The Folks at Red Wolf Inn* and *Cannibal Girls* played their grisly subject matter for laughs with jokes about spare ribs and lady fingers. The latter film starred SCTV alumni Eugene Levy and Andrea Martin and was directed by Ivan (*Ghostbusters*) Reitman. *Raw Meat* was an offbeat chiller about descendants of people trapped in a London subway tunnel who devour unsuspecting passersby. Three other cannibal movies of the 1970s and early 1980s blossomed into cult hits. The most notorious was Tobe Hooper's *The Texas Chainsaw Massacre* (1974), a ghastly tale about a family of flesh-eaters. It was condemned by critics for its violence, which was more implied than explicit. Former cowboy star Rory

Calhoun played Farmer Vincent, whose popular sausages were made from human meat, in 1980's *Motel Hell* (the *o* in Motel Hello having burned out). Cannibalism played a small but very significant role in Paul Bartel's *Eating Raoul* (1982), a black comedy about a couple who hit upon a way to finance their dream restaurant when they accidentally commit murder. *Survive!* (1976) was a nonhorror, Mexican import about plane crash survivors who resorted to eating dead fellow passengers to stay alive—a story told with better production values in 1993's *Alive*. The tragic, real-life story of the Donner party, who turned to cannibalism to avoid starvation in the harsh West, was whitewashed in the 1978 TV-movie *Donner Pass: The Road to Survival* but recounted accurately in the 1992 documentary *The Donner Party*. Anthony Hopkins won a Best Actor Oscar for his portrayal of Hannibal "The Cannibal" Lecter in Jonathan Demme's 1991 hit *The Silence of the Lambs*. See also **Ghouls; The Texas Chainsaw Massacre.** The following list excludes films featuring cannibal natives:

Sweeney Todd, the Demon Barber of Fleet Street (aka *The Demon Barber of Fleet Street*) (1936)

Mondo Cane (aka *It's a Dog's Life*) (1963)

Blood Feast (1963)

Spider Baby (aka *The Liver Eaters; Cannibal Orgy or the Maddest Story Ever Told*) (1964)

Do You Like Women? (1964)

The Undertaker and His Pals (1967)

Bloodthirsty Butchers (1970)

The Folks at Red Wolf Inn (aka *Terror at Red Wolf Inn; Terror House*) (1972)

Cannibal Girls (1972)

Raw Meat (aka *Deathline*) (1972)

The Texas Chainsaw Massacre (1974)

Survive! (1976)

Donner Pass: The Road to Survival (1978 TVM)

Motel Hell (1980)

Eating Raoul (1982)

Cannibals in the Street (aka *Invasion of the Flesh Hunters*) (1982)

Raw Force (1982)

C.H.U.D. (1984)

The Texas Chainsaw Massacre 2 (1986)

Eat the Rich (1987)

Flesh Eating Mothers (1988)

Lucky Stiff (1988)

Parents (1989)

Cannibal Women in the Avocado Jungle of Death (1989)

C.H.U.D. II: Bud the Chud (1989)

Tales From the Darkside: The Movie (1990)

The Silence of the Lambs (1991)

Delicatessen (1991)

The Donner Party (1992)

Alive (1993)

Dead/Alive (1993)

The Care Bears

Media-product tie-ins were the rage of the early 1980s, with toy companies eagerly licensing their best-selling items to TV cartoon producers and vice versa. Few products were more popular than the Care Bears, nice little pastel-colored bears with sentimental names like Wish Bear, Bedtime Bear and Tenderheart Bear. Just for a touch of realism, there was also Grumpy Bear. The Care Bears, along with My Little Pony and He-Man, were big enough to attract the attention of movie producers, too. Indeed, the first Care Bears film, a feature-length animated musical, did surprisingly well at the box office. However, the law of diminishing returns and short-lived nature of toy trends limited those nice little bears to two sequels. See also **Animated Movies (Feature-Length).**

The Care Bears Movie (1985)
The Care Bears Movie II: A New Generation (1986)
The Care Bears Adventure in Wonderland (1987)

Carry On Series

This lowbrow British comedy series made an inauspicious debut in 1958 with *Carry On Sergeant*, a silly army farce littered with bad jokes ("Your rank, soldier!" "That's a matter of opinion."). But while the critics scorched it, the public ate it up. Subsequent *Carry On* films were not sequels in a narrative sense, but they featured the same cast members (Kenneth Connor, Charles Hawtrey, Sid James) and the same vaudeville sense of humor. The series highlight was 1959's *Carry On Nurse*, which even earned respectable reviews, although it is chiefly remembered for a scene in which distinguished Wilfred Hyde-White gets a daffodil stuck up his rear end. The series got progressively racier during the 1960s (Cleopatra to Caesar: "I have seen your bust." Caesar: "I wish I could say the same.") and finally featured nudity for the first time in 1969's *Carry On Camping*. The films also suffered a sharp decline in quality (what quality there was), although no one seemed to notice since the *Carry On* movies had become a British institution by then. To its credit, the *Carry On* gang considered nothing sacred and spoofed *Cleopatra* (*Carry On Cleo*), *The Third Man* (*Carry On Spying*), *The Scarlet Pimpernel* (*Don't Lose Your Head*), *Beau Geste* (*Follow That Camel*), and *Anne of the Thousand Days* (*Carry On Henry*, which was memorably subtitled *Anne of a Thousand Lays*). The series died in the late 1970s after producing twenty-nine films — only to be revived unexpectedly in 1992 with *Carry On Columbus*, which found the famous explorer encountering streetwise Indians with Brooklyn accents. The cast featured familiar faces from the *Carry On* troupe, such as Jim Dale (tenth series entry), Jack Douglas (seventh), June Whitfield (third), and former-Dr. Who Jon Pertwee (third).

Carry On Sergeant (1958)
Carry On Nurse (1959)
Carry On Teacher (1959)
Carry On Constable (1960)
Carry On Regardless (1961)
Carry On Cruising (1962)
Carry On Cabby (1963)
Carry On Jack (aka *Carry On Venus*) (1963)
Carry On Cleo (1964)
Carry On Spying (1964)
Carry On Cowboy (1965)
Carry On Screaming (1966)
Carry On Doctor (1967)
Don't Lose Your Head (aka *Carry On Don't Lose Your Head*) (1967)
Follow That Camel (aka *Carry On Follow That Camel*) (1968)
Carry On Up the Khyber (1968)

Carry On Again Doctor (1969)
Carry On Camping (1969)
Carry On Henry (1970)
Carry On Loving (aka *One Thing on Top of Another*) (1970)
Carry On Up the Jungle (aka *Carry On Jungle Boy*) (1970)
Carry On at Your Convenience (aka *Carry On Round the Bend*) (1971)
Carry On Abroad (1972)
Carry On Matron (1972)
Carry On Girls (1973)
Carry On Dick (1974) (as in Dick Turpin, famed British outlaw)
Carry On England (1976)
Carry On Behind (1978)
Carry On Emmanuelle (1978)
Carry On Columbus (1992)

(**Note:** 1957's *Carry On Admiral* was not a part of the series.)

Carson, Billy, *see* Billy the Kid/Billy Carson

Carter, Nick

Ormond C. Smith and John Russell Coryell created this turn-of-the-century detective for *New York Weekly*. Yet, while Nick Carter seemed a sure bet for a long-running B-movie series, his screen career has been modest at best. Andre Liabel made four French serials in 1909-12, while both Edmund Lowe (a future Philo Vance) and Thomas Corrigan appeared in Nick Carter short features in the 1920s. MGM launched an updated three-film series in 1939 with Walter Pidgeon in the lead. The series was dropped when Pidgeon went on to bigger roles in bigger movies (e.g., 1941's *How Green Was My Valley*). Eddie Constantine, best known as tough detective Lemmy Caution (q.v.), played Carter in France, while Robert Conrad revived the character for American audiences in the 1972 TV-movie *The Adventures of Nick Carter*. The latter film was the pilot for a television series that never materialized. The detective reappeared unexpectedly in 1978's *Nick Carter in Prague* (aka *Dinner for Adele*), a tongue-in-cheek Czech film that's attracted a minor cult following in the United States.

Nick Carter, Master Detective (1939) (Walter Pidgeon)
Phantom Raiders (1940) (Pidgeon)
Sky Murder (1940) (Pidgeon)
License to Kill (aka *Nick Carter and the Red Club*) (1964) (Eddie Constantine)
The Adventures of Nick Carter (1972 TVM) (Robert Conrad)
Nick Carter in Prague (aka *Dinner for Adele*; *Adele Hasn't Had Her Supper Yet*)
(1978) (Michael Docolomansky)

Cartoon/Live Action Features

These films fall into two categories: Those that simply intercut "live" footage and animated sequences (e.g., *Allegro Non Troppo*) and those that show live and animated characters interacting *in the same frame*. The latter films are the more interesting, typically relying on an expensive optical trick called a traveling matte. The use of mattes can be traced back to 1925's *The Lost World*, in which special effects wizard Willis (*King Kong*) O'Brien masked out the shape of a dinosaur in a crowd scene and then inserted footage of an animated model into that "optical hole." As one might expect, Walt Disney Productions has produced the most cartoon/live action movies, featuring such memorable sequences as the carousel horse race in *Mary Poppins* and Roger Rabbit's initial transition from cartoon-world to real-world in *Who Framed Roger Rabbit?* MGM, however, rates a close second with *Anchors Aweigh* (Tom and Jerry dancing with Gene Kelly), *Dangerous When Wet* (T&J swimming with Esther Williams), and *Invitation to the Dance*. At Warner Bros., Bugs Bunny showed up in a dream sequence in Doris Day's *My Dream Is Yours* (1949). One of the most unique uses of animation was in 1968's *The Charge of the Light Brigade*, in which animated line drawings were used to convey Britain's political atmosphere. See also **Animated Movies (Feature-Length)**.

Hollywood Party (1934)
Victory Through Air Power (1943)
The Three Caballeros (1945)
Anchors Aweigh (1945)
Song of the South (1946)
So Dear to My Heart (1948)
Two Guys From Texas (1948)
My Dream Is Yours (1949)
The Four-Poster (1952)
Dangerous When Wet (1953)
The Girl Next Door (1953)
Invitation to the Dance (1957)
The Snow Queen (1959)
The Incredible Mr. Limpet (1964)
Mary Poppins (1964)
The Daydreamer (1966)
The Charge of the Light Brigade (1968)
The Phantom Tollbooth (1969)
The Picasso Summer (1969)

Bedknobs and Broomsticks (1971)
Funnyman (1971)
Two Hundred Motels (1971)
Heavy Traffic (1973)
Monty Python and the Holy Grail (1975)
Coonskin (aka Streetfight) (1975)
Allegro Non Troppo (1976)
Pete's Dragon (1977)
Gulliver's Travels (1977)
The Water Babies (1978)
9 to 5 (1980)
Xanadu (1980)
Pink Floyd—The Wall (1982)
Who Framed Roger Rabbit? (1988)
Fletch Lives (1989)
Cool World (1992)
Stay Tuned (1992)

Cartoonists

Dean Martin as a cartoonist? Only in a movie in which he steals the ideas for his comic strips from Jerry Lewis's telepathic dreams—which was precisely the plot of 1955's *Artists and Models*. In the Bob Hope comedy *That Certain Feeling*, a "ghost artist" drew a comic strip for a cartoonist who had lost his touch. James Thurber's drawings and writings inspired 1972's *The War Between Men and Women*, which starred Jack Lemmon as a half-blind cartoonist hassled by his wife's ex-husband. Two years earlier, the same material had provided the basis for the William Windom TV sitcom *My World and Welcome to It*. Michael Crawford played a cartoonist who turned into his own comic book hero in the 1981 Disney misfire *Condorman*.

Piccadilly Jim (1936)
The Girl Next Door (1953)
Artists and Models (1955)
That Certain Feeling (1956)
How to Murder Your Wife (1965)
The War Between Men and Women (1972)

Condorman (1981)
The Hand (1981)
One Crazy Summer (1986)
Slamdance (1987)
Brenda Starr (1992)
Cool World (1992)

Cassidy, Hopalong

William Boyd, the undisputed king of B-movie westerns, made sixty-six Hopalong Cassidy movies for Paramount and United Artists between 1935 and 1948. Clarence E. Mulford created the character in 1912 in a series of "old school" novels. But no one took an interest in them until veteran western producer Harry (Pop) Sherman envisioned a profitable low-budget series for Paramount. Many actors were considered for the lead role (including David Niven, according to one source), but Sherman finally settled on Boyd. A popular silent actor, Boyd was a favorite of Cecil B. DeMille and appeared in such classics as *King of Kings* (1927). A gambling scandal involving *another* William Boyd contributed to his fading star status in the early 1930s, so he welcomed the opportunity to play Hopalong. *Hop-A-Long Cassidy* (1935 — the hyphens were later dropped) was a surprise hit for Paramount and no wonder: the Cassidy westerns cost less than $100,000 and usually grossed twice that amount. Screenwriter Doris Schroeder whitewashed Mulford's original character considerably, so that the movies' Hoppy never smoked nor drank liquor. The first films sometimes ran as long as eighty-eight minutes, but later ones lasted just over an hour, which made for plenty of action. James Ellison played Jimmy Nelson, Hoppy's young sidekick at the Bar 20 ranch, with additional support by Gabby Hayes or Andy Clyde. After producing forty-one Hopalong films, Paramount sold the rights to United Artists in 1942, which released twenty-five more entries. The last twelve UA films were produced by Boyd's own Hopalong Cassidy Productions. Boyd eventually pawned almost everything he owned and bought rights to *all* the Hopalong Cassidy Westerns. He sold these to television and, when the film series ended in 1948, he began making new episodes for his TV program. Edgar Buchanan played Hoppy's TV sidekick during the series' 1949-51 run.

Hop-A-Long Cassidy (1935)	*Stagecoach War* (1940)
The Eagle's Brood (1935)	*Three Men From Texas* (1940)
Bar 20 Rides Again (1935)	*Doomed Caravan* (1941)
Call of the Prairie (1936)	*In Old Colorado* (1941)
Three on the Trail (1936)	*Border Vigilantes* (1941)
Heart of the West (1936)	*Pirates on Horseback* (1941)
Hopalong Cassidy Returns (1936)	*Wide Open Town* (1941)
Trail Dust (1936)	*Outlaws of the Desert* (1941)
Borderland (1937)	*Riders of the Timberline* (1941)
Hills of Old Wyoming (1937)	*Secret of the Wastelands* (1941)
North of the Rio Grande (1937)	*Stick to Your Guns* (1941)
Rustler's Valley (1937)	*Twilight on the Trail* (1941)
Hopalong Rides Again (1937)	*Undercover Man* (1942)
Texas Trail (1937)	*Lost Canyon* (1942)
Heart of Arizona (1938)	*Colt Comrades* (1943)
Bar 20 Justice (1938)	*Bar 20* (1943)
Pride of the West (1938)	*Hoppy Serves a Writ* (1943)
In Old Mexico (1938)	*Border Patrol* (1943)
Sunset Trail (1938)	*The Leather Burners* (1943)
The Frontiersman (1938)	*False Colors* (1943)
Partners of the Plains (1938)	*Riders of the Deadline* (1943)
Cassidy of Bar 20 (1938)	*Mystery Man* (1944)
Range War (1939)	*Forty Thieves* (1944)
Law of the Pampas (1939)	*Texas Masquerade* (1944)
Silver on the Sage (1939)	*Lumberjack* (1944)
The Renegade Trail (1939)	*The Devil's Playground* (1946)
Santa Fe Marshal (1940)	*Fool's Gold* (1947)
The Showdown (1940)	*Hoppy's Holiday* (1947)
Hidden Gold (1940)	*Marauders* (1947)

Unexpected Guest (1947)	*Strange Gamble* (1948)
Dangerous Venture (1947)	*Borrowed Trouble* (1948)
Sinister Journey (1948)	*The Dead Don't Dream* (1948)
Silent Conflict (1948)	*False Paradise* (1948)

Cats

As befits their nature, felines have maintained a subtle screen profile. While dogs (q.v.) have panted their way through major film series (see **Lassie** and **Rusty**), cats have been content with a pawful of starring roles and a few choice parts. A frisky ginger cat inherited a wretched baseball team in 1951's *Rhubarb* and turned it into a winner (with a little help from motivational publicist Ray Milland). A female cat narrated Disney's *The Three Lives of Thomasina*, a charming Scottish tale spanning but one-third of her nine lives. Other Disney feline features starred Siamese cats (*That Darn Cat!* and *Lady and the Tramp*), alien cats (*The Cat From Outer Space*), and animated cats (*The Aristocats* and *Oliver and Company*). *Gay Purr-ee* was a non-Disney feature-length cartoon with the voices of Robert Goulet and Judy Garland. Tom, the animated cat of Tom and Jerry fame, danced with Gene Kelly in *Anchors Aweigh* and swam with Esther Williams in *Dangerous When Wet*. For the best supporting feline performance, the nod goes to Art Carney's costar in 1974's *Harry and Tonto*. This bittersweet comedy about the travels of an elderly man and his cat earned Carney a Best Actor Oscar. James Bond's archnemesis Blofeld had a white Persian kitty for a pet in some of the 007 films, most notably 1971's *Diamonds Are Forever*. Gale Sondergaard played Shirley Temple's self-centered cat Tylette in the 1940 adaptation of the Oz-like fantasy *The Blue Bird*. Humans have transformed into cats (typically not the domestic variety) in the 1942 and 1982 versions of *The Cat People* and *Cat Girl* (1957). A dead girl's soul possessed a cat in 1946's *The Cat Creeps*, while an Egyptian cat goddess possessed human victims in the 1973 TV-movie *The Cat Creature*. The nastiest cats were the ones that unknowingly ate human flesh in *The Corpse Grinders* (1971) and decided they liked the taste. See also **Lions and Tigers**.

Alice in Wonderland (1933)	*That Darn Cat!* (1965)
The Black Cat (1934)	*Eye of the Cat* (1969)
The Blue Bird (1940)	*The Aristocats* (1970)
The Black Cat (1941)	*The Corpse Grinders* (1971)
Anchors Aweigh (1945)	*Alice's Adventures in Wonderland*
The Cat Creeps (1946)	(1972)
Alice in Wonderland (1950)	*The Cat Creature* (1973 TVM)
Alice in Wonderland (1951)	*Harry and Tonto* (1974)
Rhubarb (1951)	*The Blue Bird* (1976)
Dangerous When Wet (1953)	*The Cat From Outer Space* (1978)
Lady and the Tramp (1955)	*ffolkes* (aka *Assault Force*) (1980)
Bell, Book, and Candle (1958)	*Cat's Eye* (1985)
Gay Purr-ee (1962)	*The Richest Cat in the World* (1986
The Three Lives of Thomasina (1963)	TVM)
The Incredible Journey (1963)	*Oliver and Company* (1988)
Cassandra Cat (aka *When the Cat*	*The Adventures of Milo and Otis*
Comes; *The Cat*) (1963)	(1989)

Two Evil Eyes (aka Due Occhi	Strays (1991 TVM)
Diabolic) (1990)	Tom and Jerry: The Movie (1992)
Tales From the Darkside: The Movie	Homeward Bound: The Incredible
(1990)	Journey (1993)

Caution, Lemmy

American actor Eddie Constantine played Peter Cheyney's two-fisted pulp detective in a series of modest French mysteries, beginning in the early-1950s and lasting through the mid-1960s. A bit player in American films, Constantine followed his dancer wife to Paris, where he achieved minor popularity as a singer. His first Caution film, 1953's *Gun Moll*, cost a paltry $50,000 but earned impressive grosses. European audiences responded enthusiastically to his man-of-action image, which naturally transcended language barriers. Interestingly, Constantine's overseas stardom foreshadowed the 1960s European successes of other American actors such as Clint Eastwood, Charles Bronson and Lee Van Cleef. The hard-drinking, womanizing Caution made little impact in the United States, although later efforts such as *Attack of the Robots* (1962) and *Your Turn, Darling* (1963) eventually wound up on American television. Acclaimed French director Jean-Luc Godard cast Constantine as Lemmy Caution in his baffling, esoteric, futuristic "thriller" *Alphaville* (1965). It's considered the best of the Caution pictures, although it is certainly not representative of the series.

Gun Moll (aka *La Mome Vert-de-Gris*) (1953)

This Man Is Dangerous (aka *Dangerous Agent*; *Cet Homme Est Dangereaux*)
(1953)

Dames Don't Care (aka *Les Femmes s'en Balancent*) (1954)

You Dig? (aka *Vous Pigez?*) (1956)

Women Are Like That (aka *Comment qu'elle Est!*) (1960)

Attack of the Robots (aka *Cards on the Table*; *Cartes sur la Table*) (1962)

Lemmy and the Girls (aka *Ladies' Man*; *Lemmy Pour Les Dames*) (1962)

Your Turn, Darling (aka *Lemmy Caution, FBI Agent*; *You Do It, Cuties*; *A Toi
de Paire, Migonne*) (1963)

Alphaville (aka *Alphaville, une Etrange Aventure de Lemmy Caution*) (1965)

Cave People

Cavewoman to caveman in *When Dinosaurs Ruled the Earth*: "N'dye krasta m'kan neecro tedak." As any film buff with a prehistoric dictionary knows, that translates to: "Come fast. Kill evil flying monster." Those kinds of dialogue limitations have hampered storylines for prehistoric people pictures. The genre's best films have been visually arresting pieces with plots borrowed from silent films and the added excitement of a dinosaur or two (scientific accuracy being a minor concern). Hal Roach's 1940 opus *One Million B.C.* set the standard with its tale of forbidden love between Tumak (Victor Mature) of the violent Rock People and Loana (Carole Landis) of the peaceful Shell People. The dinosaurs were economically created by magnifying living lizards. *Variety* called the picture "corny" at the time of release and, indeed, it inspired no 1940s imitations. In 1950, the low-budget *Prehistoric Women* added a feminist angle and some narration (in addition to character grunts). Roger Corman's *Teenage Caveman* (1958) was obviously targeted toward young adults, which partially explains the rationale for the twist ending of revealing the past to be the future. However, Britain's Hammer Pictures deserves total credit for turning cave people epics into profitably sturdy box office performers. Its 1966 remake, *One Million Years, B.C.*, brilliantly paired a scantily clad Raquel Welch with Ray Harryhausen's impressive stop-motion dinosaurs (q.v.), thus appealing to both older and younger male viewers. Hammer followed it with *Prehistoric Women* (1967), *When Dinosaurs Ruled the Earth* (1970), and *Creatures the World Forgot* (1971). *The Tribe* was a 1974 TV-movie along the same lines, only minus the nudity and dinosaurs. Ringo Starr and his wife Barbara Bach spoofed caveman epics in the 1981 hit comedy *Caveman*. Another 1981 release, *Quest for Fire* was a big-budgeted "serious" effort, featuring a cave people language devised by novelist Anthony (*A Clockwork Orange*) Burgess. *Clan of the Cave Bear* (1985) was a dismal flop despite its best-seller origins and the presence of then-popular star Daryl Hannah. Of course, not all cave people films have been set in prehistoric times. The contemporary caveman has been around since scientists discovered one roaming about modern-day Africa in the 1927 silent comedy *The Missing Link*. Lightning revived a caveman in *Dinosaurus* (1960), Joan Crawford discovered a missing link hiding in an obscure cave in *Trog* (1970), and scientist Timothy Hutton found a Neanderthal frozen in ice in *Iceman* (1984). The overanxious scientists in *The Neanderthal Man* (1953) and *Monster on the Campus* (1958) actually turned themselves into prehistoric men. In the former film, the serum that turned Robert Shayne into a Neanderthal also transformed his dog into a vicious wolf. See also **Dinosaurs.**

The Missing Link (1927)
One Million B.C. (aka *Man and His Mate*; *The Cave Dwellers*) (1940)
Prehistoric Women (1950)
The Neanderthal Man (1953)
Monster on the Campus (1958)
Teenage Caveman (aka *Prehistoric World*) (1958)
Dinosaurus (1960)
Eegah! (1962)
One Million Years B.C. (1966)
The Oldest Profession in the World ("Prehistoric Era" sketch) (1966)
Prehistoric Women (aka *Slave Girls*) (1967)
Valley of the Dragons (1970)
Trog (1970)
When Dinosaurs Ruled the Earth (1970)

When Women Had Tails (1970)
Skullduggery (1970)
Creatures the World Forgot (1971)
Schlock (aka *The Banana Monster*) (1971)
The Creeping Flesh (1973)
The Tribe (1974 TVM)
The People That Time Forgot (1977)
Sinbad and the Eye of the Tiger (1977)
Caveman (1981)
Quest for Fire (1981)
History of the World—Part I (1981)
Iceman (1984)
Clan of the Cave Bear (1985)
Cavegirl (1985)
Link (1986)

Centerfolds

Life's been tough for girls posing in the buff. Kim Basinger played a model whose career went into a tailspin after appearing in a girlie magazine in *Katie: Portrait of a Centerfold* (1978). Apparently, the film had little impact on Basinger, who eventually *did* pose in *Playboy* (but not as the centerfold). The sad real-life story of Dorothy Stratten, a Playmate-turned-actress murdered by her former lover, reached the small screen in 1981 and the big screen two years later. Jamie Lee Curtis played Stratten in the TV-movie *Death of a Centerfold: The Dorothy Stratten Story*, while Mariel Hemingway took the lead in Bob Fosse's *Star 80* (1983). Other fact-based telefilms include 1991's *Posing: Inspired by Three Real Stories* and 1983's *Policewoman Centerfold*, the story of a lady cop who lost her job after posing for a nude layout. In a case of ideal casting, *Playboy* centerfold Erika Eleniak played a centerfold in Steven Seagal's *Under Siege* (1992). The movies have yet to exploit the plight of male nude models, once again confirming the industry's chauvinistic tendencies toward women. See also **Fashion Models; Strippers.**

The Centerfold Girls (1974)

Katie: Portrait of a Centerfold (1978 TVM)

Death of a Centerfold: The Dorothy Stratten Story (1981 TVM)

Star 80 (1983)

Policewoman Centerfold (1983 TVM)

I Married a Centerfold (1984 TVM)

Posing: Inspired by Three Real Stories (aka *I Posed for Playboy*) (1991 TVM)

Under Siege (1992)

Chainsaws

In addition to bit parts in lumberjack films (q.v.), chainsaws have made memorable appearances in a handful of horror movies—almost expressly for purposes other than cutting wood. The cannibalistic killers in *The Texas Chainsaw Massacre* movies (q.v.) used them to prepare people for dinner. Bruce Campbell discovered that chainsaws were ideal for decapitating demons in the second and third *Evil Dead* movies (q.v.). In fact, after severing his own hand (it was possessed), Campbell attached a chainsaw to his arm. Chainsaw duels were featured prominently in *Motel Hell*, *Phantasm II*, *The Texas Chainsaw Massacre 2* and the subtly titled *Hollywood Chainsaw Hookers*. The latter film featured the catchy ad line: "They charge an arm and a leg." It also starred Gunnar Hansen (Leatherface of *Texas Chainsaw Massacre* fame) as the cult leader of the chainsaw-toting prostitutes. See also **The Texas Chainsaw Massacre.**

The Texas Chainsaw Massacre (1974)

Motel Hell (1980)

The Texas Chainsaw Massacre 2 (1986)

Evil Dead 2: Dead by Dawn (aka *Evil Dead 2*) (1987)

Hollywood Chainsaw Hookers (1988)

Phantasm II (1988)

Army of Darkness (aka *Army of Darkness: Evil Dead 3*) (1993)

Chan, Charlie

Sherlock Holmes reigns as cinema's busiest sleuth, but Charlie Chan ranks a surprising—and very strong—second, with over forty mysteries to his credit. Although Earl Derr Bigger's novels were popular in the 1920s, his Hawaiian police detective was relegated to a strictly supporting role in his big-screen debut, 1926's *The House Without a Key*. He fared better in subsequent outings but didn't make an impact until Warner Oland made the part his own in 1931's *Charlie Chan Carries On*. Although Swedish by birth, Oland specialized in Oriental roles and, at one point in his career, was playing detective Chan and villain Fu Manchu (q.v.)

simultaneously. Oland brought warmth and deceiving wit to the role, masterfully phrasing words of wisdom such as: "Alibi, like dead fish, cannot stand test of time." Keye Luke usually played Charlie's Number One son, providing youth appeal and comic support, as did other sons Benson Fong and Victor Sen Yung in later entries. The Oland Chan films are considered the best of the series, with *Charlie Chan at the Opera* (costarring Boris Karloff and a young Ray Milland) as the highlight. When Oland died in 1938, American-born Sidney Toler assumed the role and continued the Twentieth Century-Fox series in capable fashion until 1942. Two years later, Toler was back as Chan in a low-budget Monogram series. On his death in 1947, he was replaced by Roland Winters, who made the last Monogram entry in 1949. Eight years later, Chan resurfaced in the form of J. Carrol Naish in a syndicated TV series called *The New Adventures of Charlie Chan*. It lasted for only thirty-nine half-hour episodes. Ross Martin, best known as Artemus Gordon on TV's *The Wild, Wild West*, made an unlikely Chan in the 1973 TV-movie *Happiness Is a Warm Clue* (aka *The Return of Charlie Chan*). Filmed for U.S. television in 1970, this attempt to revive Chan sat on the shelf for three years, showed up on British TV in 1973, and finally made its American debut on the late show in 1979. The 1981 spoof *Charlie Chan and the Curse of the Dragon Queen* received a general release, though to little avail. Critics panned it and audiences proved that they greatly preferred Oland and Toler to a feebly unfunny Peter Ustinov. The Chan character was much better parodied in Neil Simon's *Murder by Death* (1976). Two of the most potentially interesting Chan films were never made. In *The Four Star Murder Case*, Charlie would have teamed up with Philo Vance, Mr. Moto and Michael Shayne to solve one mighty tough case. *Charlie Chan at College* would have cast the Oriental detective as a visiting professor demonstrating the finer aspects of crime-solving to his students.

The House Without a Key (1926) (George Kuwa)

The Chinese Parrot (1928) (Sojin)

Behind That Curtain (1929) (E.L. Park)

The Black Camel (1931) (Warner Oland)

Charlie Chan Carries On (1931) (Oland)

Charlie Chan's Chance (1932) (Oland)

Charlie Chan's Greatest Case (1932) (Oland)

Charlie Chan's Courage (1934) (Oland)

Charlie Chan in London (1934) (Oland)

Charlie Chan in Egypt (1935) (Oland)

Charlie Chan in Shanghai (1935) (Oland)

Charlie Chan in Paris (1935) (Oland)

Charlie Chan's Secret (1936) (Oland)

Charlie Chan at the Circus (1936) (Oland)

Charlie Chan at the Opera (1936) (Oland)

Charlie Chan at the Race Track (1936) (Oland)

Charlie Chan on Broadway (1937) (Oland)

Charlie Chan at the Olympics (1937) (Oland)

Charlie Chan at Monte Carlo (1938) (Oland)

Charlie Chan in Honolulu (1938) (Sidney Toler)

Charlie Chan at Treasure Island (1939) (Toler)

Charlie Chan in Reno (1939) (Toler)

Charlie Chan in the City of Darkness (1939) (Toler)

Charlie Chan at the Wax Museum (1940) (Toler)

Charlie Chan's Murder Cruise (1940) (Toler)
Murder Over New York (1940) (Toler)
Charlie Chan in Panama (1940) (Toler)
Charlie Chan in Rio (1941) (Toler)
Dead Men Tell (1941) (Toler)
Castle in the Desert (1942) (Toler)
Charlie Chan in Black Magic (aka *Charlie Chan in Meeting at Midnight*; *Charlie Chan at Midnight*; *Black Magic*) (1944) (Toler)
Charlie Chan in the Secret Service (1944) (Toler)
The Chinese Cat (1944) (Toler)
The Jade Mask (1945) (Toler)
The Red Dragon (1945) (Toler)
The Scarlet Clue (1945) (Toler)
The Shanghai Cobra (1945) (Toler)
Shadows Over Chinatown (1946) (Toler)
Dark Alibi (1946) (Toler)
Charlie Chan in Dangerous Money (aka *Dangerous Money*) (1946) (Toler)
The Trap (1947) (Toler)
The Chinese Ring (1947) (Roland Winters)
Charlie Chan and the Golden Eye (aka *The Golden Eye*; *Mystery of the Golden Eye*) (1948) (Winters)
Docks of News Orleans (1948) (Winters)
The Feathered Serpent (1948) (Winters)
The Shanghai Chest (1948) (Winters)
Sky Dragon (1949) (Winters)
Happiness Is a Warm Clue (aka *The Return of Charlie Chan*) (1973 TVM) (Ross Martin)
Charlie Chan and the Curse of the Dragon Queen (1981) (Peter Ustinov)

Chauffeurs

Although they are privy to intimate auto conversations, chauffeurs have never acquired a cinematic stature equal to butlers (q.v.) and ladies-in-waiting. Perhaps it's because they usually live over the garage, thereby missing the essential upstairs and downstairs activities at the main house. Certainly, chauffeurs have fared poorly when it comes to romance. Both Carlo Justini and Robert Shaw mistakenly believed their female employers were interested in them in, respectively, *A Novel Affair* and *The Hireling*. Jean Simmons and chauffeur Robert Mitchum became romantically involved in *Angel Face*, but it was an unhappy affair that ended with a car zooming over a cliff. Chauffeur's daughter Audrey Hepburn endured romantic entanglements when rich brothers William Holden and Humphrey Bogart clashed over her affections in *Sabrina*. Female limo drivers have been rare in the movies, although Deborah Foreman played one in 1986's *My Chauffeur*. Jack Lenoir, who once was Wayne Rogers's real-life chauffeur, also played his driver in *Once in Paris* ... (and earned better notices than Wayne). Morgan Freeman played the cinema's best-known chauffeur in 1989's *Driving Miss Daisy*. He earned a Best Supporting Actor nomination for his performance as Hoke, Miss Daisy's (Jessica Tandy) loyal driver and steadfast friend. See also **Butlers; Maids and Housekeepers; Taxi Drivers.**

Downstairs (1932)
Merrily We Live (1938)
Native Son (1950)
Angel Face (1953)
Sabrina (aka *Sabrina Fair*) (1954)
A Novel Affair (aka *The Passionate Stranger*) (1957)
Endless Night (aka *Agatha Christie's Endless Night*) (1971)
The Hireling (1973)

Law and Disorder (1974)	*Native Son* (1986)
Once in Paris ... (1978)	*My Chauffeur* (1986)
Arthur (1981)	*Cookie* (1989)
Sunset Limousine (1983 TVM)	*Driving Miss Daisy* (1989)

Cheerleaders

When relegated to supporting roles in football (q.v.) movies and campus comedies, cheerleaders have typically been stereotyped as shallow, image-conscious individuals. Thus, one would think that movies featuring cheerleaders as principal characters would tend to paint more positive views of the primary promoters of school spirit. Instead, the post-1970 cheerleader era consisted primarily of sex comedies, slasher films, and bizarre true stories. The sex "comedies" include such notorious fare as *The Cheerleaders* (originally rated X, but since downgraded to an R) and the infamous XXX-rated *Debbie Does Dallas*. When not removing their clothes, cinematic cheerleaders often found themselves coping with killers in bloody pictures such as *Cheerleaders' Wild Weekend* and *Cheerleader Camp* (which boasted the memorable alternate title *Bloody Pom-Poms*) and the slasher film spoof *Pandemonium* (1982), set in a school for cheerleaders. Made-for-television movies have opted to present "true stories" about cheerleaders. The unexpected popularity of the Dallas Cowboy Cheerleaders was examined in two highly rated films. However, viewers showed far less interest in the Los Angeles Lakers' cheering squad. A high school cheerleader's mother plotted murder in *Willing to Kill: The Texas Cheerleader Story*, an exploitative TV drama torn from the headlines. The same fact-based incident served as the basis for HBO's dark comedy *The Positively True Adventures of the Alleged Texas Cheerleader-Murdering Mom*. Finally, Olivia Newton-John played a nice, wholesome cheerleader in *Grease*, but she ditched her pom-poms for black leather in order to keep boyfriend John Travolta. Given the fate of other movie cheerleaders, it was probably a wise decision. See also **Basketball; Football.**

The Cheerleaders (1972)	*Cheerleader Camp* (aka *Bloody Pom-*
The Pom-Pom Girls (1976)	*Poms*) (1987)
Debbie Does Dallas (1978)	*Laker Girls* (1990 TVM)
Grease (1978)	*Willing to Kill: The Texas Cheerleader*
Dallas Cowboy Cheerleaders (1979	*Story* (1992 TVM)
TVM)	*The Positively True Adventures of the*
Dallas Cowboy Cheerleaders II (1980	*Alleged Texas Cheerleader-*
TVM)	*Murdering Mom* (1993 TVM)
Pandemonium (1982)	*Flesh Gordon 2: Flesh Gordon Meets*
Cheerleaders' Wild Weekend (1985)	*the Cosmic Cheerleaders* (1993)

Chess

The game's intensity has been best captured by *Dangerous Moves*, 1985's Best Foreign Film about how two brilliant players eventually become manipulated by their own obsessions. Christopher Lambert played a chess player who becomes a murder suspect in 1992's *Knight Moves*. *Searching for Bobby Fischer* (1993) recounted the story of seven-year-old chess prodigy Josh Waitzkin. Several movies have featured memorable chess games. Max Von Sydow played a chess game with Death in Ingmar Bergman's symbolic *The Seventh Seal* (1957). Steve McQueen and Faye Dunaway practically made love over a game board in *The Thomas Crown Affair* (1968). Sherlock Holmes (Basil Rathbone) used people as chess pieces to solve the puzzle of the Musgrave Ritual in 1943's *Sherlock Holmes Faces Death*. Philo Vance (Rathbone again) clashed with a devious murderer who left a chess piece and Mother Goose rhymes as clues in S.S. Van Dine's *The Bishop Murder Case* (1930). Along similar lines, jewel thief Ryan O'Neal played a chess game with the police in 1973's *The Thief Who Came to Dinner*.

The Bishop Murder Case (1930)	*The King of Chess* (aka *Kei Wong*)
Sherlock Holmes Faces Death (1943)	(1991)
The Seventh Seal (1957)	*Knight Moves* (aka *Face to Face*)
The Thomas Crown Affair (1968)	(1992)
The Thief Who Came to Dinner (1973)	*Searching for Bobby Fischer* (1993)
The Chess Players (1977)	*The Joy Luck Club* (1993)
Dangerous Moves (1985)	

Child Custody Disputes

The commercial success of 1979's *Kramer vs. Kramer* brought the bitter struggles over child custody into close focus and undoubtedly contributed to public awareness. However, earlier movies periodically visited the same subject, often just as effectively. An obscure 1942 Paramount film, *My Heart Belongs to Daddy*, featured Martha O'Driscoll as a dancer fighting her in-laws, who maintained that her profession made her unsuitable for raising her baby. Bing Crosby gave his best nonsinging performance as a father fighting desperately to keep his son in 1957's *Man on Fire*. As in *Kramer*, *Man on Fire* painfully depicted a no-win situation, with a young boy caught in the middle. *One Potato, Two Potato* (1964) injected intriguing controversy, with Barbara Barrie as a woman who married a black man and then clashed with her ex-husband on custody of her daughter. Another variation cropped up in 1974's *Unwed Father*, in which a young man tried to gain custody of his illegitimate daughter. Post-*Kramer* theatrical films include the sensitive Australian import *Careful, He Might Hear You* (1983) and *Ernie Kovacs: Between the Laughter* (1984). The latter real-life story dealt with Kovacs's efforts to retrieve his two daughters, who were kidnapped by their mother after a child custody dispute. The television networks acquired a taste for fact-based child custody cases in the early 1990s, broadcasting films such as *Locked Up: A Mother's Rage* (1991) and *A Mother's Right: The Elizabeth Morgan Story* (1992). Overly cute Drew Barrymore sued parents Shelley Long and Ryan O'Neal for custody of herself in 1984's *Irreconcilable Differences*. That same plot took on real-life implications in two 1993 telefilms, *Gregory K* and *A Place to Be Loved*, both of which recounted the actual case of a twelve-year-old who sued to terminate his parents' custodial rights.

My Heart Belongs to Daddy (1942)	*Mark, I Love You* (1980 TVM)
The Divided Heart (1954)	*Careful, He Might Hear You* (1983)
Man on Fire (1957)	*Irreconcilable Differences* (1984)
One Potato, Two Potato (1964)	*Ernie Kovacs: Between the Laughter*
Unwed Father (1974 TVM)	(1984 TVM)
Kramer vs. Kramer (1979)	*This Child Is Mine* (1985 TVM)

The Good Father (1987)
The Good Mother (1988)
In the Best Interest of the Child (1990 TVM)
Locked Up: A Mother's Rage (1991 TVM)
In the Best Interest of the Children (1992 TVM)
Jonathan: The Boy Nobody Wanted (1992 TVM)

A Mother's Right: The Elizabeth Morgan Story (1992 TVM)
Gregory K (1993 TVM)
Desperate Rescue: The Cathy Mahone Story (1993 TVM)
A Place to Be Loved (1993 TVM)
Whose Child Is This? The War for Baby Jessica (1993 TVM)

Children of the Bride

The saga of the Becker and Hix families proves that television viewers—if not theatrical moviegoers—still have a soft spot for schmaltzy drama. The focus of this TV-movie series was Margaret Becker (Rue McClanahan), a middle-aged divorcée who fell in love with, and eventually married, younger man John Hix. In *Children of the Bride* (1990), Margaret's four adult offspring experienced difficulties coping with this unexpected development in their mother's life. Naturally, they eventually discovered that John was a swell guy. In the 1991 follow-up *Baby of the Bride*, Margaret became pregnant unexpectedly, and each of her children was forced to cope with his or her own problems: Mary had to adjust to life as a single parent; Dennis had a fling with his female boss; twice-divorced Anne was romanced by a charming policeman named Nick; and Andrew "kidnapped" his children from his ex-wife. A tidy conclusion resolved everything, and the Beckers and Hixes enjoyed two years of non-televised bliss. Then, in 1993's *Mother of the Bride*, Anne and Nick decided to get married, Margaret's ex-husband Richard (Paul Dooley) showed up suddenly, and Mary became attracted to a motorcycle-riding construction worker named Ken. Much of the cast remained the same throughout the series: McClanahan as Margaret, Kristy McNichol as Mary, Anne Bobby as Anne, and Connor O'Farrell as Andrew. Patrick Duffy played John Hix in the first film, with Ted Shackleford replacing him in the two sequels. Interestingly, Duffy and Shackleford played brothers Bobby and Gary Ewing on TV's *Dallas*. Kristy McNichol must have seemed a natural for her role, having spent four seasons on the TV series *Family*.

Children of the Bride (1990 TVM)
Baby of the Bride (1991 TVM)

Mother of the Bride (1993 TVM)

Children Raised by Animals

This theme dates back to the Roman myth about twin brothers Romulus and Remus, who were abandoned in the woods as infants and left to die, only to be found and nursed by a she-wolf. Unfortunately, this splendid legend was recounted in perfunctory terms in its only major screen version, the 1961 Italian costume epic *Duel of the Titans*. Wolves were parents again in Rudyard Kipling's *Jungle Book*, in which the young boy Mowgli joined a wolfpack after a vicious tiger separated him from his parents. Alexander Korda produced 1942's *The Jungle Book*, a lavish live-action adaptation starring the charismatic child actor Sabu (who made a career of similar roles). The Disney Studios later turned Kipling's book into a

1967 cartoon musical featuring the voices of Phil Harris and George Sanders. The life of Edgar Rice Burroughs's Tarzan (q.v.) has been detailed in many films, although his childhood among the apes was best portrayed in 1984's *Greystoke: The Legend of Tarzan, Lord of the Apes*. François Truffaut's *The Wild Child* (1969) was a fact-based story about a boy who raised himself in the woods and the doctor dedicated to "civilizing" him. The 1976 TV-movie *Stalk the Wild Child* was a thinly disguised American version about a boy raised by wolves. It was followed by a second TV-movie called *Lucan*, in which a former "wolf child" sets out to find his parents and his own identity. It served as the pilot for the 1977-78 *Lucan* TV series. Howie Mandel played a man raised by wolves in the dismal 1987 comedy *Walk Like a Man*. See also **Tarzan.**

The Jungle Book (1942)	*Stalk the Wild Child* (1976 TVM)
Zamba (1949)	*Lucan* (1977 TVM)
Duel of the Titans (1961)	*Greystoke: The Legend of Tarzan, Lord*
The Jungle Book (1967)	*of the Apes* (1984)
The Wild Child (1969)	*Walk Like a Man* (1987)

Child's Play

Director Tom Holland, who fashioned an effective vampire chiller with *Fright Night* (1985), tackled a difficult challenge with 1988's *Child's Play*. Holland burdened himself with a preposterous premise and then set about to make his audience believe it. His film opened with a shoot-out in which killer Charlie Lee Ray (Brad Dourif) takes refuge in a toy store. A dying Ray grabs an innocent-looking doll and transfers his soul to it. Shortly thereafter, a thoughtful mother (Catherine Hicks) buys the doll for her son Andy (Alex Vincent). Andy quickly realizes that this murderous doll has a life of its own, but—as usual—the adults don't believe until it's almost too late. To his credit, Holland manufactured some legitimate thrills, and he almost made Chucky the doll believable. Since *Child's Play* turned into a sleeper hit, there had to be a sequel (it's the law according to money-minded producers). *Child's Play 2* plucks traumatized Andy into a foster home while his mother recovers in an institution. Naturally, Chucky shows up at Andy's new home, despite being thoroughly mangled at the end of the first film. Alex Vincent reprised his role as Andy and Brad Dourif provided the voice again for Chucky, but John Lafia replaced Holland as director. To prove you can't keep a good villain down, Chucky came back for 1991's *Child's Play 3*, which shifted the same plot to a different setting—a military academy (q.v.)—with an older Alex. Diminishing box office returns for the third installment suggest that there will be no further series entries or a switch to direct-to-videotape releases. See also **Dolls.**

Child's Play (1988)	*Child's Play 3* (1991)
Child's Play 2 (1990)	

A Chinese Ghost Story

This wildly stylish, Hong Kong-lensed supernatural series featured such memorable monsters as the Tree Devil (with his disgustingly long tongue) and the lumbering Mountain Devil. It also mixed romance, humor, and spectacular special effects for a unique film experience. Indeed, *New York Times* film critic Walter Goodman described 1987's *A Chinese Ghost Story* as "98 minutes of bounding and bouncing, flying and flailing, slashing and slaying." The plot revolved around two travelers who took refuge from a storm in a haunted temple. During the night, they encountered a beautiful, seductive ghost and the aforementioned Tree Devil. Leslie Cheung starred in the first two films, which racked up big box office grosses in Hong Kong. The third installment did not fare quite as well as its predecessors. It featured Tony Leung Chiu-wai as a different lead character and took place a century later—still within the confines of a haunted temple. Cult horror film director Tsui Hark served as executive producer and co-wrote the screenplays.

A Chinese Ghost Story (aka *Qian Nu Youhun*) (1987)
A Chinese Ghost Story II (1990)
A Chinese Ghost Story III (aka *Sinnui Yauman III: Do Do Do*) (1991)

Christian, Dr. (Paul)

Prior to his screen debut as paternal country doctor Paul Christian, Jean Hersholt had already provided the character's radio voice and starred in a similar role in three Twentieth Century-Fox films. Daryl Zanuck was the man behind Fox's *The Country Doctor* (1936), a family drama based on the birth of the Dionne quintuplets (and featuring a brief appearance by star-to-be Tyrone Power). Hersholt scored as the family's rural physician and appeared in two sequels: *Reunion* (1936) and *Five of a Kind* (1938). A year later, Hersholt moved to RKO and initiated a new series with *Meet Dr. Christian*. Christian was the Marcus Welby of his era and, in the span of an hour, could cure an epidemic of spinal meningitis and solve a handful of personal crises for his patients. True to character, Hersholt was a great humanitarian himself and received two special Academy Awards for work with the Motion Picture Relief Fund. In 1956, the year of his death, the Academy of Motion Picture Arts and Sciences created an annual humanitarian award to be given in his name. Other *Christian* series regulars included Dorothy Lovett as the doctor's faithful nurse and Robert Baldwin as her boyfriend, the town druggist. Ring Lardner, Jr. wrote several of the scripts. In 1956, MacDonald Carey played the title role in the syndicated TV series *Dr. Christian*.

Meet Dr. Christian (1940)   *Remedy for Riches* (1940)
The Courageous Dr. Christian (1940)   *Melody for Three* (1941)
Dr. Christian Meets the Women (1940)   *They Meet Again* (1941)

Christmas

There was a time when the coming of the yuletide season promised that lesser-known holiday favorites, such as *The Cheaters* and the 1951 *A Christmas Carol* would be pulled from the vaults to air alongside annual classics such as *The Bishop's Wife*, *It's a Wonderful Life*, and *Miracle on 34th Street*. But a glut of recently produced Christmas fare, mostly made-for-TV movies, has diluted the holiday marketplace and sent the "lesser knowns" back into the film vaults. No fewer than thirty-one Christmas-oriented TV-movies were broadcast by the major networks between 1977 and 1992. Nine theatricals were also released during the same period. Ironically, the networks' heaping servings of Christmas sentiment were undoubtedly inspired by the lasting popularity of holiday classics like *It's a Wonderful Life* (which was remade for TV as 1977's *It Happened One Christmas*). As one would expect,

Charles Dickens's *A Christmas Carol* has provided the source material for the most yuletide films: *A Christmas Carol* (1938) with Reginald Owen as Scrooge, *A Christmas Carol* (1951) with Alastair Sim, the musical *Scrooge* (1970) with Albert Finney, *An American Christmas Carol* with Henry Winkler (1979 TVM), *A Christmas Carol* with George C. Scott (1984 TVM), the 1988 contemporary takeoff *Scrooged* with Bill Murray and *The Muppet Christmas Carol* (1992) (not to mention the famous cartoon short *Mr. Magoo's Christmas Carol*). Santa Claus has appeared rather less than one would think, notching appearances in *Babes in Toyland* (1961), *Santa Claus Conquers the Martians* (1964), *The Christmas That Almost Wasn't* (1966), *Santa Claus: The Movie* (1985), and *Ernest Saves Christmas* (1988). Art Carney played St. Nick in *The Night They Saved Christmas* (1984), a part he knew well as a result of his 1960 appearance in the touching "Night of the Meek" episode of the TV show *The Twilight Zone*. He starred as a drunken department store Santa who loses his job, only to find a magic bag of toys and become the real St. Nick. Of course, not everyone in a Santa suit experiences that kind of magic. Christopher Plummer played an unstable murderer who robbed a bank disguised as Santa in *The Silent Partner* (1978). A psychotic killer sported a Santa suit in the tasteless 1984 slasher film *Silent Night, Deadly Night*.

A Christmas Carol (1938)
Beyond Tomorrow (1940)
Holiday Inn (1942)
Christmas Holiday (1944)
The Cheaters (aka *The Castaway*) (1945)
Christmas in Connecticut (aka *Indiscretion*) (1945)
It's a Wonderful Life (1946)
The Bishop's Wife (1947)
Christmas Eve (aka *Sinner's Holiday*) (1947)
Miracle on 34th Street (aka *The Big Heart*) (1947)
Holiday Affair (1949)
A Christmas Carol (aka *Scrooge*) (1951)
The Lemon Drop Kid (1951)
The Holly and the Ivy (1952)
White Christmas (1954)
Babes in Toyland (1961)
Santa Claus Conquers the Martians (1964)
The Christmas That Almost Wasn't (1966)
The Christmas Tree (aka *When Wolves Cry*) (1969)
Scrooge (1970)
The Homecoming—A Christmas Story (1971 TVM)

Home for the Holidays (1972 TVM)
A Dream for Christmas (1973 TVM)
Miracle on 34th Street (1973 TVM)
Black Christmas (aka *Silent Night, Evil Night; Stranger in the House*) (1975)
Young Pioneers' Christmas (1976 TVM)
Sunshine Christmas (1977 TVM)
Christmas Miracle in Caufield, U.S.A. (aka *The Christmas Coal Mine Miracle*) (1977 TVM)
The Gathering (1977 TVM)
It Happened One Christmas (1977 TVM)
A Christmas to Remember (1978 TVM)
The Gift of Love (1978 TVM)
An American Christmas Carol (1979 TVM)
Christmas Lilies of the Field (1979 TVM)
The Gathering, Part II (1979 TVM)
The Man in the Santa Claus Suit (1979 TVM)
A Christmas Without Snow (1980 TVM)
You Better Watch Out (aka *Christmas Evil; Terror in Toyland*) (1980)

The Gift of Love: A Christmas Story (1983 TVM)

A Christmas Story (1983)

A Christmas Carol (1984 TVM)

It Came Upon a Midnight Clear (1984 TVM)

The Night They Saved Christmas (1984 TVM)

Silent Night, Deadly Night (1984)

One Magic Christmas (1985)

Santa Claus: The Movie (aka Santa Claus) (1985)

Christmas Eve (1986 TVM)

The Christmas Gift (1986 TVM)

The Christmas Star (1986 TVM)

Christmas Comes to Willow Creek (1987 TVM)

The Christmas Visitor (aka Bushfire Moon) (1987 TVM)

I'll Be Home for Christmas (1988 TVM)

Ernest Saves Christmas (1988)

Scrooged (1988)

A Very Brady Christmas (1988 TVM)

National Lampoon's Christmas Vacation (1989)

Prancer (1989)

Guess Who's Coming for Christmas? (1990 TVM)

The Kid Who Loved Christmas (1990 TVM)

Home Alone (1990)

In the Nick of Time (1991 TVM)

All I Want for Christmas (1991)

Yes, Virginia, There Is a Santa Claus (1991 TVM)

Christmas on Division Street (1991 TVM)

Miracle in the Wilderness (1991 TVM)

Christmas in Connecticut (1992 TVM)

The Man Upstairs (1992 TVM)

To Grandmother's House We Go (1992 TVM)

Home Alone 2 (1992)

The Muppet Christmas Carol (1992)

Tim Burton's The Nightmare Before Christmas (aka The Nightmare Before Christmas) (1993)

Cinerama

Former Paramount special effects technician Fred Waller invented this wide-screen process, which produces a 165-degree curved image, in the early 1950s. It evolved from an earlier Waller system called Vitarama, which used eleven synchronized projectors to create an illusion of vastness and motion on a curved theater screen. Vitarama was a big hit at the 1937 World's Fair, but its expense and technical requirements made it impractical for common use. Waller refined it over the next two decades and introduced a new version in 1952 with the travelogue film *This Is Cinerama*. The Cinerama process required a film to be shot with three cameras, one facing straight ahead and the other two slightly to the left and right of the middle camera. Three synchronized projectors then projected all three films on a curved screen simultaneously. Like *This Is Cinerama*, the early films shown in the process focused on spectacular visual effects — breathtaking roller coaster rides and soaring plane flights over the Grand Canyon. Unlike 3-D, Cinerama survived the 1950s, perhaps because its equipment restrictions limited the number of theaters that could show Cinerama films and elevated the process to special-event status. The first nontravelogue was 1962's *How the West Was Won*. Films continued to be made in Cinerama throughout the 1960s. However, technical difficulties, specifically problems with keeping the projectors synchronized, drove the development of a one-projector Cinerama process. The "new" Cinerama amounted to little more than projecting a 70mm image on a curved screen. It was abandoned in the 1970s, though expositions and amusement parks continue to exhibit popular Cinerama-like projection systems. See also **3-D; Gimmicks.**

This Is Cinerama (1952)
Cinerama Holiday (1955)
Seven Wonders of the World (1956)
Search for Paradise (1957)
South Seas Adventure (1958)
How the West Was Won (1962)
The Wonderful World of the Brothers Grimm (1962)
It's a Mad, Mad, Mad, Mad World (1963)

Circus World (1963)
The Best of Cinerama (1964)
Battle of the Bulge (1965)
Grand Prix (1966)
2001: A Space Odyssey (1968)
Ice Station Zebra (1968)
Custer of the West (1968)
Krakatoa, East of Java (aka *Volcano*) (1969)

Circuses

The allure of the big top setting has faded recently, but for four decades, it was an ideal place to find high-wire dramatics, ferocious beasts, incognito killers, and perhaps a troupe of vampires. Laughs, too, as evidenced by the number of comedies set against a circus backdrop: W.C. Fields played a ringmaster in *You Can't Cheat an Honest Man* (1939); the Marx Brothers saved a circus from bankruptcy in *At the Circus* (1939); and even Dean Martin and Jerry Lewis got into the act with *Three Ring Circus* (1954). Movie murderers have also exhibited a special fondness for circuses, as evidenced in *Charlie Chan at the Circus* (1936), *Circus of Horrors* (1960), *Psycho Circus* (1967) and *Berserk* (1968). On a classier level, James Stewart played a murder suspect hiding out as a mild-mannered clown in Cecil DeMille's 1952 extravaganza *The Greatest Show on Earth*. This multicharacter melodrama garnered a Best Picture Oscar and tallied record box office figures for Paramount. The film's successful behind-the-scenes formula was more or less copied in *The Big Circus* (1959), *The Big Show* (1961) and *Circus World* (1964). The life of the world's greatest circus showman was chronicled in 1934's *The Mighty Barnum* and 1986's *Barnum*, with Wallace Beery and Burt Lancaster in the title roles, respectively. Serious European directors have used the circus for symbolic purposes, as in Ingmar Bergman's *Sawdust and Tinsel* (1953), Federico Fellini's *La Strada* (1954), and Wim Wenders's *Wings of Desire* (1987). Four Disney pictures have taken place at least partially under the big top: *Dumbo* (1941), *Toby Tyler* (1960), *A Tiger Walks* (1964) and *The Three Lives of Thomasina* (1964). *Lady in the Dark* (1944) had a musical dream sequence set in a circus, while Rodgers and Hart's *Billy Rose's Jumbo* (1962) revolved around a circus owned by Doris Day. The circus in 1961's *Gorgo* featured a dinosaur as its main attraction. Unfortunately, it turned out to be a baby with a mad mother in hot pursuit. See also **Fairs and Carnivals.**

He Who Gets Slapped (1924)
The Circus (1928)
Dangerous Curves (1929)
Rain or Shine (1930)
Freaks (aka *Nature's Mistakes*) (1932)
Polly of the Circus (1932)
The Big Cage (1933)

The Mighty Barnum (1934)
Circus Clown (1934)
Charlie Chan at the Circus (1936)
You Can't Cheat an Honest Man (1939)
At the Circus (1939)
Chad Hanna (1940)

Dumbo (1941)
Road Show (1941)
Sunny (1941)
The Wagons Roll at Night (1941)
The Dark Tower (1943)
Lady in the Dark (1944) (dream
    sequence)
Dual Alibi (1947)
Caged Fury (1948)
The Fat Man (1951)
The Greatest Show on Earth (1952)
Encore (1952) (segment)
Sawdust and Tinsel (aka *The Naked
    Night*) (1953)
Man on a Tightrope (1953)
Three Ring Circus (aka *Jerrico, the
    Wonder Clown*) (1954)
La Strada (aka *The Road*) (1954)
Carnival Story (1954)
Ring of Fear (1954)
Trapeze (1956)
Invitation to the Dance (1957)
Merry Andrew (1958)
The Big Circus (1959)
The Flying Fontaines (1959)
Circus of Horrors (1960)
*Toby Tyler, or Ten Weeks With a
    Circus* (1960)
The Big Show (1961)

Gorgo (1961)
Hippodrome (1961)
Bimbo the Great (1961)
Billy Rose's Jumbo (aka *Jumbo*) (1962)
The Main Attraction (1962)
Circus World (aka *The Magnificent
    Showman*) (1964)
A Tiger Walks (1964)
The Three Lives of Thomasina (1964)
Rings Around the World (1967)
Psycho Circus (aka *Circus of Fear*)
    (1967)
Berserk (1968)
Vampire Circus (1971)
The Clowns (1971)
Parade (1974)
Punch and Jody (1974 TVM)
The Last Circus Show (aka *The
    Balloon Vendor*) (1974)
The Great Wallendas (1978 TVM)
When the Circus Comes to Town (1981
    TVM)
Side Show (1981 TVM)
Octopussy (1983)
Barnum (1986 TVM)
Wings of Desire (1987)
Big Top Pee Wee (1988)
Shadows and Fog (1992)

Cisco Kid

The origins of the Cisco Kid separate him from his many rival B-movie Western heroes. The Kid's sound debut was 1929's *In Old Arizona*, which had the triple distinction of being based on an O. Henry short story, featuring an Oscar-winning turn by Warner Baxter as Cisco, and introducing the popular song "My Tonia" (recorded by Nic Lucas). The film was a sizable hit for Fox, chiefly due to the expert direction of Western specialist Raoul Walsh. Baxter starred in the 1930 semisequel *The Arizona Kid* before officially reprising his Robin Hood-like Mexican outlaw in 1931's *The Cisco Kid*. *In Old Arizona* alumnus Edmund Lowe also returned as the dedicated Texas Ranger bent on capturing Cisco. After this second Cisco film, Baxter strove to avoid typecasting and appeared in musicals (*42nd Street*), biographical dramas (*Prisoner of Shark Island*), and comedies (*Daddy Long Legs*). However, by 1936, his popularity was declining and he appeared in the Cisco-like *Robin Hood of El Dorado*. Three years later, Twentieth Century-Fox hailed his comeback in *The Return of the Cisco Kid*. Yet, unlike the earlier films in the series, *Return* was a programmer, running just seventy minutes and costarring young performers like Cesar Romero. In fact, Romero stepped up into the lead role in the follow-up *The Cisco Kid and the Lady* and five subsequent films. Fox dumped the series in 1941, but four years later Monogram picked it up and installed former *Three Mesquiteers* (q.v.) supporting player Duncan Renaldo as Cisco. Renaldo starred in three films, beginning with 1945's *The Cisco Kid Returns*, before Monogram replaced him with Gilbert Roland, the only Latin actor to portray the Kid. An affable, sturdy performer, Roland made six modestly entertaining Cisco entries before Monogram ended its series. Surprisingly, United Artists revived the series in 1949 and recalled Renaldo to reprise the Mexican bandit hero. Renaldo made five entries, assisted by Leo Carillo as his chubby sidekick Pancho. In late 1950, Renaldo and Carillo transitioned from hour-long theatrical features to a half-hour syndicated TV series. *The Cisco Kid* quickly became the biggest nonnetwork hit of the 1950s. Its 156-episode run concluded in 1956, although it is still shown on television today (since the producers were smart enough to film in color).

In Old Arizona (1929) (Warner Baxter)

The Cisco Kid (1931) (Baxter)

Return of the Cisco Kid (1939) (Baxter)

The Cisco Kid and the Lady (1939) (Cesar Romero)

The Gay Caballero (1940) (Romero)

Lucky Cisco Kid (1940) (Romero)

Viva Cisco Kid (1940) (Romero)

Romance of the Rio Grande (1941) (Romero)

Ride On, Vaquero (1941) (Romero)

The Cisco Kid Returns (1945) (Duncan Renaldo)

In Old Mexico (aka *The Cisco Kid in Old Mexico*) (1945) (Renaldo)

South of the Rio Grande (1945) (Renaldo)

The Gay Cavalier (1946) (Gilbert Roland)

South of Monterey (1946) (Roland)

Beauty and the Bandit (1946) (Roland)

King of the Bandits (1947) (Roland)

Riding the California Trail (1947) (Roland)

Robin Hood of Monterey (1947) (Roland)

The Valiant Hombre (1949) (Renaldo)

The Daring Caballero (1949) (Renaldo)

The Gay Amigo (1949) (Renaldo)

Satan's Cradle (1949) (Renaldo)

The Girl From San Lorenzo (1950) (Renaldo)

Clairvoyants and Fortune-Tellers

The ability to predict the future has been a liability as often as a blessing in the movies. In 1935's *The Clairvoyant*, Claude Rains played a phony fortune-teller who discovers that his predictions—including one of his death—are coming true. A similar fate befell Akim Tamiroff in *The Great Gambini* (1937) and Edward G. Robinson in *Night Has a Thousand Eyes* (1948). Five years earlier, Robinson played a man fatally obsessed with a palm reader's uncanny predictions in the eeriest tale in Julien Duvivier's anthology *Flesh and Fantasy*. Mr. Big forcibly employed the clairvoyant Solitaire (Jane Seymour) in the 1973 Bond adventure *Live and Let Die*. Alas, 007 put an end to Solitaire's prophetic powers, since they were somehow tied to her virginity. Clairvoyants capable of predicting murders aided the police in *The Eyes of Charles Sand* (1972), *Man on a Swing* (1974) and *Eyes of Laura Mars* (1978). The 1971 TV-movie *Sweet,*

Sweet Rachel spun off the short-lived 1972 series *The Sixth Sense*, which starred Gary Collins as a psychic private investigator. Traditional gypsy and roadside fortune-tellers have had brief but memorable scenes in *The Wizard of Oz*, *The Wolf Man* and *The Leopard Man*. The finest clairvoyant comedy, Rene Clair's *It Happened Tomorrow* (1944), featured Dick Powell as a reporter who gets tomorrow's newspaper delivered a day early. Other lighthearted fortune-telling tales include Eddie Cantor's *Palmy Days* (1932) and Ealing's *The Oracle* (1952). See also **Mediums and Seances.**

The Hole in the Wall (1929)	*Sweet, Sweet Rachel* (1971 TVM)
Palmy Days (1932)	*The Eyes of Charles Sand* (1972 TVM)
The Clairvoyant (aka *The Evil Mind*) (1935)	*Visions . . .* (aka *Visions of Death*) (1972 TVM)
The Great Gambini (1937)	*Baffled* (1972 TVM)
The Wizard of Oz (1939)	*Live and Let Die* (1973)
The Wolf Man (1940)	*Man on a Swing* (1974)
The Crystal Ball (1943)	*The Premonition* (1976)
Flesh and Fantasy (1943)	*Eyes of Laura Mars* (1978)
The Leopard Man (1943)	*Mind Over Murder* (1979 TVM)
It Happened Tomorrow (1944)	*The Dead Zone* (1983)
Inner Sanctum (1948)	*The Clairvoyant* (1985)
Night Has a Thousand Eyes (1948)	*Second Sight* (1989)
The Oracle (1952)	*Black Rainbow* (1989)
Dr. Terror's House of Horrors (aka *The Blood Suckers*) (1965)	*The Butcher's Wife* (1991)
	Psychic (1992 TVM)

Class Reunions

Class reunions have reunited former sweethearts and provided a convenient grouping of classmates for revenge-minded killers. Betty Hutton and Dana Andrews played former classmates who discover love again fifteen years after college in *Spring Reunion* (1957). In *Class of '63*, a college reunion convinced Cliff Gorman that wife Joan Hackett was still in love with former flame James Brolin. And, in 1980's *Reunion*, Kevin Dobson found himself attracted to both his former high school sweetheart and her seventeen-year-old daughter. His predicament, although fraught with complexities, seems minor compared to those facing the potential slasher victims in *Slaughter High* (1986) and *Terror Stalks the Class Reunion* (1992). *National Lampoon's Class Reunion* (1982) played the classmate-killer angle for laughs (which were in short supply). In addition to class reunions, there have been a number of films about high school or college friends getting together after several years: *The Return of the Secaucus 7* (1980), *Over Forty* (aka *Beyond Forty)* (1982), *The Big Chill* (1983), *Windy City* (1984), *Peter's Friends* (1993) and *Indian Summer* (1993).

Spring Reunion (1957)	*Peggy Sue Got Married* (1986)
Class of '63 (1973 TVM)	*Something Wild* (1986)
Reunion (1980 TVM)	*Slaughter High* (1986)
National Lampoon's Class Reunion (1982)	*Terror Stalks the Class Reunion* (1992 TVM)

Coffin Ed Johnson and Grave Digger Jones

"You steal money from white folks—that's your business; you steal money from blacks, that's *my* business," warned detective Coffin Ed Johnson as he shook down a black con artist in 1970's *Cotton Comes to Harlem*. This trend-setting adaptation of Chester Himes's detective novel mixed violence, humor, nudity and racial satire to achieve predictably mixed results. The humor worked best, with most of it provided by tough, cynical Harlem detectives Coffin Ed Johnson (Raymond St. Jacques) and Grave Digger Jones (Godfrey Cambridge). As they searched for a mysterious bale of cotton, Coffin Ed and Grave Digger administered their own type of justice—exposing a crooked black evangelist, dealing with stupid white cops, and finally working out a deal with a Mafia kingpin. Through it all, they maintained their personal ethics (Coffin Ed reminded a violent mob: "We may have broken some heads, but we never broke no promises."). The film had serious flaws, including a mismatched music score and a rambling pace, but its popular success contributed substantially to the beginning of the blaxploitation (q.v.) film cycle of the 1970s. St. Jacques and Cambridge reprised their roles for the 1972 follow-up *Come Back, Charleston Blue*. Based on Himes's novel *The Heat's On*, the storyline found Grave Digger and Coffin Ed involved with a series of gruesome murders, missing razor blades, the Harlem drug trade, and a Mafia chief. This sequel failed to duplicate the first film's success, and the series apparently came to a quick conclusion. Then, nineteen years later, another Himes novel hit the screens. *A Rage in Harlem* is primarily the tale of a naive undertaker (Forest Whitaker) who falls under the spell of a provocative femme fatale (Robin Givens). She's involved with some heavy-hitting gangsters and a pair of relentless detectives—Coffin Ed Johnson (Stack Pierce) and Grave Digger Jones (George Wallace). Although relegated to supporting roles, Coffin Ed and Grave Digger boosted this entertaining action-comedy. Sadly, *A Rage in Harlem* failed to catch on with either moviegoers or videotape renters. See also **Blaxploitation Films**.

    Cotton Comes to Harlem (1970)   *A Rage in Harlem* (1991)
    Come Back, Charleston Blue (1972)

The Cohens and the Kellys

The Jewish Cohens and the Irish Kellys were feuding families in a series of seven Universal comedies that spanned the transition from silent to talking pictures. *The Cohens and the Kellys* (1926) was based on Aaron Hoffman's play *Two Blocks Away*, although the obvious similarities to Anne Nichols's Broadway hit *Abie's Irish Rose* resulted in a lawsuit. This first picture established the framework for the series, with the families being drawn together by the romance between the Kellys' son and the Cohens' daughter and the inheritance of a fortune. Jewish shopkeeper Cohen initially inherited the money, only to discover that it actually belonged to Irish cop Kelly. In the end, they became partners, setting the stage for a series of wild adventures in Africa (buying elephant tusks for a piano company), Scotland (entering the tartan business), and even Atlantic City. In most of the films, George Sidney and Vera Gorden played the Cohens with Charlie Murray and Kate Price as the Kellys. *The Cohens and Kellys in Scotland* is considered the best of the series, although *Hollywood* featured guest bits by Tom Mix, Boris Karloff and Lew Ayres. Almost forty years after the last *Cohen-Kelly* movie, the premise of feuding Jewish and Irish families popped up again in the TV series *Bridget Loves Bernie.*

The Cohens and the Kellys (1926)	*The Cohens and Kellys in Africa* (1930)
The Cohens and the Kellys in Paris (1928)	*The Cohens and Kellys in Hollywood* (1933)
The Cohens and Kellys in Atlantic City (1929)	*The Cohens and Kellys in Trouble* (1933)
The Cohens and Kellys in Scotland (1930)	

Color/B&W Features

The dramatic use of color in black-and-white films (and vice versa) attracted little interest until 1939's *The Wizard of Oz*, which transported Dorothy from monochrome Kansas into exciting, colorful Oz. The same trick was repeated in *The Blue Bird* (1940), a similar fantasy in which a black-and-white prologue gave way to a lengthy color dream sequence. The idea of filming reality in black and white and fantasy in color was neatly reversed in 1946's *Stairway to Heaven* (aka *A Matter of Life and Death*). It starred David Niven as a wounded pilot destined to die but so determined to live that he argues his case in a celestial trial. Because he wants to continue his existence in this world, the earthly segments are shown in color, while the scenes in Heaven are in black and white. Forty-one years later, Heaven reverts to color and reality to black and white in the opening of *Made in Heaven* (later in the movie, the earthly scenes acquire color, too). Less elaborate uses of color are displayed in *Portrait of Jennie, The Picture of Dorian Gray* and *The Moon and Sixpence*, three black-and-white films in which paintings appear in color. In other films: Judy Holliday drove away in a gold auto in the original black-and-white print of *The Solid Gold Cadillac*. In William Castle's gimmicky *The Tingler*, there's a brief but highly effective sequence — in which bright red blood splashes out of a black-and-white bathroom sink faucet. And in George Romero's *Martin*, a would-be teen vampire has black-and-white dreams of his earlier life as a bloodsucker.

Dixiana (1930)	*And Now My Love* (1975)
Victoria the Great (1937)	*Martin* (1978)
The Wizard of Oz (1939)	*Movie Movie* (1978)
The Blue Bird (1940)	*Stalker* (1979)
The Moon and Sixpence (1942)	*Zelig* (1983)
Stairway to Heaven (aka *A Matter of Life and Death*) (1946)	*19/19* (1985)
Portrait of Jennie (1948)	*Kiss of the Spider Woman* (1985)
I'll Never Forget You (1951)	*Mishima* (1985)
Jack and the Beanstalk (1953)	*She's Gotta Have It* (1986)
The Solid Gold Cadillac (1956)	*Made in Heaven* (1987)
The Tingler (1959)	*Radium City* (1987)
The Private Lives of Adam and Eve (1960)	*Wings of Desire* (1988)
A Man and a Woman (1966)	*D.O.A.* (1988)
If . . . (1968)	*The Navigator: A Medieval Odyssey* (1988)
	Transylvania Twist (1989)

Truth or Dare (aka *In Bed With*   *Dead Again* (1991)
   Madonna; Truth or Dare: In Bed   *Kafka* (1991)
   With Madonna) (1991)

Coma

The frightening side effects of unusual comas provided the premise for two exceptionally clever films, 1970's *The Mind of Mr. Soames* and 1983's *The Dead Zone*. Both films effectively balanced science fiction, horror and reality by concentrating on the personal traumas of the coma victims. *The Dead Zone*, adapted from Stephen King's best-seller, starred Christopher Walken as an accident victim who emerges from a five-year coma with the ability to foresee the future of those he touches. This apparent gift turned out to be a liability that drove Walken's character to commit murder to prevent a future disaster. In *The Mind of Mr. Soames*, a scientist revived a man from a thirty-year coma—which began with his birth. Thus, he was "born" as an adult with the mind of a baby. More mainstream pictures include 1978's *Coma*, with Genevieve Bujold as a dedicated doctor who discovers that the body parts of comatose patients are being auctioned in an organ black market. *Patrick* (1978) was a telekinetic teen, ala *Carrie*, who wreaked havoc while in a comatose state. *Seizure: The Story of Kathy Morris* (1980) was the real-life story of a singer's struggle to recover from a coma. See also **Suspended Animation.**

   The Clay Pigeon (1949)   *The Dead Zone* (1983)
   The Mind of Mr. Soames (1970)   *Bad Dreams* (1988)
   Coma (1978)   *Silent Night, Deadly Night III: You*
   Patrick (1978)   *Better Watch Out!* (1989)
   Seizure: The Story of Kathy Morris   *Hard to Kill* (1990)
      (1980 TVM)   *Reversal of Fortune* (1990)
   Brimstone and Treacle (1982)   *She Woke Up* (1992 TVM)

Comic Book Characters

With the notable exceptions of Superman (q.v.) and Batman, few comic book characters have encountered significant success in feature films. During the 1940s, they thrived in action-packed serials like Columbia's *Batman* and *Captain America*. A young Robert Wagner brought Prince Valiant to life in a 1954 film. Then the briefly popular 1966-68 TV series *Batman* spawned a campy, feature-length theatrical film. Both movies were intended for juvenile audiences and no sequels followed. In the mid-1970s, comic book superheroes achieved minor popularity in the form of made-for-TV movies (both *The New Original Wonder Woman* and *The Incredible Hulk* led to TV series). And then in 1978, the big-budgeted *Superman* caught the public's fancy, and three progressively less interesting, but still profitable, sequels appeared over the next decade. Meanwhile, a pair of Japanese samurai imports, based on the *Lone Wolf and Cub* comic book series, acquired a cult following in the United States. The films were *Lightning Swords of Death* and *Shogun Assassin*, and they traced the exploits of a hunted warrior who pushed his son around in an armed baby cart. Comic books, as a literature form, acquired a serious adult following in the 1980s. This ultimately led to the 1989 brooding blockbuster version of *Batman*, with Michael Keaton as the Caped Cru-

sader (sans Robin) and Jack Nicholson hamming it up as The Joker. See also
Superman; The Incredible Hulk.

Superman and the Mole Men (1951)	*Dr. Strange* (1978 TVM)
Prince Valiant (1954)	*Superman* (1978)
Batman (1966)	*Captain America* (1979 TVM)
Danger: Diabolik (1968)	*Mandrake* (1979 TVM)
The Adventures of Barry McKenzie (1972)	*Shogun Assassin* (1981)
	Swamp Thing (1982)
Barry McKenzie Holds His Own (1974)	*Howard the Duck* (1986)
	The Spirit (1987 TVM)
Wonder Woman (1974 TVM)	*Return of the Swamp Thing* (1989)
Lightning Swords of Death (1974)	*Batman* (1989)
The New Original Wonder Woman (1975 TVM)	*The Punisher* (1989)
	The Dark Avenger (1990 TVM)
The Incredible Hulk (1977 TVM)	*The Rocketeer* (1991)
Spider-Man (1977 TVM)	*Dr. Giggles* (1992)

Comic Book-Style Movies

The old E.C. horror comics have inspired four multipart movies: *Tales From the Crypt, Vault of Horror, Creepshow* and *Creepshow 2*. With its animated introductions and dark quirky humor, *Creepshow* rates as the best of these efforts.

Comic Strip Characters

Comic strips have provided a rich source of film material, serving as the basis for several popular film series. The most influential was undoubtedly Chic Young's "Blondie" (q.v.) strip, which was adapted into a twenty-seven-film series that lasted from 1938 to 1951. No other comic strip favorite has matched that level of success, although Dick Tracy, Jiggs and Maggie, Jungle Jim, Red Ryder, Dick Barton, and the Peanuts Gang (qq.v.) also earned their own film series. *Dick Tracy* and *Dennis the Menace* reached mass audiences as big-budget theatrical films in 1990 and 1993, respectively. However, other famous funnies' characters have floundered on the screen. Even an earlier Dennis the Menace movie debuted as a throwaway 1987 telefilm. A similar fate befell *Brenda Starr* (1976), *Archie: To Riverdale and Back* (1990) and *Buck Rogers in the 25th Century* (1979), although the latter made-for-TV movie actually received a theatrical distribution. The exploits of Li'l Abner and Little Orphan Annie were adapted into splashy, overblown musicals that sadly lost sight of their characters' charms. Film versions of adult comic strips have been scarce, consisting mostly of a couple of sexy heroines (*Barbarella, Modesty Blaise*) and sex-obsessed cats (*Fritz the Cat*). See also **Barton, Dick; Blondie; Jiggs and Maggie; Jungle Jim; Peanuts; Ryder, Red; Tracy, Dick.**

Little Orphan Annie (1932)	*Modesty Blaise* (1966)
Joe Palooka (1934)	*Barbarella* (aka *Barbarella, Queen of the Galaxy*) (1968)
Reg'lar Fellows (1941)	
The Sad Sack (1957)	*Fritz the Cat* (1972)
Li'l Abner (1959)	*The Nine Lives of Fritz the Cat* (1975)
Dondi (1961)	*Brenda Starr* (1976 TVM)

Buck Rogers in the 25th Century (1979)	*Dick Tracy* (1990)
Flash Gordon (1980)	*Archie: To Riverdale and Back* (1990 TVM)
Annie (1982)	*Brenda Starr* (1992)
Dennis the Menace (1987 TVM)	*Dennis the Menace* (1993)

Compilation Films (Fictional)

The birth of the "compilation film" can be traced to its widespread use by documentary filmmakers during the two World Wars. Gifted filmmakers such as Frank Capra edited selected newsreel footage to produce historical time capsules and effective propaganda pieces. In the late 1950s, former Pathé News employee Robert Youngson, who had directed the 1950 newsreel compilation *Fifty Years Before Your Eyes*, turned the compilation movie into a tool for preserving—and reviving—fictional films. His 1957 compilation *The Golden Age of Comedy* featured choice clips of silent classics starring Laurel and Hardy, Will Rogers and Harry Langdon. It revived interest in the great silent comedians, prompting Charlie Chaplin to release *The Chaplin Revue* (1958), which was simply three shorts strung together with some behind-the-scenes footage (actually, earlier Chaplin shorts had been packaged together as far back as 1938). The following year, Youngson returned with another superior silent comedy compilation, *When Comedy Was King*. In the 1960s, he raided the studios' vaults and produced *The Days of Thrills and Laughter* (1961), *Thirty Years of Fun* (1963), *MGM's Big Parade of Comedy* (1964), *Laurel and Hardy's Laughing 20's* (1965), *The Further Perils of Laurel and Hardy* (1967) and *Four Clowns* (1970). Youngson died in 1974, the same year in which Jack Haley, Jr. produced the highly successful MGM musical compilation *That's Entertainment*. Haley's film was a financial bonanza for MGM, costing next to nothing and providing glamorous publicity for the studio's fiftieth anniversary. The inevitable sequel *That's Entertainment Part 2* appeared in 1976, this one combining the musical clips with "straight" scenes (e.g., Garbo playing *Camille*). Haley added a belated third installment to his MGM compilation series with 1985's *That's Dancing*. Despite a marvelous selection of dance footage, it failed to attract the younger audiences that flocked to the contemporary hit *Flashdance* (1983). Although Youngson and Haley's compilations are the most fondly remembered, other filmmakers have utilized the format effectively. Warner Bros. compiled its best Looney Tunes cartoons and released them into the theaters as *Bugs Bunny, Superstar* (1975), *The Great American Chase* (1979), *Bugs Bunny's 3rd Movie: 1001 Rabbit Tales* (1982) and *Daffy Duck's Movie: Fantastic Island* (1983). The funniest segments from Sid Caesar's classic TV series *Your Show of Shows* surfaced in the 1973 compilation *Ten From Your Show of Shows* (1973). A year earlier, skits from British television's *Monty Python's Flying Circus* came stateside as *And Now for Something Completely Different*. Science fiction and horror film retrospectives have reached the screen as *It Came From Hollywood* (1982) and *Terror in the Aisles* (1984). *It's Showtime* (1976) was an enjoyable compilation of animal movie clips, highlighted by a canine rendition of "Singin' in the Rain."

Charlie Chaplin Carnival (1938)	*The Golden Age of Comedy* (1957)
Charlie Chaplin Cavalcade (1938)	*The Chaplin Revue* (1958)
Charlie Chaplin Festival (1938)	*When Comedy Was King* (1959)

The Days of Thrills and Laughter (1961)

Harold Lloyd's World of Comedy (1962)

Harold Lloyd's Funny Side of Life (1963)

Laugh With Max Linder (1963)

Thirty Years of Fun (1963)

The Great Chase (1963)

Marilyn (1963)

MGM's Big Parade of Comedy (1964)

The Love Goddesses (1965)

The World of Abbott and Costello (1965)

Laurel and Hardy's Laughing 20's (1965)

The Further Perils of Laurel and Hardy (1967)

The Crazy World of Laurel and Hardy (1967)

Four Clowns (1970)

And Now for Something Completely Different (1972)

Ten From Your Show of Shows (1973)

That's Entertainment (1974)

Bugs Bunny, Superstar (1975)

It's Showtime (1976)

That's Entertainment Part 2 (1976)

America at the Movies (1976)

The Great American Chase (aka The Bugs Bunny/Roadrunner Movie) (1979)

Bugs Bunny's 3rd Movie: 1001 Rabbit Tales (1982)

It Came From Hollywood (1982)

Daffy Duck's Movie: Fantastic Island (1983)

Terror in the Aisles (1984)

That's Dancing (1985)

The Puppetoon Movie (1987)

Composers (Classical)

Hollywood-produced biographies, supplemented by a handful of imports, have glossed over the history of classical music by focusing almost exclusively on a select number of composers. A French director (Julien Duvivier) made Hollywood's first major composer biography of the sound era with 1938's *The Great Waltz*, the story of Johann Strauss (the Younger) and his unforgettable "The Blue Danube." Costar/soprano Miliza Korjus and lyricist Oscar Hammerstein II turned two Strauss melodies into the popular hits "I'm in Love With Vienna" and "One Day When We Were Young." Despite the film's success, seven years elapsed before the Chopin biography *A Song to Remember* (1945) made a star of Cornel Wilde and inspired a trio of imitations. Stewart Granger played violinist virtuoso/composer Niccolo Paganini in *The Magic Bow* (1947). *Song of Love* (1947) cast Katharine Hepburn and Paul Henried as Clara and Robert Schumann and Robert Walker as their friend Johannes Brahms. Jean-Pierre Aumont played Nikolay Rimsky-Korsakov in 1947's campy *Song of Scheherezade*, which dealt primarily with the composer's infatuation with a Spanish-Moroccan dancer (Yvonne De Carlo). Occasional films about classical composers continued to appear during the next two decades. However, a new trend did not emerge until Ken Russell introduced his unconventional biographies in the early 1970s. Russell made his mark on British television in the 1960s with critically acclaimed documentaries and biographies of Wagner, Debussy and Elgar. His theatrical films have been greeted less enthusiastically due to his penchant for excess (the descriptive publicity line for his 1971 Tchaikovsky biography *The Music Lovers* was: "The story of a homosexual who married a nymphomaniac"). Russell's roller coaster style has managed to confuse his critics for years. His 1974 biopic *Mahler* earned praise for its intelligence and restraint, but the director's excesses were on display again in the following year's *Lisztomania*, a rock version of Liszt's life starring The Who's Roger Daltrey. In the post-Russell era, Czech director Milos Forman has made the biggest impact with his splendid 1984 Best Picture *Amadeus*. Peter Shaffer adapted the film from his own play about the conflict between Mozart contemporary Salieri and the Master himself.

The Great Waltz (1938) (Johann Strauss)

The Great Victor Herbert (1939)

Melody Master (1941) (Franz Schubert)

The Great Mr. Handel (1942) (George Handel)

A Song to Remember (1945) (Frederic Chopin)

The Magic Bow (1947) (Niccolo Paganini)

Song of Love (1947) (Robert Schumann)

Song of Scheherazade (1947) (Nikolay Rimsky-Korsakov)

The Great Gilbert and Sullivan (aka *The Story of Gilbert and Sullivan*) (1953) (Sir William Gilbert and Sir Arthur Sullivan)

Deep in My Heart (1954) (Sigmund Romberg)

Magic Fire (1956) (Richard Wagner)

Song Without End (1960) (Franz Liszt)

The Magnificent Rebel (1962) (Ludwig van Beethoven)

The Waltz King (1963) (Strauss)

Song of Norway (1970) (Edvard Grieg)

The Music Lovers (1971) (Peter Tchaikovsky)

The Great Waltz (1972) (Strauss)

Mahler (1974) (Gustav Mahler)

Lisztomania (1975) (Liszt)

Wagner (1983) (Wagner)

Amadeus (1984) (Wolfgang Amadeus Mozart)

Spring Symphony (1984) (Clara Schumann)

Impromptu (1991) (Chopin and Liszt)

Composers (Popular)

Few popular composers have lived long enough (or been famous enough) to see their life story reach the screen. However, there have been some noteworthy exceptions: Richard Rodgers was in his prime when 1948's *Words and Music* was released, and Cole Porter was still composing when Cary Grant played him in *Night and Day* (1945). Jerome Kern died during the filming of *Till the Clouds Roll By* (1946), and George M. Cohan passed away the year that *Yankee Doodle Dandy* was released (1942). Turn-of-the-century songwriters have proven to be popular film subjects, with Twentieth Century-Fox specializing in them in the 1940s. Victor Mature played Gay Nineties Broadway composer Paul Dresser in *My Gal Sal* (1942); singer Dick Haymes was songwriter Ernest R. Ball in Damon Runyon's *Irish Eyes Are Smiling*; and Mark Stevens played Joseph E. Howard in *I Wonder Who's Kissing Her Now* (1947). Many fields of music are represented by merely a movie or two, as evidenced by the biographies of folk songwriter Woody Guthrie (*Bound for Glory*), minstrel man Dan Emmett (*Dixie*), and marching band composer John Philip Sousa (*Stars and Stripes Forever*).

Swanee River (1939) (Stephen Foster)

My Gal Sal (1942) (Paul Dresser)

Yankee Doodle Dandy (1942) (George M. Cohan)

Dixie (1943) (Dan Emmett)

Irish Eyes Are Smiling (1944) (Ernest R. Ball)

Rhapsody in Blue (1945) (George Gershwin)

Night and Day (1945) (Cole Porter)

Till the Clouds Roll By (1946) (Jerome Kern)

I Wonder Who's Kissing Her Now (1947) (Joe Howard)

Words and Music (1948) (Rodgers and Hart)

I Dream of Jeannie (1952) (Stephen Foster)

I'll See You in My Dreams (1952) (Gus Kahn)

Stars and Stripes Forever (1953) (John Philip Sousa)

St. Louis Blues (1958) (W.C. Handy)

Bound for Glory (1976) (Woody Guthrie)

Computers

The fact that the HAL 9000 remains the best-remembered character from *2001: A Space Odyssey* is a testament to the dramatic potential of movie computers. Given a speaking voice and a significant role, the computer can effectively dominate its human costars in interesting science fiction films like *The Forbin Project* (1970). However, the early film appearances of computers gave little sign of their potential. A nuclear brain called Novac took control of a secret subterranean laboratory in 1954's *Gog*. Unfortunately, the computer's "artificial intelligence" turned out to be enemy agent programming. Humans manipulated the computers in *Desk Set* (1957) and *The Honeymoon Machine* (1961) for comedic purposes. Then in 1965, the computer took a giant step forward with Jean-Luc Godard's dense, futuristic thriller *Alphaville*. Godard presented a bleak world of emotionless people controlled by a supercomputer. Stanley Kubrick made HAL more humanlike in 1968's *2001*, giving the computer a warm personality and a friendly voice ("Everything's under control, Dave"). But HAL nevertheless took a turn for the worse and sought to eliminate his human colleagues to gain control of a space station. The supercomputer in *The Forbin Project* displayed larger-scale ambitions, setting its sights on world domination. It achieved that goal, too, by linking with its Soviet counterpart and thus controlling the defense systems for both the United States and the Soviet Union. Proteus IV, the computer in 1977's *Demon Seed*, was more concerned with propagating itself than with controlling the world. To that end, it trapped its creator's wife (Julie Christie) in her house and "raped" her. Another computer, named Edgar, didn't go that far, but it too found itself attracted to its owner's love interest in 1984's *Electric Dreams*. Less interesting computers have played small parts in many movies. College students used a computer to create a line of credit for an imaginary man in the 1971 TV-movie *Paper Man*. An electrical accident dumped a computer's memory banks into college student Kurt Russell's brain in Disney's *The Computer Wore Tennis Shoes* (1969). George Segal had a small computer surgically implanted into his brain, with horrifying results, in 1974's *The Terminal Man*. Two teens showed the power of the personal computer when they used one to create gorgeous Kelly LeBrock in 1985's *Weird Science*. See also **Androids and Cyborgs; Robots.**

Gog (1954)

Desk Set (aka *His Other Woman*) (1957)

The Invisible Boy (1957)

The Honeymoon Machine (1961)

Alphaville (1965)

Billion Dollar Brain (1967)

2001: A Space Odyssey (1968)

The Computer Wore Tennis Shoes (1969)

The Forbin Project (aka *Colossus: The Forbin Project*) (1970)

Paper Man (1971 TVM)
The Terminal Man (1974)
Dark Star (1975)
Demon Seed (1977)
Institute for Revenge (1979 TVM)
Alien (1979)
Tron (1982)
WarGames (1983)

Electric Dreams (1984)
Deadly Impact (1985)
Weird Science (1985)
Jumpin' Jack Flash (1986)
Journey to the Center of the Earth (1993 TVM)
Jackpot (aka Cybereden) (1993)
The Tower (1993)

Concert Movies

The filmed rock'n'roll concert came into vogue in the early 1970s, though technically 1969's *Monterey Pop* ushered in the new genre with lively performances by The Mamas and the Papas, Janis Joplin and others. *Woodstock* and *Gimme Shelter* are the best-known concert films, both for their music and social commentary. The Rolling Stones have starred in more movies than any other rock act, with *Gimme Shelter*, *Let's Spend the Night Together*, *The T.A.M.I. Show* and *Ladies and Gentlemen, The Rolling Stones*. Surprisingly, the genre has acquired a certain appeal for well-known, contemporary directors—Martin Scorsese directed a documentary about The Band called *The Last Waltz*, while Jonathan Demme helmed the Talking Heads' *Stop Making Sense* (1984). The latter film was one of only a handful made during the 1980s, signaling that young rock fans preferred the free footage provided by MTV. Nevertheless, concert films still appear occasionally, as evidenced by U2's 1988 release *Rattle and Hum*. Rob Reiner's *This Is Spinal Tap* tells the history of a fictitious group and is a hilarious parody of rock documentaries and concert films.

Jazz on a Summer Day (1959)
The T.A.M.I. Show (1964)
The Big T.N.T. Show (1966)
Don't Look Back (1967)
Monterey Pop (1969)
Woodstock (1970)
Gimme Shelter (1970)
Popcorn (1970)
Johnny Cash: The Man, His World, His Music (1970)
Mad Dogs and Englishman (aka Joe Cocker: Mad Dogs and Englishman) (1971)
Celebration at Big Sur (1971)
This Is Elvis! (1971)
Soul to Soul (1971)
Fillmore (1972)
Concert for Bangladesh (1972)
Let the Good Times Roll (1973)
Ladies and Gentlemen, The Rolling Stones (1975)
The Song Remains the Same (1976) (Led Zeppelin)

The Last Waltz (1977)
Rust Never Sleeps (1979) (Neil Young)
Divine Madness (1980) (Bette Midler)
Rockshow (1980) (Paul McCartney)
No Nukes (aka The Muse Concert: No Nukes) (1980)
Heartland Reggae (1980)
Emerson, Lake and Palmer in Concert (1981)
Let's Spend the Night Together (1982)
Gospel (1982)
Stop Making Sense (1984) (The Talking Heads)
Bring on the Night (1985) (Sting)
Home of the Brave (1986) (Laurie Anderson)
Hail! Hail! Rock 'n' Roll (aka Chuck Berry Hail! Hail! Rock 'n' Roll) (1987)
Rattle and Hum (1988)
Big Time (1988) (Tom Waits)
Depeche Mode 101 (1989)

Confessions . . . Series

Only the first of this feeble series of British sex farces was released in the United States. Reviews were unkind, with the *New York Times* commenting that *Confessions of a Window Cleaner* "reeks of something . . . once called Swinging London." Still, the movies are now shown regularly on pay-cable as "adults-only" features. Actor Robin Askwith was the principal series regular. Sadly, the films also featured faded British stars like Diana Dors (*Confessions of a Driving Instructor*).

Confessions of a Window Cleaner (1973)
Confessions of a Pop Singer (1975)
Confessions of a Driving Instructor (1976)
Confessions From a Holiday Camp (1977)

Corman's Poe Series

In his 1990 autobiography, low-budget auteur Roger Corman wrote: "I felt that Poe and Freud were working in different ways toward a concept of the unconscious mind, so I tried to use Freud's theories to interpret the work of Poe." Such literate aspirations may not come across in the finished films, but Corman's Poe adaptations nonetheless exemplify quality, low-budget filmmaking. The series began with 1960's *House of Usher*, a moody mixture of Poe themes produced in two weeks for a measly $270,000. The film introduced the distinguishing features of most of Corman's Poe movies: a crazed performance by Vincent Price, Daniel Haller's atmospheric period sets, Floyd Crosby's florid color photography, and a well-crafted screenplay. Indeed, all but one script were penned in part by either Richard Matheson (*Duel*) or Charles Beaumont, both *Twilight Zone* veterans. The lone exception was the final series entry, 1964's *Tomb of Ligea*, written by Robert Towne (an Oscar winner for *Chinatown*). Corman followed *Usher* with 1961's *The Pit and the Pendulum*, a clever reworking of Poe themes featuring a lively torture dungeon climax. Ray Milland replaced Vincent Price as the flat lead in 1961's *The Premature Burial*, the series' weakest entry. However, Price was back for good in Corman's follow-up, the 1962 anthology *Tales of Terror*, which also featured veteran stars Peter Lorre and Basil Rathbone. Lorre joined Price and Boris Karloff for *The Raven*, a silly but entertaining comedy bearing no relation to Poe's poem (the plot introduced Lorre as a raven — a victim of warlock Karloff's magic). *The Haunted Palace* included a fragment of the title poem, but it was really a straightforward adaptation of H.P. Lovecraft's novella *The Case of Charles Dexter Ward*. Corman produced his last two Poe films in 1964, with *The Masque of the Red Death* emerging as a critical favorite. Shot in England with a bigger budget than its predecessors (and using leftover sets from *Beckett*), *Masque* attracted attention chiefly due to Nicholas Roeg's stylish photography. Roeg, who replaced Corman's regular cameraman Crosby, went on to direct *Don't Look Now* (1973) and *The Man Who Fell to Earth* (1976). Corman concluded his Poe series after *Tomb of Ligea* because he felt (rightly so) that the films were becoming repetitive. Nevertheless, his Concorde Films tried to initiate a new Poe series over two decades later with *The Haunting of Morella* (1990). Corman did not direct these later Poe adaptations.

House of Usher (1960)
The Pit and the Pendulum (1961)
The Premature Burial (1961)
Tales of Terror (1962)

The Raven (1963)
The Haunted Palace (1963)
The Masque of the Red Death (1964)
Tomb of Ligea (1964)

Cotton Comes to Harlem, *see* Coffin Ed Johnson and Grave Digger Jones

Courts-Martial

Several fine courtroom dramas have revolved around military courts-martial. Stanley Kubrick's chilling *Paths of Glory* detailed the plight of three French soldiers tried for cowardice during World War I after their doomed mission failed. In terms of emotional power, its only rival is the incisive 1979 Australian picture *Breaker Morant*. This potent drama, set during the Boer War, also concerned three soldiers facing court-martial as scapegoats. Tom Courtenay played court-martial defendants in *Private Potter* (1962) and *King and Country* (1964). In the first film, he portrayed a soldier accused of cowardice who claimed to have seen God. In the World War I-set *King and Country*, Dirk Bogarde defended Courtenay of a desertion charge. Richard Basehart and Lee Marvin gave strong performances as soldiers facing court-martial during the Korean War in *Time Limit* (1957) and *Sergeant Ryker* (1968), respectively. Herman Wouk's Pulitzer Prize-winning novel *The Caine Mutiny* (1954) climaxed in a court-martial, with Van Johnson and Robert Francis as the naval officers who rebelled against Humphrey Bogart's neurotic Captain Queeg. The fact-based *Sergeant Matlovich vs. the U.S. Air Force* (1978) chronicled a homosexual serviceman's struggle to remain in the military. *The Winslow Boy* (1950) offered a fascinating account of the fight for a young boy's right to a trial after expulsion from a British military academy. The British officers stationed in India in *Conduct Unbecoming* (1975) conducted their own court-martial when they suspected one of the group of perverse acts. Bryan Brown, who played one of the defendants in *Breaker Morant*, played the prosecuting officer in 1990's *Blood Oath*. Bradford Dillman and Peter Graves starred in a 1966 TV series called *Court-Martial*, set during World War II.

The Winslow Boy (1950)
The Caine Mutiny (1954)
Court Martial (aka Carrington VC) (1954)
The Court Martial of Billy Mitchell (1955)
The Rack (1956)
Paths of Glory (1957)
Time Limit (1957)
Sergeant Rutledge (1960)
The Court Martial of Major Keller (1961)
Private Potter (1962)

Billy Budd (1962)
King and Country (1964)
The Man in the Middle (1964)
Sergeant Ryker (1968)
Conduct Unbecoming (1975)
Sergeant Matlovich vs. the U.S. Air Force (1978 TVM)
Breaker Morant (1979)
The Court-Martial of Jackie Robinson (1990 TVM)
Blood Oath (1990)
A Few Good Men (1992)

Crabs and Lobsters

Most movie crabs have probably appeared on dinner plates, but there have been a few exceptions. A giant pink crab, animated by special effects wizard Ray Harryhausen, had a choice scene in 1961's *Mysterious Island*. Yet even it was killed, boiled and devoured. The title creatures of *Attack of the Crab Monsters* (1956) ate human heads, which enabled them to telepathically lure more human prey for supper entrees. Still another giant crab washed ashore in 1982's *Night of the Claw* (aka *Island Claws*). The shadow of an alien crablike creature accompanied the title visitors to Earth in 1959's *Teenagers From Outer Space*. Sebastian the Crab sang the Oscar-winning song "Under the Sea" in Disney's *The Little Mermaid*. Edible, normal-sized crabs and lobsters have been the subjects of restaurant business dramas (*King Crab*), lobster fisherman sagas (*High Tide at Noon*), and even a Doris Day comedy (*It Happened to Jane*).

Port Sinister (aka *The Beast of Paradise Island*) (1952)
Attack of the Crab Monsters (1956)
High Tide at Noon (1957)
Teenagers From Outer Space (1959)
It Happened to Jane (aka *Twinkle and Shine*) (1959)
Mysterious Island (1961)
The Lost Continent (1968)
King Crab (1980 TVM)
Night of the Claw (aka *Island Claws*) (1982)
Lobster Man From Mars (1989)
The Little Mermaid (1989)

Crane, Bill

Universal made three Crane mysteries in the late 1930s as part of its Crime Club series. The intent was to develop B-movies from popular but lesser-known detectives. Author Jonathan Latimer's Bill Crane certainly fit the bill. A private eye with a drinking problem, Crane wandered through a downbeat world layered with cynicism. Such an existence would make Sam Spade and Philip Marlowe genre legends in later movies. Preston Foster played Crane.

The Westland Case (1937)
The Lady in the Morgue (1938)
The Last Warning (1938)

The Creature From the Black Lagoon

The Gill Man (as he's fondly known) was the brainchild of producer William Alland, who was inspired by a vague South American legend about a prehistoric monster that roamed the swamps. Universal Pictures spared no expense on 1954's *Creature From the Black Lagoon*, shooting the film in 3-D (q.v.) and investing $12,000 in the creature suit. The story, another reworking of "Beauty and the Beast," sends a scientific expedition down the Amazon where it discovers a man/fish creature with a fondness for human women. Like Kong, the Creature was a sympathetic monster, who simply asked to be left alone. But Universal had other other ideas. The Gill Man was back in 1955's *The Revenge of the Creature*, in which he's captured and transported to a Florida aquarium before female trouble again causes his demise. The worst was yet to come. He becomes a land mammal—thanks to unwanted surgery—in 1956's *The Creature Walks Among Us*, the final film in the trilogy. In the movie's closing scene, the Gill Man walks into the ocean, apparently aware that he will drown in the water that was once his home. Ricou Browning played the Creature in all three movies, although Ben Chapman handled the land scenes in the first film and Don Megowan was the "transformed" Creature in the last. A generic Creature (looking suspiciously like a Black Lagoon resident) surfaced in 1987's juvenile adventure *The Monster Squad*.

Creature From the Black Lagoon (1954)

The Revenge of the Creature (1955)

The Creature Walks Among Us (1956)

The Monster Squad (1987)

The Crime Doctor

Despite a past clouded by amnesia, Dr. Robert Ordway became a leading criminal psychologist — only to discover that he was once a criminal himself. Armed with "insider knowledge" of how the criminal mind works, Orday repaid society by bringing villains to justice. Such was the premise for this series of slightly offbeat detective films starring Warner Baxter as Ordway. The series originated from Max Marcin's long-running radio program and resulted in ten films over a six-year period. Baxter, an Oscar winner as the Cisco Kid (q.v.) in 1929's *In Old Arizona*, was the only actor ever to play the Crime Doctor.

The Crime Doctor (1943)

The Crime Doctor's Strangest Case (1943)

Shadows in the Night (1944)

The Crime Doctor's Courage (1945)

The Crime Doctor's Warning (1945)

The Crime Doctor's Manhunt (1946)

Just Before Dawn (1946)

The Millerson Case (1947)

The Crime Doctor's Gamble (1948)

The Crime Doctor's Diary (1949)

Critters

If you were a little, furry, fanged alien who had just hijacked a spaceship after escaping from a prison asteroid, where would you go? To Kansas, of course! The sleepy rural town of Grovers Bend, to be exact. That's the premise behind 1986's *Critters*, an easygoing science fiction/comedy that offset predictable characters with a quirky sense of humor. For example, the bounty hunters who pursued the escaped "Krites" assumed Earthling form: One took on the appearance of a video rock star and the other a dead deputy with fresh wounds — neither one blended very well with the local folks. As for the Krites, they mumbled a lot (their dialogue was subtitled) and seemed to exist to eat (humans being a favorite food). However, their intelligence level was questionable, since one unwisely ate a stick of explosive with a burning fuse. The residents of Grovers Bend eventually outwitted the Critters, only to be harassed by their hatched offspring in the disappointing 1988 follow-up *Critters 2: The Main Course*. A second sequel, 1991's *Critters 3* found the furry aliens wreaking havoc in a downtown apartment complex. The fourth installment began as an *Aliens* spoof with Charlie the bounty hunter (series regular Don Opper) and the last two Krites leaving behind Kansas and hurtling into space while in suspended animation (q.v.). Years later, a group of space salvagers discovered Charlie and the Krites and revived them aboard a space station. The film contained little humor (the "hero" died and a nice character turned cruel), and the Critters had little screen time. Still, the series must have its fans or the law of diminishing returns would have killed it long before this third sequel.

Critters (1986)

Critters 2: The Main Course (1988)

Critters 3 (1991)
Critters 4 (aka *Critters 4: They're Invading Your Space*) (1992)

Crusoe, Robinson

Daniel Defoe's classic novel about a man's struggle for survival on an isolated island influenced so many books and films that literary critics created a term for the genre: Robinsonnade. Spanish surrealist director Luis Buñuel made the best screen version, a remarkably straightforward, lyrical 1952 film starring Dan O'Herlihy. Douglas Fairbanks updated the tale as a gent whose island existence was the result of a bet in 1932's *Mr. Robinson Crusoe.* Amanda Blake played the title role in 1954's *Miss Robin Crusoe*, an unexceptional female variation, and Dick Van Dyke updated the story for children in Disney's *Lt. Robin Crusoe, USN* (1966). *Man Friday* (1976) gradually reversed the roles of master Crusoe (Peter O'Toole) and manservant Friday (Richard Roundtree). Despite its promising premise, the film deteriorated into an unpleasant affair. A more successful twist was displayed in 1964's *Robinson Crusoe on Mars*, a colorful adventure that substituted a barren planet for the typical remote island. It was remade as *Enemy Mine* in 1986 with Dennis Quaid and Lou Gossett, Jr. *Crusoe* (1989) was a return to Defoe's original, though Aidan Quinn's hero was younger than his predecessors. Many films, such as *Swept Away* (1975) and *Castaway* (1987), have borrowed the shipwrecked plot. Indeed, Defoe's original even predated Wyss's *The Swiss Family Robinson* and thus indirectly influenced film and TV variations of that novel—including *Gilligan's Island*. See also **Islands.**

Mr. Robinson Crusoe (1932)
Adventures of Robinson Crusoe (aka
  Robinson Crusoe) (1952)
Miss Robin Crusoe (1954)
Robinson Crusoe on Mars (1964)
Lt. Robin Crusoe, USN (1966)

Swept Away (aka *Swept Away by an
  Unusual Destiny in the Blue Sea of
  August*) (1975)
Man Friday (1976)
Enemy Mine (1986)
Castaway (1987)
Crusoe (1989)

Curse Series

The four films comprising this "series" are connected in name only. Actor David Keith (*An Officer and a Gentleman*) directed 1987's *The Curse*, a straightforward adaptation of an H.P. Lovecraft tale ("The Colour Out of Space") about a fallen meteorite that causes mutations. In 1989's *Curse II: The Bite*, a man was bitten by a snake, given the wrong antidote, and exposed to radiation. As one would expect, his arm turned into a snake's head. Christopher Lee starred in *Curse III: Blood Sacrifice* (1990), a conventional voodoo film originally titled *Panga*. In *Curse IV: The Ultimate Sacrifice*, a demon was unleashed from the catacombs beneath a church.

The Curse (aka *The Farm*) (1987)
Curse II: The Bite (1989)
Curse III: Blood Sacrifice (aka *Panga*) (1990)
Curse IV: The Ultimate Sacrifice (1993)

Cyclops

These one-eyed mythological Titans who forged thunderbolts for Zeus have been largely misrepresented in their few film appearances. Kirk Douglas fought one as *Ulysses* (1955), and special effects genius Ray Harryhausen brought one to life with thrilling results in his classic fantasy *The Seventh Voyage of Sinbad* (1958). However, the title creature in Bert I. Gordon's contemporary sci-fi feature *Cyclops* (1957) was just a fifty-foot-tall man (Dean Parkins) with a flab of skin covering one eye. Parkins played a similar creature in Gordon's *War of the Colossal Beast* (1958). Just to confuse matters, this latter film bore no relation to *Cyclops* (although the creatures looked quite similar), but it *was* a sequel to Gordon's non-Cyclopean picture *The Amazing Colossal Man* (1957). A gentle Cyclops warrior, considerably shorter (at about eight feet), aided Ken Marshall on a quest to save his beloved princess in *Krull* (1983). Albert Dekker played the devious *Dr. Cyclops* (1940), a mad scientist obsessed with shrinking humans. The film featured nary a Cyclops, its title being simply a reference to the doctor's poor eyesight. See also **Giants; Gorgons.**

Ulysses (1955)
Cyclops (1957)
The Seventh Voyage of Sinbad (1958)
War of the Colossal Beast (1958)

Atlas Against the Cyclops (aka *Monster From the Unknown World; Maciste nella Terror dei Ciclopi*) (1961)
Krull (1983)

Dancer, Joe

Three years after his *Baretta* series went off the air, Robert Blake returned to star as rugged private detective Joe Dancer in the 1981 TV-movie, *The Big Black Pill*, a pilot for a new show. The movie drew insufficient ratings to warrant a series, but Blake refused to give up. He played Dancer in two additional films. The effort proved fruitless, however, for a regular series still failed to materialize.

The Big Black Pill (aka *Joe Dancer*) (1981 TVM)

The Monkey Mission (1981 TVM)
Murder 1, Dancer 0 (1983 TVM)

Danger Zone

Flesh Gordon alumnus Jason Williams produced, cowrote and starred in this series about an ex-cop hunting down the nasty biker (appropriately named Grim Reaper) who killed his girlfriend. Mounted aboard his own chopper as he treks across the desert, loner hero Wade Wilson (Williams) looked and acted like he stepped out of a Western revenge picture. Interestingly, the series' third entry even involved a Western subplot in which Reaper and his gang searched for gold hidden by Quantrill's Raiders during the Civil War. *Danger Zone IV* (1992) combined recycled footage from previous entries with a ludicrous plot about scantily-clad, revenge-minded biker girls.

Danger Zone (1987)
Danger Zone II: Reaper's Revenge (1988)
Danger Zone III: Steel Horse War (1990)
Danger Zone IV: Mad Girls, Bad Girls (aka *Mad Girls, Bad Girls*) (1992)

Daninsky, Waldemar (El Hombre Lobo)

Paul Naschy, Spain's number one film star of the 1970s, created and portrayed the Polish werewolf Waldemar Daninsky—better known in his homeland as El

Hombre Lobo. Naschy's films, like the better Mexican horror movies of the 1960s, stressed atmosphere at the expense of logic. Additionally, Naschy believed in the Mexican adage that horror can be multiplied by increasing the number of monsters. El Hombre Lobo encountered vampires in *Mark of the Werewolf*, Jekyll/Hyde in *Dr. Jekyll and the Werewolf*, and aliens, a mummy, the Frankenstein Monster and Dracula in the monster all-star epic *The Man Who Came From Ummo*. Despite his European popularity, Naschy (real name Jacinto Molina) has found little fame in the United States. For its American release, 1968's 3-D *Mark of the Werewolf* was typically shown in 2-D under the misleading title *Frankenstein's Bloody Terror* and minus forty-five minutes of footage. See also **Werewolves.**

>*Mark of the Werewolf* (aka *La Marca del Hombre Lobo*; *Frankenstein's Bloody Terror*; *Hell's Creatures*) (1968)
>*Nights of the Werewolf* (aka *Las Noches del Hombre Lobo*) (1969)
>*The Werewolf's Shadow* (aka *La Noche de Walpurgis*; *The Werewolf vs. the Vampire Women*) (1970)
>*The Man Who Came From Ummo* (aka *El Hombre Que Vino de Ummo*; *Assignment Terror*; *Dracula vs. Frankenstein*) (1970)
>*Fury of the Wolfman* (aka *La Furia del Hombre Lobo*) (1970)
>*Dr. Jekyll and the Werewolf* (aka *Dr. Jekyll y el Hombre Lobo*) (1971)
>*Curse of the Devil* (aka *El Retorno de la Walpurgis*) (1973)
>*The Werewolf and the Yeti* (aka *La Maldicion de la Bestia*; *Night of the Howling Beast*) (1976)
>*The Werewolf and the Samurais* (aka *La Bestia y la Espada Magica*; *La Bestia y Los Samurais*) (1983)

Dark Shadows

Producer/director Dan Curtis has milked a lot of mileage out of his 1966-71 supernatural daytime soap *Dark Shadows*, turning it into two theatrical films, a two-part television movie, and a prime-time series revival. The original Gothic TV series owed most of its popularity to Jonathan Frid's compelling portrayal of New England vampire Barnabus Collins. His story formed the basis for *House of Dark Shadows*, a low-budget 1970 feature that also starred TV regulars Joan Bennett (Elizabeth Collins), Grayson Hall (Julia Hoffman), and Kathryn Leigh Scott (Maggie Evans). In the film's bloody climax, Barnabus encountered a fatal stake through the heart fired with a crossbow. His absence in the 1971 sequel *Night of Dark Shadows* shifted the emphasis to witchcraft and hauntings. However, audiences showed little interest in a *Dark Shadow* movie sans Barnabus. Thus, the film series—like its TV counterpart—died. Amazingly, the TV series found an afterlife in syndication and on videotape. Meanwhile, Dan Curtis, after directing *The Winds of War* and *War and Remembrance*, mounted a TV-movie revival starring Ben Cross (*Chariots of Fire*) as Barnabus. It was followed by a short-lived prime-time series also featuring Jean Simmons and Roy Thinnes. See also **Vampires.**

>*House of Dark Shadows* (1970)   *Dark Shadows* (1991 TVM)
>*Night of Dark Shadows* (1971)

Dates in Title

In addition to the *Friday the 13th* films (q.v.), other "date films" include *Saturday the 14th*, *The Night of January 16th* and *September 30, 1955*. The latter film dealt with how James Dean's death (on that date) affected a fanatical fan (Richard Thomas). See also **Year in Title**.

The Night of January 16th (1941)
D-Day the Sixth of June (1956)
September 30, 1955 (aka *9-30-55; 24 Hours of the Rebel*) (1978)
Friday the 13th (1980)

Saturday the 14th (1981)
The 32nd of December (1988)
Saturday the 14th Strikes Back (1988)
October 32nd (1992)

The Daughters of Joshua Cabe

When fur trapper Buddy Ebsen suddenly needed a "family" to hold on to his homestead, he hired a prostitute, a thief and a pickpocket to pose as his daughters. Karen Valentine, Lesley Ann Warren and Sandra Dee played the original *Daughters of Joshua Cabe* in this unexpectedly popular 1972 *ABC Movie of the Week*. Two subpar sequels followed, each featuring entirely different casts.

The Daughters of Joshua Cabe (1972 TVM)
The Daughters of Joshua Cabe Return (1975 TVM)
New Daughters of Joshua Cabe (1976 TVM)

The Dead End Kids, *see* The Bowery Boys

Deafness

The world of the deaf has received little attention in film. Like blindness (q.v.), it has been misused as a plot gimmick in syrupy romances. Opera star Mario Lanza found love with a deaf girl in the massively sentimental *For the First Time*. Loretta Young played a deaf socialite in love with poor physician Alan Ladd in the 1944 romance *And Now Tomorrow*. Five years earlier, Young had portrayed a deaf person with more conviction in *The Story of Alexander Graham Bell*. *Johnny Belinda* (1948) hinted at the unjust prejudice experienced by deaf people. The 1952 British film *The Crash of Silence* opened new vistas with its touching, semidocumentary look into the world of a deaf girl. Few films about deafness have matched its power. *Silent Victory: The Kitty O'Neil Story* (1979) was an inspirational real-life account of a deaf woman who became a successful stunt person (q.v.). The Emmy Award-winning *Love Is Never Silent* (1985) costarred Phyllis Frelich and Ed Waterstreet, acclaimed performers from the National Theatre for the Deaf. Deaf actress Marlee Matlin won a Best Actress Oscar for 1986's *Children of a Lesser God*, an unsentimental story of the love between an independent-minded deaf woman and a teacher of the deaf (William Hurt). Despite its exploitative title, 1975's *Deafula* was merely the famous vampire story told in sign language.

The Man Who Played God (aka *The Silent Voice*) (1932)
The Story of Alexander Graham Bell (aka *The Modern Miracle*) (1939)
And Now Tomorrow (1944)
Johnny Belinda (1948)

The Crash of Silence (aka *Mandy*) (1952)
Man of a Thousand Faces (1957)
For the First Time (1959)
The Miracle Worker (1962)
Gigot (1962)

The Heart Is a Lonely Hunter (1965)	*Johnny Belinda* (1982 TVM)
Psych-Out (1968)	*Hear No Evil* (1982 TVM)
Deaf Smith and Johnny Ears (aka *Los Amigos*) (1973)	*Love Is Never Silent* (1985 TVM)
	Children of a Lesser God (1986)
Deafula (1975)	*Bridge to Silence* (1989 TVM)
Silent Victory: The Kitty O'Neil Story (1979 TVM)	*See No Evil, Hear No Evil* (1989)
	Hear No Evil (1993)
And Your Name Is Jonah (1979 TVM)	*The Sound and the Silence* (1993 TVM)
The Miracle Worker (1979 TVM)	

Dear Ruth

A teenage girl pens passionate love letters to a soldier and encloses her older sister's photograph. When his leave comes due, he decides to pay her a visit. The casting of William Holden (the soldier), Joan Caulfield (the older sister), and Mona Freeman (the younger sister) propelled the routinely plotted *Dear Ruth* into one of Paramount's biggest hits of 1947. In the belated sequel, *Dear Wife* (1949), newlyweds Caulfield and Holden encountered family problems when troublesome Freeman set up Holden as a rival senatorial candidate to the girls' father (Edward Arnold). Freeman had the spotlight to herself in 1951's *Dear Brat*. Holden had gone on to bigger parts (*Sunset Boulevard*) and Caulfield to television briefly (1953's *My Favorite Husband*) and then semiretirement. See also **Letters**.

Dear Ruth (1947)	*Dear Brat* (1951)
Dear Wife (1949)	

Death Incarnate

The personification of Death has been portrayed in various ways—as a lonely romantic, a beautiful temptress, and a hideous skeleton-creature greedy for souls. Fredric March played a curious Death anxious to understand why humans cling so desperately to life in *Death Takes a Holiday* (1934). He takes a vacation to investigate the phenomenon and falls in love, while the world suffers during his leave of absence, for dying people can no longer die. Feisty Lionel Barrymore proved more than a match for Cedric Hardwicke's Mr. Brink (aka Death), literally chasing Death up a tree in the 1939 comedy *On Borrowed Time*. In Ingmar Bergman's *The Seventh Seal* (1956), Max Von Sydow played a fourteenth century knight who matches wits with Death in a game of chess. That scene was parodied in *Bill and Ted's Bogus Journey* (1991), with the two California dudes playing "His Royal Deathness" in "Clue," "Twister" and "Battleship." Death was among the uninvited guests at evil Prince Prospero's (Vincent Price) masquerade ball in Roger Corman's stylish *Masque of the Red Death* (1964). Jessica Lange made an elegant Death in Bob Fosse's *All That Jazz*, while a dreadful decaying Death swarmed anxiously about John Neville whenever he was about to give up on life in *The Adventures of Baron Munchausen*. On television, Robert Redford played Mr. Death in the memorable 1962 "Nothing in the Dark" episode of *The Twilight Zone*.

Death Takes a Holiday (1934)	*Masque of the Red Death* (1964)
On Borrowed Time (1939)	*The Devil's Bride* (aka *The Devil Rides Out*) (1968)
Orpheus (1949)	
The Seventh Seal (1956)	*Death Takes a Holiday* (1971 TVM)

All That Jazz (1979)
Monty Python's The Meaning of Life (1983)
The Adventures of Baron Munchausen (1989)

Edgar Allan Poe's Masque of the Red Death (1989)
Bill and Ted's Bogus Journey (1991)

Death Wish

Charles Bronson's biggest hit cast him as a mild-mannered architect transformed into an emotionless vigilante after a gang of punks attacked his wife and daughter. Some critics condemned the film's questionable ethics, with *N.Y. Times* reviewer Vincent Canby writing: "The movie seems to have been made for no reason except to exploit its audiences' urban paranoia and vestigial fascination with violence for its own sake." Even writer Brian Garfield, who wrote the original novel, attacked the film for advocating vigilantism. He later appealed to CBS to not broadcast the film in prime time (which it did). Despite the controversy, *Death Wish* was a blockbuster, and some tabloids even claimed that it briefly lowered the crime rate in New York City. Still, Bronson and director Michael Winner avoided making a sequel for eight years. They should have kept it that way. *Death Wish II* was an embarrassing rehash of the original, transplanted to Los Angeles. Two additional Bronson sequels were not much better. Nevertheless, in 1993, Cannon Films announced plans to produce *Death Wish V*. See also **Vigilantes**.

Death Wish (1974)
Death Wish II (1982)

Death Wish III (1985)
Death Wish IV: The Crackdown (1987)

Deathstalker

"Can you imagine what it would be like to change into Barbi Benton in two minutes?" pondered drive-in movie critic Joe Bob Briggs after viewing 1984's *Deathstalker*. Joe Bob was referring to a hilarious scene in this sword-and-sorcery (q.v.) mishmash in which an evil wizard transforms his ugly henchman into buxom Playmate Benton. Unfortunately, this inspired piece of unintentional camp turned out to be the best part of this Argentina-lensed Conan rip-off. Still, the combination of muscular men and half-naked women appealed to action-oriented videotape renters. A 1987 sequel starring former Penthouse Pet Monique Gabrielle was released directly to video. Its typical genre plot cast Gabrielle as a princess trying to regain her throne with the help of hunky John Terlesky. After a third installment with John Allen Nelson in the lead, Rick Hill — the original Deathstalker — returned for 1991's *Deathstalker IV: Match of the Titans*. Surprisingly, Hill's acting ability apparently improved during his absence from the series. After all, it takes some definite thespian skill to deliver — with a straight face — dialogue like: "I should have known — I'm always getting mixed up with princesses." See also **Sword and Sorcery**.

Deathstalker (1984)
Deathstalker II (aka Deathstalker II: Duel of the Titans) (1987)
Deathstalker and the Warriors From Hell (1989)
Deathstalker IV: Match of the Titans (aka Deathstalker IV) (1991)

Delta Force

After a superior outing in 1985's *Code of Silence*, action star Chuck Norris appeared poised to take his place beside genre stalwarts Eastwood and Bronson. The following year's *Delta Force* was intended as his final stepping stone. It featured an Academy Award-winning costar, decent production values, and a plot torn from the headlines. Unfortunately, although it earned a profit and spawned two sequels, *Delta Force* sealed Norris's fate as a performer who had reached his potential and could advance no further. *Delta Force* cast Norris as Colonel Scott McCoy, whose special forces unit undertook a mission to rescue a planeload of passengers held captive by Middle-Eastern terrorists. Lee Marvin (the aforementioned Oscar winner) played Norris's special forces sidekick, while the supporting cast included familiar TV faces such as Joey Bishop, Robert Forster, Susan Strasberg and Robert Vaughn. Both script and execution were by-the-numbers, making *Delta Force* a painfully obvious action picture with a stiff lead performance, even by Norris's standards. Still, it was superior to the 1990 follow-up, *Delta Force 2*, which pitted Norris against ruthless South American drug lords. Sadly, five people were killed in a helicopter crash during this film's production in the Philippines. Chuck bowed out of the third installment, forcing Norris fans to settle for son Mike. The Fred Williamson films *Delta Force Commando* (1987) and *Delta Force Commando Two* (1991) are not a part of the Norris series.

Delta Force (1986)
Delta Force 2 (aka *Delta Force 2: The Colombian Connection*; *Delta Force 2: Stranglehold*; *Delta Force 2: Operation Stranglehold*) (1990)
Delta Force 3: The Killing Game (1991)

Dentists

The movie dentist has experienced a checkered career since his extravagant 1924 debut in Erich von Stroheim's nine-hour marathon silent movie *Greed*. Gibson Gowland played von Stroheim's lead, an appropriately greedy lower-class dentist with an illegal practice (a fellow dentist is called "Painless" Potter). However, the bad side of dentistry is better represented by murderer Ralph Bellamy in *Footsteps in the Dark* and Nazi torture specialist Laurence Olivier (who drills holes in healthy teeth) in *Marathon Man*. Sadistic dentists have been played for laughs in both the 1960 and 1986 versions of *The Little Shop of Horrors*. Jack Nicholson was a masochistic patient in the former, while Steve Martin enthusiastically sang "I'm a Dentist" in the latter. Bob Hope played a dentist who accidentally became a gunslinging Western hero in 1948's *The Paleface*. It spawned the Hope sequel *Son of Paleface* (1952) and the Don Knotts remake *The Shakiest Gun in the West* (1968). The murder of a playboy dentist set the mystery into motion in 1985's lighthearted affair *Compromising Positions*. Government agent Peter Falk drafted dentist Alan Arkin into the spy business in *The In-Laws* (1979). Daniel Day-Lewis was a traveling dentist in the offbeat *Eversmile, New Jersey* (1989). And W.C. Fields portrayed cinema's most perverse dentist in his hilarious pre-Hays Code short *The Dentist* (1932), where his struggle to pull a tooth results in some very compromising — and funny — positions with a female patient.

Greed (1924)   *Silly Billies* (1936)
The Dentist (1932)   *Hotel Haywire* (1937)

Aren't Men Beasts! (1937)
Footsteps in the Dark (1941)
The Strawberry Blonde (1941)
The Great Moment (1944)
One Sunday Afternoon (1948)
The Paleface (1948)
The Fat Man (1951)
Son of Paleface (1952)
Bells Are Ringing (1960)
Dentist in the Chair (1960)
Come Dance With Me (1960)
The Little Shop of Horrors (1960)
Get on With It (aka *Dentist on the Job*;
 Carry On TV) (1961)

The Shakiest Gun in the West (1968)
Cactus Flower (1969)
Marathon Man (1976)
The In-Laws (1979)
Ten (1979)
Straight Through the Heart (1983)
Compromising Positions (1985)
The Little Shop of Horrors (1986)
Rocket to the Moon (1986 TVM)
Fight for Life (1987 TVM)
Eversmile, New Jersey (1989)

Desperado

NBC sought to revive the TV Western with these cliché-ridden television "movies" revolving around a young loner named McCall (Alex McArthur). Actually, each film played like an unsold TV pilot, complete with reliable guest stars such as Pernell Roberts, Robert Vaughn and Robert Foxworth. The series' premise was simple enough: After McCall guns down David Warner and a half-dozen other baddies in the first film, understanding marshal Pernell Roberts gives the would-be gunfighter a chance to clear his name. However, Roberts points out that McCall will be a fugitive from justice. So, just like David Janssen, TV's original *Fugitive*, McCall travels from town to town, helping out nice folks along the way. Mystery author Elmore Leonard wrote the screenplay for 1987's *Desperado*, and yes, the Eagles' hit song of the same name was featured prominently. Interestingly, although NBC never picked up *Desperado* as a TV series, ABC launched the similar *Young Riders* as an hour series and enjoyed minor success for a couple seasons. As for star Alex McArthur, he eventually got a TV series, but not as a cowboy. He played a spy with amnesia in the short-lived 1992 NBC series *The Fifth Corner*.

Desperado (1987 TVM)
The Return of Desperado (1988 TVM)
Desperado: Avalanche at Devil's Ridge
 (1988 TVM)

Desperado: Legacy (1989 TVM)
Desperado: The Outlaw Wars (1989
 TVM)

Deth, Jack, *see* Trancers

The Devil

Mr. Scratch, Beelzebub, Mephistopheles, Lucifer, Satan—the Devil has been known by many names throughout history. And on the screen, he has been portrayed in many guises by a diverse group of performers. Walter Huston played a cunning though admittedly likable Mr. Scratch in 1941's *All That Money Can Buy*, adapted from Stephen Vincent Benet's nineteenth-century New England variation of *Faust*. Although ultimately outwitted by lawyer Daniel Webster (Edward Arnold), Scratch displayed a sharp talent for turning the tables. When Webster demanded an American jury for his client, Scratch produced twelve of history's worst criminals and then made the point: "Dastard, liar, traitor, knave . . . Americans all." Peter Cook's George Spiggot (aka The Devil) proved equally adept at crafty tricks in 1967's *Bedazzled*, a hilarious updating of *Faust* with Dudley Moore as the woeful short-order cook who sells his soul for seven wishes. At one point, Moore's inability to be specific with his wishes results in his transformation into a nun (i.e., he wishes to be in love with a woman in a place where no men are around). The Devil has been played for comedy in less memorable films as well, by Vincent Price in *The Story of Mankind* (1957), Christopher Lee in *Poor Devil* (1973), Bill Cosby in *The Devil and Max Devlin* (1981), and George Burns (in both title roles) in *Oh God, You Devil!* (1984). The Devil, as the incarnation of evil, has taken a back seat to his disciples in most horror films. Still, Robert DeNiro made an eerie villain—one Mr. Lou Cipher—in the moody horror/mystery *Angel Heart* (1987). Soap star Susan Lucci proved that the Devil could easily be a woman in the 1984 TV-movie *Invitation to Hell*. Victor Buono made an unexpected appearance as the Devil beneath a possessed house in 1978's *The Evil*. His scenes were cut from some prints, indicating that the filmmakers were as confused as the audience about his sudden presence in a haunted house movie. Nigel Kneale's intriguing 1967 sci-fi/fantasy *Five Million Years to Earth* (see **Quatermass, Professor Bernard**) suggested that the Devil's origins were extraterrestrial. The Devil's son—the Antichrist—first gained prominence in 1976's *The Omen* (q.v.). See also **Hell; The Omen.**

The Sorrows of Satan (1927)	*Doctor Faustus* (1968)
All That Money Can Buy (aka *The Devil and Daniel Webster*) (1941)	*The Devil in Love* (1968)
	The Devil's Daughter (1972 TVM)
Cabin in the Sky (1943)	*Poor Devil* (1973 TVM)
Heaven Can Wait (1943)	*The Sentinel* (1977)
Angel on My Shoulder (1946)	*The Evil* (1978)
Alias Nick Beal (1949)	*The Devil and Max Devlin* (1981)
Meet Mr. Lucifer (1953)	*Invitation to Hell* (1984 TVM)
The Story of Mankind (1957)	*Oh God, You Devil!* (1984)
Damn Yankees (1958)	*Crossroads* (1986)
The Private Lives of Adam and Eve (1960)	*Angel Heart* (1987)
	Hunk (1987)
Bedazzled (1967)	*Prince of Darkness* (1987)
Five Million Years to Earth (aka *Quatermass and the Pit*) (1967)	*Mr. Frost* (1990)
	Switch (1991)
The Devil's Bride (aka *The Devil Rides Out*) (1968)	*Speak of the Devil* (1991)

Antichrist:

The Omen (1976)	*Child of Light, Child of Darkness* (1991 TVM)
The Chosen (aka *Holocaust 2000*) (1978)	*Servants of Twilight* (1991 TVM)
The Visitor (1979)	*Needful Things* (1993)
Fear No Evil (1981)	

Dinosaurs

The evolution of the cinematic dinosaur begins and ends with Willis O'Brien. A master of special effects photography, O'Brien perfected the stop-motion animation technique used in nearly all the memorable dinosaur sequences. After stints as a cowboy, prize fighter, and sculptor, O'Brien made his first dinosaur film in 1917, a short called *The Dinosaur and the Missing Link*. He filmed his brontosaurus (a jointed wooden skeleton covered by clay) one frame at a time, moving the model slightly between each picture to create an illusion of motion. O'Brien continued making other shorts (e.g., *The Ghost of Slumber Mountain*) and eventually landed the job of special effects creator for *The Lost World* (1925), an adaptation of Arthur Conan Doyle's novel about a journey into a prehistoric land. O'Brien's brilliant effects shine even today, especially the final sequence in which an escaped brontosaurus wreaks havoc in London. O'Brien went on to create his masterpiece in 1933's *King Kong* (q.v.), which featured a dynamic struggle between Kong and a Tyrannosaurus Rex. In 1949, he finally won an Oscar for *Mighty Joe Young*, another giant ape opus. However, his most cherished projects were never realized. These included two cowboy/ dinosaur scripts called *Creation* and *Gwangi*. O'Brien eventually sold the idea for the former film, which sadly made it to the screen as the forgotten, low-budget feature *The Beast of Hollow Mountain* (1956). However, O'Brien protege Ray Harryhausen created some superb animation sequences for the 1969 dinosaur Western *The Valley of Gwangi*. Harryhausen, the modern master of stop-action animation, was also responsible for the dinosaur that trashed the amusement park in *The Beast From 20,000 Fathoms* (1953) and the pterodactyl that snatched Raquel Welch in *One Million Years, B.C.* Of Harryhausen's rivals, Jim Danforth and David Allen have received the highest marks for their lifelike creatures in, respectively, *When Dinosaurs Ruled the Earth* (1970) and *Caveman* (1981). The high cost of stop-motion photography has limited its use over the years, and filmmakers have resorted to alternate methods for creating dinosaurs. In 1940's *One Million, B.C.*, live lizards were photographed on miniature sets. The effect was convincing enough to warrant use of that footage in countless low-budget features. In the 1950s, Japan's special effects wizard Eiji Tsuburaya perfected the man-in-a-monster suit approach with Toho's *Godzilla* films (see separate entries for Japanese monsters **Godzilla, Ghidrah, Rodan, Mothra** and **Gamera**). Director Steven Spielberg used puppets, models, computer technology and $65 million to create the impressive prehistoric beasts of 1993's *Jurassic Park*. Finally, animated dinosaurs have appeared in *Fantasia* (the creation of the world segment) and *The Land Before Time*, a children's film about lost baby dinos searching for their parents. See also **Dragons; Cave People.**

The Lost World (1925)	*King Dinosaur* (1955)
The Savage (1926)	*The Animal World* (1956)
King Kong (1933)	*The Beast of Hollow Mountain* (1956)
One Million B.C. (1940)	*The Giant Behemoth* (1959)
Fantasia (1941)	*The Lost World* (1960)
Unknown World (1948)	*Dinosaurus* (1960)
Two Lost Worlds (1950)	*Gorgo* (1961)
The Lost Continent (1951)	*Reptilicus* (1962)
The Beast From 20,000 Fathoms (1953)	*One Million Years, B.C.* (1966)
	The Valley of Gwangi (1969)

When Dinosaurs Ruled the Earth (1970)	*The Land Before Time* (1988)
The Last Dinosaur (1977 TVM)	*Adventures in Dinosaur City* (1991)
The Crater Lake Monster (1977)	*Steel Justice* (1992 TVM) (a robotic dinosaur)
Where Time Began (1978)	*Carnosaur* (1993)
Caveman (1981)	*Super Mario Bros.* (1993)
Baby . . . Secret of the Lost Legend (1985)	*Jurassic Park* (1993)
My Science Project (1985)	*We're Back!* (aka *We're Back! A Dinosaur's Story*) (1993)

Dionne Quintuplets, The, *see* Christian, Dr. (Paul)

Dirigibles

The motorized, gas-filled aircraft known as dirigibles, airships, zeppelins and blimps have made irregular screen appearances since airplanes replaced them in the 1930s. Howard Hughes's World War I aerial spectacular *Hell's Angels* (1930) confirmed the birth and signaled the death of the movie dirigible. The zeppelin raid over London, although elaborately staged, paled in comparison to the film's classic airplane dogfights. Dirigible crashes occurred at the climaxes of *The Lost Zeppelin* (1929), *Madam Satan* (1930), *Dirigible* (1931) and *Murder in the Air* (1940). The latter film, which starred Ronald Reagan as secret service agent Brass Bancroft (q.v.), was built around actual footage, obtained by industrious producer Bryan Foy, of a dirigible crashing into the ocean. The airship disaster in *Madame Satan* was preceded by a wild onboard party and followed by a happy ending. Over two decades later, a madman named Robur (Vincent Price) set out to conquer the world from his flying airship fortress, The Albatross, in the 1961 Jules Verne fantasy *Master of the World*. Two realistic films featured dirigibles in 1971. *Zeppelin* was a World War I tale of intrigue about an attempt to steal secrets from a German zeppelin factory. The fact-based *The Red Tent* chronicled a disastrous 1928 airship flight over the North Pole (a plot reminiscent of *The Lost Zeppelin*). Another fact-based drama, 1975's *The Hindenberg*, was about the 1937 New York dirigible explosion that claimed the lives of almost half the passengers and crew. Its weak narrative lead up to a chilling climax featuring actual newsreel of the Hindenberg. The familiar sight of a blimp hovering over the Super Bowl was played for suspense in 1977's *Black Sunday*, a presidential assassination thriller. James Bond grappled with a villain aboard an airship over the Golden Gate Bridge in *A View to a Kill* (1985), while Indiana Jones and his father hijacked a Nazi airplane attached to an airborne dirigible in *Indiana Jones and the Last Crusade* (1989). See also **Balloons, Hot Air.**

Zeppelin Attack on New York (1917)	*The Fabulous Baron Munchausen* (1961)
The Lost Zeppelin (1929)	
Hell's Angels (1930)	*Master of the World* (1961)
Madame Satan (1930)	*The Assassination Bureau* (1968)
Dirigible (1931)	*Zeppelin* (1971)
Murder in the Air (1940)	*The Red Tent* (1971)
The Fabulous World of Jules Verne (1958)	*Island at the Top of the World* (1974)
	The Hindenberg (1975)

Black Sunday (1977)	The Rocketeer (1991)
A View to a Kill (1985)	Little Nemo: Adventures in
Indiana Jones and the Last Crusade	Slumberland (1992)
(1989)	

The Dirty Dozen

Robert Aldrich's 1967 original was a solid World War II action film about twelve ruthless criminals offered parole in return for participating in a deadly mission behind German lines. Lee Marvin played the tough major who whipped the gang into top-notch soldiers. For the record, the original dozen were played by: John Cassavetes, Jim Brown, Telly Savalas, Donald Sutherland, Charles Bronson, Trini Lopez, Tom Busby, Colin Maitland, Al Mancini, Stuart Cooper, Ben Carruthers and Clint Walker. Although the film became MGM's number one grosser of the year, a sequel did not appear until eighteen years later—and then as a TV movie. Probably inspired by the runaway success of 1985's *Rambo*, NBC telecast *The Dirty Dozen: The Next Mission* later that year. Lee Marvin reprised his role as the Dozen's leader, and Ernest Borgnine and Richard Jaeckel returned in their original supporting roles. Telly Savalas starred in two more TV-movie sequels before the Fox network introduced the very short-lived *Dirty Dozen* TV series. Interestingly, although the original *Dirty Dozen* spawned a host of imitators in the late 1960s (e.g., *The Devil's Brigade, A Reason to Live, A Reason to Die*), the plot was borrowed from Roger Corman's 1964 quickie *The Secret Invasion*.

> *The Dirty Dozen* (1967)
> *The Dirty Dozen: The Next Mission* (1985 TVM)
> *The Dirty Dozen: The Deadly Mission* (1987 TVM)
> *The Dirty Dozen: The Fatal Mission* (1988 TVM)

Dirty Harry

Clint Eastwood created San Francisco police inspector Harry Callahan, a ruthless distributor of justice, in Don Siegel's influential 1971 action picture *Dirty Harry*. Armed with his trademark .357 magnum pistol, Eastwood/Callahan became the perfect anti-hero for the 1970s, reassuring the public that criminals above the law could—and would—be punished. Not surprisingly, the character mellowed as the series progressed, with Harry even teaming up with a female partner (Tyne Daly) in *The Enforcer*. Ironically, the series' weakest entry, *Sudden Impact*, introduced Harry's infamous quote: "Go ahead . . . Make my day." Imitators, such as Jack Palance in *One Man Jury* (1978), Sylvester Stallone in 1986's *Cobra*, and Steven Seagal in 1988's *Above the Law*, failed to duplicate Eastwood's success—perhaps because they lacked his grimacing humor.

> *Dirty Harry* (1971)   *Sudden Impact* (1983)
> *Magnum Force* (1973)   *The Dead Pool* (1988)
> *The Enforcer* (1976)

Disaster Movies

Films climaxing in disasters date back to the 1930s—to the earthquake that rocked Gable and Tracy in *San Francisco*, the storm sequence in *Hurricane*, and the locusts that stripped the fields in *The Good Earth*. All these disasters were grand spectacles but mere movie subplots. The disaster film as a genre came into vogue in the early 1970s with the releases of *Airport* and *The Poseidon Adventure*. A canny producer named Irwin Allen exploited the latter film, a tale of an upside-down ocean liner, into a box office smash ("Who will survive?" ads asked) and quickly became known as the King of Disaster Films. Allen followed it with the fiery all-star opus *The Towering Inferno*, and suddenly disaster films were all the rage. Cheap rip-offs and foreign imports filled America's screens with avalanches, volcanic eruptions and tidal waves. Then Allen's lavish disaster epic about killer bees, *The Swarm* (1978), crashed at the box office, and the fate of the genre went down with it. Allen's follow-ups, including a *Poseidon* sequel and three made-for-TV films, generated little interest. By the time 1979's *Meteor* came hurtling toward Earth, moviegoers treated it like a real disaster—avoiding it like the plague while flocking to the parody *Airplane!* Other disaster movie spoofs included *The Big Bus* (1976), a movie-within-a-movie in *Drive-In*, and the "That's Armaggedon!" segment in *Kentucky Fried Movie* (1977). See also **Airport**.

Airport (1970)	*Avalanche* (1978)
The Poseidon Adventure (1972)	*Gray Lady Down* (1978)
Earthquake (1974)	*The Swarm* (1978)
The Towering Inferno (1974)	*Beyond the Poseidon Adventure* (1979)
The Hindenberg (1975)	*Meteor* (1979)
Tidal Wave (1975)	*Airplane!* (1980)
The Big Bus (1976)	*When Time Ran Out* (aka *Volcano*)
Irwin Allen's Flood (aka *Flood!*) (1976 TVM)	(1980)
	Airplane 2: The Sequel (1982)
Irwin Allen's Fire (aka *Fire!*) (1977 TVM)	*The Night the Bridge Fell Down* (1983 TVM)

Disguises

The cinema's most renowned master of disguises was probably the murderer in John Huston's stylish murder mystery *The List of Adrian Messenger*. The film employed an interesting gimmick, too, in that the crafty criminal (Kirk Douglas) was flanked by four heavily disguised, heavyweight performers (Frank Sinatra, Tony Curtis, Robert Mitchum and Burt Lancaster). Rod Steiger wore all the disguises himself as the psychotic murderer in *No Way to Treat a Lady*, while Tony Curtis played a nice guy—and a real-life disguise specialist—in 1960's *The Great Impostor*. Several performers have disguised themselves as the opposite sex for extended periods. Ginger Rogers tried to pass for a boy to save on train fare in *The Major and the Minor* (1942), while Barbra Streisand did it to get an education in *Yentl* (1983). Her charade ran into several complications when she became engaged to Amy Irving and fell in love with best friend Mandy Patinkin. Liv Ullmann experienced a worse fate, however, when her male disguise was revealed in *Pope Joan* (1972). As for male performers, Jack Lemmon and Tony Curtis (again) donned skirts, wigs and high heels and joined an all-girls' band to elude gangsters in Billy Wilder's *Some Like It Hot*. Dustin Hoffman played a unemployed actor who became a popular soap opera actress in *Tootsie* (1982). Several performers have disguised themselves as *Charley's Aunt* in the various screen versions of Brandon Thomas's play. Movie characters noted for their disguises include Sherlock Holmes (q.v.), Inspector Neilson (John Barrymore) in the Bulldog Drummond films (q.v.), and bumbling Inspector Clouseau (see **Pink Panther Series**). It is difficult to single out a *best* disguise, but Marlene Dietrich was hardly recognizable in a key scene in *Witness for the Prosecution* (1958), and Debra Winger fooled a lot of moviegoers playing a male angel named Emmett in 1987's *Made in Heaven*, going unbilled for her performance.

Sylvia Scarlett (1935)
The Phantom Strikes Again (aka *The Gaunt Stranger*) (1938)
Hold That Co-ed (aka *Hold That Girl*) (1938)
Charley's Big-Hearted Aunt (1940)
Charley's Aunt (aka *Charley's American Aunt*) (1941)
The Major and the Minor (1942)
The Ringer (1952)
Where's Charley? (1952)
Witness for the Prosecution (1958)
Some Like It Hot (1959)
The Great Impostor (1960)
The List of Adrian Messenger (1963)
No Way to Treat a Lady (1968)

Pope Joan (aka *The Devil's Impostor*) (1972)
Sleuth (1972)
Triple Echo (1973)
Toma (1973 TVM)
Tootsie (1982)
Yentl (1983)
Her Life as a Man (1984 TVM)
Just One of the Guys (1985)
Soul Man (1986)
He's My Girl (1987)
Too Outrageous! (1987)
Darkman (1990)
Mrs. Doubtfire (1993)
M. Butterfly (1993)
The Ballad of Little Jo (1993)

District Attorney, Mr.

Like many film series of the 1940s, this one was adapted from a hit radio show. However, Republic Pictures' movies never matched the popularity of the radio programs, which were based on the career of New York D.A. (and future presidential candidate) Thomas E. Dewey. Dennis O'Keefe played young P. Cadwallader Jones in 1941's *Mr. District Attorney*, which costarred Peter Lorre. James Ellison replaced O'Keefe in 1941's *The Carter Case*, and John Hubbard played the role in 1943's *Secrets of the Underground*. Although the series failed to catch on, O'Keefe revived the role (though the character was now named Steve Bennett) in 1946's *Mr. District Attorney*. Following the failure of the film series, radio show creator Edward C. Byron set his sights on television and produced the 1951-52 small-screen series *Mr. District Attorney* starring Jay Jostyn. Following its cancellation, a 1954 syndicated series with David Brian ran for a single season.

Mr. District Attorney (1941)
The Carter Case (1941)

Secrets of the Underground (1943)
Mr. District Attorney (1946)

Doctor in the House Series

Doctor in the House, a lightweight 1954 comedy about British medical students, featured rising star Dirk Bogarde, lovely Kay Kendall, and ever-dependable Kenneth More. But character actor James Robertson Justice, as the blusterous chief surgeon Sir Lancelot Spratt, stole the show from them all. Bogarde and Justice teamed again in the follow-up, 1955's *Doctor at Sea*, which cast Dirk as a young ship's physician romancing Brigitte Bardot while tolerating the endless tirades of Captain Hogg (Justice). The third film, *Doctor at Large* (1957), gave Justice (as

Spratt again) more screen time and set the pattern for the rest of the series. Whether the handsome male lead was Bogarde, Leslie Phillips or Michael Craig, the real star was always Justice. He consistently made the *Doctor* films diverting entertainment. The 1970 British TV series *Doctor in the House* lasted for three seasons. See also **Hospitals.**

Doctor in the House (1954)	*Doctor in Distress* (1963)
Doctor at Sea (1955)	*Doctor in Clover* (1966)
Doctor at Large (1957)	*Doctor in Trouble* (1970)
Doctor in Love (1960)	

Dogs

Man's best friend has enjoyed a long and prosperous film career, both as a supporting player and a major star. A German Shepherd named Rin Tin Tin became the first canine box office attraction in silent films such as *The Clash of the Wolves* (1924) and *A Dog of the Regiment* (1930). He died in 1932, although two of his descendants went on to play the lead in the 1954-59 TV series *The Adventures of Rin Tin Tin*. Lassie (q.v.) eventually replaced Rinty as Hollywood's top dog, but other canines have also starred in their own film series, including Rusty (q.v.) and Benji (q.v.). Nick and Nora Charles's little dog Asta stole her share of scenes in *The Thin Man* (q.v.) films, as did Daisy in the *Blondie* (q.v.) movies. Walt Disney Productions seemed to specialize in dog films in the late 1950s and early 1960s. Animated tales paired two unlikely dog lovers in 1955's *Lady and the Tramp* and let loose the cinema's biggest litter in 1961's *101 Dalmations* (although, technically, the two Dalmation parents adopted most of those puppies). Mouseketeer Tommy Kirk starred in the sentimental boy-and-dog story *Old Yeller* (1957) and its more upbeat sequel, *Savage Sam* (1962). Other Disney dogs include the Irish setter in *Big Red* (1962), the three dogs (two good and one mean) in *The Incredible Journey* (1963), *The Ugly Dachshund* (1966) and the animated sniffer in *The Fox and the Hound* (1981). Some of the screen's most memorable dog pictures were derived from classic canine books like Jack London's *Call of the Wild* (1935), Ouida's *A Dog of Flanders* (1959), Albert Peyton Terhune's *Lad: A Dog* (1962), Richard Adams's *The Plague Dogs* (1982) and, of course, Eric Knight's venerable *Lassie Come Home* (1943). Mongrels easily outnumber any breed as the most popular dogs in the cinema. Still, there have been a lot of German Shepherds — the Rin Tin Tin movies, the Rusty series, *The Littlest Hobo*, *Kelly and Me*, *Won Ton Ton*, *K-9* and *We Think the World of You*. And Doberman pinschers unexpectedly became the trendy dogs of the early 1970s, appearing in movies like *They Only Kill Their Masters* (1972), *The Doberman Gang* (1972), *The Daring Dobermans* (1973) and *The Amazing Dobermans* (1976). Not all dogs have been portrayed as man's best friend. *Cujo* (1983) was about a rabid Saint Bernard dead set on devouring Dee Wallace, while *Dogs* (1976) and *The Pack* (1977) were remarkably similar thrillers about humans being stalked by wild dogs. James Brolin played a man stranded overnight in a department store — and at the mercy of vicious security dogs — in the 1973 TV-movie *Trapped*. *Devil Dog: The Hound of Hell* (1978) featured an evil, possessed pooch, while a vampire dog distinguished *Dracula's Dog* (1977). David Warner may have encountered the most frightening of all movie dogs when he threatened the safety of the Antichrist in 1976's *The Omen*. Canine fantasies have opted for a lighter tone. An ancient spell periodically turned Tommy Kirk into a lovable sheepdog in 1959's *The Shaggy Dog*. Dean Jones experienced a similar problem in the 1976 sequel *The Shaggy D.A.* A murdered German shepherd returned to Earth as private eye Rex Shepard (Dick Powell) to find his killer in 1951's hilarious *You Never Can Tell*. *Oh, Heavenly Dog!* (1980) reversed the premise and lost the laughs, despite the presence of Chevy Chase and Benji. A cast of humans portrayed the anxious dogs awaiting either new homes or death in Robert Downey's off-the-wall satire *Pound* (1970). A crafty pup named Blood communicated telepathetically with his dense human companion (Don Johnson) in the post-apocalypse satire *A Boy and His Dog* (1975). And henpecked husband Walter Abel found solace with a talking dog in *The Fabulous Joe* (1947). See also **Benji; Lassie; Rusty; The Shaggy Dog.**

The Clash of the Wolves (1924)
A Dog of the Regiment (1930)
Skippy (1931)
Lucky Dog (1933)
The Kennel Murder Case (1933)
Call of the Wild (1935)
The Voice of Bugle Ann (1936)
Storm in a Teacup (1936)
The Hound of the Baskervilles (1939)
The Biscuit Eater (1940)
Lassie Come Home (1943)
It Shouldn't Happen to a Dog (1946)
The Tender Years (1947)
The Fabulous Joe (1947)
The Emperor's Waltz (1948)
You Never Can Tell (1951)
Behave Yourself! (1951)
Bloodhounds of Broadway (1952)
Lady and the Tramp (1955)
It's a Dog's Life (aka *Bar Sinister*) (1955)
Goodbye My Lady (1956)
Kelly and Me (1957)
Old Yeller (1957)
The Man Who Wagged His Tail (1957)
The Littlest Hobo (1958)
A Dog of Flanders (1959)
The Hound of the Baskervilles (1959)
The Shaggy Dog (1959)
The Silent Call (1961)
Greyfriars Bobby (1961)
101 Dalmations (1961)
Big Red (1962)
Savage Sam (1962)
Lad: A Dog (1962)

Wild and Wonderful (1963)
The Incredible Journey (1963)
Git (1965)
The Ugly Dachshund (1966)
The Spy With a Cold Nose (1966)
Alexander (1968)
Pound (1970)
They Only Kill Their Masters (1972)
Call of the Wild (1972)
Sounder (1972)
White Fang (1972)
The Doberman Gang (1972)
The Daring Dobermans (1973)
Trapped (1973 TVM)
Where the Red Fern Grows (1974)
Digby — The Biggest Dog in the World (1974)
A Boy and His Dog (1975)
The Great Adventure (1975)
Dogpound Shuffle (aka *Spot*) (1975)
The Omen (1976)
Call of the Wild (1976 TVM)
Dogs (1976)
Won Ton Ton, the Dog Who Saved Hollywood (1976)
The Amazing Dobermans (1976)
The Shaggy D.A. (1976)
The Pack (aka *The Long Dark Night*) (1977)
Dracula's Dog (aka *Zoltan, Hound of Hell*) (1977)
Devil Dog: The Hound of Hell (1978 TVM)
C.H.O.M.P.S. (1979)
The Black Marble (1980)

Oh, Heavenly Dog! (1980)
The Courage of Kavik, the Wolf Dog
   (aka Kavik, the Wolf Dog) (1980)
The Fox and the Hound (1981)
Rottweiler (aka Dogs of Hell) (1981)
The Plague Dogs (1982)
Hear No Evil (1982 TVM)
Skeezer (1982 TVM)
White Dog (1982)
Cujo (1983)
Second Sight: A Love Story (1984
   TVM)
Love Leads the Way (1984 TVM)
Hambone and Hillie (1984)
Gus Brown and Midnight Brewster
   (1985 TVM)
A Cry in the Dark (1988)
Oliver and Company (1988)
Watchers (1988)

Pound Puppies and the Legend of Big
   Paw (1988)
K-9 (1989)
We Think the World of You (1989)
Turner and Hooch (1989)
The Adventures of Milo and Otis
   (1989)
All Dogs Go to Heaven (1989)
Watchers 2 (1990)
Baxter (1990)
White Fang (1991)
Rover Dangerfield (1991)
Bingo (1991)
Beethoven (1992)
Homeward Bound: The Incredible
   Journey (1993)
Call of the Wild (1993 TVM)
Man's Best Friend (1993)
Beethoven's 2nd (1993)

Doinel, Antoine

French director François Truffaut introduced his cinematic alter ego as an imaginative, troublemaking adolescent in 1959's *The 400 Blows*. The film also marked Truffaut's feature film debut — an impressive one that earned him a Grand Prix for direction at the Cannes Film Festival and contributed much to the success of the French "New Wave" films of the 1960s. Jean-Pierre Leaud played Antoine, a fourteen-year-old who steals and lies in defiance of adults, particularly his neglectful parents. He is finally sent to a reform school for his theft of a typewriter but manages to escape. However, Truffaut and Leaud brought Antoine back and gave him his first girlfriend in the "Antoine and Colette" episode in the 1962 anthology *Love at Twenty*. In 1968's *Stolen Kisses*, Antoine gets kicked out of the Army, becomes a night watchman, gets fired, and joins a detective agency. More importantly, he falls in love with Christine, who rejects him until he becomes interested in an older woman. Their subsequent marriage comes apart, despite the birth of a son, in 1970's *Bed and Board*. They are divorced at the beginning of 1979's *Love on the Run*, a reflective closing episode combining new footage with clips from the four previous films. Leaud was the only actor to portray Antoine Doinel.

   The 400 Blows (aka *Les Quatre Cents Coups*) (1959)
   Love at Twenty (aka *L'Amour À Vingt Ans*) (1962)
   Stolen Kisses (aka *Baiser Volés*) (1968)
   Bed and Board (aka *Domicile Conjugal*) (1970)
   Love on the Run (aka *L'Amour En Fuite*) (1979)

Dolls

Horror and fantasy filmmakers have found the most imaginative uses for dolls. A dying killer transferred his soul into a happy-looking "Chucky" doll in Tom Holland's 1988 sleeper hit *Child's Play* (q.v.). Amazingly, the film's characters — and the moviegoing public — readily took to the idea of a little doll running around an apartment wielding a knife and shouting profanities. A living doll also harassed Karen Black in the most chilling segment of 1975's *Trilogy of Terror*. Other murder-minded dolls stalked human prey in *Cathy's Curse*, a 1977 *Exorcist* clone about a possessed rag doll, and in cult director Stuart Gordon's *Dolls* (1987). Voodoo dolls have cropped up in several films, though none to better effect than in 1962's *Burn, Witch, Burn*. Teen nerds Anthony Michael Hall and Ilan Mitchell-Smith turned a Barbie doll into fetching Kelly LeBrock in the 1985 comedy *Weird Science*. The title murderer in *The Psychopath* (1966) left dolls as a calling card at the scene of his crimes. In non-horror films, dolls have been used as unlikely hiding places. Escaped fugitives fought over a doll stuffed with heroin in the 1961 drive-in picture *Wild Youth*. On a more intellectual scale, Robert Mitchum pursued two children and a doll filled with money in 1955's *The Night of the Hunter*, Charles Laughton's haunting fable of good vs. evil. Despite its title, the dolls in Tod Browning's *The Devil-Doll* (1936) were really shrunken people. The most bizarre doll film was also one of the first, 1907's *The Doll's Revenge*. It was about a little boy who destroys his sister's doll, only to have the parts reassemble themselves. The doll then grew to an alarming size and was joined by another doll; the two of them pulled the wicked boy apart and devoured him. Both *The Incredible Shrinking Man* (1957) and *The Incredible Shrinking Woman* (1981) used doll houses for temporary residences. See also **Child's Play.**

The Doll's Revenge (1907)	*Cathy's Curse* (aka *Cauchemares*)
Black Doll (1938)	(1977)
The Night of the Hunter (1955)	*The Dollmaker* (1984 TVM)
Wild Youth (aka *Naked Youth*) (1961)	*Weird Science* (1985)
Burn, Witch, Burn (aka *Night of the*	*River's Edge* (1986)
Eagle) (1962)	*Dolls* (1987)
Jack the Giant Killer (1962)	*Child's Play* (1988)
The Doll (1963)	*Dolly Dearest* (1991)
The Psychopath (1966)	*The Tommyknockers* (1993 TVM)
Trilogy of Terror (1975 TVM)	*The Baby Doll Murders* (1993)

Dolphins

Flipper, the biggest dolphin star, made the theatrical features *Flipper* (1963) and *Flipper's New Adventure* (1964) before settling into a 1964-68 TV series. Mitzi the Dolphin (who died of a heart attack in 1971 at the age of twenty-two) played Flipper on the big screen. Suzy the Dolphin replaced her in the TV version. In 1973's *Day of the Dolphin*, George C. Scott and wife Trish Van Devere taught dolphins how to speak rudimentary English ("Fa loves pa!"). Don Knotts played a meek bookkeeper who becomes an animated dolphin and joins the Navy in the charmless 1964 fantasy *The Incredible Mr. Limpet*. A deep sea diver jilted Rosanna Arquette for a pair of playful dolphins in 1988's *The Big Blue*. Given Rosanna's whiny performance, it was the right choice. See also **Fish; Sharks; Whales.**

Boy on a Dolphin (1957)	*Flipper's New Adventure* (1964)
Flipper (1963)	*The Incredible Mr. Limpet* (1964)

| *Island of the Blue Dolphins* (1964) | *The Big Blue* (1988) |
| *Day of the Dolphin* (1973) | *Splash Too* (1988 TVM) |

Dracula

Although Bram Stoker's immortal vampire novel was published in 1897, a film version was not attempted until F.W. Murnau's *Nosferatu* appeared in 1922. To avoid royalty payments, Murnau never mentioned Dracula by name. Stoker's widow nevertheless sued on the grounds of copyright infringement and some of the prints were destroyed. In 1930, Universal and Tod Browning signed horror great Lon Chaney for the title role in a film version of John Balderston and Hamilton Deane's popular stage play. However, Chaney died unexpectedly and the role went to Bela Lugosi, a screen unknown who had played Count Dracula on stage. Lugosi's compelling presence and Browning's atmospheric direction made *Dracula* a great success (it has dated rather poorly). Interestingly, a Spanish-language version was filmed concurrently on the same sets. It starred Carlos Villarias and ran twenty-nine minutes longer. Although Universal followed Browning's *Dracula* with several popular horror films (*Frankenstein*, etc.), a sequel did not appear until 1936's *Dracula's Daughter*. An offbeat love story with some fine performances, this sequel attracted little attention and was Universal's last attempt at a first-class vampire film. Seven years later, Lon Chaney, Jr. turned up as Count Alucard (spell it backwards) in Robert Siodmak's lively programmer *Son of Dracula*. Despite Chaney's miscasting, this unusual entry had its share of memorable moments — notably Dracula's transformation into mist as his coffin floated toward the surface in a swamp. The Count's Universal career ended with bit parts in 1944's *House of Frankenstein*, 1945's *House of Dracula* (played by John Carradine in both), and 1948's *Abbott and Costello Meet Frankenstein* (in which Lugosi reprised his interpretation). Except for the 1953 Turkish film *Dracula Istanbulda*, Dracula lay dormant for almost a decade. Then, Hammer Films resurrected him with style with their 1958 classic *Horror of Dracula*. As embodied by tall, imposing Christopher Lee, Dracula was a vicious, powerful, handsome vampire whose cunning was matched only by his brilliant adversary Van Helsing (superbly played by Peter Cushing). The Hammer version was a smash, but Lee (and the Count himself) was oddly missing from the equally memorable sequel *Brides of Dracula* (1960). Lee was back in 1964's *Dracula, Prince of Darkness*, but his role was brief and, amazingly, he had no dialogue. Despite occasional sparks of interest, the rest of the Hammer Dracula films were run-of-the-mill vampire features. Technically, the last was 1974's *The Legend of the Seven Golden Vampires* (aka *The Seven Brothers Meet Dracula*), but Lee's absence and an emphasis on martial arts made this hardly seem like a Dracula picture. Between the Hammer entries, Lee also appeared as Dracula in Jesus Franco's *Count Dracula* (1971), a fairly literal adaptation of Stoker's book, and a French comedy *Dracula and Son* (1976). Although Lee and Lugosi were the screen's most famous Draculas, a host of other actors have essayed the role. The usually vicious Jack Palance emphasized the Count's sympathetic side in Dan Curtis's handsome 1973 TV movie. PBS's *Count Dracula* (1978) featured Louis Jourdan in an aristocratic, sensual interpretation. Klaus Kinski was disturbing (and quite "unsensual") in Werner Herzog's 1978 remake of *Nosferatu*, while Frank Langella was surprisingly forgettable recreating his Broadway performance in 1979's big-budgeted *Dracula*. In 1992, Francis Ford Coppola mounted the stylish *Bram Stoker's Dracula*, which restored much of the novel's plot, although the Dracula-Mina romance would have shocked Stoker. See also **Vampires**.

Universal's Dracula Films

Dracula (1931) (Lugosi)
Dracula's Daughter (1936) (Gloria Holden as the daughter)
Son of Dracula (1943) (Chaney, Jr.)
House of Frankenstein (1944) (Carradine)
House of Dracula (1945) (Carradine)
Abbott and Costello Meet Frankenstein (1948) (Lugosi)

Hammer's Dracula Films

Horror of Dracula (aka *Dracula*) (1958) (Christopher Lee)
Brides of Dracula (1960) (actually, the Count is never seen)
Dracula, Prince of Darkness (1964) (Lee)
Dracula Has Risen From the Grave (1968) (Lee)
Taste the Blood of Dracula (1970) (Lee)
Scars of Dracula (1970) (Lee)
Dracula A.D. 1972 (aka *Dracula Today*) (1972) (Lee)
The Satanic Rites of Dracula (aka *Count Dracula and His Vampire Bride; Count Dracula Is Alive and Well and Living in London*) (1973) (Lee)
The Legend of the Seven Golden Vampires (aka *The Seven Brothers Meet Dracula*) (1974) (John Forbes Robertson)

Other Dracula Films

Nosferatu (1922) (Max Schreck)
Spanish Dracula (1931) (Carlos Villarias)
Dracula Istanbulda (1953) (Atif Kaptan)
Curse of Dracula (aka *Return of Dracula; The Fantastic Disappearing Man*) (1958) (Francis Lederer)
Billy the Kid vs. Dracula (1965) (Carradine)
Mad Monster Party? (1966) (puppet)
Count Dracula (1971) (Lee)
Dracula vs. Frankenstein (aka *Blood of Frankenstein*) (1972) (Zandor Vorkov)
Blacula (1972) (Charles Macaulay)
Dracula's Great Love (aka *El Grande Amore del Conde Dracula*) (1972) (Paul Naschy)
Lake of Dracula (aka *Choisu Me*) (1972) (Mori Kishida)
Dracula (1973 TVM) (Jack Palance)
Lady Dracula (aka *Legendary Curse of Lemora; Lemora, the Lady Dracula*) (1973) (Leslie Gilb)
Blood for Dracula (aka *Andy Warhol's Dracula*) (1974) (Udo Kier)
Vampira (aka *Old Dracula*) (1975) (David Niven)
Dracula and Son (1976) (Lee)
Nocturna (1978) (Carradine)

Nosferatu (1978) (Klaus Kinski)
Count Dracula (1978 TVM) (Louis Jourdan)
Dracula (1979) (Frank Langella)
The True Life of Dracula (1979) (Stefan Sileanu)
Dracula's Last Rites (1980) (Gerald Fielding)
The Monster Club (1987) (Duncan Regehr)
Bram Stoker's Dracula (1992) (Gary Oldham)
Dracula Rising (1993) (Christopher Atkins)

Dragons

The dragon has made little impact as a cinematic monster, being relegated principally to supporting roles. A splendid animated dragon dominated the fiery climax of Disney's *Sleeping Beauty* (1959), but his screen time was all too short. The same can be said of *The Reluctant Dragon* (1941), a documentary about the Disney Studios that featured a short cartoon version of Kenneth Grahame's story. Special effects genius Ray Harryhausen devised very lifelike dragons for 1958's *The Seventh Voyage of Sinbad* and 1963's *Jason and the Argonauts*. After Jason slew the seven-headed hydra in the latter film, its teeth turned into skeleton warriors which promptly attacked the mythological hero. A year earlier, fairy-tale protagonist Jack battled a sorcerer-turned-dragon in the Harryhausen-inspired fantasy *Jack the Giant Killer*. Only two films, both from Disney, have given dragons what could be called leading roles. *Pete's Dragon*, a 1977 live action/animation film, starred a friendly dragon named Elliott (animated) who helped a young boy (live action) find a loving home. Elliott, a rather plump creature with tiny wings, could make himself invisible — a rare trait for his species. In contrast to likable Elliott, Disney's *Dragonslayer* (1981) featured a hideous, fire-breathing dragon appeased only by human sacrifice. The monster and its magnificent lair were created with high-tech wizardry by George Lucas's Industrial Light and Magic Company. In terms of sheer opulence, *Dragonslayer* ranks as the dragon's finest hour. As for contemporary dragons, there really are none. One could argue that *Q the Winged Serpent* (1982) had many dragonlike qualities, but technically he was the ancient bird-god Quetzalcoatl. Likewise, the Japanese monster Ghidrah (q.v.) boasted three heads, breathed fire and flew. But whether he or any of his Japanese monster companions were dragons or unidentified dinosaurs remains a source of debate. The Philo Vance (q.v.) murder mystery *The Dragon Murder Case* (1934) revolved around a "dragon" pool where a swimmer mysteriously disappeared. Despite the presence of unusual claw prints and much talk about dragons, Vance exposed a human murderer. The medieval dragon in 1986's *Star Knight* turned out to be an alien spaceship. See also **Dinosaurs; Sea Serpents.**

The Niebelungen (1924)
The Reluctant Dragon (1941)
The Sword and the Dragon (aka *Ilya Mourometz*) (1956)
The Seventh Voyage of Sinbad (1958)
Sleeping Beauty (1959)
Goliath and the Dragon (1960)
Jack the Giant Killer (1962)

The Magic Sword (1962)
The Wonderful World of the Brothers Grimm (1962)
Captain Sinbad (1963)
Jason and the Argonauts (1963)
Ghidrah, the Three Headed Monster (1965)
Pete's Dragon (1977)

Jabberwocky (1977)	*Star Knight* (aka *The Knight of the*
Dragonslayer (1981)	*Dragon*) (1986)
The NeverEnding Story (1984)	*Erik the Viking* (1989)

Drew, Nancy

Teenage sleuth Nancy Drew has appeared in countless books by "Carolyn Keene" (a pseudonym for numerous authors who worked for supervising writers Edward Stratemeyer and daughter Harriet Adams). Yet her screen career was a surprisingly brief one, with Bonita Granville playing her in four formula B-films. Pamela Sue Martin starred in a 1977-78 TV series *The Nancy Drew Mysteries*, and Janet Louise Johnson took over the role when that show merged into *The Hardy Boys Mysteries* during the 1978-79 season.

Nancy Drew, Detective (1938)	*Nancy Drew—Reporter* (1939)
Nancy Drew and the Hidden Staircase	*Nancy Drew—Troubleshooter* (1939)
(1939)	

Drug Addiction

The United States' efforts to curb its drug addiction problems in the late 1980s brought the subject unprecedented attention in the cinema. No fewer than six major films in 1987-88 portrayed the dangers of cocaine, crack and other narcotics. Comedian Michael Keaton turned serious as a successful businessman forced to enter a clinic for treatment in *Clean and Sober* (1988). James Woods tackled a similar role, with his typical intensity, in the same year's *The Boost*. Even Michael J. Fox played against type as a nice guy turned druggie in *Bright Lights, Big City* (1988). Yet, despite the presence of these big-name stars, all three films crashed at the box office, as did *Less Than Zero* (1987) and *Bird* (1988). Faced with grim nightly newscasts of drug-related crimes, it's likely that American moviegoers preferred to avoid seeing their screen favorites as manipulated addicts. Not surprisingly, the track record of earlier drug addiction pictures has been riddled with similar failures. *The Cocaine Fiends* (1936) was ignored upon its initial release and promoted as camp in the early 1970s along with *Reefer Madness* (1936). Yet, *Cocaine Fiends* contained little material that was even unintentionally funny, being a bleak tale of a young girl whose boyfriend hooks her, and eventually her brother too, on dope. Almost two decades later, producer-director Otto Preminger tumbled censorship barriers with his powerful, highly successful *The Man With the Golden Arm* (1955). Frank Sinatra, in his finest performance, played Frankie Machine, a drummer who turns to drugs to escape pressure. A scene of Sinatra "shooting up" was deleted when the film was originally shown in Maryland (a court ruling eventually restored it). In the wake of *Golden Arm*, smaller antidrug films were released but with little impact. Cameron Mitchell played boxer-turned-addict Barney Ross in *Monkey on My Back* (1957). Teen heartthrob James Darren fell in with the wrong crowd south of the border in *The Tijuana Story* (1957). And Peter Graves battled narcotics use among truckers in *Death in Small Doses* (1957). Another wave of addiction movies began in the early 1970s, following the gradual decline of drug culture hits like Roger Corman's *The Trip* (1967). The most effective was the potent 1971 documentary *Dusty and Sweets McGee* (1971), which sadly included Billy Gray of TV's *Father Knows Best* as one of its real-life addicts.

Although drug addiction would seem to have little appeal as a comedy subject, cult director Larry Cohen broached the subject in *The Stuff* (1985), an uncomfortable satire about an addictive food. Stand-up comic Richard Pryor discussed his near-death after freebasing in his 1982 concert film *Richard Pryor Live on the Sunset Strip*. A fictionalized version of the incident also came into play in Pryor's semiautobiographical *Jo Jo Dancer, Your Life Is Calling* (1986).

The Cocaine Fiends (1936)	*I'm Dancing as Fast as I Can* (1982)
Reefer Madness (aka *Tell Your Children*; *The Burning Question*; *The Dope Addict*; *Doped Youth*; *Love Madness*) (1936)	*Desperate Lives* (1982 TVM)
	Scarface (1983)
	Cocaine: One Man's Seduction (1983 TVM)
The Man With the Golden Arm (1955)	*Torchlight* (1984)
Death in Small Doses (1957)	*The Stuff* (1985)
Monkey on My Back (1957)	*Jo Jo Dancer, Your Life Is Calling* (1986)
The Tijuana Story (1957)	
Corridors of Blood (aka *Doctor of Seven Dials*) (1958)	*Cracked Up* (1987 TVM)
	Less Than Zero (1987)
Believe in Me (1971)	*The Boost* (1988)
Dusty and Sweets McGee (1971)	*Clean and Sober* (1988)
Panic in Needle Park (1971)	*Bright Lights, Big City* (1988)
Born to Win (1971)	*Bird* (1988)
Go Ask Alice (1973 TVM)	*Drugstore Cowboy* (1989)
The Death of Richie (aka *Richie*) (1977 TVM)	*Jumpin' at the Boneyard* (1991)
	Seeds of Tragedy (1991 TVM)
A Hero Ain't Nothing But a Sandwich (1978)	*Rush* (1991)
	Light Sleeper (1992)
A Cry for Love (1980)	*Darkness Before Dawn* (1993 TVM)
Angel Dusted (1981 TVM)	*Blind Spot* (1993 TVM)

Drummond, Bulldog

Although not a detective by trade, Captain Hugh "Bulldog" Drummond was always more than willing to crack a mystery, particularly if a young attractive woman was involved. The novels (and a play) were written by H.C. (Sapper) McNeile in the 1920s. Carlyle Blackwell and Jack Buchanan portrayed Drummond in the first screen adaptations in 1922 and 1925, respectively. But the ideal Drummond proved to be Ronald Colman, who played the gentleman detective in 1929's *Bulldog Drummond* (adapted from the play) and 1934's *Bulldog Drummond Strikes Back*. The impeccable Colman brought flair and a sense of fun to the part and was ably assisted by Claud Allister or Charles Butterworth as Drummond's chum Algy. Other notable actors (e.g., Ray Milland and Ralph Richardson) played Drummond on their way to stardom, but an official series did not get underway until 1937. During the next three years, American John Howard made seven fast-moving but undistinguished series entries with Reginald Denny as Algy and E. E. Clive as his butler. The first three Howard films also featured John Barrymore, whose career was floundering, as a Scotland Yard inspector who specialized in disguises. The Howard series ended with Hugh's marriage to his long-time fianceé Phyllis in *Bulldog Drummond's Bride*. Still, Drummond showed up as a bachelor eight years later in pictures starring Ron Randell and Tom Conway (both detective movie veterans). Walter Pidgeon played a middle-aged Drummond with a prized pig in 1951's *Calling Bulldog Drummond*. And in 1967, dashing Richard Johnson updated the character in the Bondian adventure *Deadlier Than the Male*. Johnson's Drummond bore little resemblance to McNeile's original, but the movie did well enough to warrant a 1971 sequel *Some Girls Do*. It performed poorly at the box office and killed off the series. However, *Bullshot*, an unexpected British spoof, surfaced in 1982. Its hero, Captain Hugh "Bullshot" Crummond, was played by Alan Shearman, who coadapted his own stage play.

Bulldog Drummond (1929) (Ronald Colman)
Temple Tower (1930) (Kenneth McKenna)
Bulldog Drummond Strikes Back (1934) (Colman)
The Return of Bulldog Drummond (1934) (Ralph Richardson)
Bulldog Jack (aka *Alias Bulldog Drummond*) (1935) (Atholl Fleming)
Bulldog Drummond at Bay (1937) (John Lodge)
Bulldog Drummond Escapes (1937) (Ray Milland)
Bulldog Drummond Comes Back (1937) (John Howard)
Bulldog Drummond's Revenge (1937) (Howard)
Arrest Bulldog Drummond (1938) (Howard)
Bulldog Drummond in Africa (1938) (Howard)
Bulldog Drummond's Peril (1938) (Howard)
Bulldog Drummond's Secret Police (1939) (Howard)
Bulldog Drummond's Bride (1939) (Howard)
Bulldog Drummond Strikes Back (1947) (Ron Randell)
Bulldog Drummond at Bay (1947) (Randell)
The Challenge (1948) (Tom Conway)
Thirteen Lead Soldiers (1948) (Conway)
Calling Bulldog Drummond (1951) (Walter Pidgeon)
Deadlier Than the Male (1967) (Richard Johnson)
Some Girls Do (1971) (Johnson)
Bullshot (1982) (Alan Shearman)

Dupree, Paula (The Ape Woman)

After the Wolf Man's debut in 1941, Universal had gone two years without introducing a new addition to its gallery of monsters, which included Dracula, the Frankenstein Monster and the Invisible Man (all qq.v.). Thus, the studio was anxious to come up with a creature of equal popularity. Perhaps inspired by the success of Val Lewton's *The Cat People* (1942), Universal opted for a female monster—an ape woman. So, in 1943's *Captive Wild Woman*, that formidable mad scientist John Carradine employed gland transplants to change Cheela the orangutan into sultry Paula Dupree (Acquanetta). The operation was quite a success until Paula became jealous when Milburn Stone (Doc on *Gunsmoke*) failed to return her affections. That's when she turned into a murderous half-ape/half-woman (again, the plotline owes much to *Cat People* and even the earlier *Island of Lost Souls*). Paula gets gunned down during a circus stampede, but she nevertheless appeared in two sequels, played by Acquanetta again in *Jungle Woman* (1944) and by Vicky Lane in *Jungle Captive* (1945). Neither matched the tone of the original, one of Edward Dmytryk's last B-films before he made his mark with 1944's *Murder, My Sweet*. Sadly, Universal never paired Paula Dupree with the Wolf Man—they would have made an interesting couple. See also **Apes and Monkeys; Humanimals.**

Captive Wild Woman (1943) *Jungle Captive* (1945)
Jungle Woman (1944)

Durango Kid

Charles Startlett portrayed this mysterious masked rider in a long-running B-Western series for Columbia. Often described as a Robin Hood of the West, the Durango Kid used his guns more often than his guitar, thus distinguishing himself from his contemporaries, singing cowboys such as Gene Autry, Roy Rogers and Tex Ritter. Prior to acting, Startlett played football at Dartmouth, where he appeared as an extra in the 1926 Richard Dix film *The Quarterback*. The Durango Kid series ended when Startlett retired in 1953.

The Durango Kid (1940)
Return of the Durango Kid (1945)
Both Barrels Blazing (1945)
Rustlers of the Badlands (1945)
Blazing the Western Trail (1945)
Outlaws of the Rockies (1945)
Lawless Empire (1945)
Frontier Gun Law (1946)
Roaring Rangers (1946)
Gunning for Vengeance (1946)
Galloping Thunder (1946)
Two-Fisted Stranger (1946)
The Desert Horseman (1946)
Heading West (1946)
Landrush (1946)
Terror Trail (1946)
The Fighting Frontiersman (1946)
South of the Chisholm Trail (1947)
The Lone Hand Texan (1947)
West of Dodge City (1947)
Law of the Canyon (1947)
Prairie Raiders (1947)
The Stranger From Ponca City (1947)
Riders of the Lone Star (1947)
Buckaroo From Powder River (1947)
Last Days of Boot Hill (1947)
Six Gun Law (1948)
Phantom Valley (1948)
West of Sonora (1948)
Whirlwind Raiders (1948)
Blazing Across the Pecos (1948)
Trail to Laredo (1948)

El Dorado Pass (1948)
Quick on the Trigger (1948)
Challenge of the Range (1949)
Laramie (1949)
The Blazing Trail (1949)
South of Death Valley (1949)
Bandits of Eldorado (1949)
Desert Vigilante (1949)
Horsemen of the Sierras (1949)
Renegades of the Sage (1949)
Trail of the Rustlers (1950)
Outcast of Black Mesa (1950)
Texas Dynamo (1950)
Streets of Ghost Town (1950)
Across the Badlands (1950)
Raiders of Tomahawk Creek (1950)
Lightning Guns (1950)
Frontier Outpost (1950)
Prairie Roundup (1951)
Ridin' the Outlaw Trail (1951)
Fort Savage Raiders (1951)
Snake River Desperadoes (1951)
Bonanza Town (1951)
Cyclone Fury (1951)
The Kid From Amarillo (1951)
Pecos River (1951)
Smoky Canyon (1952)
The Hawk of Wild River (1952)
Laramie Mountains (1952)
The Rough Tough West (1952)
Junction City (1952)
The Kid From Broken Gun (1952)

Earthquakes

The climactic crumble experienced by Spencer Tracy and Clark Gable in 1936's *San Francisco* ranks highest on the cinematic scale for impact. However, the California quake in 1974's all-star *Earthquake* was significantly louder, since it was accompanied by a rumbling sound system dubbed "Sensurround." The most stunning footage probably belongs to the 1990 TV-movie *After the Shock*, since it includes actual news film from the 1989 San Francisco-Oakland earthquake. Aerial photographers Jackie Cooper and Cleavon Little could not convince townsfolk that an earthquake was on the way in 1974's *The Day the Earth Moved*. Dana Andrews could not figure out how to stop the monstrous quake he initiated with missile tests in *Crack in the World* (1965). And scientists could not figure out what to do with the giant insect released by an Arctic earthquake in *The Deadly Mantis* (1957). Fortunately, Superman knew how to stop an earthquake from dropping California into the Pacific and did so quite effectively in 1978's *Superman*.

San Francisco (1936)	*Earthquake* (1974)
The Sisters (1938)	*The Day the Earth Moved* (1974 TVM)
The Rains Came (1939)	*Superman* (1978)
Flame of the Barbary Coast (1945)	*Prisoners of the Lost Universe* (1983
Green Dolphin Street (1947)	TVM)
The Deadly Mantis (1957)	*After the Shock* (1990 TVM)
In Search of the Castaways (1962)	*The Big One: The Los Angeles*
The Night the World Exploded (1964)	*Earthquake* (1990 TVM)
Crack in the World (1965)	*Life on the Edge* (1992)
Short Walk to Daylight (1972 TVM)	*Miracle on I-880* (1993 TVM)

Earth's Core

Science fiction filmmakers have tended to ignore the fact that the earth's core actually consists of molten lava. In 1951's *Unknown World*, a group of scientists used a submarine-tank (called a cyclotram) to burrow 1600 miles beneath the earth's surface. Their goal was to find a safe haven from atomic bomb warfare, but instead they found a world where the human race could not reproduce. On their *Journey to the Center of the Earth* (1959), James Mason and friends uncovered a forest of mushrooms, a crystal cavern, a salt vortex, prehistoric monsters, an underground sea and a lost city. It was a marvelous showcase for the Jules Verne story, especially compared to the cut-rate 1978 Spanish version *Where Time Began*. Peter Cushing played another scientist with a drilling machine in 1976's *At the Earth's Core*, adapted from an Edgar Rice Burroughs fantasy. *Battle Beneath the Earth* (1967) did not take place at the earth's core, but it was nevertheless set far below the surface. Its imaginative premise concerned a Chinese plot to burrow tunnels from Hawaii to underneath the continental U.S. for the purpose of planting atomic bombs. *The Mole People* (1956) also featured extensive underground footage, but did not involve the earth's core. Dana Andrews set off an atomic bomb near the earth's core, causing *A Crack in the World* (1965). *The Bunker Palace Hotel* (1989) was a concrete and marble political hideaway located at the core. See also **Tunnels**.

Unknown World (1951)	*Adventure at the Center of the Earth*
Journey to the Center of the Earth	(1964)
(1959)	*A Crack in the World* (1965)

Battle Beneath the Earth (1967)
At the Earth's Core (1976)
Where Time Began (aka Trip to the
Centre of the Earth) (1978)

The Bunker Palace Hotel (1989)
Journey to the Center of the Earth (1993
TVM)

East Side Kids, *see* The Bowery Boys

Elephants

Elephants have been steadily employed bit players, stampeding through dozens of jungle pictures and prancing around numerous three-ring circuses. Starring roles have been relatively scarce but almost always memorable. Elephants sporting tutus participated in an animated ballet in the "Dance of the Hours" segment in Disney's *Fantasia* (1940). The following year, Disney introduced the world's first flying elephant in the children's classic *Dumbo*. In his only starring role without Stan Laurel, Oliver Hardy played a doctor who treated—and then couldn't get rid of—a chummy elephant in *Zenobia* (1939). Two elephants appeared in the 1942 Lupe Velez vehicle *Mexican Spitfire's Elephant* (see also **Mexican Spitfire**). The first was a toy elephant stuffed with valuable jewels, while the second was a live pink one with green polka dots. Unfortunately, the movie was filmed in black and white. The Italian comedy *Hello, Elephant* (1952) was about a schoolteacher who receives an elephant as a gift from an Indian prince. Few viewers found it funny, although the film's alternate title—*Pardon My Trunk*—still has its admirers. Sabu, who played the Indian prince, starred fifteen years earlier as the *Elephant Boy*. Other children-and-elephant movies include *The Bashful Elephant*, *Taffy and the Jungle Hunter*, and *Maya* with Jay *(Dennis the Menace)* North. On the serious side, Trevor Howard embarked on a crusade to save African elephants from greedy ivory hunters in John Huston's *The Roots of Heaven* (1958). A smashing elephant stampede played a critical part in reuniting estranged couple Peter Finch and Elizabeth Taylor in 1954's *Elephant Walk*. Burt Reynolds and Sally Field transported a pregnant elephant cross-country in the feeble 1980 comedy *Smokey and the Bandit II*. Jean de Brunhoff's beloved children's character, Babar, the King of the Elephants, made his big-screen debut in animated form in 1989's *Babar: The Movie*.

Elephant Boy (1937)
Zenobia (1939)
Fantasia (1940)
Dumbo (1941)
Mexican Spitfire's Elephant (1942)
Elephant Stampede (aka Bomba and
  the Elephant Stampede) (1951)
Hello, Elephant (aka Pardon My
  Trunk) (1952)
Elephant Walk (1954)
Jupiter's Darling (1955)
The Roots of Heaven (1958)
Elephant Gun (1959)
Hannibal (1960)

The Bashful Elephant (1962)
Billy Rose's Jumbo (aka Jumbo) (1962)
Taffy and the Jungle Hunter (1965)
Maya (1966)
Hannibal Brooks (1969)
An Elephant Called Slowly (1970)
The African Elephant (aka King of the
  Elephants) (1972)
Smokey and the Bandit II (1980)
Babar: The Movie (1989)
The Last Elephant (1990 TVM)
White Hunter, Black Heart (1990)
Madhouse (1990)

Emmanuelle

One of the few soft-core features to attract a mainstream audience, 1974's French import *Emmanuelle* cast Sylvia Kristel as the bored wife of an embassy official stationed in Thailand. The young bride was initially shocked when her freethinking husband encouraged her to explore her sexuality with other men and women. But Emmanuelle quickly proved willing to try anything once. This soft-focus adaptation of Emmanuelle Arsan's scandalous 1957 novel lacked sizzle, its success probably a product of its lush look and clever marketing campaign ("X was never like this," proclaimed the ad). Kristel reprised the lead role in *Emmanuelle— The Joys of a Woman* and *Goodbye Emmanuelle*. She appeared briefly in 1984's *Emmanuelle 4* before her character underwent plastic surgery and emerged with a different face and body (Mia Nygren). Centerfold Monique Gabrielle, a veteran of the *Deathstalker* (q.v.) series, starred in 1987's *Emmanuelle 5* but then gave way to Nathalie Uher in the following year's *Emmanuelle 6*. These six films comprise the "official" *Emmanuelle* series, but there have been many similarly titled imitations. In fact, Laura Gemser starred in so many rip-offs that these films could be treated as another series. The Gemser titles include: *Emmanuelle the Queen* (1975), *Emmanuelle in the Country* (1978), *Emmanuelle's Daughter* (1979) and many others. The British *Carry On* (q.v.) gang spoofed the *Emmanuelle* pictures with 1978's raunchy *Carry On Emmanuelle*.

Emmanuelle (1974)	*Emmanuelle 4* (1984)
Emmanuelle — The Joys of a Woman (1976)	*Emmanuelle 5* (1987)
	Emmanuelle 6 (1988)
Goodbye Emmanuelle (1979)	

End of the World/Post-Apocalypse

Pessimism sells few movie tickets, thus making the total destruction of the Earth an unpopular film subject. Nevertheless, planet Earth was wiped out by a streaking star in 1951's *When Worlds Collide*, with only a few survivors escaping to a sister planet to continue the human race. An atomic bomb blew the Earth into dust particles in 1970's *Beneath the Planet of the Apes*. Although no one escaped during that film's climax, the crafty sequel, 1971's *Escape From the Planet of the Apes*, revealed that a trio of intelligent apes had hijacked a rocket and avoided the explosion. The world's fate was left up in the air in the final scene of *The Day the Earth Caught Fire* (1962). Two newspapers awaited a final verdict before distribution, one with a headline reading "World Saved: H-bomb blasts succeed," the other declaring "World Doomed: H-bomb blasts fail." Several films such as *On the Beach* (1959) and *Testament* (1983) have ended with the human race facing ultimate extinction as a result of radioactive fallout. In contrast, the post-apocalypse genre consists of films in which a handful of humans have survived a near-catastrophic event and built a new world. Former radio writer Arch Oboler pioneered this type of film with 1951's *Five*, a talky tale of conflict among the last five people on Earth. Seen today, it's hard to gauge the film's impact, but at the time of its release, *Variety* called it "intriguing . . . but depressing in its assumption." *The World, the Flesh, and the Devil* (1959) added gloss to the same theme but is chiefly remembered for turning Manhattan into a ghost town. Similar post-apocalypse character dramas include Roger Corman's *The Day the World Ended*

(1956), the underrated vampire-plague film *The Last Man on Earth* (1964), and the TV-movie *Where Have All the People Gone?* (1974). Later low-budget films such as *A Boy and His Dog* and *The Ultimate Warrior* (both 1975) injected heavy action elements into their post-apocalypse plotlines. These led to the runaway success of 1982's *The Road Warrior* (aka *Mad Max 2*), which resulted in a slew of repetitive action films set in the barren wastelands of the future. More original views of the post-apocalypse are featured in *The War Game* (1967) and *The Bed Sitting Room* (1969). A bleak favorite at antinuke film showings, *The War Game* employs a vivid documentary style to show the devastating aftereffects of an atomic blast on London. On the other hand, *The Bed Sitting Room* makes its point with satire by showing nuclear survivors turning into furniture and pet birds. Many science fiction films have shown the Earth surviving a brush with total apocalypse, although, in a Biblical sense, none can match the close call detailed in 1988's *The Seventh Sign*. See also **Mad Max.**

When Worlds Collide (1951)
Five (1951)
The Day the World Ended (1956)
The World, the Flesh, and the Devil (1959)
On the Beach (1959)
The Day the Earth Caught Fire (1962)
Creation of the Humanoids (1962)
The Last Man on Earth (1964)
The End of August at the Hotel Ozone (aka *The End of the World at the Hotel Ozone*) (1965)
The War Game (1967)
The Bed Sitting Room (1969)
Beneath the Planet of the Apes (1970)
Glen and Randa (1971)
Doomsday Machine (1973)
Where Have All the People Gone? (1974 TVM)
A Boy and His Dog (1975)
The Ultimate Warrior (1975)
Damnation Alley (1977)
Wizards (1977)
Mad Max (1979)
Quintet (1979)
Virus (1980)

Testament (1983)
The Day After (1983)
Warlords of the 21st Century (aka *Battletruck*) (1983)
Warriors of the Wasteland (1983)
Stryker (1983)
Threads (1984 TVM)
Le Dernier Combat (1984)
Def-Con 4 (1985)
The Quiet Earth (1985)
Warriors of the Apocalypse (1985)
Wired to Kill (1986)
Radioactive Dreams (1986)
Survivor (1987)
Steel Dawn (1987)
Warlords (1988)
World Gone Wild (1988)
Badlands 2000 (1988 TVM)
Cherry 2000 (1988)
Miracle Mile (1989)
Cyborg (1989)
Hardware (1990)
The Blood of Heroes (aka *Salute of the Jugger*) (1990)
The Rapture (1991)

Episode Films, *see* Anthologies

Ernest

"Know what I mean, Vern?" asked Ernest P. Worrell in hundreds of television commercials in the 1980s. The character with the bulging eyes, gaping mouth and baseball cap was created by Nashville advertising executive John R. Cherry

III for a series of dairy commercials. But much of the character's success is owed to Jim Varney, a rubber-faced television comedian who brought Ernest to life in regional commercials that made the obnoxious know-it-all a household name. Cherry directed and cowrote 1987's *Ernest Goes to Camp*, a juvenile comedy that gave Varney a chance to make Ernest more sympathetic than his commercial incarnation—but just as clutzy. Disney's Touchstone banner picked up the independently produced film and walked away with a sleeper summer hit. In the four sequels that followed, Ernest helped Santa Claus on Christmas Eve, went to prison in place of an evil look-alike (q.v.), and battled a pesky troll on Halloween night and clashed with villains in pursuit of a Revolutionary cannon containing hidden crown jewels.

Ernest Goes to Camp (1987)	*Ernest Scared Stupid* (1991)
Ernest Saves Christmas (1988)	*Ernest Rides Again* (1993)
Ernest Goes to Jail (1990)	

Eternal Youth/Rejuvenation

The search for eternal youth has sparked movie explorations into fantastic lands as well as medically questionable scientific experiments. In 1937's *Lost Horizon*, Ronald Colman and his fellow plane crash survivors found Shangri-La, James Hilton's utopia of eternal youth, quite by accident. H. Rider Haggard's oft-filmed *She* concerned an ageless queen obsessed with exposing her reincarnated lover to the Flame of Eternal Life. Unfortunately, when she reentered the flame with him, her age caught up with her in a hurry. Oscar Wilde's aristocratic protagonist Dorian Gray sold his soul so that his portrait would age while he retained his youth in *The Picture of Dorian Gray* (1945). In the offbeat *Angel on the Amazon* (1948), an elderly woman took on the appearance of a twenty-five-year-old after a frightening encounter with a panther. Industrious individuals sought everlasting youth through medical means in *The Man in Half-Moon Street* (1944), its remake *The Man Who Could Cheat Death* (1959), *The Leech Woman* (1960), *The Wasp Woman* (1960) and *The Night Strangler* (1972). Alas, the rejuvenation methods employed in these films required their users to obtain fluids, glands or body parts from living humans. Ingrid Pitt experienced a similar problem as *Countess Dracula* (1972), who retained her youth by bathing in the blood of virgins. This gruesome tale was actually based on the life of murderess Elisabeth Bathory. On a lighter note, children flew to Never-Never Land to avoid adulthood in *Peter Pan* (1953), while a group of old-timers went to another planet to elude death in *Cocoon* (1985). Ponce de Leon never found the Fountain of Youth, but Tarzan did in 1949's *Tarzan's Magic Fountain*. It rejuvenated Cheetah into a baby chimp. Another chimpanzee caused mix ups in *Monkey Business* (1952) when he poured Cary Grant's experimental rejuvenation formula into a water cooler. Nathaniel Hawthorne's classic Fountain of Youth short story "Dr. Heideggar's Experiment" reached the screen in 1963 as a segment of *Twice Told Tales*.

The Elixir of Life (1911)	*The Picture of Dorian Gray* (1945)
She (1935)	*Angel on the Amazon* (aka *Drums*
Lost Horizon (1937)	*Along the Amazon*) (1948)
The Corpse Vanishes (1942)	*Tarzan's Magic Fountain* (1949)
The Man in Half-Moon Street (1944)	*Hurricane Island* (1951)

Monkey Business (1952)
Peter Pan (1953)
Jungle Moon Men (1955)
The Man Who Could Cheat Death (1959)
The Leech Woman (1960)
The Wasp Woman (1960)
Atom Age Vampire (1961)
Twice Told Tales (1963)
The Fat Spy (1965)
She (1965)
The Immortal (1969 TVM)
Satanik (1969)
Flesh Feast (1970)
Baron Blood (aka The Torture Chamber of Baron Blood) (1972)

The Night Strangler (1972 TVM)
Countess Dracula (1972)
Lost Horizon (1973)
The Thirsty Dead (1975)
Tuck Everlasting (1980)
Cocoon (1985)
Evil Spawn (1987)
The Rejuvenator (aka Rejuvenatrix) (1988)
Cocoon: The Return (1988)
Metamorphosis (1989)
The Spring (1990)
Death Becomes Her (1992)
Orlando (1992)
Jonny's Golden Quest (1993 TVM)

The Evil Dead

Sam Raimi was a nineteen-year-old amateur filmmaker when he and two friends decided to enter the movie industry by making a low-budget horror picture in Michigan. In 1979, they shot *Within the Woods*, a Super 8mm chiller that thrust stupid teens into an isolated cabin where they unleashed vengeful demons. Raimi and company, armed with this sample product, convinced doctors and lawyers to invest $90,000 in an expanded version. The resulting feature film, 1983's *The Evil Dead*, became an instant drive-in classic. It also earned a cult reputation in Great Britain, where copies of the videotape were seized and destroyed (although it played uncensored at the London Film Festival). *The Evil Dead* offered a highly derivative tale in which teenagers discover the Book of the Dead and then play an audio tape containing incantations that summon the demons. The lone survivor, Ash (Bruce Campbell), became the hero by default. Raimi's stylish direction and a surprisingly humorous undertone elevated *The Evil Dead* above other low-budget horror pictures. The superior 1987 sequel *Evil Dead 2* provided a delirious blend of suspense and Three Stooges' slapstick. It sent Ash into the woods again — where he naturally encountered more demons. When his hand became possessed (an absurdly funny scene), he severed it and connected a chainsaw (q.v.) to his arm. At the film's climax, he wound up in a time warp and landed in the Middle Ages. *Army of Darkness* (1993) picked up with Ash's capture by a band of bewildered knights. The plot evolved into a campy, fairly entertaining mixture of *A Connecticut Yankee in King Arthur's Court* and *Night of the Living Dead* (q.v.). The original ending, shown at the 1992 Sitges Film Festival, had our hero warp into the twenty-first century, where he found the planet in ruins. However, for its U.S. release, the ending was reshot with Ash working in a hardware store — where he has another showdown with the Evil Dead! See also **Chainsaws; Time Travel.**

The Evil Dead (1983)
Evil Dead 2: Dead by Dawn (aka Evil Dead 2) (1987)
Army of Darkness (aka Army of Darkness: Evil Dead 3) (1993)

The Exorcist

Although divergent in their approach to horror, *Rosemary's Baby* and *The Exorcist* reign jointly as the most important horror films of the 1960s and 1970s. *The Exorcist* drew huge audiences to a well-mounted exercise in intense, unsubtle, and sometimes purely visual horror. It spawned countless imitations, with the most successful being the 1974 rip-off *Beyond the Door* and the chilling 1976 box office hit *The Omen* (q.v.). Adapted by William Peter Blatty from his best-seller, *The Exorcist* pitted two priests—one of whom questions his faith—against the Devil in an all-out war over a young girl's soul. It was a straightforward story (a point overlooked by its sequels) and benefited from a fine cast: Max Von Sydow as the exorcist Father Merrin, playwright Jason Miller as his guilt-suffering assistant Father Karras, Linda Blair as twelve-year-old Regan, and Mercedes McCambridge as the voice of the Devil within Regan. However, the true stars were William Friedkin's gripping direction and the special makeup effects by Dick Smith and Rick Baker. Blatty won an Oscar for his screenplay. Naturally, *The Exorcist* begot a sequel, 1977's *Exorcist II: The Heretic*, which unexpectedly crashed at the box office—dead on arrival. The film acquired an undeserved reputation as a laughable turkey. Although certainly not a good film, it tried to maneuver the story into a different and interesting direction. The plot picked up four years after the original exorcism, with the "cured" Regan (Blair) still undergoing psychiatric treatment. Regan's newly acquired healing powers brought her to the attention of Father Lamont (Richard Burton), a priest investigating Father Merrin's death. Lamont discovered that the "Locust God" (not the Devil) still wanted control of the girl. In the confusing climax, Regan split into two people, and a horde of locusts attacked her and Lamont. They survived in the original ending, but, in a hastily reshot alternate ending, Father Lamont died. Most available prints include director John Boorman's first, more optimistic, ending. The "series" probably would have died if author Blatty had not written a fairly successful sequel novel. He wrote the screenplay and directed 1990's *Exorcist III*, an interesting but overly complex possession tale. George C. Scott starred as Kinderman, a wily detective investigating a series of murders bearing the trademark of a killer executed fifteen years earlier at the exact same time that Father Karras (Miller again) had died. Despite respectable box office earnings, *Exorcist III* apparently closed the door on additional series entries. See also **The Devil**.

The Exorcist (1973)
Exorcist II: The Heretic (1977)
Exorcist III (aka *Exorcist III: Legion*) (1990)

Eye of the Eagle

The three *Eye of the Eagle* films share few similarities: a Vietnamese (q.v.) setting, a low budget, and a common supporting actor in two of the three entries. The 1987 original involved a female newshound (Cec Verrell) who hooks up with a stalwart soldier (Bret Clark) to investigate stories about a vigilantelike "lost command" made up of POWs and MIAs. It was a far more interesting plot than the revenge tale featured in *Eye of the Eagle II: Inside the Enemy*. William Field starred as the only soldier to survive an attack when his unit's commanding officer deserts his troops. Field later learned that the same officer was a black marketeer, drug pusher and pimp—so naturally Field plotted his vengeance. In both the first and second films, Mike Monty played a supporting role as Colonel Stark. The third film went for a big-name star, but wound up with Steve Kanaly (Ray on TV's long-running *Dallas*).

Eye of the Eagle (1987)
Eye of the Eagle II: Inside the Enemy (aka *Killed in Action*; *K.I.A.*) (1989)
Eye of the Eagle 3 (1992)

Fairs and Carnivals

Fairs on film have evoked a nostalgic atmosphere of Americana, as typified by the three film versions of *State Fair*. Will Rogers starred in the original 1933 film about a family's adventures at the Iowa State Fair, but the 1945 version, boasting Rodgers and Hammerstein's only film score, remains the best remembered. The turn-of-the-century musical *Meet Me in St. Louis* (1944) ended with the opening of the 1903 World's Fair and also provided Judy Garland with one of her biggest hits, "Have Yourself a Merry Little Christmas." Elvis Presley attended the Seattle World's Fair in 1963's *It Happened at the World's Fair*. A belly dancer caused quite a sensation at the 1890's Chicago Fair in *Little Egypt* (1951). Jean Simmons's brother mysteriously disappeared without a trace at the 1889 Paris Exposition in the intriguing mystery *So Long at the Fair* (1950). And *The World of Tomorrow* (1984) provided a retrospective look at the 1939 New York World's Fair. Fairs on a smaller scale provided the settings for comedy in *Ma and Pa Kettle at the Fair* (1952) and romance in the Dan Dailey musical *Meet Me at the Fair* (1953). In contrast to frivolous fairs, carnival films have tended to offer a darker view of life. Spencer Tracy played a ruthless carnival promoter who has visions of Hell in the 1935 curio *Dante's Inferno*. Tyrone Power, in a change-of-pace role, was a heartless carny hustler who hits the big time in the spiritualism racket in *Nightmare Alley* (1947). He gets his comeuppance, however, and eventually winds up as a sideshow freak. Linda Lawson played a sideshow mermaid (q.v.) who actually believed herself to be a descendant of the murderous Sea People in Curtis Harrington's minor cult favorite *Night Tide* (1961). A spooky carnival run by the mysterious Mr. Dark invaded a quiet, Midwestern town in the underrated 1983 adaptation of Ray Bradbury's chilling *Something Wicked This Way Comes*. Stupid teenagers got themselves killed one by one after hiding out in a funhouse filled with wackos in Tobe Hooper's dreary 1981 slasher picture *The Funhouse*. Less human monsters seem to prefer amusement parks over carnivals. *The Beast From 20,000 Fathoms* (1953) was toying with the Coney Island Cyclone roller coaster when Lee Van Cleef shot him up with radioactive isotope. Godzilla (q.v.) battled his archnemesis Ghidrah (q.v.), along with several other creatures, in a children's amusement park in *Godzilla on Monster Island* (1971), one of Toho's sillier pictures. The amusement park in *Gorilla at Large* (1954) featured a murderous ape who turned out to be Anne Bancroft (!) in a gorilla suit. George Segal tracked a madman specializing in sabotaging roller coasters throughout the nation in 1977's *Rollercoaster*. It was filmed in real amusement parks (e.g., King's Dominion in Virginia) and presented in "Sensurround," a sound system that simulated rumbling vibrations during key scenes. Alfred Hitchcock's 1951 classic *Strangers on a Train* featured several amusement park scenes, including the thrilling merry-go-round climax. Likewise, the famous hall of mirrors showdown in Orson Welles's *Lady From Shanghai* took place in an amusement park crazy house. The cinema's most famous amusement park is Coney Island, which provided the setting for *Sinner's Holiday* (1930), *Coney Island* (1943), its remake *Wabash Avenue* (1950), and the aforementioned *Beast From 20,000 Fathoms* (1953). *The Third Man* featured a tense conversation between Joseph Cotten and Orson Welles atop a ferris wheel, while *Luv* opted for an awkward ferris wheel love scene. The roller coaster rumbles in *Rollercoaster* may have been deafening, but the most stomach-churning roller coaster footage still belongs to 1952's *This Is Cinerama* (see **Cinerama**), which projected its speeding dives and turns on a 165-degree curved movie screen. See also **Circuses.**

Sinner's Holiday (1930)
State Fair (1933)
Dante's Inferno (1935)
Strike Me Pink (1936)
Coney Island (1943)
Meet Me in St. Louis (1944)
State Fair (aka *It Happened One Summer*) (1945)
Nightmare Alley (1947)
Lady From Shanghai (1948)
Are You With It? (1948)
The Third Man (1949)
Wabash Avenue (1950)
So Long at the Fair (1950)
Texas Carnival (1951)
Strangers on a Train (1951)
Little Egypt (1951)
Ma and Pa Kettle at the Fair (1952)
Meet Me at the Fair (1953)
The Beast From 20,000 Fathoms (1953)
Gorilla at Large (1954)
The Glass Tomb (1955)
Dance With Me, Henry (1956)

All at Sea (1958)
Night Tide (1961)
State Fair (1962)
It Happened at the World's Fair (1963)
Roustabout (1964)
Luv (1967)
Godzilla on Monster Island (1971)
Rollercoaster (1977)
Kiss Meets the Phantom of the Park (1978 TVM)
Carny (1980)
The Funhouse (1981)
Something Wicked This Way Comes (1983)
The World of Tomorrow (1984)
Slayground (1984)
Breaking All the Rules (1985)
Funland (1986)
Ghoulies II (1987)
Two-Moon Junction (1988)
Kansas (1989)
Howling VI: The Freaks (1991)
Wild Hearts Can't Be Broken (1991)

The Falcon

Rarely has a film series been spawned from so little and turned out so different. The Falcon's only appearance in literature was Michael Arlen's "Gay Falcon," a short story about Gay Lawrence, a hard-boiled detective ("Lady, be calm . . . I don't want to get tough with you"). Yet, by the time the Falcon hit the screen in 1941 in the guise of George Sanders, he had become a charming, debonair rascal, very similar to the Saint (q.v.). The transformation was a practical one, since Sanders had just completed a series of five successful Saint features (ironically, RKO made both the Saint and Falcon series). Sometimes it was difficult to tell if Sanders was supposed to be the Saint or the Falcon—in 1941, he made one of each (*The Saint in Palm Springs* and *The Gay Falcon*). *Saint* creator Leslie Charteris also took note of the Falcon/Saint similarities and threatened RKO with a lawsuit. But the series continued with fairly enjoyable programmers like *The Falcon Takes Over*, which has the distinction of being the first screen version of Raymond Chandler's Philip Marlowe (q.v.) novel *Farewell, My Lovely*. Yet, after his third Falcon film, Sanders decided he'd had enough of the B-movie detective life. RKO was determined to save a profitable series, though, and chose to kill off Sanders's character and replace him with his brother. Such was the plot of 1942's *The Falcon's Brother*, in which Tom Conway — who *really* was Sanders's brother — played the title role. Conway slipped so smoothly into the role that the series never skipped a beat. Despite suave, British good looks and a Colmanesque voice, Conway never made the leap to stardom. Yet he made a stalwart B-movie hero, and his Falcon films were a notch above their competitors. His best effort, *The Falcon and the Coeds*, rates as a snappy mystery by any standard. Set in a girls' boarding school by a seaside cliff, it evoked a haunting atmosphere that was neatly balanced by low-key humor (pleasantly provided by three young girls instead of the typical wisecracking female reporter). Conway left the series in 1948 and was replaced by John Calvert in three additional entries. Meanwhile, Conway struggled with alcoholism in the 1950s and died of a liver ailment in 1964. Charles McGraw starred in the 1954 TV series *The Adventures of the Falcon*, which mysteriously changed the Falcon's name to Mike Waring.

The Gay Falcon (1941) (George Sanders)

A Date With the Falcon (1941) (Sanders)

The Falcon Takes Over (1942) (Sanders)

The Falcon's Brother (1942) (Sanders and Conway)

The Falcon and the Coeds (1943) (Tom Conway)

The Falcon in Danger (1943) (Conway)

The Falcon Strikes Back (1943) (Conway)

The Falcon in Hollywood (1944) (Conway)

The Falcon in Mexico (1944) (Conway)

The Falcon in San Francisco (1945) (Conway)

The Falcon Out West (1946) (Conway)

The Falcon's Adventure (1946) (Conway)

The Falcon's Alibi (1946) (Conway)

The Devil's Cargo (1948) (John Calvert)

Appointment With Murder (1948) (Calvert)

Search for Danger (1949) (Calvert)

Fashion Models

Although models have fared better in the movies than centerfolds (q.v.), they still rank among the favorite targets of psychotic killers, leering males and mutant aliens. Models were stalked by murderers in *Blood and Black Lace*, *Cover Girl Killer*, *She's Dressed to Kill*, *Lies of the Twins*, *Mind Over Murder* and *Eyes of Laura Mars*. In *Mind Over Murder* (1979), model Deborah Raffin had premonitions about her would-be killer, while *Eyes of Laura Mars* (1978) featured Faye Dunaway as a fashion photographer who "sees" through the eyes of a murderer. Plastic surgeon Albert Finney started his own investigation when his model clients began dying rather suddenly in Michael Crichton's *Looker* (1981). The most tasteless model-killer film must surely be Ray Dennis Steckler's *Hollywood Strangler Meets the Skid Row Slasher* (1979), which was retitled—quite aptly—for its video release as *The Model Killer*. When not being stalked, models have often found themselves exploited by men interested only in their outer beauty, as in cheesy drive-in movies such as *The Yum-Yum Girls* (1976) and *Game Show Models* (1977). In 1966's *Blood Beast From Outer Space*, a lecherous alien placed ads in *Bikini Girl* magazine to attract shapely models to populate his dying planet. Fortunately, some models have used their looks to their advantage. Julie Christie won a Best Actress Oscar as a model who becomes a lady of means in 1965's *Darling*. Fred Astaire transformed shy Audrey Hepburn into a glamorous model in 1957's *Funny Face*—and they fell in love along the way. Faye Dunaway, who photographed models in the aforementioned *Eyes of Laura Mars*, played one in the oddly titled *Puzzle of a Downfall Child* (1970). Finally, Jon-Eric Hexum reversed stereotypical roles in the 1983 TV-movie, *The Making of a Male Model*, which costarred Joan Collins as his mentor and lover. Kurt Russell played a male model, too, in 1980's *Amber Waves*, but it was set in a Midwestern farming town as opposed to the fashion world. See also **Centerfolds; Photographers.**

The Powers Girl (aka *Hello Beautiful*) (1942)
The Girl From Manhattan (1948)
A Life of Her Own (1950)
The Model and the Marriage Broker (1951)
Foxiest Girl in Paris (1956)
Funny Face (1957)
Cover Girl Killer (1959)
Blood and Black Lace (1964)
Darling (1965)
Blood Beast From Outer Space (aka *The Night Caller; The Night Caller from Outer Space*) (1966)
The Model Shop (1969)
Puzzle of a Downfall Child (1970)
Love Hate Love (1970 TVM)
Two People (1973)
Cover Girl Models (aka *The Models*) (1975)
The Yum-Yum Girls (1976)
Cover Girls (1977 TVM)
The Sentinel (1977)
Game Show Models (1977)

Eyes of Laura Mars (1978)
She's Dressed to Kill (aka *Someone's Killing the World's Greatest Models*) (1979 TVM)
Mind Over Murder (1979 TVM)
Hollywood Strangler Meets the Skid Row Slasher (aka *The Model Killer*) (1979)
For the Love of It (1980 TVM)
Amber Waves (1980 TVM)
Looker (1981)
Paper Dolls (1982 TVM)
Born Beautiful (1982 TVM)
Exposed (1983)
The Making of a Male Model (1983 TVM)
Jungle Warriors (1984)
Double Deal (1984)
Covergirl (1984)
Swimsuit (1989 TVM)
Lies of the Twins (1991 TVM)
Bikini Island (1991)
The Cover Girl Murders (1993)

FBI

The Federal Bureau of Investigation (FBI) has figured in the plotlines of dozens of movies. However, relatively few films have focused specifically on the organization and its employees. Before the 1970s, filmmakers portrayed the FBI as an all-powerful, incorruptible, crime-fighting machine. Some films, such as *I Was a Communist for the FBI* (1951), *Walk East on Beacon* (1952) and *The FBI Story* (1959), were produced in a documentary style that gave them an air of noble authenticity. This attitude carried over into television where Efrem Zimbalist, Jr. played the never-ruffled Inspector Erskine in the popular 1965-74 TV series *The F.B.I.* However, by the late 1970s, films began to reflect a less whitewashed view of the Bureau. Larry Cohen's *The Private Files of J. Edgar Hoover* (1977) offered a very unflattering portrait of the former FBI director. *Johnnie Mae Gibson: FBI* (1986) was a fact-based account of the tribulations experienced by the Bureau's first black female agent. Sam Shepard played an FBI agent who tries to cover up a murder on an Indian reservation in 1992's *Thunderheart*. Interestingly, *Thunderheart* director Michael Apted made a documentary, *Incident at Oglala*, about the event that inspired his fictional film. Other fact-based FBI films include *Melvin Purvis: G-Man* (1974) and its sequel *The Kansas City Massacre* (1975); *Undercover With the KKK* (1979); and *In the Line of Duty: The FBI Murders* (1988). The TV-movie *Attack on Terror: The FBI vs. the Ku Klux Klan* (1975) and the theatrical film *Mississippi Burning* (1988) were based on the same real-life case. Female agents took charge in *Johnnie Mae Gibson: FBI*, *FBI Girl* (1951), *Feds* (1988) and *The Silence of the Lambs* (1991), for which Jodie Foster won a Best Actress Oscar as special agent Clarice Starling. Keanu Reeves played the screen's only surfing FBI agent in 1991's *Point Break*. See also **Gangsters (Real-Life); In the Line of Duty; Persons in Hiding Series.**

"G" Men (1935)

FBI 99 (1945)

I Was a Communist for the FBI (1951)

FBI Girl (1951)

Walk East on Beacon (aka *The Crime of the Century*) (1952)

Down Three Dark Streets (1954)

Security Risk (1954)

The FBI Story (1959)

That Darn Cat (1965)

Who? (1974)

The FBI Story—Alvin Karpis (aka *The FBI Story—The FBI versus Alvin Karpis, Public Enemy Number One*) (1974 TVM)

Melvin Purvis: G-Man (aka *The Legend of Machine Gun Kelly*) (1974 TVM)

The Kansas City Massacre (1975 TVM)

Attack on Terror: The FBI vs. the Ku Klux Klan (1975 TVM)

The Private Files of J. Edgar Hoover (1977)

Undercover With the KKK (aka *The Freedom Riders; My Undercover Years*) (1979)

Johnnie Mae Gibson: FBI (aka *Johnnie Gibson: F.B.I.*) (1986 TVM)

Manhunter (1986)

The Wild Pair (1987)

J. Edgar Hoover (1987 TVM)

Hoover vs. the Kennedys: The Second Civil War (1987 TVM)

Feds (1988)

Mississippi Burning (1988)

The House on Carroll Street (1988)

In the Line of Duty: The FBI Murders (1988 TVM)

Mr. Hoover and I (1989)

My Blue Heaven (1990)

The Silence of the Lambs (1991)

Point Break (1991)

Thunderheart (1992)

Twins Peaks: Fire Walk With Me (1993)

Feuds, *see* **Backwoods Feuds**

Film Star Biographies

The cinema's relative youth is largely responsible for the scarcity of pre-1975 movie star screen biographies. Many of the performers who dominated the 1930s and 1940s were still making films in the 1950s and 1960s. Thus, early screen biographies focused on silent film greats such as Rudolph Valentino, Will Rogers, Buster Keaton, Jeanne Eagels and Lon Chaney (*Man of a Thousand Faces*). An interesting exception was 1955's *To Hell and Back*, in which then-current star Audie Murphy played himself. The film ignored Murphy's Hollywood career in favor of his World War II adventures as the U.S. Army's most-decorated soldier. Diana Barrymore's screen career consisted of six mediocre films made in the early 1940s. But her life story warranted a 1958 big-screen treatment when her autobiography *Too Much Too Soon* shot up the best-seller charts. The film version dwelled on the sensationalistic aspects of Ms. Barrymore's book (e.g., her struggle with alcoholism) and, in many ways, set the pattern for the exploitative biographical tomes of the 1980s. There was little that was exploitative—or interesting—about the two 1965 films called *Harlow*, in which Jean Harlow was played by Carroll Baker and Carol Lynley. However, the 1975 TV-movie *The Legend of Valentino*, while strictly a fan magazine portrait, revived interest in the lives of movie stars. Over the next two years, three movie star biographies reached the theaters: *Gable and Lombard* (1976), *W.C. Fields and Me* (1976) and *Valentino* (1977). All three hit with a thud, chiefly due to miscasting in the principal roles (e.g., James Brolin as Gable, Rod Steiger as W.C. Fields). Concurrently, made-for-TV films continued to thrive, thanks to well-chosen subjects and some genuine craftsmanship. Horror film director John Carpenter and former child star Kurt Russell combined to produce the highly rated biography *Elvis!* (1979). Loni Anderson and Arnold Schwarzenegger certainly brought the right physical qualities to their roles of Jayne Mansfield and her husband Mickey Hargitay in 1980's *The Jayne Mansfield Story*. Garson Kanin's nostalgic book *Moviola* inspired biographies of Marilyn Monroe (*This Year's Blonde*) and Greta Garbo and John Gilbert (*The Silent Lovers*). The trend burned out quickly, however, and came to an end with *Mommie Dearest*, the 1981 theatrical version of Christina Crawford's shocking best-seller about her mother, Joan, and two 1983 films about Frances Farmer (*Will There Ever Be a Morning?* and *Frances*). Performers who have played themselves in film biographies include Audie Murphy, Sophia Loren (*Sophia Loren: Her Own Story*), Shirley MacLaine (*Out on a Limb*), Ann Jillian (*The Ann Jillian Story*), Patty Duke (*Call Me Anna*) and Suzanne Somers (*Keeping Secrets*). See also **Autobiographical Films; Movies About Movies.**

Valentino (1951)
The Story of Will Rogers (1952)
The Eddie Cantor Story (1954)
To Hell and Back (1955)
The Buster Keaton Story (1957)
Man of a Thousand Faces (1957)
Jeanne Eagels (1957)
Too Much Too Soon (1958)

The George Raft Story (aka *Spin of a Coin*) (1961)
Harlow (1965)
Harlow (1965)
Funny Girl (1968) (Barbra Streisand as Fanny Brice)
Funny Lady (1975) (Streisand as Brice)

The Legend of Valentino (1975 TVM)
Gable and Lombard (1976)
W.C. Fields and Me (1976)
Goodbye, Norma Jean (1976)
Valentino (1977)
Bud and Lou (1978 TVM)
Rainbow (1978 TVM) (Andrea
    McArdle as Judy Garland)
Elvis! (1979 TVM)
Bogie — The Last Hero (aka Bogie)
    (1980 TVM)
Haywire (1980 TVM)
The Jayne Mansfield Story (1980
    TVM)
Marilyn: The Untold Story (1980
    TVM)
Sophia Loren: Her Own Story (1980
    TVM)
The Silent Lovers (1980 TVM)
This Year's Blonde (aka The Secret
    Love of Marilyn Monroe) (1980
    TVM)
The Patricia Neal Story (1981 TVM)
Mommie Dearest (1981)

Mae West (1982 TVM)
Frances (1983)
Grace Kelly (1983 TVM)
Will There Ever Be a Morning? (1983
    TVM)
My Wicked, Wicked Ways . . . The
    Legend of Errol Flynn (1985 TVM)
Out on a Limb (1987 TVM)
The Ann Jillian Story (1988 TVM)
Rock Hudson (1990 TVM)
Call Me Anna (1990 TVM)
Lucy and Desi: Before the Laughter
    (1991 TVM)
Reason for Living: The Jill Ireland
    Story (1991 TVM)
White Hot: The Mysterious Murder of
    Thelma Todd (1991 TVM)
Marilyn and Me (1991 TVM)
Keeping Secrets (1991 TVM)
Sinatra (1992 TVM)
Chaplin (1992)
Dragon: The Bruce Lee Story (1993)
Marilyn and Bobby: Her Final Affair
    (1993 TVM)

Fires and Firefighters

Crackling flames of fate have provided a central premise, an initiating spark, or a climactic turn of events for dozens of films. Chronicles of historical fires have detailed the facts behind the 1666 Great Fire of London (The Glorious Adventure), the Great Chicago Fire (In Old Chicago), and the deadly turn-of-the-century New York City blaze that changed factory fire regulations forever (The Triangle Factory Fire Scandal). Producer Irwin Allen mounted a pair of large-scale fictional films built around out-of-control flames. The Towering Inferno (1974) merged the plots of two similar books (The Tower and The Glass Inferno) into a tense tale of a burning skyscraper occupied by an all-star cast led by Paul Newman and Steve McQueen. Allen transposed the plot to an outdoor setting for his TV-movie Fire! (1977), leaving the character vignette structure intact. Another TV-movie, 1974's Terror on the 40th Floor, duplicated The Towering Inferno's fiery skyscraper plot-line to less effect. Ravaging forest fires cut a path of smoldering destruction in The Blazing Forest and Red Skies of Montana (both 1952), while providing fiery climaxes to Ring of Fire and, most memorably, Bambi. An oil blaze required four men to drive two trucks of nitroglycerin over dangerous mountain roads in the classic 1953 French thriller The Wages of Fear. Less intense dramas focusing on oil firefighters include the John Wayne picture Hellfighters (1969) and the concisely titled Oil (1977). Firefighting of a more general variety has provided the background for slapstick farce (Fireman Save My Child), romantic comedy (Roxanne), family drama (The Quinns and Backdraft), a mediocre TV series pilot (Firehouse), and a fact-based biography (*Firefighter*, the story of the L.A.F.D.'s first female member). Oscar Werner played a futuristic fireman who burned books in François Truffaut's 1966 adaptation of Ray Bradbury's *Fahrenheit 451* (the best temperature for book-incinerating). Other firestarters have set plots ablaze in *Violent Playground* (1958), *She Played With Fire* (1958), *Pyro* (1964) and *Playing With Fire* (1985). Even Paul Newman played a character with a reputation for barn-burning in Martin Ritt's *The Long, Hot Summer* (1958). Drew Barrymore played the title role in Stephen King's *Firestarter* (1984), a fanciful thriller about a little girl who inherited the power to will fires to begin. Most movie dragons (q.v.) have possessed flame-inducing breath, with the most impressive scorcher being the creature Vertithrax from Disney's 1981 fantasy *Dragonslayer*. Large-scale fires have climaxed too many movies to mention, yet it's impossible to leave out the elaborately staged burning of Atlanta in *Gone With the Wind* (1939). Likewise, the burning of Rome, best displayed in 1951's *Quo Vadis*, deserves honorable mention. On the science fiction/fantasy front, 1958's *The Flame Barrier* introduced an alien protoplasm that could melt human flesh. *Quest for Fire* (1981) sent three cave people (q.v.) in search of replacement flames when a wolf attack extinguished their only campfire. Ursula Andress lost her eternal youth (q.v.) when she stepped into the cold Flame of Eternal Life for the second time in *She* (1965). The fate of the world was undecided at the conclusion of 1962's *The Day the Earth Caught Fire*, with our planet hurtling toward the sun for an incinerating destiny.

The Glorious Adventure (1921)
Fireman Save My Child (1932)
She Loved a Fireman (1937)
In Old Chicago (1938)
The Shining Hour (1938)
Gone With the Wind (1939)
The Forest Rangers (1942)
Fires Were Started (aka *I Was a Fireman*) (1942)
The Blazing Forest (1952)
Red Skies of Montana (aka *Smoke Jumpers*) (1952)
The Wages of Fear (1953)
Inferno (1953)
Fireman Save My Child (1954)
The Flame Barrier (1958)
Maracaibo (1958)
Violent Playground (1958)
The Long, Hot Summer (1958)
She Played With Fire (aka *Fortune is a Woman*) (1958)
Ring of Fire (1961)
The Day the Earth Caught Fire (1962)
Pyro (1964)
Harvey Middleman, Fireman (1965)
Fahrenheit 451 (1966)

The Fireman's Ball (1968)
Hellfighters (1969)
The Firechasers (1970)
Firehouse (1972 TVM)
The Towering Inferno (1974)
Terror on the 40th Floor (1974 TVM)
Bug (1975)
Fire! (1977 TVM)
The Quinns (1977 TVM)
Pine Canyon Is Burning (1977 TVM)
The Storyteller (1977 TVM)
Oil (1977)
City on Fire (1979)
The Triangle Factory Fire Scandal (1979 TVM)
Don't Go in the House (1980)
Quest for Fire (1981)
Code Red (1981 TVM)
Uncommon Valor (1983 TVM)
Firestarter (1984)
The Burning Bed (1984 TVM)
The Long, Hot Summer (1985 TVM)
Playing With Fire (1985 TVM)
Firefighter (1986 TVM)
On Fire (1987 TVM)
Nice Girls Don't Explode (1987)

Roxanne (1987)
Spontaneous Combustion (1990)
Backdraft (1991)
Fire! Trapped on the 37th Floor (1991 TVM)

Barton Fink (1991)
Firestorm: 72 Hours in Oakland (1993 TVM)
Torch Song (1993 TVM)

Fish

The movies have been stocked with a small but diverse catch of fish—little ones with very sharp teeth, big ones capable of swallowing boats, and even a pair of prehistoric fish. One of these latter fish proved particularly troublesome for college professor Arthur Franz in *Monster on the Campus* (1958). Any animal coming into contact with the dead fish's fluid reversed its evolution process—Franz's dog became a wolflike creature and the professor turned into a homicidal Neanderthal man. A living, standard-issue prehistoric fish ate vacationers in the *Jaws*-inspired *Up From the Depths* (1979). No one questioned the age of the giant fish that swallowed Baron Munchausen and his mates in *The Adventures of Baron Munchausen* (1989), but judging from the contents of its "stomach," it must have been a pretty old fish. Oddly enough, the cinema's most celebrated horror movie fish is neither oversized nor prehistoric. In fact, the piranha looks rather wimpish, but its sharp teeth and carnivorous appetite have made it a popular villain's pet. Director Joe Dante made him a star with 1978's *Piranha*, a spoof strictly for horror film buffs and drive-in fanatics. The Italian-Brazilian coproduction *Killer Fish* featured a bizarre cast worthy of being fish food: Lee Majors, Karen Black, Margaux Hemingway, James Franciscus and Marisa Berenson. Prior to hitting the big time with 1984's *The Terminator*, director James Cameron fashioned the 1981 in-name-only sequel *Piranha II: The Spawning*. Kevin Kline won a Best Supporting Actor Oscar as Otto, the inept thief and raw-fish eater in the 1988 comedy hit *A Fish Called Wanda*. In Disney's *The Sword in the Stone*, magician Merlin turned himself and young King Arthur into fish. See also **Dolphins; Sharks; Whales.**

Fantasia (1940)
Monster on the Campus (1958)
The Sword in the Stone (1963)
The Day the Fish Came Out (1967)
Barracuda (aka The Lucifer Project) (1978)
Piranha (1978)
Killer Fish (aka Deadly Treasure of the Piranha) (1979)

Screamers (aka Isle of the Fishmen; Something Waits in the Dark) (1979)
Up From the Depths (1979)
Piranha II: The Spawning (1981)
A Fish Called Wanda (1988)
The Adventures of Baron Munchausen (1989)
The Little Mermaid (1989)

The Five Little Peppers

The Peppers, another wholesome family in the Hardy Family (q.v.) mold, were the subject of a brief Columbia film series. *Five Little Peppers and How They Grew* (1939), which opened to promising reviews, set the flimsy premise: Mrs. Pepper worked at a factory while her oldest daughter Polly attended the other four little Peppers. Subsequent movies attracted little attention, and the series came to an abrupt end after four entries. Dorothy Peterson starred as Mrs. Pepper. Her five offspring were played by Edith Fellows (Polly), Charles Peck (Ben), Tommy Bond

(Joey), Bobbie Larson (Dave) and Dorothy Ann Seese (Phronsie). Ronald Sinclair played the Pepper kids' rich friend Jasper, with veteran character actor Clarence Kolb as his grandfather.

Five Little Peppers and How They
Grew (1939)
Out West With the Peppers (1940)

Five Little Peppers at Home (1940)
Five Little Peppers in Trouble (1940)

Flagg and Quirt

Brawling, patriotic Marines Captain Flagg and Sergeant Quirt first clashed with one another in 1926's *What Price Glory?*, a silent screen adaptation of the Maxwell Anderson-Laurence Stallings play. Romantic lead Edmund Lowe played against type as the roughneck Quirt, with Victor McLaglen more than his match as Flagg. Set in France during World War I, this deft mixture of raucous comedy and realistic adventure found the two Marines at odds over the charms of an irresistible girl named Charmaine. The chemistry between the stars and the nonstop action (expertly directed by Raoul Walsh) made the film immensely popular. McLaglen and Lowe returned as Flagg and Quirt in three lighthearted follow-ups, all directed by Walsh. Whether they were running liquor in South America (*Hot Pepper*) or soldiering in Sweden (*Women of All Nations*), Flagg and Quirt were almost always quarreling over a woman. John Ford remade *What Price Glory?* in 1952 with James Cagney as Flagg and Dan Dailey as Quirt. The 1942 McLaglen-Lowe vehicle *Call Out the Marines* is sometimes erroneously listed as a Flagg and Quirt film. Actually, the two stars played characters named McGinnis and Curtis, and the setting was World War II.

What Price Glory? (1926)
The Cockeyed World (1929)
Women of All Nations (1931)

Hot Pepper (1933)
What Price Glory? (1952)

Floods

Floods have appeared less frequently than other motion picture disasters (see **Earthquakes; Volcanoes**), despite the increased likelihood of their natural occurrence. The biggest flood, in terms of scope, was the biblical one that set *Noah's Ark* afloat in 1929. The potential love affair between Indian aristocrat Tyrone Power and English socialite Myrna Loy was disrupted by floods, earthquakes and plague in 1939's *The Rains Came*. In *A Cry in the Wilderness* (1974), George Kennedy had himself locked inside a barn after being bitten by a rabid skunk — and then learned a flood was on the way. Not all floods are caused by rain. The gravitational pull of another planet flooded metropolitan cities all over the world — including Manhattan — in *When Worlds Collide* (1951). Enterprising (and cheap) New World Pictures reedited a 1973 Japanese film called *The Submersion of Japan* into the 1975 disaster-drama *Tidal Wave*.

Metropolis (1925)
The Johnstown Flood (1926)
Noah's Ark (1929)
The Rains Came (1939)
When Worlds Collide (1951)
Heidi and Peter (1955)

Floods of Fear (1958)
Wild River (1960)
In Search of the Castaways (1962)
Mister Moses (1965)
The Little Ark (1972)
A Cry in the Wilderness (1974 TVM)

Irwin Allen's Flood! (aka *Flood!*) (1976   *The River* (1984)
TVM)

The Fly

Before *Shogun*, there was *The Fly*. Long before his novels made him a best-selling author, James Clavell penned this 1958 cult favorite about a scientist who transforms himself into a man/fly mutation. Al (David) Hedison played the inventor of an experimental device that broke matter into molecules, transported them from one terminal to another, and then reconstructed the original object. Hedison's obsession with his invention caused him to transport himself—unaware that a house fly had buzzed into the terminal with him. The device merged the human and fly molecules, the result being a man with a fly's head and "arm" (and a fly with the corresponding human parts). The rest of the film focused on the trauma experienced by Hedison's wife (Patricia Neal). Although consistently interesting, *The Fly* does not work as a horror film because the "monster" elicits more sympathy than terror—and there's no villain. *The Return of the Fly* (1959) introduced some bad guys, but the basic plot remained the same except for an upbeat ending. The British-made film *Curse of the Fly* (1965) dealt with a matter transmission device, but otherwise bore little resemblance to the first two films. In 1986, Canadian director David Cronenberg directed a stylish rethinking of *The Fly*, with Jeff Goldblum as a scientist who mutates himself and dreams of creating a new species. It was followed by *The Fly II*, a 1989 sequel that found son Eric Stolz experiencing mutation problems before discovering how to reverse the process. See also **Teleportation.**

The Fly (1958)   *The Fly* (1986)
The Return of the Fly (1959)   *The Fly II* (1989)
The Curse of the Fly (1965)

Flying People

Flying humans have become all but extinct in the cinema. Superman and, to a lesser extent, Supergirl were common airborne sights in the late 1970s and early 1980s—but both of them were technically aliens since they hailed from the planet Krypton. Thus, the only major films in the past two decades to feature flying Earthlings have been *Condorman* (1981), *The Boy Who Could Fly* (1986) and *The Rocketeer* (1991). Michael Crawford, prior to becoming a Broadway sensation as *The Phantom of the Opera*, played a cartoonist-turned-superhero who attempted a winged flight over Paris in *Condorman*, a dismal Disney secret agent spoof produced during the studio's low point. Nick Castle's *The Boy Who Could Fly* was a tender fantasy about an apparently autistic teen who yearned to fly—and eventually soared into the clouds. Pre-1971 flights of fantasy have featured a unique brand of eccentricity. Bud Cort played a lad obsessed with donning his homemade wings and taking a flight around the Astrodome in Robert Altman's erratic satire *Brewster McCloud* (1970). The French fantasy *Fifi la Plume* (1964) concerned a thief who joined a circus as a "bird-man" and actually learned to fly. Comedian Soupy Sales starred as a "minuscule molecular particle surveillance monitor" (i.e., a janitor) who took to the air after becoming "ionized" in 1966's *Birds Do It*. A decade earlier, the Disney folks brought literature's most famous flying boy to the screen in the animated *Peter Pan* (1953). Schizophrenic Vietnam vet Matthew Modine longed to be a bird and take to the air in 1984's *Birdy*. Floating, not flying, people have also appeared in a handful of films like *Mary Poppins* (1964) and *The Fury* (1978). See also **Superman**.

Peter Pan (1953)	*Condorman* (1981)
Fifi la Plume (1964)	*Supergirl* (1984)
Birds Do It (1966)	*The Boy Who Could Fly* (1986)
Brewster McCloud (1970)	*The Rocketeer* (1991)
Superman (1978)	*Hook* (1991)

Football

Baseball may be the national pastime, but football outranks it easily as the movies' favorite team sport. Yet, unlike baseball, football has enshrined few of its legends. Its movie hall of fame has covered the careers of players Jim Thorpe (*Jim Thorpe — All American*), Brian Piccolo (*Brian's Song*), Elroy "Crazylegs" Hirsch (*Crazylegs*) and Rocky Bleier (*Fighting Back*). To their credit, football-oriented filmmakers have shown equal respect for the men on the sidelines, with profiles of real-life collegiate coaching greats Knute Rockne (*Knute Rockne, All American*), Bear Bryant (*The Bear*) and Eddie Robinson (*Grambling's White Tiger*). On the fictional front, the movies have left no football field untouched. Tom Cruise, Anthony Michael Hall and Gary Busey played high school gridiron stars in, respectively, *All the Right Moves*, *Johnny Be Good* and *Blood Sport*. The replaying of a twenty-year-old high school game was the subject of the Robin Williams comedy *The Best of Times* (1986). However, the majority of football pictures have dealt with the college game, often on a comic or musical level. Harold Lloyd starred as a clutzy student transformed into an unlikely football hero in his 1925 classic *The Freshman*. The Marx Brothers' hilarious *Horse Feathers* (1932) pitted their Huxley College team against archrival Darwin U. in one of the screen's more bizarre climactic games. Jack Oakie was the team's star and Bing Crosby a crooning college professor in the 1933 musical *College Humor*. Another gridiron musical, 1936's *Pigskin Parade*, costarred Judy Garland (in her film debut) and Jack Haley three years before *The Wizard of Oz*. Fictional pro players have experienced more stressful careers. In 1974's *The Longest Yard*, former quarterback Burt Reynolds found himself in prison leading a bunch of fellow convicts against the warden's team. Charlton Heston was another quarterback, fighting to stay in the game despite his age, in 1969's *Number One*. A similar problem plagued injury-prone Nick Nolte in *North Dallas Forty* (1979), a perceptive seriocomedy that also addressed the business end of the sport. The most enjoyable film about the realities of professional football was probably *Paper Lion* (1968), based on writer George Plimpton's best-seller about his undercover stint as a rookie for the Detroit Lions. Unpleasant pro games were featured in *Black Sunday* (terrorists planted a bomb in the blimp), *Two Minute Warning* (a sniper in the stadium) and *Superdome* (another killer on the loose). Two TV-movies about the Dallas Cowboy Cheerleaders treated women with minimal respect. However, tough-minded ladies took to the football field in *The Oklahoma City Dolls* (1981), *Quarterback Princess* (1983) and *Backfield in Motion* (1991). The cinema's most unlikely gridiron stars include the quarterbacking chimp in *Bonzo Goes to College* (1952) and the field-goal kicking mule *Gus* (1976). See also **Cheerleaders.**

The Freshman (1925)
Good News (1930)
Horse Feathers (1932)
Saturday's Millions (1933)
College Coach (1933)
College Humor (1933)
Fighting Youth (1935)
Pigskin Parade (1936)
Hold 'Em Navy (1937)
$1,000 a Touchdown (1939)
Knute Rockne, All American (1940)
Rise and Shine (1941)
Pardon My Stripe (1942)
Good News (1947)
The Spirit of West Point (1947)
Easy Living (1949)
Father Was a Fullback (1949)
Saturday's Hero (aka *Idols in the Dust*) (1951)
The Guy Who Came Back (1951)
Jim Thorpe—All American (1951)
The Rose Bowl Story (1952)
Bonzo Goes to College (1952)
The All-American (1953)
Crazylegs (aka *Crazylegs, All American*) (1953)
Son of Flubber (1963)
The Fortune Cookie (1966)
Paper Lion (1968)
Number One (1969)
M*A*S*H (1970)
Brian's Song (1970 TVM)
Footsteps (aka *Footsteps: Nice Guys Finish Last*) (1972 TVM)

A Fan's Note (1972)
Blood Sport (1973 TVM)
The Longest Yard (1974)
Gus (1976)
Two Minute Warning (1976)
Something for Joey (1977 TVM)
Black Sunday (1977)
Semi-Tough (1977)
Heaven Can Wait (1978)
Superdome (1978 TVM)
North Dallas Forty (1979)
H.O.T.S. (1979)
Coach of the Year (1980 TVM)
Fighting Back (1980 TVM)
Grambling's White Tiger (1981 TVM)
The Oklahoma City Dolls (1982 TVM)
All the Right Moves (1983)
Quarterback Princess (1983 TVM)
Off Sides (1984 TVM)
The Bear (1984)
The Best of Times (1986)
Wildcats (1986)
Everybody's All-American (1988)
Johnny Be Good (1988)
Glory Days (1988 TVM)
Triumph of the Heart: The Ricky Bell Story (1991 TVM)
Necessary Roughness (1991)
Backfield in Motion (1991 TVM)
School Ties (1992)
The Program (1993)
Rudy (1993)

Ford's Cavalry Trilogy

Director John Ford's sentimental homage to the U.S. Cavalry qualifies as a series only in the broadest sense. All three films share common themes, take place out West after the Civil War, and star John Wayne (and other Ford favorites such as Ward Bond and Victor McLaglen). However, Henry Fonda got the juicy role in *Fort Apache* (1948), which resembles Custer's final days, although it was based on James Warner Bellah's story "Massacre." Fonda played Lieutenant Colonel Owen Thursday, a Civil War general who has been demoted and shipped to a desert command post. He is a harsh disciplinarian who fails to understand his daughter, his soldiers and the Indians. When Thursday's blunders result in a

Cavalry massacre—and his own death—patriotic Captain Kirby York (Wayne) covers up for his superior and paints a gallant portrait of the dead officer. It's an odd ending to an otherwise straightforward, well-done western. Shirley Temple had one of her better adult roles as Fonda's daughter Philadelphia, and her then-husband John Agar played her love interest. Wayne dominated the second film, 1949's *She Wore a Yellow Ribbon*, which was based on two other Bellah stories: "War Party" and "Big Hunt." He played Captain Nathan Brittles, a retiring Cavalryman preparing to pass his command to young Lieutenant Flint Cahill (John Agar again). But before Brittles can step down from his responsibilities, he must intercede to thwart a war with the Indians. Again, the plot took a backseat to Ford's compassion for his characters and his breathtaking portrait of the Western frontier (as filmed by Oscar-winner Winston Hoch in Monument Valley). The trilogy's final chapter, 1950's *Rio Grande*, cast Wayne as a cavalry officer facing conflicts with a new recruit—the son he never knew. Maureen O'Hara and Victor McLaglen (who appeared in all three films) turned in fine supporting performances in the most underrated and least shown of the three films. Its songs were performed by the Sons of the Pioneers, which included future actor Ken Curtis, best known as Festus on the long-running TV series *Gunsmoke* (q.v.).

Fort Apache (1948)   *Rio Grande* (1950)
She Wore a Yellow Ribbon (1949)

Foreign Legion

P.C. Wren's 1925 adventure novel *Beau Geste* established a much-copied formula for desert tales of derring-do among soldiers in the French Foreign Legion. It was first filmed as a silent in 1926 with an all-star cast including Ronald Colman, Victor McLaglen and William Powell. This exciting story of three honor-bound brothers and a ruthless sergeant struck box office gold for Paramount, who released a hurried sequel two years later. *Beau Sabreur* was based on a Wren novel that took place within the framework of *Beau Geste*. Yet, despite the presence of William Powell and newcomer Gary Cooper, it failed to repeat its predecessor's success. Still, it fared better than another Wren-based sequel, 1931's *Beau Ideal*. Colman and McLaglen returned as Foreign Legion rivals in 1936's *Under Two Flags*, with aristocratic Rosalind Russell and commoner Claudette Colbert as the women vying for Colman's love. Its pre-*Geste* source novel had been filmed earlier in 1916 and 1922. Thirteen years after the release of Colman's 1926 *Beau Geste*, Paramount mounted a lavish scene-for-scene remake starring *Beau Sabreur* alumnus Gary Cooper, Ray Milland and Robert Preston as the brothers. Brian Donlevy outshone the leads, however, earning an Oscar nomination for his sadistic sergeant. Telly Savalas played that role in Universal's best-forgotten 1966 *Beau Geste*, which trimmed the number of brothers to two (Guy Stockwell and Doug McClure) and tacked on a happy ending. For a change of pace, Dick Powell played a contemporary American agent who joins the Foreign Legion to track down Nazis in the World War II adventure *Rogue's Regiment* (1948). Foreign Legion films in general—and *Beau Geste* in particular—have been spoofed by Laurel and Hardy (*The Flying Deuces*), Abbott and Costello (*A&C in the Foreign Legion*) and the Carry On Gang (*Follow That Camel*). Marty Feldman's *The Last Remake of Beau Geste* (1977) was an uneven affair, basically a one-joke movie about unlikely twin brothers (!) Feldman and Michael York. That same year saw the release of *March or Die*, an awkward combination of traditional Foreign Legion adventure and 1970s-style violence. It died a swift box office death. Jean-Claude Van Damme played a contemporary Legionnaire in 1990's *Lionheart*.

Beau Geste (1926)	*Ten Tall Men* (1951)
Beau Sabreur (1928)	*Flesh and the Woman* (1953)
Morocco (1930)	*Desert Legion* (1953)
Beau Ideal (1931)	*Legion of the Doomed* (1958)
Le Grand Jeu (1934)	*Beau Geste* (1966)
Under Two Flags (1936)	*Follow That Camel* (aka *Carry On*
Beau Geste (1939)	*Follow That Camel*) (1967)
The Flying Deuces (aka *Flying Aces*)	*Man of Legend* (1971)
(1939)	*The Last Remake of Beau Geste* (1977)
Rogue's Regiment (1948)	*March or Die* (1977)
Outpost in Malaya (1949)	*Renegades* (1982 TVM)
Abbott and Costello in the Foreign	*Lionheart* (aka *A.W.O.L.*; *Wrong Bet*)
Legion (1950)	(1990)

Four Daughters Series

Fanny Hurst's story "Sister Act" reached the screen in 1938 as *Four Daughters*, a vehicle designed to spotlight the Lane Sisters. The movie was a popular and artistic smash, but the sensation turned out to be a young actor named John Garfield who played Priscilla Lane's erratic suitor and eventual husband. Unfortunately, Garfield's character committed suicide, so that he was limited to a flashback role in the 1939 follow-up *Four Wives*. Undaunted, Warner Bros. paired Garfield and Lane (along with Claude Rains, who had played her father) in an unrelated but very similar picture called *Daughters Courageous* (1941). The studio then picked up with the original series, now Garfield-less and losing momentum, with 1941's *Four Mothers*. Priscilla, Rosemary and Lola Lane, along with Gale Page, played the four Lemp sisters in all three films. Claude Rains costarred with them, while Eddie Albert appeared in the last two entries.

Four Daughters (1938)	*Four Mothers* (1941)
Four Wives (1939)	

Francis, The Talking Mule

Chill Wills was the voice behind the mule and Donald O'Connor played the straight man in all but one entry in this popular Universal comedy series. The relationship between the bumbling, sincere human and the crafty (occasionally cruel) mule was established when they met in the Army in 1950's *Francis*. The running gag of the series — Francis would talk only to O'Connor, so that Donald always wound up looking crazy — naturally wore thin as the series progressed. But O'Connor, an underrated comedian, and Wills maintained a delightful rapport. The scriptwriters gave them a fair share of decent material as well, with the funniest bit being when Francis psychoanalyzed an unmotivated race horse in *Francis Goes to the Races* (1951). The series began to show signs of wear when Wills showed up in a *human* supporting role in *Francis Joins the WACs* (1954) and O'Connor played a double role in *Francis Joins the Navy* (1955). The latter film turned out to be the final one for O'Connor and Wills. But Universal was not ready to end its last profitable series. Paul Frees spoke for Francis and Mickey Rooney played the mule's sidekick in 1956's best-forgotten *Francis in the Haunted House*. It ended the series on a down note. However, just five years later, veteran *Francis* director Arthur Lubin proved that talking animals could still be funny when he introduced television audiences to that famous talking horse—Mr. Ed. See also **Talking Animals**.

Francis (1950)	*Francis Joins the WACs* (1954)
Francis Goes to the Races (1951)	*Francis in the Navy* (1955)
Francis Goes to West Point (1952)	*Francis in the Haunted House* (1956)
Francis Covers the Big Town (1953)	

Frankenstein/The Monster

The cinema's favorite mad scientist, Mary Shelley's Victor Frankenstein, has spent most of his film career in the shadow of his creation: the Frankenstein Monster. Indeed, when most people talk about Frankenstein, they are referring to the Monster, not the man. Yet both the doctor and his creation rank as two of the movies' most enduring characters. Thomas Edison's film company produced the first version of Shelley's classic, 1910's *Frankenstein*, featuring contract player Charles Ogle as a shaggy, clawed monster. Two other silent versions followed: *Life Without a Soul* (1915) and an obscure Italian picture, *The Monster of Franken-stein* (1920). A decade later, Universal Studios made Frankenstein a household name with the release of James Whale's 1931 horror classic. In Whale's version, Colin Clive played Henry Frankenstein as an intelligent but definitely irrational man of science (the name change—from Victor to Henry—has never been satisfactorily explained). Boris Karloff's man-made creature elicited both terror and sympathy, giving him a depth of character rare for a movie monster. Director Whale exploited these assets to even greater effect with his 1935 sequel *The Bride of Frankenstein*, considered by many critics as the finest of all *Frankensteins*. It also holds the distinction of being the only film in the Universal series in which the Monster spoke with his own voice. After *Bride*, Whale and Clive bowed out of the series. Nevertheless, 1939's *Son of Frankenstein* remained a superior outing in which Henry's son Wolf (Basil Rathbone) revives the Monster (Karloff), much to the delight of the mad shepherd Ygor (Bela Lugosi). These first three entries were A-pictures in every respect, but the series descended to the B-level with 1942's *The Ghost of Frankenstein*. Bela Lugosi was still around as the disturbing Ygor, but Lon Chaney, Jr. made a mediocre monster, and even reliable Cedric Hardwicke seemed uninspired as Henry's *other* son Ludwig. Universal subsequently paired the Monster with other creatures in its gallery, resulting in 1943's *Frankenstein Meets the Wolf Man* and the monster rallies *House of Frankenstein* (1944) and *House of Dracula* (1945). The Universal series ended with its self-spoof *Abbott and Costello Meet Frankenstein* (1948). However, Britain's Hammer Films revived the Frankenstein name in 1957 with its colorful, gory (for the time) adaptation *Curse of Frankenstein*. The Hammer series wisely shifted its focus from the Monster to the doctor. In a stroke of casting genius, Peter Cushing was chosen to play Victor Frankenstein; his crisp, energetic performance brought him well-deserved fame. As the series continued, Cushing developed his character, gradually becoming more ruthless but always managing to evoke a measure of pity. The lone Hammer picture to star another actor was the ill-fated 1970 satire *Horror of Frankenstein*, which presented Ralph Bates as a younger, more sexually active Victor. Although Hammer retired its series in 1974, the Frankenstein myth continued to thrive on film. Paul Morrissey directed a 1973 3-D version under the auspices of Andy Warhol called *Flesh for Frankenstein* (aka *Andy Warhol's Frankenstein*). The success of 1972's *Blacula* guaranteed the making of a blaxploitation Frankenstein. However, when *Blackenstein* appeared the following year, it lacked the style and polish of its vampire predecessor and vanished quietly. On television, the 1974 TV-movie *Frankenstein: The True Story* was a surprisingly literate adaptation with a very human-looking monster (Michael Sarrazin). It nevertheless strayed from the true story. It did feature a rare female monster (Jane Seymour), as did *Bride of Frankenstein* (Elsa Lanchester), *Frankenstein Created Woman* (Susan Denberg) and *The Bride* (Jennifer Beals). There was no real monster in 1973's *Spirit of the Beehive*, a Spanish film about a child deeply disturbed from watching Whale's original. David Carradine played a futuristic race car driver named Frankenstein in Paul Bartel's offbeat satire *Death Race 2000* (1975). *Gothic* (1986) and *Haunted Summer* (1988) dealt with the incidents surrounding Mary Shelley's writing of her novel. In the following list, the doctor, or his replacement mad scientist, is listed prior to the monster in parentheses after the film's title:

Universal Series
Frankenstein (1931) (Colin Clive/Boris Karloff)
Bride of Frankenstein (1935) (Clive/Karloff and Elsa Lanchester)
Son of Frankenstein (1939) (Basil Rathbone/Karloff)
The Ghost of Frankenstein (1942) (Cedric Hardwicke/Lon Chaney, Jr.)
Frankenstein Meets the Wolf Man (1943) (Patric Knowles/Bela Lugosi)
House of Frankenstein (aka *Chamber of Horrors*) (1944) (Karloff/Glenn Strange)
House of Dracula (1945) (Onslow Stevens/Strange)
Abbott and Costello Meet Frankenstein (1948) (Lugosi as Dracula/Strange)

Hammer Series
Curse of Frankenstein (1957) (Peter Cushing/Christopher Lee)
Revenge of Frankenstein (1958) (Cushing/Michael Gwynn)
Evil of Frankenstein (1964) (Cushing/Kiwi Kingston)
Frankenstein Created Woman (1967) (Cushing/Susan Denberg)
Frankenstein Must Be Destroyed (1969) (Cushing/Freddie Jones)
Horror of Frankenstein (1970) (Ralph Bates/Dave Prowse)
Frankenstein and the Monster From Hell (1973) (Cushing/Prowse)

Other Frankenstein films
Frankenstein (1910) (Augustus Phillips/Charles Ogle)
Life Without a Soul (1915) (William Cohill/Percy Standing)
The Monster of Frankenstein (1920) (Luciano Albertini/Umberto Guarracino)
I Was a Teenage Frankenstein (1957) (Whit Bissell/Gary Conway)
Frankenstein's Daughter (1958) (Donald Murphy/Uncredited)
Frankenstein 1970 (1958) (Boris Karloff/Mike Lane)
How to Make a Monster (1960) (Gary Conway as actor in Monster make-up)

Frankenstein Meets the Space Monster (1964) (James Karen/Robert Reilly)
Jesse James Meets Frankenstein's Daughter (1966) (Narda Onyx/Cal Bolder)
Frankenstein Conquers the World (1966)
Munster, Go Home! (1966) (Fred Gwynne as Monster-look-alike Herman
    Munster)
Mad Monster Party? (1967) (puppets)
Dr. Frankenstein on Campus (aka *Flick*) (1970) (Robin Ward as doctor who *was*
    the Monster)
The Man Who Came From Ummo (aka *El Hombre Que Vino de Ummo*;
    Assignment Terror; *Dracula vs. Frankenstein*) (1970) (Paul Naschy as
    Monster)
Lady Frankenstein (aka *La Figlia di Frankenstein*) (1971) (Joseph Cotten as
    Dr. Frankenstein)
Dracula vs. Frankenstein (aka *Blood of Frankenstein*; *They're Coming to Get
    You*) (1971) (J. Carrol Naish/John Bloom)
Frankenstein (1973 TVM) (Robert Foxworth/Bo Svenson)
Blackenstein (aka *Black Frankenstein*) (1973) (John Hart/Joe DiSue)
Flesh for Frankenstein (aka *Andy Warhol's Frankenstein*) (1973) (Udo Kier/
    Srojan Zelenovic)
Spirit of the Beehive (1973)
Frankenstein: The True Story (1974 TVM) (Leonard Whiting/Michael Sarrazin)
Young Frankenstein (1974) (Gene Wilder/Peter Boyle)
Death Race 2000 (1975)
Frankenstein: Italian Style (1977) (Gianrico Tedeschi/Aldo Maccione)
Victor Frankenstein (aka *Terror of Frankenstein*) (1977) (Leon Vitali/Pers
    Oscarsson)
Dr. Franken (1980 TVM) (Robert Vaughn/Robert Perault)
The Bride (1985) (Sting/Clancy Brown and Jennifer Beals)
Gothic (1986)
The Vindicator (aka *Frankenstein '88*) (1986) (Richard Cox/David McIlwraith)
The Monster Squad (1987) (Tom Noonan as the Monster)
Haunted Summer (1988)
Frankenhooker (1990) (James Lorinz as Jeffrey Franken/Patty Mullen as
    Elizabeth, the Monster)
Frankenstein Unbound (aka *Roger Corman's Frankenstein Unbound*) (1990)
    (Raul Julia/Nick Brimble)
Frankenstein: The College Years (1991 TVM) (Vincent Hammond as the
    Monster)
Waxworks II: Lost in Time (1991) (Martin Kemp as Baron Frankenstein)
Frankenstein (1993 TVM) (Patrick Bergin/Randy Quaid)

Friday the 13th

This modest 1980 *Halloween* (q.v.) clone has a lot to answer for — chiefly for inspiring the most successful film series of the 1980s. Who would have thought that watching teens get bumped off during summer camp would be so popular? Actually, the series' survival can be attributed to two clever ideas. First, it capitalized on 1982's 3-D craze with the gut-wrenching *Friday the 13th Part 3*. Then, after finally disposing of the indestructible killer Jason in *Friday the 13th — The Final Chapter*, it had *another* character assume Jason's identity. The series appeared to have run its course after meager returns were posted by 1989's eighth installment. However, New Line Cinema — the home of the Freddy Kreuger franchise — revived the series with 1993's *Jason Goes to Hell: The Final Friday*. A syndicated TV series *Friday the 13th* appeared in 1987. However, it owed less to Jason and more to earlier anthology shows like *Night Gallery*. See also **Slasher Movies; Summer Camps.**

Friday the 13th (1980)
Friday the 13th Part 2 (1981)
Friday the 13th Part 3 (1982)
Friday the 13th — The Final Chapter (1984)
Friday the 13th Part V: A New Beginning (1985)
Friday the 13th Part VI: Jason Lives (1986)
Friday the 13th Part VII: The New Blood (1988)
Friday the 13th Part VIII: Jason Takes Manhattan (1989)
Jason Goes to Hell: The Final Friday (1993)

Frogs

As Kermit the Frog once sang: "It ain't easy being green." That goes double for the movie business where frogs and toads have been all but forgotten (as opposed to fairy tales where frogs get some respect). The only true frog star is Kermit, who has shared top billing with Ms. Piggy in all the *Muppet* movies (q.v.). Ben Kingsley voiced the title role in 1992's *Freddie as F.R.O.7*, an animated yarn about an amphibious secret agent. Walt Disney brought Kenneth Grahame's classic *The Wind in the Willows* to the screen in animated form in the two-part feature *Ichabod and Mr. Toad* (1949). The wildly eccentric Mr. Toad came sharply to life as a result of superb animation and Eric Blore's marvelous comedic voice. (Oddly, the first half of *Ichabod and Mr. Toad* was an unrelated animated adaptation of "The Legend of Sleepy Hollow"). Although frogs and toads such as Kermit, Freddie and Mr. Toad can be charming, these green amphibians also have a dark side. The environmentally minded horror film *Frogs* (1972) carried this ominous ad line: "Millions of slimy bodies everywhere — millions of gaping mouths!" Actually, the frogs were not very frightening, though Ray Milland seemed to take offense to them. Additionally, the frogs made a strong political statement about how humans wreak havoc on the environment. The "frog monster" in 1953's *The Maze* generated more sympathy than horror. He was actually a mutant human resembling a giant frog, who hid all day in a gloomy castle and hopped around at night in a giant maze. This bizarre film featured 3-D photography (q.v.) and delightfully weird sets designed by director William Cameron Menzies. The mutants in *Hell Comes to Frogtown* were unpleasant-looking, froglike humanoids.

Ichabod and Mr. Toad (1949)
The Maze (1953)
Frogs (1972)
The Muppet Movie (1979)
Hell Comes to Frogtown (1987)
Freddie as F.R.O.7 (1992)

Fu Manchu

Warner Oland, best known as Charlie Chan, portrayed Sax Rohmer's evil Oriental mastermind in three early talkies: *The Mysterious Fu Manchu, The Return of Fu*

Manchu and *Daughter of the Dragon* (as well as a cameo in the all-star revue *Paramount on Parade*). Boris Karloff took over in 1932's *Mask of Fu Manchu*, with Myrna Loy as his equally dastardly daughter. However, a series did not result again until Christopher Lee essayed the role in 1965's entertaining *Face of Fu Manchu*, costarring Nigel Green as intrepid archnemesis Nayland Smith. Producer Harry Alan Towers followed it with four additional entries with Lee. Unfortunately, these modest efforts were hampered by poor production values and increasingly dreadful scripts. Towers also made a movie version of Sax Rohmer's *The Million Eyes of Su-Muru* (1967) and a sequel, *Rio 70*. Both films starred *Goldfinger* beauty Shirley Eaton as a female Fu called Su-Muru. In 1978, Peter Sellers played both Fu and Nayland Smith in the dismal spoof *The Fiendish Plot of Dr. Fu Manchu*. Sadly, it turned out to be Sellers's swan song. A syndicated TV series, *The Adventures of Fu Manchu* starring Glen Gordon, ran briefly in the mid-1950s.

The Mysterious Fu Manchu (1929) (Warren Oland)

The Return of Fu Manchu (1930) (Oland)

Paramount on Parade (1930) (Oland appears in a skit)

Daughter of the Dragon (1931) (Oland)

Mask of Fu Manchu (1932) (Boris Karloff)

Face of Fu Manchu (1965) (Christopher Lee)

Bride of Fu Manchu (1966) (Lee)

Blood of Fu Manchu (aka Kiss and Kill) (1968) (Lee)

Castle of Fu Manchu (aka Assignment: Istanbul) (1968) (Lee)

Vengeance of Fu Manchu (1968) (Lee)

The Fiendish Plot of Dr. Fu Manchu (1978) (Peter Sellers)

The Gambler Series

Country singer Kenny Rogers wisely banked on his easygoing charm to carry 1980's *The Gambler*, a TV-movie Western inspired by his hit song. The minimal plot starred Rogers as crafty gambler Brady Hawkes who teams up with a cowpoke (Bruce Boxleitner) on the road to lighthearted adventures. Linda Evans joined them for a 1983 sequel, and Linda Gray signed on for a third film. The fourth entry featured TV-Western heroes Wyatt Earp (Hugh O'Brien), Bat Masterson (Gene Barry) and the Rifleman (Chuck Connors). All four Gambler films scored well in the ratings, as did another song-inspired Rogers hit *Coward of the County* (1981 TVM). However, moviegoers seemed less impressed with Rogers, brushing off his 1982 theatrical feature *Six Pack* and sending it to the flop pile.

The Gambler (aka Kenny Rogers as The Gambler) (1980 TVM)

The Gambler — The Adventure Continues (aka Kenny Rogers as The Gambler — The Adventure Continues) (1983 TVM)

The Gambler III, the Legend Continues (1987 TVM)

The Gambler IV: Luck of the Draw (1991 TVM)

Gambling

With the roll of a die or the flip of a card, gambling has made fortunes, wrecked relationships, shattered reputations, and led to cold-blooded murder. The most powerful films on the subject are those dealing with compulsive gamblers. Earnest writer

Gregory Peck rescued Ava Gardner from the perils of gambling—only to catch the fever himself in 1949's *The Great Sinner*. That same year's *The Lady Gambles* was described by one critic as "a kind of *Lost Weekend* of the gaming tables." Barbara Stanwyck played the woman who sacrificed everything, including husband Robert Preston, after falling under the spell of a roulette table. She nevertheless managed to pull off a happy ending. The gambling addicts of the 1970s were less fortunate. Robert Altman's *California Split* was a depressing comedy about a pair of hopeless losers played convincingly by George Segal and Elliott Gould (the film's title is slang for cutthroat high-low poker). *The Gambler* (1975) presented the same premise, less one character and minus the humor that made *California Split* tolerable. Ladies fared even worse in made-for-TV movies, with bored housewife Shirley Jones catching gambling fever in *Winner Take All* (1975) and lonely med student's wife Valerie Bertinelli following suit in *The Seduction of Gina* (1984). In contrast to compulsive players unable to control their fate, professional gamblers know when to quit—usually. Pro poker player Steve McQueen had "The Man" (Edward G. Robinson) on the ropes in the marathon stud poker game that climaxed 1965's *The Cincinnati Kid*. But The Kid played his cards wrong and wound up with nothing (except a $5000 debt). Tony Curtis and Matt Dillon knew when to trash the cards and pocket the dice in *Mister Cory* (1957) and *The Big Town* (1987), respectively. However, neither of them hauled in winnings comparable to the loot accumulated by unlikely card shark/con artist Joanne Woodward in *Big Hand for the Little Lady* (1966). Dozens of other movies have featured professional gamblers, though their occupation has not always been of primary importance to the plot. Several films not exclusively about gambling have integrated it cleverly into their plot. A crooked card game and a subsequent lynching provoked a series of murders in the mystery-western *Five Card Stud* (1968). Vacationing married couple Julie Haggerty and Albert Brooks stopped in Las Vegas long enough for Haggerty to lose their "nest egg" in the savagely funny *Lost in America* (1985). The scene in which the frantic Brooks tries to convince casino owner Garry Marshall to return the money is a delight. It's almost as funny as the gin rummy game between bubble-headed Judy Holliday and gruff gangster Broderick Crawford in *Born Yesterday* (1950).

The Man Who Broke the Bank at Monte Carlo (1935)	*Five Card Stud* (1968)
Lady Luck (1946)	*The Gamblers* (1969)
The Lady Gambles (1949)	*California Split* (1974)
The Great Sinner (1949)	*Thursday's Game* (1974 TVM)
The Queen of Spades (1949)	*The Gambler* (1975)
Gambling House (1950)	*Winner Take All* (1975 TVM)
The Gambler and the Lady (1952)	*The Gambler* (1980 TVM)
Mississippi Gambler (1953)	*Casino* (1980 TVM)
Mister Cory (1957)	*Lookin' to Get Out* (1982)
Queen of Spades (1960)	*Stacy's Knights* (1983)
Who's Got the Action? (1962)	*The Seduction of Gina* (1984 TVM)
Bay of Angels (1962)	*Lost in America* (1985)
The Cincinnati Kid (1965)	*Fever Pitch* (1985)
Big Hand for the Little Lady (aka *Big Deal at Dodge City*) (1966)	*The Big Town* (1987)
	House of Games (1987)

Game Shows

The quintessential game show movie remains 1950's *Champagne for Caesar*, a wry satire starring Ronald Colman as a genius who practically bankrupts quiz show sponsor Vincent Price. Art Linkletter, an ideal choice, played the show's ("Masquerade for Money") obnoxious host. Mary Steenburgen appeared on a quiz show in *Melvin and Howard*, while Diane Keaton competed on the "TV Tube of Knowledge" in *The Lemon Sisters*. Arnold Schwarzenegger was an unwilling contestant on a futuristic game show in *The Running Man* (a variation on the government-sponsored hunt in 1965's *The Tenth Victim*). *Shock Treatment* (1981), the seldom-seen sequel to *The Rocky Horror Picture Show*, was an appropriately bizarre satire on television quiz programs. Radio contests were the subject of *Christmas in July* (in which Dick Powell spends the money thinking he's won the cash), *The Jackpot* (contest winner James Stewart finds his life changing for the worse), and *Ma and Pa Kettle on Vacation*. And in Woody Allen's *Radio Days*, burglars emptying out a house answer a radio quiz show question and win the homeowners new furniture.

Take It or Leave It (1944)
Champagne for Caesar (1950)
Game Show Models (1977)
Three on a Date (1978 TVM)
Melvin and Howard (1980)
Shock Treatment (1981)
For Love or Money (1984 TVM)

National Lampoon's European Vacation (1985)
The Running Man (1987)
Death Row Game Show (1987)
The Lemon Sisters (1990)
Stay Tuned (1992)

Gamera (Gammera)

Daiei Studios created this giant, flying, fanged, fire-breathing turtle to compete with rival Toho's *Godzilla* film series (q.v.). Like Godzilla, Gamera started his career as a bad guy but turned good in later installments. He was also discovered in a similar fashion, when a plane containing an atomic bomb crashed in the Arctic. The giant turtle's initial appearance was not a total surprise, however, as a scientist in the dubbed version of 1965's *Gamera* confessed: "I heard there were giant turtles that lived on the Arctic continent." Gamera flew by withdrawing into his shell and rotating like a flying saucer.

Gamera (aka *Gamera, the Invincible*; *Gammera*; *Daikaiju Gamera*) (1965)
Gamera vs. Barugon (aka *War of the Monsters*; *Gamera tai Barugon*) (1966)
Gamera vs. Gyaos (aka *Return of the Giant Monsters*; *Gamera tai Gyaos*) (1967)
Gamera vs. Outer-Space Monster Virus (aka *Destroy All Planets*; *Gamera tai Viras*) (1968)
Gamera vs. Guiron (aka *Attack of the Monsters*; *Gamera tai Guiron*) (1969)
Gamera vs. Jiger (aka *Gamera vs. Monster X*; *Gamera tai Daimaju Jaiga*) (1970)
Gamera vs. Zigra (aka *Gamera vs. the Deep Sea Monster Zigra*; *Gamera tai Shinkai Kaiju Jigura*) (1971)

Gangsters (Real-Life)

Although gangsters have been a prominent screen fixture since the 1930s, the genre's early films focused almost exclusively on fictitious bad guys. The first major picture to borrow its plot from the nation's headlines was careful to change names and slightly alter the facts. Nevertheless, everyone—including the censors—recognized that Howard Hawks's *Scarface* (1932) was the story of Al Capone. In contrast, Paramount promoted the fact-based aspects of its *Persons in Hiding* series (q.v.), which was based on a best-seller written by J. Edgar Hoover. This series of four B-movies introduced to moviegoers the blood-splattered crime careers of Bonnie Parker and Clyde Barrow (1939's *Persons in Hiding*) and Ma Barker (1940's *Queen of the Mob*). Four years later, Twentieth Century-Fox produced *Roger Touhy—Gangster*, starring Preston Foster as Capone's henchman. Fox hyped the fact that it was made in cooperation with the FBI and partially filmed at the Illinois State Penitentiary. The following year, poverty row studio Monogram mounted one of its finest films, *Dillinger*, a slick biography starring Lawrence Tierney as the 1930s most popular gangster. In a way, *Dillinger* established the gangster biopic formula for a wave of late 1950s films chronicling the careers of Machine Gun Kelly, Baby Face Nelson, Bonnie Parker and Pretty Boy Floyd. Fact-based gangster movies declined in popularity in the mid-1960s, but shot back with a vengeance with Arthur Penn's 1967 blockbuster *Bonnie and Clyde*. The success of 1972's *The Godfather* further fueled interest in gangster films of any type. Subsequently, television jumped into the genre with a quartet of snappy pictures based on the careers of the the 1930s most famous gangsters. Dale Robertson played FBI agent Melvin Purvis in two of these films, battling Machine Gun Kelly in *Melvin Purvis: G-Man* (1974) and then the Dillinger gang in *The Kansas City Massacre* (1975). The 1970s gangster film cycle ended with the theatrical box office bomb *Capone* (1975). However, real-life gangster films were on the rise again in the late 1980s, thanks to the blockbuster hit *The Untouchables* (1987) and the publicity surrounding the opening of Al Capone's secret vault (alas, the contents turned out to be rather dull). The most popular real-life gangsters on film are Al Capone (*Scarface, The Scarface Mob, The St. Valentine's Day Massacre, Capone, The Untouchables, The Revenge of Al Capone, The Lost Capone*); John Dillinger (*Dillinger, Young Dillinger, Dillinger, The Lady in Red*, the TV-movie *Dillinger*); Pretty Boy Floyd (*Pretty Boy Floyd, A Bullet for Pretty Boy, The Story of Pretty Boy Floyd*); Ma Barker (*Queen of the Mob, Ma Barker's Killer Brood, Bloody Mama*); and Bonnie Parker (*Persons in Hiding, The Bonnie Parker Story, Bonnie and Clyde, Bonnie and Clyde: The True Story*). See also **FBI; Persons in Hiding Series.**

Scarface (aka *Scarface, the Shame of a Nation*) (1932)	*Pretty Boy Floyd* (1960)
	Ma Barker's Killer Brood (1960)
Persons in Hiding (1939)	*Portrait of a Mobster* (1961)
Queen of the Mob (1940)	*Mad Dog Coll* (1961)
Roger Touhy—Gangster (1944)	*King of the Roaring 20's—The Story of Arnold Rothstein* (aka *The Big Bankroll*) (1961)
Dillinger (1945)	
Baby Face Nelson (1957)	
Machine Gun Kelly (1958)	*Young Dillinger* (1965)
The Bonnie Parker Story (1958)	*Bonnie and Clyde* (1967)
The Scarface Mob (1958)	*The St. Valentine Day's Massacre* (1967)
The FBI Story (1959)	
The Rise and Fall of Legs Diamond (1960)	*Bloody Mama* (1970)
	A Bullet for Pretty Boy (1971)

The Valachi Papers (1972)

Dillinger (1973)

The FBI Story—Alvin Karpis (aka The FBI Story—The FBI versus Alvin Karpis, Public Enemy Number One) (1974 TVM)

Melvin Purvis: G-Man (aka The Legend of Machine Gun Kelly) (1974 TVM)

Crazy Joe (1974)

The Virginia Hill Story (1974 TVM) (Bugsy Siegel's moll)

The Story of Pretty Boy Floyd (aka Pretty Boy Floyd) (1974 TVM)

Lepke (1975)

The Kansas City Massacre (1975 TVM)

Capone (1975)

The Lady in Red (1979)

The Untouchables (1987)

Nitti (1988 TVM)

The Revenge of Al Capone (1989 TVM)

The Lost Capone (1990 TVM)

Dillinger (1991 TVM)

Mobsters (1991) (Bugsy Siegel, Lucky Luciano, Meyer Lansky and Richard Costello)

Billy Bathgate (1991) (Dutch Schultz)

Bugsy (1991)

Mad Dog Coll (1992)

Hit the Dutchman (1992) (Dutch Schultz)

Bonnie and Clyde: The True Story (1992 TVM)

Genies

Genies have been common fixtures in Arabian Nights fantasy-adventures such as *Thief of Bagdad* (1940), *The Wonders of Aladdin* (1961), *A Thousand and One Nights* (1968) and *Aladdin* (1992). Rex Ingram (*Thief of Bagdad*) still rates as the cinema's most intimidating genie. However, Robin Williams, who voiced the genie for Disney's *Aladdin*, comes in a close second in terms of resourcefulness and dependability. Genies and magic lamps have also found their way into films with contemporary settings. In the 1945 musical *Where Do We Go From Here?*, Army reject Fred MacMurray found a magic lamp and asked its bumbling genie (Gene Sheldon) to get him into the armed forces. The genie complied but somehow kept putting Fred into the wrong army—in Valley Forge with Washington, on the Santa Maria with Columbus. Eric Blore was a grumpy genie in 1955's *Bowery to Bagdad*, but who wouldn't be with those overaged Bowery Boys Sach (Huntz Hall) and Slip (Leo Gorcey) around to cause trouble? Burl Ives donned the genie attire for 1964's *The Brass Bottle*, which costarred Tony Randall and Barbara Eden. Eden went on to become the most famous of all genies in the 1965-70 TV sitcom *I Dream of Jeannie* and its 1985 made-for-TV reunion movie *I Dream of Jeannie: 15 Years Later*. Not all genies are nice—the evil one in 1987's *The Outing* was out to get some teens trapped in a museum overnight. The most interesting wish granted by a genie was in the 1963 "I Dream of Genie" episode of TV's *The Twilight Zone*, in which a man given only *one* wish wishes to become a genie. A bowling trophy housed a mischievous imp in the memorably titled *Sorority Babes in the Slimeball Bowl-O-Rama* (1988).

Thief of Bagdad (1924)

Thief of Bagdad (1940)

A Thousand and One Nights (1945)

Where Do We Go From Here? (1945)

Bowery to Bagdad (1955)

The Seventh Voyage of Sinbad (1958)

The Boy and the Pirates (1960)

The Wizard of Baghdad (1960)

The Wonders of Aladdin (1961)

The Brass Bottle (1964)

A Thousand and One Nights (1968)

Aladdin (1981)

I Dream of Jeannie: 15 Years Later	*Wildest Dreams* (1987)
(1985 TVM)	*Priceless Beauty* (1988)
The Outing (1987)	*Aladdin* (1992)

Ghidrah

A giant, winged dragon with three (count 'em) fire-breathing heads, Ghidrah was "hatched" when a meteorite exploded in *Ghidrah the Three-Headed Monster* (1965). He has been the most consistently vicious Japanese monster and a formidable opponent — his three heads could battle Godzilla, Rodan and Mothra simultaneously. Ghidrah was created by master monster-maker Eiji Tsuburaya.

> *Ghidrah the Three-Headed Monster* (aka *The Greatest Battle on Earth*; *Sandai Kaiju Chikyu Saidai No Kessen*) (1965)
> *Monster Zero* (aka *Invasion of the Astro-Monsters*; *Kaiju Daisenso*) (1965)
> *Destroy All Monsters* (aka *Operation Monsterland*; *Kaiju Soshingeki*) (1968)
> *Godzilla on Monster Island* (aka *Godzilla vs. Gigan*; *Gojira tai Gaigan*) (1971)
> *Godzilla vs. King Ghidrah* (aka *Godzilla vs. King Ghidorah*) (1992)

Ghosts

Although ghost films have never been in short supply, serious ghostly dramas have been few and far between. The ghost, unlike his supernatural peers the vampire (q.v.) and the werewolf (q.v.), became strongly associated with comedy early in his career. This resulted in a stigma that has been hard to erase. Nevertheless, several of those comedies have served the ghost well, resulting in semiclassics such as *The Ghost Goes West* (1936), *Topper* (1937) and *The Ghost Breakers* (1940). Robert Donat played the title role in *The Ghost Goes West*, in which gravel-voiced Eugene Pallette purchased a castle and, unknowingly, the spirit doomed to haunt it. Cary Grant and Constance Bennett starred as the ghostly, fun-loving Kerby couple in 1937's *Topper* (q.v.). They became quite a headache for meek banker Cosmo Topper (Roland Young), who also grappled with ghosts in two sequels. A haunted house and voodoo trappings provided the atmospheric setting for *The Ghost Breakers*, a successful stage play transformed into one of Bob Hope's finest vehicles. Most comedy teams have encountered real or would-be ghosts, including Olsen and Johnson in *Ghost Catchers* (1944), Martin and Lewis in *Scared Stiff* (a 1953 remake of *The Ghost Breakers*), the Bowery Boys in *Ghost Chasers* (1951), and Abbott and Costello in *The Time of Their Lives* (1946). The latter film proved to be one of Abbott and Costello's best, with Lou and Marjorie Reynolds as a pair of frustrated Revolutionary ghosts and Bud as a mortal who tries to help them escape their earthly prison. The popularity of ghostly comedies has remained surprisingly steady over the years. In the 1980s, for example, box office duds like *Kiss Me Goodbye* (1982) and *High Spirits* (1988) were counterbalanced and overshadowed by unexpected hits like *Ghostbusters* (1984) and *Beetlejuice* (1988). Alas, serious ghost films have not fared nearly as well. *The Scoundrel* (1935) remains an obscure melodrama, despite the magnetic presence of Noel Coward as a cynical writer who returns to earth after his death. (Its lack of success may have inspired Coward's sophisticated ghostly farce *Blithe Spirit*, which appeared first as a 1941 stage play and then a 1945 movie). In the 1940s, Hollywood made a rare excursion into ghostly horror with *The Uninvited* (1944). It featured

Ray Milland, a creepy house overlooking rhythmic waves, a haunting theme by Victor Young, and a strange odor of mimosa. Oddly, it turned out to be an isolated success (there was nary a ghost in Paramount 1945's follow-up *The Unseen*). Sixteen years later, British director Jack Clayton ushered in the era of the intellectual ghost film with *The Innocents* (1961), a chilling adaptation of Henry James's *The Turn of the Screw*. This eerie tale of an unstable governess and her manipulative charges left its ghostly element up to the viewer's imagination. One could effectively argue that Deborah Kerr's governess was a little insane from the beginning or that she was driven to madness by a ghost. This same type of ambiguity could also be applied to Robert Wise's *The Haunting* and Stanley Kubrick's *The Shining* (1980). *The Legend of Hell House* (1973) was a more conventional horror film, but nevertheless a scary yarn about a nasty spirit harassing parapsychologists investigating a spooky house. *The Entity* (1983) claimed to be a fact-based story of a woman who was sexually assaulted repeatedly by a ghost. On a more pleasant note, mortal/ghost romances have been the subject of *The Ghost and Mrs. Muir*, *Sandcastles*, *Kiss Me Goodbye*, and the blockbuster hit *Ghost*. That master of gimmicks, William Castle, also produced a ghost movie. During the theatrical run of 1960's *13 Ghosts*, viewers were given cardboard glasses that allowed them to see "invisible" ghosts in the film. The ever-industrious Castle dubbed this gimmick "Illusion-O." Naturally, many ghost movies have settled for logical explanations in lieu of supernatural ones. *The Ghost of St. Michael's* (1941), for example, turned out to be a very mortal enemy agent. See also **A Chinese Ghost Story; Mediums and Seances; Poltergeist.**

The Ghost Train (1927)
The Ghost Train (1931)
The Scoundrel (1935)
The Return of Peter Grimm (1935)
The Ghost Goes West (1936)
Topper (1937)
A Christmas Carol (1938)
Happy Landing (1938)
The Ghost Breakers (1940)
Earthbound (1940)
The Ghost of St. Michael's (1941)
Hold That Ghost (1941)
The Ghost Train (1941)
The Remarkable Andrew (1942)
The Man in the Trunk (1942)
A Guy Named Joe (1943)
The Canterville Ghost (1944)
Ghost Catchers (1944)
The Uninvited (1944)
A Place of One's Own (1944)
Don't Take It to Heart (1945)
Wonder Man (1945)
Blithe Spirit (1945)
The Time of Their Lives (1946)

The Ghost and Mrs. Muir (1947)
The Ghosts of Berkeley Square (1947)
The Cockeyed Miracle (1948)
Cardboard Cavalier (1949)
A Christmas Carol (aka *Scrooge*) (1951)
Ghost Chasers (1951)
Ghost Ship (1952)
Scared Stiff (1953)
Brigadoon (1954)
The Headless Ghost (1958)
The Ghost of Dragstrip Hollow (1959)
The Invisible Creature (aka *The House on Marsh Road*) (1959)
13 Ghosts (1960)
The Innocents (1961)
The Haunting (1963)
The Ghost and Mr. Chicken (1966)
The Ghost in the Invisible Bikini (1966)
Blackbeard's Ghost (1968)
Ghosts — Italian Style (1969)
The Extraordinary Seaman (1969)
Sole Survivor (1970 TVM)

The Amazing Mr. Blunden (1972)
Sandcastles (1972 TVM)
The Legend of Hell House (1973)
Madhouse Mansion (aka Ghost Story)
    (1974)
Reflections of Murder (1974 TVM)
The Haunting of Julia (aka Full Circle)
    (1976)
Death at Love House (1976 TVM)
Empire of Passion (1978)
The Ghost of Flight 401 (1978)
Child of Glass (1978 TVM)
Dominique (aka Dominique Is Dead)
    (1978)
The Changeling (1979)
An American Christmas Carol (1979
    TVM)
The Shining (1980)
Beyond Evil (1980)
Poltergeist (1981)
Ghost Story (1981)
Don't Go to Sleep (1982 TVM)
O'Hara's Wife (1982)
Kiss Me Goodbye (1982)
The House Where Evil Dwells (1982)
The Entity (1983)

The Haunting Passion (1983 TVM)
Somewhere Tomorrow (1983)
Ghostbusters (1984)
Haunted Honeymoon (1986)
A Chinese Ghost Story (1987)
Ghost Fever (1987)
Beetlejuice (1988)
Lady in White (1988)
Ghost Town (1988)
High Spirits (1988)
Field of Dreams (1989)
Ghostbusters II (1989)
She's Back (1989)
Ghost (1990)
Ghost Dad (1990)
The Sleeping Car (1990)
Heart Condition (1990)
Ghosts Can't Do It (1990)
Cello (1990)
Escape (1990)
Truly Madly Deeply (1991)
Grave Secrets: The Legacy of Hilltop
    Drive (1992 TVM)
Love Can Be Murder (1992 TVM)
Bedevil (1993)

Ghoulies

Although considered a rip-off of *Gremlins* (1984), the original *Ghoulies* (1985) differed substantially in plot and tone—which did not necessarily make it original nor even interesting. It told the story of Jonathan Graves (Peter Liapis), a college student who drops out to renovate his deceased parents' old mansion. Unbeknownst to Jonathan, his father practiced black magic and sacrificed Jonathan's mother. The teenager discovers his father's books and falls under the spell of their power to the point that he summons the title characters (little slimy demons that admittedly resemble Gremlins). Jonathan unknowingly revives his father, who orders the ghoulies to kill most of Jonathan's friends and announces to his son that he wants to steal the boy's youth. The film was neither scary nor humorous; it was also fairly light on blood and gore, as evidenced by its PG-13 rating. The supporting cast featured some interesting faces, such as Jack (*Eraserhead*) Nance, cult actress Bobbie Bresee, and Mariska Hargitay (Jayne Mansfield's daughter), but they had little to do. The 1987 sequel, *Ghoulies II*, continued the first film's mediocrity despite a promising setting: a carnival house of horrors called Satan's Den, which was about to go out of business. The series' third entry, 1989's *Ghoulies III: Ghoulies Go to College*, added some recognizable talent: Kevin (*Invasion of the Body Snatchers*) McCarthy and Griffin O'Neal (Ryan's son). McCarthy played crusty Professor Ragnor, who summons the ghoulies to teach the campus youth a lesson. Ironically, the lukewarm reception given to the following year's *Gremlins 2: The New Batch* may have signaled the end of the *Ghoulies* series.

Ghoulies (1985)
Ghoulies II (1987)

Ghoulies III: Ghoulies Go to College
(aka *Ghoulies III*) (1989)

Ghouls

According to Muslim folklore, a ghoul is an evil spirit that robs graves and feasts upon dead flesh. Horror movies have modified that definition over the years and produced a loose variation of the term, defining a ghoul as a dead person who eats the flesh of the living. (For a discussion of noncarnivorous living dead, see **Zombies**.) Though less well known than vampires and werewolves, ghouls have been around for awhile. Boris Karloff starred in the once-lost 1933 British film *The Ghoul*. Yet, while he rose from the dead to recover a stolen jewel, he was not—technically—a ghoul. Ten years later, *The Mad Ghoul* cast the delightful George Zucco as a mad scientist whose experiments with an ancient gas turn his nice assistant, David Bruce, into a creature who feeds on fresh human hearts. However, George Romero's 1968 cult shocker *Night of the Living Dead* (q.v.) set the gory standard by which most ghoul movies are judged. Shot near Pittsburgh for less than $100,000, Romero's downbeat chiller centered around seven people trapped in a farmhouse surrounded by hungry resurrected dead people. It made little impact on its initial release, but by the early 1970s, it had emerged as a midnight movie staple and a critics' favorite. A trio of interesting ghoulish pictures appeared between 1972 and 1974, but only a few drive-in patrons saw them. Bob Clark (*A Christmas Story*) directed 1972's *Deathdream*, a reworking of "The Monkey's Paw" in which a dead Vietnam soldier returned home to eat his loved ones. The year after they produced *American Graffiti*, Gloria Katz and Willard Huyck made 1974's *Dead People*, which was reissued as *Return of the Living Dead* to capitalize on Romero's film. Italy's *Don't Open the Window* was an intriguing variation wherein a government device to kill insects transformed the dead into ghouls. By 1979, Romero had found the capital to make his long-awaited sequel *Dawn of the Dead*. This lengthy, gory, overly symbolic tale made a profit in the United States (where it was unrated) but performed exceptionally well overseas. Italian director Lucio Fulci subsequently made two Romero-inspired rip-offs: 1979's *Zombie* and 1980's *City of the Living Dead*. Meanwhile, *Night of the Living Dead* cowriter John Russo clashed with Romero on the rights to a *Living Dead* sequel. The two settled out of court, allowing Russo to make his 1985 ghoul satire *Return of the Living Dead*. Its surprise box office success overshadowed Romero's *Day of the Dead* (1985), which, prior to its commercial and critical failure, was intended as the final chapter of Romero's ghoul trilogy. Romero has since produced a remake of the original and indicated another chapter might be on the drawing board. Bill Hinzman, who played the *first* ghoul in Romero's *Living Dead* original, made an amateurish 1989 tribute dubbed *Revenge of the Living Zombies*. See also **Cannibalism; Night of the Living Dead; Zombies.**

The Mad Ghoul (1943)
Night of the Living Dead (1968)
Deathdream (aka *The Night Walk*; *Dead of Night*) (1972)

Children Shouldn't Play With Dead Things (1973)
Don't Open the Window (aka *Breakfast at the Manchester Morgue*) (1974)

Dead People (aka *Return of the Living Dead*; *Messiah of Evil*; *Revenge of the Screaming Dead*) (1974)
Dawn of the Dead (aka *Zombie*) (1979)
Zombie (aka *Zombie 2*; *Zombie Flesh-Eaters*) (1979)
Bloodeaters (1980)
City of the Living Dead (aka *Gates of Hell*) (1980)
Night of the Zombies (1983)

City of the Walking Dead (aka *Nightmare City*) (1983)
Return of the Living Dead (1985)
Day of the Dead (1985)
Return of the Living Dead II (1988)
Zombie Brigade (1988)
Redneck Zombies (1989)
Revenge of the Living Zombies (1989)
Chopper Chicks in Zombietown (1991)

Giants

Bigger has not meant better for humans of gigantic proportions. In the science fiction genre, hardly anyone has grown big because they *wanted* to. *The Amazing Colossal Man* was a victim of a plutonium explosion, while an alien caused the *Attack of the 50-Foot Woman*. Neither of those title characters dealt with his or her newfound size very well; both eventually went crazy. A major problem that plagued them, along with *The 30-Foot Bride of Candy Rock* (1959), was their wardrobe. Embarrassingly, the Colossal Man wound up wearing big diapers, while the 30-Foot Bride made a nice-looking toga out of a parachute. Producer-director Bert I. Gordon, a major proponent of rear-screen projection, specialized in giant people movies. In addition to *The Amazing Colossal Man* (1957), he produced its sequel, *War of the Colossal Beast* (1958), the very similar *Cyclops* (1957), and *Village of the Giants* (1965). The latter film, a very loose adaptation of H.G. Wells's *Food of the Gods*, starred little Ronnie Howard as a whiz kid who turns a bunch of teenagers into rowdy giants. Buddy Baer (whose nephew Max, Jr. played Jethro on *The Beverly Hillbillies*) portrayed a gigantic conquistador in 1958's *Giant From the Unknown* and Abbott and Costello's oversized nemesis in 1952's *Jack and the Beanstalk*. In Costello's only film sans Abbott, he turned his girlfriend Dorothy Provine into the aforementioned *30-Foot Bride of Candy Rock*. Richard Kiel—Jaws in the James Bond films—played the title role in *The Giant of Thunder Mountain* (1991), a wholesome family drama. See also **Little People.**

Alice in Wonderland (1951)
Jack and the Beanstalk (1952)
Cyclops (1957)
The Amazing Colossal Man (1957)
War of the Colossal Beast (1958)
Attack of the 50-Foot Woman (1958)
Giant From the Unknown (1958)

The 30-Foot Bride of Candy Rock (1959)
Village of the Giants (1965)
The Giant of Thunder Mountain (1991)
Honey, I Blew Up the Kid (1992)

Gidget

The original beach party teen was played by Sandra Dee in the 1959 eponymous opus. The first *Gidget* was semiserious, with the heroine getting somewhat involved with an older man, a beachcomber played by Cliff Robertson. The follow-ups were more lighthearted, with the spunky teen being portrayed by five different actresses. The films spawned two TV series: Sally Field's 1965-66 version and a syndicated series that cropped up in the mid-1980s. See also **Beach Party**.

Gidget (1959) (Sandra Dee)
Gidget Goes Hawaiian (1961) (Deborah Walley)
Gidget Goes to Rome (1963) (Cindy Carol)
Gidget Grows Up (1969 TVM) (Karen Valentine)
Gidget Gets Married (1972 TVM) (Monie Ellis)
Gidget's Summer Reunion (1985 TVM) (Caryn Richman)

Gildersleeve, The Great

Portly, baritone comedian Harold Peary played Throckmorton P. Gildersleeve ("Gildy") in this short-lived RKO series inspired by a hit radio show. The character first appeared in the 1941 comedy *Look Who's Laughing*, which brought together radio favorites Bergen and McCarthy and Fibber McGee and Molly. After additional appearances as Gildy in *Here We Go Again* and *Seven Days Leave* (both 1942), Peary launched his own series with 1943's *The Great Gildersleeve*. He played the unlikely "custodian" of his teenage niece Margie (Nancy Gates) and enterprising nephew Leroy (Freddie Mercer). Jane Darwell, just three years after winning an Oscar as Ma Joad in 1939's *The Grapes of Wrath*, provided maternal support as Aunt Emma. The movies never rose above program filler and usually cast Gildy as an unlikely hero—clashing with gangsters, avoiding marriage-minded spinsters, and encountering ghostly ancestors. When Gildy got into a jam (e.g., zipped in a sleeping bag with a cat and dog), he typically bellowed "Oh, Leeeeroy!" When things were going well, though, one could count on hearing his trademark giggle.

Look Who's Laughing (1941)
Here We Go Again (1942)
Seven Days Leave (1942)
The Great Gildersleeve (1943)

Gildersleeve's Bad Day (1943)
Gildersleeve on Broadway (1943)
Gildersleeve's Ghost (1944)

Gilligan's Island

During its original 1964-66 telecasts, *Gilligan's Island* scored reasonably well in the ratings opposite *The Lawrence Welk Show* and then *The Donna Reed Show*. But the series' juvenile audience eventually spelled its doom on the network. Ironically, those same viewers turned the syndicated reruns of *Gilligan's Island* into a very profitable money-making machine. The series gradually built such a large, broad-based following that it convinced NBC to reunite the cast members for 1978's *Rescue From Gilligan's Island*. With the exception of Tina Louise as Ginger, all the original castaways returned. Time had not been kind to some of the performers, but the show's fans still enjoyed watching the Minnow's passengers finally get home—only to go on a reunion cruise and land back on the island. The movie performed very well in the ratings and there was talk of reviving the series. However, dwindling audiences for two additional films put that idea to rest. See also **Television Series Reunion Films**.

Rescue From Gilligan's Island (1978 TVM)
The Castaways on Gilligan's Island (1979 TVM)
The Harlem Globetrotters on Gilligan's Island (1981 TVM)

Gimmicks

When television entered American homes in the early 1950s, Hollywood panicked. Convinced that families would stay at home to watch the small screen, filmmakers sought innovative ideas to make theatrical films different. 3-D was revived (see separate entry), widescreen processes were introduced, and William Castle lured moviegoers with gimmicks that would make a carny barker jealous. A prolific B-movie director from 1943, Castle made his first horror feature in 1958. *Macabre* was a decent, low-budget picture about a man trying to find his kidnapped daughter, who had been buried alive (q.v.). However, Castle turned it into a surprise money-maker by issuing viewers a $1000 life insurance policy from Lloyds of London — in case anyone died of fright while watching the movie. Castle followed up with 1958's *House on Haunted Hill*, starring Vincent Price and a gimmick called "emergo." Not quite as clever as its name, "emergo" was simply a skeleton on a wire that projectionists dropped over unsuspecting viewers during the film's big shock scene. *The Tingler* followed the same year, and if there's a classic gimmick, this is it. Price stars again, this time as a doctor who discovers a crustaceanlike creature that grows at the base of the spine during moments of intense fright. When you scream, the creature reduces in size and becomes harmless. However, if you're too afraid to scream, the Tingler snaps your spine, causing instant death. At the highlight of the film, Price surgically removes a Tingler, which subsequently escapes to a movie theater below him. The screen goes black and Price urges the real movie audience to "Scream! Scream for your lives!" To heighten the effect, some patrons at selected movie theatres received mild electric shocks (yes, Castle had actually wired some of the seats!). Castle's next two gimmicks were far less elaborate. For *13 Ghosts* (1960), he provided viewers with filtered glasses that allowed them to see the movie's "invisible" ghosts (he called this "Illusion-O"). And in his 1961 psycho thriller *Homicidal*, he interrupted the film with a "fright break," which told viewers that "all those too timid to take the climax will be welcomed to the Coward's Corner." Director Joe Dante paid homage to Castle with *Matinee* (1993), a nostalgic tale of a horror film producer (John Goodman) who employs elaborately named gimmicks like "Atomo-Vision." On a smaller scale, the 1991 horror-comedy *Popcorn* also spoofed Castle-type gimmicks. Although William Castle was the King of Gimmicks, others have resorted to similar tactics to draw audiences. See also **3-D**; **Cinerama**. Some of the more memorable gimmicks:

Scent of Mystery (1960). In selected theaters, over thirty aromas were piped in via plastic tubes. This was dubbed "Smell-O-Vision."

Psycho (1960). During its first run, theaters refused to admit patrons once the film started.

Ten Little Indians (1965). Featured a "murder minute" at the climax, informing viewers they had all the clues — and sixty seconds — to solve the mystery.

Chamber of Horrors (1966). Sounded the "horror horn" and showed the "fear flasher" before every murder.

Wicked, Wicked (1973). The entire movie was shown in split-screen, or as the producers proclaimed, in "Duovision."

Earthquake (1974). First of the "Sensurround" movies, whereby the soundtrack was amplified in certain scenes to cause a rumbling sensation. It also caused headaches. Other "Sensurround" movies were *Midway* (1976) and *Rollercoaster* (1977).

The Beast Must Die (1974). A "werewolf break" gave viewers time to guess the werewolf's identity.

Polyester (1981). "Odorama" provided patrons with scratch-and-sniff cards with instructions on when to scratch during the flick.

Dead Men Don't Wear Plaid (1982). Steve Martin "acted" with stars from Hollywood's golden days by intercutting footage from famous films.

Clue (1985). Released with three endings, each one identifying a different character as the murderer.

Million Dollar Mystery (1987). Viewers could win a million dollars themselves by piecing together clues provided in the film.

Godfather, The

Francis Ford Coppola and Mario Puzo's epic saga of the Corleone family spans three generations of Mafia gangsters, from the turn-of-the-century to 1980. The first two films chalked up some impressive honors — each won Best Picture — but *The Godfather Part III* slipped into film history as little more than a postscript. *The Godfather* (1972), adapted from Puzo's best-seller and starring Marlon Brando in the title role, was a "film event" from the beginning. The principal action took place between 1945 and 1955, during the final days of Don Vito's (Brando) reign as head of the powerful Corleone family. The Corleones struggled toward social and financial respectability, even as they destroyed their rivals to ensure control of their "business." It was easy to guess which son would inherit his father's throne: college-educated Michael (Al Pacino) who wanted no part of his inheritance; the violent, hot-tempered Sonny (James Caan); or the simple-minded Fredo (John Cazale). Yet, Michael's gradual transition into a strong-willed, ruthless-when-necessary gangster was the most engrossing plotline in the film. Coppola's sister Talia Shire (Adrienne in the *Rocky* films) played Don Vito's only daughter, Connie; Robert Duvall played the family's rational attorney Tom Hagen; and Diane Keaton played Michael's eventual wife Kay Adams. *The Godfather Part II* (1974), also based on Puzo's novel, told two parallel stories: Michael Corleone's attempt to take control of Las Vegas in the late 1950s and Vito Corleone's (Robert DeNiro) immigration to America and rise to Mafia power in 1917 New York. Although Pacino and other principals from the original film reprised their roles, DeNiro dominated the screen in a star-making turn for which he won a Best Supporting Actor Oscar. Film critics disagreed sharply on the merits of *The Godfather Part II*. Some found the film's divergent structure intriguing, while others echoed the views of Vincent Canby of the *New York Times*: "I can't readily imagine what Mr. Coppola and Mr. Puzo were trying to do, except to turn their first film into a long parenthesis that would fit between the halves of the new movie." Coppola must have read that quote, because he did just that seven years later with *The Godfather—The Complete Epic, 1902-1958*, a 386-minute chronological version of *The Godfather* and *The Godfather Part II* (with fifteen minutes of "never-before-seen" footage). This special edition, which played on network television and was released on videotape, appeared to be the end of the saga. However, after a string of disappointing films and financial troubles, Coppola returned to his biggest hit with 1990's *The Godfather Part III*. This stale rehash of the first two films brought back Pacino as Don Michael Corleone but neglected to surround him with an interesting story. Diane Keaton and Talia Shire, also veterans of *Part I* and *Part II*, looked concerned or bored for most of the lengthy picture's 161 minutes. Only Andy Garcia, as Michael's cocky nephew (and obvious successor), brought a fresh intensity to his role. *The Godfather Part III* earned a Best Picture nomination and middling box office results—both chiefly on the merits of the earlier films. In 1993, Coppola edited all three films together (and added still more "new footage") to create the epic videotape *The Godfather Trilogy: 1901-1980*.

    The Godfather (1972)   *The Godfather Part III* (1990)
    The Godfather Part II (1974)

Godzilla

Japan's biggest star, both literally (four hundred feet tall, two million tons) and in terms of popularity, Godzilla has starred in nineteen films since his 1954 debut. The first, and best, was *Godzilla, King of the Monsters*, in which H-bomb tests revive the prehistoric creature and equip him with radioactive breath. He leaves his native Oto island and topples most of Tokyo before an "oxygen destroyer" spells his doom. Raymond Burr costarred as a wheelchair-ridden reporter (shades of *Ironside*). The film was a smash hit in Japan and fared very well when imported to the United States in 1956. Its sequel, *Godzilla Raids Again* (1955), has caused infinite nightmares for film historians. Besides sporting the alternate titles *Godzilla's Counterattack* and *The Return of Godzilla*, it was released in the United States as *Gigantis, the Fire Monster*. Confusingly, the title monster was not a Godzilla rival, but the Big G himself. After two more movies as a baddie, Godzilla turned good monster in 1965's *Ghidrah, the Three-Headed Monster*. He continued to soften as the series progressed: He was a single parent in *Son of Godzilla* and taught a human boy about courage in *Godzilla's Revenge*. By the early 1970s, he was a shadow of his ruthless self, and the series appeared to end with *Terror of Godzilla* (aka *Terror of Mechagodzilla*). But—just to show you can't keep a good dragon down—he attempted a comeback with *Godzilla 1985*, a semi-remake of the original. It was a tremendous flop in the United States. However, the big guy made a comeback in his homeland with 1989's *Godzilla vs. Biollante*, which pitted him against a nice plant monster.

    Godzilla, King of the Monsters (aka *Godzilla*; *Gojira*) (1954)
    Godzilla Raids Again (aka *The Return of Godzilla*; *Gigantis, the Fire Monster*;
        Godzilla's Counterattack; *Gojira no Gyakushu*) (1955)
    King Kong vs. Godzilla (aka *Kingukongu tai Gojira*) (1962)
    Godzilla vs. The Thing (aka *Godzilla vs. Mothra*; *Godzilla tai Mothra*) (1964)
    Ghidrah, the Three-Headed Monster (aka *The Greatest Battle on Earth*; *Sandai*
        Kaiju Chikyu Saidai No Kessen) (1965)
    Monster Zero (aka *Invasion of the Astro-Monsters*; *Kaiju Daisenso*) (1965)
    Godzilla vs. the Sea Monster (aka *Ebriah—Terror of the Deep*; *Nankai no Dai*
        Ketto) (1966)
    Destroy All Monsters (aka *Operation Monsterland*; *Kaiju Soshingeki*) (1968)
    Son of Godzilla (aka *Gojira no Musuko*) (1968)
    Godzilla's Revenge (aka *Ord Kaiju Daishingeki*) (1969)

Godzilla on Monster Island (aka *Godzilla vs. Gigan; Gojira tai Gaigan*) (1971)
Godzilla vs. the Smog Monster (aka *Gojira tai Hedora*) (1971)
Godzilla vs. Megalon (aka *Gojira tai Megaro*) (1973)
Godzilla vs. the Bionic Monster (aka *Godzilla vs. the Cosmic Monster; Gojira tai Meka-Gojira*) (1974)
Terror of Godzilla (aka *Terror of Mechagodzilla; Meka-Gojira no Gyakusyu*) (1975)
Godzilla 1985 (1985)
Godzilla vs. Biollante (1989)
Godzilla vs. King Ghidrah (aka *Godzilla vs. King Ghidrah*) (1992)
Godzilla vs. Mothra (1992)
Godzilla vs. Mech Godzilla (1993)
(Note: Godzilla's foot also appears in the memorable animated short *Bambi Meets Godzilla*, and Bob Goldthwait dons a Godzilla suit and blunders through a miniature city in 1986's *One Crazy Summer*.)

Golf

Golf seldom ranks with its peers as a television sport, the ball being too small to follow and the game devoid of blue-collar suspense. That same handicap applies to its big screen career, resulting in but a handful of golf films. *Banning* (1967) examined (somewhat superficially) the country club set obsessed with golfing. It starred Robert Wagner as a washed-up pro who regains his self-respect and teaches the snobs a lesson. One of the stories in *Dead of Night* (1945) concerned a pair of golfing buddies who make a wager — with one of them winding up a ghost. In 1964's *Goldfinger*, James Bond introduced himself to villain Auric Goldfinger by cheating in a golf game. The President was kidnapped on a golf course in the spy spoof *In Like Flint*. And Bing Crosby and Bob Hope engaged in their favorite pastime in a sketch for 1947's Paramount all-star extravaganza *Variety Girl*. The only real-life golfer to have his story reach the silver screen was Ben Hogan, the subject of 1951's *Follow the Sun*.

The Cohens and Kellys in Scotland (1930)	*Goldfinger* (1964)
You're Telling Me (1934)	*Banning* (1967 TVM)
Carefree (1938)	*In Like Flint* (1967)
Dead of Night (1945)	*Once You Kiss a Stranger* (1969)
My Favorite Brunette (1947)	*Enter the Dragon* (1973)
Variety Girl (1947)	*Caddyshack* (1980)
Follow the Sun (1951)	*Caddyshack II* (1988)
Pat and Mike (1952)	*Dead Solid Perfect* (1988 TVM)
The Caddy (1953)	*Blades* (1989)

Gorgons

In Greek mythology, the Gorgons were female creatures who had snakes for hair and eyes that could turn men into stone. There were three Gorgon sisters: Stheno and Euryale, who were immortal, and Medusa, their well-known sibling, whose fame stems from her death at the hands of Perseus (he used a reflecting shield and a decapitating sword). Hammer Studios, Britain's "House of Horror" (and never one to worry about tradition), added a fourth sister named Magaera in its 1964 chiller *The Gorgon*. Medusa, though, still reigns as cinema's most noteworthy Gorgon. Ray Harryhausen brought her to life via stop-motion animation in 1981's *Clash of the Titans*. Tony Randall played Medusa, along with several other characters, in George Pal's juvenile fantasy *The Seven Faces of Dr. Lao* (1964). And she made a brief—and very fakey—appearance in the low-budget sand-and-sandal epic *Medusa vs. the Son of Hercules* (1962). The syndicated TV series *Swamp Thing* featured a contemporary Gorgon in its "Heart of Stone" episode. See also **Cyclops**.

Medusa vs. the Son of Hercules (1962)	*The Seven Faces of Dr. Lao* (1964)
The Gorgon (1964)	*Clash of the Titans* (1981)

Governesses and Nannies

Deborah Kerr heads an impressive group of actresses who have played governesses. She matched wits with the King of Siam (Yul Brynner) in *The King and I* (1956), fought would-be ghosts while losing her grip on sanity in *The Innocents* (1961), and "cured" troublesome teen Hayley Mills in *The Chalk Garden* (1964). However, references being what they are (and *The Innocents* episode being rather disturbing), one must recommend Julie Andrews over Ms. Kerr for employment as a governess. Andrews was a cheery, lyrical nanny who brought out the best in her charges in both *Mary Poppins* (1964) and *The Sound of Music* (1965). Bette Davis also proved capable in *All This and Heaven Too* (1940), but she was at her nastiest as *The Nanny* (1965). Other notable actresses to perform nanny duties include Ingrid Bergman (*Adam Had Four Sons*) and Katharine Hepburn (*Flame Over India*). Disney's animated *Peter Pan* (1953) featured the immortal Nana, the St. Bernard nanny. Wrestler Hulk Hogan played the title role in 1993's *Mr. Nanny*. Juliet Mills (Hayley's sister) portrayed a governess with a magic touch in the 1970-71 TV series *Nanny and the Professor*. See also **Babysitters**.

All This and Heaven Too (1940)	*The Sound of Music* (1965)
Adam Had Four Sons (1941)	*The Nanny* (1965)
Jane Eyre (1944)	*Jane Eyre* (1970 TVM)
The Unseen (1945)	*The Nightcomers* (1971)
Anna and the King of Siam (1946)	*Blue Blood* (1973)
Blanche Fury (1948)	*Miss Mary* (1986)
Peter Pan (1953)	*The Haunting of Morella* (1990)
The King and I (1956)	*The Guardian* (1990)
Flame Over India (aka *Northwest Frontier*) (1959)	*The Hand That Rocks the Cradle* (1992)
The Innocents (1961)	*Midnight's Child* (1992 TVM)
The Chalk Garden (1964)	*Mr. Nanny* (1993)
Mary Poppins (1964)	

Grave Robbers

The grisly real-life duo of William Burke and William Hare has been the subject of four films. These nineteenth-century Edinburgh grave robbers sold cadavers to medical students for dissection. When the supply of fresh corpses dried up, Burke and Hare turned to murder. Burke was accused of over a dozen murders and was hanged in 1829. Hare, who had testified against his partner, served a prison term and was later freed. On the screen, Burke was first portrayed by Boris Karloff (though the character was called Gray) in Val Lewton's 1945 adaptation of Robert Louis Stevenson's *The Body Snatcher*. Fifteen years later, Burke returned, with Hare this time, in *The Flesh and the Fiends*, a Hammer-style horror picture starring Peter Cushing. In 1971, *Burke and Hare* elevated the gruesome twosome from supporting to principal characters but lacked the style of Freddie Francis's handsome 1985 version *The Doctor and the Devils*. Other grave diggers have turned up frequently in horror films, most notably James Whale's original *Frankenstein*. Jacques Tourneur's 1964 horror spoof *A Comedy of Terrors* starred Vincent Price and Peter Lorre as budget-minded morticians who dug up graves to recover their coffins. In *Invisible Invaders*, creatures from outer space occupied the dead bodies of Earthlings and then dug themselves out of their graves.

Frankenstein (1931)
The Body Snatcher (1945)
The Greed of William Hart (1948)
The Abductors (1957)
Invisible Invaders (1959)
The Flesh and the Fiends (aka *Mania*) (1960)
The Anatomist (1961)

Mr. Sardonicus (1961)
Corridors of Blood (aka *Doctor of Seven Dials*) (1962)
A Comedy of Terrors (1964)
Burke and Hare (1971)
Dr. Jekyll and Sister Hyde (1971)
The Doctor and the Devils (1985)

Great Gildersleeve, The, *see* Gildersleeve, The Great

Gunsmoke

Four made-for-television movies followed the demise of the 1955-1975 CBS TV series. *Gunsmoke: Return to Dodge* (1987) qualifies as an official TV series reunion movie (q.v.), with Marshal Matt Dillon (James Arness) and Miss Kitty Russell (Amanda Blake) meeting up in Dodge City twelve years later. Other series regulars on-hand included Buck Taylor as gunsmith Newly O'Brien and Fran Ryan as Miss Hannah, who ran the Longbranch Saloon after Miss Kitty left Dodge. This TV-movie scored well in the ratings and prompted a 1990 sequel, *Gunsmoke: The Last Apache*, which bore a passing resemblance to John Ford's 1956 classic *The Searchers*. Matt receives a letter from an old flame (Michael Learned) whose daughter Amanda (Amy Stock-Poyton) has been kidnapped by Indians. Matt agrees to help and, in the process, learns that Amanda is his daughter, too. In 1992's *Gunsmoke: To the Last Man*, Matt, Amanda (Stock-Poyton), and her Eastern-born boyfriend fight some narrow-minded vigilantes. A fourth series entry, 1993's *Gunsmoke: The Long Ride*, found Matt searching for a look-alike outlaw killer. He encounters Ali MacGraw as a reformed prostitute along the trail. Arness made the last three films watchable (especially for *Gunsmoke* fans), but the scriptwriters seemed to have forgotten what made the TV series so successful: a large, well-defined cast of supporting characters and a willingness to focus the stories on guest stars. In its later years, the TV series *Gunsmoke* rarely built stories solely around Matt. See also **Television Series Reunion Films**.

Gunsmoke: Return to Dodge (1987 TVM)
Gunsmoke: The Last Apache (1990 TVM)

Gunsmoke: To the Last Man (1992 TVM)
Gunsmoke: The Long Ride (1993 TVM)

Gypsies

The victims of movie stereotyping, gypsies have too often been portrayed as ominous fortune-tellers or hot-blooded vagabonds. Maria Ouspenskaya created the most famous celluloid gypsy, as Maleva the fortune-teller who first informs Lon Chaney, Jr.: "Even a man who is pure in heart and says his prayers by night can become a wolf when the wolfbane blooms and the autumn moon is bright." Alas, that's exactly what happened to Lon in 1941's *The Wolf Man*, following a bite from Maleva's gypsy-werewolf son (Bela Lugosi). Although father Claude Rains put his werewolf son out of his misery, both the Wolf Man and Maleva the gypsy returned two years later for *Frankenstein Meets the Wolf Man*. The talented Ouspenskaya lost her Russian nationality in gypsy guise, but other performers have looked downright out of place. Intentional miscasting was part of the fun in 1936's *The Bohemian Girl*, which featured Stan Laurel and Oliver Hardy as unlikely gypsies. However, Jane Russell made a silly gypsy temptress in *Hot Blood* (1955), while Marlene Dietrich chewed the scenery (in entertaining fashion) in *Golden Earrings* (1947). Frank Sinatra, in heavy make-up and sporting an earring, made a gypsy cameo appearance in John Huston's gimmicky 1963 mystery *The List of Adrian Messenger*. Few films have focused on the plight of present-day gypsies. One that did was 1978's *King of the Gypsies*, an adaptation of Peter Maas's best-seller about a dying gypsy ruler (Sterling Hayden) who passes the tribe's leadership to his grandson (Eric Roberts), ignoring the birthrights of his son (Judd Hirsch). Actor Robert Duvall directed *Angelo, My Love* (1983), a curious mixture of fact and fiction set in New York City and starring a former gypsy child (Angelo Evans).

Caravan (1934)
Vanessa, Her Love Story (1935)
The Bohemian Girl (1936)
Wings of the Morning (1937)
The Hunchback of Notre Dame (1939)
The Wolf Man (1941)
Frankenstein Meets the Wolf Man (1943)
Gypsy Wildcat (1944)
Cry of the Werewolf (1944)
House of Dracula (1945)
Caravan (1946)
Madonna of the Seven Moons (1946)
Golden Earrings (1947)
Jassy (1947)
The Loves of Carmen (1948)

Gypsy Fury (1951)
Charge of the Lancers (1954)
Hot Blood (1955)
The Gypsy and the Gentleman (1957)
Babes in Toyland (1961)
The List of Adrian Messenger (1963)
From Russia With Love (1963)
Los Tarantos (1964)
Gypsy Girl (aka *Sky West and Crooked*) (1965)
The Virgin and the Gypsy (1970)
The Art of Crime (1975 TVM)
Alex and the Gypsy (1976)
King of the Gypsies (1978)
Angelo, My Love (1983)
Time of the Gypsies (1989)

Halloween

The most influential horror film of the late 1970s, this well-made psycho thriller inspired a rash of "slasher" movies (q.v.). Unfortunately, its imitators failed to realize that *Halloween* (1978) worked because of its suspense — not its gore. The thin plot concerned a babysitter and her friends who are terrorized by an emotionless psychopath on Halloween night. Donald Pleasance and Jamie Lee Curtis contributed effective performances, but the true star was John Carpenter, whose tour-de-force direction created some classic frights. Carpenter coproduced but did not direct 1981's pallid sequel *Halloween II*. *Halloween III: Season of the Witch* (1983) ignored the plot of the earlier films and opted for a clever tale about a diabolical Halloween mask manufacturer. It bombed with critics and moviegoers. Five years later, the series resumed with *Halloween IV: The Return of Michael Myers* (1988) and then *Halloween V: The Revenge of Michael Myers* (1989), non-Carpenter entries with Pleasance returning to confront the original killer. They ignored the second and third films and picked up where the original *Halloween* left off. See also **Friday the 13th; Slasher Movies.**

   Halloween (1978)
   Halloween II (1981)
   Halloween III: Season of the Witch (1983)
   Halloween IV: The Return of Michael Myers (1988)
   Halloween V: The Revenge of Michael Myers (1989)

Hammer, Mike

Mickey Spillane's rough and tough private eye has had a checkered screen career. Biff Elliott played the movies' first Hammer in the 1953 3-D flick *I, the Jury*, a pedestrian adaptation of Spillane's 1946 best-seller. Ralph Meeker also missed the mark as Hammer in Robert Aldrich's *Kiss Me Deadly* (1955), but the picture nevertheless remains a stylish film noir with a loyal cult following. Spillane took a shot at the role himself in 1963's *The Girl Hunters*, but he quickly abandoned his acting career to return to writing. To date, the most successful Hammer has been Stacy Keach, who played Hammer in the 1983 TV-movie *Murder Me, Murder You* and the subsequent series *Mickey Spillane's Mike Hammer* (later retitled *The New Mike Hammer*). In the earlier days of television, Darren McGavin starred in a 1957-58 syndicated TV series called *Mickey Spillane's Mike Hammer*.

   I, the Jury (1953) (Biff Elliott)
   Kiss Me Deadly (1955) (Ralph Meeker)
   My Gun Is Quick (1957) (Robert Bray)
   The Girl Hunters (1963) (Mickey Spillane)
   Mickey Spillane's Margin for Murder (1981 TVM) (Kevin Dobson)
   I, the Jury (1982) (Armand Assante)
   Murder Me, Murder You (1983 TVM) (Stacy Keach)
   The Return of Mickey Spillane's Mike Hammer (1986 TVM) (Keach)
   Murder Takes All (1989 TVM) (Keach)

The Happy Hooker Series

Xaviera Hollander's best-seller about her experiences as New York City's premiere madam served as the inspiration for three ill-conceived features. The original *The Happy Hooker* (1975) had pretensions of being a sly, naughty satire. But a leaden script and a miscast, red-headed Lynn Redgrave resulted in a major misfire. Blonde Joey Heatherton replaced Redgrave in *The Happy Hooker Goes to*

Washington (1977), a sex-and-politics comedy that was sexually boring and politically unfunny. Brunette Martine Beswicke finished the series with *The Happy Hooker Goes to Hollywood* (1980). The Brits proved that a funny movie could be made from the confessions of a real-life madam with 1987's *Personal Services*, an honest, sharply etched portrait of Cynthia Payne (played by Julie Walters).

   The Happy Hooker (1975)
   The Happy Hooker Goes to Washington (1977)
   The Happy Hooker Goes to Hollywood (1980)

Hardy, Andy

For a decade, the Hardys reigned as America's favorite family, and Mickey Rooney as Andy Hardy captured the public's affection as had no other teenager. His growing pains were chronicled in fifteen highly successful films released during 1937-46. The MGM series made a modest debut with *A Family Affair*, Louis Mayer's attempt to duplicate the popularity of Eugene O'Neill's family comedy-drama *Ah, Wilderness*. Mayer even reunited three stars from the 1935 film version of O'Neill's play: Lionel Barrymore, Cecilia Parker, and seventeen-year-old Mickey Rooney. To MGM's surprise, *A Family Affair* was a solid hit, prompting an immediate sequel. In *You're Only Young Once*, Lewis Stone replaced Lionel Barrymore, with Rooney and Parker (as Andy's older sister Marian) remaining as the Hardy children. Other series regulars included British actress Fay Holden as Ma, Sara Haden as Aunt Millie, and Ann Rutherford as Andy's sometime girlfriend. The cast clicked immediately, especially the chemistry between stern but understanding Judge Stone and his unpredictable son Andy. The popularity of Rooney's character became evident in the third film, 1938's *Judge Hardy's Children*, and the series shifted its focus to Andy. The plots typically centered on Andy's love life, and this afforded MGM the opportunity to build up rising stars like Judy Garland, Donna Reed, Lana Turner, Esther Williams and Kathryn Grayson. The series lost momentum during World War II, with its star in the army, and never fully recovered. Mickey was growing up, too — he was twenty-four when college student Andy encountered a pair of vivacious twins in *Andy Hardy's Blonde Trouble*. The series apparently ended in style with 1946's *Love Laughs at Andy Hardy*. However, twelve years later, *Andy Hardy Comes Home* tried to turn Rooney into an understanding father figure. This one-time revival didn't work, due to the absence of Lewis Stone (he died in 1953) and the growing popularity of television family comedies.

A Family Affair (1937)	*Andy Hardy Meets Debutante* (1940)
You're Only Young Once (1938)	*Andy Hardy's Private Secretary* (1941)
Judge Hardy's Children (1938)	*Life Begins for Andy Hardy* (1941)
Love Finds Andy Hardy (1938)	*Andy Hardy's Double Life* (1942)
Out West With the Hardys (1938)	*The Courtship of Andy Hardy* (1942)
The Hardys Ride High (1939)	*Andy Hardy's Blonde Trouble* (1944)
Judge Hardy and Son (1939)	*Love Laughs at Andy Hardy* (1946)
Andy Hardy Gets Spring Fever (1939)	*Andy Hardy Comes Home* (1958)

Having Babies Series

Title tells all in this TV-movie series about couples experiencing childbirth. The second film introduced Susan Sullivan as Dr. Julie Farr, who became the principal character in the third film. Sullivan subsequently starred in a 1978 TV series known both as *Having Babies* and *Julie Farr, M.D.* Less than three years after the show's demise, Ms. Sullivan showed up as Maggie on the long-running soap opera *Falcon Crest*. See also **Babies.**

Having Babies (aka *Giving Birth*) (1976 TVM)
Having Babies II (1977 TVM)
Having Babies III (1978 TVM)

Heaven

The cinema's view of heaven has tended to rely on soft focus and swirling mist. The most visually arresting conception along these lines is probably Michael Powell and Emeric Pressburger's *Stairway to Heaven* (1946), with its neverending staircase projecting itself from colorful Earth to black-and-white heaven. On the other hand, heaven looked very much like this world in *Made in Heaven*. In 1985's *The Heavenly Kid*, it was an ugly place filled with crowded trains and angels in frumpy clothes—no wonder the title character returned to Earth. *The Adding Machine* (1968) offered a bleak view of heaven with hellish overtones. It sent a clerk, who had murdered his boss after being replaced by a machine, to a heaven where he worked constantly with a similar machine. More humane heavenly activities have included celestial trials (*Stairway to Heaven*, *Defending Your Life* and *The Story of Mankind*), plans for armageddon (*The Horn Blows at Midnight*), and preparation of children about to be born (*The Blue Bird* and *Made in Heaven*). Some of the most prominent heavenly authority figures include Rex Ingram's "de Lawd" in *The Green Pastures* (1936), Lionel Barrymore's "Heavenly General" in *A Guy Named Joe* (1943), and Abraham Sofaer as the judge in *Stairway to Heaven*. Peter Cook as the Devil went to heaven to tell God he had won the battle for souls in the irreverent comedy *Bedazzled* (1967). Actress Diane Keaton edited movie clips and interviews into her offbeat documentary *Heaven* (1987). Purgatory was glimpsed in 1944's *Between Two Worlds*, 1985's *Impure Thoughts* and, depending on one's interpretation, 1991's *The Rapture*. See also **Angels.**

Liliom (1930)
The Green Pastures (1936)
The Blue Bird (1940)
Here Comes Mr. Jordan (1941)
A Guy Named Joe (1943)
Heaven Can Wait (1943)
The Horn Blows at Midnight (1945)
Stairway to Heaven (aka *A Matter of Life and Death*) (1946)
Down to Earth (1947)
The Bad Lord Byron (1948)
You Never Can Tell (1951)

Carousel (1956)
The Story of Mankind (1957)
The Flight That Disappeared (1961)
Bedazzled (1967)
The Adding Machine (1968)
Heaven Can Wait (1978)
Resurrection (1980)
The Heavenly Kid (1985)
Made in Heaven (1987)
Heaven (1987)
Defending Your Life (1990)
Bill and Ted's Bogus Journey (1991)

Heist/Caper Films

Jewelry stores, museums, banks, casinos and trains have been the most frequent targets of elaborately planned heists. Jules Dassin directed the two most famous jewel heist films: *Rififi* (1954) and *Topkapi* (1964). In *Rififi*, a violent ex-con recruits three specialists to stage the "perfect" heist of a jewelry store. The classic burglary sequence lasts almost thirty nail-biting minutes, with neither dialogue nor music. Dassin lightened the tone, but not the suspense, with *Topkapi*, in which the thieves set their sights on a jeweled dagger in an Istanbul museum. Although the heist sequence formed the film's centerpiece again, Peter Ustinov earned a Best Supporting Actor Oscar for his nervous performance. Though far less renowned, 1968's *Grand Slam* has its fans, who admire the $10 million diamond heist as well as Edward G. Robinson's charming performance as the professor who masterminds the intricate scheme. It's interesting to note that these three films, like many of their imitators, featured European settings and international casts. However, John Huston's seminal heist picture, 1950's *The Asphalt Jungle*, took place in the American Midwest and included a "perfect crime" that fell apart completely. It was remade in various guises as the Western *The Badlanders* (1958), *Cairo* (1963) and *Cool Breeze* (1972). Other jewel heist films include *Caper of the Golden Bulls* (1967), the two versions of *Happy New Year* (1973 and 1987), *11 Harrowhouse* (1974) and *The Hot Rock* (1972) with Robert Redford. Although jewelry thefts represent the upper-class side of the heist movie genre, carefully plotted bank robberies have generated a proportionate amount of suspense. The legendary 1950 Brinks robbery served as the basis for *Six Bridges to Cross* (1955), *Brinks: The Great Robbery* (1976) and *The Brinks Job* (1978). Meek bank clerk Alec Guinness hatched a plan to rob a truck of gold bullion in the 1951 British comedy *The Lavender Hill Mob*. In another British picture, 1960's *The League of Gentlemen*, ex-army colonel Jack Hawkins recruited some of his former soldiers to execute a bank heist. Along similar lines, Peter Falk and two Korean War buddies schemed to stage a complex bank robbery in 1971's *A Step Out of Line*. George C. Scott and cohorts didn't rob the bank—they just stole the entire building in 1974's *Bank Shot* (a sequel to *The Hot Rock* with Scott playing Redford's character!). Jim Hutton, Milton Berle and Joey Bishop broke into the U.S. mint in *Who's Minding the Mint* (1967), but their mission was to replace money that had been burned accidentally. And, as the title would indicate, the bank robbers in *The Doberman Gang* (1972) were strictly of the canine variety. In addition to banks, other attractive sources of large amounts of money have included casinos and trains. Casino robberies were staged in *Bob Le Flambeur* (1955), *5 Against the House* (1955), *Ocean's Eleven* (1960) and *They Came to Rob Las Vegas* (1968). The popularity of train robberies in films can be traced back to 1903's *The Great Train Robbery*. However, only a handful of these movies qualify as heist/caper films, such as *The Great British Train Robbery* (1967), *The Great Train Robbery* (1979) and *Buster* (1988). See also **Jewel Thieves; Trains.**

The Asphalt Jungle (1950)	*Ocean's Eleven* (1960)
The Lavender Hill Mob (1951)	*It Takes a Thief* (aka *The Challenge*)
The Great Diamond Robbery (1953)	(1960)
Rififi (1954)	*Rififi in Tokyo* (1963)
Six Bridges to Cross (1955)	*Cairo* (1963)
Bob Le Flambeur (1955)	*Topkapi* (1964)
5 Against the House (1955)	*Gambit* (1966)
The Badlanders (1958)	*The Great British Train Robbery*
The League of Gentlemen (1960)	(1967)

Who's Minding the Mint? (1967)
Caper of the Golden Bulls (aka *Carnival of Thieves*) (1967)
Grand Slam (1968)
Diamonds for Breakfast (1968)
They Came to Rob Las Vegas (1968)
The Silician Clan (1969)
The Italian Job (1969)
Perfect Friday (1970)
A Step Out of Line (1971 TVM)
Cool Breeze (1972)
The Doberman Gang (1972)
The Hot Rock (aka *How to Steal a Diamond in Four Uneasy Lessons*) (1972)
The Heist (1972 TVM)
Snow Job (1972)
Happy New Year (aka *The Happy New Year Caper*) (1973)
Bank Shot (1974)
The Great Ice Rip-Off (1974 TVM)

11 Harrowhouse (aka *Anything for Love; Fast Fortune*) (1974)
Thunderbolt and Lightfoot (1974)
Live a Little, Steal a Lot (aka *Murph the Surf; You Can't Steal Love*) (1975)
Diamonds (1975)
Target Risk (1975 TVM)
Brinks: The Great Robbery (1976 TVM)
The Brinks Job (1978)
The Great Train Robbery (aka *The First Great Train Robbery*) (1979)
The Great Bank Hoax (1979)
Happy New Year (1987)
Bellman and True (1988)
Buster (1988)
Why Me? (1990)
Sneakers (1992)
The Diamond Fleece (1992 TVM)
The Real McCoy (1993)

Helicopters

The cinema's love affair with airplanes (q.v.) has never extended to helicopters. One explanation might be that the airplane has a stronger historical background (having played a vital role in both World Wars). Yet, while the helicopter's heritage may be lacking, its airborne maneuverability would seem to make it an ideal vehicle for visually exciting chase thrillers. Television filmmakers have exploited that genre with a quartet of fast-paced features: *Birds of Prey* (1972), *Sky Heist* (1975), *Deadly Encounter* (1982) and *The Chase* (1991). The helicopter hit the big time, in terms of budget, with the 1983 theatrical release *Blue Thunder*. Yet, despite a strong cast headed by Roy Scheider and Malcolm McDowell, this cartoonish tale of a superhelicopter never generated the thrills of its small-screen counterparts (ironically, it later spawned a TV series). James Bond took to the air in helicopters built-for-one in *You Only Live Twice* (1967) and *For Your Eyes Only* (1981). Woody Allen invented a self-powered, single-seat helicopter in *A Midsummer Night's Sex Comedy* (1982), while Bruce Spence piloted another single-seater through a post-apocalyptic desert in 1981's *The Road Warrior* (aka *Mad Max 2*). See also **Airplanes**.

Battle Taxi (1955)
Flight From Ashiya (1964)
You Only Live Twice (1967)
Birds of Prey (1972 TVM)
Sky Heist (1975 TVM)
For Your Eyes Only (1981)
The Road Warrior (aka *Mad Max 2*) (1981)

Deadly Encounter (1982 TVM)
A Midsummer Night's Sex Comedy (1982)
Blue Thunder (1983)
Defense Play (1988)
Fire Birds (1990)
The Chase (1991 TVM)
Cliffhanger (1993)

Hell

No one wants to go to hell—and filmmakers have been no exception. Director Harry Lachman offered the most elaborate view, a striking ten-minute sequence of writhing souls in 1935's *Dante's Inferno*. Italian horror specialist Mario Bava created an atmospheric Hades for 1961's *Hercules in the Haunted World* (the producers apparently decided against *Hercules in Hell*). Christopher Lee, as one of Pluto's disciples, kept the seas of lava flowing and the naked girls chained. Surprisingly, the 1972 TV-movie *Haunts of the Very Rich* offered an interesting variation wherein seven people trapped on a paradise island come to realize they are in hell. See also **The Devil**.

Dante's Inferno (1935)	*Invitation to Hell* (1984 TVM)
Heaven Can Wait (1943)	*The Gate* (1987)
Angel on My Shoulder (1946)	*Hellbound: Hellraiser II* (1988)
Huis Clos (1954)	*Bill and Ted's Bogus Journey* (1991)
Hercules in the Haunted World (1961)	*Highway to Hell* (1992)
Haunts of the Very Rich (1972 TVM)	*Stay Tuned* (1992)
The Sentinel (1977)	

Hellraiser

Clive Barker's novella "The Hellbound Heart" provided the basis for 1987's *Hellraiser*, a grisly horror tale described by its author as a perverse love story. In the opening reel, Frank Cotton (Sean Chapman) unlocks the secret to a mysterious, Rubik Cube-like puzzle box called the Lamont Configuration. With its solution revealed, the box summons forth the Cenobites, a race of vile-looking, hellish creatures who torture Frank to death. However, the dead Frank, now hideously disfigured, shows up at his brother Larry's house. He convinces his former mistress, Larry's wife Julia (Clare Higgins), to obtain human flesh for his dinner—so that he can regain his human form. This blatant exercise in visual horror was distinguished by a subtle thematic twist: A woman—not a man—lures and mutilates the victims (however, unlike her typical male counterparts, Julia kills out of love). The two sequels dispensed with such thematic concerns and raised the gore quotient to appeal to hard-core horror aficionados. *Variety* called 1988's *Hellbound: Hellraiser II* a "maggotty carnival of mayhem, mutation, and dismemberment." The plot followed Larry's daughter Kristy (Ashley Laurence) as she journeyed to hell to save her father from the Cenobites and Leviathan, Lord of Hell's Labyrinth. Her clever, albeit grisly, escape gave new meaning to the phrase "putting on another face." As with the first two films, *Hellraiser III* (1992) also featured a female protagonist, a TV news reporter named Jody (Terry Farrell). In her dreams, Jody encounters the ghost of a British military officer whose experiments first unleashed the Cenobites. Concurrently, a heinous nightclub owner buys a sculpture that introduces him to Pinhead, the leader of the Cenobites. Predictably, the finale pitted Jody against Pinhead. In terms of originality, the series seems to have run its course—although that has never deterred other long-running horror series such as *Friday the 13th, The Howling* and *Nightmare on Elm Street* (qq.v.).

Hellraiser (1987)
Hellbound: Hellraiser II (1988)
Hellraiser III: Hell on Earth (1992)

Helm, Matt

In Donald Hamilton's books, secret agent Matt Helm worked as a freelance writer/photographer and drove an old pickup truck. In the movies, though, Dean Martin played him as a third-rate James Bond. Martin fumbled his way through four Helm pictures, all made between 1966-69 and costarring Stella Stevens, Ann-Margaret, Senta Berger and Elke Sommer. Tony Franciosa reprised the role for the 1975 TV-movie *Matt Helm* and a short-lived series. Franciosa's Helm was a private eye, though, instead of a secret agent.

The Silencers (1966)	*The Wrecking Crew* (1969)
Murderer's Row (1967)	*Matt Helm* (1975 TVM)
The Ambushers (1968)	

Henry Series

Character actor Raymond Walburn played Henry Latham, a rascally cheapskate with good intentions, in this minor Monogram series. The plots frequently hinged on Henry's outraged reactions to rising prices. In *Father Makes Good*, he bought a cow to avoid a milk tax. He refused to pay the butcher and took up hunting in *Father's Wild Game*. In other series entries, Henry bumbled routine jobs (e.g., accidentally burning up a toll bridge) but somehow managed to straighten things out in the end. Walter Catlett was Henry's pal Mayor Colton.

Henry the Rainmaker (1949)	*Father's Wild Game* (1951)
Leave It to Henry (1949)	*Father Takes the Air* (1951)
Father Makes Good (1950)	

Herbie, the Love Bug

Disney's longest-running film series starred a lovable Volkswagen Beetle with a mind of its own. *The Love Bug* and *Herbie Rides Again* did brisk business, but the later Herbie movies were released when Disney Productions was struggling to recapture its youthful audience. Dean Jones played Herbie's human sidekick in the first and third films and revived his role for the hour-long (!) CBS television series *Herbie, the Love Bug*. It lasted just one month before being cancelled.

The Love Bug (1969)	*Herbie Goes to Monte Carlo* (1977)
Herbie Rides Again (1974)	*Herbie Goes Bananas* (1980)

Hercules

Superdistributor Joseph E. Levine transformed *Hercules*, a modest Italian sword-and-sandal epic, into one of the biggest international hits of 1957. Steve Reeves, a former Mr. World and Mr. Universe, starred as the mythical muscle man who undertakes a series of perilous quests to win the hand of a beautiful princess (the worthy Sylva Koscina). Reeves repeated the role in the sequel *Hercules Unchained*, but bowed out after that. Since then, a succession of muscular hunks have essayed the role: Reg Park, Mark Forest, Alan Steel (real name Sergio Ciani), Gordon Scott, Arnold Schwarzenegger, and most recently Lou (*Incredible Hulk*) Ferrigno. Even muscle builder Mickey Hargitay played Herc in *The Loves of Hercules* — with wife Jayne Mansfield in support in a double role! None of these cheap programmers were particularly distinguished, although horror director Mario Bava's *Hercules in the Haunted World* presented an atmospheric view of hell.

Hercules clones proliferated, too, especially during the mid-1960s. Maciste (q.v.) and Goliath both had their own series, though it was often difficult to tell who was who. *Maciste e la Regina di Samar* wound up as *Hercules Against the Moonmen* when shown on American TV. The 1974 United Artists release *Hercules vs. Kung Fu* (aka *Mr. Hercules Against Karate*) had nothing to do with Hercules, being just another Kung Fu school "chop socky" picture. See also **Maciste**.

> *Hercules* (aka *The Labors of Hercules*; *Le Fatiche di Ercole*) (1957) (Steve Reeves)
> *Hercules Unchained* (aka *Ercole e la Regina di Lidia*) (1959) (Reeves)
> *The Loves of Hercules* (aka *Hercules and the Hydra*) (1960) (Mickey Hargitay)
> *Ulysses Against Hercules* (aka *Hercules vs. Ulysses*; *Ulysses Against the Son of Hercules*; *Ulisse contro Ercole*) (1961) (Georges Marchal)
> *The Fury of Hercules* (aka *La Furia di Ercole*) (1961) (Brad Harris)
> *Hercules in the Vale of Woe* (aka *Hercules Against Maciste in the Vale of Woe*; *Maciste Against Hercules in the Vale of Woe*; *Maciste Contro Ercole Nella Valle Dei Guai*) (1962) (Kirk Morris)
> *The Three Stooges Meet Hercules* (1962) (Samson Burke)
> *Hercules and the Captive Women* (aka *Hercules and the Haunted Women*; *Ercole alla Conquista della Atlantide*) (1963) (Reg Park)
> *Hercules, the Invincible* (aka *Ercole l'Invincibile*) (1963) (Dan Vadis)
> *Jason and the Argonauts* (1963) (Nigel Green)
> *Conquest of Mycene* (aka *Hercules Attacks*; *Hercules vs. Moloch*; *Ercole contro Moloch*) (1963) (Gordon Scott)
> *Hercules vs. the Giant Warriors* (aka *Triumph of Hercules*, *Hercules and the Ten Avengers*; *Il Trionfo di Ercole*) (1964) (Vadis)
> *Hercules Against Rome* (aka *Ercole contro Roma*) (1964) (Alan Steel)
> *Samson and the Mighty Challenge* (aka *Hercules, Maciste, Samson, and Ursus vs. the Universe*; *Ercole, Sansone, Maciste, Ursus gli Invincili*) (1964) (Steel)
> *Hercules Against the Sons of the Sun* (*Ercole contro i Figli del Sole*) (1964) (Mark Forest)
> *Hercules and the Tyrants of Babylon* (aka *Ercole contro i Tiranni di Babilonia*) (1964) (Rock Stevens)
> *Hercules in the Haunted World* (aka *Hercules vs. the Vampires*; *Hercules at the Center of the Earth*; *Ercole al Centro Delle Terra*) (1964) (Park)
> *Hercules of the Desert* (aka *La Valle dell'Eco Tonante*) (1964) (Morris)
> *Hercules, Samson, and Ulysses* (aka *Ercole Sfida Sansone*) (1965) (Morris)
> *Hercules, Prisoner of Evil* (aka *Terror of the Kirghiz*) (1967) (Park)
> *Hercules in New York* (aka *Hercules: The Movie*; *Hercules Goes Bananas*) (1970) (Arnold Schwarzenegger)
> *Hercules* (1983) (Lou Ferrigno)
> *Hercules II* (aka *The Adventures of Hercules*) (1985) (Ferrigno)

Hickok, Wild Bill, Series

Frontier marshal James Butler Hickok, aka Wild Bill, has been portrayed by many actors, but only one was popular enough to borrow his nickname permanently. Gordon Elliott became Wild Bill Elliott after trailblazing his way to fame in Columbia's 1938 serial *The Great Adventures of Wild Bill Hickok*. Two years later, Columbia resurrected Wild Bill as Wild Bill and produced an eight-film Hickok series. The series came to an end when Elliott signed with Republic in 1943 and went on to achieve his greatest success as Red Ryder (q.v.).

Prairie Schooner (aka *Through the Storm*) (1940)
Beyond the Sacramento (aka *The Power of Justice*) (1941)
The Wildcats of Tucson (aka *Promise Unfulfilled*) (1941)
Across the Sierras (aka *Welcome Stranger*) (1941)
North From the Lone Star (1941)
Hands Across the Rockies (1941)
Lone Star Vigilantes (aka *The Devil's Price*) (1942)
Bullets for Bandits (1942)

The Higgins Family

With MGM's Hardy Family (q.v.) and Twentieth Century-Fox's Jones Family (q.v.) riding high in the late 1930s, it was inevitable that low-budget Republic Pictures would initiate its own family affair. Thus, the Higgins Family series was born. For the first seven films, it was indeed a family affair with James, Lucille, and son Russell Gleason portraying Joe, Lillian and Sidney Higgins. The early entries centered on conflicts between Joe and Lillian. They wound up in divorce court in *The Higgins Family*, but a happy ending prevailed. They were at odds again in *Should Husbands Work?* with Lillian taking over Joe's job and leaving him the housework. The Gleasons, along with Harry Davenport as Grandpa, bowed out of the series after 1940's *Grandpa Goes to Town*. Roscoe Karns (Joe), Ruth Donnelly (Lil), George Ernest (Sidney) and Spencer Charters (Grandpa) took over the roles for the last two films. Interestingly, George Ernest and Russell Gleason both appeared in the Jones Family series. Ernest played young Roger Jones, while Gleason was Bonnie Jones's boyfriend and eventual husband Herbert Thompson. Russell Gleason's acting career ended suddenly when he fell from a hotel window in 1945. He was thirty-seven.

The Higgins Family (1938)   *Earl of Puddlestone* (1940)
The Covered Trailer (1939)   *Grandpa Goes to Town* (1940)
Money to Burn (1939)   *Meet the Missus* (1940)
My Wife's Relations (1939)   *Petticoat Politics* (1941)
Should Husbands Work? (1939)

The High Schoolers

The forerunner of AIP's *Beach Party* movies (q.v.), this Monogram series mixed energetic teens with popular music. Freddie Stewart and June Preisser played the main characters, bland high school lovers Freddie Trimball and Dodie Rogers. However, the series is best remembered for featuring supporting performers that TV would turn into familiar faces. Fellow-student Noel Neill went on to become Lois Lane in the hit *Superman* TV series. College professor Frank Cady became Sam Drucker on *Green Acres*. And Alan Hale, Jr., the Marine-turned-student in 1947's *Sarge Goes to College*, wound up spending several years as the Skipper on *Gilligan's Island*. If the series' movies featured dull, stereotypical plots (a big football game, class elections, etc.), the music made up for it. In addition to boasting offbeat tunes such as "Jungle Rhumba" and "Sherwood's Forest," the High

Schoolers captured captivating performances by bands like the Gene Krupa Orchestra.

High School Hero (1946)	*Vacation Days* (1947)
Junior Prom (1946)	*Campus Sleuth* (1948)
Sarge Goes to College (1947)	*Smart Politics* (1948)

Hitchhiking

Hitchhiking has come into play in dozens of "road" movies, such as 1985's *The Sure Thing* and, most memorably, 1934's *It Happened One Night*. The latter featured the now-classic scene in which Clark Gable, after trying futilely to attract a ride via the traditional thumb method, receives instruction from Claudette Colbert on how to use one's legs to better effect. The dangers of picking up hitchhikers have been explored in subtle thrillers like *Hitchhike!* and gory horror pictures like *The Hitcher*. The horror anthology *Creepshow 2* spawned the most memorable hitchhiking line, with a walking corpse following Lois Chiles around and moaning repeatedly: "Thanks for the ride, lady!" *Thumb Tripping* (1972) boasts the most hitchhiking scenes per movie with its plot about two hippies (Michael Burns and Meg Foster) hitching across the country. Many movies have revolved around characters picked up from the roadside, including *Detour* (1945), *Three Into Two Won't Go* (1969), and *Ginger in the Morning* (1973).

It Happened One Night (1934)	*Diary of a Hitchhiker* (1979 TVM)
The Devil Thumbs a Ride (1947)	*Road Games* (1981)
The Hitch-Hiker (1953)	*Vagabond* (1985)
Knife in the Water (1962)	*The Sure Thing* (1985)
Nightmare in the Sun (1964)	*The Hitcher* (1986)
Thumb Tripping (1972)	*Creepshow 2* (1987)
Hitchhike! (1974 TVM)	*Alligator Eyes* (1990)
Nightmare in Badham County (aka	*Dust Devil: The Final Cut* (1993)
Nightmare) (1976 TVM)	

Hitler

The role of Adolf Hitler has frustrated more than one good actor. Alec Guinness gave one of his lesser performances as the Nazi dictator in *Hitler: The Last Ten Days* (1973). Anthony Hopkins overplayed the part (but nevertheless won an Emmy) in the 1981 TV-movie *The Bunker*. Even reliable Richard Basehart could not overcome his basic miscasting in the low-key 1962 biography *Hitler*. Derek Jacobi probably gave the best star turn as Hitler in the epic two-part TV-movie *Inside the Third Reich* (1982). In the 1940s, character actor Robert Watson specialized in playing Hitler. In addition to starring in 1944's *The Hitler Gang*, he did cameos as Hitler in *The Devil With Hitler* (1942), *The Miracle of Morgan's Creek* (1944), *The Story of Mankind* (1957) and many others. Plots to assassinate Hitler provided the premise for *Man Hunt* (1941), its remake *Rogue Male* (1976), *Hitler: Dead or Alive* (1943), *The Strange Death of Adolf Hitler* (1943), *The Plot to Assassinate Hitler* (1955), the fact-based *Jackboot Mutiny* (1955), and *The Plot to Kill Hitler* (1990). Luther Adler played an impersonator who *did* kill Hitler and take his place in 1951's fanciful *The Magic Face*. Veronica Lake played a mad scientist who dumps a swarm of maggots on Hitler's face in the obscure gorefest *Flesh Feast*

(1970). Another deranged scientist managed to keep Hitler's head alive atop a table in 1963's dreadful *They Saved Hitler's Brain*. Ira Levin fashioned an ingenious plot about Hitler cloning in 1978's *The Boys From Brazil*. The same year's *The Lucifer Complex* found Robert Vaughn investigating another Hitler cloning plot. Charlie Chaplin treated Hitler comically in his topical farce *The Great Dictator* (1940). Comedian Gilbert Gottfried cameoed as Hitler in 1992's *Highway to Hell*. Indiana Jones got Hitler's autograph in *Indiana Jones and the Last Crusade* (1989), while Woody Allen's *Zelig* (1983) turned up in newsreel footage with the German dictator. Mel Brooks's *The Producers* (1968) featured a stage musical called "Springtime for Hitler."

The Great Dictator (1940)
Man Hunt (1941)
To Be or Not to Be (1942)
Hitler: Dead or Alive (1943)
The Strange Death of Adolf Hitler (1943)
The Hitler Gang (1944)
The Magic Face (1951)
Canaris Master Spy (1954)
The Plot to Assassinate Hitler (1955)
Jackboot Mutiny (1955)
The Last Ten Days (aka The Last Ten Days of Adolf Hitler) (1956)
Hitler (1962)
The Black Fox (1962)
They Saved Hitler's Brain (aka Madmen of Mandoras) (1963)
The Producers (1968)
Flesh Feast (1970)
Adolf Hitler: My Part in His Downfall (1972)
Hitler: The Last Ten Days (1973)

Undercovers Hero (aka Soft Beds, Hard Battles) (1973)
Rogue Male (1976 TVM)
The Boys From Brazil (1978)
The Lucifer Complex (1978)
Our Hitler, a Film From Germany (1980)
The Bunker (1981 TVM)
Inside the Third Reich (1982 TVM)
To Be or Not to Be (1983)
Zelig (1983)
Hitler's S.S.: Portrait in Evil (1985 TVM)
Dirty Dozen: The Next Mission (1985 TVM)
Indiana Jones and the Last Crusade (1989)
Elves (1989)
The Plot to Kill Hitler (1990 TVM)
Hitler's Daughter (1990 TVM)
Highway to Hell (1992)

Hockey

This game's reputation for violence would seem to make it ideal subject matter for a movie. But even during the bloody 1970s, when *The Longest Yard* (1974) and *Rollerball* (1975) glorified sports violence, hockey made little impact. Its big shot at stardom came with 1977's *Slap Shot*, which cast Paul Newman as the desperate coach of a bush-league hockey team. The film fared well at the box office, but its returns failed to inspire even a B-movie rip-off. ABC capitalized on the game's temporary popularity following the USA team's stunning upset of the Russians in the 1980 Olympics by producing a movie version titled *Miracle on Ice*. Five years later, Michael Keaton and Rob Lowe took to the ice in *Touch and Go* and *Youngblood*, respectively. Keaton's film sat on the shelf for over a year and then barely got released. Lowe's picture fizzled as well, signaling either a lack of public interest in hockey or the game's inability to attract serious filmmakers. Hockey also played a minor role in *Love Story*; Oliver (Ryan O'Neal) had a passion for playing it. Mel Gibson chased some thugs across the ice during a Los Angeles Kings hockey game in 1992's *Lethal Weapon 3*. *Friday the 13th*'s popular killer Jason made hockey masks fashionable for psychopaths. See also **Ice Skating.**

King of Hockey (1936)	*Miracle on Ice* (1981 TVM)
It's a Pleasure (1945)	*Hockey Night* (1984)
Love Story (1970)	*Generation* (1985 TVM)
Paperback Hero (1973)	*Touch and Go* (1986)
Slap Shot (1977)	*Youngblood* (1986)
The Deadliest Season (1977 TVM)	*The Cutting Edge* (1992)
The Boy Who Drank Too Much (1980 TVM)	*Lethal Weapon 3* (1992)
	The Mighty Ducks (1992)

Holmes, Sherlock

Literature's most renowned detective has certainly been one of the screen's busiest. Only Charlie Chan rivals him in number of film appearances in the sound era, and even at that, the Baker Street sleuth has been played by more actors than any detective. The first recorded screen appearance of Arthur Conan Doyle's fictional mastermind was in a 1903 silent short (very short, about a minute) called *Sherlock Holmes Baffled*. The Conan Doyle mysteries made popular silent film subjects, but a definitive Holmes interpretation did not emerge until William Gillette made *Sherlock Holmes* in 1916. The screenplay was based on Gillette's own stage play, originally performed in 1899. Ellie Norwood was the most prolific silent Holmes, appearing in seven films between 1921 and 1923. British screen veteran Clive Brook introduced Holmes to the "talkies" in 1929's *The Return of Sherlock Holmes*, an updated mystery about a retired Holmes lured into detecting again by Watson's grown daughter(!). Four other actors played Conan Doyle's sleuth from 1931-37, with Arthur Wontner garnering the most praise. Already in his mid-fifties, Wontner played an older Holmes, ably assisted by Ian Fleming (not the author) as Dr. Watson in all but one case (*The Sign of Four* with Ian Hunter). It's interesting to note that the five Wontner films were based on Conan Doyle works. Despite his success, Wontner's Holmes interpretation was eclipsed in 1939, when in a stroke of casting genius, Basil Rathbone was signed to play Holmes in Twentieth Century-Fox's lavish *The Hound of the Baskervilles*. Rathbone's crisp, energetic performance was delightfully balanced by Nigel Bruce's bumbling but endearing Watson (who in no way resembled Conan Doyle's intelligent physician/companion). *The Hound* was a rousing success, and Fox quickly followed it with *The Adventures of Sherlock Holmes*, pitting Holmes against archvillain Professor Moriarty (superbly played by the menacing George Zucco). It rates as the finest of all Holmes films. Unfortunately, Fox let the series die, and when Rathbone and Bruce reappeared as Holmes and Watson, it was for budget-minded Universal. Consisting of twelve movies shot between 1942 and 1946, the Universal series boasted updated story lines and shorter running times. Holmes battled Nazis, spies and famous murderers with sinister names like The Creeper. The series peaked with *The Scarlet Claw*, an eerie, atmospheric puzzler featuring a marsh phantom and a murderous master of disguises. Roy William Neill produced and directed most of the entries. Series regulars included Dennis Hoey as a frustrated

Inspector Lestrade and Mary Gordon as the kindly housekeeper Mrs. Hudson. When Rathbone put his violin case away for good in 1946, other actors were hesitant to take up the role. Then in 1959, Hammer Films—England's foremost horror film factory—starred Peter Cushing in a colorful adaptation of *The Hound of the Baskervilles*. It was more violent than its predecessors but handsomely mounted and boasting an excellent Watson in Andre Morell. Hammer could not secure rights for future films, although Cushing went on to play Holmes again on British television. With the Rathbone barrier broken, Holmes became a popular screen fixture again. John Neville played a dashing Holmes who encountered Jack the Ripper in *A Study in Terror* (1965), a film produced in association with Conan Doyle's son Adrian. Robert Stephens offered a complex, offbeat portrait in Billy Wilder's sly satire *The Private Life of Sherlock Holmes* (1970). Jack the Ripper reappeared to match wits with Christopher Plummer's sleuth in *Murder by Decree* (1979). The 1988 *Without a Clue* proposed the novel twist that Watson (Ben Kingsley) was the brains behind the duo and that Holmes was just an actor hired to play a part. On television, many performers have essayed the role, including Jeremy Brett, whose long-running series still appears on PBS's *Mystery!*

Rathbone/Bruce

The Hound of the Baskervilles (1939)
The Adventures of Sherlock Holmes (1939)
Sherlock Holmes and the Voice of Terror (1942)
Sherlock Holmes and the Secret Weapon (1942)
Sherlock Holmes in Washington (1943)
Sherlock Holmes Faces Death (1943)
Crazy House (1943) (cameo appearance)
The Scarlet Claw (1944)
Sherlock Holmes and the Spider Woman (aka *Spider Woman*) (1944)
The House of Fear (1945)
The Woman in Green (1945)
Pursuit to Algiers (1945)
Terror by Night (1946)
Dressed to Kill (aka *Sherlock Holmes and the Secret Code*) (1946)

Others

The Return of Sherlock Holmes (1929) (Clive Brook)
Paramount on Parade (1930) (Brook appears in a skit)
Sherlock Holmes' Fatal Hour (aka *The Sleeping Cardinal*) (1931) (Arthur
    Wontner)
The Speckled Band (1931) (Raymond Massey)
The Hound of the Baskervilles (1931) (Robert Rendel)
The Missing Rembrandt (1932) (Wontner)
The Sign of Four (1932) (Wontner)
Sherlock Holmes (1932) (Brook)
A Study in Scarlet (1933) (Reginald Owen)
The Triumph of Sherlock Holmes (1935) (Wontner)
Silver Blaze (1937) (Wontner)
The Hound of the Baskervilles (1959) (Peter Cushing)

Sherlock Holmes and the Deadly Necklace (1962) (Christopher Lee)
A Study in Terror (1965) (John Neville)
The Private Life of Sherlock Holmes (1970) (Robert Stephens)
The Hound of the Baskervilles (1972 TVM) (Stewart Granger)
The Adventures of Sherlock Holmes' Smarter Brother (1975) (Douglas Wilmer,
   Gene Wilder as the brother)
Sherlock Holmes in New York (1976 TVM) (Roger Moore)
The Seven-Per-Cent Solution (1976) (Nicol Williamson)
Murder by Decree (1979) (Christopher Plummer)
The Sign of Four (1983) (Ian Richardson)
The Hound of the Baskervilles (1983) (Ian Richardson)
Sherlock Holmes and the Masks of Death (aka *The Masks of Death*) (1984 TVM)
   (Peter Cushing)
Young Sherlock Holmes (aka *Sherlock Holmes and the Pyramid of Fear)* (1985)
   (Nicholas Rowe)
The Great Mouse Detective (aka *The Adventures of the Great Mouse Detective*)
   (1986)
The Return of Sherlock Holmes (1987 TVM) (Michael Pennington)
Without a Clue (1988) (Michael Caine as Reginald Kincaid as Holmes)
Hands of a Murderer (aka *Sherlock Holmes and the Prince of Crime*) (1990 TVM)
   (Edward Woodward)
The Crucifer of Blood (1991 TVM) (Charlton Heston)
Sherlock Holmes: Incident at Victoria Falls (1991 TVM) (Christopher Lee)
Sherlock Holmes and the Leading Lady (1991 TVM) (Lee)
Sherlock Holmes in Caracas (1992) (Jean Manuel Montesinos)
1994 Baker Street: Sherlock Holmes Returns (1993 TVM) (Anthony Higgins)
(Note: George C. Scott portrayed a man who believed himself to be Sherlock
Holmes in 1971's *They Might Be Giants*. His psychiatrist, played by Joanne Wood-
ward, was naturally named Dr. Watson. The plot was reworked in a 1976 TV
movie *The Return of the World's Greatest Detective*).

Hood, Robin

Although five silent films about Robin Hood appeared between 1909 and 1913, this
legendary outlaw did not become a hot movie property until Douglas Fairbanks
portrayed him in 1922. Since then, Robin Hood has never gone a decade without
being featured in at least one movie. Errol Flynn was the definitive Robin in the
1938 classic *The Adventures of Robin Hood*. Apparently to avoid comparison with
Flynn, no other major actor essayed the role until Richard Todd in Disney's 1952
The Story of Robin Hood. In the meantime, John Derek, Cornel Wilde and June
Laverick played the outlaw's offspring in, respectively, *Rogues of Sherwood Forest*,
Bandits of Sherwood Forest and *Son of Robin Hood* (actually daughter). Richard
Greene leapt from his successful 1955-58 *Adventures of Robin Hood* TV series
into a big-screen version, 1960's *The Sword of Sherwood Forest*. A few years later,
Disney offered an animated *Robin Hood*, depicting the characters as animals
(Robin was a fox). Sean Connery appeared as an older, wearier outlaw opposite
Audrey Hepburn's Maid Marian in the "realist" version *Robin and Marian*. *Robin
Hood: Prince of Thieves* (1991) was part adventure, part camp—but a miscast

Kevin Costner still attracted enough fans to make it a big hit. Frank Sinatra and Bing Crosby headed an all-star cast in a musical gangster variation called *Robin and the Seven Hoods* (1964). Robin has been parodied in *Time Bandits* (1981), *The Zany Adventures of Robin Hood* (1984) and in Mel Brooks's *Robin Hood: Men in Tights* (1993). The latter film was inspired by Brooks's short-lived 1975 TV series *When Things Were Rotten*.

Robin Hood (1922)	*A Challenge for Robin Hood* (1968)
The Adventures of Robin Hood (1938)	*Robin Hood* (1973)
Bandits of Sherwood Forest (1946)	*Robin and Marian* (1976)
The Prince of Thieves (1948)	*Time Bandits* (1981)
Rogues of Sherwood Forest (1950)	*The Zany Adventures of Robin Hood* (1984 TVM)
Tales of Robin Hood (1951)	
The Story of Robin Hood (1952)	*Robin Hood and the Sorcerer* (1984 TVM)
Ivanhoe (1952)	
Men of Sherwood Forest (1954)	*Robin Hood: Prince of Thieves* (1991)
Son of Robin Hood (1959)	*Robin Hood* (1991 TVM)
The Sword of Sherwood Forest (1960)	*Robin Hood: Men in Tights* (1993)

Hornleigh, Inspector

Gordon Harker and Alastair Sim played Inspector Hornleigh and Sergeant Bingham in a trio of lively British comedy-mysteries produced from 1938-40. Hans Priwin originally created the detectives for his "Monday Night at Eight" radio series. Although rarely shown on television today, the Hornleigh mysteries hold up well, mixing humor and thrills with an almost Hitchcockian flair. That should come as no surprise since two of the three films were cowritten by Frank Launder, who penned the screenplay to Hitch's *The Lady Vanishes* (1938) with Sidney Gilliat (who also worked on *Inspector Hornleigh on Holiday*). Like *The Lady Vanishes*, Launder's *Inspector Hornleigh Goes to It* (1940) climaxes on a train (q.v.). After three stints as Hornleigh's sidekick, Alastair Sim graduated to chief detective roles in the British classics *Green for Danger* (1946), cowritten and directed by Gilliat, and *An Inspector Calls* (1954).

Inspector Hornleigh (1938)	*Inspector Hornleigh Goes to It* (aka *Mail Train*) (1940)
Inspector Hornleigh on Holiday (1939)	

Horse Racing/Equitation

Mickey Rooney is the undisputed champ of horse-racing sagas with a track career spanning half a century. He played the son of a disgraced jockey in *Down the Stretch* (1936), Wallace Beery's jockey protegé in *Stablemates* (1938), a young jockey involved with crooks (and teamed with Judy Garland for the first time) in *Thoroughbreds Don't Cry* (1937), Elizabeth Taylor's young mentor in *National Velvet* (1944), the trainer of *The Black Stallion* (1979), and a horse-owner in *Lightning, the White Stallion* (1986). Surprisingly, Rooney never made a race track comedy. However, horse-racing hijinks seem to be a requirement for most comedians. The Marx Brothers produced the most memorable, 1937's *A Day at the Races*, which featured Groucho at his best as horse doctor Hugo Z. Hackenbush. Abbott and Costello raced a steed named Tea Biscuit in *It Ain't Hay* (1943). It was called *Money for Jam* in Great Britain, which one shouldn't confuse with

Money From Home (1953), another stateside horse race comedy with Dean Martin and Jerry Lewis. Hope and Crosby never raced horses in the *Road* movies, but Bob gambled on them in *Sorrowful Jones* (1949) and *The Lemon Drop Kid* (1951), while Bing backed one in Frank Capra's *Riding High* (1950). Donald O'Connor and his talking mule sidekick Francis could have made a fortune in *Francis Goes to the Races* (1951), since the race horses told Francis that they always determined the winner before the race even began. A little boy's ability to predict horse race results with amazing accuracy ended in tragedy in *The Rocking Horse Winner*, a 1949 adaptation of the D.H. Lawrence short story. Filmmakers have deemed few real-life horse-racing champions worthy of film biographies. The exceptions include a pair of exceptional horses in *The Story of Seabiscuit* (1949), *The Great Dan Patch* (1949) and *Phar Lap* (1983), the latter being Australia's most famous racing champ. Although most horse races are of the thoroughbred variety, a handful of films have explored other horse racing events: Elizabeth Taylor entered "The Pie" in the Grand National Steeplechase in *National Velvet*; father and daughter Charles Coburn and Peggy Cummins raced trotting horses in *The Green Grass of Wyoming* (1948); Tatum O'Neal and Melissa Gilbert set their sights on equestrian championships in, respectively, *International Velvet* (1978) and *Sylvester* (1985); and Gene Hackman and James Coburn were two of the riders in the grueling cross-country horse race in *Bite the Bullet* (1975). Other memorable horse-racing sequences appear in *My Fair Lady* (1964) and *Mary Poppins* (1964) in which carousel horses come to life. Film critics have pondered for years whether the title of *Million Dollar Legs* (1939) referred to the film's racehorse or its star Betty Grable.

Broadway Bill (aka *Strictly Confidential*) (1934)

Little Miss Marker (aka *The Girl in Pawn*) (1934)

Down the Stretch (1936)

Three Men on a Horse (1936)

Charlie Chan at the Race Track (1936)

A Day at the Races (1937)

Thoroughbreds Don't Cry (1937)

Racing Lady (1937)

Saratoga (1937)

Stablemates (1938)

Come on George (1939)

Million Dollar Legs (1939)

The Lady's From Kentucky (1939)

It Ain't Hay (aka *Money for Jam*) (1943)

National Velvet (1944)

Home in Indiana (1944)

The Great Mike (1944)

She Went to the Races (1945)

My Brother Talks to Horses (1946)

The Homestretch (1947)

Black Gold (1947)

The Green Grass of Wyoming (1948)

The Story of Seabiscuit (aka *Pride of Kentucky*) (1949)

The Great Dan Patch (1949)

Sorrowful Jones (1949)

Under My Skin (1949)

The Rocking Horse Winner (1949)

Boy From Indiana (1950)

The Pride of Maryland (1950)

Blue Grass of Kentucky (1950)

Riding High (1950)

Francis Goes to the Races (1951)

Blue Blood (1951)

The Galloping Major (1951)

The Lemon Drop Kid (1951)

The Rainbow Jacket (1951)

Boots Malone (1952)

Four Against Fate (aka *Derby Day*) (1952)

A Girl in Every Port (1952)

Money From Home (1953)

Fast Company (1953)

Pride of the Blue Grass (1954)	*Run for the Roses* (aka *Thoroughbred*)
The Fighting Chance (1955)	(1978)
Dry Rot (1956)	*The Black Stallion* (1979)
Glory (1956)	*My Old Man* (1979 TVM)
Photo Finish (1957)	*Little Miss Marker* (1980)
Just My Luck (1957)	*On the Right Track* (1981)
The Sad Horse (1959)	*Phar Lap* (1983)
Mary Poppins (1964)	*Sylvester* (1985)
My Fair Lady (1964)	*The Longshot* (1986)
Bite the Bullet (1975)	*Lightning, the White Stallion* (1986)
International Velvet (1978)	*Hot to Trot* (1988)
Casey's Shadow (1978)	*Let It Ride* (1989)

Horses

The horse has been a favorite film subject since Eadweard Muybridge used photography to study a horse in motion (allegedly to settle a $5000 bet) in 1872. Early horse roles were principally supporting ones, though Tom Mix's horse Tony attracted enough admirers to star in his own film, 1922's *Just Tony*. However, most early talkies either relegated horses to a mere means of transportation for cowboys or revolved around horse racing (see separate entry for a detailed discussion and list). *Kentucky* (1938) strayed from the racetrack long enough to offer a story of rival horse-breeding families. Yet it lacked the horse appeal inherent in *My Friend Flicka* (1943), a heartwarming tale of the love between a young boy (Roddy McDowell) and a mare with madness in her bloodline (*flicka* is the Swedish word for girl). McDowell and cast returned two years later with *Thunderhead — Son of Flicka*, a picturesque sequel at the end of which McDowell sets his horse free. The following year the same studio, Twentieth-Century Fox, released *Smoky*, Will James's classic horse story about the friendship between a wild stallion and a drifting cowboy (Fred MacMurray). *Smoky* and *Flicka* turned out to be highly influential films, establishing the pattern for other nonracing, person-loves-horse plots. Even John Steinbeck's *The Red Pony* (1949) offered only a minor variation, giving equal time to a purely human subplot about a boy confused over love for his father and affection for a hired hand. Two superior children-and-horse films, *Misty* (1961) and *The Black Stallion* (1979), were set partially on islands and adapted from popular juvenile novels (by Marguerite Henry and Walter Farley, respectively). *The Appaloosa* (1966) was a horse film for adults, with brooding Marlon Brando stalking the bandits who stole his steed. The only horse in *The Horse Without a Head* (1963) was a toy one hiding stolen loot. The most colorful nag was the famous Horse of a Different Color that pranced around the Emerald City in 1939's *The Wizard of Oz*. Pegasus, the mythological winged horse, took to the air with Harry Hamlin aboard in the 1981 fantasy *Clash of the Titans*. Special effects artist Ray Harryhausen created the cinema's tiniest horse in 1969's *Valley of Gwangi*. Finally, for the record, the most famous cowboy horses were as follows: Trigger (Roy Rogers), Buttermilk (Dale Evans), Champion (Gene Autry), Topper (Hopalong Cassidy), White Flash (Tex Ritter), Fritz (William S. Hart), Tarzan (Ken Maynard) and Blackjack (Allan Lane). Lane, in his post-cowboy days, provided the voice for TV's famous talking horse *Mr. Ed* (1961-65).

Just Tony (1922)
Kentucky (1938)
Sergeant Murphy (1938)
Konga, the Wild Stallion (1939)
The Wizard of Oz (1939)
Florian (1940)
My Friend Flicka (1943)
Thunderhead—Son of Flicka (1945)
Smoky (1946)
Black Beauty (1946)
The Red Stallion (1947)
King of the Wild Horses (1947)
Stallion Road (1947)
The Red Pony (1949)
Flame of Araby (1951)
The Lion and the Horse (1952)
Gypsy Colt (1954)
Black Horse Canyon (1954)
The Courage of Black Beauty (1957)
Tonka (aka A Horse Named Comanche) (1958)
King of the Wild Stallions (1959)
The Misfits (1961)
Misty (1961)
The Horse Without a Head (1963)
The Miracle of the White Stallions (1963)

Mary Poppins (1964)
Indian Paint (1964)
The Appaloosa (aka Southwest to Sonora) (1966)
Smoky (1966)
The Horse in the Gray Flannel Suit (1968)
Valley of Gwangi (1969)
Black Beauty (1971)
The Red Pony (1973 TVM)
Running Wild (1973)
Mustang Country (1976)
The Littlest Horse Thieves (aka Escape From the Dark) (1976)
Equus (1977)
The Black Stallion (1979)
Eagle's Wing (1979)
The Electric Horseman (1979)
Wild Horse Hank (1979)
Clash of the Titans (1981)
A Rare Breed (1981)
The Man From Snowy River (1982)
Danger Down Under (1988 TVM)
Wild Hearts Can't Be Broken (1991)
The Girl Who Came Late (1991)
Into the West (1992)

Hospitals

Film series about the medical profession, particularly the *Dr. Kildare* (q.v.) movies and the British *Doctor* (q.v.) comedies, have made extensive use of hospital settings. Nonseries hospital dramas reached their peak during the 1960s, their production fueled by the success of popular TV programs such as *Dr. Kildare* and *Ben Casey*. However, by the early 1970s, filmmakers had begun to view hospitals with increasing cynicism. Peter Sellers played a money-minded hospital administrator in the smutty comedy *Where Does It Hurt?* (1972). It lacked the bite of Paddy Chayefsky's *The Hospital*, a black comedy about a metropolitan medical establishment run by incompetents and housing a killer. Still, either of those was easier to digest than Frederick Wiseman's potent documentary *Hospital* (1970). A decade later, director Linday Anderson ripped into the British medical community with his irreverent hit-and-miss satire *Britannia Hospital* (1982). Other hospital-set comedies have been less ambitious, preferring to generate medical gags instead of social commentary. Nevertheless, the sight of the Carry On Gang (q.v.) carousing through a hospital is almost as frightening as it is funny. The hospital has been employed as a setting for fright films in *Halloween II* (1982), *Visiting Hours* (1982) and *Terminal Choice* (1985). The hospital in *Halloween II* rates as the creepiest—a cheap administrator's dream come true, where the staff is virtually nonexistent and the lights are turned off at every opportunity. In 1958's *Revenge of Frankenstein*, Dr. Frankenstein ran a clinic for the poor (which allowed him to amass spare body parts). Genevieve Bujold discovered a scheme in which patients were killed and their body parts sold in Michael Crichton's hospital thriller *Coma* (1978). Alastair Sim, as the witty, droll Inspector Cockrill, investigated multiple murders in a World War II hospital in the delightful 1946 mystery *Green for Danger*. See also **Doctor in the House; Nurses Series.**

Green for Danger (1946)	*The Healers* (1974 TVM)
The Sleeping City (1950)	*Medical Story* (1975)
White Corridors (1951)	*One of Our Own* (1975)
Emergency Hospital (1956)	*Coma* (1978)
Behind the Mask (1958)	*Doctors' Private Lives* (1978)
Carry On Nurse (1960)	*House Calls* (1978)
The Young Doctors (1961)	*Halloween II* (1982)
The Interns (1962)	*Visiting Hours* (1982)
A Stitch in Time (1963)	*Young Doctors in Love* (1982)
The New Interns (1964)	*Britannia Hospital* (1982)
U.M.C. (aka *Operation Heartbeat*)	*Emergency Room* (1983 TVM)
(1969 TVM)	*Terminal Choice* (1985)
Hospital (1970)	*Critical Condition* (1987)
The Hospital (1971)	*Paper Mask* (1990)
The Carey Treatment (1972)	*Deliver Them From Evil: The Taking*
Where Does It Hurt? (1972)	*of Alta View* (1992 TVM)
The Young Nurses (1973)	*Article 99* (1992)

Hotels

The hotel setting has registered as a favorite among filmmakers ever since *Grand Hotel*'s impressive guest roster made multicharacter dramas fashionable. This 1932 Best Picture, set in a Berlin hotel, featured Greta Garbo as a lonely ballerina, John Barrymore as a down-on-his-luck thief, Wallace Beery as a cold-hearted businessman, Lionel Barrymore as a dying man, and Joan Crawford as an ambitious secretary. It was officially remade with an American setting as 1945's *Weekend at the Waldorf*, but dozens of unofficial copies have borrowed the format. *Hotel Berlin* (1945), based on a novel by *Grand Hotel* author Vicki Baum, was a thinly disguised reworking bolstered by an all-star Warner Bros. cast. *Separate Tables* (1958) was set at a seaside resort and earned Oscars for Best Actor David Niven and Best Supporting Actress Wendy Hiller. The 1933 *International House* brought an eclectic group of comedians (W.C. Fields, Burns and Allen, etc.) together at an Oriental hotel in a wild plot about early television. Other all-star hotel pictures have included Arthur Hailey's *Hotel* (1967) and the Neil Simon comedies *Plaza Suite* (1971) and *California Suite* (1978). Deserts seem like unsuitable locations for hotels, but Field Marshal Rommel (Erich Von Stroheim) visited one in Billy Wilder's *Five Graves to Cairo* (1943), and Yvonne DeCarlo operated one in *Hotel Sahara* (1951). Despite the scorching sun, those hotels boasted great lifesaving offers that you just can't find at cheaper, horrific places like the Bates Motel of *Psycho* fame. While the Bates has a corner on the terror motel market, it has received some competition from the Overlook Hotel in *The Shining* (1980), *Horror*

Hotel (1960) and *Motel Hell* (1980). Jean Simmons's brother — and his hotel room — mysteriously disappeared in 1950's *So Long at the Fair*. Jean's frustration increased significantly when the hotel staff refused to acknowledge existence of the room or her brother. More pleasant hotels have provided the settings for musicals and comedies. Bing Crosby's *Holiday Inn* (1942) opened only on holidays, but still attracted quite a crowd with Bing's crooning, Fred Astaire's dancing, and Irving Berlin's catchy tunes. Bing and Danny Kaye put on a big show to save their old army colonel's hotel in 1954's *White Christmas*. Groucho played a desk clerk who had to deal with rowdy guests like Chico and Harpo in the 1929 Marx Brothers comedy *The Cocoanuts*. Nine years later, *Room Service* found Groucho and the boys sidestepping eviction from their hotel suite while desperately trying to salvage a stage play.

The Cocoanuts (1929)
Grand Hotel (1932)
International House (1933)
Hollywood Hotel (1937)
Hotel Haywire (1937)
Room Service (1938)
Hotel for Women (aka *Elsa Maxwell's Hotel for Women*) (1939)
Holiday Inn (1942)
Five Graves to Cairo (1943)
Hotel Reserve (1944)
Step Lively (1944)
Escape in the Desert (1945)
Hotel Berlin (1945)
Weekend at the Waldorf (1945)
So Long at the Fair (1950)
Hotel Sahara (1951)
White Christmas (1954)
The Girl Rush (1955)
The Green Man (1957)
Separate Tables (1958)
The Bellboy (1960)
Psycho (1960)
Horror Hotel (aka *The City of the Dead*) (1960)
Wake Me When It's Over (1960)
Man at the Carlton Tower (1961)
The Inn on the River (1962)
Tiara Tahiti (1962)

Honeymoon Hotel (1964)
The End of August at the Hotel Ozone (aka *The End of the World at the Hotel Ozone*) (1965)
Hotel (1967)
Nightmare Hotel (1970)
Plaza Suite (1971)
Snowball Express (1972)
Inn of the Damned (1974)
California Suite (1978)
Motel Hell (1980)
The Shining (1980)
Somewhere in Time (1980)
Experience Preferred . . . But Not Essential (1983 TVM)
Pink Motel (1983)
The Hotel New Hampshire (1984)
The Rosebud Beach Hotel (aka *The Big Lobby*) (1984)
Private Resort (1985)
Bates Motel (1987 TVM)
Puppet Master (1989)
Blame It on the Bellboy (1991)
Desire and Hell at Sunset Motel (1992)
Dragon Inn (1992)
Bed and Breakfast (1992)
Hotel Room (1993 TVM)
King of the Hill (1993)

House Series

This quirky series, saddled with an incongruent third entry, has juggled horror and humor with very uneven results. The original *House* (1986) starred William Katt as a depressed horror writer who moves into the title abode after his aunt vacates it via suicide. He is soon assailed by a variety of nightmarish apparitions as well as nosy neighbor George Wendt (Norm on TV's *Cheers*). *House II: The Second Story* (1987) substituted Arye Gross as the new owner but otherwise followed a similar structure. It even featured John Ratzenberger (Cliff on *Cheers*) in a memorable cameo as an electrician/adventurer. As indicated by the presence of the *Cheers* regulars, neither *House* nor *House II* harbored any pretensions as straight horror films. However, the third entry, *The Horror Show* (1989) went straight for the jugular with a slasher film plot devoid of humor. It was written by the infamous Alan Smithee (q.v.) and released outside the United States as *House III*. The humor was still missing in *House IV* (1992), a direct-to-videotape release. William Katt appeared briefly as a character with the same name as the one he played in *House*. However, it did not appear to be the same character. At any rate, he is killed in the opening reel, leaving his wife (Terri Treas) the task of battling supernatural creatures as well as dastardly human bad guys. See also **Amityville; Ghosts.**

    House (1986)
    House II: The Second Story (1987)
    The Horror Show (aka *House III*) (1989)
    House IV (1992)

The Howling

This loosely connected werewolf series continued the 1980s trend of milking a decent horror film for as many sequels as possible (see also **Halloween, Friday the 13th** and **Nightmare on Elm Street**). Joe (*Gremlins*) Dante directed 1981's *The Howling*, an affectionate mixture of gruesome horror and dark humor (peppered with inside jokes). Dee Wallace played the television newscaster who encounters a werewolf, suffers trauma, and goes to a retreat to recover. Alas, the place turns out to be crawling with bloodthirsty werewolves, and Wallace unwillingly joins the pack. The Wallace character (played by another actress) appeared fleetingly in 1984's *The Howling II: Your Sister Is a Werewolf*, a U.S.-European coproduction. This cheap-looking sequel featured a tasteless werewolf lovemaking session and excessive footage of Sybil Danning's cleavage. Wit, style, and adequate werewolf makeup were conspicuously missing. Philippe Mora's *The Howling III* shifted the locale to Down Under and introduced two tribes of Aussie "werewolves" (who carry their offspring in pouches). The tongue-in-cheek premise strove to prove that werewolves are people, too. It even featured a defected Russian ballerina who transforms into a werewolf while on stage. *Howling IV* (1988) was lensed on a shoestring budget in South Africa. Instead of pursuing another interesting tangent, it chose to rehash the original film by sending an emotionally unstable novelist to a retreat once again populated by werewolves. *Howling V: The Rebirth* (1989) resembled Agatha Christie's *Ten Little Indians*, only with a werewolf for a murderer. The last entry, 1991's *Howling VI: The Freaks*, found a lycanthrope working in a carnival sideshow run by a vampire. See also **Werewolves.**

    The Howling (1981)
    The Howling II: Your Sister Is a
       Werewolf (1984)
    The Howling III: The Marsupials
       (1987)

    Howling IV . . . The Original
       Nightmare (1988)
    Howling V: The Rebirth (1989)
    Howling VI: The Freaks (1991)

Huggetts Family

Described by film critic Leslie Halliwell as "Britain's answer to the Hardys," the Huggetts appeared in four features for Gainsborough. They were not even top-billed in their debut film, 1947's *Holiday Camp* (Jack Warner as Mr. Huggett was listed third in the cast). This charming comedy-drama, set at a highly regimented holiday resort, interwove the story of several characters. But British moviegoers favored the Huggetts, and they were given their own vehicle with 1948's *Here Come the Huggetts*. The next year, they became involved in politics and then concluded the series with a trip to Africa and an encounter with smugglers. Jack Warner and Kathleen Harrison, who played parents Joe and Ethel Huggett, continued to make films together (e.g., 1951's *A Christmas Carol*). Hazel Court played their widowed daughter Joan in *Holiday Camp*. Other Huggett children included Susan Shaw as Susan and fifteen-year-old Petula Clark as Pet. Diana Dors and David Tomlinson, who both became familiar faces to British film fans, also appeared in supporting roles.

Holiday Camp (1947)	*Vote for Huggett* (1948)
Here Come the Huggetts (1948)	*The Huggetts Abroad* (1949)

Hulot, Monsieur

Writer-director Jacques Tati introduced his alter ego in 1953's *Monsieur Hulot's Holiday*, a highly visual comedy about a middle-aged bachelor with a knack for unintentionally causing disruptions at a summer resort. The film featured minimal dialogue, inviting critics to compare Hulot to Chaplin's Tramp. Tati's later films expanded on his theme of man trapped in a technology-heavy, time-conscious world. A combination of financial problems and Tati's pursuit of perfection has severely limited his output. In addition to the four Hulot movies, he has produced only one other feature-length film, 1949's *Jour de Fête*. Tati did a cameo as Mr. Hulot in François Truffaut's *Bed and Board* (1970).

Monsieur Hulot's Holiday (1953)	*Playtime* (1967)
Mon Oncle (1958)	*Traffic* (1971)

Humanimals

Not quite human, not quite animal, and not just a werewolf — that's an apt description of a humanimal. The phrase was coined in the 1951 comedy-fantasy *You Never Can Tell* to describe animals reincarnated as humans (Dick Powell played ex-dog Rex Shepard). More loosely defined, "humanimal" includes all creatures that are animal-turned-human, human-turned-animal, or a combination of species (see **Werewolves** entry for lycanthropes and were-cats). In both *Island of Lost Souls* (1933) and *The Island of Dr. Moreau* (1977), mad scientist Moreau (Charles Laughton and Burt Lancaster, respectively) medically transformed animals into men. It was obviously not a pleasant process, as the animal-men referred to the operating room as the House of Pain. Another mad scientist (John Carradine) turned a female ape into a beautiful woman in 1943's *Captive Wild Woman* (see **Dupree, Paula**), while George Zucco tried a monkey-to-man experiment in 1942's *Dr. Renault's Secret*. Malcolm McDowell accidentally discovered a pig-man in an experimental hospital in the 1973 satire *O Lucky Man!* Similar medical experiments yielded disappointing results in bottom-of-the-barrel horror pictures like *Terror Is a Man* and *Twilight People*. Not all humanimals were produced by science or reincarnation. Puppet boy *Pinocchio* fell in with a crowd of naughty kids on Pleasure Island and they were all transformed into donkeys in Disney's version of the famous fairy tale. Two children had the power to transform themselves into bears at night in the offbeat fable *The Two Little Bears* (1961). See also **Dupree, Paula; Werewolves.**

A Blind Bargain (1922)
Island of Lost Souls (1933)
Pinocchio (1940)
Dr. Renault's Secret (1942)
The Mad Monster (1942)
Captive Wild Woman (1943)
You Never Can Tell (1951)
Terror Is a Man (aka *Blood Creature*) (1959)
The Two Little Bears (1961)

Atlantis, the Lost Continent (1961)
The Reptile (1966)
The Vulture (1967)
Twilight People (1972)
O Lucky Man! (1973)
The Island of Dr. Moreau (1977)
Oh, Heavenly Dog (1980)
Ladyhawke (1985)
Kiss of the Beast (aka *Meridian*) (1989)
Nightbreed (1990)

Hunchbacks

The most famous, of course, is that charismatic bellringer Quasimodo, created by Victor Hugo in his classic *The Hunchback of Notre Dame* and portrayed on the screen by a bevy of fine actors, most notably Lon Chaney, Sr. (1923), Charles Laughton (1939), Anthony Quinn (1957) and Anthony Hopkins (1981). Quasimodo's only rival for film popularity has been Ygor, the hunchbacked once-hanged shepherd immortalized by Bela Lugosi in *Son of Frankenstein* (1939) and *Ghost of Frankenstein* (1942) and parodied by Marty Feldman in *Young Frankenstein* (1974).

The Hunchback of Notre Dame (1923)
Son of Frankenstein (1939)
The Hunchback of Notre Dame (1939)
The Ghost of Frankenstein (1942)
House of Frankenstein (1944)
House of Dracula (1945)
Phantom From Space (1953)
Richard III (1956)
The Hunchback of Notre Dame (1957)
Revenge of Frankenstein (1958)
The Hunchback of Rome (aka *Il Gobbo*) (1960)
Mad Monster Party? (1967)
Candy (1968)
Ryan's Daughter (1970)
The Hunchback of the Morgue (1972)

Terror in the Wax Museum (1973)
Captain Kronos: Vampire Hunter (1974)
Young Frankenstein (1974)
Mr. Quilp (aka *The Old Curiosity Shop*) (1975)
The Rocky Horror Picture Show (1975)
The Hunchback of Notre Dame (1981 TVM)
Alsino and the Condor (1982)
Jean de Florette (1986)
The Name of the Rose (1986)
The Secret Garden (1987 TVM)
Big Man on Campus (1990)
The Secret Garden (1993)

Hunting Parties

A favorite pastime of the movies' idle rich, hunting parties served as social allegories in *The Shooting Party* (1984) and Jean Renoir's *The Rules of the Game* (1939). In Renoir's masterpiece, a rabbit hunt involving wealthy guests at a French chateau forms the center of the movie's structure. The hunters wait patiently, rifles in hand, for servants to beat the brush and scare rabbits from their hiding place. Then they take part in a cruel, vivid massacre of dozens of rabbits. The killing of these innocent animals – by a society they cannot comprehend – is mirrored later in the film by the accidental murder of a naive romantic. The death of a young boy during a fox hunt in 1988's *A Handful of Dust* signals the disintegration of his affluent parents' marriage. Bored European aristocrats Brigitte Bardot and Stephen Boyd visited the American West to mount a hunting expedition in Louis L'Amour's *Shalako* (1969). They found little game, but a lot of restless Apaches and an unlikely cowboy hero in Sean Connery. Errol Flynn saved an Indian chieftain during a tiger hunt in *The Charge of the Light Brigade* (1936) and lived to regret it. John Huston's gimmicky mystery *The List of Adrian Messenger* (1963) opened and closed with a fox hunt. The film's murderer, a master of disguises, plots a young boy's death but meets his own demise in the heat of the climactic hunt. Hunting parties of a different kind, led by men obsessed, comprised the plots to *Moby Dick* (1930, 1956) and *The White Buffalo* (1977).

Moby Dick (1930)	*The Hunt* (1966)
The Charge of the Light Brigade (1936)	*Shalako* (1969)
The Rules of the Game (1939)	*The White Buffalo* (1977)
Moby Dick (1956)	*The Shooting Party* (1984)
The List of Adrian Messenger (1963)	*A Handful of Dust* (1988)

Hypnotists

The hypnotist's unnerving stare, his piercing eyes aglow with flaming intensity, has been a trademark shot in almost all movies involving hypnosis. In 1909, film pioneer D.W. Griffith made *The Criminal Hypnotist*, one of the first movies in which hypnosis played a key role. A decade later, German director Robert Wiene made the highly expressionistic *The Cabinet of Dr. Caligari*, a macabre tale about a hypnotist who sends a somnambulist to commit murders. Two years later, fellow countryman Fritz Lang introduced *Dr. Mabuse* (q.v.), a criminal mastermind and hypnotist extraordinaire. The Mabuse character appeared in eight additional films, making him the screen's most enduring hypnotist. His fame has been equaled only by George du Maurier's *Svengali*, a mad Russian hypnotist whose mind-controlling eyes turned the beautiful but untalented Trilby into a singing sensation. Du Maurier's story has been filmed at least six times, with the 1931 version starring John Barrymore generally considered the finest. Jose Ferrer used hypnosis to manipulate Gene Tierney and implicate her in murder in Otto Preminger's *Whirlpool* (1949). A mesmerist employed it to control the Frankenstein Monster in *The Evil of Frankenstein* (1964). In 1953's *Invasion U.S.A.*, a man induced mass hypnosis on the patrons of a neighborhood bar so they could experience the effects of a Communist invasion. Count Dracula (q.v.) used a hypnotic look to great advantage in many of his films, although much of the effect could be attributed to his vampire charms. Hypnotism has played a major role in several reincarnation (q.v.) films, most notably *The Search for Bridey Murphy* (1956), *Spell of the Hypnotist* (1956) and the Barbra Streisand musical *On a Clear Day You Can See Forever* (1970). See also **Brainwashing; Mabuse, Dr.**

The Criminal Hypnotist (1909)
The Cabinet of Dr. Caligari (1919)
Dr. Mabuse, the Gambler (aka The Great Gambler — Image of a Generation) (1921)
Dr. Mabuse, King of Crime (aka Inferno — People of a Generation) (1922)
Running Wild (1927)
Svengali (1931)
Hypnotized (1933)
The Garden Murder Case (1936)
Night Monster (aka House of Mystery) (1942)
Calling Dr. Death (1943)
Shadows in the Night (1944)
The Frozen Ghost (1945)
The Woman in Green (1945)
Bewitched (1945)
The Seventh Veil (1945)
The Mask of Dijon (1946)
Fear in the Night (1947)
Road to Rio (1947)
Whirlpool (1949)
Invasion U.S.A. (1953)

Svengali (1954)
The Hypnotist (1956)
Nightmare (1956)
The Search for Bridey Murphy (1956)
The She Creature (1956)
Spell of the Hypnotist (1956)
Hold That Hypnotist (1957)
I Was a Teenage Werewolf (1957)
Blood of Dracula (1957)
Curse of the Demon (aka Night of the Demon) (1958)
The Hypnotic Eye (1960)
Hypnosis (aka Dummy of Death) (1963)
The Evil of Frankenstein (1964)
The Misadventures of Merlin Jones (1964)
Creature of Destruction (1968)
On a Clear Day You Can See Forever (1970)
Let's Do It Again (1975)
Svengali (1983 TVM)
Two Evil Eyes (aka Due Occhi Diabolic) (1990)

I Love a Mystery

Columbia Pictures produced this belated entry into the detective series sweep-stakes of the 1940s. Based on Carleton E. Morse's hit radio show, the *I Love a Mystery* trilogy starred Jim Bannon as investigator Jack Packard and Barton Yarborough as his crony Doc Long. Their 1945 debut film was also their best, a strange little mystery about a secret Oriental society intent on securing a businessman's head because he resembles their dead founder. The story had been previously produced on the radio program as "The Head of Jonathan Monk." Despite offbeat plotlines, the film series failed to catch on and ended in 1946. Universal Pictures tried to revive the series with the made-for-TV film *I Love a Mystery*, which featured Les Crane as Packard and David Hartman as Long. A campy spoof of the radio series, it sat on the studio's shelf for six years before being televised in 1973.

I Love a Mystery (1945)
The Devil's Mask (1946)

The Unknown (1946)
I Love a Mystery (1973 TVM)

Ice Skating

Ice skating movies fall into two categories: those starring Sonja Henie and all others. Henie, a Norwegian, won the world figure skating championship as a fifteen-year-old. At twenty-six, after three successful Olympics, she began her Twentieth Century-Fox film career opposite Don Ameche and the Ritz Brothers in 1936's *One in a Million*. Henie enjoyed a decade of popularity, skating in films such as *Thin Ice* (1938), *Second Fiddle* (1939), *Sun Valley Serenade* (1941) and *Wintertime* (1943). Other ice skating champions have ventured into films as well, although none have compared to Henie. Spunky Lynn-Holly Johnson gave a credible performance as a promising ice skater who goes blind in the sappy but effective *Ice Castles* (1979). She skated briefly in the James Bond adventure *For Your Eyes Only* (1981) but abandoned her blades to deal with unseen forces in *The Watcher in the Woods* (1980). British ice skating star Belita (real name Gladys Jepson Turner) starred in a handful of Hollywood films, such as *Ice Capades* (1941), *Silver Skates* (1943) and *Suspense* (1946). Champion skater Carol Heiss's career fared less well, her lone screen appearance being opposite Moe, Larry and Joe in 1961's *Snow White and the Three Stooges*. Olympian Tai Babilonia never made a movie, but her life and career with partner Randy Gardner formed the basis for the 1990 TV-movie *On Thin Ice: The Tai Babilonia Story*. Fictitious skaters have overcome drastic odds—and often found romance—in features such as *Champions: A Love Story* (1979 TVM), *Skate!* (1987), *Blades of Courage* (1988) and *The Cutting Edge* (1992). Angel Cary Grant taught Loretta Young and cabbie Paul Gleason how to ice skate in the 1947 fantasy *The Bishop's Wife*. Finally, Abbott and Costello set the all-time low marks for figure skating form in 1943's *Hit the Ice*. See also **Hockey; Roller Skating.**

One in a Million (1936)
Thin Ice (1938)
My Lucky Star (1938)
Second Fiddle (1939)
Ice Follies (aka *Ice Follies of 1939*)
   (1939)
Sun Valley Serenade (1941)
Ice Capades (1941)
Ice Capades Revue (1942)
Iceland (1942)
Wintertime (1943)
Silver Skates (1943)
Hit the Ice (1943)
Lake Placid Serenade (1944)

It's a Pleasure (1945)
Suspense (1946)
The Bishop's Wife (1947)
Snow White and the Three Stooges
   (1961)
Ice Castles (1979)
Champions: A Love Story (1979 TVM)
For Your Eyes Only (1981)
Skate! (1987)
Blades of Courage (1988)
On Thin Ice: The Tai Babilonia Story
   (1990 TVM)
The Cutting Edge (1992)

If . . .

If. . . (1968), *O Lucky Man!* (1973) and *Britannia Hospital* (1982) comprise director Lindsay Anderson's loosely connected, savagely satirical trilogy about rebellions against society. In *If . . .*, the most critically acclaimed of the trilogy, three boys revolt against their highly structured, often cruel, British public school. Yet, unlike Jean Vigo's 1933 classic *Zero for Conduct*, this rebellion goes to the extreme, complete with Malcolm McDowell and his fellow revolters gunning down authority figures in attendance at Speech Day. The film's surrealistic tone—is it real or fantasy?—is heightened by Anderson's alternating use of color and black and white (an economical necessity, according to him). *O Lucky Man!* narrowed the focus to one individual, an ambitious young coffee salesman (McDowell again) trying to fit into society—to be wealthy, successful and powerful. But he is manipulated by his own ambition and by those he aspires to be like. His wealthy employer frames him for a crime, he goes to prison, gets reeducated and released, tries to "help" others as he was, gets mugged by ungrateful tramps, and finally does something because he *wants* to do it. This, too, becomes an act of rebellion against a society of manipulators. The third film, *Britannia Hospital*, opted for a broader view and a more obvious target in one of society's standard institutions. McDowell and other alumni from the first two films appeared in brief roles, but *Britannia Hospital*'s heavily episodic structure made it very hit-or-miss. It has failed to achieve the faithful followings of *If . . .* and *O Lucky Man!*

> *If . . .* (1968)
> *O Lucky Man!* (1973)
> *Britannia Hospital* (1982)

Ilsa, She Wolf of the SS

Dyanne Thorpe starred in this trash trilogy, which acquired a notorious reputation for its S&M content in the mid-1970s. In *Ilsa, She Wolf of the SS*, the title character is a Nazi medical camp warden who tortures and kills female prisoners with glee. She forces the male prisoners to make love to her, then kills them brutally when none can satisfy her sexual desires. The basic premise bears a passing resemblance to 1974's *The Night Porter*, in which Dirk Bogarde and Charlotte Rampling portrayed, respectively, a former Nazi torturer and his victim, who resume their S&M relationship years later. That film may have had some social value. *Ilsa, She Wolf of the SS* is a reprehensible picture that would have faded into obscurity had critics not rebuked it so openly. Instead, the producers promptly mounted two dreadful sequels with Thorpe returning as Ilsa. The Thorpe film *Wanda, the Wicked Warden* (1977) was later retitled as both *Ilsa, the Wicked Warden* and *Ilsa — Absolute Power*. Despite obvious similarities, it was not a part of the *Ilsa* series.

> *Ilsa, She Wolf of the SS* (1974)
> *Ilsa, Harem Keeper of the Oil Sheiks* (1976)
> *Ilsa, Tigress of Siberia* (1976)

In Search of . . .

Budget-minded film company Sunn Classics pioneered the pseudodocumentary with this brief 1970s series. Its first release was its best, a faithful adaptation of Erich Von Daniken's best-seller *Chariots of the Gods?* (1974). Actually, the film had been made in Germany in 1969 and excerpts aired on American TV as the one-hour TV special *In Search of Ancient Astronauts*. Sunn picked the film up in 1974 and marketed it using a system called "four walling." This consisted of saturating the market with TV previews, renting theaters for limited runs (one or two weeks), and then keeping all box office receipts. The system worked amazingly well, with Sunn receiving large returns on minimal investments. Subsequently, it produced "documentaries" about Noah's Ark, the Shroud of Turin, mysterious "monsters" like the Yeti and Nessie, and life and death. "Real" footage was frequently intercut with fictional reenactments. And one could always count on the narrator to add some sensationalism ("Would you like to see what it's like to enter that region between life and death?"). *In Search of Dracula* (1971) was produced by another company, though it was very much in the Sunn-style.

Leonard Nimoy hosted a syndicated television program along the same lines. Dubbed *In Search of . . .*, it consisted of 144 episodes broadcast during 1976-82.

Chariots of the Gods? (1974)   *Beyond and Back* (1978)
In Search of Noah's Ark (1976)   *In Search of Historic Jesus* (1979)
The Mysterious Monsters (1976)

In the Line of Duty

NBC initiated this series of fact-based films about law enforcement officers after scoring big ratings with 1988's *In the Line of Duty: The FBI Murders*. Former TV nice guys Michael Gross (*Family Ties*) and David Soul (*Starsky and Hutch*) played against type as a pair of vicious murderers tracked down by special agent David Sheehan. Their ultimate confrontation in Miami in 1986 resulted in the bloodiest shoot-out in FBI history (and one of the most violent in TV-movie annals). The "sequels," beginning with 1990's *In the Line of Duty: A Cop for the Killing*, bore no resemblance to the original or to each other in terms of plot or characters. However, they all maintained the same gritty focus and behind-the-scenes attention to detail. In *A Cop for the Killing*, Stephen Weber became an unstable cop after his partner was murdered. Michael Gross—an FBI agent this time—went after white supremacist/murderer Gordon Rahl (Rod Steiger) in 1991's *Manhunt in the Dakotas*. Dennis Franz and Ed Begley, Jr. headlined the fourth installment, *Siege at Marion* (1992), which dealt with an FBI confrontation with a group of armed religious fanatics. *In the Line of Duty: Street War* (1992) shifted the focus back to the cop on the beat. Mario Van Peebles (*New Jack City*) starred as a New York City Housing Authority policeman who seeks revenge when his partner is killed while patrolling the drug-ridden neighborhood of their childhood. Originally scheduled to be broadcast in May 1992, it was delayed until the following fall due to the Los Angeles riots. The last entry, *In the Line of Duty: Ambush at Waco* (1993) covered ground similar to *Siege at Marion*, only this time the subject was religious cult leader David Koresh. NBC rushed the film into production—it appeared within months of the bloody shoot-out (but it did not cover the subsequent compound explosion and death of Koresh). Although variable in quality, the *In the Line of Duty* films provided a sharp, realistic contrast to contemporary escapist TV detective shows such as *Murder, She Wrote*, *Matlock*, and *Jake and the Fatman*. However, one suspects that NBC decided an occasional jolt of realism was enough—thus, its decision to go with a film series as opposed to a weekly TV series. See also **FBI**.

In the Line of Duty: The FBI Murders (1988 TVM)
In the Line of Duty: A Cop for the Killing (1990 TVM)
In the Line of Duty: Manhunt in the Dakotas (1991 TVM)
In the Line of Duty: Siege at Marion (1992 TVM)
In the Line of Duty: Street War (1992 TVM)
In the Line of Duty: Ambush at Waco (1993 TVM)

The Incredible Hulk

Comic book legend Stan Lee created the Incredible Hulk, an interesting Jekyll and Hyde (q.v.) variant, in 1962. Lee's protagonist was Dr. Bruce Banner, a scientist accidentally altered by a massive dosage of radiation. The outcome was that, when overcome with anger, the normally reserved Banner transformed into a greenish, superstrong Hulk with the dimensions of a Mr. Universe. Eventually, the Hulk would change back to Banner, who would remember nothing about his alter ego's activities. CBS brought the comic book character to TV in 1977, first in a couple of pilot movies and then as a *Fugitive*-styled series with a clever casting twist. Mild-mannered Bill Bixby played Banner, with bodybuilder Lou Ferrigno replacing him as the Hulk. The show enjoyed a modest four-year run on the basis of its juvenile audience. There have been three revival movies, the first one pairing the Hulk with Thor, another comic book superhero. See also **Comic Book Characters; Television Series Reunion Films.**

   The Incredible Hulk (1977 TVM)
   The Return of the Incredible Hulk (aka *The Return of the Hulk*) (1977 TVM)
   The Incredible Hulk Returns (1988 TVM)
   The Trial of the Incredible Hulk (1989 TVM)
   The Death of the Incredible Hulk (1990 TVM)

Inner Sanctum

Lon Chaney, Jr., starred in this generally undistinguished low-budget mystery film series, which occasionally hinted at horror. The highlights were 1944's *Weird Woman*, the first film version of Fritz Leiber's *Conjure Wife* (later remade as the superior *Burn, Witch, Burn*), and an intriguing little puzzler titled *Calling Dr. Death*. In the latter film, Chaney played a neurologist who uses hypnotism to determine if he unconsciously murdered his unfaithful wife. Inspired by a hit radio series, each movie was preceded by a warped head in a crystal ball who welcomed viewers to the Inner Sanctum (a mild version of *The Twilight Zone*). *Strange Confession* (1945) is frequently confused with Julien Duvivier's 1944 film of the same title, which is known as *The Impostor*. Oddly enough, the 1948 feature *Inner Sanctum* was not part of this series. In 1992, Victoria Principal starred in *Seduction: Three Tales From the Inner Sanctum*, a TV-movie anthology based on the radio series.

   Calling Dr. Death (1943)   *Pillow of Death* (1945)
   Dead Man's Eyes (1944)   *Strange Confession* (1945)
   Weird Woman (1944)   *Seduction: Three Tales From the Inner*
   The Frozen Ghost (1945)   *Sanctum* (1992 TVM)

Insects

Be they little specks or large enough to crush a man, insects have long been a big screen pest. Indeed, the only insect of purely noble intentions was Jiminy Cricket of *Pinocchio* fame. He was also the best six-legged singer. In most films, however, insects have been portrayed as unthinking machines of destruction. A plague of locusts stripped the wheat fields in the climax to *The Good Earth* (an effect achieved by superimposing coffee grounds over oil-covered wheat). An army of soldier ants destroyed a South American plantation in 1954's *The Naked Jungle*, although the crisis served to mend Charlton Heston and Eleanor Parker's shaky marriage. That same year introduced a colony of twelve-foot-high ants in *Them!*, the finest giant insect picture ever made. It was also the first to imply that nature was rebelling against man's misuse of radiation. Imitations quickly followed, featuring giant grasshoppers (*The Beginning of the End*) and a preying mantis (*The Deadly Mantis*). A single, regular-sized fly proved the culprit in 1958's *The Fly* (q.v.) when it interrupted an experiment and merged atomic particles with an affable scientist. Nine years later, *The Deadly Bees* started an insect film subgenre with its lively shock scenes of swarming bees stinging nice people to death. Variations gained popularity in the next decade, amid real-life reports of killer bees flying up from South America. A popular TV-movie, *The Savage Bees*, was followed by *The Bees*, Irwin Allen's big-budget bust *The Swarm*, and *Terror Out of the Sky*. In other notable insect-related features: The Devil (Peter Cook) turned Dudley Moore into a fly in one of the episodes of *Bedazzled*; the Academy Award-winning pseudodocumentary *The Hellstrom Chronicle* explored the premise that insects will one day inherit the Earth; a government device designed to kill insects raised dead humans in *Don't Open the Window* and turned them into flesh-eating ghouls; a colony of intelligent ants bred with humans to create a new superrace in *Phase IV*; the moon's inhabitants were discovered to be the insectlike Selenites in *First Men in the Moon*; and a nice, wholesome family turned out to be roaches in disguise in *Meet the Applegates*. See also **The Fly.**

The Good Earth (1937)
Pinocchio (1940)
Hoppity Goes to Town (aka *Mr. Bug Goes to Town*) (1941)
Once Upon a Time (1944)
Them! (1954)
The Naked Jungle (1954)
The Deadly Mantis (1957)
The Beginning of the End (1957)
The Fly (1958)
The Wasp Woman (1960)
Mysterious Island (1961)
First Men in the Moon (1964)
The Deadly Bees (1967)
Bedazzled (1967)
The Hellstrom Chronicle (1971)
Invasion of the Bee Girls (1973)
Phase IV (1974)
Don't Open the Window (aka *Breakfast at the Manchester Morgue*) (1974)
Killer Bees (1974 TVM)
Locusts (1974 TVM)
Bug (1975)

The Savage Bees (1976 TVM)
Empire of the Ants (1977)
Damnation Alley (1977)
Sinbad and the Eye of the Tiger (1977)
It Happened at Lakewood Manor (aka *Panic at Lakewood Manor; Ants*) (1977 TVM)
Exorcist II: The Heretic (1977)
Terror Out of the Sky (1978 TVM)
The Bees (1978)
The Swarm (1978)
The Beast Within (1982)
Creepshow (1982)
Creepers (1985)
The Nest (1988)
Honey, I Shrunk the Kids (1989)
Meet the Applegates (aka *The Applegates*) (1990)
Whispers (1990)
Popcorn (1991) (the movie-within-a-movie "Mosquito")
Matinee (1993) (the movie-within-a-movie "Mant!")

Insurance Investigators

The cinema has shown little respect for insurance investigators, typically portraying them as private eyes without steady work or as crafty con artists. Certainly, the investigators in *Mystery in Mexico, Banacek* and *Coopersmith* could have passed for private eyes if we hadn't been told they were insurance men. At least they were on the right side of the law. The insurance investigators in *Roadblock* (1951) and *She Played With Fire* (1957) were influenced by money-hungry women to turn crooked. George Kennedy played a family-oriented investigator scheming to defraud an insurance company to provide money for his loved ones in *Zigzag*. Laurence Harvey tried to swindle an insurance company, too, by faking his death in 1963's *The Running Man*, but he didn't fool insurance man Alan Bates. The TV-movie *Longstreet* (1970) served as a pilot for a TV show, as did the aforement-ioned *Coopersmith* (1992) and *Banacek* (1972). Two of the three produced regular TV series, with George Peppard as a freelance insurance investigator in *Banacek* (1972-74) and James Franciscus as a blind investigator in *Longstreet* (1971-72).

The Amazing Mr. Forrest (aka *The Gang's All Here*) (1939)	*Zigzag* (1970)
	Longstreet (1970 TVM)
Mystery in Mexico (1948)	*The Movie Murderer* (1970 TVM)
Pitfall (1948)	*The Firechasers* (1970)
Roadblock (1951)	*Banacek* (aka *Detour to Nowhere*)
Timetable (1956)	(1972 TVM)
She Played With Fire (aka *Fortune Is a Woman*) (1957)	*Lady Ice* (1973)
	The Pursuit of D.B. Cooper (1981)
Backfire (1961)	*Coopersmith* (1992 TVM)
The Running Man (1963)	*Frauds* (1993)

Invasions/Takeovers of the U.S.

The cinema has rarely dealt with the end of U.S. democracy, viewing it as a sobering premise with limited commercial appeal. In Arch Oboler's *Strange Holiday*, a businessman (Claude Rains) returned from an isolated vacation spot to discover that American Nazis had gained control of the country. The film was originally produced in 1940 for General Motors employees. GM shelved it, how-ever, and later sold it to MGM. The film sat in MGM's vaults until Rains and Oboler bought it back and released it in 1945 through a small independent com-pany. After *Strange Holiday*'s fate, it's easy to see why the enemy invasion in 1953's *Invasion U.S.A.* was framed by a plot device explaining its events as being induced by mass hypnosis. Still, the film's opening scene was undeniably powerful, with a television broadcaster reporting that an enemy task force had taken over Alaska and set off atomic bombs in Washington state. Rod Serling's *Seven Days in May* (1964) internalized the takeover attempt, focusing on a military coup to oust the U.S. president. The Russians seized an Alasakan pipeline in retaliation for a U.S. grain embargo in the two-part TV-movie *World War III* (1982). John Milius's *Red Dawn* (1984) was a pre-Glasnost adventure about a successful Com-munist invasion of the United States and a subsequent guerilla counterattack staged by patriotic teenagers. The 1987 television miniseries *Amerika* expanded the same premise into a week's worth of TV viewing. The villainous Kryptonites of *Superman II* (1981) humbled the president and trashed the White House before receiving their comeuppance from the Man of Steel. On the lighter side, the accidental grounding of a Russian submarine in New England triggered invasion rumors in the 1966 cold-war comedy *The Russians Are Coming! The Russians Are Coming!*

Strange Holiday (1945)	*Invasion U.S.A.* (1953)

Seven Days in May (1964)
The Russians Are Coming! The
Russians Are Coming! (1966)

Superman II (1981)
World War III (1982 TVM)
Red Dawn (1984)

Invisibility

The father of modern movie invisibility was John P. Fulton, a special effects photographer who engineered the ingenious optical tricks in Universal's *Invisible Man* series. The original 1933 film set a standard that was difficult even for Fulton to better. How can anyone forget the eerie scene in which Jack Griffin (Claude Rains) unwraps the bandages covering his face—only to reveal an apparently headless man? Employing double exposure and masked negatives, Fulton displayed his superb invisibility effects in six other Universal films (denoted below with *). Although no one has rivaled Fulton's trickwork, invisibility has shown up in movies with regularity since the late 1950s. The otherwise forgettable *Phantom From Space* (1953) introduced an invisible alien, a premise explored with more imagination in *Fiend Without a Face* (1958) and *Invisible Invaders* (1959). The murderous creature in 1956's *Forbidden Planet* could not be seen with the naked eye either. However, its invisibility status remains in question, since it turned to be a "mental force" generated by Walter Pidgeon. Invisible criminals proliferated in the 1960s with Edgar G. Ulmer's *The Amazing Transparent Man* (1960) and the German series entry *The Invisible Dr. Mabuse* (1961). But invisibility gradually became nothing more than a comedy gimmick in films such as Disney's *Now You See Him, Now You Don't* (1971), the 3-D *Man Who Wasn't There* (1983) and *The Invisible Kid* (1988). Two TV-movies served as pilots for "serious" series. David McCallum played an invisible scientist on the run in 1975's *The Invisible Man* and its subsequent 1975-76 series. NBC cancelled the show after half a season but still had faith in the concept. So another pilot film, *Gemini Man*, was made with Ben Murphy as a government agent who could turn invisible for fifteen minutes a day. The show debuted in September 1976—and went off in the air in one month. An earlier TV series of *The Invisible Man* ran on CBS during 1958-60. The actor playing the lead role was never revealed.

* *The Invisible Man* (1933)
* *The Invisible Man Returns* (1940)
The Body Disappears (1941)
* *The Invisible Woman* (1941)
* *Invisible Agent* (1942)
* *The Invisible Man's Revenge* (1944)
* *Abbott and Costello Meet Frankenstein* (cameo) (1948)
* *Abbott and Costello Meet the Invisible Man* (1951)
Phantom From Space (1953)
Forbidden Planet (1956)
The Invisible Boy (1957)
The New Invisible Man (aka *H.G. Wells' Invisible Man*) (1957)
Fiend Without a Face (1958)

The Invisible Avenger (aka *Bourbon St. Shadows*) (1958)
Invisible Invaders (1959)
The Amazing Transparent Man (1960)
The Invisible Dr. Mabuse (aka *The Invisible Horror*) (1961)
The Wonderful World of the Brothers Grimm (1962)
The Invisible Terror (1963)
Mad Monster Party? (1967)
Mr. Superinvisible (aka *The Invincible Invisible Man*) (1967)
Now You See Him, Now You Don't (1971)
The Invisible Man (1975 TVM)
Invisible Strangler (1976)

Gemini Man (aka Code Name: Minus One) (1976 TVM)
The Invisible Woman (1983 TVM)
The Man Who Wasn't There (1983)
The Invisible Kid (1988)
The Invisible Maniac (1990)

The Neverending Story II: The Next Chapter (1990)
Alice (1990)
Memoirs of an Invisible Man (1992)
Sleepwalkers (1992)

Iron Eagle

This modest action series has persevered solely on the strength of star Lou Gossett, Jr. The original *Iron Eagle* (1986) introduced Gossett as retired Air Force colonel Charles "Chappy" Sinclair. Chappy teams up with an eighteen-year-old hot shot pilot for a fighter jet rescue when the kid's dad is wrongly imprisoned in the Middle East. Critics found the film hokey, but it nevertheless appealed to the same moviegoers who made *Top Gun* a box office smash the same year. In 1988's Glasnost-oriented *Iron Eagle II*, Chappy — now a general — leads U.S. and Soviet pilots on a joint mission to destroy a nuclear weapons base in a fictional Middle Eastern country. The third entry, *Aces: Iron Eagle III* stole its plot from 1990's *Delta Force 2* (apparently, there is no honor among rival B-movie action series). Gossett, bodybuilder Rachel McLish, and *Magnificent Seven* (q.v.) alumnus Horst Buchholz lead a team of pilots flying vintage World War II planes on a mission to destroy a South American cocaine factory. Writer Kevin Elder had a hand in all three *Iron Eagle* scripts. Interestingly, spy movie veteran Sidney J. Furie (*The Ipcress File*) directed the first two entries, while former James Bond (q.v.) director John Glen helmed the last one. See also **Airplanes**.

Iron Eagle (1986)
Iron Eagle II (1988)
Aces: Iron Eagle III (aka Iron Eagle III) (1992)

Islands

Tropical islands have long been a favorite movie setting — and with good reason. Where else is one apt to find cannibals, wild jungle animals, pirates, buried treasure and erupting volcanoes? Monsters, too. King Kong lived on Skull Island, Godzilla visited Monster Island, Japan's favorite giant caterpillar, Mothra, was hatched on Infant Island, and an oversized pink crab harassed hungry humans on *The Mysterious Island*. Human monsters have populated islands, too, with Count Zaroff hunting people in *The Most Dangerous Game* and Dr. Moreau creating disfigured humans out of innocent animals in *Island of Lost Souls*. On the other hand, islands have also brought unlikely lovers together, as in *The Blue Lagoon, Her Jungle Love, Return to Paradise* and *Mutiny on the Bounty*. Island politics, as established by shipwreck victims, are usually pretty simple, as portrayed in *Swiss Family Robinson, Robinson Crusoe* and *Tempest*. But they can also get wildly out of hand, as in *Lord of the Flies*, William Golding's political parable about shipwrecked boys who create their own civilization. Some of the more unique uses of island settings occur in the following: *And Then There Were None* (1945), Agatha Christie's classic whodunit about nine guests trapped in an island mansion with a murderer; *The Challenge* (1970), which pits two men, each representing his country, against one another to fight World War III on an island; and Val Lewton's

Isle of the Dead (1945), an eerie horror tale about passengers quarantined on a Greek island where a dead woman seems to be alive. One unique aspect of island-set films is that they can end without warning. You never know when a volcano (*Atlantis, the Lost Continent*) or a tropical storm (*Hurricane*) is going to wipe out the whole place. See also **Crusoe, Robinson.**

Island of Lost Souls (1932)
The Most Dangerous Game (1932)
King Kong (1933)
We're Not Dressing (1934)
Hurricane (1937)
The Edge of the World (1937)
Her Jungle Love (1938)
Road to Singapore (1940)
Beyond the Blue Horizon (1942)
And Then There Were None (1945)
Isle of the Dead (1945)
On an Island With You (1948)
The Blue Lagoon (1949)
Tight Little Island (aka *Whiskey Galore*) (1949)
Return to Paradise (1953)
Attack of the Crab Monsters (1957)
Island in the Sun (1957)
Wake Me When It's Over (1960)
Swiss Family Robinson (1960)
Atlantis, the Lost Continent (1961)
The Mysterious Island (1961)
No Man Is an Island (aka *Island Escape*) (1962)
The Island (1962)
Donovan's Reef (1963)
Lord of the Flies (1963)

Island of the Blue Dolphins (1964)
Island of Terror (1966)
Hawaii (1966)
Island of the Burning Doomed (aka *Island of the Burning Damned*) (1967)
The Challenge (1970 TVM)
Godzilla on Monster Island (aka *Godzilla vs. Gigan*) (1971)
Papillon (1973)
Terminal Island (1973)
The Savage Is Loose (1974)
Islands in the Stream (1976)
The Island of Dr. Moreau (1977)
Rescue From Gilligan's Island (1978 TVM)
The Blue Lagoon (1980)
The Island (1980)
Tempest (1982)
Pascali's Island (1988)
Trouble in Paradise (1989 TVM)
Bare Essentials (1990 TVM)
Shipwrecked (1990)
And the Sea Will Tell (1991 TVM)
Return to the Blue Lagoon (1991)
Danger Island (1992 TVM)

It's Alive

Larry Cohen's 1974 low-budget shocker about a killer baby has attracted a strong cult following, chiefly due to its dual-sided view of modern morals. When his wife gives birth to a murderous mutant baby, John Ryan embarks on a personal crusade to destroy the creature. His wife pleads for the life of their "child," but Ryan feels socially responsible for all the deaths. However, when he finally confronts his son, he realizes that "it" is an innocent. He watches helplessly as the police brutally murder it. In the 1978 sequel *It Lives Again*, Ryan's character has evolved into an obsessed man fighting against a closed society that's unwilling to accept anything it cannot understand (e.g., the mutant children). Ryan dies, but converted parent Frederic Forrest carries on the crusade. Cohen returned to the theme nine years later in the barely released *It's Alive III: Island of the Alive*. A reworking of the second film, it once again portrayed the children as helpless victims of a cruel, prejudiced society.

It's Alive (1974)   *It's Alive III: Island of the Alive* (1987)
It Lives Again (aka *It's Alive II*) (1978)

Jack the Ripper

The unidentified murderer of at least five prostitutes in London's Whitechapel district in 1888, Jack the Ripper has been a screen fixture since the 1920s. He appeared briefly in a nightmare sequence in *Waxworks* (1924), in which his wax figure comes to life. And in G.W. Pabst's *Pandora's Box*, he popped up at the film's climax to deal retribution to a sinner. However, the first movie to feature Jack in a starring role was Alfred Hitchcock's 1926 adaptation of Marie Belloc Lowndes's chilling novel *The Lodger*. Unfortunately, when matinee idol Ivor Novello was cast in the title role, the ending was altered so that the Lodger turned out not to be the Ripper after all. The film was remade twice, in 1932 with Novello repeating his role (this version aka *The Phantom Fiend*) and in 1944 with Laird Cregar. The latter film was a gripping, atmospheric yarn, faithful to the book and sporting a fine, frenzied performance from Cregar. (In fact, its success resulted in Cregar playing a psychotic murderer again in 1945's *Hangover Square*.) Over the next decades, the Ripper continued to appear in B-films such as *The Curse of the Wraydons* (1946) and *Room to Let* (1950). However, the Terror of Whitechapel regained the spotlight with the release of 1959's *Jack the Ripper*. Scripted by horror veteran Jimmy Sangster (who also wrote *Room to Let*), this ordinary thriller offered no new variations. Yet, in the hands of superproducer Joseph E. Levine, it was exploited into a sensational worldwide hit that paved the way for more serious "psycho" films like *Peeping Tom* and *Psycho*. Six years later, Jack encountered Sherlock Holmes in the stylish pastiche *A Study in Terror*. This film was based on the short story "Fog," written by Conan Doyle's son Adrian. A similar fictional confrontation occurred in 1979's *Time After Time*, in which the Ripper (memorably played by David Warner) steals H.G. Wells's time machine and escapes to present-day San Francisco — where his acts of violence fit right in. In 1988's underrated *Jack's Back*, a modern-day killer replicated the Ripper's crimes in honor of Jack's 100th anniversary.

The Lodger (1926)
The Lodger (aka *The Phantom Fiend*) (1932)
The Lodger (1944)
The Curse of the Wraydons (1946)
Room to Let (1950)
Man in the Attic (1953)
Jack the Ripper (1958) (four-part anthology with one episode about the Ripper)
Jack the Ripper (1959)
A Study in Terror (1965)
Hands of the Ripper (1972) (Jack's daughter)

The Ruling Class (1972)
Knife for the Ladies (1973) (a Western variation)
Black the Ripper (1975)
Jack the Ripper (1976)
Murder by Decree (1979) (Jack meets Holmes again)
Time After Time (1979)
Bridge Across Time (aka *Arizona Ripper*) (1985 TVM)
The Ripper (1985)
Jack's Back (1988)
Jack the Ripper (1988 TVM)
Edge of Sanity (1989)

Janek, Frank

William Bayer's mystery best-seller *Switch* provided the basis for the 1985 TV-movie *Doubletake*, a grisly two-part mystery that introduced Richard Crenna as middle-aged NYC detective Lieutenant Frank Janek. The plot, which revolved around two decapitated murder victims whose heads are switched, served as a backdrop for a character study of a likable, divorced, occasionally lute-playing detective. After Janek finally commits to a relationship with younger woman Beverly D'Angelo, she observes: "You're so smart about everything else, Janek, why do you have this blind spot about women?" Indeed, Janek's love life does not fare well in this detective film series. Although he and Diahann Carroll obviously felt a strong mutual attraction in *Murder in Black and White* (1990), Janek backed away—to avoid professional conflict—after a single kiss. When engrossed in a case, Janek worked closely with dependable colleague and friend Aaron Greenberg (series regular Cliff Gorman). Novelist Bayer penned an original screenplay for 1988's *Internal Affairs*, which, like *Doubletake*, was broadcast originally as a two-part, four-hour movie. The other films filled typical two-hour time slots.

Doubletake (1985 TVM)
Internal Affairs (1988 TVM)
Murder in Black and White (1990 TVM)
Murder Times Seven (1990 TVM)
Terror on Track 9 (aka *Janek: The Grand Central Murders*) (1992 TVM)

Jaws

Despite production difficulties and what was at that time a hefty $12 million price tag, 1975's *Jaws* was pegged for blockbuster status from the start. Audiences had been carefully primed by Peter Benchley's thrilling best-seller and a publicity campaign that beached a Great White shark on the cover of *Time* magazine. The simple story of an East Coast resort transformed into a hunting ground for an insatiable shark went on to gross $133 million. Discounting ticket inflation, that made it the box office champ of all time until *Star Wars* (and eventually *E.T.*) displaced it. The inevitable sequel, *Jaws 2*, followed in 1978, with local police chief Roy Scheider, his wife Lorraine Gary and mayor Murray Hamilton returning from the original. Journeyman director Jeannot Szwarc replaced Spielberg at the helm of what was basically a rehash of the original. The shark was a female this time (spouse of the first one), but she was scary enough to earn $82.5 million in domestic rentals. No one seemed interested in making a second sequel, though a National Lampoon-style spoof, *Jaws 3 People 0*, sat on the drawing boards for awhile. Finally, in 1983, at the height of the 3-D craze (q.v.), Universal released *Jaws 3-D*. A sequel in name only, it pitted Sea World staffers Dennis Quaid and Bess Armstrong against another human-devouring shark. The 3-D effects were excellent, but the profit figures were disappointing and apparently ended the series. Unfortunately, *Jaws: The Revenge* unexpectedly surfaced in 1987. Lorraine Gary returned as Roy Scheider's widow, who has become convinced that another shark (the son of the first one?) has a personal vendetta against her family. It was nonsense from start to finish, and the entire cast, including Michael Caine, looked thoroughly embarrassed. No one went to see it, either, hopefully ending the series for good. See also **Sharks.**

Jaws (1975)

Jaws 2 (1978)

Jaws 3 (aka Jaws 3-D) (1983)

Jaws: The Revenge (1987)

Jekyll, Dr., and Mr. Hyde

Robert Louis Stevenson's dual-sided doctor has been one of the most active characters in cinema. Undoubtedly, much of his popularity stems from the challenge the double role affords actors, allowing them to run the gamut from good Dr. Jekyll to vile Mr. Hyde. Prior to 1920, no fewer than twelve silent versions appeared, ranging from Gene Gauntier's 1908 film to the comedy *Dr. Jekyll and Mr. Hyde Done to a Frazzle* (1914) to the offbeat *Miss Jekyll and Madame Hyde* (1915). Sheldon Lewis received good reviews as Jekyll/Hyde in a 1920 version for Louis B. Mayer. However, that same year he was eclipsed by John Barrymore, whose flamboyant performance would remain the standard for the next decade. Barrymore's interpretation took a back seat, though, to Frederic March's Oscar-winning portrayal in Rouben Mamoulian's *Dr. Jekyll and Mr. Hyde* (1932). This remains the definitive adaptation of Stevenson's work, with March still the only performer to win an Academy Award for a horror film. Spencer Tracy wore minimal makeup in MGM's lavish 1941 version, trying to emphasize Jekyll's emotional (as opposed to physical) transformation into Hyde. Tracy and the film received mixed reviews, inviting less-than-favorable comparisons to the March version. Subsequently, no major Jekyll/Hyde film was made until Jean Renoir's French variation, *The Testament of Dr. Cordelier* (1959). Nevertheless, Jekyll remained a popular character in lesser films. Abbott and Costello met the good doctor (as played by Boris Karloff) in 1951. In the film's funniest scene, Lou drinks Jekyll's potion and is transformed into a giant talking mouse. Louis Hayward played Jekyll's son and Gloria Talbott his daughter in a pair of unexceptional B-horror films (although Talbott's movie confused matters by making Jekyll a werewolf!). Hammer Films remade Stevenson's tale as 1960's *House of Fright* (aka *The Two Faces of Dr. Jekyll*). Naturally, the British studio stressed the story's sexual elements, but it also included a refreshing twist, presenting Henry Jekyll as a dull wimp and Hyde as a dashing, handsome devil. Hammer also deserves credit for another interesting variation, 1971's *Dr. Jekyll and Sister Hyde*, in which Ralph Bates drinks the serum and turns into Martine Beswick. Dozens of movies have featured dual-personality themes or paid homage to Stevenson's story, including 1942's *Before I Hang*, *The Nutty Professor*, Jean-Luc Godard's *Alphaville* (which featured two characters named Jekyll and Hyde), and Ken Russell's *Altered States* (1980).

Dr. Jekyll and Mr. Hyde (1920) (Sheldon Lewis)

Dr. Jekyll and Mr. Hyde (1920) (John Barrymore)

Dr. Pyckle and Mr. Pride (1925) (parody with Stan Laurel)

Dr. Jekyll and Mr. Hyde (1932)

Dr. Jekyll and Mr. Hyde (1941)

Abbott and Costello Meet Dr. Jekyll and Mr. Hyde (1951)

Son of Dr. Jekyll (1951)

Daughter of Dr. Jekyll (1957)

The Testament of Dr. Cordelier (aka *The Doctor's Horrible Experiment*) (1959)

House of Fright (aka *The Two Faces of Dr. Jekyll*) (1960)

Mad Monster Party? (1967)

Dr. Jekyll and Sister Hyde (1971)
Dr. Jekyll and the Werewolf (1971)
I, Monster (1971)
Twisted Brain (aka *Horror High*) (1974)
Dr. Black and Mr. Hyde (aka *The Watts Monster; Dr. Black and Mr. White*)
    (1976)
Dr. Heckyl and Mr. Hype (1980)
Jekyll and Hyde . . . Together Again (1982)
Edge of Sanity (1989)
Jekyll and Hyde (1990 TVM)

Jesus

The film industry's concern for reverence and its aversion to controversy have severely limited screen portraits of Jesus. In many biblical films, Christ's hand is shown or his voice is heard (as in 1959's *Ben-Hur*), but full figure shots are carefully avoided. Cecil B. DeMille mounted a tasteful story of Jesus' life with 1927's *King of Kings*, starring H.B. Warner in the title role. Nicholas Ray remade it to less effect in 1961 with thirty-six-year-old (but still youthful-looking) Jeffrey Hunter as Christ. Unkind critics promptly dubbed it *I Was a Teenage Jesus*. George Stevens recruited solemn Swedish actor Max Von Sydow to play Jesus in his excessively lavish production of *The Greatest Story Ever Told* (1965). Originally released at over four hours in length, it was cut to 141 minutes — but still flopped. However, it did receive Harvard Lampoon's Please-Don't-Put-Us-Through-De-Mille-Again Award for being the movie "which best embodied the pretensions, extravagance and blundering ineffectiveness of the traditional screen spectacular." The following year, Marxist filmmaker Pier Paolo Pasolini received the praise of both film critics and Roman Catholic leaders for his low-key, amateur-cast *The Gospel According to St. Matthew*. Other straightforward, reverent versions of Christ's life include Franco Zeffirelli's two-part, 6½ hour TV-movie *Jesus of Nazareth* (1977), the Israeli-made *Jesus* (1979), and another TV-movie, *The Day Christ Died* (1980). In 1973, the popular stage musicals *Jesus Christ, Superstar* and *Godspell* reached the screen, but neither found an eager audience. The 1979 *In Search of Historic Jesus* purported to be a documentary about the Shroud of Turin but was less than enlightening. Two films of significantly greater interest surfaced in 1988. *The Seventh Sign* mixed elements of mystery and fantasy into its plot about Jesus' (Jurgen Prochnow) return to Earth to prepare the human race for the forthcoming Apocalypse. Despite an intriguing theme, it attracted little attention, especially when compared to the exaggerated controversy surrounding Martin Scorsese's *The Last Temptation of Christ*. Fundamentalist groups tried to stop — sight unseen — this adaptation of Nikos Kazantzakis's novel, chiefly due to a dream sequence where Jesus (Willem Dafoe) was tempted by desires of the flesh. Monty Python's *Life of Brian* (1979) incurred less wrath, despite presenting a satirical tale about a poor bloke who is mistaken for Jesus and crucified (it ended with a song-and-dance number on the cross). Christ's life has been told in allegorical terms in a number of films, such as *El Topo* (1971) and *Greaser's Palace* (1972). Peter O'Toole and Peter Boyle played lunatics who believed they were Christ in, respectively, *The Ruling Class* (1971) and *The Dream Team* (1989).

Intolerance (1916)
King of Kings (1927)
Ben-Hur (1959)
King of Kings (1961)
Barabbas (1962)
The Greatest Story Ever Told (1965)
The Gospel According to St. Matthew (1966)
The Milky Way (1969)
Godspell (1973)
The Gospel Road (1973)
Jesus Christ, Superstar (1973)
The Passover Plot (1976)

Jesus of Nazareth (1977 TVM)
In Search of Historic Jesus (1979)
Jesus (1979)
The Day Christ Died (1980 TVM)
The Inquiry (1987)
The Last Temptation of Christ (1988)
The Seventh Sign (1988)
Jesus of Montreal (1989)
Child of Light, Child of Darkness (1991 TVM)
The Return (aka *Jesus Vender Tilbage*) (1992)

Jewel Thieves

The classiest of criminals, jewel thieves have long enjoyed a popularity rarely accorded to other lawbreakers. This cinematic leniency can be traced to two key points: (1) Most jewel thieves are suave, witty and good-looking (as played by David Niven, Cary Grant, etc.); and (2) jewel thieves typically steal from rich people or museums, so that the lost property is certain to be insured by large corporations that already "steal" money from the middle class. The concept of the "gentleman thief" owes much to E. W. Horung's book *The Amateur Cracksman*, which was filmed as *Raffles* in 1917 (with John Barrymore), 1925 (House Peters), 1930 (Ronald Colman), and 1940 (David Niven). Barrymore played a gentlemanly jewel thief again in the 1932 films *Arsene Lupin* (q.v.) and *Grand Hotel*. Niven continued to display an affection for other people's diamonds in *The Pink Panther* (1964) and *Rough Cut* (1980). Warren Williams and several other actors played The Lone Wolf (q.v.), a jewel-thief-turned-detective in a film series spanning the 1930s and 1940s. George Hamilton hid his tan lines under a black turtleneck in 1967's *Jack of Diamonds*. However, the cinema's most charming gentleman thief has to be Cary Grant, who portrayed a retired cat burglar chasing a copycat criminal (and Grace Kelly) in Hitchcock's *To Catch a Thief*. Hitchcock also dealt with jewel thieves, though less effectively, in his earlier *Number Seventeen* (1932). Female jewel thieves proved themselves just as effective as their male counterparts in *I Was an Adventuress* (1940), the aforementioned *To Catch a Thief*, and Lubitsch's sophisticated comedy *Trouble in Paradise* (1932). A cat burglar called The Phantom stole the Pink Panther diamond—but also encountered the ever-bumbling Inspector Clouseau—in *The Pink Panther* (1964) and *The Return of the Pink Panther* (1975). Clever thieves implemented elaborate schemes to steal the crown jewels in *The Adventures of Sherlock Holmes* (1939), *Traitor's Gate* (1965) and *The Jokers* (1966). For a discussion of movies in which the heist forms the central plot, see **Heist/Caper Films**. See also **The Lone Wolf; Lupin, Arsene; The Pink Panther.**

Raffles (1930)
Jewel Robbery (1932)
Trouble in Paradise (1932)
Grand Hotel (1932)

Number Seventeen (1932)
Arsene Lupin (1932)
Now and Forever (1934)
The Mystery of Mr. X (1934)

The Lone Wolf Returns (1935)
I Am a Thief (1935)
This Man Is News (1938)
Stolen Heaven (1938)
The Amazing Mr. Forrest (aka *The Gang's All Here*) (1939)
The Adventures of Sherlock Holmes (1939)
Raffles (1940)
Adventure in Diamonds (1940)
I Was an Adventuress (1940)
They Met in Bombay (1941)
The Peterville Diamond (1941)
A Gentleman After Dark (1942)
The Great Jewel Robber (1950)
To Catch a Thief (1955)

The Man Inside (1958)
The Greengage Summer (aka *Loss of Innocence*) (1961)
The Pink Panther (1964)
Traitor's Gate (1965)
The Jokers (1966)
That Riviera Touch (1966)
Jack of Diamonds (1967)
Deadfall (1968)
The Thief Who Came to Dinner (1973)
The Return of the Pink Panther (1975)
Rough Cut (1980)
The Great Muppet Caper (1981)
Thief of Hearts (1984)
Oddball Hall (1990)
Hudson Hawk (1991)

Jiggs and Maggie

In 1916 George McManus created this comic strip about a nouveau riche Irish couple with social aspirations. Comedian Johnny Ray played Jiggs in a series of silent two-reelers produced by Pathé Studios. The characters also appeared in a successful 1921 stage play called *Bringing Up Father*. That play served as the basis for a 1928 MGM film starring J. Farrell McDonald as the badgered Jiggs and Marie Dressler as society-minded Maggie. However, a series did not appear until budget-conscious Monogram reintroduced the characters in 1946 with another version of *Bringing Up Father*. Joe Yule (Mickey Rooney's father) and Renie Riano starred as Jiggs and Maggie in that film and four subsequent entries. Yule died in 1950, shortly after completing *Jiggs and Maggie Out West*. For sheer silliness, *Jiggs and Maggie in Society* rates as the series highlight, with Maggie taking dancing lessons from Arthur Murray and Jiggs learning etiquette from Dale Carnegie. Neil O'Malley and Agnes Moorehead also played the couple on a 1941 radio program.

Bringing Up Father (1928)
Bringing Up Father (1946)
Jiggs and Maggie in Court (1948)
Jiggs and Maggie in Society (1949)

Jiggs and Maggie in Jackpot Jitters (aka *Jackpot Jitters*) (1949)
Jiggs and Maggie Out West (1950)

Johnson, Coffin Ed, *see* Coffin Ed Johnson and Grave Digger Jones

Jones, Grave Digger, *see* Coffin Ed Johnson and Grave Digger Jones

Jones, Indiana

Steven Spielberg on *Raiders of the Lost Ark*: "The film's like popcorn, it doesn't fill you and it's easy to digest and it melts in your mouth and it's the kind of thing you can just go and chow down over and over again." That's precisely what moviegoers did with 1981's blockbuster homage to the days of serial thrills. Director Spielberg and executive producer George Lucas (who cowrote the story) received most of the credit, with the witty screenplay by Lawrence Kasdan (pre-*Big Chill*) being largely ignored. Harrison Ford, playing a part similar to Han Solo in the *Star Wars* (q.v.) films, created the whip-carrying archaeologist/adventurer who battled Nazis for the Ark of the Covenant circa 1936. For some reason, the 1984 follow-up, *Indiana Jones and the Temple of Doom*, turned out to be a prequel (q.v.) set three years before *Raiders*. The plot sent Indiana to India to fetch a magical jewel and rescue some enslaved children. The film made tons of money but incurred a surprising amount of wrath. It was criticized for being racist toward Indians, antifeminist, and overly violent for the young members of its audience. The last complaint contributed to the Motion Picture Association of America's creation of a PG-13 film rating. Spielberg and Lucas set the series on track with what they claimed would be the final entry, 1989's *Indiana Jones and the Last Crusade*. Although *Batman* eclipsed it as the year's top money-maker, the *Last Crusade* received an overwhelming thumbs up from both critics and the public. The teaming of Ford and Sean Connery as his father turned out to be pure magic — which set the rumor mill about a fourth film into motion. Ford also appeared as Indy in a 1993 episode of the *Young Indiana Jones Chronicles* TV series.

    Raiders of the Lost Ark (1981)
    Indiana Jones and the Temple of Doom (1984)
    Indiana Jones and the Last Crusade (1989)

The Jones Family

While the Hardys (q.v.) are still fondly remembered, the Joneses have been all but forgotten. Yet, Twentieth Century-Fox's Jones Family series actually came first and set the pattern for the wholesome family comedy/dramas of the late 1930s and 1940s. For the first film, 1936's *Every Saturday Night*, the family's last name was Evers. It switched to Jones that same year in *Educating Father*, the entry that set the tone for the rest of the series by putting Pa Jones in the spotlight. This emphasis on a none-too-perfect father figure is what distinguishes the Jones comedies from the Hardy pictures, which clearly belong to teenager Andy Hardy (Mickey Rooney). Veteran character actor Jed Prouty played bespectacled Pa Jones and Spring Byington, who made a career of maternal roles, was Ma. The principal Jones kids were played by Shirley Deane (oldest daughter Bonnie), Kenneth Howell (Jack), George Ernest (Roger) and June Carlson (Lucy). Bonnie Jones married her boyfriend Herbert Thompson (Russell Gleason) and became a mother in 1938's *Love on a Budget*. But stagestruck little sister Lucy remains the best remembered of the children, stealing scenes with her impersonations of Katharine Hepburn and Greta Garbo. Typical plots involved Pa's candidacy for mayor (*Hot Water*), a family vacation in Yosemite (*Back to Nature*), and an oil swindle (*Big Business*). Despite its modest popularity, the Jones Family series ended in 1940, while the Hardys lasted well into the decade. Many of the cast members, though, continued in similar movies, with Russell Gleason even appearing in the rival Higgins Family series (q.v.).

    Every Saturday Night (1936)   *Back to Nature* (1936)
    Educating Father (1936)   *Off to the Races* (1937)

Big Business (aka *The Jones Family in Big Business*) (1937)
Hot Water (1937)
Borrowing Trouble (1937)
A Trip to Paris (1938)
Love on a Budget (1938)
Safety in Numbers (1938)
Down on the Farm (1938)

The Jones Family in Hollywood (1939)
Quick Millions (aka *The Jones Family in Quick Millions*) (1939)
Everybody's Baby (1939)
Too Busy to Work (1939)
On Their Own (1940)
Young as You Feel (1940)

Josser, Jimmy

British vaudeville comedian Ernie Lotinga played the "much put upon" Jimmy Josser on the stage and in a series of shorts before making the transition to feature-length films. *P.C. Josser* (1931), an adaptation of Lotinga's play *The Police Force*, was a minor comedy about Josser's attempts to regain his job as a policeman. It pretty much set the pattern for the rest of the series, which briefly enjoyed minor popularity in its native country.

P.C. Josser (1931)
Dr. Josser KC (1931)
Josser Joins the Navy (1932)

Josser on the River (1932)
Josser in the Army (1932)
Josser on the Farm (1934)

Judges

While lawyers have garnered most of the courtroom limelight, judges have proven themselves to be more versatile outside the typical legal setting. In *The Life and Times of Judge Roy Bean* (1972), the legendary Western judge (Paul Newman) appointed himself to his post and heard cases in the local saloon. The judges in 1983's *The Star Chamber* moonlighted as vigilantes who executed criminals that avoided sentencing due to legal loopholes. Robert Van Gulick's Judge Dee, a seventh-century Oriental detective, solved his only celluloid case in the engaging 1974 TV-movie *Judge Dee and the Monastery Murders*. Female judges have been represented by Susan Hayward in *The Bachelor and the Bobby-Soxer* (1947) and Jill Clayburgh in *First Monday in October* (1981). The latter film, based on a play predating Sandra Day O'Connor's appointment, cast Clayburgh as the first woman on the Supreme Court. Arthur Hill may have played the screen's most courageous judge, as the real-life official who battled a racially prejudiced town in *Judge Horton and the Scottsboro Boys* (1976), a vivid account of the trial of nine blacks accused of raping a white woman. As Judge Hardy in the Andy Hardy series (q.v.), stern but fair Lewis Stone played a judge more often than any other performer. On the small screen, Judge Wapner listened to plaintiffs and dished out decisions on a weekday basis on *The People's Court*. See also **Courts Martial.**

Ann Vickers (1933)
Judge Priest (1934)
Angel on My Shoulder (1946)
Cass Timberlane (1947)
The Bachelor and the Bobby-Soxer (aka *Bachelor Knight*) (1947)
An Act of Murder (aka *Live for Tomorrow*) (1948)

The Judge Steps Out (1949)
The Judge and Jake Wyler (1972 TVM)
The Life and Times of Judge Roy Bean (1972)
Judge Dee and the Monastery Murders (1974 TVM)
Jury of One (aka *The Verdict*) (1974)
The Judge and the Assassin (1975)

Judge Horton and the Scottsboro Boys	*Crime of Innocence* (1985 TVM)
(1976 TVM)	*Penalty Phase* (1986 TVM)
All God's Children (1980 TVM)	*Double Standard* (1988 TVM)
First Monday in October (1981)	*Naked Lie* (1989 TVM)
The Star Chamber (1983)	

Jungle Jim

Johnny Weissmuller hung up his loincloth after 1948's *Tarzan and the Mermaids*, but he didn't stay out of the jungle for long. That same year, he moved from RKO to Columbia and kicked off a series of low-budget action pictures for producer Sam Katzman. Weissmuller's *Jungle Jim*, although based on a comic strip and radio program, was clearly inspired by Tarzan (q.v.). Sure, Jungle Jim wore clothes and spoke in complete sentences (most of the time), but the fast-paced plots (which got progressively sillier) were pure Burroughs. In the first film, Jim had a pet crow and a little dog. These "unjungle" denizens were later traded for a trusty chimp sidekick. The *Jungle Jim* films never rose above the level of backlot juvenile features, but the supporting cast sometimes included a surprising face or two, such as B-movie faves Buster Crabbe and Ray "Crash" Corrigan. The outrageousness of the plots deserves special mention, too. Jim battled "man monsters" (*Jungle Jim in the Forbidden Land*), pesky pygmies (*Jungle Moon Men*) and Nazis (*Voodoo Tiger*). In the last three films, Weissmuller dropped the Jungle Jim moniker and went by his real name. When the series ended in 1955, he moved to television and made the half-hour *Jungle Jim* syndicated series. It lasted for twenty-six episodes and costarred Martin Huston.

Jungle Jim (1948)	*Jungle Jim in the Forbidden Land*
The Lost Tribe (1949)	(1952)
Captive Girl (1950)	*Voodoo Tiger* (1952)
Mark of the Gorilla (1950)	*Killer Ape* (1953)
Pygmy Island (1950)	*Savage Mutiny* (1953)
Fury of the Congo (1951)	*Valley of the Headhunters* (1953)
Jungle Manhunt (1951)	*Jungle Maneaters* (1954)

As Johnny Weissmuller (but still considered part of Jungle Jim series):

Cannibal Attack (1954)	*Jungle Moon Men* (1955)
Devil Goddess (1955)	

The Karate Kid

Critics dubbed it a junior-league *Rocky*, but the 1984 sleeper hit *The Karate Kid* had its own winning formula built around the friendship between a gawky teen (Ralph Macchio) and a janitor/philosopher/martial artist (Noriyuki "Pat" Morita). Okay, it *was* directed by the *Rocky* veteran John Avildsen and *did* climax with a dramatic fight in the ring—but no characters were named Adrienne, Mick or Apollo. In 1986, *The Karate Kid Part II* took Morita and Macchio to the Orient with predictable results; the film was notable only for spawning Peter Cetera's number one song "The Glory of Love." Audiences snubbed a second sequel, released in 1989, which basically rehashed the original. In 1993, producer Jerry Weintraub announced a fourth installment—with a female lead replacing Macchio.

The Karate Kid (1984)
The Karate Kid Part II (1986)
The Karate Kid Part III (1989)

Karnstein Trilogy

Hammer Films, the "House of Horror" in the 1960s, saw its once-loyal audience dwindling rapidly in the early 1970s. To attract new horror fans, it updated its Christopher Lee *Dracula* (q.v.) films and introduced a new series about lesbian vampire Mircalla Karnstein. Based on Sheridan Le Fanu's novel *Carmilla*, 1970's *The Vampire Lovers* pitted veteran vampire hunter Peter Cushing against buxom Ingrid Pitt as Mircalla. In the end, she lost her head and was staked as well. She was resurrected in the form of Yutte Stensgaard for 1971's *Lust for a Vampire*, a lively sequel directed by horror veteran Jimmy Sangster. The series concluded with 1971's *Twins of Evil*, in which Mircalla (now played by Katya Keith) takes a back seat to a tale about twin village girls—one an innocent and one a vicious vampire. Again, Peter Cushing was around to provide the necessary heroics, although his character died in the process. Hammer was gasping for its dying breath, too. It produced its last theatrical film in 1974. See also **Vampires.**

The Vampire Lovers (1970)
Lust for a Vampire (aka *To Love a Vampire*) (1971)
Twins of Evil (1971)

Keate, Nurse Sarah (Sally Keating)

Mignon G. Eberhart's medically minded detective never made a successful transition from page to screen in the 1930s. In Eberhart's novels, Sarah Keate was a middle-aged nurse who solved mysteries with the assistance of young police detective Lance O'Leary. Aline MacMahon played a thirtyish Nurse Keate in 1935's *While the Patient Slept*, a Warners Bros. adaptation of a popular Eberhart novel. Guy Kibbee, who was fifty-three, portrayed Lance as a character altogether different from the one in Eberhart's books and stories. Warner Bros. subsequently used the Keate series as a training ground for promising actresses: Kay Linaker (*The Murder of Dr. Harrigan*), Marguerite Churchill (*Murder by an Aristocrat*), and Ann Sheridan (*The Patient in Room 18* and *Mystery House*). In the Linaker and Churchill movies, the heroine's name was changed to Sally Keating. Patric Knowles, another rising star, played Lance in *The Patient in Room 18.* Jane Darwell, a good choice for the spinsterish detective, played Nurse Keats (not Keate) in Twentieth Century-Fox's *The Great Hospital Mystery* (1937). Although Eberhart's Nurse Keate books resulted in strictly B-movies, she enjoyed a fine career as a mystery writer. The Mystery Writers of America gave her the prestigious Grand Master award in 1970.

While the Patient Slept (1935) (Aline MacMahon)
The Murder of Dr. Harrigan (1936) (Kay Linaker as Sally Keating)
Murder by an Aristocrat (1936) (Marguerite Churchill as Sally Keating)
The Great Hospital Mystery (1937) (Jane Darwell as Nurse Keats)
The Patient in Room 18 (1938) (Ann Sheridan)
Mystery House (1938) (Sheridan)

Keating, Sally, *see* Keate, Nurse Sarah

Kettle, Ma and Pa

Marjorie Main and Percy Kilbride made their debut as Ma and Pa Kettle in the 1947 Universal comedy *The Egg and I.* Adapted from Betty McDonald's best-seller, the picture featured Claudette Colbert as a Bostonian lass introduced to chicken farming by new hubby Fred MacMurray. The Kettles were merely supporting characters, but they were responsible for the film's funniest scenes. Universal reteamed Main and Kilbride the following year in the cornpone Donald O'Connor comedy *Feudin', Fussin' and A-Fightin'* and then turned them into stars with 1949's *Ma and Pa Kettle.* Produced for $200,000 to $400,000 each, the Kettle movies earned tidy profits for Universal through the mid-1950s. The simple series formula usually found lazy, laid-back Pa getting into unintentional mischief, while Ma ruled the Kettle brood of fifteen kids. Several entries derived humor by moving the Kettles (temporarily) to big cities. Thus, the Kettle clan visited New York (*Go to Town*), Paris (*Vacation*), and Hawaii (*Waikiki*). Richard Long played Tom, the Kettles' oldest son, and other children included Lori Nelson (Rosie) and Brett Halsey (Elwin). Pa's Indian cohort Crowbar was played by four actors: Vic Potel, Chief Yowlachie, Teddy Hart and Zachary Charles. After seven films in as many years, Percy Kilbride quit the series. There was no Pa Kettle in 1956's *The Kettles in the Ozarks*, although Arthur Hunnicutt's Uncle Sedge was mighty similar. Pa was back, though, in the guise of character actor Parker Fennelly in 1957's *The Kettles on Old MacDonald's Farm.* It turned out not only to be the last Kettle film, but also Marjorie Main's final screen role. She retired from acting and died in 1975.

The Egg and I (1947)
Ma and Pa Kettle (1949)
Ma and Pa Kettle Go to Town (1950)
Ma and Pa Kettle Back on the Farm (1951)
Ma and Pa Kettle at the Fair (1952)

Ma and Pa Kettle on Vacation (1953)
Ma and Pa Kettle at Home (1954)
Ma and Pa Kettle at Waikiki (1955)
The Kettles in the Ozarks (1956)
The Kettles on Old MacDonald's Farm (1957)

Kickboxer

Belgian martial artist Jean-Claude Van Damme clinched his niche in the 1990s action movie field with 1989's *Kickboxer.* The plot, instantly recognizable to any martial arts film enthusiast, has Van Damme swearing vengeance against a vicious Thai fighter who crippled his older brother, a world kickboxing champion. However, to beat his adversary, Van Damme must master Muay-Thai fighting, which he can learn only from the elusive Dennis Chan (Xian Chow). The outcome was never in doubt, of course, and *Kickboxer* failed to register the emotional uplift generated by *Rocky* or even *The Karate Kid.* Still, the film's popular success warranted a sequel—without the charismatic Van Damme, unfortunately. Sasha Mitchell, best known as J.R.'s illegitimate son on TV's *Dallas*, toplined 1990's *Kickboxer 2: The Road Back.* An odd choice, Mitchell did boast prior film fighting credentials, having played a boxer in the 1989 comedy-drama *Spike of Bensonhurst*. In *Kickboxer 2*, Mitchell apparently played Van Damme's younger brother, who attracts the attention of gangsters after getting behind on his gym's mortgage payments. He solves that dilemma, then heads to Rio de Janeiro for another tournament and more trouble in 1992's *Kickboxer 3: The Art of War*. Xian Chow repeated his role as Dennis Chan in both Mitchell sequels. For other martial arts series, see **American Ninja Series, Bloodfist,** and **No Retreat, No Surrender** (in which a then-unknown Van Damme appears briefly).

Kickboxer (1989)   *Kickboxer 3: The Art of War* (1992)
Kickboxer 2: The Road Back (1990)

Kildare, Dr.

The year after Joel McCrea introduced Dr. James Kildare in Paramount's *Interns Can't Take Money* (1937), MGM launched an immensely popular Kildare film series starring Lew Ayres. The supporting cast at Blair General Hospital was a potent one, featuring wheelchair-bound Lionel Barrymore as Dr. Gillespie, Laraine Day as Mary Lamont, and Nell Craig as Nurse Parker. Ayres and company made nine movies, dealing efficiently with daily medical crises and topical subjects like insulin shock. Then, in 1941, the series stunned moviegoers with *Dr. Kildare's Wedding Day*, in which Day's character was killed off. That same year, Ayres elicited a wave of bad publicity by refusing to enter the army on the grounds he was a conscientious objector. MGM promptly dropped Ayres from the Kildare series, although the actor eventually enlisted and served in combat. Rather than casting a new Kildare, MGM shifted the series focus to Barrymore with 1942's *Calling Dr. Gillespie*. Later that year, Van Johnson was introduced as *Dr. Gillespie's New Assistant*, a role he continued in four of the final five Gillespie pictures. Throughout the Kildare/Gillespie series, MGM introduced up-and-coming stars such as future *Marcus Welby* Robert Young, Donna Reed, and child star Margaret O'Brien. *Dr. Kildare* came to television in 1961 with Richard Chamberlain in the lead and Raymond Massey as Dr. Gillespie. It enjoyed high ratings and a five-year run. A half-hour syndicated program, *Young Dr. Kildare*, lasted for twenty-four episodes in 1972. See also **Hospitals; Nurses Series.**

Interns Can't Take Money (aka *You Can't Take Money*) (1937) (McCrea)
Young Dr. Kildare (1938) (Ayres)
Calling Dr. Kildare (1939) (Ayres)
The Secret of Dr. Kildare (1939) (Ayres)
Dr. Kildare Goes Home (1940) (Ayres)
Dr. Kildare's Crisis (1940) (Ayres)
Dr. Kildare's Strange Case (1940) (Ayres)
The People vs. Dr. Kildare (aka *My Life Is Yours*) (1941) (Ayres)
Dr. Kildare's Wedding Day (aka *Mary Names the Day*) (1941) (Ayres)
Dr. Kildare's Victory (1941) (aka *The Debutante and the Doctor*) (Ayres)
Calling Dr. Gillespie (1942) (Barrymore)
Dr. Gillespie's New Assistant (1942) (Barrymore)
Dr. Gillespie's Criminal Case (aka *Crazy to Kill*) (1943) (Barrymore)
Between Two Women (1944) (Barrymore)
Three Men in White (1944) (Barrymore)
Dark Delusion (aka *Cynthia's Secret*) (1947) (Barrymore)

Killer Tomatoes

Attack of the Killer Tomatoes (1979) established its reputation as one of the "worst films of all time" in a remarkably short period. Indeed, that status may have been the filmmakers' aim when they produced this sophomoric ode to low-budget, sci-fi camp. It's not as bad as one would hope—the inane title song is downright funny, and a Japanese character dubbed out-of-sync makes an amusing tribute to sci-fi imports. The 1988 sequel, *Return of the Killer Tomatoes*, starred Anthony Starke as a pizza delivery boy who develops a crush on scientist John Astin's daughter, only to discover that she's a tomato transformed into a woman! Astin returned as Professor Gangreen for 1990's *Killer Tomatoes Strike Back*. A Saturday morning animated series followed on the FOX network.

    Attack of the Killer Tomatoes (1979)
    Return of the Killer Tomatoes (1988)
    Killer Tomatoes Strike Back (1990)

King Kong

"The Eighth Wonder of the World," as showman Carl Denham proclaimed Kong in the 1933 original, was actually a three-foot model brought to life by master stop-motion animator Willis O'Brien. The marvelous O'Brien had previously performed his camera trickery on the dinosaurs (q.v.) in 1925's *The Lost World*. His post-*Kong* work included some excellent effects in the seldom-shown 1933 sequel *Son of Kong* and another giant friendly ape opus, 1949's *Mighty Joe Young*. But O'Brien's contribution accounts for just part—albeit a crucial one—of *King Kong*'s enduring success. The other critical ingredients are the film's simplistic beauty-and-the-beast theme and its ability to make Kong *a character* audiences can identify with. Subsequent Kong films floundered drastically on both counts. Japan monster movie-maker Inoshira Honda revived Kong after a twenty-nine-year hiatus for "the colossal clash of all time," 1962's *King Kong vs. Godzilla*. Featuring a man in an ape suit as Kong, it was a dull affair, of mild interest only because Kong won the fight in U.S. prints and Godzilla won in the Japanese version. Honda mounted a sequel of sorts with 1968's *King Kong Escapes*, which pitted the giant ape against a robotic replica called Mechani-Kong. At least Honda did not dare compare his film to the original *Kong*. Unfortunately, Dino De Laurentiis did just that with his $24 million man-in-ape-suit 1976 remake. *Variety* dubbed it "a brilliant remake," but most critics drubbed it, and plans for an immediate sequel were temporarily scrapped. However, that sequel finally reached the screen in 1986 as *King Kong Lives*. Kong, it turns out, had survived his fall from the World Trade Center but required a blood transfusion. Enter Mrs. Kong. This ludicrous picture turned the giant ape into a giant turkey at the box office. Nevertheless, it introduced star Linda Hamilton to the beauty-and-the-beast angle—excellent training for her 1987 TV series *Beauty and the Beast*. See also **Apes and Monkeys**.

    King Kong (1933)
    Son of Kong (1933)
    King Kong vs. Godzilla (aka
       Kingukongu tai Gojira) (1962)

    King Kong Escapes (aka *Kingukongu
       No Gyakushu*) (1968)
    King Kong (1976)
    King Kong Lives (1986)

Kojak, Theo

The fact-based film *The Marcus-Nelson Murders* (1973) introduced bald, lollipop-licking police lieutenant Theo Kojak to TV audiences. The film was adapted from Selwyn Rabb's book *Justice in the Back Room*, an account of the 1963 Wylie-Hoffert murders, which played a major role in the Supreme Court's *Miranda* decision. Savalas's Emmy-nominated portrayal resulted in the popular 1973-78 *Kojak* TV series. After a vacation from the role, Savalas revived Kojak in two TV-movies before returning on a regular basis as a revolving character in 1989 on *The ABC Saturday Mystery*. See also **Television Series Reunion Films.**

> *The Marcus-Nelson Murders* (aka *Kojak and the Marcus-Nelson Murders*) (1973 TVM)
> *Kojak: The Belarus Files* (1985 TVM)
> *Kojak: The Price of Justice* (1987 TVM)

Korean War

If not for the escapades of TV's Hawkeye Pierce and the rest of the M*A*S*H unit, the Korean War might have slipped into relative obscurity. And yet, during the days when American forces fought in Korea, the war was a popular film subject. The war films of the 1950s differed significantly in tone from their World War II counterparts of the 1940s. While escapist entertainment and glossy romances still drew crowds, many of these new pictures were grim, realistic adventures uninterested in glorifying war. Cult movie favorite Samuel Fuller produced two violent, powerful Korean War adventures in 1951: *The Steel Helmet* and *Fixed Bayonets*. The first film dealt with the war's brutal ironies, beginning with a sergeant who, because of his helmet, is the sole survivor when his unit is wiped out. The horror of war dominated *Fixed Bayonets*, as evidenced by a chilling scene where soldiers put their feet together to avoid frostbite — and one foot, already without feeling, is left out. Similar tough-minded films such as *Retreat, Hell!* (1952) and *Men in War* (1957) substituted sturdy stars (e.g., Frank Lovejoy, Robert Ryan) for big-name draws. Nevertheless, Hollywood favorites like Humphrey Bogart (*Battle Circus*) and Robert Mitchum (*One Minute to Zero*) donned fatigues long enough to fight a skirmish or two. William Holden starred as a jet pilot in love with Grace Kelly in the popular hit *Bridges at Toko-Ri* (1954) and then romanced Jennifer Jones in Hong Kong during the war in *Love Is a Many Splendored Thing* (1955). Lower-budgeted Korean War pictures provided roles for an impressive crop of rising young stars, such as Lee Marvin (*The Glory Brigade*), Charles Bronson (*Target Zero*), Robert Redford (*War Hunt*) and Michael Caine and Robert Shaw (both in *Hell in Korea*). Future best-selling author Tom Tryon (*Harvest Home*) played a soldier on shore leave from Korea in *Marines, Let's Go!* (1961). Veteran Western character actor L.Q. Jones and Alvy Moore (Mr. Kimble on *Green Acres*) had supporting roles in, respectively, *Target Zero* and *The Glory Brigade*. Two decades later, these two would team to produce and direct the science fiction cult hit *A Boy and His Dog* (1975). The effect of the Korean War back home in the States was a rare film subject, although 1951's *I Want You* dealt with it sensitively. On the other hand, 1953's *Take the High Ground* was a routine boot camp picture about soldiers undergoing intensive training prior to being shipped to Korea. The horror of war reached beyond the battlefield for the soldiers tried for treason in gripping court martial dramas such as *The Rack* (1956), *Time Limit* (1957) and *Sergeant Ryker* (1968). With exceptions like the latter film, Korean War pictures became increasingly scarce after Gregory Peck closed out the 1950s with the frightening, realistic *Pork Chop Hill*. The 1963 Kirk Douglas picture *The Hook* was a brutally effective portrait of combat. John Frankenheimer's political thriller *The Manchurian Candidate* (1962) turned a Korean vet into a brainwashed assassin. Robert Altman's film version of *M*A*S*H* (1970) showed battlefield physicians acting crazy in order to maintain their sanity in face of war's atrocities. It made a successful transition to television in 1972, where it enjoyed an eleven-year run.

Fixed Bayonets (1951)
I Want You (1951)
The Steel Helmet (1951)
A Yank in Korea (1951)
Battle Circus (1952)
Battle Zone (1952)
One Minute to Zero (1952)
Retreat, Hell! (1952)
Mission Over Korea (1953)
Combat Squad (1953)
The Glory Brigade (1953)
Sabre Jet (1953)
Torpedo Alley (1953)
Take the High Ground (1953)
Bridges at Toko-Ri (1954)
Dragonfly Squadron (1954)
Flight Nurse (1954)
Men of the Fighting Lady (1954)
Prisoner of War (1954)
Battle Taxi (1955)
Hell's Horizon (1955)
Love Is a Many Splendored Thing (1955)
Target Zero (1955)

Hell in Korea (aka *A Hill in Korea*) (1956)
Hold Back the Night (1956)
The Rack (1956)
Strange Intruder (1956)
Men in War (1957)
Time Limit (1957)
The Hunters (1958)
Jet Attack (1958)
Pork Chop Hill (1959)
Battle Flame (1959)
All the Young Men (1960)
Marines, Let's Go! (1961)
Sniper's Ridge (1961)
War Hunt (1961)
The Manchurian Candidate (1962)
The Nun and the Sergeant (1962)
War Is Hell (1963)
The Hook (1963)
Sergeant Ryker (1968)
M*A*S*H (1970)
The Reluctant Heroes (1971 TVM)
Collision Course (1975 TVM)
Inchon (1982)

Ku Klux Klan

Controversy has stalked the KKK from its inception and has naturally overflowed into its sporadic film appearances. D.W. Griffith's landmark 1915 film *Birth of a Nation* continues to incur the wrath of racial rights groups for its glorification of the KKK. Based on Thomas Dixon, Jr.'s *The Clansmen*, Griffith's film ends with a Southern family being rescued from marauding black men by heroic members of the KKK. The National Association for the Advancement of Colored People (NAACP) mounted an effective boycott of the film on its initial release. That inspired Griffith to write a defense of his film, a pamphlet entitled "The Rise and Fall of Free Speech in America." The 1936 *Black Legion* never referred to the KKK, but the racist organization that recruited Humphrey Bogart was obviously patterned after the Ku Klux Klan. *The Texans* (1938), a post-Civil War western, featured a subplot involving the KKK. It was not until 1950's *Storm Warning* that another film dealt exclusively — and frankly — with the Ku Klux Klan. Ginger Rogers starred as a woman who seeks help from liberal D.A. Ronald Reagan after learning that her sister (Doris Day) has married a racist and possibly murderous Klansman. It was far superior to the 1974 fiasco *The Klansman*, an unlikely all-star mishmash starring Richard Burton, Lee Marvin, O.J. Simpson and Linda Evans. The 1979 TV-movie *Attack on Terror: The FBI vs. the Ku Klux Klan* was an engrossing fact-based drama about the murder of three civil rights workers in Mississippi in 1964. The same case provided the basis for another fine film, 1988's Oscar-nominated picture *Mississippi Burning*. Another 1988 release, *Betrayed*, cast Debra Winger as an agent investigating a white supremist terrorist group, a topic previously addressed in the 1987 TV-movie *In the Homeland*. *Fried Green Tomatoes* (1992) and *Sommersby* (1993) featured subplots involving the KKK.

Birth of a Nation (1915)	*In the Homeland* (1987 TVM)
Black Legion (1936)	*Betrayed* (1988)
The Texans (1938)	*Mississippi Burning* (1988)
Storm Warning (1950)	*Unconquered* (1989 TVM)
The FBI Story (1959)	*Cross of Fire* (1989 TVM)
The Black Klansman (1966)	*Murder in Mississippi* (1990 TVM)
The Klansman (1974)	*Line of Fire: The Morris Dees Story*
Attack on Terror: The FBI vs. the Ku	(1991 TVM)
Klux Klan (1975 TVM)	*Fried Green Tomatoes* (1992)
Brotherhood of Death (1976)	*Sommersby* (1993)
Undercover With the KKK (aka *The*	
Freedom Riders; *My Undercover*	
Years With the KKK) (1979 TVM)	

Labor Unions and Strikes

Images of defiant workers and waving picket signs can powerfully transcend the themes of even mediocre films. In the hands of a Sergei Eisenstein, the result can be chilling, as was the case with *Strike* (1924), the famed director's gripping account of a 1912 revolt against working conditions in czarist Russia. Equally compelling was John Sayles's *Matewan* (1987), the fact-based story of a West Virginia coal mine labor dispute circa 1920 that erupted into violence and bloodletting. British films, such as 1944's *The Agitator* and 1960's *The Angry Silence*, have best explored the roles played by powerful individuals on both sides of the picket fence. The latter film concerned a worker ostracized by his peers for refusing to join a walkout. The British even satirized their labor problems with 1960's cunning farce *I'm All Right, Jack*. It was much more adroitly handled than 1958's *Never Steal Anything Small*, an uncomfortable American musical starring James Cagney as a crooked labor leader. In 1992, Jack Nicholson and James Woods starred, respectively, in the union leader biographies *Hoffa* and *Teamster Boss: The Jackie Presser Story*.

Strike (1924)	*Black Fury* (1935)
Metropolis (1925)	*The Agitator* (1944)
The Guns of Loos (1927)	*The Whistle at Eaton Falls* (aka *Richer*
The Revolt of the Fishermen (1934)	*Than the Earth*) (1951)

Salt of the Earth (1953)
Inside Detroit (1956)
The Garment Jungle (1957)
The Pajama Game (1957)
Never Steal Anything Small (1958)
The Big Operator (aka Anatomy of a
  Syndicate) (1959)
The Angry Silence (1960)
I'm All Right, Jack (1960)
Men of Brazil (1960)
Flame in the Streets (1961)
Jessica (1962)
Adalen 31 (1969)
Ramparts of Clay (1971)
Harlan County, U.S.A. (1977)

Sleeping Dogs (1977)
Blue Collar (1978)
F.I.S.T. (1978)
Norma Rae (1979)
Power (1980 TVM)
Keeping On (1981 TVM)
A Matter of Sex (1984 TVM)
The Killing Floor (1984 TVM)
Matewan (1987)
Last Exit to Brooklyn (1989)
American Dream (1989)
Teamster Boss: The Jackie Presser
  Story (1992 TVM)
Hoffa (1992)

Lassie

The caring collie made her debut in 1943's *Lassie, Come Home*, one of the finest of all dog (q.v.) movies. Eric Knight wrote the original novel about a family forced to part with its cherished collie, which manages to overcome all obstacles and return to them. The MGM cast was an exceptional one: established child star Roddy McDowell, promising eleven-year-old Elizabeth Taylor, plus adults Donald Crisp, Nigel Bruce and Elsa Lanchester. Pal, a male collie, played Lassie. Donald Crisp, Nigel Bruce and Pal returned in the 1945 follow-up *Son of Lassie*, with Peter Lawford and June Lockhart (shades of foreshadowing) playing adult versions of McDowell and Taylor. Elizabeth Taylor was back, however, for the following year's *Courage of Lassie*, a confusing entry in which the dog (played by Pal again) was actually called Bill, not Lassie. Fortunately, Lassie was Lassie in 1948's *The Hills of Home*, a colorful entry that reunited Crisp and the collie and featured the always enjoyable Edmund Gwenn and a young Janet Leigh. MGM's last three Lassie entries were unremarkable programmers, although 1949's *The Sun Comes Up* was notable as Jeanette MacDonald's final film appearance. In 1954, Lassie embarked on a long-running, immensely popular TV series. During the original 1954-71 *Lassie* run, the collie was paired with an assortment of owners, including Jeff (Tommy Rettig), Timmy and his Mom (Jon Provost and June Lockhart), and Corey the forest ranger (Robert Bray). See also **Dogs**.

Lassie, Come Home (1943)
Son of Lassie (1945)
Courage of Lassie (1946)
The Hills of Home (1948)
Challenge for Lassie (1949)

The Sun Comes Up (1949)
The Painted Hills (1951)
Lassie's Great Adventure (1963)
The Magic of Lassie (1978)

Lemon Popsicle Series

Former Cannon Films moguls Menahem Golan and Yorum Globus produced this Israeli series of nostalgic teen sex comedies. The films proved to be immensely popular in Europe, inspiring Cannon to produce an Americanized version in 1981, appropriately titled *The Last American Virgin*. Boaz Davidson directed this variation as well as the first four *Popsicle* films.

Lemon Popsicle (1978)
Lemon Popsicle II (aka *Greasy Kids Stuff*) (1979)
Lemon Popsicle III: Let's Go to Paris (aka *Hot Bubblegum*) (1980)
The Last American Virgin (1981)
Lemon Popsicle IV (aka *Private Popsicle*) (1982)
Lemon Popsicle V (aka *Baby Love*) (1983)
Lemon Popsicle VI (aka *Up Your Anchor*) (1984)
Lemon Popsicle VII (aka *Young Love*) (1987)

Lethal Weapon

The continuing popularity of a film series almost always hinges on its ability to evolve over time. Even the Bond films modified their popular formula by emphasizing gadgetry and humor significantly more as the series progressed. On a smaller scale, the three-film *Lethal Weapon* series has also evolved — perhaps explaining why the films have thrived at the box office, while a *48 HRS* sequel received a series-killing, lukewarm reception. In the first *Lethal Weapon* (1987), detective Roger Murtaugh (Danny Glover), a stable, black family man, gets a new partner: white, single and dangerously short-fused Martin Riggs (Mel Gibson). As they bicker through the inevitable shoot-outs and explosions, Murtaugh and Riggs develop a mutual respect — a classic buddy action film (q.v.) premise. The formula was altered for 1989's *Lethal Weapon 2*, which stressed character development and humor, while maintaining enough fistfights and gunplay to please action fans. Joe Pesci provided most of the laughs, with a hyperactive turn as Leo Getz, a money-laundering bank accountant requiring witness protection from the detective odd couple. Pesci popped up again in *Lethal Weapon 3* (1992), which introduced Rene Russo as a karate-kicking internal affairs investigator who catches Riggs's eye. Their unusual romance, Glover's easygoing charm, and Pesci's comic outbursts helped the film generate $80 million in North American box office rentals. The *Lethal Weapon* films were spoofed with mediocre results in 1993's *National Lampoon's Loaded Weapon 1*. See also **Buddy Action Films.**

Lethal Weapon (1987)   *Lethal Weapon 3* (1992)
Lethal Weapon 2 (1989)

Letters

Letters have brought lovers together, torn marriages apart, incriminated the innocent, blackmailed the guilty, and caused endless misunderstandings. Pen pals James Stewart and Margaret Sullavan fell in love through their letters, not realizing they were coworkers in *The Shop Around the Corner* (1940). A little girl sent her mother's photo to her own lonely soldier pen pal in *Never Say Goodbye* (1946), never suspecting that he would come visiting. Similar pen pal deceptions occurred in 1945's *A Letter for Evie* and the 1947 hit comedy *Dear Ruth* (q.v.). One cannot always be certain of the identity of a letter's author. *Cyrano de Bergerac* (Jose Ferrer) wrote poignant love letters to the beautiful Roxanne but signed the name of his hapless friend Christian in the 1950 adaptation of Edmund Rostand's celebrated play. Jennifer Jones suffered amnesia in *Love Letters* (1945) after learning that her wartime love letters were not written by her fiancé. The deceiving letters penned by the devious Marquise de Merteuil (Glenn Close) in *Dangerous Liaisons* (1988) eventually led to the death of her lover (John Malkovitch). Celeste Holm provided the voice of the authoress of *A Letter to Three Wives* (1949), in which three ladies learn that one of their husbands has run off with Holm's character. Paul Lukas played a converted Nazi incriminated by false letters sent by a former friend in *Address Unknown* (1944). Loretta Young tried to retrieve another incriminating letter, one framing her for murder, in 1951's *Cause for Alarm*. Pat Boone was similarly panic-stricken over a hard-to-retrieve letter in the British comedy *Never Put It in Writing* (1964). An unsigned love note dropped into a high school locker revealed numerous hidden feelings in the pleasant 1985 comedy *Secret Admirer*. Misdirected letters reaching their destination after a year-long delay provided the premise for the three-part TV-movie *The Letters* and its sequel *Letters From Three Lovers* (both 1973). *84 Charing Cross Road* (1987) traced the charming twenty-year letter-writing relationship between a New York book lover (Anne Bancroft) and a British book dealer (Anthony Hopkins). See also **Dear Ruth; Postal Carriers.**

The Strong Man (1926)
Poison Pen (1939)
The Shop Around the Corner (1940)
The Letter (1940)
Address Unknown (1944)
Love Letters (1945)
A Letter for Evie (1945)
Never Say Goodbye (1946)
The Captive Heart (1946)
Dear Ruth (1947)
The Lost Moment (1947)
Letter From an Unknown Woman (1948)
A Letter to Three Wives (1949)
Cyrano de Bergerac (1950)
Cause for Alarm (1951)
The 13th Letter (1951)
Demoniaque (1958)
Fate Takes a Hand (1961)
Never Put It in Writing (1964)
Dear Brigitte (1965)
The Go-Between (1971)
The Letters (1973 TVM)
Letters From Three Lovers (1973 TVM)
No Sex Please, We're British (1973)
Dirty Tricks (1980)
Touched by Love (aka *To Elvis, With Love*) (1980)
The Letter (1982 TVM)
Love Letters (aka *My Love Letters*) (1983)
A Letter to Three Wives (1985 TVM)
Secret Admirer (1985)
84 Charing Cross Road (1987)
Dangerous Liaisons (1988)
The Anonymous Letter (aka *El Anonimo*) (1990)

Librarians

It's been difficult for movie librarians to move away from their stereotyped image as shy, conservative bookworms. Despite their star power, Greer Garson (*Adventure*), June Allyson (*Good News*), Shirley Jones (*The Music Man*), and Barbara Eden (*The Seven Faces of Dr. Lao*) did little to alter the stereotype. In contrast, Bette Davis portrayed a fiery librarian fired for her refusal to censor a book on communism in 1956's *Storm Center*. Jewish college dropout-turned-librarian Richard Benjamin ignored social conventions in his pursuit of country club heiress Ali MacGraw in the film version of Philip Roth's frank best-seller *Goodbye, Columbus* (1969). Meek librarian Jason Robards, Jr. turned out to be the only person in town with enough courage and will power to confront the mysterious Mr. Dark in Ray Bradbury's chilling, turn-of-the-century fantasy *Something Wicked This Way Comes* (1983). In the 1974 oddity *Mr. Sycamore*, Robards played a mailman with a crush on librarian Jean Simmons and a bizarre desire to become a tree.

Scandal Street (1938)	*Only Two Can Play* (1962)
Adventure (1945)	*The Seven Faces of Dr. Lao* (1964)
Good News (1947)	*Goodbye, Columbus* (1969)
Katie Did It (1951)	*Mr. Sycamore* (1974)
Storm Center (1956)	*Something Wicked This Way Comes*
Desk Set (aka *His Other Woman*)	(1983)
(1957)	*Off Beat* (1986)
The Music Man (1962)	*The Gun in Betty Lou's Handbag* (1992)

Lighthouses

Not surprisingly, horror and fantasy films have made the best use of lighthouse settings. Adrienne Barbeau operated a lighthouse radio station in John Carpenter's *The Fog* (1980)—at least until pirate ghosts with grappling hooks forced her to abandon the broadcast booth and seek refuge on the top of the cylindrical structure. People-eating plants harassed lighthouse resident Janette Scott in 1963's *Day of the Triffids*. She discovered that, like most plants, triffids don't care for salt water. In fantasy films, a lighthouse played a prominent role during the climactic storm in *Portrait of Jennie* (1948), and Michael Redgrave's life changed for the better after he experienced ghostly visions in his lighthouse home in *Thunder Rock* (1942). The dull side of lighthouse living was displayed in *The Light at the Edge of the World* (1971), in which lighthouse-keeper Kirk Douglas fights boring pirates (led by Yul Brynner) for the affections of boring Samantha Eggar. The sweet side found Shirley Temple brightening up lighthouse-keeper Guy Kibbee's life in *Captain January* (1936).

Lighthouse by the Sea (1925)	*A Summer Place* (1959)
Captain January (1936)	*Day of the Triffids* (1963)
Sh! The Octopus (1938)	*The Light at the Edge of the World*
Thunder Rock (1942)	(1971)
Seven Miles From Alcatraz (1942)	*Pete's Dragon* (1977)
A Stolen Life (1946)	*The Fog* (1980)
Portrait of Jennie (1948)	*Eye of the Needle* (1981)
The Monster of Piedras Blancas (1958)	*Final Analysis* (1992)

Lions and Tigers

The big cats have alternated effectively between roles as cuddly, playful felines and vicious, merciless maneaters. In the former category, one must begin with Bert Lahr's lovable Cowardly Lion from *The Wizard of Oz* (1939), who was too afraid to be ferocious ("I'm just a dandy lion"). In the wonderful screwball comedy *Bringing Up Baby* (1938), Katharine Hepburn "lost" Baby, her pet lion. To catch Baby, Hepburn and Cary Grant roam through the woods singing the big cat's favorite tune: "I can't give you anything but love—Baby." *Fluffy* and *Clarence, the Cross-Eyed Lion* (both 1965) were harmless pets, too, though their tendency to frighten strangers provided much of the films' humor. Clarence was even popular enough to warrant his own 1966-69 TV series *Daktari*. However, as its title suggests, the series devoted more time to Clarence's veterinarian (q.v.) owner Marshall Thompson. Lions peaked in popularity with the release of 1966's family hit *Born Free*, the engrossing true story of a husband and wife's efforts to train their domesticated lioness to fend for herself in the wilds of Africa. A belated sequel, *Living Free*, followed in 1972, accompanied two years later by a short-lived *Born Free* TV series. In contrast to these friendly lions, other features, such as 1981's *Savage Harvest*, have portrayed big cats as powerful, silent killers. Escaped animals in urban settings have proven to be a continuing problem ever since a black leopard slipped away from Jean Brooks during a publicity stunt in 1943's *The Leopard Man*. Films employing a similar premise include 1964's *A Tiger Walks* and two 1978 TV-movies, *Maneaters Are Loose!* and *The Beasts Are on the Streets*. The 1953 jungle adventure *Bwana Devil* introduced the cinema's first 3-D cat and promised to "put a lion in your lap." Stop-action animator Ray Harryhausen created a saber-toothed tiger for his colorful fantasy *Sinbad and the Eye of the Tiger* (1977). No discussion of big cats would be complete without mentioning the animated pencil-thin panther with the pink skin that hams his way through the opening credits of Blake Edwards's *Pink Panther* (q.v.) films. See also **Cats**.

East of Java (1935)
Bringing Up Baby (1938)
The Wizard of Oz (1939)
The Jungle Book (1942)
The Leopard Man (1943)
Maneater of Kumaon (1948)
Samson and Delilah (1949)
Androcles and the Lion (1952)
Fearless Fagan (1952)
The Horse and the Lion (1952)
Track of the Cat (1954)
The African Lion (1955)
The Flute and the Arrow (1957)
Harry Black and the Tiger (aka *Harry Black*) (1958)
Jungle Cat (1960)
Ursus in the Valley of Lions (1961)
The Lion (1962)
Rampage (1963)
A Tiger Walks (1964)
Fluffy (1965)

Clarence, the Cross-Eyed Lion (1965)
Born Free (1966)
The Cat (aka *Cat!*) (1966)
The Jungle Book (1967)
Charlie, the Lonesome Cougar (1968)
Living Free (1972)
Napoleon and Samantha (1972)
Maneater (1973 TVM)
When the North Wind Blows (1974)
Christian the Lion (1976)
Sinbad and the Eye of the Tiger (1977)
Maneaters Are Loose! (1978 TVM)
The Beasts Are on the Streets (1978 TVM)
Night Creature (aka *Out of the Darkness*) (1978)
Savage Harvest (1981)
The White Lions (1981)
Cheetah and Friends (aka *Cheetah*) (1989)

Little House on the Prairie

Michael Landon executive produced and starred in the 1974 TV-movie *Little House on the Prairie*, a wholesome drama about a pioneer family based on the writings of Laura Ingalls Wilder. The telefilm spawned a very successful 1974-83 TV series that featured Landon as Charles Ingalls, Karen Grassle as his wife Caroline, and Melissa Gilbert and Melissa Sue Anderson as daughters Laura and Mary. Twins Lindsay and Sidney Greenbush alternated as the youngest child

Carrie. The show's characters evolved significantly over the years (e.g., Mary went blind; daughter Grace was born), and Landon left the series in 1982 (the title changing to *Little House: A New Beginning*). Without Landon, the series folded — only to be revived in the form of three TV-movie "specials." Landon directed and appeared in the first and third postseries pictures. The town of Walnut Grove was blown up in *The Last Farewell*, leaving Landon free to play an angel in his *Highway to Heaven* series. See also **Television Series Reunion Films.**

Little House on the Prairie (1974 TVM)
Little House on the Prairie: Look Back to Yesterday (1983 TVM)
Little House: Bless All the Dear Children (1984 TVM)
Little House: The Last Farewell (1984 TVM)

Little People

They come in all sizes — they may be as minute as an atom or as tall as four feet. So, in that respect, little people is a pretty big category. The tiniest person was probably *The Incredible Shrinking Man*. At the conclusion of Richard Matheson's philosophical 1957 science-fiction film, the hero continued to shrink until he could literally see atomic particles. In both *Fantastic Voyage* and *Innerspace*, people were reduced in size until they could be injected into the bloodstreams of normal-sized folks. Considerably bigger, say around three or four inches in height, were the scientists in *Dr. Cyclops*, the Liliputians in film adaptations of *Gulliver's Travels*, and the title character in *tom thumb*. *Dr. Cyclops* has evolved into something of a cult classic, being the first picture in which little people are harassed by a cat, a chicken, raindrops and the like. Finally, there are the "little people" of folklore — leprechauns, gnomes and mischievous dwarfs. They have appeared in numerous movies, typically in charming, playful roles. Of course, not all movies involving little people are fantastic in nature. In *The Tin Drum*, a child injures himself (becoming a dwarf) so that he can never grow up. Dwarf-sized killers figure prominently in Nicholas Roeg's *Don't Look Now* and David Cronenberg's bizarre chiller *The Brood*. See also **Giants.**

Minute-Sized People
Fantastic Voyage (1966)   *Innerspace* (1987)

Under Five Inches
The Devil Doll (1936)   *Help!* (1965)
Gulliver's Travels (1939)   *The Borrowers* (1973 TVM)
Dr. Cyclops (1940)   *Don't Be Afraid of the Dark* (1973
Peter Pan (1953)   TVM)
Girl in His Pocket (1957)   *Gulliver's Travels* (1977)
The Incredible Shrinking Man (1957)   *The Incredible Shrinking Woman*
Attack of the Puppet People (1958)   (1981)
The Seventh Voyage of Sinbad (1958)   *Here Come the Littles* (1985)
tom thumb (1958)   *Willow* (1988)
The Three Worlds of Gulliver (1960)   *Honey, I Shrunk the Kids* (1989)
Babes in Toyland (1961)   *Dollman* (1991)
Mothra (1962)   *FernGully . . . The Last Rainforest*
Ghidrah, the Three-Headed Monster   (aka *FernGully*) (1992)
  (1965)

Leprechauns, Gnomes, Dwarfs, Midgets

Snow White and the Seven Dwarfs
  (1938)
The Terror of Tiny Town (1938)
The Luck of the Irish (1948)
It's a Small World (1950)
Darby O'Gill and the Little People
  (1959)
Jack the Giant Killer (1962)
The Gnomemobile (1967)
Even Dwarfs Started Small (1968)
Finian's Rainbow (1968)

Don't Look Now (1973)
Little Cigars (1973)
The Brood (1979)
The Tin Drum (1979)
Under the Rainbow (1981)
Time Bandits (1981)
Dance of the Dwarfs (aka *Jungle Heat*)
  (1983)
Willow (1988)
Leprechaun (1993)

The Little Tough Guys, *see* The Bowery Boys

The Living Dead, *see* Ghouls; Night of the Living Dead

The Lone Wolf

Michael Lanyard, better known as The Lone Wolf, was a jewel thief-turned-detective created by Louis Joseph Vance in 1914. The character led a lively screen life, being played by eight actors over a span of twenty-nine years. Bert Lytell (a one-time Boston Blackie) starred as Lanyard in five silent films, starting with 1917's *The Lone Wolf*. Other actors followed in his footsteps, including Jack Holt and Henry B. Walthall. However, it was Lytell who returned to the role one last time for the first Lone Wolf "talkie," 1930's *Last of the Lone Wolf*. Five years later, Melvyn Douglas made a promising debut as Lanyard in Columbia's *The Lone Wolf Returns*. With Douglas too much in demand for other roles, Czech import Francis Lederer took over for 1938's *The Lone Wolf in Paris*. He was replaced the following year by Warren William in *The Lone Wolf Spy Hunt*. William, a veteran "gentleman detective," had previously played both Philo Vance (q.v.) and Perry Mason (q.v.). He was an actor in search of a role to call his own — and he found it with Michael Lanyard. William made nine *Lone Wolf* films, with Eric Blore providing reliable comedy relief as his valet/sidekick. The series was a showcase for promising Columbia starlets, and William's leading ladies included Rita Hayworth and Ida Lupino. William retired from the series after 1943's *Passport to Suez*. Gerald Mohr played Lanyard in three films during 1946-47, and ex-Bulldog Drummond (q.v.) Ron Randell starred in the series finale, 1949's *The Lone Wolf and His Lady*. Like most B-movie detectives, the Lone Wolf found a home on television, where Louis Hayward played him in a thirty-nine-episode 1953 series known as both *The Lone Wolf* and *Streets of Danger*.

The Lone Wolf (1917) (Lytell)
False Faces (1919) (Lytell)
The Lone Wolf Returns (1926) (Lytell)
Alias the Lone Wolf (1927) (Lytell)
The Lone Wolf's Daughter (1929) (Lytell)
Last of the Lone Wolf (1930) (Lytell)
Cheaters at Play (1932) (Thomas Meighan)
The Lone Wolf Returns (1935) (Douglas)

The Lone Wolf in Paris (1938) (Lederer)
The Lone Wolf's Spy Hunt (1939) (William)
The Lone Wolf Meets a Lady (1940) (William)
The Lone Wolf Strikes (1940) (William)
The Lone Wolf Keeps a Date (1941) (William)
The Lone Wolf Takes a Chance (1941) (William)
Secrets of the Lone Wolf (1941) (William)
Counter-Espionage (1942) (William)
One Dangerous Night (1943) (William)
Passport to Suez (1943) (William)
The Notorious Lone Wolf (1946) (Mohr)
The Lone Wolf in London (1947) (Mohr)
The Lone Wolf in Mexico (1947) (Mohr)
The Lone Wolf and His Lady (1949) (Randell)

Long Running Times

U.S.-released theatrical features with running times longer than three hours have been rare, especially prior to the 1950s. Erich Von Stroheim's original, unreleased version of his 1924 silent classic *Greed* fitted onto forty-two reels (approximately nine hours' worth of film). MGM production head Irving Thalberg insisted on cuts, and Von Stroheim and friend Rex Ingram deleted six reels of footage. Still not satisfied, Thalberg hired June Mathis to cut eight more reels. By the time it was released, *Greed* boasted a scant 150 minutes. Existing prints run even shorter at 110 minutes. Amazingly, just four years later, Von Stroheim made *The Wedding March*, which clocked in at 196 minutes. It was released in two parts and failed miserably at the box office. Leni Riefenstahl's *Olympia*, an epic documentary of the 1936 Olympic Games in Berlin, was also released in two parts (118 minutes and 107 minutes). However, MGM released all 179 minutes of 1936's *The Great Ziegfeld* in one lump sum. This biopic of legendary showman Flo Ziegfeld ranked as Hollywood's longest talkie film until *Gone With the Wind* (yet another MGM release) topped it by 41 minutes in 1939. Despite *GWTW*'s success, Hollywood refrained from overwhelming wartime audiences with lengthy films. Short features cost less and made tidy profits. The studios' perspective changed, though, in the 1950s when television was seen as a growing threat to theatrical movies. Gimmicks such as 3-D (q.v.) and Cinemascope came into vogue—and so did lengthy theatrical epics. In 1956 alone, *The Ten Commandants*, *Giant* and *War and Peace* were released. If a viewer watched them on a triple feature (thankfully they were never billed together), he'd be watching movies for over ten hours! This trend of long running times continued through the mid-1960s, with an average of two or three epic films being released yearly. No one genre dominated the releases, though biblical pictures such as *The Ten Commandments*, *Ben-Hur*, and *The Greatest Story Ever Told* seemed to hold an edge. Still, there were long war films (*The Longest Day*), long comedies (*It's a Mad, Mad, Mad, Mad World*) and long musicals (*Star!*). The number of lengthy releases gradually decreased through the 1970s and 1980s, as budget-minded theater owners realized longer movies meant fewer showings and therefore less profit. Television's ability to broadcast multiple-part movies on successive nights also made it a desirable viewer alternative to sitting in a movie theater for over three hours. Thus, as the miniseries thrived, the long movies faded. A final note: Many long films were trimmed after preview showings of their original releases and thus now exist in multiple versions. Various cuts of 1970's *Ryan's Daughter* run 206 minutes, 192 minutes and 176 minutes. Only the original running times are listed below:

Greed (1924) 570m (approximately)

Napoleon (1927) 235m

The Wedding March (1928) 196m

Olympia (aka *Olympische Spiele*) (1936) 225m

The Great Ziegfeld (1936) 179m

Gone With the Wind (1939) 220m

Children of Paradise (1944) 195m

Aan (aka *Savage Princess*) (1952) 190m

The Seven Samurai (1954) 200m

A Star Is Born (1954) 181m

The Ten Commandments (1956) 220m

Giant (1956) 201m

War and Peace (1956) 208m

Raintree County (1957) 187m

Les Miserables (1957) 210m

Ben-Hur (1959) 212m

The Big Fisherman (1959) 180m

The Alamo (1960) 192m

Knights of the Teutonic Order (1960) 180m

Exodus (1960) 213m

Pepe (1960) 195m

Rocco and His Brothers (1960) 180m

Spartacus (1960) 196m

El Cid (1961) 184m

Judgment at Nuremberg (1961) 190m

The Longest Day (1962) 180m

Mutiny on the Bounty (1962) 185m

Cleopatra (1962) 243m

Lawrence of Arabia (1962) 222m

It's a Mad, Mad, Mad, Mad World (1963) 192m

The Leopard (1963) 195m

The Fall of the Roman Empire (1964) 187m

Doctor Zhivago (1965) 180m

The Greatest Story Ever Told (1965) 225m

Hawaii (1966) 189m

The Sand Pebbles (1966) 193m

Camelot (1967) 180m

Star! (1968) 194m

War and Peace (1968) 373m

Ryan's Daughter (1970) 206m

Nicholas and Alexander (1971) 183m

Fiddler on the Roof (1971) 181m

Ludwig (1972) 246m

The Iceman Cometh (1973) 239m

The Godfather, Part II (1974) 200m

Barry Lyndon (1975) 183m

The Memory of Justice (1976) 278m

The Sorrow and the Pity (1976) 260m

1900 (1976) 243m

Mohammed, Messenger of God (aka *The Message*) (1977) 180m

Renaldo and Clara (1978) 232m

The Deer Hunter (1978) 183m

Heaven's Gate (1980) 225m

Reds (1981) 199m

Gandhi (1982) 188m

Fanny and Alexander (1983) 197m

The Right Stuff (1983) 193m

Once Upon a Time in America (1984) 227m

Shoah (1985) 570m

Little Dorrit (1988) 360m (aka *Nobody's Fault* 182m/*Little Dorrit's Story* 178m)

Dances With Wolves (1990) 183m

JFK (1991) 188m

At Play in the Fields of the Lord (1991) 187m

Idiot (1992) 185m

Gettysburg (1993) 254m

Long Titles

Long movie titles (ten words or more) have posed nightmarish problems to film publicists and theater owners. Imagine trying to get the complete twenty-four-word title to Peter Brooks's *Marat/Sade* on a marquee at a multiscreen complex! To solve this obvious dilemma, most long-titled films have been given shorter alternate names. Thus, Lina Wertmuller's *Swept Away by an Unusual Destiny in the Blue Sea of August* (1975) is more commonly referred to as simply *Swept Away*. Indeed, Wertmuller fans may be the only ones who know the film's full title. Not surprisingly, the reasons behind most long titles remain a mystery. However, schlockmeister Roger Corman offers a simple explanation for the first sixteen-word American film title, 1957's *The Saga of the Viking Women and Their Voyage to the Waters of the Great Sea Serpent*. He claims that he came up with "the longest title in the history of motion pictures" because he was unable to think up a one- or two-word title to describe his film's plot. Corman's attitude toward the title was very tongue-in-cheek. He opened his film with a shot of a book's front page reading "The Saga of the Viking Women, etc." If Corman pioneered the long title, Stanley Kubrick made it fashionable by subtitling 1964's *Dr. Strangelove* as *Or, How I Learned to Stop Worrying and Love the Bomb*. Subsequently, alternate titles appeared on major studio pictures like Roman Polanski's *The Fearless Vampire Killers* (1967) and *Those Magnificent Men in Their Flying Machines* (1965). The banner year for long titles was 1967, with three lengthy ones averaging out to 17.7 words each. Long titles have been rare since Lina Wertmuller turned more conventional in the late 1970s.

The Saga of the Viking Women and Their Voyage to the Waters of the Great Sea Serpent (aka The Viking Women and the Sea Serpent) (1957)

The Incredibly Strange Creatures Who Stopped Living and Became Mixed Up Zombies (aka The Teenage Psycho Meets Bloody Mary) (1963)

Dr. Strangelove; or, How I Learned to Stop Worrying and Love the Bomb (1964)

Those Magnificent Men in Their Flying Machines, or How I Flew From London to Paris in 25 Hours and 11 Minutes (1965)

A Funny Thing Happened on the Way to the Forum (1966)

The Fearless Vampire Killers; or Pardon Me, But Your Teeth Are in My Neck (1967)

Oh Dad, Poor Dad, Mama's Hung You in the Closet and I'm Feeling So Sad (1967)

Persecution and Assassination of Jean-Paul Marat as Performed by the Inmates of the Asylum of Charenton Under the Direction of the Marquis de Sade (aka Marat/Sade) (1967)

Why Would Anyone Want to Kill a Nice Girl Like You? (1969)

Can Hieronymus Merkin Ever Forget Mercy Humpe and Find True Happiness? (1969)

Gas-s-s-s (aka Gas-s-s-s . . . Or, It May Be Necessary to Destroy the World in Order to Save It) (1970)

Who Is Harry Kellerman and Why Is He Saying Those Terrible Things About Me? (1971)

You've Got to Walk It Like You Talk It or You'll Lose the Beat (1971)

Everything You Always Wanted to Know About Sex (But Were Afraid to Ask) (1972)

I Could Never Have Sex With Anyone Who Has So Little Respect for My Husband (1973)

Swept Away by an Unusual Destiny in the Blue Sea of August (aka *Swept Away*) (1975)

The Effect of Gamma Rays on Man-in-the-Moon Marigolds (1976)

Buffalo Bill and the Indians, or Sitting Bull's History Lesson (1976)

The End of the World in Our Usual Bed in a Night Full of Rain (aka *A Night Full of Rain*) (1978)

Come Back to the Five and Dime, Jimmy Dean, Jimmy Dean (1982)

A Joke of Destiny in Wait Around the Corner Like a Bandit (aka *A Joke of Destiny*) (1983)

Summer Night With Greek Profile, Almond Eyes, and Scent of Basil (aka *Summer Night*) (1987)

The Return of the Six Million Dollar Man and the Bionic Woman (1987 TVM)

The Decline of Western Civilization Part II: The Metal Years (1988)

The Search for Signs of Intelligent Life in the Universe (1991)

I Can Make You Love Me: The Stalking of Laura Black (1993 TVM)

Longstocking, Pippi

Swedish children's author Astrid Lindgren introduced Pippi Longstocking, a rather unconventional nine-year-old orphan, in a 1945 novel. In all, Lindgren wrote three books about the pigtailed, redheaded Pippi, who possesses superhuman strength, defies adults, and tells tall tales that may or may not be true (her father supposedly lives on an island as a "cannibal king"). Swedish director Olle Hellbron brought Pippi to the screen in the early 1970s in a four-film series starring Inger Nilsson. These movies rank as the most irritating and obnoxious children's films in cinema history. However, if viewed from the perspective of a pseudointellectual film critic, the *Pippi* pictures can at least be appreciated as political statements on the advantages of anarchy. The Hellbron-Nilsson films were shot in 1969 but released over several years. A new, bigger-budgeted version appeared in 1988, complete with a publicized talent hunt for a new Pippi (Tami Erin). Despite energetic musical numbers and some familiar performers (e.g., Eileen Brennan), the new Pippi was not much of an improvement over the old Pippi. Mercifully, a new series did not materialize.

Pippi Longstocking (1969)
Pippi in the South Seas (1970)
Pippi on the Run (1970)

Pippi Goes on Board (1971)
The New Adventures of Pippi Longstocking (1988)

Look-Alikes

Although very similar to twins (q.v.), this category addresses movies with characters that look alike but remain distinctly unrelated. The two most famous sets of movie look-alikes were adapted from Anthony Hope's *The Prisoner of Zenda* and Mark Twain's *The Prince and the Pauper*. In the oft-filmed *Prisoner of Zenda*, a gallant gentleman—a dead ringer for a recently kidnapped king—impersonates the monarch in order to save Ruritania. *Moon Over Parador* (1988) borrowed the plot and updated it to contemporary Latin America. Twain's tale of a young prince who playfully trades places with a look-alike pauper has been filmed many times. The best adaptation was the rousing 1937 version starring Errol Flynn, but Disney fashioned an adequate remake, and an all-star rendition appeared in 1978 under the deceiving title of *Crossed Swords*. In other films, look-alikes have been played for laughs or as part of devious espionage plots. Danny Kaye played look-alikes in both *On the Double* and *On the Riviera*, while Bob Hope was the spitting image of a clever secret agent in *My Favorite Spy*. Yul Brynner had dual roles in the overly complicated thriller *The Double Man*, playing an East German mole who underwent plastic surgery and special grooming to replace a CIA agent. Sometimes the government convinces actors (or ordinary look-alikes) to double for VIPs. Thus, the real Winston Churchill was not assassinated in *The Eagle Has Landed*, and an actor was persuaded to pose as General Montgomery for diversion purposes in the World War II action picture *I Was Monty's Double*. That's also how space officials tried to cover up the death of an astronaut in the 1972 TV-movie *The Astronaut*. An interesting variation on the look-alike premise is the Doppelgänger. Literally translated from the German as "double-goer," a Doppelgänger is often a ghostly double of a living person. In the "William Wilson" segment of 1968's *Spirits of the Dead*, the protagonist murdered the mysterious stranger who had been following him—only to find out it was himself. In the 1969 science fiction puzzler *Journey to the Far Side of the Sun*, Roy Thinnes played an an astronaut who landed on a parallel Earth and thereby exchanged places with an exact duplicate of himself (see also **Parallel Worlds**). Timothy Hutton and Bruce Campbell "split" into two people in, respectively, *The Dark Half* and *Army of Darkness* (both 1993). While Doppelgängers may be look-alikes who are *the same person*, clones are look-alikes derived from the same genes but nonetheless separate entities. Laurence Olivier tracked down little Hitler clones in Ira Levin's ingenious *The Boys From Brazil*. Robert Forster cloned himself and ran into all kinds of trouble in *The Darker Side of Terror*. Additional clones turned up in 1978's *The Clone Master* and 1983's *Anna to the Infinite Power*. Kim Novak played a look-alike in Hitchcock's *Vertigo* who turned out not to be a look-alike after all. Contrary to its title, *The Lookalike* (1990) was actually a twin and therefore does not belong in this category. See also **Twins**.

The Phantom President (1932)	*Stolen Face* (1952)
All the King's Horses (1934)	*The Four-Sided Triangle* (1953)
The Whole Town's Talking (1935)	*Flesh and the Woman* (1953)
Honolulu (1937)	*The Most Wanted Man in the World*
The Prince and the Pauper (1937)	(aka *The Most Wanted Man*)
The Prisoner of Zenda (1937)	(1953)
So You Won't Talk (1940)	*Mad About Men* (1954)
The Saint's Double Trouble (1940)	*Francis in the Navy* (1955)
Berlin Correspondent (1942)	*Invasion of the Body Snatchers* (1956)
Pardon My Past (1945)	*I Was Monty's Double* (1958)
The Forbidden Street (aka *Britannia*	*The Square Peg* (1958)
Mews) (1948)	*Vertigo* (1958)
Callaway Went Thataway (1951)	*The Scapegoat* (1959)
My Favorite Spy (1951)	*On the Double* (1961)
The Man With My Face (1951)	*The Double Man* (1967)
On the Riviera (1951)	*Spirits of the Dead* (the segment
The Prisoner of Zenda (1952)	"William Wilson") (1968)
The Brigand (1952)	*It's Your Move* (1968)

Journey to the Far Side of the Sun (aka
  Doppelgänger) (1969)
The Man Who Haunted Himself (1970)
Diamonds Are Forever (1971)
The Astronaut (1972 TVM)
The Stranger (1973 TVM)
Royal Flash (1975)
Obsession (1976)
Casanova and Co. (1976)
The Eagle Has Landed (1977)
End of the World (1977)
Crossed Swords (1978)
The Boys From Brazil (1978)
Parts: The Clonus Horror (1978)
The Clone Master (1978 TVM)
The Darker Side of Terror (1979 TVM)
The Wild, Wild West Revisited (1979
  TVM)

The Prisoner of Zenda (1979)
Anna to the Infinite Power (1983)
Dark Mansions (1986 TVM)
Double Switch (1987 TVM)
Moon Over Parador (1988)
Julia and Julia (1988)
Bullseye! (1989)
Ernest Goes to Jail (1990)
The Lookalike (1990 TVM)
Double Edge (1992 TVM)
Army of Darkness (aka *Army of
  Darkness: Evil Dead 3*) (1993)
Dave (1993)
The Dark Half (1993)
Doppelgänger (aka *Doppelgänger: The
  Evil Within*) (1993)

Lottery

Lottery tickets have brought lovers together, torn friends apart, and led to contemplations of murder. Strangers Ronald Colman and Ginger Rogers purchased a ticket together in 1940's *Lucky Partners* and, after a court dispute, wound up confessing their love to each other. David Niven played a film star who agreed to be a lottery prize in 1953's *The Love Lottery* (1953), as did Jeanette MacDonald in 1930's *The Lottery Bride*. Misplaced or stolen lottery tickets caused frantic confusion of the comedy kind in *Uptown Saturday Night* (1974) and Rene Clair's *Le Million* (1931). In *Babette's Feast* (1987), cook extraordinaire Stephane Audran used lottery winnings to show her gratitude to her employers for giving her a home. She spent all the money on a lavish feast—which also provided her with a final chance to practice her culinary art. In the 1966 black comedy *The Wrong Box*, John Mills and family sought to murder Ralph Richardson and win a tontine, a form of lottery in which the surviving player receives all the money. Michael Keaton uncovered a crooked lottery run by John Davidson in the 1987 flop *The Squeeze*. *29th Street* (1991) told the true story of actor Frank Pesce, who won the first New York State Lottery in 1976. Chloe Webb played a mentally retarded young woman who wins a lottery in 1991's *Lucky Day*.

The Lottery Bride (1930)
Le Million (1931)
La Belle Equipe (1936)
Lucky Partners (1940)
Three Strangers (1945)
Dual Alibi (1947)
The Love Lottery (1953)
The Wrong Box (1966)

Uptown Saturday Night (1974)
Fox and His Friends (1975)
Lots of Luck (1985 TVM)
Babette's Feast (1987)
The Squeeze (1987)
29th Street (1991)
Lucky Day (1991 TVM)
Loser (1991)

Lumberjacks

With the trademark crack of falling trees and shouts of "timber!" films about the rugged men who run lumber camps have tended toward sprawling outdoor melodrama. Howard Hawks and William Wyler fashioned a reliable formula with 1936's *Come and Get It*, Edna Ferber's tale of conflict between lumber tycoon Edward Arnold, his son Joel McCrea, and the woman they both loved, Frances Farmer. The 1938 film *Valley of the Giants* offered the now-familiar tale about a ruthless lumber man attempting to strip California of its redwood forests. The same story was previously filmed in 1919 and 1927 and remade as the 1952 Kirk Douglas vehicle *The Big Trees*. Wayne Morris, the man who thwarted Charles Bickford in *Valley of the Giants*, fought to save a lumber camp in 1950's *The Tougher They Come*. Paul Newman's *Sometimes a Great Notion* focused on the hardships endured by a family of lumberjacks after they defied a local strike. *Fire in the Sky* (1993) recounted real-life lumberjack Travis Walton's claims that he was "probed" by aliens.

Come and Get It (aka *Roaring Timber*) (1936)
God's Country and the Woman (1936)
Valley of the Giants (1938)
Moon Over Burma (1940)
Lumberjack (1944)
The Tougher They Come (1950)
The Blazing Forest (1952)
The Big Trees (1952)
Timberjack (1955)
Spoilers of the Forest (1957)
Girl in the Woods (1958)
Guns of the Timberland (aka *Stampeded*) (1960)
Freckles (1960)
Sometimes a Great Notion (aka *Never Give an Inch*) (1971)
Trouble in High Timber Country (1980 TVM)
The Journey of Natty Gann (1985)
Fire in the Sky (1993)

Lupin, Arsene

In Maurice Leblanc's short stories, this French jewel thief (q.v.) was a product of the Parisian streets. However, he became quite a polished gentleman on the screen, especially as portrayed by John Barrymore in 1932's *Arsene Lupin*. Brother Lionel Barrymore starred as Lupin's detective nemesis, and Karen Mortley turned up naked in Lupin's bed (pre-Hays Code) as an undercover police agent. Melvyn Douglas played Lupin in the belated MGM sequel, 1938's entertaining *Arsene Lupin Returns*. Interestingly, both Douglas and costar Warren William also played thief-turned-detective The Lone Wolf (q.v.). Although a Lupin film series never materialized, a French television program did appear in the 1970s.

Arsene Lupin (1932)
Arsene Lupin Returns (1938)
Enter Arsene Lupin (1944)
The Adventures of Arsene Lupin (1957)

Lynching

Fritz Lang's *Fury* (1936) rattled Depression Era moviegoers with its powerful depiction of contemporary mob violence. Spencer Tracy portrayed the innocent stranger locked up in a small jail after being charged with kidnapping a young girl. When an incensed mob's lynching effort fails, it burns the jail. However, Tracy's character escapes unseen and lives to administer his own justice/revenge. William Wellman's *The Ox-Bow Incident* (1943), based on Walter Van Tilburg Clark's Western novel, shifted the emphasis from the victim to the lynchers. Again, a mob (in this case, a posse) passes judgment based on weak circumstantial evidence. However, those who oppose the lynching, like drifters Henry Fonda and Harry Morgan, are too passive to make their arguments convincing. Despite these fine films, the most powerful statement against mob violence remains 1950's underrated *The Sound of Fury*. Based on Joe Pagano's novel *The Condemned*, it followed the first half of *Fury*'s plotline before developing into a chilling morality tale. In this case, the accused—Frank Lovejoy and Lloyd Bridges—really are guilty. In fact, Bridge's character murdered a boy in cold blood. But after whipping the townspeople into a frenzy, even journalist Richard Carlson is shocked to see the two criminals hanged in the town square. Other films about lynching lack the conviction of these three, although *The Hanging Tree* (1959) effectively proposed that greed can quench even the bloodthirstiest mob. Of course, not all lynchings result in deaths, as evidenced by Clint Eastwood surviving his own hanging and setting out on a path of revenge in the 1968 Western *Hang 'Em High*.

Fury (1936)
Young Mr. Lincoln (1939)
The Ox-Bow Incident (1943)
Intruder in the Dust (1949)
The Sound of Fury (aka Try and Get Me) (1950)

The Woman They Almost Lynched (1953)
The Young Land (1957)
The Hanging Tree (1959)
Five Card Stud (1968)
Hang 'Em High (1968)

Mabuse, Dr.

Norbert Jacques's criminal mastermind was the subject of three motion picture classics and an offbeat, low-budget film series. Famed director Fritz Lang and his screenwriter wife Thea Von Harbou introduced Mabuse to German audiences in 1921 with *Dr. Mabuse, the Gambler*. Rudolf Klein-Rogge, Von Harbou's ex-husband, starred as the crazed genius and master hypnotist bent on world domination. The same team completed a "second part," titled *Dr. Mabuse, King of Crime*, the following year. The two parts were intended to be shown on consecutive evenings and are frequently listed as one film. For their 1927 U.S. release, the films were heavily cut and edited into a single feature *The Fatal Passions*. Lang and Von Harbou resurrected Mabuse for 1932's *The Testament of Dr. Mabuse*, which was banned for its anti-Hitler statements. Lang subsequently left Germany, while Von Harbou stayed behind. Following a successful career in the United States, Lang returned to Germany (West Germany) in 1960 to make *The Thousand Eyes of Dr. Mabuse*, his directorial swan song, for producer Artur Brauner. Even without Lang, Brauner continued the series for five more films starring Wolfgang Preiss as Mabuse. In 1990, director Claude Chabrol made *Dr. M*, whose villain Dr. Marsfelt (Alan Bates) and plot were "inspired by Norbert Jacques' novel *Mabuse der Spieler*." The Mabusian storyline has Dr. M causing Berlin residents to commit suicide by sending out subliminal messages on TV.

Dr. Mabuse, the Gambler (aka The Great Gambler—Image of a Generation; Dr. Mabuse, der Spieler) (1921)

Dr. Mabuse, King of Crime (aka *Inferno — People of a Generation*; *Inferno — Menschen der Zeit*) (1922)

The Testament of Dr. Mabuse (aka *The Last Will of Dr. Mabuse*; *The Crimes of Dr. Mabuse*; *Das Testament des Dr. Mabuse*) (1932)

The Thousand Eyes of Dr. Mabuse (aka *Eyes of Evil*; *Die Tausend Augen des Dr. Mabuse*) (1960)

The Invisible Dr. Mabuse (aka *Die Unsichtbaren Krallen des Dr. Mabuse*) (1961)

The Return of Dr. Mabuse (aka *Phantom Fiend*; *Im Stahlnetz des Dr. Mabuse*) (1961)

The Testament of Dr. Mabuse (aka *The Terror of Dr. Mabuse*; *Das Testament des Dr. Mabuse*) (1962)

Dr. Mabuse vs. Scotland Yard (aka *Scotland Yard Hunts Dr. Mabuse*; *Scotland Yard Jagt Dr. Mabuse*) (1963)

The Secret of Dr. Mabuse (aka *Dr. Mabuse's Ray of Death*; *Die Todesstrahlen des Dr. Mabuse*) (1964)

Dr. M (aka *Club Extinction*) (1990)

Maciste

A muscular Italian hero in the Hercules (q.v.) mold, Maciste remains anonymous in this country although over a dozen films about him have received U.S. release. The culprits behind this unintentional conspiracy have been American distributors, who changed the original Maciste titles (and subsequently dubbed the dialogue) to misrepresent the films' hero as more widely known musclemen like Hercules, Goliath or Samson. Thus, *Maciste alla Corte del Gran Khan* became *Samson and the Seven Miracles of the World*, while *Maciste e la Regina di Samar* became *Hercules Against the Moon Men*. One of the few imports to retain Maciste in its title was 1964's sand-and-sandal spoof *Maciste Against Hercules in the Vale of Woe*. Not suprisingly, that film was later retitled *Hercules in the Vale of Woe*, thus dropping Maciste into anonymity again. To confuse matters even further, brawny actors Mark Forest, Reg Park, Kirk Morris and Alan Steel (aka Sergio Ciani) all played Hercules as well as Maciste.

Maciste in Hell (aka *Maciste all'Inferno*) (1926) (Umberto Guarracino)

Son of Samson (aka *Maciste the Mighty*; *Maciste nella Valle dei Re*) (1960) (Mark Forest)

The Witch's Curse (aka *Maciste all'Inferno*) (1960) (Kirk Morris)

Molemen vs. the Son of Hercules (aka *The Strongest Man in the World*; *Maciste l'Uomo Piu Forte del Mondo*) (1961) (Forest)

Atlas Against the Cyclops (aka *Monster From the Unknown World*; *Maciste nella Terror dei Ciclopi*) (1961) (Mitchell Gordon)

Colossus and the Headhunters (aka *Maciste Contro i Cacciatori de Teste*) (1962) (Kirk Morris)

Death in the Arena (aka *Colossus of the Arena*; *Maciste il Gladiatore Più Forte del Mondo*) (1962) (Forest)

Fire Monsters Against the Son of Hercules (aka *Colossus of the Stone Age*; *Maciste Contro i Monstri*) (1962) (Reg Park)

Triumph of the Sons of Hercules (aka *El Trionfo di Maciste*) (1962) (Morris)

Goliath and the Sins of Babylon (aka *Maciste l'Eroe Più Grande del Mondo*)
(1963) (Forest)
Samson and the Slave Queen (aka *Zorro Contro Maciste*) (1963) (Alan Steel)
Samson vs. the Giant King (aka *Giant of the Lost Tomb*; *Maciste alla Corte dello Zar*) (1963) (Morris)
Samson and the Seven Miracles of the World (aka *Maciste alla Corte del Gran Khan*) (1963) (Gordon Scott)
Goliath and the Vampires (aka *The Vampires*; *Maciste Contro il Vampiro*) (1964) (Scott)
Hercules in the Vale of Woe (aka *Maciste Against Hercules in the Vale of Woe*) (1964)
Maciste, Spartan Gladiator (aka *Maciste, Gladiatore di Sparta*) (1964) (Forest)
Hercules of the Desert (aka *La Valle dell'Eco Tonante*) (1964) (Morris)
Samson and the Mighty Challenge (aka *Hercules, Maciste, Samson, and Ursus Against the Universe*; *Ercole, Sansone, Maciste, Ursus: gli Invincibli*) (1964)
Samson in King Solomon's Mines (aka *Maciste nelle Miniere de Re Salomone*) (1964) (Park)
Hercules Against the Moon Men (aka *Maciste Contro gli Uomini Della Luna*; *Maciste e la Regina di Samar*) (1964) (Steel)
Hercules Against the Barbarians (aka *Maciste nell'Inferno di Genghis Khan*) (1964) (Forest)

Mad Max

The Australian-imported *Mad Max* movies not only made a star of Mel Gibson, but they also managed to make the near-impossible transition from drive-in cult status to mainstream major hits. *Mad Max* (1979) starred Gibson as the title character, a futuristic cop who patrols a post-apocalyptic world populated with motorcycle gangs and other riffraff. When his partner and family are murdered, Max becomes a one-man vigilante force and wipes out the "Glory Riders." From the beginning, director/cowriter George Miller's film found favor with science fiction and action fans, but it attracted little critical attention. Undoubtedly, the release of some *dubbed* prints (in which even Gibson spoke with someone else's voice) limited its appeal. That all changed with the superior sequel, 1981's *The Road Warrior* in which Gibson and Miller transformed Max into a mythic warrior. Critics jumped on the bandwagon ("Apocalypse Pow!" proclaimed *Time*), and Gibson's career began a rapid ascent. He was an established star when he returned to his homeland for 1985's *Mad Max Beyond Thunderdome*. This slick rehash of *Road Warrior*, bolstered by the presence of rock queen Tina Turner, racked up impressive box office figures — but nevertheless lacked the enduring popularity of *Road Warrior*. See also **End of the World/Post-Apocalypse**.

Mad Max (1979)
The Road Warrior (aka *Mad Max 2*) (1981)
Mad Max Beyond Thunderdome (1985)

Magicians

Even though its running time was a scant two minutes, 1896's *Conjuring a Lady at the Robert Houdin's* holds a unique double distinction among magician films.

In addition to containing one of the first filmed magic tricks, it spotlighted the moviemaking talents of former conjuror and cinema pioneer Georges Méliès. Unlike this landmark work, other magician movies have often forgotten that the cinema is a magical medium. They have been largely content to pass off the magician as a devious trickster or bland do-gooder. In 1946's *The Strange Mr. Gregory*, Edmund Lowe played a magician/hypnotist who pretended to be dead to win the affections of Jean Rogers. Vincent Price was a nineteenth-century illusionist who went mad in the well-titled *The Mad Magician* (1954). He sought revenge on his cheating wife (Eva Gabor) and other magicians by murdering them with his famous tricks (the imaginative murder angle was repeated in later Price films like *The Abominable Dr. Phibes* and *Theatre of Blood*). Satanic cult leader Niall MacGinnis performed Halloween magic shows for the kiddies in the classic *Curse of the Demon* (1958) and then explained to Dana Andrews the critical distinctions between black and white magic. On the other hand, heroic magicians have been far less interesting. *Chandu the Magician*, culled from a 1932 serial, sent Edmund Lowe (again) against Bela Lugosi's evil Roxor (oddly, Bela showed up as Chandu two years later in another serial). In TV-movies, Christopher George's escape artist in *Escape* (1970) and Bill Bixby's illusionist in *The Magician* (1973) both helped people in trouble—that's TV talk for detective work. Bixby's film served as the pilot for a shortlived 1973-74 TV series. Neither Laurel and Hardy nor Jerry Lewis could mix magic and comedy to much effect in, respectively, *A-Haunting We Will Go* (1942) and *The Geisha Boy* (1958). However, Tommy Smothers had some amusing scenes in *Get to Know Your Rabbit* (1972), and Woody Allen lost his mother at a magic show in his *New York Stories* segment (1989). Tony Curtis and Paul Michael Glaser played the famous magician/escape artist Harry Houdini in 1953 and 1976 films. Ingmar Bergman explored the mystical side of magic in *The Magician* (1958), a haunting tale about an illusionist detained by villagers unconvinced by his magical powers.

Conjuring a Lady at Robert Houdin's (1896)	*Two on a Guillotine* (1965)
The Phantom of Paris (1931)	*The Mysterious Magician* (1965)
Chandu, the Magician (1932)	*Escape* (1970 TVM)
Lady in Distress (aka *A Window in London*) (1939)	*Get to Know Your Rabbit* (1972)
A-Haunting We Will Go (1942)	*The Golden Voyage of Sinbad* (1973)
The Strange Mr. Gregory (1946)	*The Magician* (1973 TVM)
Houdini (1953)	*The Great Houdinis* (1976 TVM)
The Mad Magician (1954)	*The Magician of Lublin* (1979)
Curse of the Demon (aka *Night of the Demon*) (1958)	*Mandrake* (1979 TVM)
The Geisha Boy (1958)	*The Escape Artist* (1982)
The Magician (1958)	*Bagdad Cafe* (1988)
	New York Stories (1989)
	Waiting for the Light (1990)
	Shadows and Fog (1992)

The Magnificent Seven

John Sturges's 1960 remake of the Japanese classic *Seven Samurai* has grown in popularity over the years, becoming—according to *TV Guide*—one of the most frequently shown movies on television. The original seven gunfighters hired to protect a Mexican village were (and this is a great "list" question in its own right): Yul Brynner, Steve McQueen, James Coburn, Robert Vaughn, Charles Bronson, Brad Dexter and Horst Buchholz. Only Yul returned for the first sequel, 1966's *Return of the Seven*. But Elmer Bernstein's great music score (best known as the Marlboro theme) was used in all four *Seven* films. The original plot has been recycled extensively and transplanted to contemporary Arizona (the 1985 TVM *Command 5*), the Middle East (1968's *The Invincible Six*), and outer space (1980's *Battle Beyond the Stars*). *The Adventures of the Magnificent 6½* (1988) was a children's variation.

The Magnificent Seven (1960)	*Guns of the Magnificent Seven* (1969)
Return of the Seven (1966)	*The Magnificent Seven Ride* (1972)

Maids and Housekeepers

Although they typically form the backbone of celluloid domestic staffs, maids and housekeepers have labored in the shadow of butlers. For example, while the 1930s featured prime butler roles in *Ruggles of Red Gap* (1935) and *My Man Godfrey* (1936), maids and housekeepers were relegated to minor — albeit essential — roles in the 1939 releases *Rules of the Game*, *The Cat and the Canary* and *Gone With the Wind*. Of course, Hattie McDaniel won a Best Supporting Actress Oscar for her role as Mammy in *GWTW* (an honor not bestowed on a performer playing a butler until John Geilgud's Best Supporting Actor award for 1981's *Arthur*). Gale Sondergaard created the prototype for sinister domestics in *The Cat and the Canary*. However, Judith Anderson refined the evil housekeeper role with her chilling portrayal of Mrs. Danvers in Alfred Hitchcock's *Rebecca* (1940). Anderson received a well-deserved Oscar nomination but lost to Jane Darwell's good-natured Ma in *The Grapes of Wrath*. Loretta Young won a Best Actress Oscar for 1947's *The Farmer's Daughter*, in which she played a Swedish maid who falls in love with her employer and then runs against him for Congress. Other maids who married, or had affairs with, their employers were featured in *Common Clay* (1930), *Jassy* (1947) and *Houseboat* (1958). In the latter film, Sophia Loren was a socialite posing as a housekeeper for Cary Grant. Likewise, Ally Sheedy was a spoiled rich girl working as a domestic in 1987's *Maid to Order*. In contrast, *That Funny Feeling* (1965) cast Sandra Dee as a maid intent on hiding her occupation from her new boyfriend. She moves into her employer's swank apartment — not realizing that her boyfriend is her employer. Men have taken their turns as maids, although not too successfully, in movies such as 1982's *Maid in America* (with Alex Karras) and 1990's *The Maid* (with Martin Sheen). Maids have fared extremely well on television in the series *Hazel* (1961-66), *Grindl* (1963-64), *The Good Life* (1971-72), and most memorably, *Upstairs, Downstairs* (1971-75). Although there was never a film series about a maid, Maisie (q.v.) worked as one in *Maisie Was a Lady* (1940), and Mary Gordon cleaned up after Sherlock Holmes (q.v.) in the Rathbone/Bruce film series. See also **Butlers; Chauffeurs.**

Common Clay (1930)	*Rules of the Game* (1939)
Downstairs (1932)	*The Cat and the Canary* (1939)
Servants' Entrance (1934)	*Gone With the Wind* (1939)
If You Could Only Cook (1935)	*Rebecca* (1940)
Maid's Night Out (1938)	*Maisie Was a Lady* (1940)

His Butler's Sister (1943)	The Maids (1975)
Standing Room Only (1944)	A Matter of Time (1976)
Mrs. Parkington (1944)	That Obscure Object of Desire (1977)
Diary of a Chambermaid (1946)	Private Lessons (1981)
The Farmer's Daughter (1947)	Maid in America (1982 TVM)
Jassy (1947)	In the White City (1983)
Footsteps in the Fog (1955)	Loyalties (1986)
Papa, Mama, the Maid and I (1956)	A Judgment in Stone (aka The
Houseboat (1958)	Housekeeper) (1986)
Upstairs and Downstairs (1959)	Maid to Order (1987)
Diary of a Chambermaid (1964)	The Maid (1990)
That Funny Feeling (1965)	Maid for Each Other (1992 TVM)
For Love of Ivy (1968)	Remains of the Day (1993)

Maisie

The year 1939 was a banner year for MGM, featuring the releases of *Gone With the Wind*, *The Wizard of Oz* and *Goodbye, Mr. Chips*. So it's no wonder that no one remembers it as the year Ann Sothern made her debut as Maisie, a tough, spunky girl with a heart of gold. At age thirty, Sothern was already a B-movie veteran, having played similar roles for both Columbia and RKO. Robert Young (as a ranch hand!) costarred with her in the first series entry, *Maisie*. A few months later, Sothern was back in *Congo Maisie*, a revamped version of the Clark Gable-Jean Harlow sizzler *Red Dust*. Eight more Maisie adventures appeared between 1940 and 1947, making the title character the busiest single woman in the movies. She was a maid in *Maisie Was a Lady*, a police detective in *Undercover Maisie*, and an aircraft factory worker in *Swing Shift Maisie*. Sothern's film career slacked off during the 1950s and she turned to television, experiencing modest success with *Private Secretary* and *The Ann Sothern Show*.

Maisie (1939)	Swingshift Maisie (aka The Girl in
Congo Maisie (1939)	Overalls) (1943)
Gold Rush Maisie (1940)	Maisie Goes to Reno (aka You Can't
Maisie Was a Lady (1940)	Do That to Me) (1944)
Ringside Maisie (aka Cash and Carry)	Up Goes Maisie (aka Up She Goes)
(1941)	(1945)
Maisie Gets Her Man (aka She Got Her	Undercover Maisie (1947)
Man) (1942)	

Malibu Express

Husband-and-wife team Andy and Arlene Sidaris masterminded this B-movie series, an R-rated variation of *Charlie's Angels* featuring one fewer female lead but much more flesh. Hunky Darby Hinton starred as Texan troubleshooter Cody Abilene in the series' first installment, 1985's *Malibu Express* (the title being the name of Cody's yacht). Set in Hawaii, it offset poor acting with some lively action footage staged by Andy Sidaris, a former Emmy-winning director for *ABC's Wide World of Sports*. Former soap star Steve Bond played another Abilene — enforcement agent Travis — in the 1987 follow-up *Picasso Trigger*. Although he made a bland lead, former *Playboy* Playmates Dona Speir and Hope Marie Carlton attracted attention as Donna and Taryn, a pair of freelance flyers. Ronn Moss took over as cousin Rowdy Abilene in *Hard Ticket to Hawaii* (1988), but Speir and Carlton's supporting characters received a hefty amount of screen time. Not surprisingly, they headlined 1989's *Savage Beach*, which featured a meatier story and less gratuitous nudity. Carlton bowed out after this installment. Thus, Speir sported a new partner, Roberta Vasquez as Nicole, in 1990's *Guns*, which had the distinction of casting Erik Estrada as a baddie. Speir, Vasquez and Estrada returned for 1991's *Do or Die*, although Estrada played a different character (a good guy). The Karate Kid's former mentor, Pat Morita, took over as villain. The principal villains in 1992's *Hard Hunted* were played by movie-star offspring R.J. Moore (Roger's son) and Tony Peck (Gregory's son). Although the *Malibu Express* films never attracted much attention at the box office, the action/jiggle formula found a steady audience on videotape.

Malibu Express (1985)	*Guns* (1990)
Picasso Trigger (1987)	*Do or Die* (1991)
Hard Ticket to Hawaii (1988)	*Hard Hunted* (1992)
Savage Beach (1989)	*Fit to Kill* (1993)

A Man Called Horse

Richard Harris starred in this offbeat western about an English aristocrat captured by Sioux Indians in 1825. He suffers torture, learns to live with his captors, grows to understand them, and becomes their leader. The film was based on Dorothy M. Johnson's 1950 *Collier*'s story and featured the harrowing Sun Vow ritual, which required Indian males to be suspended by clamps inserted in their pectoral muscles. Although Harris's character returned to civilization at the film's end, he came back to help his Indian friends in 1976's *The Return of a Man Called Horse*. This sequel lacked the box office zip of its predecessor, but that did not deter the belated release of a third film, 1983's *Triumphs of a Man Called Horse*, which starred Harris and Michael Beck as his son.

A Man Called Horse (1970)
The Return of a Man Called Horse (1976)
Triumphs of a Man Called Horse (1983)

The Man From U.N.C.L.E.

NBC introduced this lighthearted spy TV series in 1964, shortly after the third James Bond thriller, *Goldfinger*, struck the mother lode at the national box office. U.N.C.L.E. stood for United Network Command for Law and Enforcement and was run by gruff, fatherly Mr. Waverly (Leo G. Carroll). The agency's top two agents were American Napoleon Solo (Robert Vaughn) and Russian Illya Kuryakin (David McCallum). (The fact that Americans and Russians were fighting together for world peace made *The Man From U.N.C.L.E.* the first *Glasnost* TV series.) The show was an immediate hit, especially with the younger set, and inspired MGM to release a big-screen feature, *To Trap a Spy*, in 1965. Actually, it had originally been shown as a 1964 TV episode called "The Vulcan Affair," but fans didn't seem to mind that they had seen it before. Seven additional movies were released between 1965-68. Meanwhile, the television edition spun off the short-lived series *The Girl From U.N.C.L.E.* (starring Stefanie Powers) and dropped in the ratings after peaking at No. 13 for the year in the 1965-66 season. The series was cancelled in January 1968 and replaced by *Rowan and Martin's Laugh-In*. A reunion TV-movie, *The Return of the Man From U.N.C.L.E.*, surfaced in 1983. See also **Television Series Reunion Films.**

To Trap a Spy (1965)	*The Spy in the Green Hat* (1967)
One of Our Spies Is Missing (1966)	*The Helicopter Spies* (1968)
One Spy Too Many (1966)	*How to Steal the World* (1968)
The Spy With My Face (1966)	*The Return of the Man From*
The Karate Killers (1967)	*U.N.C.L.E.* (1983 TVM)

The Man With No Name

Clint Eastwood first portrayed this laconic gunslinger in 1964's *A Fistful of Dollars*, Sergio Leone's spaghetti-Western version of Akira Kurosawa's samurai epic *Yojimbo*. Although it's not actually specified, Eastwood apparently played the same character in Leone's follow-ups *For a Few Dollars More* and *The Good, the Bad, and the Ugly* (Clint was the Good, Lee Van Cleef the Bad, and Eli Wallach the Ugly). Clint may have played the role in other Westerns, too (e.g., *High Plains Drifter*, *Pale Rider*). Given his subtle acting style, it's hard to tell.

A Fistful of Dollars (1964)	*The Good, the Bad, and the Ugly* (1967)
For a Few Dollars More (1965)	

Marlowe, Philip

The screen exploits of Raymond Chandler's tough, cynical private eye make for fascinating trivia. The first adaptation of a Marlowe mystery (*Farewell, My Lovely*) was tailored for George Sanders as 1942's *The Falcon Takes Over*, an entry in the long-running Falcon (q.v.) film series. That same year, the Philip Marlowe novel *The High Window* was adapted for detective Michael Shayne (q.v.) as *Time to Kill*. Two years later, Marlowe finally reached the screen in the guise of Dick Powell, who made the switch from crooner to tough guy in *Murder, My Sweet*, another version of *Farewell, My Lovely*. Powell was terrific as Marlowe, setting a standard that even Bogart couldn't surpass in 1946's *The Big Sleep*. Later that year, actor-director Robert Montgomery filmed *The Lady in the Lake* in first person, showing audiences everything as Marlowe saw it. It was a novel experiment (e.g., kisses filled the screen, the camera rocked back after a punch to Marlowe's face), but ultimately it was more irritating than interesting. George Montgomery (no relation to Robert) played Marlowe in 1947's *The Brasher Doubloon*, the second version of Chandler's *The High Window*. There were no Marlowe films in the 1950s, but James Garner played the part in 1969's *Marlowe* (which featured Bruce Lee as a minor villain). Elliott Gould played an unrecognizable Marlowe in Robert Altman's 1973 *The Long Goodbye*. And in the late 1970s, a weary-looking Robert Mitchum played the detective in *Farewell, My Lovely* (set in the 1940s) and *The Big Sleep* (updated to the present). Ironically, the only Marlowe novel never filmed was *Playback*, which was originally an unsold Chandler screenplay.

Murder, My Sweet (1944)	*Marlowe* (1969)
The Big Sleep (1946)	*The Long Goodbye* (1973)
The Lady in the Lake (1946)	*Farewell, My Lovely* (1975)
The Brasher Doubloon (1947)	*The Big Sleep* (1978)

Marple, Miss Jane

Agatha Christie's sharp-witted spinster enjoyed modest success in the 1960s when Margaret Rutherford's *Murder, She Said* sparked a four-film series. Ms. Rutherford also made a cameo appearance as Miss Marple opposite Tony Randall's Hercule Poirot (q.v.) in 1966's *The Alphabet Murders*. In 1980, Angela Lansbury (pre-*Murder, She Wrote*) made a delightful Jane Marple in *The Mirror Crack'd* but sadly did not return for an encore. That made it possible for Helen Hayes to star as Miss Marple in a pair of entertaining, if easily forgotten, made-for-TV mysteries.

Murder, She Said (1962)	*The Mirror Crack'd* (1980)
Murder at the Gallop (1963)	*A Caribbean Mystery* (1983 TVM)
Murder Ahoy! (1964)	*Murder With Mirrors* (1985 TVM)
Murder Most Foul (1965)	

Marriage Brokers and Dating Services

The arrangement of marriages is a dangerous profession that requires an understanding of love and compatibility to ensure success. As a result, it's a rare occupation both in real life and in film. Still, the cinema has featured a handful of marriage brokers. Thelma Ritter played Cupid for X-ray technician Scott Brady and model Jeanne Crain in *The Model and the Marriage Broker*. Shirley Booth and Barbra Streisand each played the grand dame of marriage brokers—Miss Dolly Levi—in, respectively, *The Matchmaker* and its musical remake *Hello, Dolly!* Charles Boyer proved that men could be matchmakers (though not successful ones, apparently) in 1963's *Love Is a Ball*. His attempts to use Glenn Ford to push Hope Lange into Ricardo Montalban's arms resulted in a Ford-Lange romance. Michael Callan and Paula Prentiss played marriage brokers who discover they have unknowingly arranged a series of illegal marriages in the 1969 TV-movie comedy *In Name Only*. Dating services, not marriage brokers, paired unlikely couples in *Promise Him Anything*, *The Love Tapes*, *Lonely Hearts* and *The Whole Truth*.

The Model and the Marriage Broker (1951)	*Fiddler on the Roof* (1971)
The Matchmaker (1958)	*Promise Him Anything* (1974 TVM)
Love Is a Ball (aka *All This and Money Too*) (1963)	*The Love Tapes* (1980 TVM)
Hello, Dolly! (1969)	*Lonely Hearts* (1983)
In Name Only (1969 TVM)	*Crossing Delancy* (1988)
	Ladykiller (1992 TVM)
	The Whole Truth (1992)

The Marseilles Trilogy

The characters of Marcel Pagnol's French trilogy of *Marius*, *Fanny* and *Cesar* have maintained universal appeal ever since their first appearances. Thus, in addition to the trilogy, they have appeared (sometimes under different names) in German, Italian and American features based on Pagnol's works. Pagnol was a rising French playwright when Paramount expressed interest in filming his 1929 hit play *Marius*. The movie version, with Alexander Korda directing from a Pagnol screenplay, was released in 1931. Pierre Fresnay played Marius, who dreams of a life at sea although he has fallen in love with Fanny (Orane Demazis). Fanny tries to make Marius jealous by flirting with the rich, middle-aged Panisse, a friend of Marius's father Cesar (Raimu). Eventually, she and Marius make love, but even that cannot cure Marius's wanderlust. Fanny sacrifices her own happiness, and Marius leaves for the sea. Marc Allegret directed the second chapter, 1932's *Fanny*, which Pagnol again adapted from his play. Fanny, who has become pregnant with Marius's child, agrees to marry Panisse. Cesar becomes upset with this arrangement, but eventually agrees to be the child's godfather. After two years at sea, Marius returns and wants Fanny and the child. Panisse won't give the child up and Fanny, although she still loves Marius, again sacrifices her own happiness – this time for her son. Pagnol wrote an original screenplay and directed the final installment, 1936's *Cesar*. Set seventeen years later, it opens with the death of Panisse. Fanny tells her eighteen-year-old son Cesariot that Marius, not Panisse, was his father. With Cesar's help, Cesariot seeks out his father and eventually reunites Fanny, Marius and Cesar. While film critics preferred the first and last films, *Fanny* attained the greatest popularity at the time of its release. It was remade in Italy in 1933, in Germany in 1934 (with Emil Jannings), and in the United States in 1938 as *Port of Seven Seas*. The latter film made little impression despite a solid cast of Wallace Beery, Frank Morgan and Maureen O'Sullivan. In 1961, producer Joshua Logan condensed the trilogy into *Fanny*, a colorful but overlong reworking. The film reunited *Gigi* stars Leslie Caron (as Fanny) and Maurice Chevalier (as Panisse) and added Charles Boyer (Cesar) and Horst Buchholz (Marius). Unfortunately, Logan's ownership of the rights to *Fanny* prevented Pagnol's trilogy from being shown outside France for several years. Jacques Demy's charming musical *The Umbrellas of Cherbourg* (1964) borrowed and updated *Fanny*'s plot.

Marius (1931)
Fanny (1932)
Fanny (1933) (Italian remake)
Fanny (1934) (German remake)

Cesar (1936)
Port of Seven Seas (1938)
Fanny (1961)

Marsh, Abel

Lane Slate wrote a theatrical film and two made-for-TV movies featuring contemporary small-town sheriff Abel Marsh. James Garner played Marsh on the big screen in 1972's *They Only Kill Their Masters*, a sly mystery about a Doberman with apparently murderous tendencies. The film emphasized offbeat humor and Garner's laid-back charm over action or suspense, and it made little impact at the box office. Five years later, however, Slate resurrected Abel Marsh in the form of Andy Griffith, who played the plaid-shirted detective in two TV-movies: *The Girl in the Empty Grave* (1977) and *Deadly Game* (1977). The purpose of these films was to launch an Abel Marsh TV series for Griffith, but further Marsh mysteries never materialized. Interestingly, Griffith starred in an earlier TV-movie, 1974's *Winter Kill*, which was "inspired" by *They Only Kill Their Masters* but not written by Slate. *Winter Kill* featured Griffith as a ski resort sheriff (named Sam McNeill) investigating mysterious murders. It, too, was a failed pilot for a TV series. Griffith, of course, finally turned in his sheriff's badge and found TV series success in 1986 as a lawyer in *Matlock*.

They Only Kill Their Masters (1972)
Deadly Game (1977 TVM)

The Girl in the Empty Grave (1977 TVM)

Mason, Perry

Raymond Burr will always be Perry Mason for millions of mystery fans, but Erle Stanley Gardner's lawyer/detective hit the big screen twenty years before the long-running TV series. Warren William was a sharp-witted, gourmet-minded Mason in four Warner Bros. films, beginning with 1934's *The Case of the Howling Dog*. William seemed a natural for the part, having already played that urbane sleuth Philo Vance (q.v.), and soon destined to play the Lone Wolf (q.v.), a jewel thief and detective. In fact, William's Mason did so much detection that it was easy to forget he was a lawyer; some entries were devoid of courtroom scenes. Two of William's films are of special interest. *The Case of the Curious Bride* featured superstar-to-be Errol Flynn as a murder victim and Donald Woods, a future Perry Mason, in another supporting role. *The Case of the Velvet Claws* found Mason and secretary Della Street (Claire Dodd) married and trying to take a honeymoon! Comic actor Allen Jenkins played Perry's detective assistant Spudsy (*not* Paul) Drake. In 1936, former Sam Spade Ricardo Cortez replaced William in *The Case of the Black Cat*, and Donald Woods finished the Warner series with 1937's *The Case of the Stuttering Bishop*. The *Perry Mason* TV series debuted in 1957 and enjoyed a nine-year run on CBS. Burr played the lead, of course, with Barbara Hale as Della Street, William Hopper as detective Paul Drake, William Talman as prosecuting attorney Hamilton Burger, and Ray Collins as police Lieutenant Arthur Tragg (Collins died prior to the 1965-66 season). In 1973, CBS revived the show as *The New Adventures of Perry Mason* starring Monte Markham, but it folded after half a season. Then, in 1985, NBC brought back Burr in the TV-movie *Perry Mason Returns*, reuniting him with Hale and introducing William Katt (Hale's real-life son) as Paul Drake's son. The film's ratings went through the roof, and a series of equally high-rated made-for-TV movies quickly evolved. See also **Television Series Reunion Films.**

The Case of the Howling Dog (1934) (Warren William)
The Case of the Curious Bride (1935) (William)
The Case of the Lucky Legs (1935) (William)
The Case of the Velvet Claws (1936) (William)
The Case of the Black Cat (1936) (Ricardo Cortez)
The Case of the Stuttering Bishop (1937) (Donald Woods)

Raymond Burr TV-Movies

Perry Mason Returns (1985 TVM)
Perry Mason: The Case of the Notorious Nun (1986 TVM)
Perry Mason: The Case of the Shooting Star (1986 TVM)
Perry Mason and the Case of the Sinister Spirit (1987 TVM)
Perry Mason: The Case of the Lost Love (1987 TVM)
Perry Mason: The Case of the Murdered Madam (1987 TVM)
Perry Mason: The Case of the Scandalous Scoundrel (1987 TVM)
Perry Mason: The Case of the Avenging Ace (1988 TVM)
Perry Mason: The Case of the Lady in the Lake (1988 TVM)
Perry Mason: The Case of the All-Star Assassin (1989 TVM)
Perry Mason: The Case of the Lethal Lesson (1989 TVM)
Perry Mason: The Case of the Musical Murder (1989 TVM)

Perry Mason: The Case of the Poison Pen (1990 TVM)
Perry Mason: The Case of the Silenced Singer (1990 TVM)
Perry Mason: The Case of the Desperate Deception (1990 TVM)
Perry Mason: The Case of the Defiant Daughter (1990 TVM)
Perry Mason: The Case of the Ruthless Reporter (1991 TVM)
Perry Mason: The Case of the Maligned Mobster (1991 TVM)
Perry Mason: The Case of the Glass Coffin (1991 TVM)
Perry Mason: The Case of the Fatal Fashion (1991 TVM)
Perry Mason: The Case of the Fatal Framing (1992 TVM)
Perry Mason: The Case of the Reckless Romeo (1992 TVM)
Perry Mason: The Case of the Heartbroken Bride (1992 TVM)
Perry Mason: The Case of the Skin Deep Scandal (1993 TVM)
Perry Mason: The Case of the Tell-Tale Talk Show Host (1993 TVM)
Perry Mason: The Case of the Killer Kiss (1993 TVM)

Matadors/Bullfights

Blood and Sand reigns as the best-remembered bullfight film, chiefly because the 1922 and 1941 versions provided screen favorites Rudolph Valentino and Tyrone Power with one of their best roles. Vicente Blanco Ibáñiz wrote the original story in 1908, and Tom Cushing adapted it for the stage in 1921. The following year, Valentino starred as the young matador who rises from poverty to stardom in the bullring, only to fall victim to the charms of an irresistible temptress (Nita Naldi). The matador died in the Ibáñiz story, but the Valentino version was altered so that his faithful wife nursed him to recovery from near-death. The Tyrone Power remake followed the original closely (with Rita Hayworth as the seducer) but restored the climactic death scene in the bullring. Ex-matador Budd Boetticher, a technical advisor on the Power film, subsequently became a director and made three films about the perils of the bullring and the lifestyles of those who enter it. His semiautobiographical *The Bullfighter and the Lady* (1951) starred Robert Stack as an American (like Boetticher) in Mexico who convinces a famous matador (Gilbert Roland) to help him become a bullfighter. Boetticher followed it with 1955's *The Magnificent Matador*, which cast Anthony Quinn as an aging matador who trains his illegitimate son for the ring despite premonitions of death. Boetticher left Hollywood in 1960 to make a documentary in Mexico about the legendary bullfighter Carlos Arruza. The venture proved disastrous, with the producer/director facing endless personal and production problems. The film was finally completed in 1967 and released in 1972 as *Arruza*. Not surprisingly, bullfighting has been played for laughs in a number of films. In the 1945 comedy *The Bullfighters*, bumbling detectives Laurel and Hardy discovered that Stan resembled a famous matador. Naturally, he wound up facing an unpleasant-looking bull in the ring. A similar fate befell Lou Costello in the 1948 Abbott and Costello comedy *Mexican Hayride*. In 1956's *Around the World in Eighty Days*, Cantilfas entered the bullring so he and David Niven could borrow Gilbert Roland's yacht. In one of the livelier scenes in 1957's *The Sun Also Rises*, Errol Flynn and Eddie Albert played rompish drunks who posed the dangerous question: "Bully, bully, where's the bull?" Esther Williams(!) played an unlikely-looking female matador in the

1947 musical *Fiesta*. Still, she looked at ease with the role compared to the Volks-wagen-turned-matador in *Herbie Goes Bananas*.

Blood and Sand (1922)
The Kid From Spain (1932)
The Trumpet Blows (1934)
Blood and Sand (1941)
Masquerade in Mexico (1945)
The Bullfighters (1945)
Fiesta (1947)
Mexican Hayride (1948)
The Bullfighter and the Lady (1951)
The Brave Bulls (1951)
The Magnificent Matador (aka *The Brave and the Beautiful*) (1955)

Around the World in Eighty Days (1956)
The Sun Also Rises (1957)
Fun in Acapulco (1963)
The Bobo (1967)
Arruza (1972)
Herbie Goes Bananas (1980)
Bolero (1984)
Matador (1986)

Matchmakers, *see* Marriage Brokers and Dating Services

Meatballs

Five years before 1984's *Ghostbusters* lined their pockets with gold, comedian Bill Murray and director Ivan Reitman made this Canadian sleeper about life in a summer camp. Despite an abundance of teen comedy stereotypes, it was raunchy, occasionally schmaltzy, and pretty funny when Murray was around. Wisely, Murray went on to bigger roles and avoided further association with Camp Sasquatch in *Meatballs II*, *Meatballs III* and *Meatballs 4*. John Laroquette, Sally Kellerman, Patrick Dempsey and Corey Feldman were not as selective. See also **Summer Camp.**

Meatballs (1979)
Meatball II (1983)

Meatballs III (1987)
Meatballs 4 (1992)

Mediums and Seances

The movies have treated mediums with both respect and disdain. Sadly, in movies where they get the most footage, mediums are typically portrayed as charlatans. In 1947's *Nightmare Alley*, Tyrone Power gave one of his best performances as a sideshow hustler who becomes a financially successful spiritualist through trickery and deceit. He is eventually exposed as a fraud and winds up back in the carnival as "the geek." Along similar lines, Turhan Bey played *The Amazing Mr. X* (1948), a fake spiritualist who plots with a "dead man" to dupe the man's wife. And in *Seance on a Wet Afternoon* (1964), an unbalanced medium (Kim Stanley) hatches a plot to kidnap a child and then hold a seance that will reveal the child's whereabouts. Real-life magician (q.v.) Harry Houdini spent the latter portion of his life exposing fake spiritualists, a pastime explored briefly in 1953's *Houdini*. In the 1990 box office smash *Ghost*, Whoopi Goldberg won a Best Supporting Actress Oscar as a fake medium who becomes a real one when Patrick Swayze's spirit returns to protect his wife Demi Moore. Margaret Rutherford played an eccentric but legitimate medium in *Blithe Spirit* (1945), as did spunky Zelda Rubinstein in 1982's *Poltergeist* (q.v.). Claire Bloom was a psychic and Julie Harris a lonely spinster in 1963's eerie classic *The Haunting*, in which one (or both?) of them seemed to attract (or cause?) supernatural happenings in an old mansion. Seances have played minor parts in many ghost (q.v.) movies, with some of the most memorable appearing in *The Uninvited, Curse of the Demon* and Abbott and Costello's *The Time of Their Lives*. See also **Clairvoyants and Fortune-Tellers; Ghosts.**

Palmy Days (1932)
Miracles for Sale (1939)
The Spell of Amy Nugent (aka
   Spellbound; Passing Clouds) (1940)
The Uninvited (1940)
Blithe Spirit (1945)
The Time of Their Lives (1946)
Nightmare Alley (1947)
The Amazing Mr. X (aka *The
   Spiritualist*) (1948)
The Medium (1951)
Houdini (1953)

Curse of the Demon (aka *Night of the
   Demon*) (1958)
13 Ghosts (1960)
The Haunting (1963)
Seance on a Wet Afternoon (1964)
The Legend of Hell House (1973)
Family Plot (1976)
The Manitou (1978)
Poltergeist (1982)
Grave Secrets (1989)
Ghost (1990)

Mermaids

Mermaid movies seem to come in waves, with 1947's *Miranda* sparking the first volley. It starred Glynis Johns as a comely mermaid who rescues a drowning physician on a Cornwall holiday. To show his gratitude, the doctor takes the mermaid back to London, where she moves in with him and his wife and decides that she prefers the sophisticated land-life. This light comedic concoction inspired a 1954 sequel, *Mad About Men*, in which mermaid Johns trades places with a look-alike (q.v.) human. In the meantime, producer-writer Nunnally Johnson mounted an American imitation of *Miranda* with 1948's *Mr. Peabody and the Mermaid*. William Powell played a man in the midst of a midlife crisis who hooks mermaid Ann Blyth while on a fishing trip. Complications ensue when he takes her back and deposits her in a fish pond near his beach house. A gap of five years separated *Mad About Men* from the next group of mermaid movies. *Mermaids and Sea Robbers* (1959), a Japanese import, and *The Mermaids of Tiburon* (1962) were low-grade fantasies with no redeeming traits. Curtis Harrington's *Night Tide* (1961) was an atmospheric yarn about a sailor (Dennis Hopper) who meets an odd girl (Linda Lawson) who plays a mermaid in a carnival sideshow. She claims to be a descendant of the "sea people," who must kill during a full moon. Far less compelling was 1965's *Beach Blanket Bingo*, which featured a subplot involving a mermaid played by Marta Kristen (the oldest daughter in TV's *Lost in Space*). Almost twenty years later, a mermaid subplot in Bill Forsyth's charming Scottish fantasy *Local Hero* (1983) initiated another round of mermaid movies. The following year's *Splash* was a solid sleeper hit about a young man (Tom Hanks) reunited with the fetching mermaid (Daryl Hannah) who rescued him from drowning as a boy. Ariel the mermaid also fell in love with the human prince she rescued in Disney's 1989 animated version of *The Little Mermaid*. Cher donned flippers to attend a costume party in 1990's *Mermaids*.

Miranda (1947)
Mr. Peabody and the Mermaid (1948)

Hans Christian Andersen (the "Little
   Mermaid" sequence) (1952)

Peter Pan (1953)
Mad About Men (1954)
Mermaids and Sea Robbers (1959)
Don't Give Up the Ship (1959)
Night Tide (1961)
The Mermaids of Tiburon (aka *The Aqua Sex*) (1962)

Beach Blanket Bingo (1965)
Local Hero (1983)
Splash (1984)
Splash Too (1988 TVM)
The Little Mermaid (1989)
Hook (1991)

Mexican Spitfire

By the time she was thirty, spicy Latin American actress Lupe Velez had experienced a flirtation with stardom (opposite Douglas Fairbanks in 1927's *The Gaucho*), a scandalous romance with Gary Cooper, and an unhappy marriage to Johnny Weissmuller. Her career was in a slow tailspin when she made a lightweight 1939 comedy called *The Girl From Mexico*. Donald Woods starred as a young advertising executive who falls for a fiery Latin entertainer (Velez) while dealing with his own devious Uncle Matt (Leon Errol). To everyone's surprise, the movie's success spawned a *Mexican Spitfire* series. Although Velez was the star, Errol stole the show at every turn, playing both Uncle Matt and a delightful drunken Englishman named Lord Epping. Sometimes, the antics got a wee silly—one entry featured a live pink elephant with green polka dots. Sadly, the series ended abruptly in 1944 with Velez's elaborately staged sleeping-pill suicide. (**Note:** Although both Velez and Errol appeared in 1941's *Six Lessons From Madame La Zonga*, it was not a *Spitfire* entry.)

The Girl From Mexico (1939)
Mexican Spitfire (1939)
Mexican Spitfire Out West (1940)
Mexican Spitfire at Sea (1941)
Mexican Spitfire's Baby (1941)

Mexican Spitfire Sees a Ghost (1942)
Mexican Spitfire's Elephant (1942)
Mexican Spitfire's Blessed Event (1943)

Military Academies

As one would expect, the United States Military Academy—better known as West Point—has provided the bulk of military school settings. West Point stories have ranged from inspirational sport sagas (*The Spirit of West Point*) to musical revues (*West Point Story*) to true-life dramas (*The Silence* and *Dress Gray*). Ask any cadet about his favorite West Point film and he will probably answer *The Long Gray Line*, a sentimental tale about an athletic trainer (Tyrone Power) and his wife (Maureen O'Hara) who become an institution at the school. West Point comedies have been rare, though Francis the Talking Mule tutored Donald O'Connor in 1952's *Francis Goes to West Point*, and females invaded the academy in the 1979 TV-movie *Women of West Point*. An "illegal" woman caused Eddie Albert quite a bit of trouble at the Virginia Military Institute in the 1940 comedy *Brother Rat*. The woman turned out to be his pregnant wife (Jane Bryan), a fact he had hidden from school officials who did not accept married cadets. It was remade as the musical *About Face* with Eddie Bracken in 1952. Not surprisingly, controversial dramas have taken place in fictitious military schools. Ben Gazarra played a sadistic cadet with a dominating hold over classmates in 1957's *The Strange One*, adapted from Calder Willingham's novel *End as a Man*. (*Sorority Girl*, a female version of the same novel, was also released in 1957.) In 1981's *Taps*, Timothy Hutton led a group of fellow cadets, including Sean Penn and Tom Cruise, in a revolt against school officials trying to turn their beloved academy into a condominium. David Keith battled modern-day prejudice at a Southern military academy in 1983's *The Lords of Discipline*. The most unlikely military school is the one run by an order of nuns in the Charlton Heston picture *The Private War of Major Benson*. See also **Boarding Schools**.

Tom Brown of Culver (1932)	*Francis Goes to West Point* (1952)
Flirtation Walk (1934)	*The Long Gray Line* (1955)
Dinky (1935)	*The Private War of Major Benson*
Navy Blue and Gold (1937)	(1955)
The Duke of West Point (1938)	*The Strange One* (aka *End as a Man*)
Lord Jeff (1938)	(1957)
Spirit of Culver (1939)	*The Silence* (1975 TVM)
Brother Rat (1940)	*Women of West Point* (1979 TVM)
They Died With Their Boots On (1941)	*Up the Academy* (1980)
Ten Gentlemen From West Point	*Taps* (1981)
(1942)	*Evilspeak* (1982)
Best Foot Forward (1943)	*The Lords of Discipline* (1983)
The Spirit of West Point (1947)	*Hard Knox* (1984 TVM)
Beyond Glory (1948)	*Dress Gray* (1986 TVM)
West Point Story (aka *Fine and Dandy*)	*Combat High* (1986 TVM)
(1950)	*Child's Play 3* (1991)
About Face (1952)	

Mirrors

Employed principally in fantasy films, mirrors have also been used effectively in comic sequences and climactic confrontations. An imaginary mirror was the gimmick in *Duck Soup*, in which Harpo Marx posed as Groucho's reflection, mimicking perfectly his brother's every movement. Errol Flynn and Donald Woods, both attired in Santa suits, repeated the "no mirror" trick in 1946's *Never Say Goodbye* (as did Lucille Ball and Harpo Marx in TV's *I Love Lucy*). A man's reflection stepped out of a mirror to offer advice to his owner in the 1936 comedy *The Man in the Mirror*. And a magician's trick mirror saved Woody Allen from the strangler in 1992's *Shadows and Fog*. Orson Welles confronted murderess Rita Hayworth in a carnival hall of mirrors in the gripping climax of Welles's *Lady From Shanghai* (1948). In a similar fashion, Bruce Lee outdueled villain Shih Kien in a chamber of mirrors in the 1973 martial arts classic *Enter the Dragon*. However, fantasy films have used mirrors most imaginatively, beginning with the Wicked Witch's magic mirror in Disney's *Snow White and the Seven Dwarfs* (1937). In 1945's *Dead of Night*, an antique mirror haunted a happy husband by reflecting the room of its previous owner—a jealous gent who strangled his wife. Another old mirror allowed Bradford Dillman to return from the dead to visit fiancée Linda Day George in the 1969 TV-movie *Fear No Evil*. On a more intellectual scale, a mirror provided the door between Earth and the Zone (a sort of Heaven/Hell) in Jean Cocteau's eerie classic *Orpheus* (1949). For the most bizarre use of mirrors, it's hard to beat *The Boogeyman*, a 1980 sleeper about a shard of broken mirror that turned people into killers. Finally, mirrors have exposed quite a few vampires to those smart enough to know that the bloodsuckers cast no reflection.

Duck Soup (1933)
The Man in the Mirror (1936)
Snow White and the Seven Dwarfs (1937)
Kitty Foyle (1940)
Dead of Night (1945)
Never Say Goodbye (1946)
Fear in the Night (1947)
Lady From Shanghai (1948)
Orpheus (1949)
Nightmare (1956)
The Witch's Mirror (1960)
The Devil's Bride (aka *The Devil Rides Out*) (1968)

Fear No Evil (1969 TVM)
Enter the Dragon (1973)
The Boogeyman (aka *The Boogey Man*) (1980)
The Mirror Crack'd (1980)
Come Back to the Five and Dime, Jimmy Dean, Jimmy Dean (1982)
Big Business (1988)
Fright Night 2 (1989)
Curse of the Blue Lights (1989)
Mirror, Mirror (1990)
Shadows and Fog (1992)

Missing in Action

This 1984 Chuck Norris action picture cashed in on the public's "new patriotism" and shot to the top of the box office charts. In many ways, it paved the way for 1985's *Rambo: First Blood Part II*, with a plot that sent Colonel Norris back into Vietnam to rescue some buddies imprisoned in a P.O.W. camp. It was followed by a prequel and then a sequel. *Missing in Action 2: The Beginning* (1985), which was actually filmed *before* the earlier film, focused on Norris's P.O.W. escape. *Braddock: Missing in Action III* (1988) had Norris returning to Vietnam again, this time to save his own son. Neither of these two films attained the popularity of the original. See also **Prisoners of War; Vietnam.**

Missing in Action (1984)
Missing in Action 2: The Beginning (1985)
Braddock: Missing in Action III (1988)

Mobile Homes

Not many movie residents have lived in mobile home parks. Dick Powell and Rhonda Fleming called the Clover Trailer Park home in *Cry Danger*, but their place of residence had little to do with the plot. The same can be said of mobile home dwellers Jamie Lee Curtis (*Grandview, U.S.A.*), John Travolta and Debra Winger (*Urban Cowboy*), Bette Midler (*Jinxed!*) and Holly Hunter and Nicholas Cage (*Raising Arizona*). The first half of 1984's delightful *The Last Starfighter* took place in an atmospheric trailer park where an ugly alien tried to liquidate a teen video game expert. Two wonderful comedies dealt with couples who took their trailers on the road. In *The Long, Long Trailer* (1954), Lucille Ball and Desi Arnaz went on their honeymoon in a particularly troublesome trailer. Yuppies Albert Brooks and Julie Haggerty gave up the "rat race" for an enlightening life on the road in *Lost in America* (1985). However, they didn't count on Haggerty losing their nest egg on their first stop—at a casino in Las Vegas.

Cry Danger (1951)
The Long, Long Trailer (1954)

Anatomy of a Murder (1959)
Pretty Poison (1968)

Urban Cowboy (1980)	*Lost in America* (1985)
Jinxed! (1982)	*Raising Arizona* (1987)
Grandview, U.S.A. (1984)	*Pals* (1987 TVM)
The Last Starfighter (1984)	*Gas, Food, Lodging* (1992)

Models, *see* Fashion Models

Monks

In comparison to priests and nuns, monks have been poorly represented in films. The only monks to achieve celebrity status have been Friar Tuck of Robin Hood (q.v.) fame and Rasputin, the Russian monk whose alleged healing powers gained him influence over the imperial family. This colorful character has attracted many performers, most notably Christopher Lee (*Rasputin — The Mad Monk*), Tom Baker (*Nicholas and Alexandra*), Edmund Purdom (*Nights of Rasputin*) and, in the definitive performance, Lionel Barrymore (*Rasputin and the Empress*). The portly frame of Friar Tuck has been inhabited by even more actors, though Eugene Pallette's portrayal in 1938's *The Adventures of Robin Hood* outshines all others. With the exception of Rasputin, other film biographies of monks have been of the saintly variety. Both Franco Zeffirelli's *Brother Sun, Sister Moon* (1973) and the earlier *Francis of Assisi* (1961) told how St. Francis of Assisi founded the Franciscan order of monks. The 1974 *Luther* was a straightforward adaptation of John Osborne's play about the founder of Protestantism. In fictional films, Harrison Ford and Sean Connery encountered an ancient monk who guarded the Holy Grail in the 1989 blockbuster *Indiana Jones and the Last Crusade*. Three years earlier, Connery solved a series of devious murders in a thirteenth-century Italian monastery in *The Name of the Rose*. It was not, however, the first monastery mystery. That distinction belongs to the offbeat 1974 TV-movie *Judge Dee and the Monastery Murders*, which was set in seventh-century China. Another Chinese monastery appeared briefly in 1972's TV-movie *Kung Fu*, the pilot for the 1972-75 series about a fugitive Buddhist monk in the American West. The most unusual monks have been played by Charles Boyer (opposite Marlene Dietrich in *The Garden of Allah*), Marty Feldman (*In God We Trust*), and Edward G. Robinson (as a gangster who reforms in *Brother Orchid*). Contrary to its title, the 1969 TV-movie *The Monk* had nothing to do with monks. George Maharis played a private eye named Gus Monk. See also **Nuns; Popes and Cardinals.**

Rasputin and the Empress (1932)	*Kung Fu* (1972 TVM)
The Garden of Allah (1936)	*Brother Son, Sister Moon* (1973)
The Adventures of Robin Hood (1938)	*Luther* (1974)
Brother Orchid (1940)	*Judge Dee and the Monastery Murders*
Letters From My Windmill (1954)	(1974 TVM)
Nights of Rasputin (1960)	*In God We Trust* (1980)
Francis of Assisi (1961)	*The Name of the Rose* (1986)
Rasputin — The Mad Monk (1966)	*Indiana Jones and the Last Crusade*
I Killed Rasputin (1967)	(1989)
Nicholas and Alexandra (1971)	

Mothra

Toho Studios, the home of Godzilla, introduced this giant female caterpillar (and occasional moth) in 1962. Her debut film marked a turning point in the studio's Japanese monster series: It was the first movie to be shot in color and feature a sympathetic creature. Of course, Mothra wreaked plenty of havoc, just like her predecessors Godzilla (q.v.) and Rodan (q.v.). However, the carnage was a justified response to the kidnapping of two fairies from Mothra's home island. Mothra's next appearance was in 1964's *Godzilla vs. the Thing*, in which the radioactive "King of Monsters" destroyed the giant caterpillar. However, an egg hatched to unleash two baby giant caterpillars who wove a web of silk around Godzilla and rendered him helpless. Thus, the Mothras that appear in subsequent films are either children or grandchildren of the original Mothra—it's never made clear. The giant caterpillar's film appearances decreased after Godzilla made the switch from bad guy to good in 1965's *Ghidrah, the Three-Headed Monster*. See also **The Alilenas (The Peanuts Sister).**

> *Mothra* (aka *Mosura*) (1962)
> *Godzilla vs. the Thing* (aka *Godzilla vs. Mothra*; *Gojira tai Mothra*) (1964)
> *Ghidrah the Three-Headed Monster* (aka *the Greatest Battle on Earth*; *Sandai Kaiju Chikyu Saidai No Kessen*) (1965)
> *Godzilla vs. the Sea Monster* (aka *Ebriah — Terror of the Deep*; *Nankai no Dai Ketto*) (1966)
> *Destroy All Monsters* (aka *Operation Monsterland*; *Kaiju Soshingeki*) (1968)
> *Godzilla's Revenge* (aka *Ord Kaiju Daishingeki*) (1969)
> *Godzilla vs. Mothra* (1992)

Moto, Mr.

J.P. Marquand's Japanese sleuth was a brilliant thinker, a master of disguises, and a martial arts expert. That description does not exactly bring Peter Lorre to mind, but he nevertheless made a fine movie Moto. He made eight films in a two-year period, beginning with 1937's *Think Fast, Mr. Moto*. The series ended abruptly in 1939, its demise usually attributed to the United States' growing disenchantment with Japan's World War II activities. In 1965, an unexpected update, *The Return of Mr. Moto*, appeared with movie heavy Henry Silva as Moto. This new Moto bore little resemblance to Marquand's detective, and the movie died at the box office. The only other "actor" to play Mr. Moto was Porky Pig in the 1939 cartoon "Porky's Movie Mystery."

> *Think Fast, Mr. Moto* (1937)
> *Mr. Moto's Gamble* (1938)
> *Mr. Moto Takes a Chance* (1938)
> *The Mysterious Mr. Moto* (1938)
> *Thank You, Mr. Moto* (1938)
>
> *Mr. Moto on Danger Island* (1939)
> *Mr. Moto's Last Warning* (1939)
> *Mr. Moto Takes a Vacation* (1939)
> *The Return of Mr. Moto* (1965)

Motorcycle Gangs

Sheriff's daughter to motorcycle gang leader Marlon Brando: "What are you rebelling against?" Brando: "What ya got?" That simple line of dialogue from 1953's *The Wild One* summarizes the attitude of pointless rebellion that would eventually spark the motorcycle gang films of the late 1960s and early 1970s. Considering the popularity of Brando's film with youth audiences of the 1950s, it's amazing that the genre was not born earlier. In all likelihood, however, audiences were not yet prepared to accept antiestablishment criminals as their idols. Thus, the teen bikers in 1957's *Motorcycle Gang* were presented as a "bad crowd" to be avoided by nice teens. Likewise, Oliver Reed and his fellow "Teddy Boys" had no redeeming features in Joseph Losey's science fiction cult film *These Are the Damned* (1962). Harvey Lembeck brought a little humanity—and a disarming ridiculousness—to his role of gang leader Eric Von Zipper in 1963's *Beach Party* (q.v.) and its sequels. Three years later, the biker anti-hero roared onto the screen in the guise of leather-clad, joint-smoking, Hell's Angel leader Peter Fonda in Roger Corman's *The Wild Angels*, about which Hollis Alpert of the *Saturday Review* wrote: It "strings together such incidents as the invasion of a hospital and the rape of a Negro nurse, a gang fight, and an orgy in a church . . . the film is faulty, and in a sense, irresponsible." Still, many mid-1960s teenagers identified with the angry, ultimately pessimistic attitudes of Fonda's Heavenly Blues and Bruce Dern's Loser. Cheaper, cruder biker films filled drive-in screens in the wake of *Wild Angels*'s success. At their best, these exploitation films provided steady work for rising talents such as Jack Nicholson (*Hell's Angels on Wheels*, *Rebel Rousers*), Harry Dean Stanton (*The Miniskirt Mob*), Tyne Daly (*Angel Unchained*), Bruce Dern (*The Cycle Savages, Rebel Rousers*) and disc jockey Casey Kasem (*Wild Wheels*). The worst films were the ones that capitalized on returning Vietnam veterans, such as *Angels From Hell* and *The Angry Breed*. An interesting exception was 1967's *Born Losers*, which introduced a peace-loving, former Green Beret named Billy Jack (Tom Laughlin). Four years later, Laughlin revived the character for the influential, nonbiker sleeper hit *Billy Jack* (q.v.). Still, few motorcycle gang films strayed from the *Wild Angels*'s violence-drugs-orgy formula, although female bikers took charge effectively in *The Miniskirt Mob, She-Devils on Wheels* and *Angels' Wild Women*, and supernatural twists livened up *Werewolves on Wheels* and *Psychomania* (the latter concerning bikers revived from the dead). In 1973, the motorcycle gang movie craze gave way to other blossoming, low-budget genres like the martial arts imports and blaxploitation (q.v.) pictures. Ironically, the most influential biker film of the 1966-72 period turned out to be Dennis Hopper and Peter Fonda's 1967 sleeper smash *Easy Rider*—and it was not about motorcycle gangs. Post-1972 film appearances by biker gangs have been rare. A hapless gang incurred the wrath of Clint Eastwood in his comedy hit *Every Which Way But Loose*. Don Murray reunited his old gang to get rid of some contemporary punks in the 1981 TV-movie *Return of the Rebels*. Ed Harris played King Arthur to a traveling group of jousting bikers in George Romero's heavy-handed parable *Knightriders* (1981). On television, *Monty Python's Flying Circus* presented a hilarious skit about a gang of vicious, motorcycle-riding grannies.

The Wild One (1953)	*Born Losers* (1967)
Motorcycle Gang (1957)	*Hell's Angels on Wheels* (1967)
These Are the Damned (aka *The Damned*) (1962)	*Rebel Rousers* (1967)
	The Glory Stompers (1967)
Beach Party (1963)	*Angels From Hell* (1968)
Motor Psycho (1965)	*Girl on a Motorcycle* (aka *Naked Under Leather*) (1968)
The Wild Angels (1966)	

The Miniskirt Mob (1968)
She-Devils on Wheels (1968)
The Savage Seven (1968)
The Angry Breed (1969)
The Cycle Savages (1969)
Wild Wheels (1969)
Angels Die Hard (1970)
Hell's Bloody Angels (aka The Fakers;
    Smashing the Crime Syndicate)
    (1970)
Angel Unchained (1970)
The Black Angels (1970)
C.C. and Company (1971)
Chrome and Hot Leather (1971)
Psychomania (1971)
The Hard Ride (1971)
The Peace Killers (1971)
The Jesus Trip (1971)
Werewolves on Wheels (1971)

Angels' Wild Women (1972)
The Dirt Gang (1972)
Hex (1973)
The Northville Cemetery Massacre
    (1976)
Every Which Way But Loose (1978)
Dawn of the Dead (1979)
Hog Wild (1980)
Return of the Rebels (1981 TVM)
The Loveless (1981)
Knightriders (1981)
Hear No Evil (1982 TVM)
Hell's Angels Forever (1983)
Eye of the Tiger (1986)
Nam Angels (1989)
Easy Wheels (1989)
Chopper Chicks in Zombietown (1990)
Masters of Menace (1990)
The Last Riders (1990)

Mountain Climbing

No fictional film has been able to match 1953's *Conquest of Everest* in terms of portraying the awesome beauty and never-ending danger of mountain climbing. Sadly, this gripping chronicle of Edmund Hillary's Everest expedition lost the Best Documentary Oscar to Disney's *The Living Desert*. On the dramatic front, Glenn Ford led a group of climbers intent on scaling the Swiss Alps in *The White Tower* (1950). In *Cliffhanger* (1993), Sylvester Stallone flexed his muscles as a Rocky Mountain Rescue pro who grapples with a gang of money-hungry villains. James MacArthur played a young man intent on conquering a peak called the Citadel (actually the Matterhorn) in the 1959 Disney adventure *Third Man on the Mountain*. *Five Days One Summer* and *The Mountain* ended with mountain climbing tragedies. In the latter film, Spencer Tracy followed greedy brother Robert Wagner up the slopes to prevent the looting of plane wreckage. Numerous films have boasted extensive mountain climbing footage, ranging from the scaling of the German fortress in *The Guns of Navarone* to the Clint Eastwood spy adventure *The Eiger Sanction* to the James Bond picture *For Your Eyes Only*.

The White Tower (1950)
Conquest of Everest (1953)
The Mountain (1956)
The Abominable Snowman of the
    Himalayas (1958)
Third Man on the Mountain (1959)
The Guns of Navarone (1961)
Climb an Angry Mountain (1972
    TVM)
The Eiger Sanction (1975)

High Ice (1980 TVM)
The Constant Factor (1980)
For Your Eyes Only (1981)
Five Days One Summer (1982)
A Breed Apart (1984)
Storm and Sorrow (1990 TVM)
Scream of Stone (1991)
K2 (1992)
Cliffhanger (1993)

Mounties

Television has treated the Royal Canadian Mounted Police far more generously than the cinema. *Sergeant Preston of the Yukon* and *Dudley Doright* may have done little for Mountie prestige, but they still accounted for some brief popularity. On the big screen, Mountie musicals and a handful of modest adventures have attracted minimal attention. Cecil DeMille saluted the Royal Mounted with his lavish *Northwest Mounted Police* (1940), starring Gary Cooper and Robert Preston. Critic Otis Ferguson called it "two hours of colour, killing, kindness and magnificent country" (Oregon and Hollywood, not Canada). Despite racking up Paramount's biggest grosses of the year, DeMille's film inspired no imitations. Instead, Warner Bros. offered Errol Flynn as a contemporary Mountie tracking a Nazi across Canada in *Northern Pursuit* (1943). *Death Hunt* (1981) followed a similar plotline, with Mountie Lee Marvin hunting down trapper-murder suspect Charles Bronson. The gentle side of married Mountie life was covered in the 1949 Dick Powell-Evelyn Keyes vehicle *Mrs. Mike*. The only true Mountie musical remains *Rose Marie*, which was first filmed without the music as a 1928 silent picture. In 1936, Nelson Eddy and Jeanette MacDonald lent their voices to the operatic songs and enjoyed one of their biggest hits. Howard Keel and Ann Blyth remade *Rose Marie*, with less success, in 1954. Little Shirley Temple sang a bit as *Susannah of the Mounties* (1939), and B-movie series Mountie *Renfrew* (q.v.) could always be counted on for a song if the bad guys were behind bars. The most offbeat casting for a Mountie belongs to Tom Smothers, who played one in the *Friday the 13th* spoof *Pandemonium* (1982). Jean-Claude Van Damme made an unlikely Mountie who went undercover as a prison inmate in 1990's *Death Warrant*. See also **Renfrew of the Royal Mounted.**

Rose Marie (1936)	*Fort Vengeance* (1953)
King of the Royal Mounted (1936)	*Missile Base at Taniak* (aka *Canadian*
O'Malley of the Mounted (1936)	*Mounties vs. Atomic Invaders*)
Renfrew of the Royal Mounted (1937)	(1953)
The Girl of the Golden West (1938)	*Rose Marie* (1954)
Susannah of the Mounties (1939)	*Yukon Vengeance* (1954)
Northwest Mounted Police (1940)	*The Canadians* (1961)
Northern Pursuit (1943)	*Alien Thunder* (aka *Dan Candy's Law*)
R.C.M.P. and the Treasure of Genghis	(1973)
Khan (1948)	*Death Hunt* (1981)
Mrs. Mike (1949)	*Pandemonium* (1982)
Pony Soldier (aka *MacDonald of the*	*Death Warrant* (1990)
Canadian Mounted) (1952)	*Conspiracy of Silence* (1991 TVM)

Movie Theaters

Films about movie theaters fall into three general subject categories: cinemas, projectionists and drive-ins. Cinemas have been the principal subject of only a handful of films. A young couple inherited and subsequently managed a rundown theater in the 1957 British comedy *The Smallest Show on Earth*. The 1989 Oscar winner *Cinema Paradiso* lovingly depicted a young boy's obsession with the only movie theater in his small Italian village. A projectionist and a concession girl tried to save a closed theater by raising mushrooms in it and selling them in *Coming Up Roses* (1986). Movie characters came to life—and walked off the screen—in *The Purple Rose of Cairo* (1985) and *Last Action Hero* (1993). Woody Allen and Bette Midler made out in a movie theater showing the solemn *Salaam Bombay* in *Scenes From a Mall* (1991). *The Hard Way* (1991) featured a climactic shoot-out in a theater showing one of star Michael J. Fox's movies. In Lamberto Bava's *Demons* (1985), a movie prop on display in the lobby unleashed a horde of nasty demons on a theater-full of unsuspecting patrons. Along similar lines, mischievous gremlins briefly invaded a movie theater in 1990's *Gremlins 2: The New Batch*. The men that show the movies were the subject of *Merton of the Movies* (1947), *The Projectionist* (1971), *The Picture Show Man* (1977) and Buster Keaton's classic *Sherlock Jr.* (1924). In the latter film, Buster ran down the aisle in one scene and stepped into the movie on the screen, obviously serving as the inspiration for Woody Allen's reverse trick in *Purple Rose*. Drive-in theaters served as the principal setting for two cult favorites, *Targets* (1968) and *Dead End Drive-In* (1986). The low-budget *Targets* starred Boris Karloff as a has-been horror star promoting his latest picture at a drive-in where a mentally unstable sniper begins randomly killing moviegoers. The Australian oddity *Dead End Drive-In* took place at a futuristic drive-in where patrons are not allowed to leave once they enter. Their tires are stolen during the movies. Drive-in owner Todd Tomorrow (Tab Hunter) specialized in showing esoteric triple-features in John Waters's campy *Polyester* (1981). The following films are either about movie theaters or feature key scenes set in movie theaters:

Sherlock Jr. (1924)
The Good Fairy (1935)
Sabotage (aka *A Woman Alone*) (1936)
Contraband (aka *Blackout*) (1940)
Merton of the Movies (1947)
White Heat (1949)
Singin' in the Rain (1952)
The Smallest Show on Earth (aka *Big Time Operators*) (1957)
The Blob (1958)
The Tingler (1959)
Crime Does Not Pay (aka *The Gentle Art of Murder*) (1962)
Targets (1968)
The Last Picture Show (1971)
The Projectionist (1971)
Drive-In (1976)
Drive-In Massacre (1976)
Ruby (1977)
The Picture Show Man (1977)
Grease (1978)
The Meateater (1978)

Something Short of Paradise (1979)
Polyester (1981)
Night of the Comet (1984)
Demons (1985)
The Purple Rose of Cairo (1985)
Desperately Seeking Susan (1985)
Coming Up Roses (1986)
Dead End Drive-In (1986)
Anguish (1987)
American Drive-In (1987)
Who Framed Roger Rabbit? (1988)
Invasion Earth: The Aliens Are Here (1988)
Cinema Paradiso (1989)
Apartment Zero (1989)
Gremlins 2: The New Batch (1990)
Popcorn (1991)
Scenes From a Mall (1991)
The Hard Way (1991)
Into the West (1992)
Matinee (1993)
Last Action Hero (1993)

Movies About Movies

The film industry's love affair with itself has been a long-term relationship, though frequently a stormy one. The inhabitants of Tinseltown have stereotypically portrayed themselves as ruthless producers, crazed directors, alcoholic actors and ambitious starlets. Still, the best of these movies have provided an entertaining behind-the-scenes look at filmmaking and/or the gossip scene. An occasional film has actually delved into the psyche of movie makers. The first talking picture to seriously tackle the subject was 1932's *What Price Hollywood?*, George Cukor's tragic tale of a director who transforms a waitress into a star while he slides into alcoholism. The same plot, with Fredric March as an established star and Janet Gaynor as a promising newcomer, surfaced in 1937 as the now-classic *A Star Is Born*. Joel McCrea played a film director who felt he had lost touch with his audience, so he set out to learn about them in Preston Sturges's seriocomic *Sullivan's Travels* (1941). World War II kept the movies about movies lighthearted, leaving it to the 1950s to introduce a bitter view of Hollywood. Gloria Swanson was overpowering as a faded star desperate for public adoration in Billy Wilder's wry *Sunset Boulevard* (1950). Kirk Douglas portrayed an ambitious producer with a bad habit of stepping on people in Vincente Minnelli's hugely entertaining *The Bad and the Beautiful* (1952). Still, even Hollywood insiders liked the film, honoring it with five Oscars, including Best Supporting Actress for Gloria Grahame. The 1954 remake of *A Star Is Born* was even more effective than the original, thanks to James Mason's searing performance as a washed-up star. *The Goddess* (1958), a downbeat, thinly disguised biography of Marilyn Monroe, signaled the continuation of "realistic" films about Hollywood, a trend that blossomed in the 1960s. That decade produced a line of trashy but often enjoyable fare about filmmaking: *Two Weeks in Another Town* (1962) with Kirk Douglas again, *The Carpetbaggers* (1964), *The Oscar* (1966) and *The Movie-Maker* (1967 TVM). "Serious" movies about the industry decreased over the next two decades, though even satiric features like *The Stunt Man* (1980) and *S.O.B.* (1981) offered darkly cynical views of Hollywood. More mainstream comedies have poked gentle fun at the people behind the movies. A host of deft comedians have employed film studio settings, including Buster Keaton in *Movie Crazy* (1932), Olsen and Johnson in *Hellzapoppin* (1941), Red Skelton in *Merton of the Movies* (1947), Bud and Lou in *Abbott and Costello Meet the Keystone Kops* (1955) and Jerry Lewis in *The Errand Boy* (1961). Woody Allen's *The Purple Rose of Cairo* (1985) was about a movie character who stepped off the screen and caused all kinds of complications. The early days of filmmaking were remembered fondly in *Singin' in the Rain* (1952) and *Nickelodeon* (1976). On the other side of the Atlantic, England produced *The Magic Box* (1951), an all-star biography of film pioneer William Friese-Greene. Joseph Losey's *Finger of Guilt* (1956) offered a rare look inside a British film studio. French New Wave directors Jean-Luc Godard and François Truffaut paid homage to their craft with *Contempt* (1963) and *Day for Night* (1973). Federico Fellini's semiautobiographical *8½* (1963) explored the mind of fantasy-ridden director Marcello Mastroianni. The title was a reference to the number of movies Fellini had previously made. See also **Film Star Biographies.**

The Studio Murder Mystery (1929)	*What Price Hollywood?* (1932)
Movie Crazy (1932)	*Once in a Lifetime* (1932)

Bombshell (aka *Blonde Bombshell*) (1933)
The Death Kiss (1933)
A Star Is Born (1937)
Stand-In (1937)
Hollywood Cavalcade (1939)
The Bank Dick (aka *The Bank Detective*) (1940)
Sullivan's Travels (1941)
Hellzapoppin (1941)
The Reluctant Dragon (1941)
World Premiere (1941)
Crazy House (1943)
The Falcon in Hollywood (1944)
Merton of the Movies (1947)
It's a Great Feeling (1949)
You're My Everything (1949)
Sunset Boulevard (1950)
The Magic Box (1951)
Hollywood Story (1951)
The Bad and the Beautiful (1952)
Singin' in the Rain (1952)
The Star (1952)
A Star Is Born (1954)
Susan Slept Here (1954)
Abbott and Costello Meet the Keystone Kops (1955)
Finger of Guilt (aka The *Intimate Stranger*) (1956)
The Goddess (1958)
Paradise Alley (aka *Stars in the Back Yard*) (1961)
The Errand Boy (1961)
Two Weeks in Another Town (1962)
Contempt (1963)
8½ (1963)
The Carpetbaggers (1964)
The Oscar (1966)
After the Fox (1966)
The Movie-Maker (1967 TVM)
Everything for Sale (1968)
The Legend of Lylah Clare (1968)
David Holzman's Diary (1968)
Alex in Wonderland (1970)
Bombay Talkie (1970)
The Movie Murderer (1970 TVM)

The Last Movie (aka *Chinchero*) (1971)
Day for Night (1973)
The Sex Symbol (1974 TVM)
Day of the Locust (1975)
Hollywood Boulevard (1976)
The Last Tycoon (1976)
Nickelodeon (1976)
The World's Greatest Lover (1977)
Evening in Byzantium (1978 TVM)
The Users (1978)
An Almost Perfect Affair (1979)
The Stunt Man (1980)
The Dream Merchants (1980 TVM)
Loose Shoes (aka *Coming Attractions*) (1980)
S.O.B. (1981)
Burden of Dreams (1982)
Passion (1982)
Strangers Kiss (1983)
Love Scenes (1984)
Special Effects (1984)
The Last Horror Film (1984)
The Purple Rose of Cairo (1985)
Means and Ends (1985)
Malice in Wonderland (1985 TVM)
I Hate Actors (1986)
Overnight (1986)
Smart Alec (aka *The Movie Maker*) (1986)
Sweet Liberty (1986)
Good Morning, Babylon (1987)
The Big Picture (1989)
Sexbomb (1989)
Stardumb (1990)
Twisted Obsession (1990)
Postcards From the Edge (1990)
Barton Fink (1991)
The Inner Circle (1991)
The Player (1992)
Double Threat (1992)
Matinee (1993)
Torch Song (1993 TVM)
Last Action Hero (1993)
My Life's in Turnaround (1993)
The Pickle (1993)

Movies Without Dialogue

Since the advent of "talkies," movies without dialogue have been screen oddities. Charlie Chaplin, who felt uncomfortable with dialogue, resisted making a talking picture until 1940's *The Great Dictator*. Thus, his two classic comedies of the 1930s, *City Lights* and *Modern Times*, were both sans dialogue, their soundtracks consisting solely of sounds and music. Given Chaplin's success as a silent film-maker, these "nontalkies" were taken in stride. That was not the case with 1952's *The Thief*, an unusual mainstream experiment devised by producer Clarence Greene and director Russell Rouse. This dialogueless film cast Ray Milland as an enemy spy pursued by the FBI. Initially intriguing, *The Thief*'s gimmick grows tiresome and becomes a forced irritation. A similar fate befell Gene Kelly's *Invitation to the Dance* (1957), an ambitious attempt to tell three stories completely in dance. Obviously, the movie puzzled MGM's head brass, who delayed its release for five years. A handful of foreign films have bypassed all language barriers by telling their plots completely in visuals. French director-writer-star Jacques Tati's *Mr. Hulot's Holiday* (1953) continues to charm international audiences with its winning visual humor. Poetic visual splendor replaced dialogue in Kaneto Shindo's *The Island* (1962), the low-key story of a solitary family inhabiting a tiny isle. *Le Bal* (1982) told the story of a ballroom through fifty years of dancing. Back in the United States, Mel Brooks spoofed Hollywood of the 1920s in his wacky 1976 comedy *Silent Movie* (in which mime Marcel Marceau had the film's single line of dialogue). Eleanor Antin directed *The Last Night of Rasputin* (1989) and *The Man Without a World* (1992), both of which look like vintage black-and-white silent films. Many movies have employed minimal dialogue to great effect, such as Cornel Wilde's thrilling adventure film *The Naked Prey* (1966).

City Lights (1931)
Modern Times (1936)
The Thief (1952)
Mr. Hulot's Holiday (aka *Monsieur Hulot's Holiday*) (1953)
Invitation to the Dance (1957)
The Island (aka *Hadaka no Shima*) (1962)

Silent Movie (1976)
Le Bal (1982)
Le Dernier Combat (1984)
Sidewalk Stories (1987)
Missing Link (1989)
The Last Night of Rasputin (1989)
A Bullet in the Head (1990)
The Man Without a World (1992)

Multiple Personalities

The subject of schizophrenia resulting in multiple personalities has enabled several fine performers to display their acting versatility. Ronald Colman won his only Oscar for portraying a psychologically unstable Shakespearean actor who begins to play Othello for real in 1947's *A Double Life*. Joanne Woodward also won an Oscar for her career-breakthrough performance as a woman with three personalities in 1957's *The Three Faces of Eve*. Almost two decades later, Woodward played the psychiatrist to Sally Field's *Sybil* in the fact-based story of a young woman plagued by seventeen distinct personalities. The film also provided Field with her acting breakthrough, proving her TV days as "The Flying Nun" were behind her. Hitchcock's *Psycho* (1960) ended with the once-shocking revelation that Norman Bates was *also* his mother. In the seldom-shown 1945 thriller *Bewitched*, Phyllis Thaxter murdered a man as one personality but remembered nothing about it as her other self. And in *Three Nuts in Search of a Bolt* (1964), three neurotics hired an unemployed actor to visit a psychiatrist for them. When he acts out all their neuroses, the psychiatrist diagnoses him as a victim of multiple personality! See also **Psychiatrists.**

Bewitched (1945)
A Double Life (1947)
Lizzie (1957)
The Three Faces of Eve (1957)
Psycho (1960)
Three Nuts in Search of a Bolt (1964)
The Boston Strangler (1968)
Sybil (1976 TVM)

The Strange Possession of Mrs. Oliver (1977 TVM)
The Five of Me (1981 TVM)
Loose Cannons (1990)
Voices Within: The Lives of Truddie Chase (1990 TVM)
Femme Fatale (1991)
Raising Cain (1992)

Multiple Roles

The challenge of playing three or more roles in the same film has appealed to very few performers. It is also likely that the profession's more serious actors have viewed the ploy as mere gimmickry. For whichever reason, it has been a rare screen occurrence. Peter Sellers played at least three roles in each of three movies. He first performed the trick for the 1959 comedy sleeper *The Mouse That Roared*, appearing as the picture's hero, as a count, and as the Grand Duchess of Fenwick. Five years later, he landed his most famous triple role as U.S. President Muffey, Captain Mandrake, and Nazi scientist Dr. Strangelove in Stanley Kubrick's cold war satire *Dr. Strangelove, or How I Learned to Stop Worrying and Love the Bomb* (1964). In the twilight of his career, Seller took on six roles in the barely released comedy *Undercovers Hero* (1975). Second to Sellers is America's own Jerry Lewis, who must have decided he was ready for bigger numbers after his double role in *The Nutty Professor* (1963). Lewis played five roles in 1966's *Three on a Couch* and seven roles in 1965's *The Family Jewels*. The latter film was obviously patterned after the droll British classic *Kind Hearts and Coronets* (1949), which featured marvelous Alec Guinness as eight murder tims. Except for Malcolm McDowell, the principal cast of the sparkling British satire *O Lucky Man!* (1973) appeared in multiple roles. In a similar vein, the members of the Monty Python comedy troupe have essayed a variety of roles in their pictures, particularly *Monty Python and the Holy Grail* (1974) and *The Life of Brian* (1979).

Kind Hearts and Coronets (1949) (Alec Guinness)
Watch the Birdie (1950) (Red Skelton)
The Mouse That Roared (1959) (Peter Sellers)
Dr. Strangelove, or How I Learned to Stop Worrying and Love the Bomb (1964) (Peter Sellers)
The Seven Faces of Dr. Lao (1964) (Tony Randall)
The Family Jewels (1965) (Jerry Lewis)
Three on a Couch (1966) (Jerry Lewis)
Arabella (1969) (Terry-Thomas)
O Lucky Man! (1973)
Monty Python and the Holy Grail (1974)
Undercovers Hero (aka *Soft Beds and Hard Battles*) (1975) (Peter Sellers)
Hot Lead and Cold Feet (1978) (Jim Dale)

The Man in the Santa Claus Suit (1978 TVM) (Fred Astaire)
Circle of Iron (aka *The Silent Flute*) (1978) (David Carradine)
The Life of Brian (1979) (Monty Python Troupe)
Cracking Up (aka *Smorgasbord*) (1983) (Jerry Lewis)
Cheech and Chong's Corsican Brothers (1984) (Cheech and Chong)
Joe vs. the Volcano (1990) (Meg Ryan)
Seduction: Three Tales From the Inner Sanctum (1992 TVM) (Victoria Principal and John Terry)

The Mummy

With facial features swathed in bandages (or wrinkles) and a vocabulary limited to growls, the Mummy lacked the personality of his cinematic peers: Dracula, the Frankenstein Monster, and the Wolf Man (q.q.v.). For most of his career, he has been used as a slow-moving killing machine. He did not start out that way, though. Karl Freund's *The Mummy* (1932) was a haunting film about reincarnation and eternal love. As the mummified priest Imhotep, Boris Karloff appeared only briefly in Jack Pierce's famous mummy makeup. He spent most of the film in his reincarnated form, playing a menacing Egyptian archaeologist. In a fitting climax, he was reduced to dust when the heroine called upon the ancient god Isis. Oddly, the Mummy was not revived until 1940, when former cowboy star Tom Tyler replaced Karloff in *The Mummy's Hand*, the first of a low-budget series. Lon Chaney, Jr. took over the role (the Mummy having undergone a name change, from Imhotep to Kharis) for three additional installments. None of these films rose above the routine, although *The Mummy's Curse* offered a different setting (the Louisiana Bayou), and the heroine actually turned into a mummy in *The Mummy's Ghost*. The official Universal series ended in 1944, although the studio brought back the Gauzed One (played by Eddie Powell) for one final fling in 1955's *Abbott and Costello Meet the Mummy*, one of the comedy duo's last efforts. After lying dormant for a couple years, the Mummy turned up in Mexico and Britain almost simultaneously. Like most Mexican horror films of the late 1950s, Rafael Portillo's *The Aztec Mummy* (1957) boasted fine black-and-white photography and, despite an absurd plot, recalled the eerie atmosphere of Universal's 1940s features. The title mummy, named Popoca, did well enough to inspire a series of Aztec Mummy movies, which still crop up on television today. Meanwhile, fresh on the heels of its *Dracula* success, Britain's Hammer Studios produced a colorful remake of *The Mummy* (1959). Transplanting the story to England in 1895, this version profited from Peter Cushing's steady performance as an intrepid archaeologist and Christopher Lee's imposing presence as the movies' quickest-footed Mummy. Despite good notices, Hammer waited five years before continuing the series. It was hardly worth the effort, since two of the three sequels were cheap programmers. The other, however, was 1972's *Blood From the Mummy's Tomb*, an adaptation of Bram Stoker's story "Jewel of the Seven Stars" and a welcome return to the literate approach of Freund's original film. The same story served as the basis for 1980's *The Awakening*, an expensive—but less effective—version starring Charlton Heston and Stephanie Zimbalist. Spanish horror star Paul Naschy, who has played more monsters than anybody, took his turn in the bandages for *The Mummy's Revenge* (1973). And in 1982's ridiculous *Timewalker*, a nasty mummy is revealed to be a misunderstood alien who just wanted to go home. Shades of *E.T.*

Universal's Mummy
The Mummy (1932)
The Mummy's Hand (1940)
The Mummy's Tomb (1942)
The Mummy's Curse (1944)

The Mummy's Ghost (1944)
Abbott and Costello Meet the Mummy (1955)

The Aztec Mummy
The Aztec Mummy (aka *La Momia*; *La Momia Azteca*) (1957)
Robot vs. the Aztec Mummy (aka *La Momia Azteca Contra el Robot Humano*) (1959)

Curse of the Aztec Mummy (aka *La Maldicion de la Momia Azteca*) (1959)
Wrestling Women vs. the Aztec Mummy (aka *La Luchadoras Contra la Momia*) (1964)

Hammer's Mummy
The Mummy (1959)
Curse of the Mummy's Tomb (1964)
The Mummy's Shroud (1967)

Blood From the Mummy's Tomb (1972)

Others
The Egyptian Mummy (1914)
Eyes of the Mummy (1918)
The Pharaoh's Curse (1956)
Curse of the Faceless Man (1958) (very Mummy-like)
Attack of the Mayan Mummy (1963)

The Mummy's Revenge (1973)
The Awakening (1980)
Timewalker (1982)
The Monster Squad (1987)
Tales From the Darkside: The Movie (1990)

The Muppets

Kermit the Frog and Miss Piggy were established television stars and pop icons when they and their furry friends made the leap to the big screen in 1979's *The Muppet Movie*. Film industry watchers expected a guaranteed audience of loyal children, but the film's widespread success came as a surprise. The 1981 sequel *The Great Muppet Caper* pitted the gang against jewel thieves (q.v.) who had stolen the Fabulous Baseball Diamond. It outperformed its predecessor at domestic box offices, earning a nifty $16 million. Muppet creator Jim Henson interrupted the series in 1982 to produce *The Dark Crystal*, a more conventional "quest fantasy" with puppets. He returned to the Muppets with 1984's *The Muppets Take Manhattan*, in which Kermit took his college musical to the Great White Way. Its box office receipts were disappointing, and another theatrical feature did not appear until 1992's *The Muppet Christmas Carol*. Sadly, Henson died in the interim. He coined the phrase "muppet" in the 1950s to describe a combination of "marionette" and "puppet." See also **Puppets**.

The Muppet Movie (1979)
The Great Muppet Caper (1981)
The Muppets Take Manhattan (1984)
The Muppet Christmas Carol (1992)

My Favorite . . . Series

Bob Hope made the three *My Favorite* . . . films at the peak of his Paramount career. Technically, he played a different character in each film, but that seems irrelevant considering that Hope acted pretty much the same in all his movies (although there were exceptions, such as 1957's *Beau James*). The series' premise had Bob encountering mysterious women who got him involved in murder mysteries and spy intrigue. In *My Favorite Blonde*, he meets Madeleine Carroll (already a spy movie veteran after 1935's *The 39 Steps*) on a train and winds up helping her elude Nazi agents. *My Favorite Brunette* turned out to be Bob's *Road* movie (q.v.) costar Dorothy Lamour, who lures him into a hilarious mystery spoof revolving around a photo taken by Bob's "keyhole camera." The supporting cast included an amusing Peter Lorre and a cameo by Bing Crosby as a prison executioner. This entry also featured one of Hope's funniest scenes, in which the villains administer truth serum to him. The final series entry was 1951's *My Favorite Spy*, which paired him with the gorgeous Hedy Lamarr in a spy spoof casting Bob as a comedian posing as a tough secret agent. The *My Favorite* . . . films hold up very well despite numerous in-jokes certain to be lost on many contemporary viewers.

My Favorite Blonde (1942)   *My Favorite Spy* (1951)
My Favorite Brunette (1947)

National Lampoon's Vacation Series

The leisure-time exploits of the Griswold Family formed the basis for three *Vacation* films cowritten by prolific producer-writer John Hughes (*Home Alone*). Hughes based the first film (loosely, one hopes) on his magazine article "Vacation '56," a satirical remembrance of a family trip. The plot sent the Griswolds on a wild, sometimes wacky, odyssey across the United States in search of the theme park Wally World. The family consisted of parents Clark (Chevy Chase) and Ellen (Beverly D'Angelo), son Rusty (Anthony Michael Hall) and daughter Audrey (Dana Barron). They met other relatives, including uncouth cousin Eddie (Randy Quaid), along the way. Capitalizing on Chase's silly *Saturday Night Live* persona, *National Lampoon's Vacation* (1983) signaled Hughes's arrival as a producer with a Midas touch (he followed this hit with *Sixteen Candles* and *The Breakfast Club*). However, critics and moviegoers were unkind to the dreadful 1985 sequel, *National Lampoon's European Vacation*, in which the Griswolds — dressed as pigs — win a transcontinental vacation on the TV quiz show *Pig in a Poke*. Chase and D'Angelo returned as the parents, but Jason Lively took over as Rusty and Dana Hill as Audrey. The Griswolds fared much better by staying home for the holidays in 1989's *National Lampoon's Christmas Vacation*. This second sequel mixed a little sentiment with the irreverent humor, most of which was supplied by the unexpected arrival of cousin Eddie (Quaid again). Chase and D'Angelo returned for *Christmas Vacation*; their children were played by Johnny Galecki and Juliette Lewis (two years away from her Oscar-nominated performance in *Cape Fear*).

National Lampoon's Vacation (1983)

National Lampoon's European Vacation (1985)

National Lampoon's Christmas Vacation (1989)

Neutron

Neutron was one of three Mexican wrestler superheroes to enjoy South-of-the-Border popularity in the 1960s. Silver-masked Santo (q.v.) was the undisputed king, but Neutron held his own against latecomer rival The Blue Demon (q.v.). Mexico's America Studios shot the first three Neutron films in 1960, starting with *Neutron, the Black Masked*. This introductory effort pitted the wrestler against evil Dr. Caronte and his neutron bomb. Caronte returned in both *Neutron vs. the Amazing Dr. Caronte* and *Neutron Against the Death Robots*. In the United States, the films were released out of order and sometimes shown as serials. This latter oddity occurred because the films were originally made in three parts and later edited together. This was a necessity for the filmmakers, since Mexican labor agreements allowed America Studios to produce short features only. See also **The Blue Demon; Santo; Wrestling.**

Neutron, the Black Masked (aka *Neutron el Enmascarado Negro*) (1960)
Neutron vs. the Amazing Dr. Caronte (aka *Neutron Contra el Doctor Caronte*) (1960)
Neutron Against the Death Robots (aka *Los Automatas de la Muerte*) (1961)
Neutron Battles the Karate Assassins (1962)
Neutron vs. the Maniac (aka *Neutron and the Cosmic Bomb*) (1962)
Neutron Traps the Invisible Killers (1963)

Night of the Living Dead

Commenting on the scenes of "ghouls" devouring human flesh in 1968's *Night of the Living Dead*, director George Romero once wrote: "I was delighted when one of our investors, who happened to be in the meat packing business, turned up on the set one day with a sackful of animal innards which made the sequences seem so real." The film was shot outside of Pittsburgh over a span of nine months for the rock-bottom price of $118,000. *Night* was panned by the few critics who saw it during its original 1968 release. However, Romero and the film gained some recognition after a glowing *Village Voice* review in 1969 and a 1970 screening at the Museum of Modern Art. Theaters began showing it as a midnight feature in 1971, and its status as a cult classic grew quickly. Romero's subsequent films made little money, and he experienced difficulty in financing a sequel. However, with the help of Italian horror filmmaker Dario Argento, he produced 1979's *Dawn of the Dead*. Not surprisingly, the film was hailed by some critics as a brilliant analogy of our times and condemned by others as a violent, pretentious time waster. Both *Night* and *Dawn* dealt with the resurrection of dead people who feed upon the flesh of the living. The former film confined the action to seven people trapped in an isolated farmhouse. They *all* die. *Dawn* began in an urban setting before moving its four central characters to an abandoned shopping mall (the scene of many obvious analogies). Although *Dawn of the Dead* was released without a rating (Romero feared it would be given an X), it performed well both in the United States and abroad (interestingly, as part of their deal, Argento recut the film for its European release). Romero's long-awaited final installment, *Day of the Dead*, appeared in 1985 and was greeted with much disappointment. Rather than concluding the trilogy (either plotwise or thematically), it opted for a 1950s-style story of understanding scientists trying to prevent the military from killing all the ghouls. It naturally left plenty of room for a fourth *Dead* picture. Meanwhile, Romero produced a 1990 color remake of the original *Night of the Living Dead*, with makeup expert Tom Savini handling the directing chores. See also **Ghouls.**

Night of the Living Dead (1968)   *Day of the Dead* (1985)
Dawn of the Dead (1979)   *Night of the Living Dead* (1990)

Nightmare on Elm Street

With a black felt hat, a red-and-green striped sweater, and a right-hand glove with steel "finger knives," Freddy Kreuger can hardly be considered a stylish dresser. Still, that has not deterred him from overtaking Jason (see **Friday the 13th**) as the 1980s' most popular killer of teens. The 1984 *Nightmare on Elm Street* introduced Mr. Kreuger (Robert Englund), a janitor at Springwood High with a special interest in kidnapping and murdering teens. The law finally caught up with him, but a court freed him on a technicality. This inspired some vigilante parents to track him down and fry him in a boiler room. In revenge, he invaded the dreams of the parents' children and dispensed with them in ghastly fashion. In a *Time* interview, director Wes Craven offered his explanation for the film's unexpected popularity among teens: "Freddy is the most ruthless primal father. The adult who wants to slash down the next generation." The films' flippant humor may have also contributed to "Freddymania." In one scene, Freddy bashes an aspiring teen actress's head into a TV set and then quips: "This is it, Jennifer, your big break in TV." Englund has been the only performer to appear in all six entries, though Heather Langenkamp played the heroine in the first and third films. The last entry, 1991's *Freddy's Dead: The Final Nightmare* boasted a ten-minute finale shown in 3-D (q.v.). A syndicated hour-long TV anthology dubbed *Freddy's Nightmares* ran for a few seasons in the late 1980s. Englund introduced the stories and occasionally appeared in them (including the first, a prequel to the original film, directed by Tobe Hooper). Finally, Freddy's hand made a cameo appearance at the climax of 1993's *Jason Goes to Hell: The Final Friday*. See also **Slasher Movies.**

Nightmare on Elm Street (1984)
Nightmare on Elm Street II: Freddy's Revenge (1986)
Nightmare on Elm Street III: The Dream Warriors (1987)
Nightmare on Elm Street IV: The Dream Master (1988)
Nightmare on Elm Street V: The Dream Child (1989)
Freddy's Dead: The Final Nightmare (1991)

1918 Trilogy

Playwright Horton Foote (*Tender Mercies, The Trip to Bountiful*) wrote these three understated films, in which the storylines unfold in reverse chronological order. That is, each succeeding film went further back in time to reveal incidents in the characters' pasts. The first installment, *1918*, introduced Horace Robedaux (William Converse-Roberts), his wife Elizabeth (Hallie Foote), and their baby, who live in the little town of Harrison, Texas, where Horace runs a dry-cleaning store. The plot consisted of several touching vignettes that climaxed with a subplot about an epidemic that brings tragedy to the townspeople. The second film, *On Valentine's Day*, took place in 1917, a year after Horace and Elizabeth's elopement—an event that resulted in the silent treatment from her parents. The final entry, *Convicts*, took place on a sugar plantation in 1902, with a young Horace (Lukas Haas) befriending the chain gang laborers. All three movies were produced in association with PBS's *American Playhouse*. In fact, *1918* and *On Valentine's Day* were broadcast together as *Story of a Marriage*. The three movies were based on Foote's autobiographical nine-play cycle *An Orphan's Home*. Hallie Foote is Horton's daughter. Matthew Broderick played her rakish brother, strictly in a supporting role, in the first two films.

1918 (1984)   *Convicts* (1991)
On Valentine's Day (1986)

No Retreat, No Surrender

Frequently described as a *Karate Kid/Rocky IV* hybrid rip-off, 1985's *No Retreat, No Surrender* starred Kurt McKinney as Jason, a young Seattle lad who must battle a ruthless Russian in a martial arts showdown. Our hero is bright enough to know he needs a good coach to prepare him for the big fight, but, sadly, Pat Morita (the Karate Kid's mentor) is nowhere to be found. Luckily, Bruce Lee's ghost has the time to give the kid some pointers. In front of a meager crowd (in what appears to be a school gym), Kurt outkicks and punches his Russian opponent — who turns out to be Jean-Claude Van Damme (who would go on to become the 1990s' answer to Bruce Lee). Understandably, the belated 1989 sequel dispensed with Jason altogether and shifted the action to Bangkok. This time, Loren Avedon played the lead character, a nice guy named Scott who gets really mad when his Vietnamese girlfriend is kidnapped by some of her father's enemies. Scott recruits a couple of friends (including Queen of Kung Fu Cynthia Rothrock) and mounts a rescue in which he winds up challenging Russian killer Matthias Hues (this "Soviet bad guy" angle is apparently the thematic link to the original film). Avedon returned for 1990's *No Retreat, No Surrender III: Blood Brothers*, in which he and his bickering brother (Keith Vitali) go their separate ways as they avenge their father's death at the hands of terrorists. Although the last two films were slightly better than the first, this subpar action series will be best remembered for introducing Van Damme to American audiences. For other martial arts series, see **American Ninja Series**, **Bloodfist**, and **Kickboxer**.

No Retreat, No Surrender (1985)
No Retreat, No Surrender II (1989)
No Retreat, No Surrender III: Blood Brothers (1990)

North Pole/South Pole

The North Pole may be best known as Santa's home, but in the movies, it's been home to a variety of unpleasant creatures. An atomic explosion in the Arctic awoke *The Beast From 20,000 Fathoms*. Both *Frankenstein: The True Story*, and the Swedish *Terror of Frankenstein* (aka *Victor Frankenstein*) restored the original ending of Mary Shelley's novel, in which the Monster was stranded in the frozen wastelands. In Howard Hawks's 1951 sci-fi classic *The Thing (From Another World)*, an unfriendly alien tried to devour a group of scientists at an Arctic research station. On the plus side, the North Pole was also where Superman built his personal fortress (and "honeymooned" with Lois Lane) in *Superman II*. The South Pole, despite having a continental advantage in terms of mass, has been the setting for fewer movies. *Scott of the Antarctic* chronicled the exploits of real-life explorer Robert Scott. George Maharis and Bobby Morse explored ways to get women to their isolated residence in *Quick Before It Melts*. John Carpenter transplanted his 1982 remake of *The Thing* from the North Pole to the South Pole. Only two scientists survived in this version, with the fate of the alien (he may be one of the survivors) heavily in doubt.

North

S.O.S. Iceberg (1933)
She (1935)
The Thing (From Another World) (1951)
The Beast From 20,000 Fathoms (1953)
The Perfect Furlough (aka *Strictly for Pleasure*) (1958)
The Atomic Submarine (1959)
Voyage to the Bottom of the Sea (1961)
Ice Station Zebra (1968)

Frankenstein: The True Story (1973 TVM)
Island at the Top of the World (1974)
Victor Frankenstein (aka *Terror of Frankenstein*) (1977)
Superman II (1980)
Cook and Peary: The Race to the Pole (1983 TVM)
Santa Claus, the Movie (1985)
Ordeal in the Arctic (1993 TVM)

South

The Secret Land (1948)
Scott of the Antarctic (1948)
The Land Unknown (1957)
Quick Before It Melts (1964)

Cry of the Penguins (aka *Mr. Forbush and the Penguins*) (1971)
The Thing (1982)
Antarctica (1983)

Nostradamus

Mexican horror movie veteran German Robles played a descendant of the prophet Nostradamus (now a vampire) in a ten-part, South-of-the-Border serial. In the United States, it was edited into four feature films, dubbed in English, and released directly to television. The prophecies of the original Nostradamus reached the screen in exploitative splendor with the 1974 Japanese import *The Last Days of Planet Earth* (aka *Prophecies of Nostradamus: Catastrophe 1999*).

Blood of Nostradamus (aka *La Sangre de Nostradamus*) (1960)
Curse of Nostradamus (aka *La Maldición de Nostradamus*) (1960)
The Monster Demolisher (aka *Nostradamus y el Destructor de Monstruos*) (1960)
The Genii of Darkness (aka *Nostradamus, el Genio de las Tinieblas*) (1960)

Nuns

The call of the convent and life within its walls have provided filmmakers with a wealth of varied plotlines. Young would-be nuns have frequently been forced to choose between the convent and the man they love, a problem confronted by Helen Hayes in *The White Sister* (1933), Julie Andrews in *The Sound of Music* (1965), and Mary Tyler Moore in *Change of Habit* (1969). Deborah Kerr and her fellow nuns faced a crisis of faith at a remote Himalayan mission in Powell and Pressburger's hypnotic *Black Narcissus* (1946). Vanessa Redgrave's deranged nun in Ken Russell's *The Devils* (1971) provided the testimony necessary to burn outspoken priest Oliver Reed for practicing witchcraft. More conventional nuns have dealt with more humane problems: Rosalind Russell played the real-life nurse who initiated treatment for polio in *Sister Kenny* (1946); Celeste Holm and Loretta Young earned Oscar nominations as French nuns trying to build a children's hospital in *Come to the Stable* (1949); and Bonnie Franklin founded a home for women prison parolees in *Sister Margaret and the Saturday Night Ladies* (1987). Movie nuns have often been paired with unruly types, whom they typically reform. These unlikely pairings include nun Deborah Kerr and soldier Robert Mitchum in *Heaven Knows, Mr. Allison* (1957), Robert Webber and Anna Sten in *The Nun and the Sergeant* (1962), detective David Janssen and Susannah York in *The Golden Gate Murders* (1979), and gunfighter Clint Eastwood and Shirley MacLaine in *Two Mules for Sister Sara* (1970). In the last film, however, Ms. MacLaine turned out to be a prostitute disguised as a nun. Although not disguised, Dudley Moore wound up in a nun's habit in the fiendishly funny Faust spoof *Bedazzled* (1967). Tricked by the Devil (Peter Cook), Moore was transformed into a sister in the Order of the Leaping Nuns. The serious side of being a nun has been examined vividly by Fred Zinnemann in *The Nun's Story* (1959) and French director Alain Cavalier in *Therese* (1986). The most troubled nun was the one played by Meg Tilly in *Agnes of God* (1985), the story of a young nun accused of killing a child she claims was immaculately conceived. See also **Monks; Popes and Cardinals.**

The White Sister (1933)	*Where Angels Go, Trouble Follows* (1968)
Song of Bernadette (1943)	
Till We Meet Again (1944)	*Change of Habit* (1969)
The Bells of St. Mary's (1945)	*Two Mules for Sister Sara* (1970)
Black Narcissus (1946)	*Weekend of Terror* (1970 TVM)
Sister Kenny (1946)	*Madron* (1970)
Come to the Stable (1949)	*The Devils* (1971)
Thunder on the Hill (aka *Bonaventure*) (1951)	*The Weekend Nun* (aka *Matter of the Heart*) (1972 TVM)
Appointment With Danger (1951)	*Airport 1975* (1974)
Anna (1951)	*In This House of Brede* (1975 TVM)
Heaven Knows, Mr. Allison (1957)	*Nasty Habits* (1976)
Sea Wife (1957)	*The Golden Gate Murders* (aka *Specter on the Bridge*) (1979 TVM)
The Miracle (1959)	*The Runner Stumbles* (1979)
The Nun's Story (1959)	*Dixie: Changing Habits* (1983 TVM)
Conspiracy of Hearts (1960)	*Choices of the Heart* (aka *In December the Roses Will Bloom Again*) (1983 TVM)
The Devil and the Nun (aka *Mother Joan of the Angels*) (1960)	
Viridiana (1961)	*Dark Habits* (1983)
The Nun and the Sergeant (1962)	*September Gun* (1983 TVM)
Lilies of the Field (1963)	*Shattered Vows* (1984 TVM)
The Little Nuns (1965)	*Agnes of God* (1985)
The Nun (1965)	*Sacred Hearts* (1985)
The Sound of Music (1965)	*Therese* (1986)
The Singing Nun (1966)	*Sister Margaret and the Saturday Night Ladies* (1987 TVM)
The Trouble With Angels (1966)	
Bedazzled (1967)	*Angel in Green* (1987)

Nuns on the Run (1990)	*Sister Act* (1992)
Child of Light, Child of Darkness (1991 TVM)	*The Nun and the Bandit* (1992)
	Walls and Bridges (1992)
Hudson Hawk (1991)	*Sister Act 2: Back in the Habit* (1993)
Freejack (1992)	

Nurses Series

B-movie mogul Roger Corman developed this R-rated, loosely connected film series for the drive-in crowd. After leaving American International Pictures in the late 1960s, Corman started his own production/distribution company, New World Pictures. He served as executive producer on New World's first movie, 1970's *The Student Nurses*. Directed by drive-in cult favorite Stephanie Rothman, this surprisingly unexploitative picture featured strong female characters and even some topical issues (e.g., abortion). One of its stars, Elaine Giftos, used it as a stepping stone for the 1970-71 TV series *The Interns*. Neither Corman nor Rothman had a hand in the other series films, which dealt with nothing more topical than waterbeds. The casts changed from film to film, although Corman movie veteran Dick Miller appeared in the last three entries. Future Oscar nominee Sally (*Anna*) Kirkland starred in *The Young Nurses*. See also **Hospitals**; **Kildare, Dr.**

The Student Nurses (1970)	*The Young Nurses* (aka *Emergency*
Private Duty Nurses (1972)	*Nurses*) (1973)
Night Call Nurses (1972)	*Candy Stripe Nurses* (1974)

Octopuses and Squids

The first octopus film of note, 1938's *Sh! The Octopus*, was ironically an adaptation of the stage play *The Gorilla*. That typifies the lack of respect shown to these homely creatures throughout most of their screen careers. A giant squid made a memorable splash in Cecil B. DeMille's *Reap the Wild Wind* (1942). Twelve years later, an even bigger squid attacked the submarine *Nautilus* during an intense storm sequence in Disney's *20,000 Leagues Under the Sea*. This was the squid's finest hour, its memorable death coming at the hands of Kirk Douglas (who harpooned it in the eye). Deep sea diver Bob Hope wrestled an oversized squid for laughs in *The Road to Bali* (1952). Special effects wizard Ray Harryhausen created a giant "octopus" for *It Came From Beneath the Sea*. Due to budget constraints, Harryhausen trimmed off two tentacles and subsequently dubbed his creation a "sexopus." The submarine *Seaview* electrocuted another giant octopus in *Voyage to the Bottom of the Sea*. Killer whales rescued a seaside resort from a similar menace in 1976's low-budget, *Jaws*-inspired rip-off *Tentacles*. Lovely Maud Adam kept a venomous octopus for a pet in the 1983 James Bond adventure *Octopussy*, while Esther Williams swam an underwater ballet with an animated octopus in 1953's *Dangerous When Wet*. Ghosts brought a cardboard squid to life in a hotel in 1988's *High Spirits*.

Sh! The Octopus (1938)	*The Road to Bali* (1952)
Reap the Wild Wind (1942)	*Dangerous When Wet* (1953)
The Magic Voyage of Sinbad (aka *Sadko*) (1952)	*Beneath the Twelve Mile Reef* (1953)
	20,000 Leagues Under the Sea (1954)

Monster From the Ocean Floor (1954)	*King Kong vs. Godzilla* (1962)
It Came From Beneath the Sea (1955)	*Octaman* (1971)
The Bride of the Monster (1956)	*Tentacles* (1976)
The Fabulous World of Jules Verne (1958)	*Warlords of Atlantis* (1978)
	Octopussy (1983)
Don't Give Up the Ship (1959)	*High Spirits* (1988)
Mysterious Island (1961)	*The Little Mermaid* (1989)
Voyage to the Bottom of the Sea (1961)	

Oh, God

It took George Burns eighty-one years to find the role he will best be remembered for, but it was a heavenly part as the unlikely incarnation (complete with trademark cigar) of the Deity in *Oh, God!* (1977). This gentle, uplifting fantasy blossomed into a substantial hit and ultimately begot two sequels. *Oh, God! Book II* (1980) rehashed the original film and added a little girl and globs of sentiment. *Oh God! You Devil* (1984) was a contemporary version of *Faust* with Ted Wass as a singer who sells his soul and Burns in a dual role as God and the Devil.

Oh, God! (1977)	*Oh God! You Devil* (aka *Oh, God! Book*
Oh, God! Book II (1980)	*III*) (1984)

Oil Wells

The sight of thick, black fluid gushing forth from the ground was a familiar one on the theater screens of the 1950s. How can anyone forget the classic scene where ecstatic, oil-soaked James Dean strikes black gold in 1956's *Giant*? Yet, even before *Giant*, viewers in the 1950s had the option of pulling for nice guy James Stewart to strike oil off the Louisiana Coast (*Thunder Bay*), hooting against oily villains like Gene Barry (*The Houston Story*), or simply pondering what former elephant-boy Sabu was even doing on an oil field (*Jaguar*). Pre-1950s fare offered more typical wildcatter heroes in the guise of Spencer Tracy, Clark Gable (both in *Boom Town*) and Richard Arlen (*Wildcat*). A notable exception was 1937's *High, Wide, and Handsome*, a nostalgic Hammerstein-Kern musical with Randolph Scott as an oil driller. Oil women have been scarce, though Faye Dunaway (with a little help from George C. Scott) proved more than tough enough to handle nasty Jack Palance in 1973's *Oklahoma Crude*. John Wayne fought oil fires for a living in *The Hellfighters* (1969), as did Cornel Wilde in *Maracaibo* (1958). A blazing oil fire sent four drifters on a deadly journey over mountainous roads in trucks carrying nitroglycerine in Henri Clouzot's *The Wages of Fear* (1952) and its remake *Sorcerer* (1977).

Flaming Gold (1933)	*The Wages of Fear* (1952)
Oil for the Lamps of China (1935)	*Thunder Bay* (1953)
High, Wide, and Handsome (1937)	*Blowing Wild* (1953)
Boom Town (1940)	*Lucy Gallant* (1955)
Flowing Gold (1940)	*The Houston Story* (1956)
Wildcat (1942)	*Giant* (1956)
Black Gold (1947)	*Jaguar* (1956)
Tulsa (1949)	*The Magnificent Roughnecks* (1956)
The Big Gusher (1951)	*Joe Dakota* (1957)

Maracaibo (1958)	*Oil* (1977)
Black Gold (1963)	*Sorcerer* (1977)
The Hellfighters (1969)	*Roughnecks* (1980 TVM)
Five Easy Pieces (1970)	*The Intruder Within* (1981 TVM)
Oklahoma Crude (1973)	*Dallas: The Early Years* (1986 TVM)
Oceans of Fire (1976 TVM)	

Olympics

Documentaries, fact-based dramas, and fictitious tales of inspiring athletic feats have revolved around the greatest event in international sports. Leni Riefenstahl's *Olympia* (1936), a vivid record of the 1936 Berlin games, remains an unparalleled tribute to the athletes and the spirit of the games — all this despite an underlying theme praising Nazism. Kon Ichikawa's mesmerizing *Tokyo Olympiad* (1966) was trimmed from 170 minutes to 93 for its U.S. release, though the shortened version still included the dynamic volleyball match between the women of Japan and the Soviet Union. *Visions of Eight* (1973) featured segments by eight international directors (including Ichikawa again). Most critics found it disappointing, except for John Schlesinger's dramatic feature on the grueling marathon. Film biographies of inspirational Olympic athletes have been devoted to runner Jim Thorpe (*Jim Thorpe—All American*), decathlete Bob Mathias (*The Bob Mathias Story*), track star Wilma Rudolph (*Wilma*), the 1980 U.S. hockey team (*Miracle on Ice*), runner Billy Mills (*Running Brave*), gymnast Nadia Comaneci (*Nadia*), and Jesse Owens (*The Jesse Owens Story*). The 1976 TV-movie *21 Hours at Munich* recreated the tragic terrorist killings that cast a dark cloud over the 1972 Olympics. Another TV-movie, *The First Olympics—Athens 1896* (1984), chronicled the events that led up to the first modern-day games. The 1962 *It Happened in Athens* offered a fictitious view of the same events, placing special emphasis on Jayne Mansfield as an actress who agrees to marry the winner of the marathon. Earl Derr Bigger's proverb-quoting detective Charlie Chan (q.v.) uncovered a murder plot at the Berlin Games in 1937's *Charlie Chan at the Olympics*. Charlie's No. 1 son (Keye Luke) was even a member of the U.S. swimming team. Jim Hutton played an Olympic walker in the 1966 romantic comedy *Walk, Don't Run*, which found him in overcrowded Tokyo sharing an apartment with Samantha Eggar and matchmaker Cary Grant. A ninety-pound weakling sent off for a weight-lifting program and grew up to be a muscular Olympic hammer thrower in 1956's charming British film *Wee Geordie*. *The Golden Moment: An Olympic Love Story* (1980) found an American decathlete (David Keith) falling in love with a Russian gymnast (Stephanie Zimbalist) at the 1980 Moscow games — which the U.S. boycotted after this TV-movie was made. The 1978 *Special Olympics* was a heartwarming story of a mentally retarded youngster who found fulfillment playing sports and enters the Special Olympics.

Million Dollar Legs (1932)	*Jim Thorpe—All American* (aka *Man*
Olympia (aka *Olympische Spiele*)	*of Bronze*) (1951)
(1936)	*The Bob Mathias Story* (aka *The*
One in a Million (1936)	*Flaming Torch*) (1954)
Charlie Chan at the Olympics	*Wee Geordie* (aka *Geordie*) (1956)
(1937)	*It Happened in Athens* (1962)

Tokyo Olympiad (1966)
Walk, Don't Run (1966)
Downhill Racer (1969)
The Games (1970)
Visions of Eight (1973)
21 Hours at Munich (1976 TVM)
The Loneliest Runner (1976)
Wilma (1977)
Special Olympics (aka A Special Kind
   of Love) (1978 TVM)
Animalympics (1979)
The Top of the Hill (1980 TVM)
The Golden Moment: An Olympic Love
   Story (1980 TVM)

Swan Song (1980 TVM)
Miracle on Ice (1981 TVM)
Personal Best (1982)
Running Brave (1983)
Nadia (1984 TVM)
The Jesse Owens Story (1984 TVM)
The First Olympics—Athens 1896
   (1984 TVM)
Going for the Gold: The Bill Johnson
   Story (1985 TVM)
16 Days of Glory (1986)
Reach for the Sky (1991)
Alex (1993)
Cool Runnings (1993)

The Omen

This 1976 movie about the coming of the Antichrist was a slick, well-done chiller, bolstered by crisp performances by Gregory Peck and David Warner. Yet, despite its merits and box office popularity, it hardly warranted a series, even a short-lived one. *Damien—Omen II* was a predictable follow-up, showing Damien coping with teen problems by killing people. The series apparently ended with *The Final Conflict*, which had Damien dabbling in politics. However, ten years later, the TV-movie *Omen IV: The Awakening* introduced the hellish adopted daughter of a politician. See also **The Devil.**

The Omen (1976)
Damien—Omen II (1978)
The Final Conflict (1981)
Omen IV: The Awakening (1991 TVM)

Outlaws (Real-Life Western)

Jesse James and Billy the Kid easily outdistance their peers as the most oft-filmed outlaws in American cinema. In James's case, his celluloid fame is deserved, since his legendary exploits are backed up with the famous ill-fated Northfield, Minnesota, bank robbery. Billy the Kid, however, was a minor bandit gunned down in an ambush at the age of twenty-one. His real name was Henry McCarty, though he was also known as William H. Bonney. On the screen, Billy has been portrayed as a wronged hero, a psychopath and a vampire killer. Western veteran Johnny Mack Brown starred as the talkies' first Kid in 1930's *Billy the Kid*, a lavish MGM production originally shown in 70mm. It was remade a decade later in Technicolor with Robert Taylor, dumping his romantic image, in the title role. In contrast to these big-budget efforts, Billy was also the subject of a minor 1939 Roy Rogers picture (*Billy the Kid Returns*) and 1940's *Billy the Kid Outlawed*, the first of a PRC series starring Bob Steele and later Buster Crabbe (see **Billy the Kid/Billy Carson**). Jane Russell's cleavage overshadowed Billy's story in Howard Hughes's much-publicized, long-delayed *The Outlaw* (1943). It was the Kid's last prestigious picture until Paul Newman played him in Arthur Penn's psychological

Western *The Left-Handed Gun* (1958), based on a TV-play by Gore Vidal (which was remade for cable-TV in 1989). Billy the Kid's subsequent film appearances have ranged from ambitious to awful. Sam Peckinpah's *Pat Garrett and Billy the Kid* (1973) promised to examine the relationship between lawman Garrett and ex-crony Billy. However, miscasting (Kris Kristofferson as Billy) and an overemphasis on violence spelled box office failure and critical doom. Billy discovered his girlfriend's uncle (John Carradine) was a vampire in *Billy the Kid vs. Dracula* (1966), a movie not as dreadful as its title—but close. Emilio Estevez made Billy a romantic antihero in the 1988 "brat pack" western *Young Guns*, which drew audiences despite an abundance of critical pans. Despite these frequent appearances, Billy still ranks second to Jesse James in number of films. James's career first received lavish treatment with Twentieth Century-Fox's colorful *Jesse James* (1939), starring Tyrone Power as Jesse and Henry Fonda as brother Frank. Fonda reprised his role in Fritz Lang's superior 1940 sequel *The Return of Frank James*, one of the finest outlaw pictures. Jesse was a common fixture in the programmer Westerns of the 1950s. He was portrayed by Dale Robertson (*Fighting Man of the Plains*), Audie Murphy (*Kansas Raiders*), Willard Parker (*The Great Jesse James Raid*), Robert Wagner (*The True Story of Jesse James*), Ray Stricklyn (*Young Jesse James*) and others. Even Bob Hope was mistaken for the famous outlaw in *Alias Jesse James* (1959), one of his funniest comedies. In 1966, while Billy fought Dracula on one half of a double bill, Jesse saw a pal turned into a bald monster in *Jesse James Meets Frankenstein's Daughter*. Writer-director Philip Kaufman stressed factual detail over interesting narrative in 1972's *The Great Northfield, Minnesota Raid*, which featured Robert Duvall as Jesse and Cliff Robertson as Cole Younger. Both characters also appeared in Walter Hill's stylish outlaw saga *The Long Riders* (1980), a family affair starring Stacy and James Keach as Jesse and Frank James; David, Keith and Robert Carradine as the Younger Brothers; and Dennis and Randy Quaid as the lesser-known Mills Brothers. The Younger Brothers were paired with the Jameses in other pictures as well, such as *The Great Missouri Raid* (1950) and *The Intruders* (1970). It's interesting to note that Audie Murphy is the only actor to have played both Billy the Kid and Jesse James, and he did it in the same year, starring in 1950's *The Kid From Texas* and *Kansas Raiders*. Belle Starr, the only female outlaw to achieve notoriety, has been portrayed by Gene Tierney (*Belle Starr*, 1941), Jane Russell (*Montana Belle*), and Elizabeth Montgomery (*Belle Starr*, 1980). Paul Newman and Robert Redford brought fame to a couple of minor outlaws with their 1969 smash *Butch Cassidy and the Sundance Kid*. William Katt and Tom Berenger starred in a 1979 prequel *Butch and Sundance: The Early Days*. In made-for-TV movies, the Sundance Kid's woman was played by Elizabeth Montgomery in 1974's *Mrs. Sundance* and Katharine Ross (recreating her role from the Newman-Redford picture) in 1976's *Wanted: The Sundance Woman*. Other outlaw gangs appearing in multiple features include the Clantons (*Law and Order, Gunfight at the OK Corral, Hour of the Gun*) and the Daltons (*The Last Day, The Last Ride of the Dalton Gang*). On the small screen, Clu Gulager played Billy the Kid opposite Barry Sullivan's Pat Garrett in the 1960-62 series *The Tall Man*, while Christopher Jones starred in 1965-66's *The Legend of Jesse James*. In the following list, the outlaw's name appears in parentheses unless specified in the title. See also **Billy the Kid/Billy Carson**.

Billy the Kid (aka *The Highwayman Rides*) (1930)
Law and Order (1932) (Clantons)
Jesse James (1939)
Billy the Kid Returns (1939)
Billy the Kid (1940)
Billy the Kid Outlawed (1940)
When the Daltons Rode (1940)
The Return of Frank James (1940)
Belle Starr (1941)
The Outlaw (1943) (Billy the Kid)
My Darling Clementine (1946) (Clantons)
Belle Starr's Daughter (1947)
Fighting Man of the Plains (1949) (Jesse James)
The Younger Brothers (1949)
I Shot Jesse James (1949)
The Kid From Texas (1950) (Billy the Kid)
Kansas Raiders (1950) (Jesse James)
The Great Missouri Raid (1950) (James and Younger Brothers)
Best of the Badmen (1951) (Jeff Clanton)
Montana Belle (1952) (Belle Starr)
The Great Jesse James Raid (1953)
Jesse James vs. the Daltons (1954)
Jesse James' Women (1954)
The Law vs. Billy the Kid (1954)
The Parson and the Outlaw (1955) (Billy the Kid)
The True Story of Jesse James (1956)
Hell's Crossroad (1957) (Jesse James)
Gunfight at the OK Corral (1957) (Clantons)
The Dalton Girls (1957)
Badman's Country (1958) (Butch Cassidy)
The Left-Handed Gun (1958) (Billy the Kid)
Alias Jesse James (1959)
Young Jesse James (1960)
Billy the Kid vs. Dracula (1966)
Jesse James Meets Frankenstein's Daughter (1966)
Hour of the Gun (1967) (Clantons)
Butch Cassidy and the Sundance Kid (1969)
The Intruders (1970 TVM) (James and Youngers)
Chisum (1970) (Billy the Kid)
Doc (1971) (Clantons)
Dirty Little Billy (1972)
The Great Northfield, Minnesota Raid (1972) (James and Youngers)
Pat Garrett and Billy the Kid (1973)
Mrs. Sundance (1974 TVM)
The Last Day (1975 TVM) (Daltons)
Wanted: The Sundance Woman (aka *Mrs. Sundance Rides Again*) (1976 TVM)
Go West, Young Girl (1978 TVM) (Billy the Kid)
Butch and Sundance: The Early Days (1979)
The Last Ride of the Dalton Gang (1979 TVM)
Cattle Annie and Little Britches (1980) (Daltons)
The Long Riders (1980) (James and Youngers)
Belle Starr (1980 TVM)
The Grey Fox (1982) (Bill Miner)
The Last Days of Frank and Jesse James (1986 TVM)
Young Guns (1988) (Billy the Kid)
Billy the Kid (aka *Gore Vidal's Billy the Kid*) (1989 TVM)
Young Guns II (1990) (Billy the Kid)

Painted People

Covering one's body with paint is not exactly a healthy thing to do. In fact, it resulted in the death of one of the asylum inmates in *Bedlam* (1946), though the institution's vicious director (Boris Karloff) seemed rather undisturbed. Bond villain Auric Goldfinger killed 007's girlfriend (Shirley Eaton) by covering her in his trademark gold in 1964's *Goldfinger*. In contrast, partially painted people have led healthier lives. Marlene Dietrich sported a pair of painted legs for her famous dance scene in *Kismet* (1944). On the kinkier side, Britt Ekland exposed her painted breasts in *Scandal* (1989), while jungle natives dipped Bo Derek in an ugly shade of off-white in *Tarzan, the Ape Man* (1981). See also **Tattoos.**

Kismet (aka *Oriental Dream*) (1944)	*Slave of the Cannibal God* (1977)
	Tarzan, the Ape Man (1981)
Bedlam (1946)	*Scandal* (1989)
Goldfinger (1964)	

Painters

The post-Impressionists of the late nineteenth century dominate film biographies of painters, primarily due to the influences of Vincent Van Gogh and Paul Gaugin. The 1956 *Lust for Life*, based on an Irving Stone book, was a colorful portrait of Van Gogh's tormented life. Kirk Douglas played the Dutch painter, with Anthony Quinn earning a Best Supporting Actor Oscar as his friend Gaugin. The unusual 1987 Australian tribute, *Vincent*, consisted mostly of Van Gogh's paintings accompanied by John Hurt's affective readings of his letters. Gaugin's life provided Somerset Maugham with the basis for his novel *The Moon and Sixpence*, which was filmed in 1942. George Sanders played the stockbroker who left his family to pursue painting and wound up dying of leprosy on a South Seas island. The Hays Office, the film industry's censorship watchdog, required that some of the film's nude paintings be toned down by adding leaves or flowers to cover appropriate body parts. Two Gaugin biographies surfaced in the 1980s. The 1980 TV-movie *Gaugin the Savage* boasted fine production values, including on-location footage of France and Tahiti, but a miscast David Carradine doomed the venture. Donald Sutherland made an appropriately passionate Gaugin in 1987's *Wolf at the Door*, a slow-moving account of Gaugin's brief return from Tahiti. Aside from Gaugin and Van Gogh, biographies of painters have been scarce and sporadic. Alexander Korda produced 1936's *Rembrandt*, an opulent version of the Dutch painter's life featuring a classic Charles Laughton performance. John Huston's *Moulin Rouge* (1953) fictionalized the life of dwarfish French painter Toulouse-Lautrec (Jose Ferrer). Yet, the film remains fondly remembered for its atmospheric nineteenth-century Montmartre setting and an elaborate cancan sequence. A Picasso biography has somehow eluded filmmakers, although the Cubist painter created a canvas on screen for French director Henri-Georges Clouzot in 1955's *The Mystery of Picasso*. *The Picasso Summer* in 1969 starred Albert Finney and Yvette Mimieux as a vacationing couple who set off in search of the famous artist. It sat on the studio shelf for some time before debuting in the United States as a late-night network movie. Despite its promising title, *The Adventures of Picasso* was a 1978 oddball Swedish comedy. In addition to providing biographical material for filmmakers, painters have contributed to the behind-the-scenes art of cinema. Spanish artist Salvador Dalí designed a haunting, surrealistic dream sequence for Alfred Hitchcock's *Spellbound* (1945). The special effects crew of 1947's *The Private Affairs of Bel Ami* claimed that Van Gogh's canvas *The Garden of the Vicarage at Nuenen* gave them the idea of using plastic to create "dry rain." See also **Paintings.**

Rembrandt (1936)

The Moon and Sixpence (1942) (Paul Gaugin)

Kitty (1945) (Cecil Kellaway as Gainsborough in bit role)

Moulin Rouge (1953) (Toulouse-Lautrec)

The Mystery of Picasso (1955)

Lust for Life (1956) (Van Gogh and Gaugin)

The Lovers of Montparnasse (aka Montparnasse 19) (1957) (Modigliani)

The Naked Maja (1959) (Francisco Goya)

The Agony and the Ecstasy (1965) (Michaelangelo)

El Greco (1966)

The Picasso Summer (1969)

Savage Messiah (1972) (Henri Gautier)

The Adventures of Picasso (1978)

Gaugin the Savage (1980 TVM)

The Rothko Conspiracy (1983 TVM) (Mark Rothko)

Carravaggio (1986)

Wolf at the Door (1987) (Paul Gaugin)

Vincent — The Life and Death of Vincent Van Gogh (aka Vincent) (1987)

Vincent (1988)

My Left Foot (1989) (Christy Brown)

Vincent and Theo (1990 TVM) (Van Gogh)

A Season of Giants (1991 TVM) (Raphael, Michelangelo, Da Vinci)

Van Gogh (1991)

The Van Gogh Wake (aka La Passion Van Gogh) (1993)

Paintings

Canvases have figured prominently in an odd assortment of horror films, fantasies, mysteries and comedies. At least three films have been based on Oscar Wilde's wickedly clever *The Picture of Dorian Gray*, the story of a vile Victorian rake whose portrait ages while he retains his youth. The 1945 version remains the best-remembered, with the portrait appearing in color in an otherwise black-and-white film. Joseph Cotten played a struggling artist who paints a masterpiece after falling in love with a ghost in the marvelous 1948 fantasy *Portrait of Jennie*. Again, the film reverted to color for the closing shot of Cotten's painting. Dana Andrews fell in love with the portrait of Gene Tierney hanging over her mantle in Otto Preminger's stylish 1944 mystery *Laura*. That perceptive sleuth Sherlock Holmes cracked the case of *The Hound of the Baskervilles* by examining a painting of Sir Hugo Baskerville and deducing that an unlikely suspect was actually a murderous relative. A theft of a painting provided the excuse for the 1930 Marx Brothers romp *Animal Crackers*. In the 1942 British comedy *Much Too Shy*, George Formby played an unfortunate handyman whose paintings of his clients wound up at an advertising agency — with nude bodies added to them. A demonic portrait hanging in a museum required New York City to call for Bill Murray, Dan Aykroyd and Harold Ramis in 1989's blockbuster comedy *Ghostbusters II*. See also **Painters**.

Animal Crackers (1930)

The Hound of the Baskervilles (1939) (see **Sherlock Holmes** for other versions)

Much Too Shy (1942)

Laura (1944)

The Picture of Dorian Gray (1945)

Portrait of Jennie (1948)

The Fake (1958)

Now You See It, Now You Don't (1967 TVM)

The Picture of Dorian Gray (1973 TVM)

The Sins of Dorian Gray (1983 TVM)   *Ghostbusters II* (1989)
Hot Paint (1988 TVM)

Palmer, Harry

Michael Caine played Len Deighton's Cockney thief-turned-disenchanted-spy three times, beginning with 1965's *The Ipcress File*. While other spy movies strove to imitate the Bond films (q.v.), the Palmer series played up its differences. Harry wore thick glasses, enjoyed cooking, and complained about his dirty profession. However, like 007, he had a weak spot for the ladies. Guy Doleman played Palmer's blackmailing superior, while Oscar Homolka was memorable as a Russian officer in the last two films. Fans argue over which entry was the best, though everyone agrees that *The Billion Dollar Brain* (directed by maverick director Ken Russell) was the weakest. Deighton's character remained nameless in the novels.

The Ipcress File (1965)   *The Billion Dollar Brain* (1967)
Funeral in Berlin (1966)

Parallel Worlds

Few filmmakers have been attracted to the complex concept of a character floating back and forth between two mirrored worlds. Astronaut Roy Thinnes discovered a twin Earth on his *Journey to the Far Side of the Sun* (1969). It took him awhile to figure out that he had exchanged places with his exact duplicate. The 1973 TV-movie *The Stranger* was an unofficial remake with Glenn Corbett as the baffled astronaut. Kathleen Turner's trips between two parallel worlds left her so confused that she murdered the wrong man in 1987's *Julia and Julia*. Tom Bell's journey into another dimension, courtesy of an explosion, enabled him to save a dying girl's life in *Quest for Love* (1971). A more common variation on the parallel world theme incorporates time travel, as when Lindsay Wagner transported herself into another age whenever she put on an old dress in 1979's *The Two Worlds of Jennie Logan*. See also **Look-Alikes; Time Travel.**

Journey to the Far Side of the Sun (aka   *Julia and Julia* (1987)
    Doppelgänger) (1969)   *Paperhouse* (1988)
Quest for Love (1971)   *Cool World* (1992)
The Stranger (1973 TVM)   *Super Mario Bros.* (1993)
The Two Worlds of Jennie Logan (1979
    TVM)

Peanuts

Charles Schulz's lovable "Peanuts" characters leapt from the comic pages to theater screens with 1969's *A Boy Named Charlie Brown*, a full-length animated feature with songs by Rod McKuen. After three more films, Charlie, Snoopy, Lucy, Linus, and the rest of the gang gave up their screen careers and concentrated on their long-running, apparently never-ending series of TV specials. See also **Animated Movies (Feature-Length); Comic Strip Characters.**

A Boy Named Charlie Brown (1969)
Snoopy, Come Home (1972)
Race for Your Life, Charlie Brown (1977)
Bon Voyage, Charlie Brown (and Don't Come Back) (1980)

Penitentiary Series

The 1979 film *Penitentiary* was the first installment in the saga of Too Sweet, an unjustly imprisoned black convict reformed by boxing. Written, produced and directed by Jamaa Fanaka, the film earned a reputation as a minor league *Rocky* (q.v.), although its gritty approach was praised. Fanaka and star Leon Isaac Kennedy continued with two disappointing sequels, *Penitentiary 2* (1982) and *Penitentiary 3* (1987). The *Rocky* similarities became blatant in these films, right down to the presence of *Rocky III* alumnus Mr. T in *Penitentiary 2*. Kennedy and his then-wife, sportscaster/model Jayne Kennedy, also made a 1981 remake of the 1947 boxing classic *Body and Soul*. See also **Boxing**.

Penitentiary (1979)   *Penitentiary 3* (1987)

Penitentiary 2 (1982)

Penrod

Booth Tarkington wrote three books about Penrod Schofield, "The Worst Boy in Town," who consistently stirred up trouble in a quiet, Midwestern town circa 1914. Gordon Griffith appeared in a 1922 version, and Ben Alexander took over as Penrod in the following year's *Penrod and Sam*. The latter film was remade by Warner Bros. in 1931 with Leon Janney in the lead and Dorothy Peterson (later Mrs. Pepper in the *Five Little Peppers* series) as his mother. However, Warner's official Penrod series began in 1937 with the third version of *Penrod and Sam*, with Bobby Mauch as a much nicer boy. This movie also updated the setting, making Penrod the head of a Junior G-Men Club (which met in a barn just like Our Gang). Bobby's twin brother, Billy, joined the cast for the last two films: *Penrod and His Twin Brother* and *Penrod's Double Trouble* (both 1938). The Mauch Twins, who had their greatest success in Errol Flynn's *The Prince and the Pauper* (1937), virtually disappeared from films in the 1940s. However, Penrod showed up again — in diluted form — in two Doris Day musicals: *Moonlight Bay* (1951) and *By the Light of the Silvery Moon* (1953). These films restored the earlier setting but relegated Penrod to a supporting character and changed his name to Wesley. He was played by Billy Gray, best known as Bud on TV's *Father Knows Best*.

Penrod (1922)   *Penrod and His Twin Brother* (1938)

Penrod and Sam (1923)   *Penrod's Double Trouble* (1938)

Penrod and Sam (1931)   *Moonlight Bay* (1951)

Penrod and Sam (1937)   *By the Light of the Silvery Moon* (1953)

People Hunters/Human Prey

The premise of hunting human prey for sport was explored vividly in Richard Connell's famous short story "The Most Dangerous Game." Connell's story about ruthless hunter Count Zaroff has been filmed "officially" as *The Most Dangerous Game* (1932), *A Game of Death* (1946), *Run for the Sun* (1956) and *Blood Lust* (1966). The 1932 version is best remembered, chiefly for Leslie Banks's campy, despicable villain. Future nice guy Alan Alda played a mad, crippled Vietnam veteran who tracked down a harmless couple trapped on his island in *To Kill a Clown*. In the 1973 TV-movie *Maneater*, Richard Basehart portrayed a deranged animal trainer who unleashed two hungry tigers on four visitors. One of the more interesting variations on Connell's plot has people stalking each other as part of a socially acceptable pastime, a twist featured in *The Tenth Victim* (1965) and Stephen King's *The Running Man* (1987). Perhaps the finest film about people hunters was Cornel Wilde's gripping 1966 adventure *The Naked Prey*. Director Wilde played a safari guide, the only survivor of a native ambush, who is freed by his captors and then methodically tracked down. No other film matches this one for showing how self-survival can force a man to evolve into a killer as brutal as his pursuers.

The Most Dangerous Game (1932)	*Open Season* (1974)
A Game of Death (1946)	*Savages* (1974 TVM)
Johnny Allegro (1949)	*Escape 2000* (aka *Turkey Shoot*) (1981)
Run for the Sun (1956)	*The Running Man* (1987)
The Tenth Victim (1965)	*Predator* (1987)
The Naked Prey (1966)	*Lethal Woman* (1989)
Blood Lust (1966)	*Deadly Game* (1991 TVM)
Woman Hunt (1972)	*Do or Die* (1991)
To Kill a Clown (1972)	*Hard Target* (1993)
Maneater (1973 TVM)	

Personal Ads

Filmmakers have typically used personal ad columns to bring unlikely lovers together. After reading the personals and suffering amnesia, bored yuppie house-wife Rosanna Arquette wound up with practical projectionist Aidan Quinn in *Desperately Seeking Susan* (1985). Recently divorced Bill Schuppert thought he had found the perfect companion in 1981's *The Personals* — until she turned out to be married. In 1981's *I Sent a Letter to My Love*, a lonely woman discovered romance by taking up correspondence with a man listed in the personals. In a bittersweet twist, he turned out to be her paralyzed brother. A serial murderer used the personals to attract victims in the 1989 thriller *Sea of Love*.

Snares (aka *Personal Column; Plèges*) (1939)	*Classified Love* (1987 TVM)
	Sea of Love (1989)
The Personals (1981)	*Personals* (1990 TVM)
I Sent a Letter to My Love (1981)	*Single White Female* (1992)
Desperately Seeking Susan (1985)	*Dying to Love You* (1993 TVM)
The Perfect Match (1987)	

Persons in Hiding Series

J. Edgar Hoover's nonfiction best-seller *Persons in Hiding* provided the basis for this modest Paramount four-film gangster series. Actually, Courtney Riley Cooper ghostwrote the book, but the FBI director's name sold the copies and gave the series what marquee value it possessed. The best entries were the first and last, tight thrillers featuring a potent combination of rising and veteran stars (e.g., Richard Denning, William Frawley, J. Carrol Naish, Robert Ryan, Ralph Bellamy, Jack Carson and Hedda Hopper). The 1939 *Persons in Hiding* traced the exploits of Bonnie Parker (later of *Bonnie and Clyde* fame), while 1940's *Queen of the Mob* was based on the career of Ma Barker. See also **Gangsters (Real-Life)**.

Persons in Hiding (1939)	*Parole Fixer* (1940)
Undercover Doctor (1939)	*Queen of the Mob* (1940)

Peyton Place

Grace Metalious's cynical small town exposé made quite an impact when released in 1957. Its 1961 sequel, *Return to Peyton Place*, was a more conventional soap opera, but it did well enough to inspire a television series. The show premiered in 1964 and became an immediate runaway hit. It ran two or three times weekly for five years, thanks largely to an all-star cast featuring Dorothy Malone, Mia Farrow, Ryan O'Neal and Ruth Warrick (pre-*All My Children*). *Murder in Peyton Place*, a 1977 made-for-TV movie, killed off Allison MacKenzie and Rodney Harrington (Farrow and O'Neal in the TV series) but reunited regulars Malone and Ed Nelson. *Peyton Place: The Next Generation* (1985), another TV movie, was a feeble attempt to drum up interest for a new series.

Peyton Place (1957)
Return to Peyton Place (1961)
Murder in Peyton Place (1977 TVM)
Peyton Place: The Next Generation (1985 TVM)

Photographers

News photographers, army photographers, fashion photographers, amateur shutterbugs — photography is a wide field that has interested filmmakers on a regular basis. Photojournalists in volatile environments played key supporting roles in the 1983 films *Under Fire* and *The Year of Living Dangerously*. The latter film featured Linda Hunt in a Best Supporting Oscar performance as a philosophizing *male* photographer in 1965 Indonesia. Nick Nolte played a photojournalist in contemporary Nicaragua in *Under Fire*, while 1986's *Salvador* starred James Woods as a cynical freelance photographer unable to distance himself from his subjects. *84 Charlie Mopic* is the Army job classification for a motion picture cameraman. This 1989 film showed viewers the Vietnam War through his eyes — or rather, through his camera. The photographer is glimpsed only when he hands his motion picture camera to someone else to engage in a little horseplay. Most female camera clickers in the movies have been fashion photographers, such as Faye Dunaway in *Eyes of Laura Mars* and Pam Grier in *Friday Foster*. Photographer Claudette Colbert unexpectedly fell in love with subway digger Fred MacMurray in the 1943 comedy *No Time for Love*. In other comic escapades, Buster Keaton starred in the classic 1928 comedy *The Cameraman*. It was remade, much less effectively, with Red Skelton as 1950's *Watch the Birdie*. Allegedly, an uncredited Keaton supervised many of the gags. Bob Hope played a photographer-turned-detective in *My Favorite Brunette* (which was Dorothy Lamour, of course). The source of Bob's trouble was not Dorothy, but a valuable picture taken with his "keyhole camera." Photographers have not fared well in horror films. David Warner was one of the first to realize that little Damien was not an angelic child in 1976's *The Omen*. Unfortunately, that knowledge lost him his head in the film's goriest sequence. In Michael Powell's cult classic *Peeping Tom* (1960), Carl Boehm played a deranged photographer obsessed with capturing his murder victims on film at the precise moment of their deaths. Scientist Robert Stephens invented a camera that could capture one's spirit as it leaves the body in 1972's intriguing *The Asphyx*. Michelangelo Antonioni's *Blow-Up* (1966) remains the most overrated movie about a photographer. It took a promising premise (David Hemmings unintentionally photographs what may be a murder) and burdened it with heavy-handed symbolism. See also **Fashion Models.**

The Cameraman (1928)	*Little Murders* (1971)
Picture Snatcher (1933)	*The Asphyx* (1972)
Murder in Greenwich Village (1937)	*Friday Foster* (1975)
Dust Be My Destiny (1939)	*The Omen* (1976)
China Girl (1942)	*Eyes of Laura Mars* (1978)
Escape From Crime (1942)	*Girlfriends* (1978)
Hit the Ice (1943)	*Georgia, Georgia* (1982)
No Time for Love (1943)	*Under Fire* (1983)
Double Exposure (1944)	*The Year of Living Dangerously* (1983)
Lover Come Back (aka *When Lovers Meet*) (1946)	*No Small Affair* (1984)
My Favorite Brunette (1947)	*Salvador* (1986)
Watch the Birdie (1950)	*The Fantasist* (1986)
I Love Melvin (1953)	*The Girl in the Picture* (1986)
Rear Window (1954)	*Double Exposure* (1989)
Joe Butterfly (1957)	*84 Charlie Mopic* (1989)
Funny Face (1957)	*Margaret Bourke-White* (1989 TVM)
Peeping Tom (1960)	*Somebody Has to Shoot the Picture* (1990 TVM)
A Girl Named Tamiko (1962)	*Curiosity Kills* (1990 TVM)
If a Man Answers (1962)	*In the Cold of the Night* (1990)
Blow-Up (1966)	*Drop Dead Gorgeous* (1991 TVM)
Negatives (1968)	*The Public Eye* (1992)
Live a Little, Love a Little (1968)	*Lethal Exposure* (1993 TVM)
La Prisonnière (1969)	

Pianists

While movie violinists (q.v.) have been limited to classical settings and trumpet players (q.v.) to jazz scenes, movie pianists have crossed all musical boundaries. The film appearances of a divergent group of real-life musicians confirms this point: Ignace Jan Paderewski and Liberace played the classics in, respectively, *Moonlight Sonata* (1937) and *Sincerely Yours* (1955); Ray Charles opted for the blues in *Blues for Lovers* (1964); and contemporary singer/pianist Charles Aznavour mixed jazz and popular music in *Shoot the Piano Player* (1960), as did Barry Manilow in *Copacabana* (1985). A wide variety of physical impairments and emotional problems have plagued pianists. Liberace went deaf in *Sincerely Yours*, while blind piano players were the subject of *Night Song* (1947), *Torch Song* (1953), and Charles's *Blues for Lovers*. Jack Nicholson abandoned a promising career as a concert pianist to become an aimless drifter in *Five Easy Pieces* (1970). The pianists in *Shoot the Piano Player* and *Fingers* — the first a washed-up concert performer, the second a promising star — both became involved with gangsters. A dying concert pianist tried to possess Alan Alda's body in the Satanic thriller *The Mephisto Waltz* (1971). That was a mild problem, however, compared to Peter Lorre's struggles with the severed hand of a piano player in *The Beast With Five Fingers* (1946). Still, the incredibly weird Dr. Seuss fantasy *The 5,000 Fingers of Dr. T* (1953) rates as the most terrifying pianist film. Little Tommy Rettig starred as a boy who dreams that his vicious piano teacher has imprisoned him and 499 other boys in a castle where they play a giant piano all day long. In comparison, the troubled young piano players of *Madame Sousatzka* and *Running on Empty* (both 1988) had it easy. Richard Dreyfuss and Amy Irving played young adults going for the same career-making prize while falling in love in *The Competition* (1980). Two teenage groupies stalked pianist Peter Sellers wherever he went in *The World of Henry Orient* (1964). No discussion of piano players would be complete without at least mentioning Dooley Wilson as Sam in *Casablanca* (1942). Although they were not pianists, Tom Hanks and Robert Loggia danced out a catchy rendition of "Chopsticks" on a giant piano in *Big* (1988). See also **Trumpet Players; Violinists.**

Moonlight Sonata (1937)
Stolen Heaven (1938)
When Tomorrow Comes (1939)
The Great Lie (1941)
That Uncertain Feeling (1941)
Casablanca (1942)
The Constant Nymph (1943)
Love Story (aka *A Lady Surrenders*) (1944)
The Seventh Veil (1945)
The Beast With Five Fingers (1946)
Detour (1946)
Carnegie Hall (1947)
Night Song (1947)
Letter From an Unknown Woman (1948)
A Kiss in the Dark (1949)
Too Young to Kiss (1951)
Strange Fascination (1952)
The 5,000 Fingers of Dr. T (1953)
Torch Song (1953)
Rhapsody (1954)
Sincerely Yours (1955)
The Eddy Duchin Story (1956)
Julie (1956)
Shoot the Piano Player (aka *Shoot the Pianist*) (1960)
The Hands of Orlac (aka *Hands of the Strangler*) (1960)
The World of Henry Orient (1964)
Blues for Lovers (aka *Ballad in Blue*) (1964)
The Battle of the Villa Fiorita (aka *Affair at the Villa Fiorita*) (1964)
30 Is a Dangerous Age, Cynthia (1968)
The Story of a Woman (1969)
Five Easy Pieces (1970)
The Mephisto Waltz (1971)
Autumn Sonata (1978)
Fingers (1978)
Practice Makes Perfect (1978)
The Competition (1980)
Copacabana (1985 TVM)
Ghost of a Chance (1987 TVM)
Madame Sousatzka (1988)
Running on Empty (1988)
Matters of the Heart (1990 TVM)
The Fabulous Baker Boys (1990)
Winter in Lisbon (1990)
The Pianist (1991)
The Accompanist (aka *L'Accompagnatrice*) (1992)
The Piano (1993)

Pickpockets

The colorful pickpockets of Charles Dickens's *Oliver Twist* have reached the screen in five official adaptations, with David Lean's 1948 version and Carol Reed's 1968 musical attracting the most admirers. George C. Scott played Fagin in the 1982 TV-movie. Coincidentally, Scott's one-time wife Trish Van Devere played one of master pickpocket James Coburn's new recruits in 1973's *Harry in Your Pocket*. Ginger Rogers played another lady pickpocket in the 1946 comedy *Heartbeat*, while *Thick as Thieves* (1991) featured a brother-and-sister pickpocket team who unwisely select an undercover cop as their target. A movie extra disrupted pickpocket Ben Gazzara's plans in the Italian-made comedy *The Passionate Thief* (1960). Pickpocket

Richard Widmark inadvertently thwarted enemy spies by stealing valuable microfilm in Samuel Fuller's *Pickup on South Street* (1953). Finally, French director Robert Bresson produced the cinema's most philosophical essay on the subject with 1959's *Pickpocket*.

Oliver Twist (1922)	*Oliver* (1968)
Oliver Twist (1933)	*The Daughters of Joshua Cabe* (1972
Heartbeat (1946)	TVM)
Oliver Twist (1948)	*Harry in Your Pocket* (1973)
Pickup on South Street (1953)	*Oliver Twist* (1982 TVM)
Pickpocket (1959)	*Thick as Thieves* (1991)
The Passionate Thief (1960)	*Life With Mikey* (1993)

Pigs

Leading roles for pigs have been few and far between — and limited to animated features. The principal characters in the 1955 British adaptation of George Orwell's satire *Animal Farm* were two pigs named Napoleon and Snowball. E.B. White's children's classic *Charlotte's Web* (1973) focused on a friendship between a matronly spider and a shy pig. In supporting roles, real-life pigs have stolen their fair share of scenes. A frolicking contraband porker upstaged Maggie Smith and Michael Palin in the deft food-rationing comedy *A Private Function* (1985). Michael J. Fox acquired a pet pig named Jasmine in 1991's *Doc Hollywood*. A talking pig popped up opposite Pee Wee Herman in 1988's *Big Top Pee Wee*. In the horror genre, a giant killer pig stalked the Australian countryside in 1984's *Razorback*, while an ad for 1982's *Pigs* proclaimed: "They'll eat anything so she had the perfect method to dispose of her victims." The daffy and dangerous Annie Wilks (Kathy Bates) named her pet pig after her favorite romance novel heroine in Stephen King's *Misery* (1990). Bizarre man/pig love relationships were explored in *Futz* and Pier Paolo Pasolini's *Pigsty* (both 1969). People were transformed into pigs in *Ulysses* (1955), *O Lucky Man!* (1973) and *Elvira — Mistress of the Dark* (1988). Hugh "Bulldog" Drummond (Walter Pidgeon) retired from sleuthing to raise pigs in 1951's *Calling Bulldog Drummond*. Animated shorts have featured Pooh's friend Piglet and that world-famous stuttering pig Porky. A 1911 silent short boasted the interesting title *The Electrified Pig*. On television, no pig has been able to compete with Arnold Ziffel of *Green Acres* fame.

Calling Bulldog Drummond (1951)	*Razorback* (1984)
Animal Farm (1955)	*A Private Function* (1985)
Ulysses (1955)	*Elvira — Mistress of the Dark* (1988)
Pigsty (aka *Pig Pen; Porcile*) (1969)	*The Milagro Beanfield War* (1988)
Futz (1969)	*Big Top Pee Wee* (1988)
Charlotte's Web (1973)	*Return to Green Acres* (1990 TVM)
O Lucky Man! (1973)	*Misery* (1990)
Pigs (1982)	*Doc Hollywood* (1991)
Evilspeak (1982)	*Leon the Pig Farmer* (1992)

Pinball/Video Games

Brooke Shields as a pinball player? The movie was 1978's *Tilt*, and Shields, age thirteen, played a wandering pinball wizard who mounted a challenge against champ Charles Durning. The "tension-filled" pinball matches bore no resemblance to Paul Newman's pool scenes in *The Hustler* or Steve McQueen's poker games in *The Cincinnati Kid*. Three years prior to *Tilt*, flamboyant director Ken Russell brought The Who's rock opera *Tommy* to the screen. The rock group's lead singer Roger Daltry recreated his stage role as "the deaf, dumb, and blind kid who sure plays a mean pinball." Elton John appeared as his opponent, the Pinball Wizard. The ultimate video game movie was Disney's *Tron* (1982), a visually marvelous but dramatically empty high-tech adventure. Jeff Bridges starred as a computer genius sucked into a computer and forced to play a "real" video game for his survival. Cocky video gamemaster Emilio Estevez also wound up inside a video game in one of the segments of the 1983 horror anthology *Nightmares*. In 1984's *The Last Starfighter*, aliens used an Earth-bound video game to test fighter-pilot skills to assist in recruiting warriors to save their dying planet.

Tommy (1975)	*Nightmares* (1983)
Tilt (1978)	*Joysticks* (aka *Video Madness*) (1983)
Pick-Up Summer (aka *Pinball Summer; Pinball Pick-up*) (1981)	*The Last Starfighter* (1984)
	The Wizard (1989)
Tron (1982)	*Super Mario Bros.* (1993)
Never Say Never Again (1983)	

The Pink Panther

Blake Edwards's 1964 comedy *The Pink Panther* was a mildly amusing all-star farce about a jewel thief called the Phantom trying to steal the famous Pink Panther diamond. It starred David Niven, Claudia Cardinale and Robert Wagner, and it introduced Peter Sellers as that classic bumbling detective Inspector Clouseau. Thanks to Sellers's hilarious performance, the movie was a hit and he and Edwards reteamed for the 1964 sequel *A Shot in the Dark*. It's the best of all Clouseau movies and marked the debuts of eventual series regulars Herbert Lom (as Clouseau's boss/nemesis) and Burt Kwouk (as the kung fu-minded valet Kato). Surprisingly, another Sellers/Clouseau comedy did not appear for a decade. In the meantime, Alan Arkin starred in *Inspector Clouseau*, a 1968 flop *not* directed by Edwards. But Sellers and Edwards revived both their careers with *The Return of the Pink Panther*, the surprise hit of summer 1975. After two more popular entries, Sellers died in 1980. Nevertheless, outtakes of him were edited into the shoddily constructed *The Trail of the Pink Panther*. It was a well-deserved box office disaster, as was *The Curse of the Pink Panther* with Ted Wass following in Sellers's footsteps. The persistent Edwards tried to resurrect the series a decade later with 1993's *Son of the Pink Panther*, which starred Italian comedian Roberto Benigni as Clouseau's bumbling, illegitimate son.

The Pink Panther (1964)	*The Revenge of the Pink Panther* (1978)
A Shot in the Dark (1964)	*The Trail of the Pink Panther* (1982)
The Return of the Pink Panther (1975)	*The Curse of the Pink Panther* (1983)
The Pink Panther Strikes Again (1976)	*Son of the Pink Panther* (1993)

Pirates

The jolly roger has been a screen fixture since before Douglas Fairbanks, Sr. took to the high seas in 1926's colorful *The Black Pirate*. In fact, Robert Louis Stevenson's immortal pirate Long John Silver appeared in an adaptation of *Treasure Island* six years earlier. In the talking film era, Errol Flynn probably logged the most appearances as a pirate. He played Rafael Sabatini's gentlemanly buccaneer in 1935's *Captain Blood*—the role that made him an overnight star. Flynn also played a queen's privateer in *The Sea Hawk*, a British spy among pirates in *Against All Flags*, and a Scottish nobleman-turned-temporary-pirate in *The Master of Ballantrae*. Long John Silver easily outdistanced his closest rival, Sabatini's Peter Blood, as the screen's busiest pirate. He was portrayed most memorably by Wallace Beery (1934), Robert Newton (1950 and 1954) and Orson Welles (1972). Female pirates have been scarce, but Maureen O'Hara proved a fiery match for Flynn in *Against All Flags*. Other lady pirate captains were featured in *Anne of the Indies*, *The Pirate Queen* and *Queen of the Pirates*. Pirate musicals have proven to be dismal box office failures, despite the presence of some heavyweight talent. RKO's *The Dancing Pirate* (1936) was an early Technicolor film (as was the aforementioned *Black Pirate*) featuring a music score by Rodgers and Hart. The 1948 Gene Kelly-Judy Garland musical *The Pirate* is fondly remembered for its fancy footwork (courtesy of Kelly and the Nicholas Brothers) and catchy tunes like "Be a Clown." *The Pirate Movie* (1982) was an inept rip-off of Gilbert and Sullivan's operetta *The Pirates of Penzance*, which reached the screen itself the following year. To the astonishment of music lovers, it fared little better financially than its predecessor. Pirate comedies have included the obvious (*Abbott and Costello Meet Captain Kidd*), the offbeat (*Blackbeard's Ghost*) and the inane (*Yellowbeard*). Modern-day pirates harassed David Warner in *The Island*, and futuristic pirates sought water, not treasure, in *Ice Pirates*.

The Black Pirate (1926)
Old Ironsides (1926)
Treasure Island (1934)
Captain Blood (1935)
The Dancing Pirate (1936)
The Buccaneer (1938)
The Sea Hawk (1940)
The Black Swan (1942)
The Princess and the Pirate (1944)
Captain Kidd (1945)
The Spanish Main (1945)
Pirates of Monterey (1947)
The Pirate (1948)
Old Mother Riley's Jungle Treasure (1949)
Buccaneer's Girl (1950)
Fortunes of Captain Blood (1950)
Last of the Buccaneers (1950)
Treasure Island (1950)
Anne of the Indies (1951)
Double Crossbones (1951)
The Pirate Queen (1951)
Against All Flags (1952)

Abbott and Costello Meet Captain Kidd (1952)
Blackbeard the Pirate (1952)
Captain Pirate (1952)
Caribbean (aka *Caribbean Gold*) (1952)
The Crimson Pirate (1952)
Yankee Buccaneer (1952)
Peter Pan (1953)
The Master of Ballantrae (1953)
Prince of Pirates (1953)
Raiders of the Seven Seas (1953)
Yankee Pasha (1954)
His Majesty O'Keefe (1954)
Long John Silver (1954)
Pirates of Tripoli (1955)
The Buccaneer (1958)
Queen of the Pirates (1960)
The Boy and the Pirates (1960)
Morgan the Pirate (1961)
The Pirate and Slave Girl (1961)
Pirates of Tortuga (1961)
The Son of Captain Blood (1962)

Tiger of the Seven Seas (1962)
Pirates of Blood River (1962)
Hero's Island (1962)
Fury at Smugglers Bay (1963)
Devil-Ship Pirates (1964)
A High Wind in Jamaica (1965)
The King's Pirate (1967)
The Rover (1967)
Blackbird's Ghost (1968)
When Eight Bells Toll (1971)
Treasure Island (1972)
Ghost in the Noonday Sun (1973)
Scalawag (1973)

Swashbuckler (aka The Scarlet
   Buccaneer) (1976)
The Island (1980)
The Pirate Movie (1982)
Pirates of Penzance (1983)
Yellowbeard (1983)
Ice Pirates (1984)
Pirates (1986)
The Princess Bride (1987)
Shipwrecked (1990)
Treasure Island (1990 TVM)
Hook (1991)

Planet of the Apes

In its 1968 review, *Variety* called *Planet of the Apes* an "intriguing blend of chilling satire, a sometimes ludicrous juxtaposition of human and ape mores, optimism and pessimism." It's a fitting description for an unusual series that featured both brilliant plot twists and incredibly dull science fiction. Rod Serling wrote the original film, adapting Pierre (*Bridge Over the River Kwai*) Boulle's satirical novel. Charlton Heston starred as an astronaut who is hurled into a time warp and lands on a planet where intelligent apes are masters over men. In the film's climactic closing scene, Heston found the remains of the Statue of Liberty and realized that he had seen man's future on planet Earth. Critics raved over Serling's witty screenplay, but most of the publicity centered on John Chambers' brilliant ape make-up (which won a special Oscar). Two years later, a dull sequel, *Beneath the Planet of the Apes*, ended with the detonation of an atomic bomb that destroyed the world—and apparently the series. However, when it scored at the box office, producer Arthur P. Jacobs and screenwriter Paul Dehn revived the series with a crafty twist. *Escape From the Planet of the Apes* revealed that two nice apes (Roddy McDowall and Kim Hunter) escaped from the exploding Earth in a spaceship and entered into the same time warp that Heston encountered. They land on Earth circa 1971 and run afoul of human prejudice. However, before they are murdered, they smuggle their infant son to safety. He grows up and, in the fourth film *Conquest of the Planet of the Apes*, leads an ape revolt. In the final series entry, 1973's mediocre *Battle for the Planet of the Apes*, the time line came full circle and ended where *Planet of the Apes* began. A year later, an hour-long TV series was launched, with McDowall repeating his original role. It bombed in the ratings and became a midseason casualty, although the pilot episode, *Back to the Planet of the Apes*, was later released as a TV-movie. A Saturday morning cartoon version also surfaced during the 1975-76 TV season. See also **Apes and Monkeys**.

Planet of the Apes (1968)
Beneath the Planet of the Apes (1970)
Escape From the Planet of the Apes
   (1971)
Conquest of the Planet of the Apes
   (1972)

Battle for the Planet of the Apes (1973)
Back to the Planet of the Apes (1974
   TVM)
Forgotten City of the Planet of the Apes
   (1974 TVM culled from series
   episodes)

Plants

Perhaps because of their decorative and unthinking nature, plants have been greatly ignored by filmmakers. In fact, prior to the 1950s, they were restricted to bit roles — nothing they could really sink their roots into. A rare flower, which bloomed only in the moonlight, was featured prominently in 1935's *Werewolf of London*. Called the marifesa, it could cure lycanthropy, but — ironically — Henry Hull was bitten by a werewolf while searching for the flower. In the 1940s, Egyptian high priests used a brew made from tana leaves to periodically revive the Mummy (q.v.). But the first abnormal plants of note appeared in *The Wizard of Oz* (1939), in which Dorothy and the Scarecrow encountered a grove of apple trees who didn't like their fruit to be picked. Later in the film, they experienced the effects of sleep-inducing poppies. Arguably, the most renowned plant movie is 1951's *The Thing From Another World* (subsequently shortened to *The Thing*). It starred an alien frequently described (even in the movie) as a giant carrot (actually, his shape seemed inspired by the Frankenstein Monster). He was electrocuted — one could say "cooked" — at the film's climax. Alien pods invaded a small California community and systematically replaced its residents with look-alikes (q.v.) in Don Siegel's *Invasion of the Body Snatchers* (1956). Less memorable vegetation movies of the 1950s included *From Hell It Came*, in which radiation created a silly-looking tree monster, and *Voodoo Island*, which featured a "woman-eating cobra plant." B-movie mogul Roger Corman gave the screen its most charismatic plant with his campy cult classic *The Little Shop of Horrors* (1960). It was about a nerd named Seymour Krelboined who nurtures a mysterious plant that grows to human size and periodically craves people for dinner, screaming: "Feed me! Feed me! I'm hungry!" It spawned an Off-Broadway musical in 1982 and a big-budget remake in 1986. The plants in John Wyndham's *The Day of the Triffids* couldn't talk, but they could communicate via shrill sounds. In many ways, *Triffids* is the ultimate plant movie. At a height of ten feet, the poisonous, people-eating *Triffids* were a menacing crop, indeed. And unlike in other plant pictures, there wasn't just one monster in *Triffids*, it was a large-scale invasion. Talking trees appeared in *Babes in Toyland* (1961) and *Monty Python and the Holy Grail* (1975). A meteorite caused Stephen King to turn into a plant in 1982's *Creepshow*. And a mad scientist crossbred humans and plants to create *The Mutations* (1973).

The Werewolf of London (1935)
The Wizard of Oz (1939)
The Thing (1951)
Fury of the Congo (1951)
Invasion of the Body Snatchers (1956)
From Hell It Came (1957)
Voodoo Island (1957)
The Woman Eater (1959)
The Little Shop of Horrors (1960)
Babes in Toyland (1961)
The Day of the Triffids (1963)
Dr. Terror's House of Horrors (1964)
Maneater of Hydra (aka *Island of the Doomed*) (1966)

Navy vs. the Night Monsters (1966)
Please Don't Eat My Mother (1972)
The Mutations (1973)
Mr. Sycamore (1974)
Monty Python and the Holy Grail (1975)
The Kirlian Witness (aka *The Plants Are Watching*) (1978)
Nick Carter in Prague (aka *Dinner for Adele; Adele Hasn't Had Her Supper Yet*) (1978)
Invasion of the Body Snatchers (1978)
Attack of the Killer Tomatoes (1978)
Creepshow (1982)

The Little Shop of Horrors (1986)   *The Guardian* (1990)
Godzilla vs. Biollante (1989)

Plastic Surgery

Movie surgeons have wasted little time on routine face-lifts and nose jobs (though Steve Martin pleaded for a nose alteration in 1987's *Roxanne*). Instead, they have concentrated far more on extensive plastic surgery, frequently resulting in horror movie plots. In 1935's *The Raven*, Bela Lugosi played a Poe-reciting surgeon who turned gangster Boris Karloff's face into a hideous mass of scar tissue. Karloff exacted his revenge by escorting Lugosi to the torture chamber in the film's climax. However, the most common plastic surgery plot involves the scientist who murders innocent bystanders in order to rebuild the facial features of a loved one. Georges Franju's chilling *The Horror Chamber of Dr. Faustus* is considered the classic example of this type. Rock Hudson probably underwent the most elaborate make-over in John Frankenheimer's *Seconds*. He played an elderly millionaire who emerged from high-tech surgery as a new, younger man—only to find out later that the price was too steep. *The Girl Most Likely to . . .* uncovered a vein of dark humor in its story of a mistreated ugly duckling (Stockard Channing) transformed into a revenge-minded beauty. A car accident, plastic surgery and a mean mother kept lovers Kathleen Quinlan and Stephen Collins apart in *The Promise*, a rare change-of-face romance.

The Raven (1935)	*Ash Wednesday* (1973)
A Woman's Face (1941)	*Who?* (1974)
Black Dragons (1942)	*Scalpel* (aka *False Face*) (1976)
Dark Passage (1948)	*Rabid* (1977)
Stolen Face (1952)	*The Promise* (1978)
Jail Bait (1954)	*Mirror, Mirror* (1979 TVM)
The Mirror Has Two Faces (aka *Le Miroir a Deux Faces*) (1958)	*The Man With Bogart's Face* (aka *Sam Marlowe, Private Eye*) (1980)
The Face of Terror (1959)	*Looker* (1981)
Circus of Horrors (1960)	*The Jigsaw Man* (1984)
The Awful Dr. Orloff (1961)	*Why Me* (1984 TVM)
The Horror Chamber of Dr. Faustus (aka *Eyes Without a Face*) (1962)	*Emmanuelle 4* (1984)
Seconds (1966)	*Batman* (1989)
Corruption (1968)	*Johnny Handsome* (1989)
The Groundstar Conspiracy (1972)	*Doc Hollywood* (1991)
The Girl Most Likely to . . . (1973 TVM)	*Shattered* (1991)
	Death Becomes Her (1992)

Poe, Edgar Allan, *see* Corman's Poe Series

Poirot, Hercule

Agatha Christie's Belgian sleuth was brought to the screen in the guise of British actor Austin Trevor in the early 1930s in mysteries like *Alibi* and *Lord Edgware Dies*. Decades later, Tony Randall (*The Alphabet Murders*) and Albert Finney (*Murder on the Orient Express*) took shots at playing Poirot. However, Christie fans quibbled with those interpretations, and an acceptable Poirot was not discovered until Peter Ustinov made the role his own, beginning with 1978's *Death on the Nile*. Sadly, the quality of the Ustinov/Poirot films declined gradually after his second film, *Evil Under the Sun* (1982). But Ustinov remained entertaining in spite of the progressively worsening conditions. Hercule Poirot was also among the many detectives spoofed in Neil Simon's *Murder by Death* (1976).

Alibi (1931) (Austin Trevor)

Black Coffee (1931) (Trevor)

Lord Edgware Dies (1934) (Trevor)

The Alphabet Murders (aka *The ABC Murders*) (1966) (Tony Randall)

Murder on the Orient Express (1974) (Albert Finney)

Death on the Nile (1978) (Peter Ustinov)

Evil Under the Sun (1982) (Ustinov)

Thirteen at Dinner (1985 TVM) (Ustinov)

Dead Man's Folly (1986 TVM) (Ustinov)

Murder in Three Acts (1986 TVM) (Ustinov)

Appointment With Death (1988) (Ustinov)

Police Academy

An unexpected commercial success, the *Police Academy* series has proven to be the 1980s answer to Britain's *Carry On* comedies (q.v.) of the 1960s. Both series manufactured low-brow humor that moviegoers thrived on and critics found distasteful. The 1984 *Police Academy* naturally set the tone for the rest, focusing on a class of unlikely police recruits led by smart guy Steve Guttenberg, former football player Bubba Smith, and human noise machine Michael Winslow. Unpredictable stand-up comic Bobcat Goldthwait joined the series for the third and fourth entries. After the fourth film, Guttenberg graduated to bigger roles (1987's monster hit *Three Men and a Baby*), and Smith bowed out temporarily. Only Winslow remained for all six entries. *Night Patrol* (1985) was a worthless rip-off boasting a bizarre cast headed by Linda Blair, Pat Paulsen and Billy Barty.

Police Academy (1984)

Police Academy 2 (1985)

Police Academy 3: Back in Training (1986)

Police Academy 4: Citizens on Patrol (1987)

Police Academy 5: Assignment Miami Beach (1988)

Police Academy 6: City Under Siege (1989)

Police Story Series

The three *Police Story* films, featuring martial arts stylist Jackie Chan, are no relation to the 1973-77 U.S. television anthology series (nor the TV-movies based on it). Instead, the Chan films were fast-paced action pictures, emphasizing their star's athletic prowess, comic touch and incredible stunts. Chan once said: "The audience comes in the theater to see Jackie Chan — not the double. That's why I do my own stunts." His daredevil antics are legendary. In one sequence in *Police Story II*, Chan jumped off a building onto a fast-moving truck, leaped over to a passing bus, and then dived into a second-story window. No insurance company will issue him a policy, especially after a fall in *Armor of God* resulted in a cracked skull requiring extensive surgery. In addition to acting and choreographing the action scenes, Chan directed the first two *Police Story* films. Tony Kwei Lai (aka

Stanley Tong) took over for the third entry, which paired Chan with a no-nonsense female partner. Despite superb action scenes and clever bits of humor, Chan's films have never attracted much attention in the United States. His two American-made movies, 1980's *The Big Brawl* (aka *Battle Creek Brawl*) and 1985's *The Protector*, failed to showcase Chan as well as his own Hong Kong features.

Police Story (aka *Jackie Chan's Police*	*Police Story II* (1988)
Story; *Police Force*) (1985)	*Police Story III: Supercop* (1992)

Pool

Paul Newman's second tour through the world of smoke-filled pool halls finally resulted in his first Academy Award, as Best Actor for 1986's *The Color of Money*. Newman played Eddie Felson, a smooth veteran pool shark he introduced as an ambitious youth fifteen years earlier in *The Hustler*. Eddie's match against the legendary Minnesota Fats (Jackie Gleason) in the 1961 picture easily ranks as pool's finest moment in the movies. But other actors have also taken their shot at the eight ball: James Coburn in *The Baltimore Bullet*, Whoopi Goldberg in *Kiss Shot*, and Johnny Cash in *The Baron and the Kid*, a TV-movie inspired by his country hit "The Baron."

The Hustler (1961)	*The Color of Money* (1986)
The Baltimore Bullet (1980)	*Kiss Shot* (1989 TVM)
The Baron and the Kid (1984 TVM)	

Popes and Cardinals

Cardinal Richelieu, who virtually ruled France from 1624-42, has been the cinema's most prominent senior church figure. George Arliss portrayed him as an unscrupulous scoundrel in *Cardinal Richelieu* (1935), while others who have donned the red robe include Nigel du Brulier in *The Three Musketeers* (1935) and *The Man in the Iron Mask* (1939), Raymond Massey in *Under the Red Robe* (1937), Christopher Logue in *The Devils* (1971), and Charlton Heston in *The Three Musketeers* (1974) and *The Four Musketeers* (1975). *Guilty of Treason* (1949) was a fact-based account of the trial of Cardinal Mindszenty, while *The Cardinal* (1963) offered a fictitious tale of a young American's (Tom Tryon) rise to prominence within the church. Few actors have portrayed popes, although Albert Finney had the lead in the 1984 TV-movie *Pope John Paul II* and Anthony Quinn ruled from the Vatican in *Shoes of a Fisherman* (1968). The 1964 documentary *A Man Named John* traced the accomplishments of Pope John XXIII. A plot to assassinate the Pope lurked behind the comedy bits in Chevy Chase's *Foul Play* (1978). Finally, Liv Ullmann disguised herself as a man to reach the papacy in 1972's *Pope Joan*. See also **Monks; Nuns.**

Cardinal Richelieu (1935)	*Becket* (1964)
The Three Musketeers (1935)	*Shoes of a Fisherman* (1968)
Under the Red Robe (1937)	*The Devils* (1971)
The Man in the Iron Mask (1939)	*Pope Joan* (aka *The Devil's Impostor*)
Guilty of Treason (1949)	(1972)
Never Take No for an Answer (1951)	*Brother Sun, Sister Moon* (1973)
The Cardinal (1963)	*The Abdication* (1974)
A Man Named John (1964)	*The Three Musketeers* (1974)

The Four Musketeers (1975)
Foul Play (1978)
From a Far Country: Pope John Paul II (1981 TVM)
Pope John Paul II (1984 TVM)

Saving Grace (1986)
The Godfather, Part III (1990)
The Pope Must Die (aka The Pope Must Diet) (1991)
Sister Act (1992)

Porky's

Shortly before he made the delightful family favorite A Christmas Story, director Bob Clark filmed this 1982 Canadian-made comedy smash about horny teens in Florida circa 1954. The majority of the action centered around Porky's, a bar/brothel located just across the county line. Most critics called Porky's smutty and pointless, but a *lot* of teens saw it. Perhaps it was the timing, for the 1983 sequel, *Porky's II: The Next Day*, lacked the box office fire despite reteaming teen leads Dan Monahan, Mark Herrier and Wyatt Knight. The same trio showed up in a third installment that attracted little attention.

Porky's (1982)
Porky's II: The Next Day (1983)

Porky's Revenge (1985)

Postal Carriers

Just as librarians (q.v.) have been stereotyped as drabbily-dressed spinsters, postal carriers have struggled with their clichéd portrayals as mild-mannered unmarried men. However, in those rare films in which postal characters have been given major roles, they have proven themselves to be an eclectic lot, rarely mild-mannered and sometimes downright peculiar. The pleasant Mr. Potts turned out to be a devious murderer who almost outwitted Sherlock Holmes in 1944's The Scarlet Claw. Of course, Potts was actually an actor named Ramson who killed the real postman and assumed his identity (nevertheless, Ransom/Potts delivered the mail, making him a postal carrier). In another murder mystery, the British Green for Danger, a postman provided a critical clue in uncovering an operating room killer. Alan Ladd played a postal inspector in Appointment With Danger (1951), while Eli Wallach played a postman-turned-kidnapper in the 1967 satire The Tiger Makes Out. French comedian Jacques Tati, best known for his Mr. Hulot (q.v.) movies, played a mailman in 1949's delightful Jour de Fete. On a more bizarre level, postman Jason Robards, Jr. wanted to turn into a tree in 1974's Mr. Sycamore! A family of cannibals devoured the mailman in the offbeat horror-comedy Spider Baby (1964). Finally, no discussion of postal carriers would be complete without mentioning Cliff Clavin (John Ratzenberger), the bar-bound know-it-all on Cheers. See also **Letters**.

The Scarlet Claw (1944)
Green for Danger (1946)
Jour de Fête (aka The Big Day) (1949)
The Barefoot Mailman (1951)
Appointment With Danger (1951)
Postman's Knock (1961)
Spider Baby (aka Spider Baby, or the Maddest Story Ever Told; The Liver Eaters) (1964)

The Tiger Makes Out (1967)
Mr. Sycamore (1974)
Queen of the Stardust Ballroom (1975 TVM)
Harry's War (1981)
Stepfather II (aka Stepfather II: Make Room for Daddy) (1989)
The Tommyknockers (1993 TVM)

Prequels

A prequel is the opposite of a sequel, in that its narrative takes place earlier than in the original film. For example, German filmmaker Paul Wegener destroyed the Golem, a stone statue brought to life, in 1914's *The Golem: Monster of Fate*. However, six years later, Wegener went back and told the story of the Golem's origin in *The Golem: How He Came to Be*. The 1926 Foreign Legion classic *Beau Geste* inspired two partial prequels, as the plots of *Beau Sabreur* (1928) and *Beau Ideal* (1931) took place in the same time frame as — instead of prior to — the original film. However, the first Hollywood prequel was 1948's *Another Part of the Forest*, which depicted the early days of the ruthless Hubbard family first introduced in 1941's *The Little Foxes*. Dan Duryea (as Leo Hubbard) was the only holdover from the original film's cast. Sporadic prequels (e.g., 1966's *Nevada Smith*) and "partial prequels" (e.g., 1950's *The Fortunes of Captain Blood*) appeared throughout the 1950s and 1960s. However, it was not until the sequel-crazy early 1980s that the prequel attracted much attention. Even then, however, prequels typically performed poorly at the box office, as evidenced by flops such as *Butch and Sundance: The Early Days* (1979). A noteworthy exception, of course, was *Indiana Jones and the Temple of Doom* (1984), a blockbuster prequel to *Raiders of the Lost Ark* (1981). The longest gap between prequel and original is the twenty-three years that separated the 1977 adaptation of Henry Handel Richardson's *The Getting of Wisdom* from the 1954 version of his later novel *Rhapsody*. Of course, *Wide Sargasso Sea* (1993) could also claim that distinction, depending on whether one considers it a prequel to the 1944 or the 1971 *Jane Eyre*. Sometimes, the distinction between prequel and original becomes a bit confusing. The Chuck Norris action picture *Missing in Action II: The Beginning* (1985) was actually filmed before *Missing in Action* (1984). It became a prequel only when the producers decided to release the second film first. (**Note:** The 1986 TV-movie *Dallas: The Early Years* was similar to a prequel, in that it took place chronologically prior to the television series *Dallas*.) In the following list, the prequel is listed in the left column, with the original film listed to the right.

The Golem: How He Came to Be (aka *Der Golem, Wie Er in die Welt Kam*) (1920)	*The Golem: Monster of Fate* (aka *Der Golem*) (1914)
Beau Sabreur (1928)	*Beau Geste* (1926)
Beau Ideal (1931)	*Beau Geste* (1926)
Another Part of the Forest (1948)	*The Little Foxes* (1941)
The Fortunes of Captain Blood (1950)	*Captain Blood* (1935)
Nevada Smith (1966)	*The Carpetbaggers* (1964)
The Nightcomers (1972)	*The Innocents* (1961)
The Getting of Wisdom (1977)	*Rhapsody* (1954)
Butch and Sundance: The Early Days (1979)	*Butch Cassidy and the Sundance Kid* (1969)
Zulu Dawn (1979)	*Zulu* (1964)
Bálint Fábián's Encounter With God (1980)	*Hungarians* (1979)
Amityville II: The Possession (1982)	*The Amityville Horror* (1979)
Indiana Jones and the Temple of Doom (1984)	*Raiders of the Lost Ark* (1981)

Missing in Action 2: The Beginning (1985)	*Missing in Action* (1984)
On Valentine's Day (1986)	*1918* (1984)
The Rainbow (1989)	*Women in Love* (1970)
A Better Tomorrow III (aka *Love and Death in Saigon*) (1989)	*A Better Tomorrow* (1986)
Psycho IV: The Beginning (1990 TVM)	*Psycho* (1960)
Puppet Master III: Toulon's Revenge (1991)	*Puppet Master* (1989)
Wide Sargasso Sea (1993)	*Jane Eyre* (1944; 1971)

Presidents (U.S.)

The cinema has not treated all presidents equally, but then neither has American history. Abraham Lincoln, according to Guinness, has appeared as a character in over 150 films, far more than any other president. Actor Frank McGlynn specialized in portraying Lincoln for most of his career, beginning with 1915's *The Life of Abraham Lincoln* and continuing in bit roles in films like *The Littlest Rebel* (1935), *The Prisoner of Shark Island* (1936) and *The Plainsman* (1937). Most Lincoln biographies have been reverent sagas starring distinguished performers such as Walter Huston (1930's *Abraham Lincoln*), Henry Fonda (*Young Abe Lincoln*) and Raymond Massey (*Abe Lincoln in Illinois*). In 1951, *The Tall Target* offered a suspenseful change of pace, with Dick Powell as a detective (named John Kennedy!) trying to thwart an 1861 assassination attempt on Lincoln. In an even greater fictional elaboration, *The Lincoln Conspiracy* (1977) proposed that assassin John Wilkes Booth was conspiring with members of the U.S. Senate. Ronald Reagan ranks second to Lincoln in number of film appearances—but only because he really was an actor. More legitimate screen appearances have been logged by Andrew Jackson and John F. Kennedy, both of whom have been the subjects of several film biographies. Jackson's exploits in the War of 1812 played a major role in both versions of *The Buccaneer* (1938 and 1958). The scandal surrounding his alleged adulterous affair with future-wife Rachel Robards formed the basis for *The Gorgeous Hussy* (1936) and *The President's Lady* (1953). Interestingly, Charlton Heston played Jackson in both *The President's Lady* and *The Buccaneer* (1958). William Holden befriended Jackson's ghost in the unremarkable 1942 fantasy *The Remarkable Andrew*. Kennedy's pre-presidential adventures as a patrol torpedo boat commander were played for escapist entertainment in 1963's *PT 109*, with Cliff Robertson in the lead. The 1977 TV-movie *Johnny, We Hardly Knew Ye* dealt with Kennedy's first try for public office, while 1984's *Prince Jack* was an inconsequential chronicle about the Kennedy clan. Other Kennedy-related pictures include the documentary *John F. Kennedy: Years of Lightning, Day of Drums* (1966), the assassination thriller *Executive Action* (1973), *Jacqueline Bouvier Kennedy* (1982), *Hoover vs. the Kennedys: The Second Civil War* (1987) and Oliver Stone's conspiracy drama *JFK* (1991). In 1991's *Point Break*, bank robbers calling themselves the President Gang wore rubber masks of Reagan, Carter, Nixon and Johnson. Fictional presidents have been portrayed in many films, several of which have cast our nation's leader into intriguing situations. President Henry Fonda ordered the destruction of New York City in order to avoid a war with the Soviet

Union in 1964's *Fail Safe*. That same year, military officer Burt Lancaster plotted a coup to overthrow President Fredric March in *Seven Days in May*. In 1971 TV-movies, a top presidential advisor disappeared in *Vanished*, which more or less prepared viewers for *The President's Plane Is Missing*. The President has also been kidnapped by lethal ladies (*In Like Flint*), terrorists (*The Kidnapping of the President*), and futuristic New York City convicts (*Escape From New York*). Polly Bergen played the country's first female commander-in-chief in the 1964 comedy *Kisses for My President*. James Earl Jones portrayed a black senator thrust into the Oval Office when the President is killed in *The Man* (1972). The following list includes only films specifically about presidents or featuring them in prominent roles (for instance, although George Washington has been a minor character in over a dozen movies, those films are not listed). The president's name is shown in parentheses if it is not apparent from the title; some are about fictitious presidents.

Abraham Lincoln (1930)
The Phantom President (1932)
Gabriel Over the White House (1933)
The Gorgeous Hussy (1936) (Jackson)
First Lady (1937)
This Is My Affair (aka *His Affair*) (1937) (McKinley)
The Buccaneer (1938) (Jackson)
Young Mr. Lincoln (1939)
Abe Lincoln in Illinois (1940)
Tennessee Johnson (aka *The Man on America's Conscience*) (1942) (Andrew Johnson)
The Remarkable Andrew (1942) (Jackson)
Wilson (1944)
Magnificent Doll (1946) (Madison)
The Tall Target (1951) (Lincoln)
The President's Lady (1953) (Jackson)
Suddenly (1954)
The Buccaneer (1958) (Jackson)
Sunrise at Campobello (1960) (Franklin Roosevelt)
Advise and Consent (1962)
PT 109 (1963) (Kennedy)
The Best Man (1964)
Kisses for My President (1964)
Seven Days in May (1964)
Fail Safe (1964)
The Eleanor Roosevelt Story (1965)
John F. Kennedy: Years of Lightning, Day of Drums (1966)
In Like Flint (1967)

The Virgin President (1968) (Fillmore spoof)
The Great Man's Whiskers (1971 TVM) (Lincoln)
Vanished (1971 TVM)
The President's Plane Is Missing (1971 TVM)
The Man (1972)
Hail to the Chief (aka *Hail; Washington, B.C.*) (1973)
Executive Action (1973) (Kennedy)
Collision Course (1975 TVM) (Truman)
Give 'Em Hell, Harry! (1975) (Truman)
The Wind and the Lion (1975) (Theodore Roosevelt)
Eleanor and Franklin (1976 TVM) (Franklin Roosevelt)
The Lincoln Conspiracy (1977)
Johnny, We Hardly Knew Ye (1977 TVM) (Kennedy)
F.D.R. – The Last Year (1980 TVM)
First Family (1980)
The Kidnapping of the President (1980)
Escape From New York (1981)
Jacqueline Bouvier Kennedy (1982 TVM)
Eleanor Roosevelt, First Lady of the World (1982 TVM)
The Indomitable Teddy Roosevelt (1983)
Prince Jack (1984) (Kennedy)

Secret Honor: The Last Testament of
  Richard M. Nixon (1984 TVM)
The Betty Ford Story (1987 TVM)
Assassination (1987)
Hoover vs. the Kennedys: The Second
  Civil War (1987 TVM)
LBJ: The Early Years (1987 TVM)

Gore Vidal's Lincoln (1988 TVM)
The Final Days (1989 TVM) (Nixon)
The Perfect Tribute (1991 TVM)
  (Abraham Lincoln)
JFK (1991)
Dave (1993)
JFK: Reckless Youth (1993 TVM)

Presley, Elvis

It used to be that the cinema endured a waiting period before spinning off biographical films about deceased personalities. The FDR biography *Sunrise at Campobello*
(1960) did not appear until fifteen years after the former president's death. Evi-
dently, the film industry deemed Elvis Presley's life more marketable. Less than
two years after Presley's death, ABC ushered in *Elvis*, the made-for-TV story of his
life. Over the next ten years, five additional Presley-related films appeared amid
rumors that the "King" still lived. None of these films surpassed ABC's *Elvis*, a
solid picture directed by talented horror specialist John Carpenter and starring an
effective Kurt Russell in the title role. North Carolina filmmaker Earl Owensby's
Living Legend (1980) made no claims about being based on Elvis's life. But the plot
similarities and the presence of Elvis's last girlfriend, Ginger Alden, left little doubt
as to the picture's intent. The same year's *Touched by Love* was a fact-based story
about the pen-pal relationship between a young girl with cerebral palsy and Presley.
Don Johnson made an unlikely Elvis in the 1981 TV-movie *Elvis and the Beauty
Queen*, the story of Presley's five-year relationship with Linda Thompson (Stephanie Zimbalist). Elvis's only wife, Priscilla Presley, executive-produced 1988's
Elvis and Me, the TV version of her best-seller. David Keith was Elvis in 1989's
box office bomb *Heartbreak Hotel*, a light-hearted, fictionalized account of Presley's
friendship with a teenaged boy. Presley also played himself in his final two screen
appearances: the behind-the-scenes documentary *Elvis: That's the Way It Is* (1970)
and the concert film *Elvis on Tour* (1972). Finally, *Honeymoon in Vegas* (1992) featured a troupe of flashily dressed skydivers called the Flying Elvises.

Elvis: That's the Way It Is (1970)
Elvis on Tour (1972)
Elvis (1979 TVM)
Living Legend (1980)
Touched by Love (aka To Elvis, With
  Love) (1980)
Elvis and the Beauty Queen (1981
  TVM)

Elvis and Me (1988 TVM)
Heartbreak Hotel (1989)
Honeymoon in Vegas (1992)
Elvis and the Colonel: The Untold Story
  (1993 TVM)
The Woman Who Loved Elvis (1993
  TVM)

Prisoners of War

POW films fall into three basic camps: German, Japanese and Vietnamese. Each
of these groups features an Oscar winner of some sort. William Holden won a
Best Actor Oscar for his portrayal of a cynical prisoner wrongly tagged an informer
in Billy Wilder's *Stalag 17* (1953). Although not among the first POW films, Wilder's movie combined humor, suspense, and an assortment of motley characters
to create a much-imitated formula. *The Password Is Courage*, one of several mid-

1960s POW pictures, was based on the real-life exploits of Sergeant-Major Charles Coward, who made a military career out of escaping from German camps. *Von Ryan's Express* (1965) opened in a POW camp but expanded into a perilous train journey through Nazi-occupied territory. Allied prisoners escaped during a climactic soccer game with a Nazi team in *Victory* (1981), while less athletic prisoners built a glider in the 1971 TV-movie *Birdmen*. *The Great Escape* (1963) made a star of Steve McQueen, while rolling up enough ticket receipts to make it the most profitable POW film of the last three decades. It was cowritten by James (*Shogun*) Clavell, whose novel *King Rat* reached the screen in 1965. Set in a Japanese POW camp, it chronicled the rise and fall of a manipulating con artist (George Segal). However, the best-remembered Japanese-set POW film remains David Lean's *The Bridge on the River Kwai* (1957). It earned Oscars for Best Picture, Best Director and Best Actor, the latter honoring Alec Guinness's portrayal of a stubborn, manipulated British officer. Other Japanese prison camp films include *The Purple Heart* (1944), *Escape to Mindinao* (1968), *Merry Christmas, Mr. Lawrence* (1983) and *Empire of the Sun* (1987). *The Deer Hunter*, the 1978 Oscar winner for Best Picture, was partially set in a Vietnamese POW camp where prisoners were subjected to a chilling game of Russian roulette. *When Hell Was in Session* (1979) was a grim account of a Navy officer held prisoner for seven years in North Vietnam. However, *Missing in Action II* (1985), *P.O.W. The Escape* (1986) and *The Hanoi Hilton* (1987) used Vietnamese prison camps strictly for their topical exploitation value. A handful of films have dealt with female POW camps, most notably *Two Thousand Women* (1944), *Three Came Home* (1950), *A Town Like Alice* (1956) and *Women of Valor* (1986). Although most movie POWs seem to be American or British, there have been exceptions. Jean Renoir's antiwar classic *Grand Illusion* (1937) focused on French prisoners during World War I. *Until Hell Is Frozen* (1960) was set in a Russian camp, and *The McKenzie Break* (1970) had captured Germans escaping from a Scottish POW camp. Television introduced the infamous POW camp sitcom *Hogan's Heroes* in 1965. It enjoyed a six-year run and a profitable afterlife in syndication. See also **Prisons**.

Everything Is Thunder (1936)
Grand Illusion (aka *La Grande Illusion*) (1937)
The Cross of Lorraine (1943)
Two Thousand Women (1944)
The Purple Heart (1944)
The Captive Heart (1948)
Act of Violence (1949)
The Wooden Soldier (1950)
Three Came Home (1950)
Stalag 17 (1953)
Break to Freedom (aka *Albert RN*) (1953)
The Bamboo Prison (1954)
Prisoner of War (1954)
A Town Like Alice (aka *Rape of Malaya*) (1956)

The Bridge on the River Kwai (1957)
The Colditz Story (1957)
The Camp on Blood Island (1958)
Breakout (aka *Danger Within*) (1958)
Until Hell Is Frozen (1960)
A Coming-Out Party (aka *A Very Important Person*) (1961)
The Manchurian Candidate (1962)
The Great Escape (1963)
The Password Is Courage (1963)
Von Ryan's Express (1965)
King Rat (1965)
Escape to Mindinao (1968)
The McKenzie Break (1970)
Birdmen (aka *Escape of the Birdmen*) (1971 TVM)
The Deer Hunter (1978)

Escape to Athena (1979)
When Hell Was in Session (1979 TVM)
Victory (1981)
Merry Christmas, Mr. Lawrence (1983)
Missing in Action 2: The Beginning (1985)

Women of Valor (1986 TVM)
Opposing Force (aka Hellcamp) (1986)
P.O.W. The Escape (aka Behind Enemy Lines) (1986)
Empire of the Sun (1987)
The Hanoi Hilton (1987)
The Last P.O.W.?: The Bobby Garwood Story (1993 TVM)

Prisons

The most engrossing accounts of life behind bars are those based on real-life exploits. Robert Stroud, a prisoner who became a leading ornithologist, was portrayed in Oscar-nominated fashion by Burt Lancaster in *Birdman of Alcatraz* (1962) and by Art Carney in *Alcatraz: The Whole Shocking Story* (1980). The appeals to prevent the execution of Caryl Chessman, a rapist/murderer known as the "Lover's Lane Bandit," were the subject of 1955's *Cell 2455, Death Row* and 1977's *Kill Me If You Can*. *Papillon* chronicled Henri Charrière's thrilling escape from Devil's Island. *Escape From Alcatraz* (1979) was inspired by a daring 1962 breakout engineered by convict Frank Norris (Clint Eastwood). As the aforementioned films indicate, Alcatraz rates as the cinema's busiest real-life prison. Other actual penitentiaries that have provided movie settings include Sing Sing (*20,000 Years in Sing Sing, Castle on the Hudson*), San Quentin (*Duffy of San Quentin, Women of San Quentin*) and Folsom (*Inside the Walls of Folsom Prison*). Foreign prisons have proven to be harrowing places, especially as depicted in *Midnight Express* (1978), *Kiss of the Spider Woman* (1985), *Jacobo Timerman: Prisoner Without a Name, Cell Without a Number* (1983) and *Dadah Is Death* (1988). Not all movie prisons have been surrounded by four walls. Futuristic New York City was envisioned as a prison in John Carpenter's *Escape From New York* (1981). A similar premise was explored earlier in 1973's *Terminal Island*, which was set in a futuristic coed penal colony off the coast of California. The prison in the 1993 Australian film *Fortress* was built thirty stories underground. An entire planet was used as a prison in 1985's *Space Rage*. Women prison pictures date back to 1931, although 1950's *Caged* remains the best remembered. However, its most disturbing scene (a prisoner gets her head shaved) seems tame by today's standards. Since Jonathan Demme's drive-in feature *Caged Heat* earned critical kudos in 1974, exploitative "women in prison" films have proliferated. Linda Blair was lusted after by both fellow female inmates and male guards in *Chained Heat* (1983) after being sexually assaulted with a broom handle in the 1974 made-for-TV film *Born Innocent*. Other women prison movies include *The Weak and the Wicked* (1953), *School for Unclaimed Girls* (1969), *The Concrete Jungle* (1982) and *Reform School Girls* (1986). Although most inmates have concentrated solely on escaping from prison, Peter Sellers was concerned with how to break out and then back into one in the 1960 comedy *Two Way Stretch*. Convict Noel Coward led a luxurious prison life — and even masterminded elaborate crimes — in 1969's *The Italian Job*. See also **Penitentiary Series.**

The Big House (1930)
Ladies of the Big House (1931)

The Criminal Code (1931)
The Last Mile (1932)

Hold 'Em Jail (1932)
20,000 Years in Sing-Sing (1933)
Ladies They Talk About (1933)
San Quentin (1937)
Alcatraz Island (1937)
King of Alcatraz (1938)
Blackwell's Island (1939)
The Big Guy (1939)
Castle on the Hudson (aka *Years Without Days*) (1940)
San Quentin (1946)
Brute Force (1947)
Prison Warden (1949)
White Heat (1949)
Caged (1950)
Inside the Walls of Folsom Prison (1951)
Hellgate (1952)
The Weak and the Wicked (1953)
Riot in Cell Block Eleven (1954)
The Steel Cage (1954)
Duffy of San Quentin (1954)
Betrayed Women (1955)
Cell 2455, Death Row (1955)
Women's Prison (1955)
Gang Busters (1955)
Hold Back Tomorrow (1955)
Unchained (1955)
Behind the High Wall (1956)
Girls in Prison (1956)
Jailhouse Rock (1957)
Escape From San Quentin (1957)
The Last Mile (1958)
Two Way Stretch (1960)
Birdman of Alcatraz (1962)
The Concrete Jungle (aka *The Criminal*) (1962)
Convicts Four (aka *Reprieve*) (1962)
House of Women (1962)
The Hill (1965)
Cool Hand Luke (1967)
99 Women (1969)
School for Unclaimed Girls (aka *The Smashing Birds I Used to Know*; *House of Unclaimed Women*) (1969)
Riot (1969)

Breakout (1970)
There Was a Crooked Man (1970)
The Glass House (aka *Truman Capote's The Glass House*) (1972 TVM)
The Hot Box (1972)
Sweet Sugar (aka *Chaingang Girls*) (1972)
Papillon (1973)
Terminal Island (1973)
Caged Heat (*Renegade Girls*) (1974)
Breakout (1975)
Short Eyes (aka *Slammer*) (1977)
Kill Me If You Can (1977 TVM)
Midnight Express (1978)
Escape From Alcatraz (1979)
Penitentiary (1979)
Alcatraz: The Whole Shocking Story (1980 TVM)
Attica (1980 TVM)
Brubaker (1980)
Stir Crazy (1980)
Inmates: A Love Story (1981 TVM)
Escape From New York (1981)
The Concrete Jungle (1982)
Love Child (1982)
Dangerous Company (1982 TVM)
Bad Boys (1983)
Women of San Quentin (1983 TVM)
Chained Heat (1983)
Jacobo Timerman: Prisoner Without a Name, Cell Without a Number (aka *Prisoner Without a Name, Cell Without a Number*) (1983 TVM)
Beyond the Walls (1984)
Mrs. Soffel (1984)
Kiss of the Spider Woman (1985)
Space Rage (1985)
Doin' Time (1985)
Star Slammer: The Escape (aka *Prison Ship*) (1986)
Vendetta (1986)
The Naked Cage (1986)
Reform School Girls (1986)
Prison for Children (1987 TVM)
Weeds (1987)
Dadah Is Death (1988 TVM)

Prison (1988)	*Death Warrant* (1990)
Lock Up (1989)	*Bloodfist III: Forced to Fight* (1992)
Caged Fury (1989)	*Alien³* (1992)
Prison Stories: Women on the Inside	*American Me* (1992)
(1990 TVM)	*Fortress* (1993)
Ernest Goes to Jail (1990)	*Last Light* (1993 TVM)

Prom Night

The original entry in this slasher film series toplined the scream queen of the early 1980s — Jamie Lee Curtis. Like many slasher films, it featured a killer seeking revenge for an earlier crime (in this case, the death of Jamie Lee's little sister). Despite above-average acting for this genre, *Prom Night* hardly warranted a sequel. However, the popularity of horror videotapes toward the end of the decade sent low-budget producers clamoring for recognizable titles. *Hello Mary Lou: Prom Night II* (1987) lifted its plot shamelessly from Stephen King's *Carrie*: At her 1957 high school prom, senior class party girl Mary Lou gets mysteriously elected prom queen. Alas, a good time does not await her — she winds up burning in flames on the dance floor. Thirty years later, her vengeful spirit returns, and the student body of Hamilton High quickly becomes less populous. A second sequel covered similar ground with Mary Lou popping up again to possess another teen. The fourth installment dropped Mary Lou in favor of a vengeful male spirit, making it a series entry in name only. See also **Slasher Movies.**

Prom Night (1980)

Hello Mary Lou: Prom Night II (1987)

Prom Night III: The Last Kiss (1989)

Prom Night IV: Deliver Us From Evil (1991)

Psychiatrists

Sympathetic, homicidal, crazy — psychiatrists and the occasional psychologist have run the gamut of screen characters. Michael Caine played a murderous shrink in desperate need of psychiatric help himself in *Dressed to Kill*. Surprisingly, women psychiatrists have proven even more adept at murder. Psychology professor Loretta Young accidentally killed a student and then covered her crime in 1949's *The Accused*. Manipulated psychiatrist Lindsay Crouse went over the edge in the final scene of *House of Games* (1987) and unexpectedly shot Joe Mantegna. In Hitchcock's *Spellbound*, Gregory Peck played an amnesiac who *thought* he was a prominent psychiatrist. Dan Aykroyd was a patient masquerading as a radio talk show psychiatrist in *The Couch Trip*. The world's most famous psychiatrist, Sigmund Freud, had his life chronicled in 1962's *Freud* (with Montgomery Clift in the lead role). Alan Arkin played Freud to Nicol Williamson's Sherlock Holmes in the stylish 1976 adaptation of Nicholas Meyers's *The Seven-Per-Cent Solution*. And Alec Guinness took his turn as Freud, having imaginary conversations with contemporary psychiatrist Dudley Moore in *Lovesick*. Fred Astaire made a most unlikely psychiatrist in the Astaire-Rogers musical *Carefree*. Brian Cox and Anthony Hopkins each played the cinema's creepiest psychologist, the cannibalistic Hannibal Lecter, in the movies *Manhunter* (1986) and *The Silence of the Lambs*

(1991). John Vernon had the best line as a psychiatrist in 1982's *Airplane II: The Sequel*. When a lawyer asked him to give his impression of the defendant, he replied: "I'm sorry, I don't do impressions. My expertise is in psychiatry." See also **Hypnotists; Multiple Personalities.**

Carefree (1938)
The Cat People (1942)
Lady in a Jam (1942)
She Wouldn't Say Yes (1945)
Shock (1946)
The Dark Past (1948)
The Accused (1949)
The Astonished Heart (1950)
Bedtime for Bonzo (1951)
Teresa (1951)
Sleeping Tiger (1954)
The Cobweb (1955)
The Three Faces of Eve (1957)
The Undead (1957)
Oh Men! Oh Women! (1957)
Stop Me Before I Kill! (aka *The Full Treatment*) (1961)
Mix Me a Person (1961)
The Couch (1962)
Pressure Point (1962)
Freud (1962)
David and Lisa (1962)
Tender Is the Night (1962)
Captain Newman, M.D. (1963)
Blindfold (1965)
Three on a Couch (1966)
The President's Analyst (1967)
The Impossible Years (1968)
Coming Apart (1969)
Dial Hot Line (1969 TVM)
The Psychiatrist: God Bless the Children (aka *Children of the Lotus Eater*) (1970 TVM)
They Might Be Giants (1971)
Klute (1971)
Dark Places (1972)
Diagnosis: Murder (1975)

One Flew Over the Cuckoo's Nest (1975)
The Seven-Per-Cent Solution (1976)
Sybil (1976 TVM)
Face to Face (1976)
Equus (1977)
Beyond Reason (1977)
High Anxiety (1977)
Dressed to Kill (1980)
Simon (1980)
Ordinary People (1980)
Phobia (1980)
Still of the Night (1982)
Zelig (1983)
Lovesick (1983)
Private Sessions (1985 TVM)
Manhunter (1986)
Beyond Therapy (1987)
A Different Affair (1987 TVM)
House of Games (1987)
The Couch Trip (1988)
Jack's Back (1988)
The Dream Team (1989)
Disturbed (1991)
The Silence of the Lambs (1991)
Victim of Love (1991 TVM)
What About Bob? (1991)
Red Wind (1991 TVM)
Love Kills (1991 TVM)
The Prince of Tides (1991)
Final Analysis (1992)
Whispers in the Dark (1992)
Raising Cain (1992)
Loving Lulu (1992)
Relentless: Mind of a Killer (1993 TVM)

Psycho

In François Truffaut's 1967 interview book *Hitchcock*, Hitch offered this explanation for making *Psycho*: "I think that the thing that appealed to me and made me decide to do the picture was the suddenness of the murder in the shower, coming, as it were, out of the blue. That was about all." Shot on a backlot with Hitchcock's

TV series crew, *Psycho* was a clever shocker about meek hotel owner Norman Bates (Anthony Perkins), who periodically assumed his dead mother's identity and became a jealous murderess. This inexpensive picture made its famed director a wealthy man and eventually became Hitch's best-known film to a generation of baby boomers. Even when his film career began to decline after failures like *Torn Curtain* (1966) and *Topaz* (1969), Hitchcock resisted a *Psycho* sequel. Yet, just three years after Hitchcock's death, the inevitable *Psycho II* was released. In an attempt to out-twist its predecessor, this sequel revealed that, despite dual personalities, alleged murderer Norman Bates (Perkins) was not as mad as most people thought. Perkins directed and starred in the 1986 follow-up *Psycho III*, which proved to be an uneasy mixture of dark humor and studio-inserted gore. The 1987 TV-movie *Bates Motel* strove for a lighter touch but failed to find one. It starred Bud Cort (Harold in *Harold and Maude*) as a former mental patient who inherited the motel from fellow ex-inmate Norman Bates. A second TV-movie, 1990's *Psycho IV: The Beginning*, starred former *E.T.* youngster Henry Thomas as a young Norman.

Psycho (1960)	*Bates Motel* (1987 TVM)
Psycho II (1983)	*Psycho IV: The Beginning* (1990 TVM)
Psycho III (1986)	

Puppet Master

Following on the heels of 1987's *Dolls*, 1989's *Puppet Master* tried to generate terror by transforming harmless toys into murderous little monsters. The film's prologue opens in 1939 at the Bodega Bay Inn (an apparent reference to Hitchcock's *The Birds*). Elderly puppeteer Andre Toulon (William Hickey) has discovered an ancient secret for breathing life into inanimate objects. However, fearing that his discovery will be exploited for evil, Toulon hides his work and commits suicide. Fifty years later, four psychics journey to the now-isolated hotel to investigate the death of a colleague who had been obsessed with Toulon. Shortly thereafter, a quartet of homicidal puppets — with colorful names like Pinhead, Tunneler, and Ms. Leech — begin bumping off the psychics in gruesome fashion. Despite its predictability and overemphasis on gore, horror aficionados made *Puppet Master* a popular videotape rental. A 1990 sequel rehashed most of the original's elements, although it was enlivened by a mysterious stranger wrapped in gauze and sporting sunglasses ala Claude Rains in *The Invisible Man*. The series then took an unexpected turn by producing a cleverly plotted prequel (q.v.). *Puppet Master III: Toulon's Revenge* (1991) essentially turned the killer-puppets into heroes by pitting them against the ruthless Nazis responsible for the murder of Andre Toulon's wife. As with the earlier films, the special effects were somewhat interesting. However, the puppets never really generated terror — they could be outmaneuvered and kicked out of the way too easily. See also **Puppets**.

Puppet Master (1989)	*Puppet Master III: Toulon's Revenge*
Puppet Master II (1990)	(1991)

Puppets

Puppetry, as the sole means of telling a story, has garnered little interest in the cinema. Except for Jiri Trnka's *A Midsummer Night's Dream* (1958), most all-puppet features have been aimed strictly at juveniles. Early efforts, such as *Willy McBean and His Magic Machine* (1965) and *Mad Monster Party?* (1967), were viewed as low-cost alternatives to animation. The James Bond-style 1966 British TV puppet series *Thunderbirds* attracted a more sophisticated audience. It inspired two theatrical features, *Thunderbirds Are Go* (1966) and *Thunderbird 6* (1968). American puppeteer Jim Henson hit box office gold in the early 1980s with movies using characters from his television series *The Muppet Show* (q.v.). However, his elaborate 1983 non-Muppet, puppet fantasy, *The Dark Crystal*, baffled Miss Piggy fans and was only modestly successful. Charming puppet sequences have graced a handful of films, most notably the Cary Grant/Katharine Hepburn romantic comedy *Holiday* (1938) and the family musicals *The Sound of Music* (1965) and *Lilli* (1953). In the latter film, Leslie Caron sang "Hi Lilli, Hi Lo" with a quartet of puppets and later danced a semiballet with life-sized puppet replicas. In the 1931 Marx Brothers comedy *Monkey Business*, Harpo pretended to be a puppet. A good fairy transformed a puppet-boy into a real boy in Disney's classic *Pinocchio* (1940). The TV-movie *Special People* (1984) told the true-life story of a puppet troupe composed of mentally handicapped young people. Master mime Marcel Marceau played a puppeteer who could revive the dead in the disturbing 1974 fantasy *Shanks*. Murderous puppeteers have appeared in *The Falcon Strikes Back* (1943) and *Bluebeard* (1944). A crazy scientist reduced humans to puppet size in schlockmeister Bert I. Gordon's *Attack of the Puppet People* (1958). See also **The Muppets; Puppet Master.**

Monkey Business (1931)
Holiday (1938)
Pinocchio (1940)
The Falcon Strikes Back (1943)
Bluebeard (1944)
The Forbidden Street (aka *Britannia Mews*) (1948)
Lilli (1953)
tom thumb (1958)
A Midsummer Night's Dream (1958)
Attack of the Puppet People (1958)

The Sound of Music (1965)
Willy McBean and His Magic Machine (1965)
Thunderbirds Are Go (1966)
Mad Monster Party? (1967)
Thunderbird 6 (1968)
Shanks (1974)
Side Show (1981 TVM)
The Dark Crystal (1983)
Special People (1984 TVM)
Puppet Master (1988)

Quatermass, Professor Bernard

The intrepid, brilliant, sometimes eccentric scientist Bernard Quatermass made his initial appearance on TV in Nigel Kneale's 1954 three-hour BBC serial *The Quatermass Experiment*. The program, about an astronaut who returns to Earth and evolves into a "vegetable monster," was phenomenally successful. A bigscreen version was naturally in order and it came in 1955, courtesy of a struggling studio called Hammer Films. Hammer promptly replaced Reginald Tate, TV's Quatermass, with American Brian Donlevy—the biggest star it could afford—and dubbed the film *The Creeping Unknown* for its American showings. Despite Donlevy's lackluster performance, the movie was a hit, and the sequel *Enemy From Space* (aka *Quatermass II*) was released in 1957. It was also based on a Kneale TV serial and Donlevy again ousted the small-screen lead (John Robinson). A ten-year hiatus followed, then Hammer revived the series in grand fashion with

1967's *Five Million Years to Earth* (aka *Quatermass and the Pit*). A unique blend of science fiction and gothic horror, it boasted a fine lead performance by Scottish actor Andrew Keir and an ingenious premise ("As far as anybody is," concludes a Quatermass emphatically, "we're the Martians."). Quatermass's next and final appearance was in the 1979 serial *Quatermass*. Distinguished actor John Mills took his turn as Quatermass, whose demise at the end of the film signaled an end to the series. This 200-minute TV miniseries was trimmed to 107 minutes and given a limited theatrical release as *The Quatermass Conclusion*.

> *The Creeping Unknown* (aka *The Quatermass Experiment*; *The Quatermass Xperiment*) (1955)
> *Enemy From Space* (aka *Quatermass II*) (1957)
> *Five Million Years to Earth* (aka *Quatermass and the Pit*) (1967)
> *The Quatermass Conclusion* (aka *Quatermass*) (1979)

Queen, Ellery

A unique literary creation, Ellery Queen is famous as both a fictional detective and a best-selling "author" (as a pseudonym for cousins Frederic Dannay and Manfred B. Lee). His film career, however, has been an unequivocal disaster. Donald Cook made an uninspired Queen in 1935's *The Spanish Cape Mystery*. A year later, he was followed by comedian Eddie Quillan in *The Mandarin Mystery*. Columbia launched an official series in 1940 by casting Ralph Bellamy as *Ellery Queen, Master Detective*. Charley Grapewin played Ellery's police inspector father, Richard Queen. These movies relied heavily on comic relief, and Bellamy's clumsy detective resembled the literary Queen in name only. After four mysteries, sturdy William Gargan replaced Bellamy for three additional films. In the 1950s, four actors played Queen on television. Richard Hart was Ellery in 1950's *The Adventures of Ellery Queen*. He died in 1951 and was replaced by Lee Bowman until the series was cancelled in 1952. In 1954, Hugh Marlowe starred in a syndicated TV series also titled *The Adventures of Ellery Queen* (aka *Mystery Is My Business*). George Nader popped up as Queen in a 1958-59 series called *The Further Adventures of Ellery Queen* (aka *Ellery Queen*). Peter Lawford made the screen's worst Queen in the 1971 TV-movie *Ellery Queen: Don't Look Behind You*, while Jim Hutton and David Wayne played Ellery and Inspector Queen, respectively, in another made-for-TV mystery, 1975's *Ellery Queen* (aka *Too Many Suspects*). Hutton's film evolved into an entertaining weekly series that lasted a year. Queen's story "Ten Days Wonder" (which did not feature Queen the detective) was made into a 1972 film starring Orson Welles and Anthony Perkins.

> *The Spanish Cape Mystery* (1935) (Donald Cook)
> *The Mandarin Mystery* (1936) (Eddie Quillan)
> *Ellery Queen, Master Detective* (1940) (Ralph Bellamy)
> *Ellery Queen and the Murder Ring* (1941) (Bellamy)
> *Ellery Queen and the Perfect Crime* (1941) (Bellamy)
> *Ellery Queen's Penthouse Mystery* (1941) (Bellamy)
> *A Close Call for Ellery Queen* (1942) (William Gargan)
> *Enemy Agents Meet Ellery Queen* (1942) (Gargan)
> *A Desperate Chance for Ellery Queen* (1942) (Gargan)
> *Ellery Queen: Don't Look Behind You* (1971 TVM) (Peter Lawford)

Ellery Queen (aka *Too Many Suspects*) (1975 TVM) (Jim Hutton)

Rabbits

Despite their ability to reproduce in massive numbers, bunnies have been pretty scarce in the cinema. The Disney children's classic *Bambi* made a star out of Thumper the rabbit. Another animated feature, 1978's *Watership Down*, offered a literary fable about a warren of rabbits seeking a new home. Bugs Bunny, the cinema's only Oscar-winning rabbit, has a few theatrical cartoon compilations (q.v.) to his name. And, naturally, one must not forget James Stewart's six-foot, invisible rabbit chum in *Harvey*. A 1965 spy spoof called *The Nasty Rabbit* featured the unforgettable song "The Jackrabbit Shuffle." The picture's plot revolved around virus-carrying rabbits. Still, they were bunnies without malice, unlike the nasty ones—standing four feet tall and weighing 150 pounds—that terrorized Janet Leigh in 1972's *Night of the Lepus* (surely a movie she'd like to forget). In *The Lemon Sisters* (1990), Elliott Gould created "taffits"—taffy rabbits—but found few buyers. *Rabbit Run, The Rabbit Trap, Bunny Lake is Missing* and *Bunny O'Hare* were rabbit films in name only. Ditto for *A Bunny's Tale*, which was about Gloria Steinem's undercover stint as a *Playboy* bunny.

Alice in Wonderland (1933)
The Rules of the Game (1939)
Bambi (1942)
Song of the South (with Brer Rabbit) (1946)
Harvey (1950)
Alice in Wonderland (1951)
The Nasty Rabbit (aka *Spies a Go Go*) (1965)
Get to Know Your Rabbit (1972)
Night of the Lepus (1972)

Monty Python and the Holy Grail (1975)
Bugs Bunny, Superstar (1975)
Watership Down (1978)
The Bugs Bunny/Roadrunner Movie (1979)
The Adventures of the American Rabbit (1986)
Jean de Florette (1986)
Who Framed Roger Rabbit? (1988)

Racing, *see* Auto Racing; Horse Racing

Radio

During the Great Depression, movies ranked as the second most popular form of entertainment—with radio firmly entrenched in the number one position. Surprisingly, the film industry promoted its rival, with dozens of films set behind the scenes of radio programs. Many of these films were built around the era's big radio singing stars, such as Dick Powell in *Twenty Million Sweethearts* (1934) and Bing Crosby in the series-inspiring *The Big Broadcast* (1932). On the dramatic side, *Two Against the World* (1936) starred Humphrey Bogart as a moralistic radio station manager. Mystery radio shows provided the background for real murders in the Abbott and Costello comedy *Who Done It?* (1942) and the Claude Rains vehicle *The Unsuspected* (1947). Few films have been principally about radio stations. Paul Newman played a drifter-turned-d.j. who gains fame broadcasting on the right-wing radio station *WUSA* (1970). A rock station's management rebelled against its uptight parent company in the 1978 satire *FM*, which laid the groundwork for the broader 1978-82 TV sitcom *WKRP in Cincinnati*. Disc jockeys have appeared as principal characters in the guise of Clint Eastwood (*Play Misty for Me*), Adrienne Barbeau (*The Fog*), Wolfman Jack (*American Graffiti*), Bill Paterson (*Comfort and Joy*), Robin Williams (*Good Morning, Vietnam*), and Tim McIntire (*American Hot Wax*). The latter two movies chronicled the lives of real-life d.j.'s Adrian Cronauer and rock 'n' roll legend Alan Freed. Oliver Stone's *Talk Radio* (1988) was practically a one-man show about a controversial radio talk show host, but it was not the first film on the subject. Call-in radio programs were integral to the plots of Jack Nicholson's *The King of Marvin Gardens* (1972) and George Romero's vampire chiller *Martin* (1978). Of course, not all radio broadcasts have originated from Earth. *Orpheus* (1949) and *Christine* (1983) both featured cars equipped with radios that picked up otherworldly signals. Celestial broadcasts were the subject of *Red Planet Mars* (1952) and *The Next Voice You Hear* (1950), which costarred Nancy Davis Reagan. Both these films conveyed optimistic religious messages, although their heavy-handed approach limited their showings. Radio's subtler influence on its listening audience was explored in *Music Hath Charms* (1935) and Woody Allen's *Radio Days* (1987). The former film showed how a dance band's music played different roles in the lives of those listening to it. In contrast, radio's ability to incite hysteria was powerfully displayed in 1975's *The Night That Panicked America*, a fact-based drama about Orson Welles's 1938 "War of the Worlds" broadcast.

The Big Broadcast (1932)
Death at Broadcasting House (1934)
Music Hath Charms (1935)
Two Against the World (aka *One Fatal Hour*; *The Case of Mrs. Pembroke*) (1936)
Love Is on the Air (1937)
The Great American Broadcast (1940)
Wake Up and Live (1942)
Who Done It? (1942)
I'll Tell the World (1945)
The Falcon's Alibi (1946)
Where There's Life (1947)
The Unsuspected (1947)
Orpheus (1949)
The Next Voice You Hear (1950)
Red Planet Mars (1952)
WUSA (1970)
Play Misty for Me (1971)

The King of Marvin Gardens (1972)
The Night That Panicked America (1975 TVM)
American Hot Wax (1978)
FM (1978)
Martin (1978)
On the Air Live With Captain Midnight (aka *Captain Midnight*) (1979)
Radio On (1979)
The Fog (1980)
Christine (1983)
Comfort and Joy (1984)
Radio Days (1987)
Good Morning, Vietnam (1987)
Talk Radio (1988)
Pump Up the Volume (1990)
Straight Talk (1992)

Rambo

Rambo named after a poet? University of Iowa professor David Morrell, who created one-man army John Rambo in his novel *First Blood*, claims that he derived his hero's name from nineteenth century symbolist poet Arthur Rimbaud. But when Morrell sold the film rights to his book for $90,000, it's doubtful if he envisioned bare-chested, muscle-rippling Sylvester Stallone as his character. Stallone, though, was anxious to break away from his *Rocky* image when he was offered the chance to do *First Blood*. The 1982 film introduced Rambo as a misunderstood drifter, a former Green Beret, who runs afoul of a redneck sheriff in a small town. Despite substituting explosions for punches, Rambo and Rocky are very much alike—two underdogs fighting apparently insurmountable odds to make a point. The picture proved to be Stallone's first non-*Rocky* hit. His 1985 sequel, *Rambo: First Blood Part II*, sent its hunky hero into Cambodia in search of POWs. Stallone brilliantly capitalized on a new wave of patriotism, and the sequel's grosses went through the roof. Again, the actor portrayed Rambo as a soldier betrayed at every turn and yet still patriotic to his country. That tone changed with 1988's *Rambo III*, which paired Rambo with his trusty ex-commander (Richard Crenna) and made him less of a loner fighting the establishment. The public noticed the difference. It made a lot of quick cash, but failed to follow the highly profitable path of its predecessors.

    First Blood (1982)   *Rambo III* (1988)
    Rambo: First Blood Part II (1985)

The Range Busters

Monogram Pictures launched this low-budget western series in an effort to duplicate rival Republic's successful *Three Mesquiteers* (q.v.) films. John "Dusty" King joined former Mesquiteers Ray "Crash" Corrigan and Max Terhune to form Monogram's cowboy trio. Their adventures followed the Mesquiteers closely, even to the point of mixing Old West stories with contemporary adventures (e.g., the boys clashed with Nazis in 1943's *Cowboy Commandos* and the Japanese in *Texas to Bataan*). A more interesting series might have focused on the stars' varied backgrounds: Corrigan was a stunt daredevil, Terhune a former ventriloquist, and King a band vocalist.

The Range Busters (1940)	*Thunder River Feud* (1942)
Trailing Double Trouble (1940)	*Boot Hill Bandits* (1942)
West of Pinto Basin (1940)	*Texas Trouble Shooters* (1942)
Trail of the Silver Spurs (1941)	*Texas to Bataan* (1942)
The Kid's Last Ride (1941)	*Trail Riders* (1942)
Tumbledown Ranch in Arizona (1941)	*Two Fisted Justice* (1943)
Wrangler's Roost (1941)	*The Haunted Ranch* (1943)
Fugitive Valley (1941)	*Land of Hunted Men* (1943)
Saddle Mountain Roundup (1941)	*Cowboy Commandos* (1943)
Tonto Basin Outlaws (1941)	*Black Market Business* (1943)
Underground Rustlers (1941)	*Bullets and Saddles* (1943)

Rats, *see* Rodents

Reincarnation

The definitive film on this intriguing subject has yet to be made. In the past, reincarnation has been chiefly employed in comedies and low-budget efforts that emphasized its sensationalistic values. The first of these latter films was 1956's *The Search for Bridey Murphy*, an adaptation of Morey Bernstein's allegedly fact-based best-seller about a housewife who reveals under hypnosis that she led another life two hundred years earlier. This dreary, uninvolving tale captured the public's fancy and imitations followed in rapid succession. *Spell of the Hypnotist* (1956), Roger Corman's *The Undead* (1957) and the Bowery Boys' *Hold That Hypnotist* (1957) all concerned people who learned of previous existences through hypnotism. Corman's movie, shot in a refurbished supermarket, was the best of the bunch, mixing witch trials and time travel elements with its reincarnation plot. Hypnotism also played a prominent role in the only reincarnation musical comedy, Barbra Streisand's *On a Clear Day You Can See Forever*. Men were reincarnated as women in *Goodbye, Charlie* (1964), *Cleo/Leo* (1989) and *Switch* (1991). Finally, no discussion on celebrity reincarnation would be complete without mentioning Shirley MacLaine, who espoused her beliefs in *Out on a Limb* (1987), a TV-movie based on her autobiographical best-seller. In *Defending Your Life* (1991), Shirley introduced people to their past lives at the heavenly Past Lives Pavilion. See also **The Mummy**.

She (1935)	*Audrey Rose* (1977)
Corridor of Mirrors (1948)	*Oh, Heavenly Dog!* (1980)
You Never Can Tell (1951)	*All of Me* (1984)
The Search for Bridey Murphy (1956)	*Deja Vu* (1985)
Spell of the Hypnotist (aka *Fright*) (1956)	*Out on a Limb* (1987 TVM)
	Chances Are (1989)
I've Lived Before (1956)	*Manika: The Girl Who Lived Twice* (1989)
Hold That Hypnotist (1957)	
The She Creature (1957)	*Cleo/Leo* (1989)
The Undead (1957)	*Identity Crisis* (1990)
Goodbye, Charlie (1964)	*Switch* (1991)
She (1965)	*Defending Your Life* (1991)
On a Clear Day You Can See Forever (1970)	*Hi Honey, I'm Dead* (1991 TVM)
The Reincarnation of Peter Proud (1975)	

Remakes of Foreign Films

The problems inherent in remaking foreign films into English-language pictures have both intrigued and frustrated filmmakers. No rule of thumb has met with steady success. John Sturges translated Akiro Kurosawa's classic *The Seven Samurai* (1954) into the enduringly popular American Western *The Magnificent Seven* (1960). Likewise, Italian "spaghetti-Western" king Sergio Leone also exploited the samurai/Western link and turned Kurosawa's *Yojimbo* (1961) into Clint Eastwood's breakthrough film, *A Fistful of Dollars* (1964). But Martin Ritt's *The Outrage* (1964), a philosophical Western remake of Kurosawa's *Rashomon* (1951), missed the tone of the Japanese original and bored audiences and critics equally. Although Kurosawa's films have been popular targets for remakes, American and British filmmakers have shown a special fondness for the French cinema. Julien Duvivier's *Pépé Le Moko* (1937) was remade as *Algiers* just a year after its release. The remake incorporated the same setting and plot and even cast a Frenchman in the lead—Charles Boyer as the charming gangster originally created by Jean Gabin. French thrillers from the 1940s and 1950s have been turned into little films (*Midnight Episode*) and costly bombs (*Sorcerer*). The popularity of French light comedies in the 1970s and 1980s inspired a slew of Americanized versions. Most of these state-side remakes compared poorly with their continental counterparts and fizzled at the box office. Big name stars did not help either. Walter Matthau and Jack Lemmon looked out of place in *Buddy, Buddy* (1981), while Richard Pryor floundered in *The Toy* (1982). However, the surprise successes of 1986's *Down and Out in Beverly Hills*, 1987's *Three Men and a Baby* and, to a lesser degree, 1989's *Cousins*, have ensured that the French cinema will continue to be raided for remake properties. Occasionally, the original director has even helmed the English-language version, as did Francis Veber (*Les Fugitifs*; *Three Fugitives*), Roger Vadim (*And God Created Woman*) and George Sluizer (*The Vanishing*). Interestingly, not all remakes have gone the direct route of foreign film into English-language film. Bergman's *Smiles of a Summer Night* (1955) and Fellini's *Nights of Cabiria* (1957) stopped at Broadway long enough to be transformed into the hit musicals *A Little Night Music* and *Sweet Charity*. Thus, the film versions of these musicals are indirect remakes of the original movies. Along similar lines, one could argue that Fritz Lang's *Human Desire* (1954) was based solely on Emile Zola's novel *La Bête Humaine* and not on Jean Renoir's 1938 adaptation of Zola's book. Occasionally, this question of whether a film is or is not a remake becomes a matter of opinion. Many critics consider Curtis Harrington's *Games* (1967) a remake of Clouzot's *Les Diaboliques*, although the films differ substantially in setting and premise (perhaps it's more a variation than a remake). Likewise, Claude Lelouch's *Another Man, Another Chance* (1977) is often listed as a Western remake of his own contemporary romance *A Man and a Woman* (1966) since the plots of both films are about a widow and widower falling in love. That's a pretty common plot, allowing one to argue that 1968's *With Six You Get Eggroll* was an earlier remake of Lelouch's original. Occasionally, foreign countries have remade American films, as in the case of 1957's *The Burglar* and 1971's *La Casse* (aka *The Burglars*). In the following list, the remakes are listed chronologically on the left with the original films shown on the right.

Port of Seven Seas (1938)	*Fanny* (1932)
Algiers (1938)	*Pépé Le Moko* (1937)
A Woman's Face (1941)	*En Kvinnas Ansikte* (1938)
Scarlet Street (1945)	*La Chienne* (1931)
The Unfinished Dance (1947)	*Ballerina* (1938)
The Long Night (1947)	*Le Jour se Leve* (aka *Daybreak*) (1939)
Midnight Episode (1951)	*Monsieur le Souris* (aka *Midnight in Paris*) (1947)
The Thirteenth Letter (1951)	*Le Corbeau* (aka *The Raven*) (1948)
Human Desire (1954)	*La Bête Humaine* (aka *The Human Beast*; *Judas Was a Woman*) (1938)
The Magnificent Seven (1960)	*The Seven Samurai* (aka *Shichinin no Samurai*) (1954)
The Outrage (1964)	*Rashomon* (1951)
A Fistful of Dollars (1964)	*Yojimbo* (1961)
Games (1967)	*Les Diaboliques* (aka *Diabolique*) (1955)
Cop-Out (1968)	*Les Inconnus dans la Maison* (aka *Strangers in the House*) (1949)

Sweet Charity (1969)

Another Man, Another Chance (1977)

Sorcerer (1977)

Which Way Is Up? (1977)

A Little Night Music (1978)

Dear Detective (1979 TVM)

Willie and Phil (1980)

Buddy, Buddy (1981)

Kiss Me Goodbye (1982)

The Toy (1982)

Breathless (1983)

The Lost Honor of Kathryn Beck (aka Act of Passion) (1984 TVM)

Crackers (1984)

The Woman in Red (1984)

Blame It on Rio (1984)

The Man With One Red Shoe (1985)

Down and Out in Beverly Hills (1986)

Happy New Year (1987)

Three Men and a Baby (1987)

Dangerous Liaisons (1988)

And God Created Woman (1988)

Three Fugitives (1989)

Cousins (1989)

Baby Cakes (1989 TVM)

Men Don't Leave (1990)

Nights of Cabiria (aka Le Notti di Cabiria) (1957)

A Man and a Woman (aka Un Homme et une Femme) (1966)

The Wages of Fear (aka La Salaire de la Peur) (1953)

The Seduction of Mimi (aka Mimi Metallurgico Ferito nell'Onore) (1974)

Smiles of a Summer Night (aka Sommarnattens Leende) (1955)

Dear Detective (aka Tendre Poulet; Dear Inspector) (1978)

Jules and Jim (aka Jules et Jim) (1961)

A Pain in the A-- (aka L'Emmerdeur) (1974)

Dona Flor and Her Two Husbands (aka Dona Flor e Seurs Dois Maridos) (1977)

Le Jouet (1976)

À Bout de Souffle (aka Breathless) (1960)

The Lost Honor of Katharina Blum (aka Die Verlorene Ehre der Katharina Blum) (1975)

Big Deal on Madonna Street (aka I Soliti Ignoti) (1958)

Pardon Mon Affaire (aka Un Elephant ça Troupe Enormement) (1976)

One Wild Moment (aka Un Moment D' Egarement) (1977)

The Tall Blond Man With One Black Shoe (aka Le Grand Blond Avec Une Chaussure Noire) (1972)

Boudu Saved From Drowning (aka Boudu Sauvé des Eaux) (1932)

Happy New Year (aka La Nonne Anné; The Happy New Year Caper) (1973)

Three Men and a Cradle (aka Trois Hommes et un Couffin) (1985)

Les Liaisons Dangereuses (aka Dangerous Meetings) (1959)

Et Dieu . . . Créa La Femme (aka And God Created Woman) (1957)

Les Fugitifs (1986)

Cousin, Cousine (1975)

Zuckerbaby (aka Sugarbaby) (1985)

Continue (Life Goes On) (1981)

Paradise (1991)

Pure Luck (1991)

Scent of a Woman (1992)

Sommersby (1993)

The Vanishing (1993)

Point of No Return (1993)

The Big Road (aka *Le Grand Chemin*; *The Grand Highway*) (1987)

Le Chevre (aka *The Goat*) (1981)

Profumo di Donna (1974)

The Return of Martin Guerre (aka *Le Retour de Martin Guerre*) (1982)

The Vanishing (aka *Spoorloos*) (1988)

La Femme Nikita (aka *Nikita*) (1991)

Renfrew of the Royal Mounted

Renfrew the singing Mountie had already appeared in Laurie York Erskine's books and on the radio before Monogram gave him his own film series. James Newill, a singer on the Burns and Allen radio show, played Sergeant Renfrew and always found time to sing a sturdy tune or two like "Mounted Men." Lightning the Dog accompanied him on his first trek, but Dave O'Brien became Renfrew's regular sidekick Kelly beginning with 1939's *Crashing Thru*. The plots were naturally action-oriented and somewhat lacking in plausibility (in *Sky Bandits*, the bad guys hijacked a plane carrying an experimental death ray). Newill later became one of the *Texas Rangers* (q.v.), creating the role that Tex Ritter would later play. See also **Mounties**.

Renfrew of the Royal Mounted (1937)

On the Great White Trail (aka *Renfrew of the Royal Mounted on the Great White Trail*; *Renfrew on the Great White Trail*) (1938)

Crashing Thru (1939)

Fighting Mad (1939)

Danger Ahead (1940)

Yukon Flight (1940)

Murder on the Yukon (1940)

The Sky Bandits (1940)

Revenge of the Nerds

In a clever bit of role reversal, the *Nerd* films portrayed nerdism as cool and yuppiedom as bogus. Unfortunately, most of the series' good ideas can be found in the first film, a likable 1984 comedy about a nerd fraternity formed by friends Lewis (Robert Carradine), Gilbert (Anthony Edwards) and Booger (Curtis Armstrong). The 1987 sequel followed Lewis and Booger to Fort Lauderdale for some bland hijinks at a United Fraternity Conference. Edwards appeared briefly as Gilbert. A belated third installment, the made-for-TV *Revenge of the Nerds III: The Next Generation* (1992), squandered a promising premise. Set several years later, it revealed that Lewis had become . . . a yuppie, right down to the BMW with the LEWSTER license plate. Fortunately, he reverted to his old self when his nerdish nephew Harold encountered yuppie trouble at Adams College. Carradine and Armstrong reprised their roles as Lewis and Booger.

Revenge of the Nerds (1984)

Revenge of the Nerds II: Nerds in Paradise (1987)

Revenge of the Nerds III: The Next Generation (1992 TVM)

Revere, Johnny

John Paul (Johnny) Revere was another sturdy Western hero in the typical Republic Pictures mold. Eddie Dew played him in the first two films, getting comic support from Gene Autry's usual sidekick Smiley Burnette. Robert Mitchum played a bit part in 1943's *Beyond the Last Frontier*, but Dew's second entry, *Raiders of Sunset Pass*, was much more interesting. A sort of feminist Western, it pitted a group of tough ladies (dubbed the Women's Army of the Plains, or WAPs) against some male rustlers during World War II. Western series veteran Bob Livingston (see **The Three Mesquiteers**) replaced Dew in the final two entries.

> *Beyond the Last Frontier* (1943)   *Pride of the Plains* (1944)
> *Raiders of Sunset Pass* (1943)   *Beneath Western Skies* (1944)

Riley, Dexter

Kurt Russell played this energetic, quick-thinking college student in a trilogy of Disney comedies produced in the 1970s. In each film, the easygoing Dexter acquired some superhuman trait while enjoying campus life at Medfield College. An electrical accident gave him super intelligence in *The Computer Wore Tennis Shoes*. He accidentally discovered an invisibility potion in *Now You See Him, Now You Don't*. A lab experiment gave him incredible strength in *The Strongest Man in the World*. Other series regulars included: Joe Flynn as Dexter's nemesis Dean Higgins; Cesar Romero as gangster A.J. Arno (who wanted to steal the inventions); and William Schallert as nice Professor Quigley. Interestingly, Dexter bore a strong resemblance to an earlier Disney campus hero, Merlin Jones (Tommy Kirk), who appeared in *The Misadventures of Merlin Jones* (1964) and *The Monkey's Uncle* (1965).

> *The Computer Wore Tennis Shoes* (1969)
> *Now You See Him, Now You Don't* (1972)
> *The Strongest Man in the World* (1975)

Riley, Old Mother

Donning a gray wig, a frumpy dress, and a plaid-colored shaw, British comedian Arthur Lucan transformed himself into Old Mother Riley, a spunky Irish washerwoman, in fifteen features between 1937 and 1952. Katie MacShane, Lucan's wife, played Old Mother Riley's daughter. The two had created the characters in a vaudeville sketch called "Bridget's Night Out." Despite their popularity in Britain, the movies never caught on in the United States, although 1952's *My Son, the Vampire* (aka *Old Mother Riley Meets the Vampire*) finally showed up on American screens in 1963. By then, Lucan had been dead for nine years and costar Bela Lugosi for seven.

> *Old Mother Riley* (aka *The Original*
>   *Old Mother Riley*; *The Return of*
>   *Old Mother Riley*) (1937)
> *Old Mother Riley in Paris* (1938)
> *Old Mother Riley Joins Up* (1939)
> *Old Mother Riley MP* (1939)
> *Old Mother Riley in Business* (1940)
> *Old Mother Riley's Ghosts* (1940)
> *Old Mother Riley's Circus* (1941)
> *Old Mother Riley in Society* (1942)
> *Old Mother Riley Detective* (1943)
>
> *Old Mother Riley Overseas* (1943)
> *Old Mother Riley at Home* (1944)
> *Old Mother Riley Headmistress* (1945)
> *Old Mother Riley's New Venture* (aka
>   *Old Mother Riley's New Look*)
>   (1947)
> *Old Mother Riley's Jungle Treasure*
>   (aka *Jungle Treasure*) (1949)
> *My Son, the Vampire* (aka *Old Mother*
>   *Riley Meets the Vampire*; *Vampires*
>   *Over London*) (1952)

Road Movies

The Road to Singapore was originally written for George Burns and Gracie Allen. When they turned it down, it was revamped as a "buddy comedy" for Fred Mac-Murray and Jack Oakie. But prior commitments kept MacMurray and Oakie tied up, so Paramount—in a stroke of casting magic—paired Bing Crosby and Bob Hope for their musical comedy debut. Their initial *Road* picture (*Singapore*) was a huge success, but when seen today, it clearly lacks the wacky humor that made the series memorable. Everyone has his or her favorite *Road* picture, but it's hard to top the bizarre Alaskan outing, *Road to Utopia*, which featured animated fish, the Paramount mountain, and the only ending in which Bob got the girl (well, sort of). Dorothy Lamour costarred in all but *Hong Kong*, in which she made only a cameo appearance, leaving the female lead to a young Joan Collins.

Road to Singapore (1940)	*Road to Rio* (1947)
Road to Zanibar (1941)	*Road to Bali* (1952)
Road to Morocco (1942)	*Road to Hong Kong* (1962)
Road to Utopia (1945)	

Robin Hood, *see* Hood, Robin

Robots

For purposes of categorization, robots are defined as machines that require guidance to function *and* that look distinctively different from humans. Humanlike machines capable of independent thought are discussed under the **Androids and Cyborgs** entry. Although it is a difficult distinction to draw, there are obvious differences between *Forbidden Planet*'s Robbie the Robot and the androids played by Rutger Hauer and Daryl Hannah in *Blade Runner*. The robot's origin in film can be traced back to early silent films like *The Electric Servant* (1909). Yet, while the Golem thrived in the early 1920s and the Frankenstein Monster ruled in the 1930s, robots were restricted to sporadic appearances in serials such as *The Phantom Empire* and *The Undersea Kingdom*. The robot's relative anonymity finally ended with 1951's *The Day the Earth Stood Still*. This superior science fiction saga worked on many levels, but remains fondly remembered for introducing the first robot "star": Gort. Standing twelve-feet tall with no facial features nor visible joints, Gort was a rather imposing "mechanical man," especially when he opened his visor and unleashed his disintegration ray on a helpless tank. Gort could not talk, however, and that certainly placed some constraints on his personality. MGM corrected that quirk with its contribution to the robotic race, the ever-helpful—and talking—Robby the Robot. After his popular debut in 1956's *Forbidden Planet*, Robby turned up again in a larger role in *The Invisible Boy* (1957), in which a computer temporarily converted him to evil. Except for guest appearances, Robby retired after *The Invisible Boy*, although a robot bearing an amazing resemblance to him later joined the cast of TV's 1965-68 *Lost in Space* series. No other robotic stars emerged until 1977, when George Lucas's *Star Wars* introduced that charismatic robotic pair: C3PO and R2D2. Their skyrocketing popularity, especially among the younger set, revitalized interest in robots and accounted for their major supporting roles in films such as *The Black Hole* and *Buck Rogers in the 25th Century* (both 1979). In other robot films of interest: The robot "drones" Huey and Dewey in 1971's *Silent Running* appear to be the forerunners to R2D2's design. Lightning struck a meek little robot, No. 5, and brought him "alive" in *Short Circuit* (1986). Both King Kong (q.v.) and Godzilla (q.v.) fought robot versions of themselves in, respectively, *King Kong Escapes* (1968) and *Terror of Godzilla* (1975). *Tobor, the Great* (1954) had the catchiest robot name (spell it backwards). See also **Androids and Cyborgs; Computers.**

The Electric Servant (1909)	*Buck Rogers in the 25th Century*
The Day the Earth Stood Still (1951)	(1979)
Robot Monster (1953)	*The Black Hole* (1979)
Gog (1954)	*C.H.O.M.P.S.* (1979)
Target Earth (1954)	*Runaway* (1984)
Tobor, the Great (1954)	*Chopping Mall* (1986)
Forbidden Planet (1956)	*Short Circuit* (1986)
The Invisible Boy (1957)	*Space Camp* (1986)
Attack of the Robots (1962)	*Robot Holocaust* (1987)
King Kong Escapes (1968)	*Too Much* (1987)
Silent Running (1971)	*Short Circuit 2* (1988)
Terror of Godzilla (1975)	*Robot Jox* (1990)
Star Wars (1977)	*Steel Justice* (1992 TVM)

Rocky

In 1976, an unknown character actor named Sylvester Stallone wrote a script (in three-and-half days, reputedly) about a mediocre, small-time boxer who gets a shot at the world championship. Producers Irwin Winkler and Robert Chartoff offered Stallone $300,000 for the screenplay, but the actor held out for $75,000, a percentage of the profits, and the lead role. He got what he wanted—and the rest is history. A simple picture, *Rocky* boasted a memorable cast: Talia Shire as Rocky's shy girlfriend; Burt Young as her obnoxious, hustling brother; Burgess Meredith as Rocky's grizzled manager; and Carl Weathers as cocky heavyweight champion Apollo Creed. Rocky lost the title bout (in a split decision), but audiences loved the film's old-fashioned emotion. It went on to gross $55 million and won an Academy Award for Best Picture. Subsequently, Stallone tried his hand at other movies, but none approached the success of *Rocky*. Thus, the inevitable sequel, *Rocky II*, appeared in 1979. A rehash of the original, it had Rocky winning a rematch with Creed and almost losing his wife due to medical complications. Although it was a box office smash, Stallone vowed it would be the last Rocky picture. Nevertheless, no one was surprised when *Rocky III* was released in 1982. Probably the cleverest film in the series, it traced Rocky's decline as a champion, capped by a humiliating defeat at the hands of ruthless Clubber Lang (Mr. T) and the death of faithful manager Meredith. Encouraged by former opponent and newfound friend Apollo Creed, Rocky recaptured that "eye of the tiger" and beat Clubber into a pulp. Again, Stallone insisted this was the last of the series, but the box office receipts led him to a different decision. The dismal *Rocky IV* followed in 1985, with Rocky avenging Creed's death at the hands of a heartless Russian "fighting machine" (Dolph Lundgren). Critics panned it, but audiences made it another hit, thereby leaving the door open for *Rocky V* (1990). Even audiences avoided this fifth outing, in which a retired Rocky trained a young boxer. See also **Boxing**.

Rocky (1976)	*Rocky IV* (1985)
Rocky II (1979)	*Rocky V* (1990)
Rocky III (1982)	

Rodan

This pterodactyl-like creature with supersonic wing speed made an illustrious debut in 1956's *Rodan*. However, he never achieved the popularity of Godzilla (q.v.) or even Mothra (q.v.) and was quickly relegated to a supporting player in the mid-1960s Japanese "monsteramas." One of the reasons for Rodan's lesser fame might have been his weapon arsenal. While Godzilla boasted fiery breath and Mothra a cocoon-producing fluid, Rodan dispensed with foes (and buildings) by simply flapping his gigantic wings.

Rodan (1956)

Monster Zero (aka *Invasion of the Astro-Monsters*; *Kaiju Daisenso*) (1965)

Ghidrah the Three-Headed Monster (aka *The Greatest Battle on Earth*; *Sandai Kaiju Chikyu Saidai No Kessen*) (1965)

Destroy All Monsters (aka *Operation Monsterland*; *Kaiju Soshingeki*) (1968)

Rodents

Rats have had an image problem in the movies, typically being pictured as untrustworthy. There have been exceptions, of course, such as the lovable rat family in the animated feature *The Secret of NIMH* (1982). And technically, the people-killing rats in *Willard* (1971) and *Ben* (1972) did not dispose of anyone who didn't deserve it. In fact, *Ben* was basically a heartwarming story of the friendship between a boy and his rat (and, lest we forget, this film featured Michael Jackson's popular hit "Ben"). Giant rats have populated horror films such as *Food of the Gods* (1976) and *Deadly Eyes* (1982). Sondra Locke's *Ratboy* (1986) was a sympathetic film about a disfigured boy who resembled a rat, while the Russian import *The Redeemer* (1977) was about rat people disguising themselves in order to infiltrate the human race. Chuck Norris killed a rat with his teeth in *Missing in Action 2* (1985), while people tramped through rat-infested chambers in *Inferno* (1978) and *Indiana Jones and the Last Crusade* (1989). On the other hand, mice on film have been portrayed as cute, charming creatures, especially in animated form. Thoughtful mice helped *Cinderella* get ready for the ball in Disney's 1950 version of the fairy tale. Adventurous mice formed The Mouse Rescue Aid Society in *The Rescuers* (1977). A sleuthing mouse resembling Sherlock Holmes matched wits with a devious rat (Professor Ratigan) in 1986's *The Great Mouse Detective*. One of the biggest holiday hits of 1986, *An American Tail*, concerned the plight of two immigrant mice children in turn-of-the-century New York City. Finally, people were turned into mice in *Abbott and Costello Meet Dr. Jekyll and Mr. Hyde* (1953) and Roald Dahl's delightful children's fantasy *The Witches* (1990). See also **Teenage Mutant Ninja Turtles**.

Cinderella (1950)	*Lady and the Tramp* (1955)
Abbott and Costello Meet Dr. Jekyll and Mr. Hyde (1953)	*The Pied Piper of Hamlin* (1957 TVM)
	Willard (1971)

The Rats Are Coming, the Werewolves
    Are Here (1972)
Ben (1972)
The Pied Piper (1972)
The Missing Are Deadly (1974 TVM)
Food of the Gods (1976)
The Mouse and His Child (1977)
The Redeemer (1977)
The Rescuers (1977)
Inferno (1978)
Rock 'n' Roll High School (1979)
Deadly Eyes (aka The Rats) (1982)
The Secret of NIMH (1982)
Of Unknown Origin (1983)
Nightmares (1983)

Missing in Action 2: The Beginning
    (1985)
An American Tail (1986)
Ratboy (1986)
The Great Mouse Detective (aka The
    Adventures of the Great Mouse
    Detective) (1986)
Indiana Jones and the Last Crusade
    (1989)
Gnaw: Food of the Gods II (1989)
The Witches (1990)
Teenage Mutant Ninja Turtles (1990)
An American Tail: Fievel Goes West
    (1991)

Rodeos

Few filmmakers seemed interested in the rodeo setting prior to the 1970s. A handful of B-films, including the 3-D effort *Arena*, emerged in the 1950s. However, the rodeo gained more exposure through a bit part in 1956's *Bus Stop*, in which Don Murray played a naive rodeo star visiting the big city for the first time and struggling to understand urban conventions. Thirteen years later, *The Wild Bunch*, with its theme of the aging cowboy as a symbol of social change, revived interest in the contemporary cowboy. Subsequently, four features about aging rodeo stars appeared in 1972, all starring veteran performers well into their forties or older: Richard Widmark (age fifty-eight in *When the Legends Die*); Cliff Robertson (forty-seven in *J.W. Coop*); James Coburn (forty-four in *The Honkers*); and Steve McQueen (forty-two in *Junior Bonner*). The latter film was made by *Wild Bunch*-director Sam Peckinpah. The plight of the younger rodeo wrangler was explored in *Riding Tall*, yet another 1972 release. It starred Andrew Prine as a rodeo rider coping with conventional love problems. The 1980 TV-movie *Rodeo Girl* was the true story of world champion rodeo star Sue Pirtle. The 1974 documentary *The Great American Cowboy* told the story of rodeo legend Larry Mahan. Scott Glenn, who rode a mechanical bull in *Urban Cowboy* (1981), encountered a mean rodeo bull named Thunderbolt in *My Heroes Have Always Been Cowboys* (1991).

The Cowboy and the Lady (1938)
A Lady Takes a Chance (aka The
    Cowboy and the Girl) (1943)
Rodeo (1952)
The Lusty Men (1952)
Bronco Buster (1952)
Arena (1953)
Bus Stop (aka The Wrong Kind of Girl)
    (1956)
Born Reckless (1959)
Stay Away Joe (1968)
Black Rodeo (1971)

The Honkers (1972)
Junior Bonner (1972)
J.W. Coop (1972)
When the Legends Die (1972)
Riding Tall (aka Squares) (1972)
Cotter (1973)
The Great American Cowboy (1974)
Goldenrod (1977 TVM)
Rodeo Girl (1980 TVM)
My Heroes Have Always Been Cowboys
    (1991)

Rohmer's Comedies and Proverbs

Eric Rohmer initiated this new series in 1980 after completing his "Six Moral Tales" (q.v.) and two nonseries excursions, *The Marquise of O* and *Perceval*. Although less thematically linked than the "Moral Tales," Rohmer's "Comedies and Proverbs" extended the filmmaker's views on love, loneliness and irony. In *The Aviator's Wife* (1980), a man pining for the title character forgot her after falling for an attractive student — whom he later discovered in the arms of another man as well. In *The Perfect Marriage* (1982), a woman tried to persuade a man that she would make the perfect wife and he would make the perfect husband, only to find out the man had been engaged to another all along. As with his "Moral Tales" series, critics ignored the early entries and heaped praise on later ones, such as the international hit *Pauline at the Beach* (1982), *Boyfriends and Girlfriends* (1988) and *Summer* (1986). The original title of the latter film, *Le Rayon Vert*, actually translates as *The Green Ray*, referring to a "flash of green" seen in rare sunsets in southern climates. Keeping with the series' theme, it opened with a proverb from Rimbaud: "Ah, let the season start/ When fancy takes the heart." See also **Rohmer's Moral Tales**.

The Aviator's Wife (aka *La Femme de l'Aviateur*) (1980)
The Perfect Marriage (aka *Le Beau Marriage*) (1982)
Pauline at the Beach (aka *Pauline à la Plage*) (1982)
Full Moon in Paris (aka *Les Nuits de la Pleine Lune*) (1984)
Summer (aka *Le Rayon Vert*; *The Green Ray*) (1986)
Boyfriends and Girlfriends (aka *L'Ami de Mon Amie*; *My Girlfriend's Boyfriend*) (1988)

Rohmer's Moral Tales

Eric Rohmer was best known as a writer and editor for the prestigious cinema journal *Cahiers du Cinéma* when he set out to make a series of films linked by a common theme. His initial effort, the 1962 short *La Boulangère de Monceau*, established the premise for what would eventually comprise a six-film series. A young man about to commit to one woman meets a second woman who causes him to question his original choice. Rohmer expanded on that premise in 1963's hour-long *Suzanne's Profession*, but the series attracted little attention until his fourth entry, 1969's *My Night at Maud's*, garnered international raves. Rohmer completed his "Six Moral Tales" in 1972 with *Chloe in the Afternoon*. In the 1980s, he embarked on his "Comedies and Proverbs" (also referred to as "Parables") series. See also **Rohmer's Comedies and Proverbs**.

La Boulangère de Monceau (1962)
Suzanne's Profession (aka *La Carriere de Suzanne*) (1963)
La Collectioneuse (1967)
My Night at Maud's (aka *Ma Nuit chez Maud*) (1969)
Claire's Knee (aka *Le Genou de Claire*) (1970)
Chloe in the Afternoon (aka *L'Amour, l'après-midi*; *Love in the Afternoon*) (1972)

Roller Skating/Skateboards

On the silver screen, roller skating has never enjoyed the popularity of ice skating, although trendy filmmakers have tried to capitalize on both roller derby and roller disco fads. At the height of the roller derby craze in the early 1970s, Raquel Welch donned knee pads and a helmet for her rough-and-tumble title role in *Kansas City Bomber* (1972), the saga of a derby queen. A more enlightening look at those roller skating ladies was provided in the previous year's documentary *Derby*. James Caan participated in a futuristic, and even more violent, variation of roller derby in *Rollerball* (1975). The most unlikely champion roller skater was probably Mickey Rooney, who strapped on skates for 1950's *The Fireball*. The most graceful skaters were Fred Astaire and Ginger Rogers, who performed a roller skate dance number to "Let's Call the Whole Thing Off" in 1937's *Shall We Dance*. Later dancers have naturally lacked their polish. Scott Baio and Dorothy Stratten took to the disco dance floor on roller skates in *Skatetown, U.S.A.*, as did Linda Blair in *Roller Boogie* (1979). Mercifully, both movies slid out of theaters in no time. More interesting uses of roller skates can be found in *Return to Oz* (1985) and *Solarbabies*. In the former film, a gang of skating humanoids called The Wheelers pestered Dorothy. The futuristic teens in *Solarbabies* (1986) used skates as their primary means of transportation. Movies featuring skateboards include *Skateboard, Thrashin', Gleaming the Cube* and even *Back to the Future*. Bill Murray's *Loose Shoes* included a trailer for the make-believe movie "Skateboarders From Hell." See also **Back to the Future; Ice Skating**.

Shall We Dance (1937)	*The Personals* (1981)
The Fireball (1950)	*Return to Oz* (1985)
It's Always Fair Weather (1955)	*Back to the Future* (1985)
Derby (1971)	*Roller Blade* (1986)
Kansas City Bomber (1972)	*Solarbabies* (1986)
Unholy Rollers (1972)	*Thrashin'* (1986)
Roll, Freddy, Roll (1974 TVM)	*Madame Sousatzka* (1988)
Rollerball (1975)	*Gleaming the Cube* (1989)
Rollerbabies (1976)	*Roller Blade Warriors* (1989)
Skateboard (1977)	*Hook* (1991)
Skatetown U.S.A. (1977)	*Prayer of the Rollerboys* (1991)
Roller Boogie (1979)	*Airborne* (1993)
Xanadu (1980)	
Loose Shoes (aka *Coming Attractions*) (1980)	

Room at the Top

This dour 1958 drama is best remembered for its frank attitude toward sex, its depressing northern England setting, and Simone Signoret's Oscar-winning performance as an ambitious young man's mistress. Laurence Harvey played Joe Lampton, the working-class lad determined to get to the top at all costs—even the death of his lover. Harvey returned to the role in 1965's *Life at the Top*, his character's ambition now replaced by disillusionment. Kenneth Haigh starred as Lampton in a popular 1971-73 British TV series called *Man at the Top*. It subsequently led to a third film, 1975's *Man at the Top*, the dramatics now transformed into big business soap opera. John Braine wrote the original novel.

Room at the Top (1958)	*Man at the Top* (1975)
Life at the Top (1965)	

The Rough Riders

Despite its title, this Monogram series had nothing to do with the early days of Teddy Roosevelt. Instead, it was just another Western series starring veteran screen cowboy Buck Jones. Jones had been Universal's major Western hero in the 1930s, but he was fading when Monogram cast him with Tim McCoy and Raymond Hatton as *The Rough Riders*. The trio played U.S. marshals with a penchant for infiltrating outlaw gangs. The series ended abruptly in 1942 when Jones died in the Cocoanut Grove nightclub fire while on a U.S. Savings Bonds campaign. Jones had escaped from the building but was overcome by the flames when he returned to help others.

Arizona Bound (1941)
The Man From Bodie (1941)
Forbidden Trails (1941)
Below the Border (1942)

Ghost Town Law (1942)
Down Texas Way (1942)
Riders of the West (1942)
West of the Law (1942)

Running

The melodic strains of the *Chariots of Fire* theme automatically bring to mind the vision of barefoot runners gliding across a sandy beach. That, plus the fact it won the 1981 Best Picture Oscar, makes *Chariots* the most well-known running film, but other pictures have covered the sport with equal depth. The 1962 *Loneliness of the Long Distance Runner* made Tom Courtenay a star for his portrayal of a lonely lad who finds solace in pounding a cross-country course. *See How She Runs* (1978), *Running* (1979) and *On the Edge* (1985) were more conventional examinations of the runner's psyche, dealing with the obsession and motivation that make some athletes push themselves to the limit. Olympic runners have been profiled in the documentary *Visions of Eight*, the biographies *Running Brave* (Billy Mills), *Babe* (Babe Didrikson) and *The Jesse Owens Story*, and the fictional features *The Loneliest Runner*, *The Games*, *Goldengirl* and *Personal Best*.

Loneliness of the Long Distance
    Runner (1962)
Billie (1965)
The Games (1970)
Visions of Eight (1973)
Babe (1975 TVM)
Marathon Man (1976)
The Loneliest Runner (1976 TVM)
See How She Runs (1978 TVM)
Goldengirl (1979)
Running (1979)

The Jericho Mile (1979 TVM)
Three Hundred Miles for Stephanie
    (1980 TVM)
Chariots of Fire (1981)
Personal Best (1982)
Running Brave (1983)
The Terry Fox Story (1983 TVM)
Courage (aka *Raw Courage*) (1984)
The Jesse Owens Story (1984 TVM)
On the Edge (1985)
China Run (1987)

Rusty

Rusty was Columbia's answer to canine rival Lassie in this affable boy-and-dog series of the late 1940s. Al Martin wrote the series opener, 1945's *Adventures of Rusty*, which introduced Ted Donaldson as young Danny Mitchell and Rusty as his faithful German Shepherd, a former police dog. John Litel, best known as Henry Aldrich's (q.v.) dad, played Danny's father in the first three films before being replaced by Tom Powers. Ann Doran was Danny's stepmother. The stories usually centered on Danny's personal problems (e.g., misunderstandings with Dad in *For the Love of Rusty*), but it was Rusty who consistently saved the day. See also **Dogs**.

Adventures of Rusty (1945)	*My Dog Rusty* (1948)
The Return of Rusty (1946)	*Rusty Leads the Way* (1948)
Son of Rusty (1947)	*Rusty Saves a Life* (1949)
For the Love of Rusty (1948)	*Rusty's Birthday* (1950)

Ryder, Red

Republic Pictures first brought Fred Harmon's comic strip Western hero to the screen in the 1940 serial *The Adventures of Red Ryder*. Star Don Barry took the nickname "Red" and kept it for the rest of his career, but he was not Republic's choice to headline a Red Ryder film series. That distinction went to Wild Bill Elliott, a veteran B-Western star Republic lured away from Columbia in 1943. Elliott had acquired *his* nickname "Wild Bill" while playing Wild Bill Hickok (q.v.) in an earlier serial and series. Gabby Hayes played Elliott's grizzled sidekick in the first two Ryder pictures, 1944's *Tucson Raiders* and *Marshal of Reno*. But he was eventually dropped, allowing young Bobby Blake (Robert Blake of TV's *Baretta*) to assume the sidekick role as the Indian boy Little Beaver. After sixteen films, Republic promoted Elliott to bigger pictures and signed Allan "Rocky" Lane to play Red. Lane had been a contract player since 1929 at Fox, Warners and RKO before joining Republic as a serial star in 1940. His transition into the Ryder films went smoothly, assisted by Blake who provided continuity as Little Beaver. Lane played Red seven times before the Ryder series moved to Eagle Lion in 1949. After his acting career ended in 1961, Lane provided the voice of TV's "Mr. Ed." The Eagle Lion pictures starred Jim Bannon, best known as detective Jack Packard in Columbia's short-lived *I Love a Mystery* (q.v.) series. Don Reynolds co-starred as Little Beaver. Plagued by legal problems involving rights to the source comic strip, the Eagle Lion *Red Ryder* series folded within a year.

    Tucson Raiders (1944) (Bill Elliott)
    Marshal of Reno (1944) (Elliott)
    Vigilantes of Dodge City (1944) (Elliott)
    Cheyenne Wildcat (1944) (Elliott)
    The San Antonio Kid (1944) (Elliott)
    Sheriff of Las Vegas (1944) (Elliott)
    Marshal of Laredo (1945) (Elliott)
    Lone Texas Ranger (1945) (Elliott)
    The Great Stagecoach Robbery (1945) (Elliott)
    Phantom of the Plains (1945) (Elliott)
    Colorado Pioneers (1945) (Elliott)
    Wagon Wheels Westward (1945) (Elliott)
    Sun Valley Cyclone (1946) (Elliott)
    Sheriff of Redwood Valley (1946) (Elliott)
    California Gold Rush (1946) (Elliott)
    Conquest of Cheyenne (1946) (Elliott)
    Santa Fe Uprising (1946) (Allan Lane)
    Stagecoach to Denver (1946) (Lane)

Homesteaders of Paradise Valley (1947) (Lane)
Rustlers of Devil's Canyon (1947) (Lane)
Vigilantes of Boom Town (1947) (Lane)
Marshal of Cripple Creek (1947) (Lane)
Oregon Trail Scouts (1947) (Lane)
The Fighting Redhead (1949) (Jim Bannon)
The Cowboy and the Prizefighter (1949) (Bannon)
Roll, Thunder, Roll (1949) (Bannon)
Ride, Ryder, Ride (1949) (Bannon)

Sabata

When Clint Eastwood abandoned the Italian "spaghetti Westerns" that made him an international star in the 1960's, Lee Van Cleef stepped right into his boots. Van Cleef had the necessary credentials—he had played opposite Eastwood in two of the three "Man With No Name" (q.v.) films: *For a Few Dollars More* (1965) and *The Good, the Bad, and the Ugly* (1967). Furthermore, Van Cleef made the perfect antihero, and his well-groomed mustache and classy duds contrasted nicely with Eastwood's scruffy character. Thus, by all accounts, 1970's *Sabata* should have made Van Cleef a superstar. However, that never occurred, although *Sabata* enhanced Van Cleef's popularity among European moviegoers. His character—a friendly variation of his earlier bad guys—gambled freely, shot people without remorse, and broke the law if it suited his purpose. He also carried gimmicky guns (e.g., a derringer that fired an extra bullet from the handle). The year after *Sabata* was released, a film called *Adios, Sabata* appeared in theaters. At first glance, it looked like a sequel, with Yul Brynner replacing Van Cleef in the title role. However, it was actually a completely different film titled *Indigo Black* (or *Indio Black sai che to dico: sei un Gran Figlio . . .*). Its producers redubbed the film, changing the name of Brynner's character from Black to Sabata. This is confusing, to say the least, since Yul wore a black outfit (including an unbuttoned shirt, which would never be found in Sabata's wardrobe). Interestingly, Van Cleef and Eastwood pursued a character named Indio in *For a Few Dollars More*. As for the real Sabata, Van Cleef came back to play him in 1972's *The Return of Sabata*. Gianfranco Parolini—a director with a fetish for quick zooms—helmed all three films, and Ignazio Spalla played supporting roles.

Sabata (1970)
Adios, Sabata (aka *Indigo Black*) (1971)
The Return of Sabata (1972)

The Saint

Leslie Charteris's dapper adventurer Simon Templar walked a thin line between crime and the law. His calling card featured a stick figure with a halo, thus explaining his moniker, the Saint. The movies never alluded much to the Saint's criminal tendencies—he was strictly a good guy with a mischievous streak. George Sanders was the screen's busiest Saint, although Louis Hayward and Hugh Sinclair each starred in two movies. Jean Marais played the class-conscious sleuth on the French screen. In the 1960s, Roger Moore made the role his own with a highly successful TV series that even spawned a theatrical film (composed of two episodes). Although Moore's show ended in 1969, fellow Brit Ian Ogilvy starred in a short-lived revival series, *The Return of the Saint*, nine years later. In 1993, shortly before Charteris's death, producer Robert Evans announced plans to mount a big-budget Saint motion picture.

The Saint in New York (1938) (Louis Hayward)
The Saint in London (1939) (George Sanders)
The Saint Strikes Back (1939) (Sanders)
The Saint's Double Trouble (1940) (Sanders)
The Saint Takes Over (1940) (Sanders)
The Saint in Palm Springs (1941) (Sanders)
The Saint Meets the Tiger (1941) (Hugh Sinclair)
The Saint's Vacation (1941) (Sinclair)
The Saint's Girl Friday (1953) (aka *The Saint Returns*) (Hayward)
The Fiction-Makers (1968 TVM) (Roger Moore)
The Saint and the Brave Goose (1981 TVM) (Ian Ogilvy)

St. Trinian's

An unruly girls' school where young ladies spent more time studying betting sheets than history, St. Trinian's provided the setting for a popular series of British farces spanning twenty-six years. The directing-writing team of Frank Launder and Sidney Gilliat created the series, but it was droll comic genius Alastair Sim who made the first entries consistently entertaining. Actually, Launder, Gilliat and Sim had teamed up earlier for 1950's *The Happiest Days of Your Life*, a riotous comedy about a girls' school (St. Swithin) that was accidentally "displaced" into a boys' school (Nutbourne). Sim and Margaret Rutherford played the respective heads of the schools, but they generously devoted screen time to their youthful, mischievous costars. *The Belles of St. Trinian's* (1954) initiated the series proper and introduced a swarm of rebellious girls that made St. Swithin's look like a charm school. Sim was doubly delightful as both the headmistress (in drag, of course) and her brother. Sim also appeared, albeit too briefly, in 1958's follow-up *Blue Murder at St. Trinian's*, in which a jewel thief on the lam wishes he had never stumbled into the "perfect hiding place." Launder and Gilliat produced two additional lackluster entries without Sim. The series apparently ended with 1966's *The Great St. Trinian's Train Robbery*. However, Launder returned to the school fourteen years later for *The Wildcats of St. Trinian's*, a time-capsule comedy that failed to find an audience. Gilliat served as a production consultant but did not have an active role in the writing chores. Launder and Gilliat broke into the movies as writers in the 1930s. They penned the screenplay for Hitchcock's classic *The Lady Vanishes* (1937) as well as some of the Inspector Hornleigh (q.v.) films. See also **Boarding Schools.**

The Belles of St. Trinian's (1954)
Blue Murder at St. Trinian's (1958)
The Pure Hell of St. Trinian's (1961)
The Great St. Trinian's Train Robbery (1966)
The Wildcats of St. Trinian's (1980)

Sanders, Commissioner Harry

Prolific mystery writer Edgar Wallace created Commissioner Sanders—a stern administrator stationed in Africa—in 1911's *Sanders of the River*. However, in their lavish 1935 film version, Alexander and Zoltan Korda made Sanders a mellower character and relegated him to a supporting role. Paul Robeson took top billing as Bosambo, a native chief loyal to the British and a friend of Sanders's (Leslie Banks). The plot pitted Sanders against ruthless traders, while Bosambo confronted a rebellious rival chief. The film is remembered chiefly for its striking on-location photography and its unintentionally depressing view of British colonialism. Although the film did not spawn a sequel, Francis Gerard penned the novel *Return of Sanders of the River* in 1939. Three decades later, British actor Richard Todd starred as Sanders in two inexpensive B-pictures. The first Todd film, 1963's *Sanders of the River*, was a loose adaptation that found Sanders investigating a murder in an African hospital. The 1964 follow-up, *Coast of Skeletons*, found Sanders encountering a gang of diamond-seeking heavies in southwest Africa. Sanders's creator Edgar Wallace wrote over 170 novels during his career, many of which were adapted by German filmmakers in the 1950s. Wallace also wrote the original story for the 1933 classic *King Kong* (q.v.).

Sanders of the River (aka *Bosambo*) (1935)
Sanders of the River (aka *Death Drums Along the River*) (1963)
Coast of Skeletons (1964)

Santo

The origin of this Mexican wrestling superhero remains somewhat hazy, though it may date as far back as 1952's *El Enmascarado de Plata* (aka *The Silver Mask*). Regardless, Santo donned his head-covering mask for the longest-running film series in Mexican cinema. These wild, action-packed films peaked in popularity during the 1960s, a decade in which the Silver-Masked wrestler fought a plethora of vampires, zombies, witches, man-made monsters and other wrestlers. Originally, the "movies" were made as serials for Mexican television. But due to the scarce number of television markets, they were ultimately edited into features and released to neighborhood theaters. The actor behind Santo's silver mask was never billed, although Rodolfo Guzman Huerta and Eric del Castillo are generally credited as the principal Santos. Yet, with the wrestler's facial features hidden, one could never be certain about his real-life identity. Rival wrestlers The Blue Demon (q.v.) and Neutron (q.v.) were introduced in the early 1960s. Neutron made little impact, but the Blue Demon eventually costarred with Santo in 1968's *Santo Against Blue Demon in Atlantis*. Its success led to additional wrestler pairings, culminating in the Mexican monster extravaganza *Santo and Blue Demon vs. the Monsters* — which pitted the tag team against three vampires, a mummy, a cyclops, a Frankenstein monster, a mad doctor, and a robot double of the Blue Demon. The Santo films never strayed from their juvenile plotlines, despite gradually stressing sexual content, which had become obligatory by the late 1960s. Santo remained relatively unknown in the United States until cable networks gave him new exposure in the 1980s. Even then, Santo faced an identity crisis since some dubbed prints referred to him as Samson. See also **The Blue Demon; Neutron; Wrestling.**

Santo Contra Hombres Infernales (1958)
Santo vs. the Zombies (aka *Invasion of the Zombies*; *Santo Contra los Zombies*) (1961)

Samson vs. the Vampire Women (aka *Santo Contra las Mujeres Vampiro*) (1961)
Santo vs. the King of Crime (aka *Santo Contra el Rey de Crimen*) (1963)
Santo in the Hotel of the Dead (aka *Santo en el Hotel de la Muerte*) (1963)
Santo Against the Diabolical Brain (aka *Santo Contra el Cerebro Diabólico; El Cerebro del Mal*) (1963)
Samson in the Wax Museum (aka *Santo en el Museo de Cera*) (1963)
Santo Attacks the Witches (aka *The Witches Attack; Santo Ataca; Atacan las Brujas*) (1965)
Santo vs. Baron Brakola (aka *Santro Contra el Baron Brakola*) (1966)
Santo vs. the Strangler (aka *Santo Contra el Estrangulador*) (1966)
Profanadores de Tumbas (1966)
The Ghost of the Strangler (aka *Espectro del Estrangulador; Santo Contra el Espectro*) (1967)
Santo vs. the Martian Invasion (aka *Santo vs. Invasion de los Marcianos*) (1967)
Santo Against Blue Demon in Atlantis (aka *Santo Contra Blue Demon en la Atlántida*) (1968)
The Diabolical Hatchet (aka *El Hacha Diabólica*) (1968)
The World of the Dead (aka *El Mundo de los Muertos*) (1969)
Santo in the Revenge of the Vampire Women (aka *Santo en la Venganza de las Mujeres Vampiro*) (1969)
Santo and Dracula's Treasure (aka *The Vampire and Sex; El Vampiro y el Sexo*) (1969)
Santo and Blue Demon vs. the Monsters (aka *Santo y Blue Demon Contra los Monstruos*) (1971)
Murderers From Other Worlds (aka *Asesinos de Otros Mundos*) (1971)
Suicide Mission (aka *Misión Suicida*) (1971)
Santo Against the Daughter of Frankenstein (aka *The Daughter of Frankenstein; Santo Contra la Hija de Frankenstein*) (1972)
Santo in the Mummy's Revenge (aka *Santo en la Venganza de la Momia*) (1972)
Santo Against the Black Magic (aka *Santo Contra la Magia Negra*) (1972)
Santo vs. Capulina (1972)
Santo and Blue Demon vs. Dracula and the Wolf Man (aka *Santo y Blue Demon Contra Dracula y el Hombre Lobo*) (1973)
Pafnucio Santo (1976)

Sartana

While most spaghetti-Western gunfighters killed for revenge or profit, Sartana served a higher justice as an "Angel of Death." Sometimes he pitted evil against evil, giving men of greed just enough rope to hang themselves. However, he typically rendered his final verdict with his deadly aim. John (Gianni) Garko played the Western vigilante in five films, with George Hilton taking over for a final entry. Spaghetti-Western enthusiasts recognize the six Garko/Hilton films as the "official" series. However, there were many other Italian-made Westerns featuring a character named Sartana. To make matters more confusing, Garko played a different character named Sartana in the 1967 movie *One Thousand Dollars on the Black*. That film was released two years later with a new title (*Sartana's Blood at Sundown*) and promoted as one of the Sartana films. Despite their popularity in Europe, the Sartana films never achieved the American success of the Sergio Leone-Clint Eastwood "Man With No Name" movies (q.v.) nor the later Trinity series (q.v.).

Sartana (aka *Se Incontri Sartana Prega per la Tua Morte*; *If You Meet Sartana . . . Pray for Your Death*; *Gunfighters Die Harder*) (1968) (John Garko)

I Am Sartana . . . Your Angel of Death (aka *Sono Sartana, il Vostro Becchino*; *Sartana and the Gravedigger*) (1969) (Garko)

Sartana Kills Them All (aka *Lo Irritarono . . . e Sartana Fece Piazza Pulita*) (1970) (Garko)

Light the Fuze . . . Sartana Is Coming (aka *Una Nuvola di Porvere . . . un Grido di Morte Arriva Sartana*) (1971) (Garko)

Have a Good Funeral, My Friend . . . Sartana Will Pay (aka *Buon Funerale, Amigos . . . Paga Sartana*) (1971) (Garko)

I Am Sartana . . . Trade Your Guns for a Coffin (aka *C'è Sartana, Vendi la Pistola e Comprati la Bara*) (1972) (George Hilton)

Scanners

A marketing campaign emphasizing its eye-popping visual effects turned 1981's *Scanners* into a modest mainstream hit for Canadian cult director David Cronenberg. Thematically, this science fiction thriller differed little from Cronenberg's previous and subsequent films, all of which revolved around human metamorphosis (e.g., an operation turned a woman into a blood-seeking killer in 1977's *Rabid*; an experiment transformed a man into a mutant in 1986's *The Fly*). In *Scanners*, a drug has created a race of humans with telekinetic powers who roam as social outcasts through a city of the near-future. There are good scanners and bad ones — and two opposing brothers engage in a climactic telekinetic showdown that results in eyeballs spurting out of their sockets. Despite such occasional descents into visual gore, *Scanners* emerged as a stylish film with a sound following. Yet, as Cronenberg progressed to bigger-budgeted films, the likelihood of a *Scanners* sequel appeared to fade forever. However, in the early 1990s, executive producer Pierre David revived interest in *Scanners* and mounted two made-in-Canada sequels, both directed by Christian Duguay. *Scanners II: The New Order* (1991) sacrificed original storytelling for visual flair. Once again, a good scanner tracked down a bad one and saved other scanners from a power-hungry "normal" human. The only new element was a drug addiction theme (we learned that scanners could be controlled by an addictive drug that relieved their mental pain). *Scanners III: The Takeover* (1992) featured an evil female scanner who learns that she can "scan" normal humans via television. Her brother, who has found peace in a Buddhist monastery, returns to thwart her. While neither of these *Scanners* sequels found much favor at the U.S. box office, they nevertheless did a decent business on videotape. See also **Telekinesis.**

Scanners (1981)   *Scanners III: The Takeover* (1992)
Scanners II: The New Order (1991)

Sea Serpents

Judging from their reluctance to be photographed, one might assume that sea serpents are shy creatures. Filmmakers have certainly honored the creatures' privacy. *The Secret of the Loch*, a mild 1934 British comedy, and 1982's *The Loch Ness Horror* may be the only feature films exclusively about the Loch Ness Monster. Holmes encountered "Nessie" in *The Private Life of Sherlock Holmes* (1970), but he revealed "the serpent" to be a mechanical trick. Nessie was one of *The Mysterious Monsters* (1976) addressed in the exploitative Sunn Classics "documentary." And a tiny fish grew into Nessie in one of the magical moments in George Pal's 1964 fantasy *The Seven Faces of Dr. Lao*. Some of the suspects in *The Dragon Murder Case* (1934) pointed to murder evidence that suggested a sea serpent, but Philo Vance knew better and later identified a human culprit. Quests for sea serpents opened *20,000 Leagues Under the Sea* (1954), *The Viking Women and the Sea Serpent* (1957) and quite naturally, *The Quest* (1986). Timothy Bottoms and Ray Milland found what they were looking for in *The Sea Serpent* (1986), a film they would surely like to forget. See also **Dragons**.

The Secret of the Loch (1934)	*The Mysterious Monsters* (1976)
The Dragon Murder Case (1934)	*The Loch Ness Horror* (1982)
The Viking Women and the Sea	*The Sea Serpent* (1986)
Serpent (1957)	*The Quest* (1986)
The Seven Faces of Dr. Lao (1964)	*Freddie as F.R.O.7* (1992)
The Private Life of Sherlock Holmes	
(1970)	

Secret Service Series, *see* Bancroft, Brass

Serials Into Features

The practice of condensing movie serials into feature films was pioneered in the 1930s by a small company called Mascot Pictures. A major producer of early serials, Mascot discovered it could get twice the value out of its serials by also rereleasing highlights as feature films. Thus, the 1933 John Wayne Western serial *The Three Musketeers* was recut and released as *Desert Command*. A rival studio, Principal, squeezed *two* feature films out of its Bela Lugosi serial *The Return of Chandu* (1934). The first four chapters were condensed into the film *The Return of Chandu*, while the last eight chapters were edited into another feature called *Chandu on Magic Island*. In a unique reversal, Burroughs-Tarzan Enterprises edited its 1935 feature film *The New Adventures of Tarzan* (aka *Tarzan and the Green Goddess*) into a twelve-chapter serial in a desperate attempt to compete with MGM's Tarzan (q.v.). The company reasoned that theater owners uninterested in showing the feature version might be induced to play the serial version. The ploy did not work. In 1936, Universal released its first *Flash Gordon* serial, an expensive ($350,000 according to most sources) space opera that earned a fervent following. Inspired by Orson Welles's famous "War of the Worlds" radio broadcast and the success of the serial sequel *Flash Gordon's Trip to Mars*, Universal released two Flash Gordon feature versions in 1938. *Trip to Mars* was condensed into *Mars Attacks the World*, while the original *Flash Gordon* became *Rocketship*. Confusingly, the footage from these serials, a third Flash Gordon entry, and a Buck Rogers serial have been reedited into other feature versions as well. For example, *Trip to Mars* can be viewed as the 99-minute *Deadly Ray From Mars* in addition to the aforementioned 101-minute *Mars Attacks the World*. Although Universal encountered great success with its Flash Gordon serials, little Republic Pictures eventually became the most popular producer of serials. Throughout the 1940s and midway through the 1950s, Republic filled matinee screens with exciting chapters of *Spy Smasher* (1942), *Captain America* (1944) and *Panther Girl of the Kongo* (1955). The television series format contributed greatly to the death of theatrical serials in the mid-1950s. However, in 1965, Columbia revived interest in serials by mounting a limited release of its 1943 *Batman* serial. This, along with the 1966 *Batman* TV series, inspired Republic to condense twenty-six of its best serials and release them directly to television. In the following list, the serials are listed chronologically on the left, with the feature versions shown on the right.

The Three Musketeers (1933)	*Desert Command*
The Return of Chandu (1934)	*The Return of Chandu; Chandu on Magic Island*
The New Adventures of Tarzan (1935)	*The New Adventures of Tarzan*
Darkest Africa (1936)	*Batmen of Africa* (aka *King of Jungleland*)
Undersea Kingdom (1936)	*Sharad of Atlantis*
Robinson Crusoe of Clipper Island (1936)	*Robinson Crusoe of Mystery Island*
Flash Gordon (1936)	*Rocketship; Spaceship to the Unknown; Space Soldiers; Atomic Rocketship*
Zorro Rides Again (1937)	*Zorro Rides Again*
Fighting Devil Dogs (1938)	*Torpedo of Doom*
Flash Gordon's Trip to Mars (1938)	*Mars Attacks the World; Deadly Ray From Mars*
Hawk of the Wilderness (1938)	*Lost Island of Kioga*
Buck Rogers (1939)	*Planet Outlaws; Destination Saturn*
Flash Gordon Conquers the Universe (1940)	*Purple Death From Outer Space; Perils From the Planet Mongo; Space Soldiers Conquer the Universe*
The Mysterious Dr. Satan (1940)	*Dr. Satan's Robot*
Spy Smasher (1940)	*Spy Smasher Returns*
The Perils of Nyoka (1942)	*Nyoka and the Lost Secrets of Hippocrates*
G-Men vs. the Black Dragon (1943)	*Black Dragon of Manzanar*
The Masked Marvel (1943)	*Sakima and the Masked Marvel*
The Tiger Woman (1944)	*Jungle Gold*
Manhunt of Mystery Island (1945)	*Captain Mephisto and the Transformation Machine*
Federal Operator 99 (1945)	*FBI 99*
The Purple Monster Strikes (1945)	*D-Day on Mars*
The Crimson Ghost (1946)	*Cyclotrode "X"*
The Black Widow (1947)	*Sombra, the Spider Woman*
Dangers of the Canadian Mounted (1948)	*R.C.M.P. and the Treasure of Genghis Khan*

G-Men Never Forget (1948)	Code 645
Federal Agents vs. Underworld, Inc. (1948)	Golden Hands of Kurigal
King of the Rocket Men (1949)	Lost Planet Airmen
The Invisible Monster (1950)	Slaves of the Invisible Monster
Flying Disc Man From Mars (1951)	Missile Monsters
Radar Men From the Moon (1952)	Retik, the Moon Menace
Zombies of the Stratosphere (1952)	Satan's Satellites
Jungle Drums of Africa (1952)	U-238 and the Witch
Canadian Mounties vs. Atomic Invaders (1953)	Missile Base at Taniak
Trader Tom of the China Seas (1954)	Target: Sea of China
Panther Girl of the Kongo (1955)	The Claw Monsters

Sewers

Until olfactory films can be refined (see "Smellovision" under **Gimmicks**), sewer settings will be underappreciated. Still, the dark catacombs that lurk beneath urban areas have served the horror film well, providing an atmospheric retreat for people-shy monsters. The *Phantom of the Opera* played piano and plotted murder in his tastefully decorated sewer lair. To his dismay, Christine, the unwilling object of his affections, found it a loathsome place. Rats are a common sight in sewers, so naturally 1972's *Ben*, a tale about a misunderstood rodent and his young human friend, featured extensive sewer footage. Other more horrific sewer residents include the giant ants in *Them!* (1954), the killer baby in *It's Alive* (1974), and the title creatures in *Alligator* (1980) and the 1988 remake of *The Blob*. The 1984 film *C.H.U.D.* (that's Cannibalistic Humanoid Underground Dwellers) was about a mutant race that lived in the sewers by day and sought surface victims at night. It was obviously inspired by the H.P. Lovecraft short story "Pickman's Model," which was adapted into a chilling segment on Rod Serling's 1970-73 TV series *Night Gallery*. *The Third Man* (1949) featured a memorable scene in which Harry Lime (Orson Welles) is chased through a Vienna sewer. Lex Luthor's sewer lair in *Superman* (1978) looked very posh, possibly setting a new standard for screen supervillains. And a band of Christians trekked through the Caesar Augustus Memorial Sewer in Monty Python's *Life of Brian* (1979). See also **Teenage Mutant Ninja Turtles.**

Les Misérables (1935)	The Blues Brothers (1980)
The Phantom of the Opera (1943)	C.H.U.D. (1984)
The Third Man (1949)	Underworld (aka Transmutations) (1985)
Them! (1954)	
Kanal (aka They Loved Life; Sewer) (1956)	The Vindicator (aka Frankenstein '88) (1986)
Who's Minding the Mint? (1967)	Wild Thing (1987)
Ben (1972)	Something Is Out There (1988 TVM)
It's Alive! (1974)	The Blob (1988)
Superman (1978)	Cyborg (1989)
Life of Brian (1979)	Ghostbusters II (1989)
Alligator (1980)	Teenage Mutant Ninja Turtles (1990)

The Rainbow Thief (1990)	*Jonny's Golden Quest* (1993 TVM)
It (1990 TVM)	*Super Mario Bros.* (1993)

Sex Change

Exploitation films have frequently tackled subjects considered taboo even by serious filmmakers. Thus, it is not surprising that the first films to address men undergoing surgical operations to become women (and vice versa) were drive-in second features. Edward J. Woods, Jr., director of the infamous *Plan Nine From Outer Space*, broached the subject back in 1953 with *Glen or Glenda?* A shoddily constructed film (like most of Woods's), it told the stories of transvestite Glen and ex-marine Alan who becomes Ann. Although undoubtedly inept, the film was nevertheless ahead of its time in terms of subject matter. Seventeen years later, United Artists released the low-budget filler *The Christine Jorgensen Story* (1970), the alleged facts behind "the world's first sex change operation." That same year, Gore Vidal's satiric sex-change novel *Myra Breckinridge* reached the screen, with film critic Rex Reed as Myron who becomes surgically transformed into Raquel Welch as Myra! The film drowned in its own tastelessness despite a memorable cast and a decent budget. The obscure British picture *I Want What I Want* (1972) treated the subject with much greater respect. Both critics and audiences responded well to 1975's *Dog Day Afternoon*, the story of a man who stages a bank robbery to pay for his male lover's sex-change operation. Karen Black shocked her diner companions by revealing she was once a man in *Come Back to the 5 and Dime, Jimmy Dean, Jimmy Dean* (1982). The 1986 TV-movie *Second Serve* was the biography of surgeon Richard Raskins who became tennis player Renee Richards (Lynn Redgrave played both roles). Two other movies have dealt with non-surgical change of sexes. Young Dr. Jekyll (Ralph Bates) downed his formula and transformed into an evil woman (Martine Beswicke) in Hammer Films' sly 1972 variation *Dr. Jekyll and Sister Hyde*. A fourteen-year-old girl wished to become a boy—and did—in the 1986 fantasy *Something Special*.

Glen or Glenda? (aka *I Changed My Sex*; *I Led Two Lives*; *He or She?*) (1953)	*Come Back to the 5 and Dime, Jimmy Dean, Jimmy Dean* (1982)
The Christine Jorgensen Story (1970)	*The World According to Garp* (1982)
Myra Breckinridge (1970)	*Second Serve* (1986 TVM)
I Want What I Want (1972)	*Something Special* (aka *Willy/Milly*; *I Was a Teenage Boy*) (1986)
Dr. Jekyll and Sister Hyde (1972)	*Sleepaway Camp II: Unhappy Campers* (1988)
Dog Day Afternoon (1975)	*Cleo/Leo* (1989)
Let Me Die a Woman (1979)	
The Woman Inside (1981)	

Shadow, The

"Who knows what evil lurks in the hearts of men?" The Shadow knew—and this mysterious do-gooder dealt out his own brand of justice in a series of immensely popular pulp novels, a radio program, and a handful of films. Created by Maxwell Grant (real name Walter Gibson) in 1931, the Shadow sent his agents into the underworld to infiltrate the ganglords. When they got into trouble, the Shadow—revolvers blazing at his side—came out of the darkness to rescue them. Grant established in an early novel that the Shadow *was not* wealthy socialite Lamont Cranston. Nevertheless, both on radio and in the movies, Cranston and The Shadow were synonymous. Former silent film star Rod La Rocque brought the Shadow to the screen in 1937's *The Shadow Strikes* and 1938's *International Crime*. La Rocque retired from acting in the early 1940s and entered into a successful real estate career. Monogram Pictures revived the Shadow for a 1946 three-film series starring serial star Kane ("Spy Smasher") Richmond. The Shadow's last film appearance was in Republic's 1958 picture *The Invisible Avenger*, a New Orleans-set mystery starring Richard Derr, which was rereleased in 1962 as *Bourbon Street Shadows*. In 1993, director Russell (*Highlander*) Mulcahy announced plans to produce a big-budget Shadow feature.

The Shadow Strikes (1937) (Rod La Rocque)
International Crime (1938) (La Rocque)
Behind the Mask (1946) (Kane Richmond)
The Shadow Returns (1946) (Richmond)
The Missing Lady (1946) (Richmond)
The Invisible Avenger (aka *Bourbon Street Shadows*) (1958) (Richard Derr)

Shaft

A slick, violent action picture about a supercool black private eye, 1971's *Shaft* ignited the "blaxploitation" craze while enjoying its own mainstream success. Ernest Tidyman's screenplay practically turned John Shaft into a black male stereotype (a tough dude described in the theme song as a "sex machine"). But Richard Roundtree's rugged performance and Gordon Park's gritty direction gave the film a new look much copied by other black filmmakers. Isaac Hayes's hit theme won an Oscar (despite having minimal words) and eventually landed him a starring role in the 1974 movie *Truck Turner*. Roundtree appeared in both *Shaft* sequels and then made the jump to television. His ninety-minute *Shaft* TV series rotated with *The CBS Tuesday Night Movie* and a James Stewart lawyer show called *Hawkins*. The TV version whitewashed the Shaft character (less violence, no sex) and caught the cancellation axe after one season. See also **Blaxploitation Films.**

Shaft (1971)   *Shaft in Africa* (1973)
Shaft's Big Score (1972)

The Shaggy Dog

An ancient curse and a magical ring made Tommy Kirk his own best friend as the boy-turned-dog in 1959's *The Shaggy Dog*. This amusing variation on the werewolf theme established a juvenile formula that worked very well for Disney during the 1960s (e.g., *Son of Flubber, The Misadventures of Merlin Jones*). The film also provided major roles for future child superstars Annette Funicello and Tommy Kirk, while costarring Fred MacMurray and Tim Considine a year before *My Three Sons*. Dean Jones portrayed Kirk's character as an adult in 1976's *The Shaggy D.A.* The 1987 TV-movie *The Return of the Shaggy Dog* ignored the second film, being a direct sequel to the 1959 original. See also **Dogs; Humanimals.**

The Shaggy Dog (1959)   *The Return of the Shaggy Dog* (1987
The Shaggy D.A. (1976)   TVM)

Sharks

Except for bit parts, sharks had a hard time finding movie roles prior to 1975's *Jaws* (q.v.). *Killer Shark* (1950) put Roddy McDowell aboard a shark-hunting vessel but offered little excitement. Victor Mature became concerned about the way sharks gobbled up navy flyers in 1956's *The Sharkfighters*. He eventually devised a shark repellent, derived from octopus ink, that turned away even the hungriest underwater predator. *Blue Water, White Death* was a striking 1971 documentary about the Great White shark. It failed to find an audience until four years later after the release of *Jaws*. Naturally, the phenomenal success of Steven Spielberg's blockbuster inspired a host of imitators. The 1982 *Great White* was so similar to *Jaws* that Universal Pictures went to court and acquired an injunction to remove the rip-off from circulation. *Mako: The Jaws of Death* offered a refreshing twist on the post-*Jaws* shark genre, with Richard Jaeckel as a man trying to protect sharks from people who would exploit them. See also **Dolphins; Fish; Jaws; Whales.**

Killer Shark (1950)
The Sharkfighters (1956)
Tiko and the Shark (1965)
Shark! (aka *Maneater*) (1969)
Blue Water, White Death (1971)
Shark's Treasure (1974)
Jaws (1975)

Mako: The Jaws of Death (aka *The Jaws of Death*) (1976)
Shark Kill (1976 TVM)
Tintorera — Bloody Waters (1977)
Great White (1982)
Mission of the Shark (1991 TVM)

Shayne, Michael

Brett Halliday's two-fisted private eye made his film debut with 1941's *Michael Shayne, Detective*. Lloyd Nolan, a veteran tough guy, starred as Shayne in seven films from 1941-42. Hugh Beaumont, best known as Ward Cleaver on TV's *Leave It to Beaver*, reprised Shayne for five additional features in 1946-47. Although these fast-paced mysteries never rose above the programmer level, they paved the way for more serious private eye films, such as the 1944 Philip Marlowe vehicle *Murder, My Sweet*. Ironically, the Shayne movie *Time to Kill* was based on the Marlowe novel *The High Window*. Richard Denning starred in the *Michael Shayne* TV series in 1960-61.

Michael Shayne, Detective (1941) (Lloyd Nolan)
Blue, White, and Perfect (1941) (Nolan)
Dressed to Kill (1941) (Nolan)
Sleepers West (1941) (Nolan)
Just Off Broadway (1942) (Nolan)
The Man Who Would Not Die (1942) (Nolan)
Time to Kill (1942) (Nolan)
Blonde for a Day (1946) (Hugh Beaumont)
Larceny in Her Heart (1946) (Beaumont)
Murder Is My Business (1946) (Beaumont)
Three on a Ticket (1947) (Beaumont)
Too Many Winners (1947) (Beaumont)

Shopping Malls, *see* Stores

Silent Night, Deadly Night

Film ads showing a murderous Santa Claus created a minor controversy when *Silent Night, Deadly Night* was released in 1984. Actually, this low-budget slasher picture did not depict Santa as a killer — the knife-wielding murderer turned out to be just a psycho dressed up like St. Nick. Still, the ploy generated plenty of free publicity for a film that otherwise would have sunk into obscurity. Instead, it spawned a series. The 1987 *Silent Night, Deadly Night Part II* recycled a large chunk of the original's footage before setting up the first killer's baby brother, Ricky, as another Santa-dressed slasher. Ricky emerged from a six-year coma in *SN, DN III: You Better Watch Out!* (1989). It's considered the highlight of the series (though not necessarily a good film), chiefly due to the efforts of once-promising director Monte Hellman (*Two-Lane Blacktop*). The films *Silent Night, Bloody Night* (1972) and *Silent Night, Evil Night* (1974) are not a part of this series. See also **Slasher Movies.**

Silent Night, Deadly Night (1984)
Silent Night, Deadly Night Part II (1987)
Silent Night, Deadly Night III: You Better Watch Out! (1989)
Silent Night, Deadly Night IV: Initiation (1990)
Silent Night, Deadly Night V: The Toymaker (1991)

Sinbad the Sailor

This Arabian Nights adventurer owes his film fame to producer Charles Schneer and special effects creator Ray Harryhausen, who made Sinbad the subject of a colorful movie trilogy. The first of the three films, 1958's *The Seventh Voyage of Sinbad*, was a marvelous fantasy, though its plot must have confused Sinbad purists. It combined Sinbad's encounter with a two-headed roc (which actually occurred on the sailor's second voyage) with his climactic clash with a cyclops (the subject of his third voyage). Naturally, none of this bothered filmgoers enraptured with Harryhausen's spectacular special effects — a fire-breathing dragon, a four-armed siren, and a classic swordfight between Sinbad and a skeleton. Surprisingly, although *The Seventh Voyage* turned an impressive profit, Schneer and Harryhausen waited sixteen years to mount a sequel. *The Golden Voyage of Sinbad* was a stylish rehash that featured a new Sinbad (John Phillip Law replacing Kerwin Matthews) and a bevy of eye-popping special effects. Although Harryhausen failed to top his earlier skeleton swordfight, he still wove visual magic with a six-armed statue come-to-life (q.v.) and a clash between a centaur and a griffin. *The Golden Voyage*'s warm reception led to 1977's *Sinbad and the Eye of the Tiger*, which was, in comparison to its predecessors, a disappointment. Patrick Wayne played a leaden Sinbad, and Harryhausen's creatures were less fantastic (e.g., a saber-toothed tiger, a walrus, and a chess-playing baboon). It turned out to be Schneer and Harryhausen's last Sinbad voyage. There have been other celluloid Sinbads, of course, including Douglas Fairbanks, Jr.'s entertaining *Sinbad the Sailor*, 1963's *Captain Sinbad* with Guy Williams (Disney's TV "Zorro"), and *Sinbad and the Seven Seas* with Lou Ferrigno (the green half of TV's *The Incredible Hulk*). Gene

Kelly danced with Hanna-Barbera cartoon characters in the "Sinbad" segment of 1957's *Invitation to the Dance*.

Sinbad the Sailor (1947)	*Captain Sinbad* (1963)
Son of Sinbad (1955)	*The Golden Voyage of Sinbad* (1974)
Invitation to the Dance (1957)	*Sinbad and the Eye of the Tiger* (1977)
The Seventh Voyage of Sinbad (1958)	*Sinbad and the Seven Seas* (1990)

Six Million Dollar Man

Martin Caidin's novel *Cyborg* inspired the 1973 TV-movie and subsequent 1974-78 TV series *The Six Million Dollar Man*. Lee Majors starred as Steve Austin, a critically injured astronaut who had certain body parts replaced by "atomic-powered electromechanical devices." The end result was a superhero — part human, part machine (but not nearly as interesting as *Robocop*). He acquired a bionic girlfriend in 1975, when tennis pro Jaime Sommers (Lindsay Wagner) met with a skydiving accident. She proved too popular for just one man, so she got her own show, *The Bionic Woman*, in 1976. It went off the air in 1978, a few months after the final telecast of *The Six Million Dollar Man*. However, just to show you can't keep a bionic pair down for good — and in the wake of the hit movie *Robocop* — Steve and Jaime were reunited for 1987's *The Return of the Six Million Dollar Man and the Bionic Woman*. It proved to be a ratings hit, thus inspiring a second postseries movie pitting the twosome against a bionic villain. See also **Androids and Cyborgs**.

The Six Million Dollar Man (1973 TVM)
The Return of the Six Million Dollar Man and the Bionic Woman (1987 TVM)
Bionic Showdown: The Six Million Dollar Man and the Bionic Woman (1989 TVM)

Skiing

Fictional Olympic skiers have been portrayed in the movies as obsessive, self-centered types, as exemplified by Robert Redford's character in *Downhill Racer* (1969) and Wayne Rogers in *The Top of the Hill* (1980). Real-life Olympic skiers-turned-actors have chosen more likable roles, though that's done little to extend their brief film careers. Olympic great Jean-Claude Killy starred in the 1972 heist film *Snow Job*, earning high marks for his slalom skills and low ones for his acting. Suzy ("Chapstick") Chaffee's role was strictly a supporting one in the 1978 TV-movie *Ski Lift to Death*.

Non-Olympic real-life skiers have appeared in the documentaries *Last of the Ski Bums* (1969) and *The Man Who Skied Down Everest* (1976). The latter film, which chronicled the exploits of Japanese skier Yuichiro Miura, won an Oscar for Best Documentary. *Ski Bums* was a less serious affair about the joys of skiing, produced by the makers of the classic surfing documentary *The Endless Summer*. The James Bond spy thrillers have exhibited a special flair for ski scenes. A lengthy, breathtaking ski sequence, among the finest chases in the entire series, forms the centerpiece of 1969's *On Her Majesty's Secret Service*. A shorter chase opened 1977's *The Spy Who Loved Me*, ending with Bond skiing off a cliff and releasing a parachute. Bond was back on the slopes, to less effect, in 1985's *A View to a Kill*. The fact-based drama *Going for the Gold: The Bill Johnson Story*

(1985) chronicled the life of the 1984 Olympic downhill champion. A skiing accident proved to be the turning point in a weekend among friends in Alan Alda's 1981 comedy-drama *The Four Seasons*. A life-threatening accident ended the career of 1956 Olympic hopeful Jill Kilmont in the fact-based *The Other Side of the Mountain* (1975). And a childhood skiing accident accounted for Gregory Peck's amnesia in Hitchcock's *Spellbound*. On a cheerier note, the Beatles frolicked on the slopes to the tune of "Ticket to Ride" in Richard Lester's hectic 1965 farce *Help!*

The Man Who Knew Too Much (1934)	*The Man Who Skied Down Everest*
I Met Him in Paris (1937)	(1976)
Two-Faced Woman (1941)	*The Spy Who Loved Me* (1977)
Sun Valley Serenade (1941)	*The Deadly Triangle* (aka *Crisis in*
Spellbound (1945)	*Sun Valley*) (1977 TVM)
The Duchess of Idaho (1950)	*Ski Lift to Death* (1978 TVM)
Ski Troop Attack (1960)	*Lost and Found* (1979)
The Pink Panther (1964)	*The Top of the Hill* (1980 TVM)
Help! (1965)	*Swan Song* (1980 TVM)
Ski Party (1965)	*The Four Seasons* (1981)
Caprice (1967)	*Hot Dog . . . The Movie* (1984)
The Double Man (1967)	*Just the Way You Are* (1984)
Ski on the Wild Side (1967)	*Better Off Dead* (1985)
Last of the Ski Bums (1969)	*A View to a Kill* (1985)
On Her Majesty's Secret Service (1969)	*Going for the Gold: The Bill Johnson*
Ski Fever (1969)	*Story* (1985 TVM)
Downhill Racer (1969)	*Fire and Ice* (1987)
The Ski Bum (1971)	*Striker's Mountain* (1987 TVM)
The Ski Raiders (1972)	*Ski Patrol* (1990)
Snow Job (1972)	*Ski School* (1990)
Snowball Express (1972)	*Born to Ski* (1991)
The Other Side of the Mountain (aka *A*	
Window to the Sky) (1975)	

Skydiving

Strictly defined, skydiving is the sport of parachuting from airplanes and performing various body maneuvers before pulling the ripcord. Legitimate cinema skydivers have included an odd assortment of performers, ranging from Raquel Welch to Burt Lancaster to Patrick Swayze to Frankie and Annette. In *Fathom*, skydiver Ms. Welch landed in the midst of a lighthearted spy caper. John Frankenheimer's *The Gypsy Moths* took a more serious view, although it occasionally dipped into soap opera despite the presence of Burt Lancaster and Deborah Kerr. Unlikely FBI agent Patrick Swayze jumped from a plane on a dare from thrill-seeker/bank robber Sam Elliott in *Point Break*. Even Frankie Avalon and Annette Funicello took the plunge in *Beach Blanket Bingo* (in the same film, Linda Evans took credit for someone else's jump). However, the most unlikely group of skydivers was probably the Flying Elvises—and non-Elvis Nicolas Cage—who landed just outside the Bally Casino in the climax to *Honeymoon in Vegas*. Technically, James Bond (Roger Moore) was not parachuting for the fun of it in *Moonraker*'s pretitle sequence. However, his freefall fight with *Jaws* (Richard Kiel) certainly deserves an honorable mention. Likewise, parachuting (not skydiving) played a significant role in the Jerry Lewis-Dean Martin comedy *Jumping Jacks* and has been featured briefly in other military movies such as *Objective Burma, Where Eagles Dare* and *Red Dawn.* Poor Eddie Albert spent most of the *The Longest Day* hanging from a parachute stuck in a tree.

Jumping Jacks (1952)	*The Gyspy Moths* (1969)
Beach Blanket Bingo (1965)	*Moonraker* (1979)
Fathom (1967)	*Fandango* (1985)
Thin Air (aka *The Body Stealers*;	*Point Break* (1991)
Invasion of the Body Stealers)	*Honeymoon in Vegas* (1992)
(1968)	

Slasher Movies

A subgenre of the psycho thriller, the slasher movie enjoyed tremendous popularity among young adults during the 1978-83 period. John Carpenter's *Halloween* (1978) is generally considered the prototype, introducing what would become the mandatory ingredients: sexually active teenage protagonists, a conspicuous absence of adults, gory murders (the higher the body count, the better), and a seemingly indestructible killer. Despite a low budget and frail storyline, Carpenter's incredibly tense direction brought *Halloween* (q.v.) critical acclaim as well as box office millions. Amazingly, imitations were slow to follow (although the grisly-titled *Driller Killer* was released the next year). Then in 1980, Sean S. Cunningham exploited a routine thriller called *Friday the 13th* (q.v.) into a box office smash. (Nine years earlier, Cunningham had produced the infamous shocker *Last House on the Left*.) Unlike Carpenter's movie, *Friday the 13th* garnered few favorable reviews, but its lucrative grosses did not go unnoticed by low-budget filmmakers. Slasher films flooded the nation's screens during 1981, exhibiting a special fondness for titles involving holidays. Yet, with the exception of the *Friday the 13th* series, slasher films began to fade temporarily in 1983, primarily a victim of their own lack of originality. The genre was practically dead in its grave when Wes Craven (who directed *Last House on the Left*) introduced a razor-fingered killer named Freddy Krueger in 1984's *Nightmare on Elm Street* (q.v.). The *Elm Street* and *Friday the 13th* series maintained their core audiences into the early 1990s, though the time between releases lengthened. Both film series spawned television series and numerous imitations. See also **Friday the 13th; Halloween; Nightmare on Elm Street; Prom Night; Silent Night, Deadly Night; Sleepaway Camp; Slumber Party Massacre.**

Halloween (1978)	*The Final Terror* (1981)
The Driller Killer (1979)	*Funhouse* (1981)
Friday the 13th (1980)	*Graduation Day* (1981)
Mother's Day (1980)	*Happy Birthday to Me* (1981)
Prom Night (1980)	*My Bloody Valentine* (1981)
Silent Scream (1980)	*New Year's Evil* (1981)
Terror Train (1980)	*Night School* (1981)
The Burning (1981)	*Road Games* (1981)
Final Exam (1981)	*Student Bodies* (1981)

Slumber Party Massacre (1982)
Death Valley (1982)
The House on Sorority Row (1983)
Deadly Lessons (1983)
Nightmare on Elm Street (1984)
Silent Night, Deadly Night (1984)
Splatter University (1985)
Slaughter High (1986)

April Fool's Day (1986)
Bad Dreams (1988)
Cheerleader Camp (aka Bloody Pom Poms) (1988)
Shocker (1989)
Cutting Class (1989)
Darkroom (1990)
There's Nothing Out There (1991)

Sleepaway Camp

In the wake of the *Friday the 13th* (q.v.) films, 1983's *Sleepaway Camp* emerged as a weak carbon copy about another bloody killer running amok among teenage campers. However, when its sequels appeared five years later, they shifted the emphasis from gore to black humor. Shot back to back, *Sleepaway Camp II: Unhappy Campers* (1988) and *Sleepaway Camp III: Teenage Wasteland* both starred Pamela Springsteen (Bruce's sister) as the murder-minded camp counselor. Just in case any viewers had actually seen the original—in which the stalker was a man—*Unhappy Campers* explained that the killer had undergone a sex change (q.v.) operation. The transformation gave the murderer a much-needed sense of humor, as she dispatched one-liners along with the inhabitants of Camp New Horizons. In addition to Springsteen, these sequels featured other interesting casting choices. Michael J. Pollard, an Oscar nominee for *Bonnie and Clyde*, played the loony head counselor in *Unhappy Campers*. Tracy Griffith, Melanie's sister, turned up as a camper in that film, while Renee Estevez, Emilio's sister, had a supporting role in *Teenage Wasteland*. See also **Slasher Movies; Summer Camp.**

Sleepaway Camp (1983)
Sleepaway Camp II: Unhappy Campers (1988)
Sleepaway Camp III: Teenage Wasteland (1989)

Slumber Party Massacre

Feminist author Rita Mae Brown penned the script for 1982's *Slumber Party Massacre*, an unexceptional slasher film (q.v.) featuring a driller killer. Amy Jones, fresh from studying film at MIT, rescued Brown's screenplay (originally titled *Don't Open the Door*) from the file cabinets of Roger Corman's New World Pictures. Yet, despite its female author and director, *Slumber Party Massacre* exploited young girls in true stereotypical slasher film fashion. Nevertheless, it still managed to turn a nifty profit during the genre's low period. Five years later, on the heels of 1986's similar *Sorority House Massacre*, a *Slumber Party Massacre* sequel appeared, featuring Crystal Bernard of the TV series *Wings* in a major role. It found a niche in home video rentals and paved the way for a third installment starring Brittain Frye as Ken the killer and, in a minor role, former Playmate Hope Marie Carlton of *Malibu Express* (q.v.) fame. See also **Slasher Movies.**

Slumber Party Massacre (1982)
Slumber Party Massacre II (1987)
Slumber Party Massacre III (1990)

Smithee, Allen/Alan

When a director or writer wishes his name to be withdrawn from a movie—for whatever reason—he must petition the Director's or Writer's Guild of America (providing he's a member, of course). If the Guild grants his request, his credit is assigned to a fictitious person named Allen (or Alan) Smithee. At least, this has been the standard practice since 1967, when Smithee "replaced" Robert Totten and Don Siegel as directors of *Death of a Gunfighter*. In that instance, both Totten and Siegel alleged that star Richard Widmark had interfered with their creative control of the picture. Prior to the "Smithee rule," George Cukor had his name removed from 1947's *Desire Me*. Its credits simply did not list a director.

> *Death of a Gunfighter* (1967) (directors: Totten and Siegel)
> *Fade-in* (1968) (director: Jud Taylor)
> *The Challenge* (1970 TVM) (director unknown)
> *City in Fear* (1980 TVM) (director: Jud Taylor)
> *Fun and Games* (1980 TVM) (director: Paul Bogart)
> *Student Bodies* (1981) (producer: Michael Ritchie)
> *Moonlight* (1982 TVM) (directors: Jackie Cooper and Rod Holcomb)
> *Dune*—TV version (1984) (director: David Lynch)
> *Stitches* (1985) (director: Rod Holcomb)
> *Appointment With Fear* (1985) (director: Ramzi Thomas)
> *Let's Get Harry* (1986) (director: Stuart Rosenberg)
> *Dalton: Code of Vengeance II* (1986 TVM) (director unknown)
> *I Love N.Y.* (1987) (director: Gioanni Bozzacchi)
> *Ghost Fever* (1987) (director: Lee Madden)
> *Morgan Stewart's Coming Home* (1987) (director: Paul Aaron)
> *Riviera* (1987 TVM) (director: John Frankenheimer)
> *The Horror Show* (aka *House III*) (1989) (writer unknown)
> *The Shrimp on the Barbie* (1990) (director: Michael Gottlieb)
> *Starfire* (aka *Solar Crisis*; *Crisis 2050*) (1990) (director: Richard Sarafian)
> *Bloodsucking Pharaohs in Pittsburgh* (1991) (director unknown)
> *Fatal Charm* (1992 TVM) (director: Fritz Kiersch)

Smokey and the Bandit

Burt Reynolds's star power peaked with this 1977 road comedy in which he, then-girlfriend Sally Field, and Jackie Gleason seem to be having *more* fun than the audience. Burt played a bootlegger who spends the entire film eluding redneck sheriff Gleason, while having a good ol' time with chum Jerry Reed and perky passenger Field. The humor was so tongue-in-cheek that Burt almost seemed to be winking at the audience after every line. The formula provided more of the same with 1980's *Smokey and the Bandit II*, only this time it tasted a little stale, despite the presence of a baby elephant. *Smokey and the Bandit III* (1983) was a misguided attempt to make a Burt Reynolds film without Burt. Initially, Jackie Gleason played a double role, as the pursued and the pursuer. When this confused preview audiences, it was reshot with sheriff Gleason chasing Jerry Reed. By that point, no one really cared either way.

> *Smokey and the Bandit* (1977)   *Smokey and the Bandit III* (1983)
> *Smokey and the Bandit II* (1980)

SnakeEater

Jack "Soldier" Kelly (Lorenzo Lamas) was, according to a police detective crony, the "rebellious type, doesn't like authority figures." So naturally, this former marine and undercover agent had trouble battling criminals within the confines of the law—especially when some crazed hillbillies murdered his parents and kidnapped his sister. The inaugural film in this Canadian-lensed series started out as a tongue-in-cheek action picture but quickly degenerated into an uninteresting revenge tale. Lamas displayed his athletic talents, but not his acting ones. He did sport a catchy belt buckle depicting a snake (a SnakeEater, one character explains, is a special type of elite marine). The 1991 sequel opened with Soldier in a mental hospital, where he was sent for examination following his violent vigilante acts. He soon escaped, however, and set out to combat a drug kingpin. As evidenced by his delight in demolishing a biker gang in *SnakeEater III*, Soldier Kelly still needs to find more sedate ways to express himself.

    SnakeEater (1989)
    SnakeEater II—The Drug Buster (1991)
    SnakeEater III . . . His Law (1992)

Snakes

Snakes have led a charismatic screen existence, often stealing pictures on the basis of a scene or two. A wispy snake made a brief guest appearance in the 1931 Sherlock Holmes mystery *The Speckled Band*, but the picture nevertheless remained named after the viper. Likewise, the snake pit scene in *Raiders of the Lost Ark* (1981) made a lasting impression despite its brevity. A solitary snake, such as the Black Mambo in *Venom* (1982), has wreaked as much havoc as a slew of them slithering rampantly throughout a submarine, as in *Fer-de-Lance* (1974). A shy teenager conjured up giant snakes to kill her thoughtless classmates in 1978's *Jennifer*. *Stanley* (1972) used his influence on regular-sized snakes, with just as much effect. A Mayan curse turned a Cornish lass into a snake-woman in 1966's *The Reptile*, while Strother Martin's experiments slowly transformed Dirk Benedict into a king cobra in 1973's *Ssssss* ("Don't say it, hiss it!" said the ads). Amanda Donohoe boasted some ugly fangs in *Lair of the White Worm* (1988), but the film's real monster turned out to be the hideous snake god she worshiped. The only one of *The Seven Faces of Dr. Lao* (1964) *not* played by Tony Randall was the animated serpent. However, Bob Fosse did play a hissing snake in the 1974 fantasy *The Little Prince*.

The Speckled Band (1931)	*Fer-de-Lance* (1974 TVM)
The Lady Eve (1941)	*The Little Prince* (1974)
Cobra Woman (1944)	*Jennifer* (aka *Jennifer, the Snake*
Cult of the Cobra (1955)	*Goddess*) (1978)
The Seven Faces of Dr. Lao (1964)	*Raiders of the Lost Ark* (1981)
The Reptile (1966)	*Venom* (1982)
The Jungle Book (1967)	*Jaws of Satan* (aka *King Cobra*) (1982)
Snake People (aka *Isle of the Snake*	*Spasms* (1983)
People) (1968)	*Hard Ticket to Hawaii* (1987)
Stanley (1972)	*Lair of the White Worm* (1988)
Ssssss (1973)	*Fair Game* (1989)

Soap Operas

Daytime dramas, a potentially rich source for satire, have been underutilized by big screenscripters. Still, soap opera settings provided two fine performers, Beryl Reid and Dustin Hoffman, with meaty parts. *The Killing of Sister George* (1968) cast Reid as an aging actress who suspects that her once-popular soap opera character is about to be dropped permanently from the series. The film, based on Frank Marcus's play, dealt frankly with the main character's lesbianism—it was originally rated X. It also provided American viewers with a rare glimpse behind the scenes of British television (where soaps such as *Coronation Street* thrive). Compared to *Sister George*, *Tootsie* (1982) generated far less controversy—although Hoffman's character spent most of the film disguised as a woman so he could act on a soap (which certainly provided an interesting subtext). The comedy misfire *Delirious* (1991) wasted a witty premise: Soap writer John Candy bumped his head and wound up in his own fictional daytime drama (complete with veteran soap actress Emma Samms). Peter Falk played a writer of radio daytime drama in 1990's *Tune in Tomorrow.* . . . Mary McDonnell portrayed a soap star who became paralyzed in 1992's *Passion Fish*, while clairvoyant Demi Moore provided advice to a soap star in *The Butcher's Wife* (1991). Several real-life soap stars, including Demi Moore and Janine Turner of *General Hospital*, had cameos in the lame 1982 comedy *Young Doctors in Love*. On the flip side, *Peyton Place* (1961) (q.v.), a big-screen, all-star soap, spawned two television versions: the nighttime serial *Peyton Place* (1964-69) and the daytime drama *Return to Peyton Place* (1972-74). See also **Television**.

Phffft! (1954)	*Delirious* (1991)
The Killing of Sister George (1968)	*Soapdish* (1991)
Tootsie (1982)	*Passion Fish* (1992)
Tune in Tomorrow . . . (1990)	*Perry Mason: The Case of the Killer*
The Butcher's Wife (1991)	*Kiss* (1993 TVM)

Soccer

Probably the most popular sport worldwide, soccer has only recently made strides in endearing itself to American athletes and fans. The shortage of English-language soccer films reflects the game's relative obscurity in the United States prior to the 1980s. Great Britain produced soccer films such as *The Winning Goal* (1920) and *The Ball of Fortune* (1926) in the days of silent cinema. In 1942's *One of Our Aircraft Is Missing*, one of the bomber's crewmembers was a famous fictitious soccer player. A few other scattered British releases also surfaced in the 1930s and 1950s. However, in countries like Czechoslovakia and Brazil, where soccer reigns supreme, a flood of soccer films reached the public in the decades following World War II. None of these films received a major U.S. release. However, the game gained some American exposure when Sylvester Stallone headed an all-star cast, including former soccer great Pele, in the 1981 POW/soccer adventure *Victory*. That same year saw the release of Bill Forsyth's charming Scottish comedy *Gregory's Girl*, in which an incompetent goalie pursues a hot-shot female soccer teammate. An animated animal soccer game was played in the Disney 1971 fantasy *Bedknobs and Broomsticks*.

The Winning Goal (1920)	*The Ball of Fortune* (1926)

The Great Arsenal Stadium Mystery (1939)
One of Our Aircraft Is Missing (1942)
The Great Game (1953)
Small Town Story (1953)
Bloomfield (1969)
The Goalie's Anxiety at the Penalty Kick (1971)

Bedknobs and Broomsticks (1971)
The Hero (1972)
Yesterday's Hero (1979)
Victory (aka Escape to Victory) (1981)
Gregory's Girl (1981)
Hotshot (1987)
Ladybugs (1992)

Somewhere Series

War-weary British audiences of the 1940s found the *Somewhere* films agreeably silly in spite of their nonexistent plots and sloppy production values. The movies consisted mostly of old, loosely connected vaudeville sketches performed by dancehall veterans like Frank Randle, Harry Korris and Robbie Vincent. The lowbrow humor frequently bordered on tastelessness, making the *Somewhere* films the forerunners of the *Carry On* (q.v.) comedies of the late 1950s and 1960s. Ironically, Randle made a 1949 non-*Somewhere* film called *What a Carry On*.

Somewhere in England (1940)
Somewhere in Camp (1942)
Somewhere on Leave (1942)

Somewhere in Civvies (1943)
Somewhere in Politics (1949)

South Pole, *see* North Pole/South Pole

Spiders

Is it their shape? Their four pairs of eyes? The fact that some are deadly poisonous? It's hard to figure out why the movies have cast good-natured spiders as vile henchmen or oversized people-eaters. Nevertheless, silly-looking giant spiders appeared in *The Spider* (1958), *The Lost World* (1960), *Son of Godzilla* (1968) and *Giant Spider Invasion* (1975). Jungle Jim (q.v.) chased a big one that produced a valuable drug in 1951's *Fury of the Congo*. Raquel Welch ran in the opposite direction of another giant web-spinner, created with precision by special effects expert Ray Harryhausen in *One Million Years B.C.* (1966). Scientist Leo G. Carroll's artificial food was responsible for creating the most famous oversized spider in 1955's *Tarantula*. The spider killed by Grant Williams with a straight pin in *The Incredible Shrinking Man* ran a close second, even though it was not really giant (but certainly appeared that way to the incredibly small Williams). Man/fly David Hedison also encountered a little spider that probably looked big to him in 1958's *The Fly*. Unfortunately, he did not have access to a handy pin. Normal-sized spiders have been used for evil purposes by satanists (*The Devil's Bride*) and crafty murderers. Indeed, Gale Sondergaard employed spiders to make her murders look like suicides in 1944's *Spider Woman*. She might have escaped detection if not for the presence of that master sleuth Sherlock Holmes (Basil Rathbone). Interestingly, Sondergaard also starred in a 1946 film called *The Spider Woman Strikes Back*—but she played a different character and there were no spiders! Meanwhile, Holmes (Peter Cushing this time) saved Henry Baskerville from a deadly tarantula in 1959's *The Hound of the Baskervilles*. For the most part, though, solitary little spiders have posed little trouble. A thousand or more? That's a different story altogether, as evidenced by the invasions detailed in *Kingdom of the Spiders* (1977), *Tarantulas: The Deadly Cargo* (1977 TVM) and *Arachnaphobia* (1990). Tom Selleck met up with a robot spider in the 1982 science fiction thriller *Runaway*. And—at last—a nice spider got a starring role in the animated adaptation of E.B. White's children's classic *Charlotte's Web*. See also **The Fly; Insects.**

Spider Woman (aka *Sherlock Holmes and the Spider Woman*) (1944)

Sombra, the Spider Woman (aka *The Black Widow*) (1947)

Fury of the Congo (1951)

Tarantula (1955)

The Incredible Shrinking Man (1957)

The Spider (aka *Earth vs. the Spider*) (1958)

The Fly (1958)

The Hound of the Baskervilles (1959)

The Lost World (1960)

One Million Years B.C. (1966)

The Devil's Bride (aka *The Devil Rides Out*) (1967)

Son of Godzilla (1968)

Charlotte's Web (1973)

Giant Spider Invasion (1975)

Spider-Man (1977 TVM)

Kingdom of the Spiders (1977)

Tarantulas: The Deadly Cargo (1977 TVM)

Runaway (1982)

Arachnaphobia (1990)

An American Tail: Fievel Goes West (1991)

Star Trek

The road from cancelled TV series to phenomenally successful film series is a bizarre one, traveled only by the *Starship Enterprise*. Gene Roddenberry's science fiction TV series debuted on NBC in 1966. Science fiction fans embraced it, but it was a consistent ratings loser opposite veteran series like *My Three Sons* and *Bewitched*. An enthusiastic write-in campaign saved it from cancellation after its second season, but the series was axed after its third year in 1969. Shortly thereafter, its seventy-eight episodes went into syndication and began playing almost daily on local TV stations. By 1974, the show had developed a dizzyingly loyal cult following (dubbed "trekkies") that honored stars William Shatner (Kirk) and Leonard Nimoy (Spock) at national conventions and urged Roddenberry to revive the series. Roddenberry tried just that. He had laid the groundwork for a *Star Trek* made-for-TV movie (and pilot for a new series) when George Lucas's *Star Wars* went through the box office roof in 1977. Eager to duplicate *Star Wars*'s receipts, Paramount decided to turn its *Star Trek* movie into a lavish theatrical space opera. The $40-million *Star Trek—The Motion Picture* was rushed into theaters just in time for Christmas 1979. Trekkies made it a hit, but the reviews were mixed, with critics and fans complaining of an overemphasis on special effects. However, best-selling writer-turned-director Nicholas Meyer set the film series on track with the 1982 sequel *Star Trek II: The Wrath of Khan*. Jack Soward's script resurrected super-villain Khan (Ricardo Montalban) from the TV episode "Space Seed" and climaxed with Spock's "death." Leonard Nimoy took over the directing reins for *Star Trek III: The Search for Spock* (1984) and *Star Trek IV: The Voyage Home* (1986), both of which were praised for capturing the flavor of the series. After helming the non-*Trek* smash *Three Men and a Baby* (1987), Nimoy handed over *Star Trek* directing chores to his costar. William Shatner directed and cowrote the story for 1989's *Star Trek V: The Final Frontier*, which opened strongly enough to temporarily oust *Indiana Jones and the Last*

Crusade from number one on *Variety*'s box office charts. Its popularity was short-lived, however, as even faithful fans found it a plodding, unexciting trek with old friends. The *Enterprise* crew returned two years later with the satisfying, though unremarkable, *Star Trek VI: The Undiscovered Country*. Its sentimental ending hinted that this installment was the last for the original cast. Roddenberry launched *Star Trek: The Next Generation*, a syndicated TV series with a cast of newcomers, in 1987.

Star Trek — The Motion Picture (1979)
Star Trek II: The Wrath of Khan (1982)
Star Trek III: The Search for Spock (1984)
Star Trek IV: The Voyage Home (1986)
Star Trek V: The Final Frontier (1989)
Star Trek VI: The Undiscovered Country (1991)

Star Wars

George Lucas's tremendously popular space adventure trilogy has developed its own mythos in an amazingly short period of time. When *Variety* predicted a "huge outlook" for *Star Wars* back in 1977, it turned out to be the venerable trade paper's grossest understatement. But the film's greatest impact was not in dollars, but in influencing the near-future of American cinema. Like another late 1970s hit, *Halloween* (q.v.), *Star Wars* fostered dozens of imitations, such as *Battle Beyond the Stars* (1980), *Spacehunter* (1983), *The Ice Pirates* (1984) and the Mel Brooks spoof *Spaceballs* (1986). However, whereas *Halloween* impacted on a specific genre, Lucas's mixture of adventure and morals carried over into non-science fiction films — most notably his and Steven Spielberg's *Indiana Jones* (q.v.) movies. Curiously, Lucas's interest in the *Star Wars* films seemed to diminish as the series progressed. He turned over the directing reins to Irvin Kershner on 1980's *The Empire Strikes Back* (arguably the best) and to Richard Marquand on 1983's *Return of the Jedi*. Despite insisting that the trilogy was the middle three chapters of a longer series, Lucas has shown no intention of making additional, framing films. He did, nonetheless, give the furry and friendly little Ewoks (introduced in *Return*) two TV-movie adventures. Although oriented toward the juvenile audience, these small-screen sequels boasted the usual excellent production values and a reasonable amount of charm. The major theatrical stars — Harrison Ford, Mark Hamill, Carrie Fisher — were naturally missing.

Star Wars (1977)
The Empire Strikes Back (1980)
Return of the Jedi (1983)

The Ewok Adventure (1984 TVM)
Ewoks: The Battle for Endor (1985 TVM)

Statues Come to Life

German director/actor Paul Wegener gave the cinema its first living statue with his 1914 horror classic *The Golem: Monster of Fate* and its 1920 prequel *The Golem: How He Came to Be*. These films were based on a Jewish myth about a rabbi who brought to life a giant man of clay to protect persecuted Jews. However, when the rabbi lost control of his creation, a young girl destroyed it by removing the Star of David from its chest. The same story served as the basis for Julian Duvivier's *Golem* (1936), the French television film *Le Golem* (1966), and an updated

British version called *It* (1966) starring Roddy McDowell. An interesting Japanese variation, *Majin, Monster of Terror* (1966) told the story of a giant stone god summoned to wreak vengeance on those who displaced a kingdom's rightful rulers. Two sequels, *The Return of Majin* and *Majin Strikes Again*, also appeared in 1966. Bill Murray, Dan Aykroyd and Harold Ramis used "positive slime" to bring the Statue of Liberty to life to battle evil in 1989's *Ghostbusters II*. Not all living statues have been of the giant variety, nor have they been necessarily humanlike. Ava Gardner played a storefront statue of Venus who became a living mortal in 1948's *One Touch of Venus*. Yet another Venus statue came to life in the form of game show hostess Vanna White in the 1988 TV-movie *The Goddess of Love*. A contemporary witch sent a giant stone eagle to dispense with a college professor and his wife in the intelligent 1962 fantasy *Burn, Witch, Burn*. Statues turned into people and people into statues in Jean Cocteau's stylized *Blood of a Poet* (1930). See **Gorgons** for other movies where people have been transformed into statues.

> *The Golem: Monster of Fate* (aka *Der Golem*) (1914)
>
> *The Golem: How He Came to Be* (aka *Der Golem, Wie Er in die Welt Kam*) (1920)
>
> *Blood of a Poet* (aka *Le Sang d'un Poete*) (1930)
>
> *One Touch of Venus* (1948)
>
> *The Miracle* (1959)
>
> *Burn, Witch, Burn* (aka *Night of the Eagle*) (1962)
>
> *Jason and the Argonauts* (1963)
>
> *It* (1966)
>
> *Majin, Monster of Terror* (aka *Majin, the Hideous Monster; Daimajin*) (1966)
>
> *Majin Strikes Again* (aka *Daimajin Gyakushu*) (1966)
>
> *The Return of Majin* (aka *The Return of Giant Majin; Daimajin Ikaru*) (1966)
>
> *The Golden Voyage of Sinbad* (1973)
>
> *Mannequin* (1987)
>
> *Creepshow 2* (1987)
>
> *The Goddess of Love* (1988 TVM)
>
> *Ghostbusters II* (1989)

The Stepfather Series

One good movie does not make a good series. *The Stepfather* (1987) was an effective sleeper featuring an outstanding performance from Terry O'Quinn as a psychopath. The film starts with a family squabble which results in the father's massacre of the rest of the family. It seems that Dad (O'Quinn) wants a perfect family and will settle for nothing less. He departs calmly for another city where he romances a young mother and takes on a new family—complete with suspicious stepdaughter. The unnecessary 1989 sequel revealed that O'Quinn's character had survived the first film, only to be imprisoned in an asylum. He promptly escapes, sets up business as a marriage counselor (of all things!), and begins romancing another young widow. Wisely, O'Quinn bowed out of the series after this installment. Robert Wightman replaced him for the 1992 made-for-cable *Stepfather III*, in which the killer undergoes plastic surgery (thus explaining the new face) and pursues Priscilla Barnes. As with the second film, it offered no new deviations on the original idea. Unfortunately, that's not always a prerequisite for ending a film series, as evidenced by the plethora of low-budget series such as *Sleepaway Camp* and *Silent Night, Deadly Night* (qq.v.).

> The Stepfather (1987)
> Stepfather II (aka Stepfather II: Make Room for Daddy) (1989)
> Stepfather III (1992 TVM)

The Stepford Wives

A dark satire disguised as a horror film, 1975's *The Stepford Wives* took male chauvinism to outrageous extremes. Katharine Ross starred as a young wife who accompanies her husband to their new home in the quiet suburban town of Stepford, Connecticut. Ross soon begins to notice something odd about her fellow females. Slowly, she discovers that the husbands of Stepford are "trading in" their human wives for obedient robotic replicas. Unlike another adaptation of an Ira Levin novel, *Rosemary's Baby* (1968), *The Stepford Wives* did not burn up the box office. However, like *Rosemary's Baby*, it did spawn a made-for-TV sequel. In *Revenge of the Stepford Wives* (1980), Sharon Gless played a TV reporter who uncovers another dark suburban secret about Stepford. Apparently, no one listened to her, for Don Murray moved his family there in another TV-movie sequel, 1987's *The Stepford Children*. In this slight variation, the Stepford men seek to replace their troublesome kids with well-behaved robots. Fortunately, the series ended before the Stepford pets could be replaced. See also **Androids and Cyborgs**.

> The Stepford Wives (1975)
> Revenge of the Stepford Wives (1980 TVM)
> The Stepford Children (1987 TVM)

Stevens, Cat

Not to be confused with the same-named singer, this double-crossing con artist and gunfighter appeared in a spaghetti-Western trilogy directed by Giuseppe Colizzi. Terrence Hill (real name Mario Girotti) played Cat in all three entries, although he would later find far greater fame and fortune as the lead in the Trinity series (q.v.). The first Cat Stevens entry, 1966's *God Forgives, I Don't*, was notable for pairing the handsome Hill with gruff, burly Bud Spencer (real name Carlo Pedersoli). Hill and Spencer went on to enjoy great success as an Italian "Odd Couple," starring together in all three Cat Stevens entries, the two best Trinity films, and even contemporary action comedies such as *All the Way, Boys* (1973) and *Watch Out, We're Mad* (1974). See also **Trinity**.

> God Forgives, I Don't (aka Dio Perdona . . . Io No!; Blood River) (1966)
> Ace High (I Quattro dell'Ave Maria; Revenge at El Paso; Four Gunmen of Ave Maria) (1967)
> Boot Hill (aka La Collina degli Stivali) (1969)

Stores

Where would you shop for a vicious dog, a flesh-eating ghoul or a mannequin-come-to-life? If you lived in a movie, you could walk down to the nearest department store and find these unusual items and more. Stores have provided colorful background settings for a number of films. Few movies, however, have confined themselves to a store setting for the bulk of their running times. In 1973's *Trapped*, James Brolin recovered from a mugging to find himself locked overnight in a department store—in the company of a nasty, people-eating security dog. Still, that sounds preferable to the shopping mall in 1979's *Dawn of the Dead*, which was populated by flesh-eating ghouls (q.v.) and a gang of crazy bikers. Other mall-bound movies featured similar horrific elements: killer security robots in *Chopping Mall* (1986) and inept dialogue between Woody Allen and Bette Midler in *Scenes From a Mall* (1991). Movies less confined to their store settings have induced an impressive list of Hollywood stars to step behind the counters: James Stewart and Margaret Sullavan (*The Shop Around the Corner*), Rod Steiger (*The Pawnbroker*), Ginger Rogers (*Bachelor Mother*) and Gene Hackman (*All Night Long*). The Marx Brothers and Jerry Lewis wreaked havoc on department stores in, respectively, *The Big Store* and *Who's Minding the Store?* Rock Hudson, in one of his first roles, played a store detective in 1950's *I Was a Shoplifter*. Bob Hoskins played a pet shop owner who moonlighted as a private detective in *Shattered* (1991). Talia Shire also worked in a pet store before she married Sylvester Stallone in *Rocky* (1976), while Rod Taylor and Tippi Hedren met in a pet shop at the beginning of *The Birds* (1963). However, the most famous specialty store probably remains Mr. Mushnik's flower shop, better known as *The Little Shop of Horrors* (1960). It gained fame as the home of the Audrey II, the world's most famous people-devouring plant.

Shop Angel (1932)	*The Shop on Main Street* (aka *The*
Sweepings (1933)	*Shop on High Street*) (1965)
Employees' Entrance (1933)	*The Pawnbroker* (1965)
The Nitwits (1935)	*Trapped* (1973 TVM)
Bachelor Mother (1939)	*Fire Sale* (1977)
The Shop Around the Corner (1940)	*The Girls in the Office* (1979 TVM)
The Big Store (1941)	*Dawn of the Dead* (1979)
The Devil and Miss Jones (1941)	*All Night Long* (1981)
Miracle on 34th Street (aka *The Big*	*Chopping Mall* (aka *Killbots*) (1986)
Heart) (1947)	*The Little Shop of Horrors* (1986)
One Touch of Venus (1948)	*Mannequin* (1987)
I Was a Shoplifter (1950)	*Lady Beware* (1987)
Trouble in Store (1953)	*Big* (1988)
Bundle of Joy (1956)	*Scenes From a Mall* (1991)
The Little Shop of Horrors (1960)	*Career Opportunities* (1991)
Who's Minding the Store? (1963)	*To Be the Best* (1992 TVM)

Strippers

Strippers have appeared in the background of many films but have been the subject of few. Celebrated stripper/actress/author Gypsy Rose Lee had a hand in four films about strippers. Her mystery novel *The G-String Murders* was adapted for the screen as the 1943 Barbara Stanwyck vehicle *Lady of Burlesque*. This potentially grisly story about a backstage strangler wisely mixed in comedy elements. In Britain, it sported the more exploitative title *Striptease Lady*. Lee's play *Doll Face*, about a burlesque queen with Broadway ambitions, was turned into the same-titled 1945 film. Likewise, her autobiography *Gypsy* spawned a hit Broadway musical and a 1962 movie version. Finally, she appeared in a supporting role in 1963's *The Stripper*. Based on William Inge's play *A Loss of Roses*, it starred a miscast Joanne Woodward as a former stripper seeking a new life and becoming involved with a nineteen-year-old. Danish actress Britt Ekland played an Amish girl-turned-stripper in William Friedkin's fond homage to old-time burlesque *The Night They Raided Minsky's* (1968). Other actresses who have played strippers include Goldie Hawn (*CrissCross*), Melanie Griffith (*Fear City*) and Sherilyn Fenn (*Ruby*). The serious side of striptease was explored in 1986's *Stripper*, a surprisingly straightforward, nonexploitative documentary about three professional strippers entering a Las Vegas contest. Naturally, B-movie directors have exploited striptease for its cheesecake value. Drive-in filler of this kind has ranged from disgusting tripe like 1987's *Stripped to Kill* to modestly amusing fodder like Stephanie Rothman's *The Working Girls*. The latter film, a pay-TV favorite, featured Cassandra Petersen (TV horror hostess Elvira) as a part-time stripper. Male strippers have not received equal time, although Christopher Atkins played one in 1983's best-forgotten *A Night in Heaven*. His leading lady was Lesley Ann Warren, an ecdysiast herself in 1982's *Portrait of a Stripper*.

Lady of Burlesque (aka *Striptease Lady*) (1943)	*Portrait of a Stripper* (1982 TVM)
	A Night in Heaven (1983)
Delightfully Dangerous (1945)	*Fear City* (1984)
Doll Face (1945)	*Little Treasure* (1985)
Lady Godiva Rides Again (1951)	*Stripper* (1986)
Sex Kittens Go to College (aka *The Beauty and the Robot*) (1960)	*Kandyland* (1987)
A Cold Wind in August (1961)	*Stripped to Kill* (1987)
Danger by My Side (1962)	*Ladykillers* (1988 TVM)
Gypsy (1962)	*Dance of the Damned* (1989)
The Stripper (aka *Woman of Summer*) (1963)	*Stripped to Kill 2* (1989)
	Blaze (1989)
The Night They Raided Minsky's (1968)	*CrissCross* (1992)
	Ruby (1992)
The Working Girls (1973)	*Somebody's Daughter* (1992 TVM)
Between the Lines (1977)	*Candy the Stripper* (1993)

Stunt People

Films about stunt people naturally tend to emphasize action over intellect, as in 1978's *Hooper*, an easygoing Burt Reynolds vehicle about an aging stuntman contemplating one last death-defying feat. In both *Stunt Seven* (1979) and *Stunts Unlimited* (1980), the government sent stunt experts on top-secret rescue missions. No one bothered to question the logic behind substituting Hollywood union men for military-trained specialists. The engrossing real-life story of a deaf stuntwoman was the subject of *Silent Victory: The Kitty O'Neil Story* (1979). In 1980, *The Stunt Man* offered a thought-provoking yarn about a desperate fugitive (Steve Railsback) hired by a crazy film director (Peter O'Toole) to perform dangerously real stunts. On television, Lee Majors played a stuntman who tracked down bail jumpers on the side in *The Fall Guy*. A lunatic casting director somehow concluded that the Dave Clark Five would be just right as the fun-loving stuntmen in 1965's *Having a Wild Weekend.*

Lucky Devils (1932)
Palm Springs Weekend (1963)
Having a Wild Weekend (aka *Catch Us If You Can*) (1965)
Stuntman (1968)
Night Moves (1975)
Hollywood Boulevard (1976)
Stunts (aka *Who Is Killing the Stuntmen?*) (1977)

Hooper (1978)
Texas Detour (1978)
Silent Victory: The Kitty O'Neil Story (1979 TVM)
Stunt Seven (1979 TVM)
Stunts Unlimited (1980 TVM)
The Stunt Man (1980)

Submarines

Tense war melodramas and fanciful science fiction adventures have made the most effective use of submarine settings. The 1938 *Submarine Patrol* was a routine World War I actioner that unknowingly paved the way for later World War II star-studded efforts. In 1943 alone, Cary Grant navigated a submarine into Japanese waters in *Destination Tokyo*; Humphrey Bogart took on the Germans in *Action in the North Atlantic*; John Mills helmed a British sub in *We Dive at Dawn*; and Tyrone Power clashed with Dana Andrews in *Crash Dive*. The popularity of sub war dramas decreased in the 1950s, but big name stars still kept them afloat at the box office. Sub officers Clark Gable and Burt Lancaster engaged in a bitter conflict in 1958's *Run Silent, Run Deep*. That same year, Glenn Ford was given a mission to destroy a Japanese ship carrying his family in *Torpedo Run*. The only World War II films to survive into the 1960s were epic-scale features like *The Longest Day* (1962) and *Battle of the Bulge* (1965). The submarine war film disappeared into obscurity until the German-made *Das Boot* (*The Boat*) unexpectedly surfaced to wow art-house audiences in 1981. An incredibly tense, claustrophobic thriller, it traced the final days of a doomed German submarine during World War II. In contrast to the realism of war, futuristic submarines have appeared principally in escapist entertainment. Two Jules Verne novels provided the basis for the best-known submarine fantasies. Disney's 1954 adaptation of *20,000 Leagues Under the Sea* remains a splendid spectacle for children of all ages, highlighted by a thrilling attack by a giant squid. Verne's sequel *Mysterious Island* has been filmed twice, first as a loose adaptation in 1929 and later as a compact 1961 adventure (which actually contained little footage of the famous submarine *Nautilus*). Irwin Allen, in his pre-disaster movie days, produced 1961's *Voyage to the Bottom of Sea*, which starred Walter Pidgeon as commander of the submarine *Seaview*. The wild plot pitted the *Seaview* against a giant octopus, on-board saboteurs, and a radiation belt threatening to burn the Earth to a crisp. The *Seaview*, with Richard Basehart replacing Pidgeon, transitioned to television as the 1964-68 series *Voyage to the Bottom of the Sea*. The most elaborate submarine was probably the supership featured in the 1963 Japanese fantasy *Atragon* — it could travel underwater, on land or in the air! Animated Beatles sailed aboard 1968's *Yellow Submarine* (which is where they all lived). In 1966's *Batman*, the Penguin, the Riddler, the Joker and the Cat Woman plotted mischief from within a penguin-shaped submarine. James Bond used a minisub in *Thunderball* (1965), while a full-sized submarine was stolen in the 1977 Bond adventure *The Spy Who Loved Me*. Herpephobes should avoid *Fer-de-Lance*, a 1974 TV-movie about snakes slithering rampantly about a damaged submarine.

Mysterious Island (1929)
The Devil and the Deep (1932)
Hell Below (1933)
Submarine D-1 (1937)
Submarine Patrol (1938)
Escape to Glory (aka *Submarine Zone*) (1940)
Crash Dive (1943)
Destination Tokyo (1943)
We Dive at Dawn (1943)
Action in the North Atlantic (1943)
The Damned (1947)
Operation Disaster (aka *Morning Departure*) (1950)
Hell and High Water (1954)
20,000 Leagues Under the Sea (1954)
Above Us the Waves (1956)
The Deep Six (1958)
Run Silent, Run Deep (1958)
The Silent Enemy (1958)
Torpedo Run (1958)
Atomic Submarine (1959)
On the Beach (1959)
Operation Pellicoat (1959)
Up Periscope (1959)
Atlantis, the Lost Continent (1960)

Mysterious Island (1961)
Voyage to the Bottom of the Sea (1961)
Mystery Submarine (aka *Decoy*) (1962)
Atragon (1963)
The Bedford Incident (1965)
Around the World Under the Sea (1966)
The Russians Are Coming! The Russians Are Coming! (1966)
Batman (1966)
Assault on the Wayne (1966 TVM)
Yellow Submarine (1968)
Submarine X-1 (1968)
Nobody's Perfect (1968)
Ice Station Zebra (1969)
Latitude Zero (1969)
The Land That Time Forgot (1974)
Fer-de-Lance (1974 TVM)
The Spy Who Loved Me (1977)
Gray Lady Down (1978)
Das Boot (aka *The Boat*) (1981)
The Fifth Missile (1986)
The Abyss (1989)
The Hunt for Red October (1990)
Full Fathom Five (1990)
Endless Descent (1991)

Subways

Underground trains have been underutilized as film settings, principally because their frequent stops and passenger turnover prohibit the development of an involved plot. Nevertheless, French director Luc Bresson fashioned a stylish tale about contemporary underground denizens in 1985's *Subway*. The underrated horror film *Raw Meat* was about the trapped survivors of a London subway disaster and their descendants—who evolved into cannibals. Vicious Robert Shaw and cronies hijacked a NYC subway and held the passengers for ransom in the 1974 thriller *The Taking of Pelham One Two Three*. Exciting subway chase sequences appeared in *Predator 2, Highlander 2: The Quickening, Eve of Destruction* and *Lethal Weapon 3*. The difficulties of getting a seat on the morning subway were explored in the 1950 comedy *Pretty Baby*. Youth gangs harassed subway passengers in *The Warriors* (1979) and *We're Fighting Back* (1981). Subway workers figured prominently in the plots of *No Time for Love* (1943) and *Sugarbaby* (1985). The remains of an alien spaceship were unearthed during a subway station excavation in the clever science-fiction fantasy *Five Million Years to Earth* (1967). See also **Trains**.

No Time for Love (1943)
Pretty Baby (1950)
Dutchman (1966)
Five Million Years to Earth (aka
    Quatermass and the Pit) (1967)
The Incident (1967)
Short Walk to Daylight (1972 TVM)
Raw Meat (aka Deathline) (1973)
The Taking of Pelham One Two Three
    (1974)

The Warriors (1979)
We're Fighting Back (1981)
Subway (1985)
Sugar Baby (1985)
Predator 2 (1990)
Highlander 2: The Quickening (1991)
Eve of Destruction (1991)
Lethal Weapon 3 (1992)

Suicide

Although suicide has played an integral role in dozens of features, films expressly about it fall into two general categories. The first includes movies in which someone attempts to thwart a potential suicide. In 1951's *Fourteen Hours*, Richard Basehart spent the better part of a day on a skyscraper's ledge as likable policeman Paul Douglas and others (including Grace Kelly) tried to talk him out of taking the plunge. While Basehart's character fell into a net and lived, Sissy Spacek succeeded in killing herself in 1986's *'Night, Mother*, despite desperate pleas from parent Anne Bancroft. An angel named Clarence dissuaded James Stewart from suicide in Frank Capra's perennial holiday offering *It's a Wonderful Life* (1946). Paralyzed Richard Dreyfuss fought a hospital staff for his right to die in the powerful *Whose Life Is It Anyway?* (1981). The second category of suicide films revolves around how a loved one's suicide affects the living. Families and friends dealt with devastating teenage suicides in *Silence of the Heart* (1984), *Surviving* (1985) and *Permanent Record* (1988). Angie Dickinson played a woman trying to rebuild her life after her husband took his in *The Suicide's Wife* (1979). On the lighter side, suicide has been played for laughs in a handful of offbeat comedies. After tightening a noose around his neck in *Reuben, Reuben*, poet Tom Conti changed his mind—only to have a dog burst into the room and knock his chair out from under him. Bud Cort delighted in staging elaborate fake suicides in the cult classic *Harold and Maude* (1971). In 1978's *The End*, a dying man unable to commit suicide decides he needs professional help with his death. Would-be suicide victims met and fell in love in *Paris in Spring* (1935) and *Tulips* (1981). And four middle-aged men decided to commit group suicide by eating themselves to death in the French farce *La Grande Bouffe* (1973). Several films have climaxed in shocking suicides. *Guyana Tragedy: The Story of Jim Jones* (1980) ended with the bizarre mass suicide staged in the late 1970s by the Rev. Jones and his cult followers. A murderess (Jean Simmons) rejected by her lover (Robert Mitchum) backed their car off a cliff in Otto Preminger's *Angel Face* (1953). In 1948's *The Red Shoes*, a ballerina confronted with choosing between art and love plunges to her death. Ship steward Edmund Gwenn explained the ultimate fate of suicide victims to the dead passengers aboard his ship in *Between Two Worlds* (1944).

Dangerous Corner (1934)
Paris in Spring (aka Paris Love Song)
    (1935)
Between Two Worlds (1944)

It's a Wonderful Life (1946)
The Red Shoes (1948)
Fourteen Hours (1951)
Angel Face (1953)

The Slender Thread (1965)
The Art of Love (1965)
Harold and Maude (1971)
La Grande Bouffe (1973)
The End (1978)
Leap Into the Void (1979)
The Suicide's Wife (aka A New Life)
   (1979 TVM)
Guyana Tragedy: The Story of Jim
   Jones (1980 TVM)
Tulips (1981)
Whose Life Is It Anyway? (1981)

The Eyes, the Mouth (1982)
Reuben, Reuben (1983)
Right of Way (1983 TVM)
Silence of the Heart (1984 TVM)
A Reason to Live (1985 TVM)
Mishima (1985)
Surviving (1985 TVM)
'Night Mother (1986)
Permanent Record (1988)
Retribution (1988)
Last Wish (1992 TVM)
Woman on the Ledge (1993 TVM)

Summer Camp

Summer camp settings seem to foster rivalries, love affairs and pranks among their teen residents. Rivals Kristy McNichol and Tatum O'Neal wagered with each other on who would lose her virginity first at the summer camp in *Little Darlings* (1980). On a broader scale, the boys and girls of Camp Sasquatch challenged the rich kids' camp across the river to an absurd athletic contest in *Meatballs* (q.v.) (1979). And the Peanuts Gang (q.v.) got involved in a river race in *Race for Your Life, Charlie Brown* (1977). Michael J. Fox and Nancy McKeon found summer camp love in the 1975 TV-movie comedy *Poison Ivy*. A more honest relationship, between a disfigured teenage boy and a blind girl, took place at the summer camp in *Mask* (1985). The 1987 *Ernest Goes to Camp* dispensed with any pretensions of plot and focused on the antics of a bumbling counselor and his practical joke-prone charges. Hayley Mills played a pair of twins who meet accidentally at a summer camp and wind up reuniting their divorced parents in *The Parent Trap* (1961). *The Acorn People* (1981) was a heartwarming story about a camp for severely handicapped youngsters. Murders galore took place at the isolated summer camps in the *Friday the 13th* films (q.v.), *The Burning* (1981) and *Summer Camp Nightmare* (1987). See also **Friday the 13th; Meatballs; Sleepaway Camp.**

Make a Wish (1937)
The Under-Pup (1939)
There's Magic in Music (1941)
Summer Love (1958)
Beware of Children (1961)
The Parent Trap (1961)
Please Sir (1971)
Poison Ivy (1975 TVM)
Race for Your Life, Charlie Brown
   (1977)
Piranha (1978)
Meatballs (1979)
Friday the 13th (1980)
Little Darlings (1980)

Gorp (1980)
The Burning (1981)
The Acorn People (1981 TVM)
Oddballs (1983)
Sleepaway Camp (1983)
Mask (1985)
Party Camp (1986)
Ernest Goes to Camp (1987)
Summer Camp Nightmare (aka The
   Butterfly Revolution) (1987)
Camp Cucamonga (1990 TVM)
Princes in Exile (1991 TVM)
Indian Summer (1993)

Superfly

One of the most successful blaxploitation (q.v.) films of the early 1970s, *Superfly* remains a morally ambiguous tale about a black drug dealer who double-crosses his cronies, goes "straight," and jets off to Italy. Youngblood Priest (Ron O'Neal) dresses sharply and always acts cool. He's a charming drug lord, especially compared to the scum surrounding him (this apparently justifies his actions). Despite its questionable social values, the film clicked at the box office and with critics who admired its hip style. Composer Curtis Mayfield scored two top ten singles with "Freddie's Dead" and "Superfly." O'Neal took the directorial reins for the inevitable sequel, 1973's *Superfly T.N.T.* This meandering follow-up found a disenchanted Priest running guns to help an oppressed African country. It faded quickly at theaters and relegated O'Neal to supporting roles. A third entry, *The Return of Superfly*, unexpectedly surfaced in 1990. Nathan Purdee took over as Priest, who returns from exile in Paris to get even with his old gang. Mayfield completed the music score shortly before his death. See also **Blaxploitation Films**.

Superfly (1972)   *The Return of Superfly* (1990)
Superfly T.N.T. (1973)

Superman

"You'll believe a man can fly!" proclaimed the ads when *Superman* was released in 1978. Millions of moviegoers did just that, making the Man of Steel's celebrated screen return the first of a profitable series. Actually, Superman made his first feature-length movie appearance in 1951 in the guise of stocky George Reeves. *Superman and the Mole Men* (1951) was a low-budget independent feature aimed at the juvenile trade. It would have likely remained a B-movie oddity, except that its minor success resulted in the phenomenal, syndicated TV series *The Adventures of Superman*. In all, 104 half-hour episodes were broadcast originally between 1952 and 1957. Reeves starred as Clark Kent/Superman, with Phyllis Coates and later Noel Neill as Lois Lane, Jack Larson as Jimmy Olsen, and John Hamilton as Perry White. Despite obvious budget limitations, the series made the most of its special effects. Later episodes were even filmed in color, a television rarity in the 1950s. Sadly, Reeves became typecast by the role and had difficulty finding work, a fact that may have attributed to his 1959 suicide. The Superman character, created by writer Jerry Siegel and artist Joe Shuster, first appeared in comic book form in 1939. Bud Collyer provided the voice of Superman for a 1940-1951 radio series. Kirk Allyn also played the Man of Steel in 1948 and 1950 serials (and can be seen as Lois Lane's father in the TV-expanded version of 1978's *Superman*). But with the 1978 smash *Superman*, Christopher Reeve made the role his own for a generation of comic book lovers. Much of the 1981 sequel *Superman II* was filmed simultaneously with the first film, partially accounting for the original's $55 million price tag. Whereas *Superman* dealt with the Man of Steel's origin and introduced the supporting characters, *Superman II* promptly pitted our hero against three vicious outlaws from his own planet. The romance between Lois Lane (Margot Kidder) and Clark Kent/Superman was also developed, to the extent that they consummated their relationship. The series took an inexplicable turn for the worse with 1983's *Superman III*, which boasted the additional marquee value of Richard Pryor. Margot Kidder made a brief appearance as Lois Lane, but

Superman's love interest was old flame Lana Lang (Annette O'Toole). Reeve balked at starring in a fourth film, so executive producers Ilya and Alexander Salkind brought *Supergirl* to the screen in 1984. Casting an unknown (as they did with Reeve), the Salkinds failed to create another star in girl-next-door Helen Slater. The silly plot and Faye Dunaway's hammy villainess were a far cry from *Superman II*. The only cast holdover from the *Superman* films was Marc McClure as Jimmy Olsen. The failure of *Supergirl* apparently ended the series. However, Cannon Films acquired distribution rights from Warner Bros. and lured Reeve back into the fold. The actor wrote the story and directed some scenes in 1987's *Superman IV: The Quest for Peace*. Despite the presence of Gene Hackman (returning as Lex Luthor) and a token appearance by Kidder, *Superman IV* was a victim of shoddy special effects and a pretentious plot. It sent Superman packing for an indefinite vacation from the movies. See also **Comic Book Characters.**

Superman and the Mole Men (1951)	*Supergirl* (1984)
Superman (1978)	*Superman IV: The Quest for Peace*
Superman II (1981)	(1987)
Superman III (1983)	

Surfing

The quest for the Big Wave was a constant teenage concern in the lightweight *Gidget* (q.v.) and *Beach Party* (q.v.) movies of the 1960s. However, serious surfers had little opportunity to promote their sport prior to Bruce Brown's 1966 documentary *The Endless Summer*. This lyrical homage to the beauties and dangers of surfing earned critical raves and a loyal cult following. Dramatic films have been far less interesting. The 1978 *Big Wednesday* traced the lives of surfing buddies Jan-Michael Vincent, William Katt and Gary Busey from the mid-1960s to the late 1970s. *Shimmering Light* (1978) sent Beau Bridges to Australia in search of the Big Wave. *North Shore* (1987) starred Matt Adler as a cocky surfer eager to challenge the famed Oahu waves in Hawaii. David Dukes played a man permanently paralyzed by a surfing accident in the 1979 TV-movie *Some Kind of Miracle*. The 1987 *Beach Party* reunion film *Back to the Beach* featured Frankie Avalon staging a surfing duel against a wonderfully tacky rear-screen wave. Australian filmmaker-star Yahoo Serious had Albert Einstein inventing the first surfboard and riding a few waves in the offbeat 1989 comedy *Young Einstein*.

Ride the Wild Surf (1964)	*North Shore* (1987)
The Endless Summer (1966)	*Back to the Beach* (1987)
Pacific Vibrations (1971)	*Surf Nazis Must Die* (1987)
Big Wednesday (aka *Summer of*	*Aloha Summer* (1988)
Innocence) (1978)	*Under the Boardwalk* (1988)
Shimmering Light (1978 TVM)	*Young Einstein* (1989)
California Dreaming (1979)	*Red Surf* (1990)
Some Kind of Miracle (1979 TVM)	*Point Break* (1990)
Top Secret! (1984)	*Surf Ninjas* (1993)

Surrogate Motherhood

Television movies have frequently borrowed their stories from the headlines, with no better example than the four films about surrogate motherhood broadcast between 1979 and 1988. The celebrated case of *Baby M* garnered the most attention, but earlier efforts explored the same territory with less fanfare. In fact, *The Seeding of Sarah Burns* (1979) was a fictional drama with remarkable similarities to *Baby M.* Kay Lenz played the woman who underwent an embryo transplant and then had second thoughts about giving up the baby. Two 1982 TV-movies covered the same ground, with Susan Dey and Stephanie Zimbalist as the surrogate mothers in *The Gift of Life* and *Tomorrow's Child.* The 1984 theatrical release *The Surrogate* dispensed with emotional crises in favor of a whodunit plot. *Private Practices: The Story of a Sex Surrogate* (1986) was a detailed documentary on the subject. Along similar lines, a sterile wife and her spouse hired a young woman to conceive a child with the husband in 1970's *The Baby Maker.* See also **Babies.**

The Baby Maker (1970)	*Private Practices: The Story of a Sex*
The Seeding of Sarah Burns (1979	*Surrogate* (1986)
TVM)	*Baby M* (1988 TVM)
Tomorrow's Child (aka *Genesis*) (1982	*Waiting* (1990)
TVM)	*The Handmaid's Tale* (1990)
The Gift of Life (1982 TVM)	*Moment of Truth: A Child Too Many*
The Surrogate (1984)	(1993 TVM)

Suspended Animation

If one is to believe science fiction cinema, the most popular method for inducing suspended animation is to freeze living cells. The Frankenstein Monster was discovered frozen in ice, and subsequently revived to full strength in both *The House of Frankenstein* (1944) and *The Evil of Frankenstein* (1964). Likewise, a Neanderthal Man encased in ice was thawed in Fred Schepisi's heavy-handed social parable *Iceman* (1984). Warped scientist Dana Andrews tried to bring back frozen Nazis in 1967's *The Frozen Dead.* And a man frozen through cryogenic means returned to life as a killer in Wes Craven's offbeat 1985 TV-movie *Chiller.* *Star Trek* creator Gene Roddenberry produced three TV pilot films about a twentieth century man awakened from suspended animation to find himself in the future. Alex Cord starred in *Genesis II* (1973), with John Saxon playing the lead in both *Planet Earth* (1974) and *Strange New World* (1975). None of these TV-movies resulted in a weekly series. Actually, the 1939 *Buck Rogers* serial was probably the first "film" to use suspended animation as a means of placing contemporary man into the future. It was reedited into two feature films (1953's *Planet Outlaws* and 1965's *Destination Saturn*) and later remade as 1979's *Buck Rogers in the 25th Century.* Woody Allen borrowed the basic premise for comedic purposes in 1973's *Sleeper.* Other interesting uses of suspended animation have appeared in *This Island Earth* (1954) and *In Like Flint* (1967). The aliens in the former film were among the first to use suspended animation as a method for enabling living beings to endure unbearably long space voyages. The villains in *Flint* suspended a golf game long enough to replace the real president with a look-alike substitute. On television, the 1967-68 sitcom *The Second Hundred Years* was about a thirty-three-year-old man who was frozen in a glacier in 1900, only to thaw out sixty-seven years later and encounter his now elderly son. See also **Coma.**

The House of Frankenstein (1944)	*Dinosaurus* (1960)
This Island Earth (1954)	*Frozen Alive* (1964)

The Evil of Frankenstein (1964)
Kiss the Girls and Make Them Die
(1966)
In Like Flint (1967)
The Frozen Dead (1967)
Sleeper (1973)
Genesis II (1973 TVM)
Planet Earth (1974 TVM)
Live Again, Die Again (1974 TVM)
Strange New World (1975 TVM)

Buck Rogers in the 25th Century
(1979)
Iceman (1984)
Chiller (1985 TVM)
Aliens (1986)
Late for Dinner (1991)
The Chilling (1991)
Critters 4 (aka *Critters 4: They're
Invading Your Space*) (1992)
Forever Young (1992)

Swamps

Sun-baked bodies trudging slowly through murky waters. Bloodsucking leeches clinging to human flesh. The crisp snap of an alligator's jaws. These are familiar sights and sounds in movie swamps, which have been used chiefly as convenient hideouts, treacherous short-cuts, and unlikely long-term residences. In Jean Renoir's *Swamp Water* (1941), Dana Andrews chased his dog into a Georgia swamp and discovered the secret hiding place of an alleged murderer (Walter Brennan). He also discovered Brennan's lonely daughter Ann Baxter and, eventually, the real murderers (who met their fate in a pit of quicksand). Brennan repeated his role for the 1952 remake *Lure of the Wilderness*. Richard Gere and Kim Basinger took a short-cut through the Louisiana swamps to elude pursuers in 1986's *No Mercy*. In contrast, Michael Beck and hostage Lee Remick took a Carolina swamp route to avoid the law in the 1984 TV-movie *Rearview Mirror*. Barbara Hershey won a Cannes Best Actress Award in 1987's *Shy People* as a Bayou widow whose life is disrupted by an unexpected visit from city relative Jill Clayburgh. Hershey's swampy residence reflected her character's internal strength and emotional isolation. No hidden meanings were behind the swamp setting in *Gator Bait*, a drive-in quickie about a Cajun girl (former Playmate Claudia Jennings) navigating a zippy launch to avoid lusty Bayou males. Nine National Guardsmen wound up fighting unfriendly Cajuns in the *Deliverance*-inspired *Southern Comfort* (1981). The Mouse Rescue Aid Society ventured into a threatening swamp to find a helpless child mouse in Disney's 1977 animated feature *The Rescuers*. The 1982 *Swamp Thing*, based on a cult comic book, was about a good scientist transformed into a half-man, half-plant monstrosity. He ventured out of the marshy waters to periodically rescue girlfriend Adrienne Barbeau from the clutches of evil scientist Louis Jourdan. The plot was essentially repeated in the 1989 sequel *Return of the Swamp Thing*, in which Jourdan returned as the villain and Heather Locklear replaced Barbeau.

Swamp Water (aka *The Man Who
Came Back*) (1941)
Strangler of the Swamp (1946)
Swamp Fire (1946)
Lure of the Wilderness (1952)
Cry of the Hunted (1953)
Swamp Women (aka *Swamp
Diamonds; Cruel Swamp*) (1955)

Lure of the Swamp (1957)
Attack of the Giant Leeches (aka *The
Giant Leeches*) (1959)
Curse of the Swamp Creature (1966)
Frogs (1972)
Live and Let Die (1973)
Gator Bait (1976)
The Rescuers (1977)

Southern Comfort (1981)   Down by Law (1986)
Swamp Thing (1982)   Shy People (1987)
Rearview Mirror (1984 TVM)   Return of the Swamp Thing (1989)
No Mercy (1986)

Sword and Sorcery

Although its literary basis dates back to the 1930s, the sword and sorcery genre of the 1980s probably owes its cinematic inspiration to George Lucas's *Star Wars* (1977) and *The Empire Strikes Back* (1980). Han Solo and Luke Skywalker, while lacking the physical attributes of muscular heroes, together formed the basic mold of an ironic adventurer sent forth on a preordained quest. However, the genre proper — complete with muscle-bulging hunks and heavy swords — began with 1982's *Conan the Barbarian*. Robert E. Howard wrote seventeen Conan stories, which appeared in the *Weird Tales* pulp magazine between 1932-36 (four others were published posthumously). John Milius's film version offered little more than a straightforward telling of Conan's beginnings, but it made a star of Arnold Schwarzenegger and inspired a sequel as well as a rash of imitators. One rip-off, *The Sword and the Sorcerer*, starring TV stars-to-be Lee Horsley (*Matt Houston*) and Kathleen Beller (*Dynasty*), actually beat *Conan* to the theaters. More typical imitations included an ineptly made Italian series starring former *Tarzan* Miles O'Keefe as a silly beefcake hero named Ator (q.v.). Despite attempts to infuse the genre with good-natured camp (Don Coscarelli's *Beastmaster*) or elaborate production design (Peter Yate's *Krull*), the sword and sorcery craze died softly in 1985 with *Red Sonja*, a box office failure despite the potentially potent pairing of Arnold Schwarzenegger and Brigitte Nielsen. See also **Ator; Deathstalker.**

Hawk the Slayer (1980)   Conan the Destroyer (1984)
The Sword and the Sorcerer (1982) Red Sonja (1985)
Conan the Barbarian (1982)   Amazons (1986)
Sorceress (1982)   Iron Warrior (1987)
Beastmaster (1983)   The Barbarians (1987)
Krull (1983)   Wizard of the Lost Kingdom II (1989)
Yor — the Hunter From the Future   Wizards of the Demon Sword (1991)
   (1983)   October 32nd (1992)
Ator the Fighting Eagle (1983)

Talking Animals

Talking animals have been a screen oddity, with the exceptions of Francis the Talking Mule (q.v.) and various animated critters. Bing Crosby and Bob Hope's wacky *Road* comedies featured a talking fish in *Road to Utopia* and a pair of conversing camels in *Road to Morocco*. Another talking camel made a cameo in the adventure spoof *Slave Girl* (1947). Walter Abel had a talking dog in *The Fabulous Joe* (1947), Mickey Rooney a conversant duck in *Everything's Ducky* (1961), Pee Wee Herman a prose-producing pig in *Big Top Pee Wee* (1988), and Bob Goldthwait a chattering horse in *Hot to Trot* (1988). Another talking horse named Renaldo had a brief scene in 1988's *High Spirits*. Don Johnson could speak telepathically with his dog Blood in Harlan Ellison's science fiction satire *A Boy and His Dog* (1975). No discussion of talking animals would be complete without mentioning

TV's famous talking horse *Mr. Ed*. See also **Francis the Talking Mule.**

Road to Morocco (1942)	*A Boy and His Dog* (1975)
Road to Utopia (1945)	*Hot to Trot* (1988)
Slave Girl (1947)	*Big Top Pee Wee* (1988)
The Fabulous Joe (1947)	*High Spirits* (1988)
Everything's Ducky (1961)	

Tammy

A wholesome backwoods teenager, Tammy managed to charm the socks off of everyone she met. Her adventures were mild, to say the least, but nevertheless influential. They set the stage for similar fodder such as *Gidget* (q.v.) and thus proved there was a lucrative market for teen-oriented, non-horror pictures (a fact exploited by AIP's *Beach Party* series). Twenty-five-year-old Debbie Reynolds, already an established star, created the role in 1957's *Tammy and the Bachelor*. She also sang the memorable title tune, which hit number one on *Billboard*'s pop chart in July 1957. Sandra Dee, after introducing Gidget two years earlier, played Tammy in two sequels, with John Gavin and Peter Fonda as her love interests. A half-hour sitcom starring Debbie Watson debuted in September 1965 and lasted a single season. Four of its episodes were edited into an eighty-seven-minute movie and released theatrically as *Tammy and the Millionaire*.

Tammy and the Bachelor (aka *Tammy*) (1957) (Debbie Reynolds)
Tammy Tell Me True (1961) (Sandra Dee)
Tammy and the Doctor (1963) (Dee)
Tammy and the Millionaire (1967) (Debbie Watson)

Tarzan

Edgar Rice Burroughs's muscular jungle hero has shown remarkable endurance since his film debut in 1918. He has survived ill-conceived character changes, gross miscastings, and cheap-looking backlot jungles. Elmo Lincoln, a D.W. Griffith player who had appeared in *Birth of a Nation*, was the first actor to don the loincloth in 1918's *Tarzan of the Apes*. From the beginning, Burroughs stressed that he wanted the film to be a faithful adaptation. Yet, despite his presence during filming, the plot strayed slightly from the book—a problem that would plague Burroughs on a much larger scale in future Tarzan pictures. The movie performed well at the box office, and a less successful sequel, *Romance of Tarzan*, came out later that year. Burroughs reaped little profit from these films and sold the rights to subsequent novels to other producers. During the silent era: Goldwyn distributed *The Revenge of Tarzan* (1920); National Film Corporation turned the novel *Son of Tarzan* into a 1921 serial; Elmo Lincoln reprised the role for another serial, *The Adventures of Tarzan* (1921) and Film Booking Offices (later RKO Radio) released *Tarzan and the Golden Lion* (1927). The star of the latter picture, Jim Pierce, married Burroughs's daughter Joan, and they later played Tarzan and Jane in a radio series. Following two more Tarzan serials in the early 1930s, Irving Thalberg acquired series rights for MGM. *Tarzan, the Ape Man* (1932) was a lavish jungle epic. It made a film star of former Olympic swimming champion Johnny Weissmuller but also unfortunately dispensed with Burroughs's conception of Tarzan as an educated man. Weissmuller's Tarzan spoke in broken English ("Tarzan—Jane") and never strayed from his beloved jungle in his series debut. Still, audiences loved the wild animal thrills and the romance between primitive Tarzan and civilized Jane (Maureen O'Sullivan). MGM mounted an even more impressive sequel in 1934's *Tarzan and His Mate*, which most critics consider Weissmuller's finest Tarzan epic. MGM produced four more Tarzan entries, introducing Johnny Sheffield as Boy in 1939's *Tarzan Finds a Son!* and concluding the series with 1942's *Tarzan's New York Adventure*. Although MGM's Tarzan films dominated the 1930s, other independent efforts competed against them. Sol Lesser, who had acquired an option from Burroughs through a third party, signed Buster Crabbe for *Tarzan the Fearless* (1933). It was edited into two different versions, so theater owners could show it as a seventy-one-minute feature or as a serial. The same fate befell 1935's *The New Adventures of Tarzan*. This historic oddity was produced by Burroughs's own company, thus ensuring that Tarzan acted like an educated man. Herman Brix, later known as Bruce Bennett, played the lead. Initially available as a feature or serial, the film was recut *again* in 1938 and released with the new title *Tarzan and the Green Goddess*. A third non-MGM effort, 1938's *Tarzan's Revenge*, offered minimal backlot thrills and a lackluster hero as played by Glenn Morris. MGM may have felt these low-budget rivals weakened the box office attraction of their films. However, RKO did not hesitate to grab Weissmuller and launch its own Tarzan series in 1943. Johnny Sheffield accompanied Weissmuller to RKO, but Maureen O'Sullivan bowed out as Jane. There was no Jane—but lots of Nazis—in RKO's first entry, *Tarzan Triumphs*. The film marked Sol Lesser's return as a Tarzan producer and he eventually installed Brenda Joyce as the series' new Jane. Although relying heavily on stock footage, the RKO films drew steady business. Johnny Sheffield, who had outgrown his role as Boy, left the series after 1947's *Tarzan and the Huntress*. Monogram immediately signed him to play Bomba, the Jungle Boy (q.v.). Weissmuller turned in his loincloth the following year, after Lesser refused to give him a percentage of the profits. Producer Sam Katzman grabbed Weissmuller for the lead in his Jungle Jim (q.v.) series. Bland Lex Barker replaced Weissmuller for the five remaining RKO pictures, beginning with 1949's *Tarzan's Magic Fountain*. When Barker balked at signing a multipicture contract, Lesser dropped him in favor of muscular Gordon Scott, a former lifeguard with no acting experience. Scott's first Tarzan picture, *Tarzan's Hidden Jungle* (1955), was RKO's last. Unperturbed, industrious producer Lesser took Scott and the series to MGM and unleashed the first Technicolor Tarzan adventure with 1957's *Tarzan and the Lost Safari*. Lesser and Scott also did *Tarzan's Fight for Life* (1958) for MGM and then made three TV pilots that were edited into *Tarzan and the Trappers* (1958). The latter films fared poorly, and Lesser sold his film and TV series rights to Sy Weintraub in 1959. Weintraub produced four superior Tarzan films, the first two starring Scott and the last two introducing stunt man and veteran actor Jock Mahoney. The Mahoney films featured exotic locales, vibrant colors, and a literate interpretation by the star. Unfortunately, Mahoney stepped aside after his second film and the Weintraub series took a turn for the worse. Mahoney's replacement, former Rams linebacker Mike Henry, had the right physique, but his performance doomed 1966's *Tarzan and the Valley of Gold* and two sequels. Henry turned down Weintraub's TV series, allowing Ron Ely to become the small screen's first Tarzan. The series debuted in 1966 and enjoyed a two-year run. In 1970, unsuspecting moviegoers were lured to the theaters to see *Tarzan's Jungle Rebellion* and *Tarzan's Deadly Silence*, two features compiled from TV series episodes. Except for an R-rated cartoon spoof, *Shame of the Jungle* (1975), the 1970s was a quiet decade for Tarzan. In 1981, John and Bo Derek produced the unintentionally funny *Tarzan, the Ape Man*, devoting more screen time to Bo's frequently nude Jane than to Miles O'Keefe's hunky Tarzan. In contrast, 1984's *Greystoke: The Legend of Tarzan, Lord of the Apes* made a legitimate stab at transferring Burroughs's novel to the screen intact. Tarzan's childhood in the jungle was depicted splendidly, but his eventual trip to England brought the picture to a standstill. Christopher Lambert made a fine Tarzan, while Andie McDowell's voice as Jane was dubbed by actress Glenn Close. Five years later, Tarzan unexpectedly reappeared in *Tarzan in Manhattan*, an ill-conceived TV-movie with Jane as a taxi driver. It was funnier, in a sad sort of way, than Jimmy Durante's appearance as "Schnarzan" in the 1934 movie industry spoof *Hollywood Party*.

Tarzan of the Apes (1918) (Elmo Lincoln)
Romance of Tarzan (1918) (Lincoln)
The Revenge of Tarzan (1920) (Gene Pollar)
Tarzan and the Golden Lion (1927) (Jim Pierce)
Tarzan, the Ape Man (1932) (Johnny Weissmuller)
Tarzan the Fearless (1933) (Buster Crabbe)
Tarzan and His Mate (1934) (Weissmuller)
The New Adventures of Tarzan (aka *Tarzan's New Adventure*; reedited in 1938
    as *Tarzan and the Green Goddess*) (1935) (Herman Brix aka Bruce Bennett)
Tarzan Escapes (1936) (Weissmuller)
Tarzan's Revenge (1938) (Glenn Morris)
Tarzan Finds a Son! (1939) (Weissmuller)
Tarzan's Secret Treasure (1941) (Weissmuller)
Tarzan's New York Adventure (1942) (Weissmuller)
Tarzan Triumphs (1943) (Weissmuller)
Tarzan's Desert Mystery (1943) (Weissmuller)
Tarzan and the Amazons (1945) (Weissmuller)
Tarzan and the Leopard Woman (1946) (Weissmuller)
Tarzan and the Huntress (1947) (Weissmuller)
Tarzan and the Mermaids (1948) (Weissmuller)
Tarzan's Magic Fountain (1949) (Lex Barker)
Tarzan and the Slave Girl (1950) (Barker)
Tarzan's Peril (aka *Tarzan and the Jungle Queen*) (1951) (Barker)
Tarzan's Savage Fury (1952) (Barker)
Tarzan and the She-Devil (1953) (Barker)
Tarzan's Hidden Jungle (1955) (Gordon Scott)
Tarzan and the Lost Safari (1957) (Scott)
Tarzan's Fight for Life (1958) (Scott)
Tarzan and the Trappers (1958) (Scott)
Tarzan's Greatest Adventure (1959) (Scott)
Tarzan, the Ape Man (1959) (Denny Miller)
Tarzan the Magnificent (1960) (Scott)

Tarzan Goes to India (1962) (Jock Mahoney)
Tarzan's Three Challenges (1963) (Mahoney)
Tarzan and the Valley of Gold (1966) (Mike Henry)
Tarzan and the Great River (1967) (Henry)
Tarzan and the Jungle Boy (1968) (Henry)
Tarzan's Jungle Rebellion (1970) (Ron Ely)
Tarzan's Deadly Silence (1970) (Ely)
Shame of the Jungle (1975) (voice of Johnny Weissmuller, Jr.)
Tarzan, the Ape Man (1981) (Miles O'Keefe)
Greystoke: The Legend of Tarzan, Lord of the Apes (1984) (Christopher Lambert)
Tarzan in Manhattan (1989 TVM) (Joe Lara)

Tattoos

The most tattooed characters in cinema history are probably *The Illustrated Man* (1969) and Queequeg of *Moby Dick* (1956) fame. As to which of these has the most tattoos, well, that's difficult to determine, although Queequeg may get the edge on the basis of his tattooed face. Still, one could make an argument in favor of the Illustrated Man. His face may have been unmarked, but his tattoos did move and tell stories. In other films: Burt Lancaster sported *The Rose Tattoo* (1955) on his chest, symbolizing his "sexual prowess" and also reminding widow Anna Magnani of her deceased husband. Bruce Dern played a wacko artist in 1981's *Tattoo* who kidnaps Maud Adams so he can tattoo her entire body. It was written by Joyce Buñuel, Luis's daughter. Tattoos have been used less dramatically for concealing treasure maps, as in *The Stranger and the Gunfighter* (1976). See also **Painted People.**

The Rose Tattoo (1955)	*Tattoo* (1981)
Moby Dick (1956)	*Octopussy* (1983)
The Illustrated Man (1969)	*Double Exposure* (1989)
The Golden Voyage of Sinbad (1973)	*Cape Fear* (1991)
Get Charlie Tully (1976)	*The Piano* (1993)
The Stranger and the Gunfighter (1976)	*The Son-in-Law* (1993)

Taxi Drivers

Colorful cabbies have appeared as memorable supporting characters in dozens of movies and have been played by an impressive group of veteran character actors. James Gleason drove Loretta Young and angel Cary Grant to a frozen lake in *The Bishop's Wife* (1947) and wound up ice skating with them. Streetwise cabbie Ernest Borgnine navigated Kurt Russell through the hazardous ruins of futuristic Manhattan in the science fiction adventure *Escape From New York* (1981). Yaphet Kotto played the unfortunate cab driver stuck with taking self-confessed murderer David Janssen to Mexico in the suspense-drama *Night Chase* (1970). Ricardo Cortez was one of the first actors to play a taxi driver in a leading role, starring opposite Barbara Stanwyck in 1931's *Ten Cents a Dance* (a rare directorial effort by Lionel Barrymore). Other star performers who have played cabbies include George Raft (*Pick-up*), Red Skelton (*The Yellow Cab Man*) and Fred Astaire (*The Purple Taxi*). In the respective box office bombs *Rhinestone* (1984) and *Die Laughing* (1980), Sylvester Stallone and Robby Benson proved that taxi drivers can't sing professionally. Lady cabbies have been represented on-screen by Beulah Bondi in *She's a Soldier Too* (1944) and Sophia Loren in *Aurora* (1984). In the 1989 TV-movie *Tarzan in Manhattan*, Jane turned out to be a cab driver! Britain's long-running *Carry On* comedy film series (q.v.) featured the appropriately titled entry *Carry On Cabby* (1963). The 1981 animated feature *Heavy Metal* included a segment about a futuristic NYC cab driver. *Total Recall* (1990) featured both a murderous mutant cab driver and a robotic "Johnnycab." *D.C. Cab* (1983) was an episodic comedy about a cab company, obviously inspired by the 1978-83 *Taxi* TV series. The best-remembered cabbie performance remains Robert DeNiro's splendid portrait of unbalanced Vietnam vet Travis Bickle in Martin Scorsese's *Taxi Driver* (1976). See also **Chauffeurs.**

Ten Cents a Dance (1931)
Taxi (1932)
Pick-up (1933)
The Big City (aka *Skyscraper Wilderness*) (1937)
She's a Soldier Too (1944)
Two O'Clock Courage (1945)
Two Guys From Milwaukee (1946)
The Bishop's Wife (1947)
The Yellow Cab Man (1950)
Taxi (1953)
99 River Street (1953)
The Catered Affair (aka *Wedding Breakfast*) (1956)
Carry On Cabby (1963)
Night Chase (aka *The Man in the Back Seat*) (1970 TVM)
Pigeons (aka *The Sidelong Glances of a Pigeon Kicker*) (1971)
Law and Disorder (1974)
Taxi Driver (1976)
Adventures of a Taxi Driver (1976)
The Purple Taxi (1977)
Love in a Taxi (1980)

Die Laughing (1980)
The Princess and the Cabbie (1981 TVM)
Escape From New York (1981)
Heavy Metal (1981)
Chan Is Missing (1982)
Hit and Run (aka *Revenge Squad*) (1982)
D.C. Cab (1983)
Signal 7 (1983)
Rhinestone (1984)
Aurora (1984 TVM)
I-Man (1986 TVM)
Graveyard Shift (1987)
Ernest Saves Christmas (1988)
Tarzan in Manhattan (1989 TVM)
Wired (1989)
Look Who's Talking (1989)
Total Recall (1990)
Breathing Under Water (1991)
The Tune (1992)
Night on Earth (1992)
My Life's in Turnaround (1993)

Teenage Mutant Ninja Turtles

This quartet of karate-chopping, pizza-eating, turtle do-gooders first appeared in Peter Laird and Kevin Eastman's underground comic books (q.v.) in 1984. They were media stars and popular toy characters long before their film debut in 1990. However, few film industry analysts predicted that their self-titled film opus would earn over $100 million in the United States alone. The origin of the turtles goes like this: They were flushed down the toilet and discovered in the sewer (q.v.) by an exiled ninja master named Splinter. When a toxic slime seeps into the sewer system, the turtles mutate into "half-teens," and Splinter becomes a rat. He teaches them martial arts (they learn to devour pizza and ice cream on their own) so they can battle the evil Foot Clan. The turtles are named after Renaissance artists: Raphael, Leonardo, Michelangelo and Donatello. Although an animated film was planned at one time, the turtles' screen debut was a live-action film for which Jim Henson's Creature Shop designed the costumes. Judith Hoag costarred as TV reporter April O'Neil, who befriends the turtles (but proves that humans are boring compared to turtle teens). Paige Turco replaced Hoag for the 1991 sequel, which also featured David Warner as the scientist who created the ooze. Turco and the Turtle Quartet traveled back in time to feudal Japan in 1993's *Teenage Mutant Ninja Turtles III*. Mark Caso, as Leonardo, was the only actor to play a Turtle in all three films. The Turtles made a cameo appearance in the 1993 buddy cop spoof *National Lampoon's Loaded Weapon 1*.

> *Teenage Mutant Ninja Turtles* (1990)
> *Teenage Mutant Ninja Turtles II: The Secret of the Ooze* (1991)
> *Teenage Mutant Ninja Turtles III* (aka *Teenage Mutant Ninja Turtles III: The Turtles Are Back . . . In Time*) (1993)

Telekinesis (Psychokinesis, or PK)

Movie teenagers have displayed a special knack for acquiring telekinesis, the power to move objects with the mind. Sissy Spacek showed just how much havoc a mistreated, revenge-minded, telekinetic teen could wreak in the 1976 adaptation of Stephen King's *Carrie*. She veered cars off course, sent knives flying through the air, and demolished a high school gym with a fire hose. Imitations were bound to follow, and Brian De Palma produced an interesting one with 1978's *The Fury*, which offered two telekinetic teens — one good (Amy Irving) and one gone bad (Andrew Stevens). In contrast, the telekinetic teen comedy *Zapped!* (1982) offered a trite plot about a horny guy (Willie Aames) who takes a perverse interest in friend Scott Baio's newly acquired talent. A young boy and a teenage girl used their telekinetic powers to battle a demon and the hockey-masked Jason, respectively, in the 1988 films *Cameron's Closet* and *Friday the 13th Part VII — The New Blood*. As for adults, some playful gods endowed meek Roland Young with temporary telekinetic powers in the H.G. Wells fantasy *The Man Who Could Work Miracles*. In George Pal's underrated 1968 thriller *The Power*, scientist George Hamilton tracked down a mysterious telekinetic killer capable of changing his appearance by controlling people's minds (which made him devilishly difficult to find). Chevy Chase explored the frivolous side of telekinesis as an air traffic controller in the mild 1981 comedy *Modern Problems*. Richard Burton played the most destructive — and lazy — telekinetic villain by causing all sorts of disasters from his hospital bed in *The Medusa Touch* (1978). See also **Scanners**.

The Man Who Could Work Miracles (1936)	*Scanners* (1981)
	Zapped! (1982)
The Power (1968)	*Firestarter* (1984)
Carrie (1976)	*Cameron's Closet* (1988)
The Man With the Power (1977 TVM)	*Friday the 13th Part VII — The New Blood* (1988)
The Fury (1978)	
The Medusa Touch (1978)	*Firehead* (1991)
Modern Problems (1981)	*The Lawnmower Man* (1992)

Telephones

Although telephones have played bit parts in thousands of movies, a few particularly memorable roles are called to mind. A foreign agent used the telephone (and a Robert Frost poem) to activate brainwashed killers in *Telefon*. A party line brought Doris Day and Rock Hudson together in *Pillow Talk*. Judy Holliday ran a telephone answering service called Susanswerphone in the otherwise forgettable musical comedy *Bells Are Ringing*. And Barbara Stanwyck inadvertently learned of her own proposed murder via the phone in *Sorry, Wrong Number*. Telephone numbers have been played for drama in the fact-based *Call Northside 777* and for strained chuckles in the goofy *Transylvania 6-5000*. James Coburn was almost killed in a phone booth in *The Carey Treatment*, while Christopher Reeve used booths for dressing rooms in the *Superman* movies. Telephones were employed as spur-of-the-moment murder weapons in *The Naked Kiss* and *The Stepfather*. Clever premeditated murderers found ingenious uses for phones in *The Invisible Killer* and *Murder by Phone*. Devious Vincent Price bumped off a victim with a spiked telephone receiver in *Dr. Phibes Rises Again*.

The Invisible Killer (1940)
Call Northside 777 (aka *Calling Northside 777*) (1948)
For the Love of Mary (1948)
Sorry, Wrong Number (1948)
Southside 1-1000 (1950)
Chicago Calling (1951)
Dial M for Murder (1954)
Pillow Talk (1959)
Bells Are Ringing (1960)
The Naked Kiss (1964)
I Saw What You Did (1965)
The Slender Thread (1965)
Boy, Did I Get a Wrong Number! (1966)
Dial Hot Line (1969 TVM)
The Day the Hot Line Got Hot (1969)
Dr. Phibes Rises Again (1972)
When Michael Calls (1972 TVM)
The Secret Night Caller (1975 TVM)
Telefon (1977)
When a Stranger Calls (1979)

Don't Answer the Phone (1980)
Murder by Phone (aka *Bells*) (1980)
Dial M for Murder (1981 TVM)
E.T. the Extra-Terrestrial (1982)
Hotline (1982 TVM)
Transylvania 6-5000 (1985)
The Stepfather (1987)
Call Me (1988)
The Telephone (1988)
976-EVIL (1989)
Party Line (1989)
Dial: Help (1989)
Bill and Ted's Excellent Adventure (1989)
Murder on Line One (aka *Helpline*) (1990)
Julia Has Two Lovers (1991)
Intimate Stranger (1991)
The Phone Call (1991)
Bill & Ted's Bogus Journey (1991)
The Sound and the Silence (1993 TVM)

Teleportation

Science fiction buffs have defined teleportation as the process of almost instantaneously transmitting matter from one place to another. This is usually accomplished by breaking down an animal or object into its molecules, transporting the molecules through space, and then reassembling them. Edward Page Mitchell may have been the first writer to decribe the process in his 1877 short story "The Man Without a Body." In the *Star Trek* (q.v.) TV series and films, the crew of the *Starship Enterprise* used a teleporter as a routine mode of travel. The Delambre and Brundle families had a terrible time with teleportation experiments in *The Fly* (q.v.) movies. Andre Delambre initiated the problems by unknowingly allowing a fly to sneak into the teleportation booth with him. Their molecules merged — resulting in a disgusting combination of man/fly (and also fly/man). Bryant Halliday encountered a slightly different problem in 1966's *The Projected Man*. His "projection device" transported him successfully, but it also charred half his face and endowed him with a deadly electric touch. See also **The Fly; Star Trek.**

The Fly (1958)
The Projected Man (1966)
Willy Wonka and the Chocolate Factory (1971)
Star Trek — The Motion Picture (1979)

Television

Even before television's success threatened the popularity of theatrical movies, the big screen all but ignored the little screen. The 1933 comedy *International House* used an early television experiment as the premise for jamming an all-star cast into a Chinese hotel. The stars included W.C. Fields, George Burns and Gracie Allen, Bela Lugosi, and — appearing in a TV broadcast — Rudy Vallee and Cab Calloway. On a smaller scale, comedians operated a pirate TV station out of a castle in 1939's *Band Waggon*, which was inspired by a hit British radio series. Amazingly, this lighthearted comedy was considerably ahead of its time, for pirate TV broadcasts were not further explored until 1983's *Videodrome* and 1986's *Riders of the Storm*. During the 1950s, the early days of network TV provided the setting for fluffy comedies like *Two Gals and a Guy* and *Simon and Laura*. A noteworthy exception was 1956's *The Great Man*, a scathing look at a much-loved TV personality revealed by Jose Ferrer to have been an unscrupulous, egotistical heel. The decade also produced Arch Obler's *The Twonky* (1953), a bizarre satire that remains an oddity after almost four decades. The title creature was a futuristic robot that began running Hans Conried's life after becoming accidentally trapped inside the man's TV set. The sarcastic *Variety* review commented that the "thought is posed that Twonky can reduce mankind to automatons" — a charge television is still facing today. Indeed, by the mid-1970s, television was ingrained as an integral part of American society, prompting renewed interest in movies about TV. *The Groove Tube* (1974) was the first of several movies consisting of loosely connected comedy sketches built around television. *The Front* (1976) and *My Favorite Year* (1982) evoked nostalgia toward the early days of television. The former film skillfully covered a dark period in TV history — the blacklisting of writers accused of Communist activities. Ethics in the television industry have been addressed principally in films about network TV news. News broadcasts were packaged as entertainment in 1976's *Network*, while news reporter William Hurt faked an emotional tear for the camera in 1987's *Broadcast News*. The 1983 TV-movie *Special Bulletin* looked just like a news broadcast, with anchors Ed Flanders and Kathryn Walker keeping viewers informed about a terrorist group threatening to destroy Charleston, South Carolina, with a nuclear bomb. The film simulated the feel of a real broadcast so well that the final outcome carried a shattering, terrifying jolt. Horror filmmakers have used television to temporarily house transient ghosts, demons and extraterrestrials in *Poltergeist, Demons 2* and

Terrorvision, respectively. None of those was nearly as frightening as David Cronenburg's powerful horror/satire *Videodrome*, which cast James Woods as a broadcast executive metamorphosed into a television/man (at one point, he slips a videotape into a newly formed slot in his stomach). This overly complex film (was it all a hallucination?) disgusted most moviegoers and died quickly at the box office. The 1985 *Explorers*, while not a movie about television, featured aliens who learned everything they knew about humans from watching Earth TV—a frightening premise when one thinks about it. The 1985 comedy-drama *Static* was about a young man who claimed to have invented a television capable of tuning in Heaven. See also **Soap Operas.**

International House (1933)	*Videodrome* (1983)
Murder by Television (1935)	*Special Bulletin* (1983 TVM)
Band Waggon (1939)	*The Record* (1984)
Two Gals and a Guy (1951)	*The Ratings Game* (1984 TVM)
The Twonky (1953)	*Static* (1985)
Meet Mr. Lucifer (1953)	*Reckless Disregard* (1985 TVM)
The Glass Web (1953)	*Ginger and Fred* (1985)
Simon and Laura (1955)	*America* (1986)
The Great Man (1956)	*News at Eleven* (1986 TVM)
A Face in the Crowd (1957)	*Terrorvision* (1986)
The Gazebo (1959)	*Riders of the Storm* (aka *The American*
The Thrill of It All (1963)	*Way*) (1986)
Panic Button (1964)	*Broadcast News* (1987)
The Barefoot Executive (1971)	*Pass the Ammo* (1988)
The Love Machine (1971)	*Switching Channels* (1988)
The Groove Tube (1974)	*Demons 2* (1988)
The Front (1976)	*The Brain* (1988)
Network (1976)	*UHF* (1989)
Tunnelvision (1976)	*Shocker* (1989)
Telethon (1977 TVM)	*Instant Karma* (1990)
KGOD (aka *Pray TV*) (1980)	*Avalon* (1990)
Deathwatch (1980)	*Soapdish* (1991)
My Favorite Year (1982)	*Wayne's World* (1992)
This Is . . . Kate Bennett (1982 TVM)	*Secrets* (1992 TVM)
Wrong Is Right (1982)	*Stay Tuned* (1992)
Poltergeist (1982)	*Exclusive* (1992 TVM)

Television-Expanded Films

Television has long practiced the "art" of dicing up theatrical films to fit a specified time period or to delete material its censors deemed unacceptable. However, the equally offensive practice of expanding theatrical films for television showings did not gain widespread popularity with the networks until the mid-1970s. That's when network executives realized that it was cheaper to add leftover footage to an existing film than to pay for new programming. Thus, instead of one night of *Superman*, they could add enough footage to stretch its impressive ratings over two nights. In the case of *Superman*, the new scenes did allow film buffs to glimpse Kirk Allyn (Superman in the movie serials) and Noel Neill (Lois in the TV series) as Lois Lane's parents. However, other TV expansions have been less thoughtful. The James Bond adventure *On Her Majesty's Secret Service* was expanded by simply tacking the climactic ski chase onto the front of the film, adding a voiceover, and repeating the same scene (in its proper sequence) later in the broadcast. Director Gene Palmer shot almost an hour of new footage, complete with new cast, for the network TV broadcast of the already-inflated *Two Minute Warning*. Alas, one cannot blame the networks alone. Director David Lynch had his name removed from the credits of *Dune* when the movie was lengthened for its syndicated showing. On the other hand, Francis Ford Coppola played a central role in altering his *Godfather* films for a special television broadcast. He intercut scenes from the 175-minute *The Godfather* (1972) and 200-minute *The Godfather, Part II* (1974), added footage from the cutting room floor, and produced the mammoth 475-minute *The Godfather Saga*. In addition to expanding movies for television, distributors have begun to release alternate versions of the same film in limited theatrical releases and/or on videotape/laserdisc. This practice is nothing new — Steven Spielberg's *Close Encounters of the Third Kind — The Special Edition* followed his original 1977 version three years later. Recent alternate versions have included *Blade Runner, JFK, The Abyss* and *Basic Instinct*.

Requiem for a Heavyweight (1962)	*The Concorde: Airport '77* (aka *Airport*
The Evil of Frankenstein (1964)	*'77*) (1977)
Secret Ceremony (1968)	*Superman* (1978)
On Her Majesty's Secret Service (1969)	*Dune* (1984)
Jeremy (1973)	*Cry Freedom* (1987)
Earthquake (1974)	*Sea of Love* (1989)
Two Minute Warning (1976)	*Dances With Wolves* (1990)
The Godfather Saga (1977)	*Backdraft* (1991)
The Deep (1977)	

Television Movie Sequels to Theatrical Films

ABC-TV pioneered the concept of the television movie sequel with 1974's *Mrs. Sundance*, a small-screen continuation of 1969's *Butch Cassidy and the Sundance Kid*. Elizabeth Montgomery replaced Katharine Ross in the role of Etta Place, the Sundance Kid's widow and the new quarry of ruthless bounty hunters. Although produced by Twentieth Century-Fox, who made the original, *Mrs. Sundance* caused no confusion in regard to its origin — it looked and played like a made-for-TV movie, right down to the perfectly timed commercial breaks. Interestingly, just two years later, Twentieth Century-Fox convinced Katharine Ross to recreate the role for *Wanted: The Sundance Woman*, another TV sequel. This version ignored *Mrs. Sundance* (which no doubt confused some meticulous viewers) and involved Etta with Mexican rebel Pancho Villa. Ross was one of a handful of performers to play the same role in both a theatrical film and its TV-movie sequel. George C. Scott repeated his Oscar-winning 1970 portrayal of General George Patton for the 1986 TV film *The Last Days of Patton*. Lee Marvin returned as the leader of *The Dirty Dozen* in *The Dirty Dozen: Next Mission*. Carol Kane and Robert Carradine repeated their theatrical roles in, respectively, *When a Stranger Calls Back* (1993) and *Revenge of the Nerds III: The Next Generation* (1992). And Barry Newman played lawyer Tony Petrocelli on the big screen in *The Lawyer* (1970) and on the small screen in *Night Games* (1974). The latter served as a pilot for Newman's short-lived TV series *Petrocelli*. Other TV-movie sequels have also doubled as pilots for prospective series, such as *Matt Helm, Nevada Smith, True Grit, Serpico: The Deadly Game* and *Our Man Flint: Dead on Target*. In some of these features, the only connection with the original feature was the name of the main character. Dean Martin's Matt Helm was a boozing super secret agent, while Tony Franciosa's TV incarnation was a wisecracking private eye with a steady girlfriend. The longest gap between a theatrical film and its made-for-TV sequel was forty-four years—from 1946's *It's a Wonderful Life* to 1990's *Clarence. The Dirty Dozen* has spawned the most TV sequels: three and still counting. In the following list, the TV-movies are listed chronologically in the left column with the theatrical film on the right (if a theatrical series, the last series entry is shown):

Mrs. Sundance (1974 TVM)	*Butch Cassidy and the Sundance Kid* (1969)
Sidekicks (1974 TVM)	*Skin Game* (1971)
Night Games (1974 TVM)	*The Lawyer* (1970)
Nick and Nora (1975 TVM)	*Song of the Thin Man* (1947)
Matt Helm (1975 TVM)	*The Wrecking Crew* (1969)
Nevada Smith (1975 TVM)	*Nevada Smith* (1966)
Look What's Happened to Rosemary's Baby (aka *Rosemary's Baby II*) (1976 TVM)	*Rosemary's Baby* (1968)
Wanted: The Sundance Woman (aka *Mrs. Sundance Rides Again*) (1976 TVM)	*Butch Cassidy and the Sundance Kid* (1969)
Our Man Flint: Dead on Target (1976 TVM)	*Our Man Flint* (1966)
Serpico: The Deadly Game (1976 TVM)	*Serpico* (1973)
A Matter of Wife . . . and Death (1976 TVM)	*Shamus* (1973)
The Girl in the Empty Grave (1977 TVM)	*They Only Kill Their Masters* (1972)
True Grit (1978 TVM)	*True Grit* (1969)
A Real American Hero (1978 TVM)	*Final Chapter—Walking Tall* (1973)
Christmas Lilies of the Field (1979 TVM)	*Lilies of the Field* (1963)
High Noon II: The Return of Will Kane (1980 TVM)	*High Noon* (1952)
Revenge of the Stepford Wives (1980 TVM)	*The Stepford Wives* (1975)
Trackdown: Finding the Goodbar Killer (1983 TVM)	*Looking for Mr. Goodbar* (1977)
The Jerk Too (1984 TVM)	*The Jerk* (1979)
The Dirty Dozen: The Next Mission (1985 TVM)	*The Dirty Dozen* (1967)
Popeye Doyle (1986 TVM)	*The French Connection II* (1975)

The Parent Trap II (1986 TVM)	*The Parent Trap* (1961)
The Last Days of Patton (1986 TVM)	*Patton* (1970)
The Return of the Shaggy Dog (1987 TVM)	*The Shaggy D.A.* (1976)
Bates Motel (1987 TVM)	*Psycho III* (1986)
The Dirty Dozen: The Deadly Mission (1987 TVM)	*The Dirty Dozen* (1967)
If It's Tuesday, It Still Must Be Belgium (1987 TVM)	*If It's Tuesday, It Must Be Belgium* (1969)
The Great Escape II: The Untold Story (1988 TVM)	*The Great Escape* (1963)
Amityville: The Evil Escapes (1989 TVM)	*Amityville 3-D* (1983)
Clarence (1990 TVM)	*It's a Wonderful Life* (1946)
Omen IV: The Awakening (1991 TVM)	*The Final Conflict* (1981)
Revenge of the Nerds III: The Next Generation (1992)	*Revenge of the Nerds II: Nerds in Paradise* (1987)
Stepfather III (1992 TVM)	*Stepfather II* (aka *Stepfather II: Make Room for Daddy*) (1989)
When a Stranger Calls Back (1993 TVM)	*When a Stranger Calls* (1979)

Note: The 1989 TV-movie *Get Smart, Again* was obviously intended as a television series reunion movie (q.v.) and thus is not listed as a sequel to 1980's *The Nude Bomb* (aka *The Return of Maxwell Smart*).

Television Series Reunion Films

A wave of nostalgia washed over television viewers of the 1980s, making small screen movies based on old television series the most significant TV-movie trend of the decade. The nostalgia went beyond mere revival of a TV show's premise, for, in almost all cases, the made-for-TV movies reunited some of the series' original cast members. The 1969 *Dragnet* could lay claim to being the first TV series reunion film. It was based on the then-running 1967-70 *Dragnet* series, which was an updated revival of the original 1952-59 *Dragnet*. Jack Webb starred as police sergeant Joe Friday in the movie and both runs of the series. *The New Maverick* (1978) reunited James Garner and Jack Kelly as freewheeling brothers Bret and Bart Maverick, roles they originated in the popular 1957-62 Western series. However, the purpose of the 1978 TV-movie was to launch a new show starring Charles Frank as their nephew Ben (the series *Young Maverick* ran very briefly in 1979). On the other hand, 1977's *Father Knows Best Reunion* and 1978's *Rescue From Gilligan's Island* offered nothing new, just pure nostalgia with the original cast members returning (except for Tina Louise as Ginger Grant in the latter film). Their successful ratings (*Gilligan* resulted in two sequels) initiated a steady growth in the number of TV series reunion films. Interestingly, the *Gilligan's Island* TV series was only a modest hit during its 1964-67 run, cracking the top twenty shows only once. The series gained tremendous popularity, especially among young viewers, through syndicated repeats running on local stations. Subsequently, syndication success became a criterion for determining if a series had potential as a reunion film, thus accounting for TV-movies based on *The Brady Bunch*, *The Munsters* and *I Dream of Jeannie*. Indeed, hit series have not always resulted in hit movies. *The Return of the Beverly Hillbillies* (1981) was a painful reunion highlighted by the absence of series regulars Irene Ryan (Granny), Max Baer, Jr. (Jethro), and Raymond Bailey (Mr. Drysdale). Without the 1960s spy movie genre to spoof, 1983's *The Return of the Man From U.N.C.L.E.* came across as dry and dated, despite the presence of stars Robert Vaughn and David McCallum. In contrast, Raymond Burr's triumphant *Perry Mason Returns* (1985) was a well-conceived update that inaugurated a series of highly rated Perry Mason (q.v.) TV-movies. The longest gap between a series' last year and its reunion film was the twenty-eight years separating the 1959-63 series *The Untouchables* from 1991's *The Return of Eliot Ness*. Twenty-seven years separated the series *Peter Gunn* from the 1989 TV-movie — however, the TV-movie *Peter Gunn* was a reunion only in that Blake Edwards produced and directed both movie and show. Peter Strauss and an all new cast replaced Craig Stevens and the other series regulars. Michael Landon, Jr. was the only link between his father's *Bonanza* series and 1988's *Bonanza: The Next Generation*. The 1987 *Police Story: The Freeway Killing* was an oddity — a revival of an anthology TV show. In the following list, only the first reunion film is shown (e.g., see **Gilligan's Island** for a list of other movies based on the series). See also **Gunsmoke; The Incredible Hulk; Kojak, Theo; Little House on the Prairie; The Man From U.N.C.L.E.; Mason, Perry; The Six Million Dollar Man; Theatrical Films Based on Television Series; The Waltons;** and **Welby, Marcus.**

Dragnet (1969 TVM)
Father Knows Best Reunion (1977 TVM)
The New Maverick (1978 TVM)
Rescue From Gilligan's Island (1978 TVM)
The Return of the Mod Squad (1979 TVM)
The Wild, Wild West Revisited (1979 TVM)
The Return of Frank Cannon (1980 TVM)
The Brady Girls Get Married (1981 TVM)
The Munsters' Revenge (1981 TVM)
The Return of the Beverly Hillbillies (1981 TVM)
A Wedding on Walton's Mountain (1982 TVM)
The Return of the Man From U.N.C.L.E. (1983 TVM)
Still the Beaver (1983 TVM)
The Return of Marcus Welby (1984 TVM)
I Dream of Jeannie: 15 Years Later (1985 TVM)
Kojack: The Belarus File (1985 TVM)
Perry Mason Returns (1985 TVM)
Kung Fu: The Movie (1986 TVM)
Return to Mayberry (1986 TVM)
Eight Is Enough: A Family Reunion (1987 TVM)
Gunsmoke: Return to Dodge (1987 TVM)
The Return of the Six Million Dollar Man and the Bionic Woman (1987 TVM)
Police Story: The Freeway Killing (1987 TVM)

Still Crazy Like a Fox (1987 TVM)
Bonanza: The Next Generation (1988 TVM)
Bring Me the Head of Dobie Gillis (1988 TVM)
The Incredible Hulk Returns (1988 TVM)
The Return of Ben Casey (1988 TVM)
Get Smart Again (1989 TVM)
Peter Gunn (1989 TVM)
The Return of Sam McCloud (1989 TVM)
The Love Boat: A Valentine Voyage (1990 TVM)
Return to Green Acres (1990 TVM)
Knight Rider 2000 (1991 TVM)
The Return of Eliot Ness (1991 TVM)
Dynasty: The Reunion (1991 TVM)
I Still Dream of Jeannie (1991 TVM)
Back on the Streets of San Francisco (1992 TVM)
Jonny's Golden Quest (1993 TVM)
The Return of Ironside (1993 TVM)
The Odd Couple: Together Again (1993 TVM)

Tennis

Tennis and golf (q.v.) have failed to interest many filmmakers, perhaps because the two sports were once viewed as leisurely activities reserved for the country club set. Director Ida Lupino lent a feminist slant to 1951's *Hard, Fast and Beautiful*, an overwrought drama about a domineering mother who pushed her daughter toward tennis stardom. The 1978 TV biography *Little Mo* told the story of teen Grand Slam champion Maureen Connelly, who died after a long struggle with cancer. Two theatrical tennis movies were released the following year and both flopped badly. *Racquet* starred Bert Convey as a tennis pro who used sex to get what he wanted, while *Players* featured Dean Paul Martin as a promising player forced to choose between the game and a woman (Ali MacGraw). Real-life tennis stars Pancho Gonzalez (*Players*) and Bobby Riggs (*Racquet*) lent the movies a touch of credibility. *Spring Fever* (1983) simply recruited a real player to play the lead role, but teenaged Carling Bassett showed no promise as an actress (of course, neither did the rest of the cast, which included Susan Anton as the girl's mother). The 1986 *Second Serve* examined the fascinating real-life saga of Richard Raskins, the male surgeon who underwent a sex-change operation and became tennis player Renee Richards. Tennis games have served as memorable set pieces in several movies. Monsieur Hulot (q.v.) experienced a great deal of trouble with the game in one of the funniest scenes in *Monsieur Hulot's Holiday*. A troupe of mimics played an imaginary game of tennis in the symbolic denouement of *Blow-Up*. And in Alfred Hitchcock's *Strangers on a Train*, tennis player Farley Granger rushes through a big match so he can stop psychopath Robert Walker from murdering again.

You Can't Cheat an Honest Man (1939) (table tennis)
Come to the Stable (1949)
Hard, Fast and Beautiful (1951)
Strangers on a Train (1951)
Monsieur Hulot's Holiday (1953)
Dial M for Murder (1954)
Blow-Up (1966)

The High Commissioner (aka Nobody
  Runs Forever) (1968)
The Christian Licorice Store (1971)
Little Mo (1978 TVM)
Racquet (1979)

Players (1979)
Spring Fever (1983)
Second Serve (1986 TVM)
Jocks (aka Road Trip) (1987)
Nobody's Perfect (1990)

The Texas Chainsaw Massacre

This gruesome 1974 shocker was loosely based on the case of real-life Wisconsin
mass murderer Ed Gein, whose exploits also provided the basis for *Psycho* (1960)
and *Deranged* (1974). Shot on a small budget in Texas, the film traced the plight
of a group of young people stranded near an isolated farmhouse run by three crazy
cannibalistic brothers and their all-but-dead grandfather. As directed by Tobe
Hooper, *Chainsaw Massacre* turned into a derivative exercise in shock, recalling
Hershell Gordon Lewis's *Two Thousand Maniacs* (1964) and George Romero's
Night of the Living Dead (1968). Still, the film attracted a faithful cult following
and eventually provided Hooper with a ticket to mainstream Hollywood (e.g.,
1982's *Poltergeist*). After flirting with the big time, Hooper returned belatedly to
his Texan roots for 1986's *The Texas Chainsaw Massacre II*. Jim Siedow reprised
his role as one of the crazy Sawyer brothers, but Bill Moseley replaced fan favorite
Gunnar Hansen as the chainsaw-wielding brother Leatherface. As if to compen-
sate, Dennis Hopper joined the cast as Lefty Enright, a Texas Ranger who carried
a chainsaw in his holster. Despite its attempts at black humor, the film found
little favor with horror fans. Nevertheless, New Line Cinema rolled out a third
installment, *Leatherface: Texas Chainsaw Massacre III*, four years later. Jeff Burr
replaced Hooper as director, and R.A. Mihailoff played the title role. It too faded
quickly at the box office. See also **Chainsaws**.

  The Texas Chainsaw Massacre (1974)
  The Texas Chainsaw Massacre II (1986)
  Leatherface: Texas Chainsaw Massacre III (1990)

The Texas Rangers

This was another routine Western series (once again built around three lawmen)
until Tex Ritter joined the cast in 1944. The original lineup consisted of Dave
O'Brien, Guy Wilkerson and James Newill, best known as the singing Mountie
of the *Renfrew* series (q.v.). Ritter replaced Newill after *Brand of the Devil* and
distinguished the films with his familiar voice. Ironically, Ritter's biggest hit song
occurred in a Western in which he did not star—1952's *High Noon*. Eagle Lion
reissued the Texas Ranger pictures, with different titles, in the late 1940s.

  Rangers Take Over (1943)
  Bad Men of Thunder Gap (aka
    Thundergap Outlaws) (1943)
  West of Texas (aka Shootin' Irons)
    (1943)
  Border Buckaroos (1943)
  Fighting Valley (1943)
  Trail of Terror (1944)
  The Return of the Rangers (1944)

  Boss of the Rawhide (1944)
  Gunsmoke Mesa (1944)
  Outlaw Roundup (1944)
  Guns of the Law (1944)
  The Pinto Bandit (1944)
  Spook Town (1944)
  Brand of the Devil (1944)
  Gangsters of the Frontier (1944)
  Dead or Alive (1944)

The Whispering Skull (1944)   Three in the Saddle (1945)
Marked for Murder (1945)   Frontier Fugitives (1945)
Enemy of the Law (1945)   Flaming Bullets (1945)

Theatrical Films Based on TV Series

The reasons why some TV series have been developed into theatrical films, while others have not, defy logic. Surprisingly, television ratings have rarely been a criterion. The 1964-66 sitcom *The Munsters* was hardly a ratings hit, but that did not deter Universal from releasing a 1966 theatrical version dubbed *Munster, Go Home*. Likewise, the Saturday morning kiddie show *H.R. Pufnstuf* seemed an odd choice for a big-screen musical when 1970's *Pufnstuf* appeared in theaters. Ironically, both the *Pufnstuf* and *Munsters* TV series were cancelled almost simultaneously with the release of their feature film versions. Cult television shows have fared far better as theatrical films. The gothic soap opera *Dark Shadows* had a built-in audience of loyal fans when the movie *House of Dark Shadows* premiered in 1967. It did well enough to inspire a second picture, 1971's *Night of Dark Shadows*. The classic TV series *Star Trek* performed dismally in the ratings (ranking fifty-two in its best season) during its original 1966-69 run. However, by the time an expensive big-screen version was mounted in 1979, the show had turned into a national phenomenon thanks to syndicated showings on local TV stations. The *Star Trek* (q.v.) film series initiated by *Star Trek — The Motion Picture* easily outdistances all other TV series-inspired films in terms of both box office returns and popularity. Its closest competition comes from Jim Henson's Muppets (q.v.), which used the syndicated *Muppet Show* as a springboard for four theatrical features beginning with 1979's *The Muppet Movie*. On British television, three of the Quatermass (q.v.) science fiction serials were remade as theatrical movies, and the 1970-75 comedy series *On the Buses* inspired a 1971 big-screen version. The longest span between a series' last season and its theatrical version was the twenty-six years that separated *The Fugitive* (1963-67) from the 1993 big screen version starring Harrison Ford. The most successful movie based on a television flop was 1988's *The Naked Gun*, which evolved from the very short-lived comedy series *Police Squad* (1982). *The Man From U.N.C.L.E.* movies (q.v.) were not "new" theatrical films but merely episodes of the TV series edited together. The 1992 TV-movie *Boris and Natasha* is included since it was produced originally for theatrical release. See also **Dark Shadows; The Man From U.N.C.L.E.; The Muppets; Star Trek.**

Here Come the Nelsons (1952)
Our Miss Brooks (1956)
The Lone Ranger (1956)
The Creeping Unknown (aka The
   Quatermass Xperiment) (1956)
The Lineup (1958) (based on San
   Francisco Beat)
McHale's Navy (1964)
Munster, Go Home (1966)
A Man Called Flintstone (1966)
Batman (1966)
Gunn (1967)

House of Dark Shadows (1967)
Pufnstuf (1970)
On the Buses (1971) (from a British
   series)
Dad's Army (1971) (from a British
   series)
Doomwatch (1972) (from a British
   series)
Callan (1974) (from a British series)
Sweeney! (1976) (from a British
   series)
Star Trek — The Motion Picture (1979)

Doing Time (1979) (from a British series)
The Muppet Movie (1979)
The Blues Brothers (1980) (based on Saturday Night Live)
The Gong Show Movie (1980)
The Nude Bomb (aka The Return of Maxwell Smart) (1980)
Twilight Zone — The Movie (1983)
Smurfs and the Magic Flute (1984)
Dragnet (1987)
Masters of the Universe (1987)
The Naked Gun (1988)
Jetsons: The Movie (1990)

Tales From the Dark Side: The Movie (1990)
Duck Tales: The Movie — Treasure of the Lost Lamp (1990)
The Addams Family (1991)
Boris and Natasha (1992 TVM) (based on The Adventures of Rocky and Bullwinkle)
Wayne's World (1992) (based on Saturday Night Live)
Coneheads (1993) (based on Saturday Night Live)
The Fugitive (1993)
The Beverly Hillbillies (1993)

The Thin Man

In the 1930s and 1940s, one detective film series stood above all the others. With two big stars in the leads and plenty of MGM gloss, the six Thin Man mysteries clearly separated themselves from their B-movie competitors. These were "A" efforts and marketed as such, with new entries released only at two- or three-year intervals. The first film, based on Dashiell Hammett's novel, cast William Powell and Myrna Loy as wealthy, amateur detectives Nick and Nora Charles. Powell already had extensive detective film experience, having played Philo Vance (q.v.) in four films for Paramount and Warner Bros. But unlike the urbane Vance, Nick Charles afforded Powell the opportunity to display his gift for light comedy. Myrna Loy provided the perfect foil, becoming a role model for spunky film heroines. The third family member was Asta, Nick and Nora's faithful and mischievous fox terrier. Nick, Jr. made his series debut in the third entry, Another Thin Man (actually the title made little sense since the "thin man" was a murder victim played by Edward Ellis in the first film). The quality of the mysteries declined as the series progressed, but the films remained popular due to the Charles's sophisticated relationship, a natural blend of good-natured insults and honest affection. As with the Hardy series (q.v.), MGM used the Thin Man films as a training ground for its brightest acting prospects: James Stewart (playing against type) in After the Thin Man, Donna Reed in Shadow of the Thin Man, and Gloria Grahame and Dean Stockwell (as Nick, Jr.) in Song of the Thin Man. Peter Lawford and Phyllis Kirk played Nick and Nora on television, enjoying a modest run with their 1957-59 series The Thin Man. Craig Stevens (TV's Peter Gunn) and Jo Ann Pflug tried to update the characters in the charmless 1975 TV-movie Nick and Nora. The Charleses were among the detectives spoofed in Neil Simon's Murder by Death (1976).

The Thin Man (1934)
After the Thin Man (1936)
Another Thin Man (1939)
Shadow of the Thin Man (1941)

The Thin Man Goes Home (1944)
Song of the Thin Man (1947)
Nick and Nora (1975 TVM)

3-D

Three-dimensional, or stereoscopic, films create an illusion of depth by filtering the image separately for each eye. This is usually accomplished by requiring viewers to wear cardboard glasses with clear polarized lenses or lenses tinted red and blue-green (the latter process is called anaglyphic 3-D). Although experimental 3-D films date back to 1915, the depth process was largely ignored until the early 1950s. Faced with the growing popularity of television, movie moguls felt that something new was needed to lure patrons back to the theaters. The astonishing success of Arch Obler's low-budget, three-dimensional jungle adventure *Bwana Devil* ("A lion in your lap!" proclaimed the poster) convinced Hollywood that 3-D was the answer to its problems. Over forty stereoscopic films were released between 1953 and 1954. Arguably, the finest was 1953's *House of Wax*, which launched Vincent Price's horror career by casting him as a mad sculptor who made wax figures from his murder victims. Unfortunately, quality efforts such as *House of Wax* and *It Came From Outer Space* were quickly overshadowed by technically inept, let's-make-a-buck features like *Robot Monster* and *Cat Women of the Moon*. By 1955, the 3-D craze had ended, brought to an early death by the popularity of less expensive wide-screen processes like Cinemascope (which also offered something TV couldn't). Attempts to revive 3-D proved fruitless for almost two decades. Then, in 1969, the unexpected success of *The Stewardesses*, a low-budget sex picture, inspired a fleeting interest in 3-D again. However, as in the 1950s, poor quality 3-D movies flooded the market and snuffed out the chances of a big comeback. But just to prove you can't keep a good idea down, 3-D surfaced once more in the early 1980s with the release of a ludicrous Italian Western dubbed *Comin' at Ya*. This time, the major studios jumped on the bandwagon and produced big-budget features like *Jaws 3* and *Metalstorm*. Despite a few legitimate hits (e.g., *Friday the 13th Part 3*), 3-D never really captured the public's fancy and faded within a year. Nevertheless, the 1980s craze did produce the first 3-D feature-length cartoon, 1985's *Starchaser: The Legend of Orin*. The climax to 1991's *Freddy's Dead: The Final Nightmare* was shown in Freddyvision—a catchy term for 3-D. See also **Cinerama; Gimmicks.**

Bwana Devil (1952)
Arena (1953)
The Charge at Feather River (1953)
Devil's Canyon (1953)
Fatal Desire (1953)
Money From Home (1953)
The Moonlighter (1953)
Fort Ti (1953)
Flight to Tangier (1953)
Hondo (1953)
House of Wax (1953)
I, the Jury (1953)
It Came From Outer Space (1953)
Invaders From Mars (1953)
Inferno (1953)
Kiss Me Kate (1953)

Man in the Dark (1953)
Miss Sadie Thompson (1953)
The Maze (1953)
Outlaw Territory (aka *Hannah Lee*) (1953)
Robot Monster (1953)
Sangaree (1953)
Wings of the Hawk (1953)
Second Chance (1953)
The Stranger Wore a Gun (1953)
Cat Women of the Moon (aka *Rocket to the Moon*) (1954)
Creature From the Black Lagoon (1954)
Dial M for Murder (1954)
Drums of Tahiti (1954)

The French Line (1954

Gog (1954)

Gorilla at Large (1954)

The Mad Magician (1954)

Phantom of the Rue Morgue (1954)

Taza, Son of Cochise (1954)

Son of Sinbad (1954)

Eyes of Hell (aka The Mask) (1961)

The Bubble (aka Fantastic Invasion of
   Planet Earth) (1966)

The Mark of the Werewolf (aka
   Frankenstein's Bloody Terror)
   (1968)

The Stewardesses (1969)

Three Dimensions of Greta (1972)

The Flesh and Blood Show (aka
   Asylum of the Insane) (1972)

Andy Warhol's Frankenstein (aka
   Flesh for Frankenstein) (1973)

The Playmates (1973)

A*P*E (1976)

The Surfer Girls (1980)

Comin' at Ya! (1981)

Rottweiler (aka Dogs of Hell) (1981)

Friday the 13th Part 3 (1982)

Treasure of the Four Crowns (1982)

Parasite (1982)

Jaws 3 (aka Jaws 3-D) (1983)

The Man Who Wasn't There (1983)

Metalstorm: The Destruction of Jared-
   Syn (1983)

Spacehunter: Adventures in the
   Forbidden Zone (1983)

Tales of the Third Dimension (1984)

Silent Madness (aka Omega Factor;
   Night Killer) (1984)

Hit the Road Running (1984)

Starchaser: The Legend of Orin (1985)

Blonde Emmanuelle in 3-D (1990)

Freddy's Dead: The Final Nightmare
   (1991)

The Three Mesquiteers

Republic Pictures introduced *The Three Mesquiteers* in 1936, the year after Paramount released the first of its highly profitable *Hopalong Cassidy* (q.v.) Westerns. Popular western novelist William Colt MacDonald created the three Dumas-inspired do-gooders: Stony Brooke, the trio's hot-tempered leader; Tucson Smith, his more rational friend and frequent romantic rival; and Lullaby Joslin, the easygoing comedian of the group. The plots frequently shifted from the Civil War period to more contemporary settings. Their first film, for example, found the Mesquiteers helping World War I vets whose settlement on government-leased land was opposed by unreasonable cattlemen. The original Mesquiteer line-up featured Ray "Crash" Corrigan as Tucson, Robert Livingston as Stony, and Syd Saylor as Lullaby. Max Terhune replaced Saylor in the second film, and it's this cast—Corrigan, Livingston and Terhune—that's best remembered. Other performers, though, also spent time in the saddle. Ralph Temp temporarily replaced Livingston, and an upcoming actor named John Wayne played Stony for a while. A cowboy singer named Dick Weston had a musical number in 1937's *Wild Horse Rodeo*. Weston later became a Western star in his own right—after changing his name to Roy Rogers. Duncan Renaldo, best known as the Cisco Kid (q.v.), joined the cast in 1939 for a brief stint as a new character named Rico. Meanwhile, Corrigan, Livingston and Terhune moved to other studios and launched new series. Corrigan and Terhune joined John "Dusty" King to form *The Range Busters* (q.v.) for Monogram. Livingston teamed up with Al "Fuzzy" St. John in PRC's *The Lone Rider* movies. These series and many similar ones owe much to the "Western trio" premise fostered by the first Mesquiteer pictures.

Law of the 45's (1935)   Powdersmoke Range (1935)

The Three Mesquiteers (1936)
Ghost Town Gold (1936)
Roarin' Lead (1936)
Riders of the Whistling Skull (1937)
Hit the Saddle (1937)
Gunsmoke Ranch (1937)
Come On, Cowboys (1937)
Range Defenders (1937)
Heart of the Rockies (1937)
The Trigger Trio (1937)
Wild Horse Rodeo (1937)
The Purple Vigilantes (1938)
Call the Mesquiteers (1938)
Outlaws of Sonora (1938)
Riders of the Black Hills (1938)
Heroes of the Hills (1938)
Pals of the Saddle (1938)
Overland Stage Raiders (1938)
Santa Fe Stampede (1938)
Red River Range (1938)
The Night Riders (1939)
Three Texas Steers (1939)
Wyoming Outlaws (1939)
New Frontier (1939)
The Kansas Terrors (1939)

Cowboys From Texas (1939)
Heroes of the Saddle (1940)
Pioneers of the West (1940)
Covered Wagon Days (1940)
Rocky Mountain Rangers (1940)
Oklahoma Renegades (1940)
Under Texas Skies (1940)
The Trail Blazers (1940)
Lone Star Raiders (1940)
Prairie Pioneers (1941)
Saddlemates (1941)
Gangs of Sonora (1941)
Outlaws of the Cherokee Trail (1941)
Gauchos of El Dorado (1941)
West of Cimarron (1941)
Code of the Outlaw (1942)
Raiders of the Range (1942)
Westward Ho (1942)
The Phantom Plainsmen (1942)
Shadows on the Sage (1942)
Valley of Hunted Men (1942)
Thundering Trails (1943)
The Blocked Trail (1943)
Santa Fe Scouts (1943)
Riders of the Rio Grande (1943)

Three Mothers Trilogy

Stephen King once confessed that 1977's *Suspiria*, the first of this horrific would-be trilogy, was one of his "guilty pleasures, in part because it treated us to an entire girls' school being bombarded by a rain of maggots at dinner ... good stuff." Italian horror stylist Dario Argento allegedly based the films on an essay by Thomas De Quincey entitled "Levana and Our Ladies of Sorrow." The "ladies" are the three wicked sisters who produce the sorrows of the world: Mater Suspiriorum (Mother of Sighs); Mater Tenebrarum (Mother of Darkness); and Mater Lachrymarum (Mother of Tears). Although its English-language title suggests that *Tenebrae* (1982) is part of the "trilogy," there is strong evidence to suggest otherwise. The plot features no supernatural elements, focusing on a murderer replicating crimes from author Tony Franciosa's novel (which is titled *Tenebrae*). Thus, Argento fans still await a third film to conclude the trilogy.

Suspiria (1977)
Inferno (1980)
Tenebrae (aka Tenebres; Unsane) (1982)

The Three Musketeers

Alexandre Dumas's novels *The Three Musketeers*, *Twenty Years After* and *The Man in the Iron Mask* have provided a rich source for cinematic swashbucklers. Silent versions of *The Three Musketeers* appeared in 1911, 1913, 1914 and 1921. The 1921 adaptation starred Douglas Fairbanks, Sr. in one of his most memorable roles as D'Artagnan. It was so successful that Fairbanks took another turn as D'Artagnan in 1929's *The Iron Mask*. Other actors have donned the hot-headed Gascon's sword, but none has made a lasting impression. Character actor Walter Abel was miscast in 1935's *The Three Musketeers*. Don Ameche's 1939 version was played for laughs, with the Ritz Brothers as the trio of Athos, Porthos and Aramis. Gene Kelly gave an energetic performance in the lavish 1948 adaptation, but he lacked the necessary charisma. Warren William and Michael York may be the best post-Fairbanks D'Artagnans due to their different interpretations. In 1939's *The Man in the Iron Mask*, William portrayed D'Artagnan as a middle-aged swordsman, while York made him an awkward youth anxious to be a musketeer in Richard Lester's *The Three Musketeers* (1974). Interestingly, a number of coincidences surround the directors and performers in the *Musketeer* movies. There's a Frankenstein connection between James Whale's *The Man in the Iron Mask* (1939) and Rowland V. Lee's *The Three Musketeers* (1935). Whale directed Boris Karloff in *Frankenstein* and *The Bride of Frankenstein*, while Lee directed Karloff's last appearance as the Monster in *Son of Frankenstein*. Louis Hayward played the lead role in the 1939 *Man in the Iron Mask* but switched to the part of D'Artagnan for *Lady in the Iron Mask* (1952). Eugene Pallette, who played the musketeer Aramis in the 1921 *Three Musketeers*, is best remembered as Friar Tuck in Errol Flynn's *The Adventures of Robin Hood*. One of his costars in that film was Alan Hale, Sr., (as Little John), who played the musketeer Porthos in Whale's *The Three Musketeers*. His son, Alan Hale, Jr., played Porthos in *Lady in the Iron Mask* and *The Fifth Musketeer* and the son of Porthos in *At Sword's Point*. That same film featured Cornel Wilde as D'Artagnan's son, Dan O'Herlihy as Aramis's son, and Maureen O'Hara as Athos's daughter. Richard Lester filmed his *The Three Musketeers* and *The Four Musketeers* in 1973, but they were released in 1974 and 1975 respectively. The same cast reunited fifteen years later for 1989's *The Return of the Musketeers*. It played theatrically in Europe but debuted in the United States on a cable network two years later. In 1993, no doubt inspired by the success of 1991's *Robin Hood: Prince of Thieves*, Disney mounted a light-hearted adaptation of Dumas's novel. Since the film boasted a bevy of hot young performers, the trade papers dubbed it "Young Guns in Tights."

The Three Musketeers (1921)
The Iron Mask (1929)
The Three Musketeers (1935)
The Three Musketeers (1939)
The Man in the Iron Mask (1939)
The Three Musketeers (1948)
Lady in the Iron Mask (1952)
At Sword's Point (1952)
Sword of D'Artagnan (1952)
The Three Musketeers (1953)
The Three Musketeers (1961)

The Secret Mark of D'Artagnan (1962)
The Three Musketeers (The Queen's Diamonds) (1974)
The Four Musketeers (The Revenge of Milady) (1975)
The Man in the Iron Mask (1977 TVM)
The Fifth Musketeer (1979)
The Return of the Musketeers (1989)
The Three Musketeers (1993)

Three Smart Girls

Teen star Deanna Durbin made her feature film debut in 1936's *Three Smart Girls*, a sentimental comedy about the efforts of three sisters to reunite their separated parents. Nan Grey and Barbara Read played the other two sisters. Helen Parrish replaced Read in the 1939 follow-up *Three Smart Girls Grow Up*, which focused on Deanna's plans to marry off her older sisters. This fluffy sequel gave the eighteen-year-old Durbin one of her biggest recording hits with "Because." She reprised the Penelope Craig character one more time, as an adult, in the more serious World War II romance *Hers to Hold* (1943).

Three Smart Girls (1936)	*Hers to Hold* (1943)
Three Smart Girls Grow Up (1939)	

Tibbs, Virgil

An urbane black detective from Philadelphia, Tibbs first appeared as a fish out of water in the 1967 Best Picture *In the Heat of the Night* (1967), a mystery set in a racially prejudiced Southern town. Rod Steiger won a Best Actor Oscar as the town's sheriff, but it was Tibbs, as portrayed by Sidney Poitier, who came back for a sequel. *They Call Me MISTER Tibbs* (1970) sent Tibbs to San Francisco to solve a homicide. He was still there in 1971, working with a vigilante group to crack a drug ring in *The Organization*. That was the last Tibbs film, except for a 1988 TV version (and series pilot) of *In the Heat of the Night* starring Howard Rollins as Virgil Tibbs.

In the Heat of the Night (1967)	*The Organization* (1971)
They Call Me MISTER Tibbs (1970)	*In the Heat of the Night* (1988 TVM)

Time Travel

The subject of time has long fascinated filmmakers, as evidenced by 1910's *The Times Are Out of Joint*, an obscure science fiction feature about a clock that manipulates time by accelerating motion. Generally, however, movies about time travel fall into three categories: traveling into the past, traveling into the future, and traveling from the future back to present day. The first category is by far the most common, dating back to Mark Twain's *A Connecticut Yankee in King Arthur's Court*. Twain's novel alone has been filmed four times: as a silent film, a Will Rogers comedy, a Bing Crosby musical, and a Disney feature (mysteriously titled *Unidentified Flying Oddball*). Leslie Howard traveled back to eighteenth-century England in *Berkeley Square*, as did Tyrone Power in the remake *I'll Never Forget You*, while Christopher Reeve willed himself back to turn-of-the-century America in *Somewhere in Time*. All three fell in love with beautiful ladies, lost them temporarily, and then were reunited in one way or another. Spacecrafts accidentally stumbled through time warps in *World Without End* (1956) and *Planet of the Apes* (1968). In 1986's *Star Trek IV: The Voyage Home*, the *Enterprise* used warp speed to go back in time to save some whales. Curious scientists have naturally preferred to travel to the future, as in *The Time Travelers* (1964) and George Pal's 1960 adaptation of H.G. Wells's *The Time Machine*. A cornered Jack the Ripper used Wells's time machine to make a quick escape to modern-day San Francisco in Nicholas Meyer's stylish thriller *Time After Time* (1979). Finally, inhabitants of the future have sought to change their course of events by traveling back to the present day in *Cyborg 2087* (1966), its partial remake *The Terminator* (1984) and *Trancers* (1985). *Cyborg 2087*, an underrated cheapie, cast Michael Rennie as a cyborg assigned to stop the creation of his own "race." Other time-related movies of interest include 1944's *It Happened Tomorrow* (a reporter acquires tomorrow's newspaper today), 1947's *Repeat Performance* (two people live a year over again), 1956's *The Atomic Man* (a scientist moves 7.5 seconds ahead of everyone else) and 1963's *The Jetty* (a man remembers his own future death). See also **Back to the Future; Planet of the Apes; Trancers.**

A Connecticut Yankee in King Arthur's Court (1921)
A Connecticut Yankee in King Arthur's Court (1931)
Berkeley Square (1933)
Time Flies (1944)
Fiddlers Three (1944)
Where Do We Go From Here? (1945)
Repeat Performance (1947)
A Connecticut Yankee in King Arthur's Court (1949)
I'll Never Forget You (aka *The House in the Square*) (1951)
The Atomic Man (aka *Timeslip*) (1956)
World Without End (1956)
The 30-Foot Bride of Candy Rock (1959)
Beyond the Time Barrier (1960)
The Time Machine (1960)
The Jetty (aka *La Jetée*; *The Pier*) (1963)
The Time Travelers (1964)
Dr. Who and the Daleks (1965)
Willy McBean and His Magic Machine (1965)
Cyborg 2087 (1966)
Daleks — Invasion Earth 2150 A.D. (aka *Invasion Earth 2150 A.D.*) (1966)
Journey to the Center of Time (1967)
Planet of the Apes (1968)
A Witch Without a Broom (1968)
Hu-Man (1975)
Time Travelers (1976)
The Time Machine (1978 TVM)
Jubilee (1978)
Time After Time (1979)
Unidentified Flying Oddball (1979)
The Day Time Ended (aka *Time Warp*) (1980)

The Final Countdown (1980)
Somewhere in Time (1980)
Time Bandits (1981)
Through the Magic Pyramid (1981 TVM)
Timerider (1983)
The Philadelphia Experiment (1984)
The Terminator (1984)
The Cold Room (1984 TVM)
Arthur the King (1985 TVM)
The Blue Yonder (aka *Time Flyer*) (1985 TVM)
Trancers (aka *Future Cop*) (1985)
My Science Project (1985)
Back to the Future (1985)
Biggles: Adventures in Time (aka *Biggles*) (1986)
Peggy Sue Got Married (1986)
Star Trek IV: The Voyage Home (1986)
The Time Guardian (1987)
Timestalkers (1987 TVM)
Out of Time (1988 TVM)
Light Years (1988)
Earth*Star Voyager (1988 TVM)
The Navigator: A Medieval Odyssey (1988)
Bill and Ted's Excellent Adventure (1989)
Quantum Leap (1989 TVM)
Time Trackers (1989)
Millennium (1989)
Turn Back the Clock (1989 TVM)
Frankenstein Unbound (aka *Roger Corman's Frankenstein Unbound*) (1990)
Running Against Time (1990 TVM)
Spirit of '76 (1991)
Warlock (1991)
Beastmaster 2: Through the Portal of Time (1991)

Titanic

Both *Titanic* and *A Night to Remember* chronicled the human drama surrounding the 1912 luxury liner disaster. *S.O.S. Titanic* was a made-for-TV rehash, while

Raise the Titanic! was a dull adaptation of Clive Cussler's best-seller about salvaging the sunken ship. The *Titanic* returned as a ghost ship, complete with spooky passengers, in 1989's *Ghostbusters II*.

Titanic (1953)   *Raise the Titanic!* (1980)
A Night to Remember (1958)   *Ghostbusters II* (1989)
S.O.S. Titanic (1979 TVM)

Topper

George and Marion Kerby were a fun-loving couple until a car crash put a premature end to their earthly existence. Required to perform a good deed to earn admittance into Heaven, the ghostly Kerbys turned their attention to meek banker Cosmo Topper. Cosmo's subsequent problems with George and Marion generated most of the laughs in 1937's *Topper*. The film was a guaranteed success, with Cary Grant, Constance Bennett and Roland Young in the principal roles. Bennett and Young returned for the 1939 sequel *Topper Takes a Trip*, which found Marion badgering Cosmo on his Riviera vacation. Only Young (and Billie Burke as Mrs. Topper) remained for 1941's *Topper Returns*. It drew poor comparisons with the first two films but has since come to be regarded as a first-rate haunted house comedy. It also gave Burke a chance to shine with some wacky dialogue: "My, my, it's strange how it's always cold in the winter and warm in the summer, isn't it?" Leo G. Carroll played Cosmo in the 1953-56 TV series *Topper*, with Robert Sterling and Anne Jeffreys as the Kerbys. Kate Jackson and then-husband Andrew Stevens produced and starred (as the Kerbys) in a lackluster 1979 TV-movie, costarring Jack Warden as Cosmo Topper. In 1983's *Somewhere Tomorrow*, a lonely teenage girl watched *Topper*, bumped her head, and then met a boy ghost. See also **Ghosts**.

Topper (1937)   *Topper Returns* (1941)
Topper Takes a Trip (1939)   *Topper* (1979 TVM)

Tora-san

The longest-running film series in the world remains virtually unknown to English-language moviegoers. Yet the *Tora-san* films have appealed to faithful Japanese fans for over twenty years and forty-five episodes. Amazingly, the title character has always been played by the same actor, Kiyoshi Atsumi, and all but two of the entries were directed by Yoji Yamada. The popularity of the films can be traced to the lovable title character, Tora-san (a colloquial reference to Torajiro Kuruma), whom *Variety* once described as "a none-too-bright, bumbling but streetwise peddler who most often fouls up the plot and lets the woman get away." A middle-aged bachelor, Tora-san travels throughout Japan when not living with his aunt and uncle. He also spends time with his sister's family, especially nephew Mitsuo (Hidetaka Yoshioka). Now a teenager, Mitsuo's relationship with Tora-san has become a focal point of recent series entries—a development credited with introducing the films to a wider, more youthful audience in the late 1980s. Star Kiyoshi Atsumi was forty-two when the series debut entry, *Tora-san, Our Lovable Tramp* (*Otoko Wa Tsurai Yo*), was released in 1969. He appeared in an average of two *Tora-san* films annually from 1969-87, before the production pace decreased to one per year. According to some sources, he outranks the Emperor as the most recognizable face in Japan.

Tora-san, Our Lovable Tramp (1969)
Tora-san's Cherished Mother (1969)
Tora-san: His Tender Love (1970)
Tora-san's Grand Scheme (1970)
Tora-san's Runaway (1970)
Tora-san's Shattered Romance (1971)
Tora-san, the Good Samaritan (1971)
Tora-san's Love Call (1971)
Tora-san's Dear Old Home (1972)
Tora-san's Dream-Come-True (1972)
Tora-san's Forget-Me-Not (1973)
Tora-san Loves an Artist (1973)
Tora-san's Lovesick (1974)
Tora-san's Lullaby (1974)
Tora-san Meets the Songstress Again (1975)
Tora-san, the Intellect (1975)
Tora-san's Sunrise and Sunset (1976)
Tora-san's Heart of Gold (1976)
Tora-san Meets His Lordship (1977)
Tora-san Plays Cupid (1977)
Stage-Struck Tora-san (1978)
Talk-of-the-Town Tora-san (1978)
Tora-san, the Watchmaker (1979)
Tora-san's Dream of Spring (1979)

Tora-san's Tropical Fever (1980)
Foster Day, Tora-san (1980)
Tora-san's Many-Splintered Love (1981)
Tora-san's Promise (1981)
Hearts and Flowers for Tora-san (1982)
Tora-san, the Expert (1982)
Tora-san's Song of Love (1983)
Tora-san Goes Religious (1983)
Marriage Counselor Tora-san (1984)
Tora-san's Forbidden Love (1984)
Tora-san, the Go-Between (1985)
Tora-san's Island Encounter (1985)
Tora-san's Bluebird Fantasy (1986)
Tora-san Goes North (1987)
Tora-san Plays Daddy (1987)
Tora-san's Salad Date Memorial (1988)
Tora-san Goes to Vienna (1989)
Tora-san, My Uncle (1989)
Tora-san Takes a Vacation (1990)
Tora-san Confesses (1991)
Tora-san Makes Excuses (1992)

The Toxic Avenger

Melvin Ferd, Tromaville's town "nerd," worked as a janitor at the local health club, where he regularly incurred the ridicule of the club's snobbish clientele. After a particularly degrading experience, he jumped out a second-story window and landed in a vat of chemical toxins. This accident transformed meek Melvin into a muscular, green, disfigured superhero (resembling Swamp Thing). All this happened in the first twenty minutes of 1985's *The Toxic Avenger*, a hopeless comedy that found a video audience and evolved into a campy, low-budget series. The rest of the first picture found the Toxic Avenger, janitor's mop in hand, beating up bad guys and falling in love with a blind blonde named Sara. Mark Torgi played Melvin, while Mitchell Cohen took over as Toxie (with Kenneth Kessler providing the voice). The Troma Team (yes, the studio named the film's town after itself) waited four years to produce *The Toxic Avenger Part II*. The gap between installments must have confused the Troma staff, for in *Part II*, Melvin's last name had changed to Junko and Sara (still blonde and blind) had become Claire. The plot sent Toxie to Tokyo to find his father, while the evil Apocalypse, Inc. took over Tromaville. Ron Fazio and John Altamura teamed up as Toxie. They also headlined the same year's *The Toxic Avenger Part III: The Last Temptation of Toxie*, an effort described by *Variety* as a "toxic stew that, in no particular order, mixes lots of entrails, half-naked women and sound effects plucked from the Three Stooges."

The Toxic Avenger (1985)	*The Toxic Avenger Part III: The Last*
The Toxic Avenger Part II (1989)	*Temptation of Toxie* (1989)

Tracy, Dick

Chester Gould's comic strip police detective had been the subject of four 1937-41 Republic serials before RKO decided he had potential as a B-film series hero. Former tough guy Morgan Conway brought Tracy alive in 1946's *Dick Tracy* and 1947's *Dick Tracy vs. Cueball*, a pair of lively action pictures balanced nicely by a sense of humor. The scripts stayed close to the comic strip characters, with Anne Jeffreys as Tess Trueheart, Esther Howard as Filthy Flora of the Dripping Dagger Inn, and Ian Keith as Vitamin Flintheart. Ralph Byrd, who had played the detective for Republic, took over the role in the last two films in the series. Since they appeared when film series were declining in popularity, the Tracy films are all but forgotten today. That's a shame, for they featured some very colorful villains: Mike Mazurki's Spitface (*Dick Tracy*), Dick Wessel's Cueball, Jack Lambert's The Claw (*Dick Tracy's Dilemma*), and Boris Karloff's Gruesome. In 1990, Warren Beatty mounted a visually exciting screen adaptation, but—despite casting Madonna as a femme fatale and featuring some catchy Stephen Sondheim songs—it was a rather dull affair. See also **Comic Strip Characters**.

Dick Tracy (aka *Spitface*) (1946)	*Dick Tracy Meets Gruesome* (aka *Dick*
Dick Tracy vs. Cueball (1947)	*Tracy's Amazing Adventure*)
Dick Tracy's Dilemma (aka *Mark of*	(1947)
the Claw) (1947)	*Dick Tracy* (1990)

Trail Blazers, The

Monogram Pictures was the home of the B-Western in the 1940s. The budget-minded studio was already producing The Rough Riders (q.v.) and The Range Busters (q.v.) films when it introduced the Trail Blazers series in 1943. Monogram signed the three biggest names available (at budget price) and wound up with cowboy greats Hoot Gibson, Ken Maynard and Bob Steele. Gibson and Maynard had retired in the 1930s, but Monogram lured them back to the screen even though they were fifty-one and forty-eight, respectively. After just seven pictures, the series came to an end, and Gibson and Maynard closed out their film careers except for occasional appearances.

Blazing Guns (1943)	*Death Valley Rangers* (1944)
The Law Rides Again (1943)	*Outlaw Trail* (1944)
Wild Horse Stampede (1943)	*Westward Bound* (1944)
Arizona Whirlwind (1944)	

Trailers, *see* Mobile Homes

Trains

Trains have long been a favorite setting for tense dramas and mysteries, primarily because the close confines force character interaction by restricting movement beyond a limited area. Mysteries that have taken place almost entirely on trains include the Basil Rathbone Sherlock Holmes entry *Terror by Night* and the 1974 all-star adaptation of Agatha Christie's *Murder on the Orient Express*. Two of Alfred Hitchcock's most famous works are set aboard trains: A little old lady who's really a spy (Dame May Whitty) got kidnapped in *The Lady Vanishes*, while Robert Walker and Farley Granger swapped murders in a chilling scene in *Strangers on a Train*. Trains were hijacked and used as getaway vehicles in *Runaway Train* (Jon Voight and Eric Roberts as convicts) and *Von Ryan's Express* (with Frank Sinatra and fellow escaped POWs speeding through Germany to freedom). A thawed-out primeval monster and a demented Cossack (Telly Savalas) wreaked havoc aboard the *Horror Express* — thank heavens sturdy hero Peter Cushing was a passenger! However, that's nothing compared to the deadly virus threatening Sophia Loren and Burt Lancaster as they raced through Europe in *The Cassandra Crossing*. It's enough to make one revel in fluffier (and far more entertaining) outings like the Gene Wilder-Richard Pryor action-comedy *The Silver Streak*. See also **Subways**. The following movies either take place on trains or feature memorable train scenes:

The Iron Horse (1924)
Number Seventeen (1932)
The Phantom Express (1932)
Shanghai Express (1932)
Rome Express (1932)
Union Depot (1932)
The Silver Streak (1934)
Twentieth Century (1934)
Streamline Express (1935)
Florida Special (1936)
Night Mail (1936)
California Straight Ahead (1937)
La Bête Humaine (aka *The Human Beast*) (1938)
The Lady Vanishes (1938)
Union Pacific (1939)
Night Train to Munich (aka *Night Train*) (1940)
Broadway Limited (1941)
Lady on a Train (1945)
One Way to Love (1945)
Terror by Night (1946)
Sleeping Car to Trieste (1948)
Berlin Express (1948)
Train of Events (1949)
Peking Express (1951)
Strangers on a Train (1951)
Diplomatic Courier (1952)
The Narrow Margin (1952)
Terror on a Train (aka *Time Bomb*) (1952)

The Titfield Thunderbolt (1953)
The Paris Express (aka *The Man Who Watched the Trains Go By*) (1953)
Human Desire (1954)
The Great Locomotive Chase (aka *Andrews' Raiders*) (1956)
Flame Over India (aka *Northwest Frontier*) (1959)
Night Train (1959)
Train Robbery Confidential (1962)
From Russia With Love (the most memorable of several James Bond train scenes) (1963)
Stop Train 349 (1964)
Dr. Terror's House of Horrors (1965)
The Sleeping Car Murders (1965)
The Train (1965)
Von Ryan's Express (1965)
Trans-Europe Express (1966)
Closely Watched Trains (1966)
The Great St. Trinian's Train Robbery (1966)
The Great British Train Robbery (1967)
Istanbul Express (1968)
Boxcar Bertha (1972)
Horror Express (aka *Panic on the Trans-Siberian Express*) (1972)
Emperor of the North (aka *Emperor of the North Pole*) (1973)
The Train Robbers (1973)

Hijack (1973 TVM)
Runaway! (aka *The Runaway Train*)
   (1973 TVM)
Murder on the Orient Express (1974)
Breakheart Pass (1976)
The Silver Streak (1976)
The Cassandra Crossing (1977)
The Stationmaster's Wife (1977)
Julia (1977)
The Great Train Robbery (aka *The
   First Great Train Robbery*) (1979)
Avalanche Express (1979)
Disaster on the Coastliner (1979 TVM)
Hanging by a Thread (1979 TVM)
The Lady Vanishes (1979)

Cafe Express (1980)
Terror Train (1980)
Chattanooga Choo Choo (1984)
Romance on the Orient Express (1985
   TVM)
Runaway Train (1985)
Stand by Me (1986)
Planes, Trains, and Automobiles
   (1987)
Throw Momma From the Train (1987)
The Sleeping Car (1990)
Back to the Future III (1990)
Narrow Margin (1990)
The Railway Station Man (1992 TVM)

Trancers

The law of diminishing returns applies to this low-budget series, which got off to a promising — if derivative — beginning. *Trancers* (1985) starred Tim Thomerson as Jack Deth, a twenty-fourth-century hard-boiled cop (shades of Harrison Ford in *Blade Runner*) who chases a villain back through time to prevent him from killing the father of a future government leader (shades of the previous year's *Terminator*). Deth's task was complicated by the title creatures, zombielike humans with extraordinary strength and the ability to withstand a handful of bullets at close range (it usually took four or five shots to down a trancer). The film had its admirers, chiefly due to its light touch and quick pace. Director Charles Band tried to mount a follow-up as a segment in the three-part feature *Pulse Pounders*, but the project was never completed. Instead, Thomerson encored as Deth in 1991's *Trancers II*, an unsurprising sequel featuring perennial bad guy Richard Lynch as the brother of the original film's villain. The film's saving grace was Deth's attempts to deal with two wives — one from the present (Helen Hunt) and one from the future (Megan Ward). The third installment, 1992's *Trancers III*, explained how trancers were first created (with a drug invented by Colonel "Daddy" Muthuh) and ended Deth's marriage with his present-day wife. However, its primary purpose was obviously to set up further entries in the series. In its closing scene, the high council paired Deth with a new partner (an odd-looking android named Shark) and appointed him "peace-keeping emissary of time and space." See also **Time Travel**.

Trancers (aka *Future Cop*) (1985)
Trancers II (aka *Trancers II: The Return of Jack Deth*) (1991)
Trancers III (aka *Trancers III: Deth Lives*) (1992)

Traveling Salespersons

The exploits of those who earn their living selling door-to-door have been played mostly for laughs. Lady vendors have proven far more adept than their male counterparts at peddling products: Joan Blondell sold booze-flavored toothpaste in *The Traveling Saleslady* (1935); Joan Davis tried to convince Westerners they needed soap in *The Traveling Saleswoman* (1950); Ginger Rogers marketed girdles in *The First Travelling Saleslady* (1956); Phyllis Diller pushed pianolas in *Did You Hear the One About the Traveling Saleslady?* (1968); and Lucille Ball specialized in cosmetics as *The Fuller Brush Girl* (1950). Red Skelton had one of his best roles as *The Fuller Brush Man* (1948), the hit that inspired Ball's similarly titled sequel. Lou Costello played an incompetent vacuum cleaner salesman in 1946's *Little Giant*, as did Jimmy Durante and Phil Silvers in *You're in the Army Now* (1941). Both comedies featured the patented scene in which dirt is dumped on a clean carpet for an unsuccessful vacuum demonstration. Serious films about traveling salesmen include the 1951 and 1985 adaptations of Arthur Miller's searing stage play *Death of a Salesman*. The 1960 *Never Let Go* was about a salesman victimized by car thieves. Steve Martin played a Depression-era sheet-music salesman in the offbeat dramatic musical *Pennies From Heaven* (1981).

The Traveling Saleslady (1935)	*Never Let Go* (1960)
You're in the Army Now (1941)	*Did You Hear the One About the*
Little Giant (aka *On the Carpet*) (1946)	*Traveling Saleslady?* (1968)
The Emperor Waltz (1948)	*The Strange Vengenace of Rosalie*
The Fuller Brush Man (aka *That Mad*	(1972)
Mr. Jones) (1948)	*O Lucky Man!* (1973)
The Traveling Saleswoman (1950)	*Naughty Wives* (1974)
The Fuller Brush Girl (aka *The Affairs*	*Pennies From Heaven* (1981)
of Sally) (1950)	*Death of a Salesman* (1985 TVM)
Death of a Salesman (1951)	*Tin Men* (1987)
The Bigamist (1953)	*Traveling Man* (1989 TVM)
The First Travelling Saleslady (1956)	

Trinity

Terrence Hill (aka Mario Girotti) had established himself as a rising Italian star by the late 1960s. After promising supporting roles in quality dramas like Visconti's *The Leopard* (1963), Hill switched to leading roles in spaghetti Westerns such as the Cat Stevens (q.v.) films, which paired him with Bud Spencer (aka Carlo Pedersoli). The blonde, handsome Hill and dark-haired, burly Spencer quickly became the Odd Couple of spaghetti Westerns. Their reputations were sealed with the international success of 1970's *They Call Me Trinity*, a spirited romp featuring Hill as a lazy, quick-drawing rascal named Trinity and Spencer as his surly, cattle-thief-turned-sheriff brother Bambino. The 1972 sequel, *Trinity Is Still My Name*, was funnier and also bigger at the box office, especially in Italy where it was a huge hit. These were the only *Trinity* pictures featuring the Hill-Spencer team, although they made several other movies together. Hill made 1971's *Trinity Sees Red* without Spencer; it was a humorless Western that bore no resemblance to the other *Trinity* movies. In the final "official" series entry, *Trinity Plus the Clown and a Guitar*, George Hilton replaced Hill in the lead role. There are several other spaghetti Westerns with heroes named Trinity, but they do not appear to be *the* Trinity. Hill played a Trinity-like character in the 1974 Henry Fonda Western *My Name Is Nobody*. He has remained a popular star in his homeland. In 1991, Hill directed and starred in *Lucky Luke*, a Western comedy along the same lines as the *Trinity* films. See also **Stevens, Cat.**

They Call Me Trinity (aka *Lo Chiamavano Trinita*) (1970) (Hill)
Trinity Sees Red (aka *La Collera del Vento*; *Trinita Voit Rouge*) (1971) (Hill)
Trinity Is Still My Name (aka *Continuavano a Chiamarlo Trinita*) (1972) (Hill)
Trinity Plus the Clown and a Guitar (aka *Prima Ti Suono e Poi Ti Sparo*; *First I Play You . . . Then I Shoot You)* (1975) (Hilton)

Truck Drivers

Truckers have been stereotyped as macho men of action, particularly during the 1970s. Typical roles featured country singer Jerry Reed playing a good ole boy trucker in *High-Ballin'* (1978), Claude Akins and Frank Converse as no-nonsense truck drivers in *In Tandem* (1974), and Kris Kristofferson as the leader in charge of a *Convoy* (1978). Lady truckers have been virtually ignored, although a few females have nevertheless proven themselves as tough as their male counterparts. Kim Darby and Annie Potts played spunky women truckers in *Flatbed Annie and Sweetiepie: Lady Truckers* (1979), as did Deborah Raffin in *Willa* (1979) and Helen Shaver in *High-Ballin'*. Few big-name stars have been attracted to truck-driving roles, although Humphrey Bogart was behind a rig's wheel in *They Drive by Night* (1940). James Cagney, while still on the road to stardom, drove a truck as the *St. Louis Kid* (1934). The most existential truckers were the ones driving nitroglycerin over dangerous mountain roads in 1953's *The Wages of Fear* and its 1977 remake *Sorcerer*. The most mysterious one was the unseen rig driver who tried to run Dennis Weaver off the road in Steven Spielberg's 1971 TV-movie *Duel*. The TV series *Movin' On* and *B.J. and the Bear* both evolved from made-for-TV movies. In the latter series, the "Bear" was a mischievous, truck-ridin' chimpanzee.

Quick Millions (1931)
St. Louis Kid (1934)
California Straight Ahead (1937)
They Drive by Night (aka *The Road to Frisco*) (1940)
Desperate (1947)
Thieves' Highway (1949)
The Wages of Fear (1953)
Death in Small Doses (1957)
The Long Haul (1957)
The Big Gamble (1960)
Moonfire (1970)
Duel (1971 TVM)
Deadhead Miles (1972)
In Tandem (aka *Movin' On*) (1974 TVM)
White Line Fever (1975)
The Great Smokey Roadblock (aka *The Last of the Cowboys*) (1976)
Breaker! Breaker! (1977)

Handle With Care (aka *Citizen's Band*) (1977)
Sorcerer (1977)
F.I.S.T. (1978)
High-Ballin' (1978)
Steel Cowboy (1978 TVM)
Convoy (1978)
B.J. and the Bear (1978 TVM)
Flatbed Annie and Sweetiepie: Lady Truckers (aka *Flatbed Annie*) (1979 TVM)
Willa (1979 TVM)
Coast to Coast (1980)
Road Games (1981)
Brothers-in-Law (1985 TVM)
Big Trouble in Little China (1986)
Killing Machine (1986)
Rolling Vengeance (1987)
Driving Force (1989)
Think Big (1990)

Trumpet Players

Young trumpet players have been portrayed as brash, compulsive musicians by Kirk Douglas in *Young Man With a Horn* (1950) and Steve McQueen in *Love With the Proper Stranger* (1963). Burt Young was a down-on-his-luck trumpeteer who befriended a terminally ill youth in the maudlin *Uncle Joe Shannon* (1978). Carole Lombard rescued Fred MacMurray from the skids in 1937's *Swing High, Swing Low*. Danny Kaye played real-life bandleader/trumpet player Red Nichols in *The Five Pennies*. He even played a duet with Louis Armstrong, whose story reached the TV screen in 1976's *Louis Armstrong—Chicago Style*. Ben Vereen starred as "Satchmo." See also **Pianists; Violinists.**

Swing High, Swing Low (1937)	*Louis Armstrong—Chicago Style*
Young Man With a Horn (1950)	(1976 TVM)
The Five Pennies (1959)	*Uncle Joe Shannon* (1978)
Love With the Proper Stranger (1963)	*Mo' Better Blues* (1990)
Dr. Terror's House of Horrors (1964)	*Dingo* (1991)
A Man Called Adam (1966)	*The Mambo Kings* (1992)

Tunnels

Tunnels have been a common fixture in POW (q.v.) sagas such as *The Wooden Horse* (1950) and, of course, *The Great Escape* (1963). The Germans built secret tunnels, too, though a British spy thwarted their efforts in *The W Plan* (1930). John Garfield masterminded a tunnel through a cemetery to assassinate a Cuban official in 1949's *We Were Strangers*. On a considerably larger scale, the 1933 German film *The Tunnel* was about the construction of a tunnel connecting Europe and the United States. It was remade in Britain as 1935's *Transatlantic Tunnel*. A Chinese army tried to "burrow" its way into the United States to mount an invasion in *Battle Beneath the Earth* (1968). In 1988's *The Navigator*, some medieval villagers enter a tunnel to escape from the Black Plague—and wind up in twentieth-century New Zealand! Several films have featured "tunnels of love," while TV even offered a 1966-67 *Time Tunnel* series.

The W Plan (1930)	*The Great Escape* (1963)
The Tunnel (aka *Der Tunnel*) (1933)	*Battle Beneath the Earth* (1968)
Transatlantic Tunnel (aka *The*	*Berlin Tunnel 21* (1981 TVM)
Tunnel) (1935)	*The Navigator: A Medieval Odyssey*
Tycoon (1947)	(aka *The Navigator*) (1988)
We Were Strangers (1949)	*Criminal Act* (1989)
The Wooden Horse (1950)	*Tunnel Child* (aka *Tunnelkind*) (1990)
The Hole (1959)	

Twins

The most frequent use of twins has been to portray good and evil, as in *Dead Ringer* and *The Dark Mirror* (featuring Bette Davis and Olivia de Havilland, respectively, in double roles). But comedies of mistaken identities have been popular, too. Hayley Mills swapped places with her sister (Hayley Mills, too) and reunited their divorced parents in *The Parent Trap*. In a neat technical trick, the two Hayleys even sang a duet. Two sets of twins separated at birth caused all kinds of confusion in *Start the Revolution Without Me* and *Big Business*. Horror movies such as Brian De Palma's *Sisters* and cult favorite *Basket Case* have featured Siamese twins in murderous roles. In *Whispers* (1990), twins were made to believe they were one person. In contrast, *Seduction: Three Tales From the Inner Sanctum* (1992) had Victoria Principal acting like twins as part of a sexual fantasy game. Finally, in *The Miracle of Morgan's Creek*, Betty Hutton gave birth to sextuplets, which certainly seems to fit this category in spirit. See also **Basket Case; Look-Alikes.**

Freaks (aka *Nature's Mistakes*) (1932)
Strangers in Love (1932)
The Sphinx (1933)
The Black Room (1935)
Our Relations (1936)
Man of Affairs (aka *His Lordship*) (1936)
A Stolen Life (1938)
The Man in the Iron Mask (1939)
The Boys From Syracuse (1940)
Among the Living (1941)
Two-Faced Woman (1941)
Keep 'Em Flying (1941)
The Corsican Brothers (1941)
The Dark Mirror (1942)
Nazi Agent (1942)
Dead Men Walk (1943)
Cobra Woman (1944)
Here Come the Waves (1944)
Miracle of Morgan's Creek (1944)
Wonder Man (1945)
A Stolen Life (1946)
The Guilty (1947)
Dual Alibi (1947)
Campus Honeymoon (1948)
Chained for Life (1950)
I Cover the Underworld (1955)
House of Numbers (1957)
The Girl in the Kremlin (1957)
Duel of the Titans (1961)
The Parent Trap (1961)
Dead Ringer (aka *Dead Image*) (1964)
Open the Door and See All the People (1964)
Cat Ballou (1965)

Start the Revolution Without Me (1970)
Twins of Evil (vampires, to be exact) (1972)
The Other (1972)
Sisters (1973)
Twin Detectives (1976 TVM)
The Man in the Iron Mask (1977 TVM)
Zorro, the Gay Blade (1981)
Basket Case (1982)
The Dark Mirror (1984 TVM)
Slapstick (*Of Another Kind*) (1984)
Cheech and Chong's The Corsican Brothers (1984)
Brotherly Love (1985 TVM)
Deceptions (1985 TVM)
The Covenant (1985 TVM)
Killer in the Mirror (1986 TVM)
Double Agent (1987 TVM)
Nightmare at Shadow Woods (1987)
Big Business (1988)
Dead Ringers (1988)
Dominick and Eugene (1988)
Take Two (1988)
Jack's Back (1988)
Twins (1988)
The Krays (1990)
Whispers (1990)
The Lookalike (1990 TVM)
A Kiss Before Dying (1991)
Lies of the Twins (1991 TVM)
Double Impact (1991)
Killing Streets (1991)
Double Trouble (1991)

Two-Headed Creatures

The old adage that two heads are better than one has never held true for the movies. The first two-headed monster movie of note, 1959's U.S./Japanese coproduction *The Manster* (aka *The Split*), concerned a reporter who grew a second head after a mad scientist injected him with an experimental serum. Eventually, the man/beast split apart totally and the parts fought each other. Bruce Dern transplanted a head onto a new body in the aptly titled *The Incredible Two-Headed Transplant* (1971). That film was quickly eclipsed by the following year's *The Thing With Two Heads* — the heads belonging to Ray Milland and Rosey Grier. The theme of two men — one white, one black — connected to each other was better explored in the Tony Curtis-Sidney Poitier chase drama *The Defiant Ones*. But, on strictly visual terms, the sight of Milland and Grier jammed together in one big suit remains a whole lot more fun to watch. An ad man working on a pimple cream campaign grew an obnoxious second head in Bruce Robinson's black comedy *How to Get Ahead in Advertising* (1989). Finally, *Ghidrah, the Three-Headed Monster* (q.v.) deserves special mention since he sported the minimum requirement of two heads.

The Seventh Voyage of Sinbad (1958)	*The Thing With Two Heads* (1972)
The Manster (1959)	*Monty Python and the Holy Grail*
The Magic Sword (1962)	(1974)
Jack the Giant Killer (1962)	*Willow* (1988)
The Incredible Two-Headed	*How to Get Ahead in Advertising*
Transplant (1971)	(1989)

U.N.C.L.E., *see* The Man From U.N.C.L.E.

Uptown Saturday Night

Sidney Poitier directed Bill Cosby and himself in this silly 1974 comedy about two friends, a stolen lottery ticket, and a *Godfather*-like gangster (Harry Belafonte). In the 1985 follow-up *Let's Do It Again*, they used hypnosis to turn Jimmie Walker (from TV's *Good Times*) into an unlikely boxer. The final installment, 1977's *A Piece of the Action*, balanced the laughs with a more serious plot about ghetto kids. Technically, Poitier and Cosby played different characters in each film, but audiences did not seem to notice.

Uptown Saturday Night (1974)	*A Piece of the Action* (1977)
Let's Do It Again (1975)	

Vampires

With his sexuality, air of mystery and aristocratic manners, the vampire has long been a favorite subject of filmmakers. Count Dracula and his descendants dominated the 1930s and 1940s (see **Dracula** entry for details). However, there were some notable exceptions, such as 1932's *Vampyr* (aka *The Strange Adventure of David Gray*) and 1943's *The Return of the Vampire*. Directed by Carl Dreyer, *Vampyr* is a wonderfully atmospheric but slow-moving classic, while *Return* is of interest solely because it featured Bela Lugosi as a very Dracula-like character stalking victims in World War II England. The vampire was generally ignored through the mid-1950s, although *Old Mother Riley Meets the Vampire* (aka *My Son, the Vampire*) sadly marked Lugosi's last appearance as one of the undead. However, vampire movies made a resounding comeback in 1957-58. Herman Cohen, the man responsible for *I Was a Teenage Frankenstein*, made 1957's teen-oriented *Blood of Dracula* (in which a young girl is made to believe she's a vampire). That same year, German Robles made his debut as Count Lavud in the Mexican movie *The Vampire*, and John Beals took pills to grow fangs in *Mark of the Vampire* (not to be confused with Lugosi's 1935 film of the same title). In 1958, Jimmy Sangster wrote two vampire films — the competent *Blood of the Vampire* and Hammer Films' landmark *Horror of Dracula* (aka *Dracula*), arguably the most influential of all vampire movies. The Hammer approach, with its blatant emphasis on Dracula's sexual attraction, put vampirism in a new light. Hammer continued that trend with 1960's *Brides of Dracula*, another fine effort in which Baron Meinster (not the Count) preys upon a girls' boarding school. French director Roger Vadim offered *Blood and Roses* in 1960, a less subtle variation of the sexuality theme featuring a lesbian vampire. Naturally, other countries tried to cash in on the vampire's newfound popularity. The United States contributed a vampire Western, *Curse of the Undead* (1959), Italy produced *The Vampire and the Ballerina* (1960), and Mexico added *The World of Vampires* (1960). Hammer returned to its favorite subject in 1963 with *Kiss of the Vampire*, a well-acted, though unsurprising, bloodsucking tale. A year later, Vincent Price fought a world infected by a vampire plague in Italy's *The Last Man on Earth*, an underrated adaptation of Richard Matheson's chilling novel *I Am Legend*. Yet, despite these lively efforts, the vampire was becoming anemic at the box office by the late 1960s. Hence, some new twists were introduced to draw back the dwindling audience. Hammer Studios resurrected lesbian vampires with its 1970-71 Karnstein trilogy (q.v.) *The Vampire Lovers*, *Lust for a Vampire* and *Twins of Evil*. Robert Quarry played a contemporary vampire confronted by hippies in 1971's *Count Yorga, Vampire*. And in another contemporary-set tale, William Marshall played a Black African prince who is bitten by Dracula and becomes *Blacula*. Despite modest success, these films failed to ignite a major revival, and the vampire sank quietly into his grave, except for occasional trips to the blood bank (e.g., Dan Curtis's high-rated 1971 TV-movie *The Night Stalker* and the 1979 spoof *Love at First Bite*). By the early 1980s, the vampire was lost amid the slasher films made in the wake of *Halloween* and *Friday the 13th*. But, just to show you can't keep a good bloodsucker down, he was revived yet again in a rash of youth-oriented pictures like *Fright Night* (1985), *The Lost Boys* and *Near Dark* (both 1987). These movies proved that the vampire, although clearly not the box office champ he once was, remained a force to be reckoned with. The villainous ladies in *Lair of the White Worm* and *The Kiss* (both 1988), while technically not vampires, exhibited similar neck-biting traits. People thought they were vampires in *Vampire's Kiss* (1989) and *A Vampire in Paradise* (1991). *Variety* noted that the title vehicle in 1990's *I Bought a Vampire Motorcycle* "runs on blood, doesn't function in daylight, recoils from crucifixes, and consumes humans and animals." See also **Dracula; Karnstein Trilogy.**

Vampyr (aka *The Strange Adventure of David Gray*) (1932)

The Return of the Vampire (1943)

The Vampire's Ghost (1943)

Dead Men Walk (1943)

My Son, the Vampire (aka *Old Mother Riley Meets the Vampire*; *Vampires Over London*) (1952)

Mark of the Vampire (aka *The Vampire*) (1957)

Blood of Dracula (1957)

The Vampire (aka *El Vampiro*) (1957)

The Vampire's Coffin (aka *El Ataud del Coffin*) (1958)

Blood of the Vampire (1958)

Uncle Was a Vampire (1959)

Curse of the Undead (1959)
The World of Vampires (aka El Mundo de los Vampiros) (1960)
Blood and Roses (1960)
The Vampire and the Ballerina (1960)
Slaughter of the Vampires (aka Curse of the Blood Ghouls) (1961)
Kiss of the Vampire (aka Kiss of Evil) (1963)
The Last Man on Earth (1964)
Goliath and the Vampires (aka The Vampires) (1964)
Planet of the Vampires (aka The Demon Planet) (1965)
Munster, Go Home! (1966)
Planet of Blood (aka Queen of Blood) (1966)
Track of the Vampire (aka Blood Bath) (1966)
The Fearless Vampire Killers; or Pardon Me, But Your Teeth Are in My Neck (1967)
House of Dark Shadows (1970)
Vampire Men of the Lost Planet (1970)
The House That Dripped Blood (1970)
Count Yorga, Vampire (1971)
The Velvet Vampire (aka Cemetery Girls) (1971)
The Return of Count Yorga (1971)
The Bloodsuckers (aka Incense for the Damned) (1971)
The Night Stalker (1971 TVM)
Daughters of Darkness (1971)
Vampire Circus (1971)
Blacula (1972)
The Bloody Vampire (1972)
The Deathmaster (1972)
Scream, Blacula, Scream (1973)
Captain Kronos: Vampire Hunter (aka Kronos) (1974)
Spermula (1975)
Martin (1978)
Love at First Bite (1979)

Vampire Hookers (aka Sensuous Vampires) (1979)
Vampire (1979 TVM)
Last Rites (aka Dracula's Last Rites) (1980)
I, Desire (1982 TVM)
The Hunger (1983)
Fright Night (1985)
Lifeforce (1985)
Once Bitten (1985)
Vamp (1986)
Near Dark (1987)
The Lost Boys (1987)
Graveyard Shift (1987)
Dance of the Damned (1988)
The Vampire at Midnight (1988)
The Understudy: Graveyard Shift II (1988)
My Best Friend Is a Vampire (1988)
Fright Night Part 2 (1989)
Vampire's Kiss (1989)
Thirst (1989)
Nightlife (1989 TVM)
Beverly Hills Vamp (1989)
Dracula's Widow (1989)
Transylvania Twist (1989)
To Die For (1989)
Daughter of Darkness (1990 TVM)
I Bought a Vampire Motorcycle (1990)
Sundown: The Vampire in Retreat (aka Sundown) (1990)
Subspecies (1990)
Pale Blood (1990)
Son of Darkness: To Die For II (1991)
Blood Ties (1991 TVM)
Howling VI: The Freaks (1991)
Buffy, the Vampire Slayer (1992)
Vampire Hunter D (1992)
Innocent Blood (1992)
A Vampire in Paradise (aka Un Vampire au Paradis) (1992)
To Sleep With a Vampire (1992)
Tale of a Vampire (1993)

Vance, Philo

S.S. Van Dine's dapper, erudite sleuth never made much of a hit on the screen. William Powell first played the part, enjoying modest success in four mysteries.

Ironically, although Powell looked the part, he lacked the briskness of manner that made Vance such a memorable literary character, and his portrayal is somewhat overrated. In his pre-Holmes days, Basil Rathbone made a more effective Vance in the slowly paced but cleverly plotted *The Bishop Murder Case* (the murderer wrote nursery rhymes containing clues about the identity of his next victim). Perhaps the best Vance was Warren William, whose white-gloves-and-cane portrayal sparkled in 1934's *The Dragon Murder Case*. Based on a Van Dine novel, this underrated puzzler found Vance investigating a young man's apparent drowning in a mysterious pool (haunted by a sea serpent?). William reprised the role in 1939's *The Gracie Allen Murder Case*, a comedy-mystery written for Allen by Van Dine. Other actors played the part, but none could make it their own. Later Vance films such as *Philo Vance's Secret Mission* and *Philo Vance's Gamble* were Vance films in name only—their detectives were clearly closer to Philip Marlowe (q.v.).

The Canary Murder Case (1929) (William Powell)
The Greene Murder Case (1929) (Powell)
The Benson Murder Case (1930) (Powell)
Paramount on Parade (1930) (Powell appears in a skit)
The Bishop Murder Case (1930) (Basil Rathbone)
The Kennel Murder Case (1933) (Powell)
The Dragon Murder Case (1934) (Warren William)
The Casino Murder Case (1935) (Paul Lukas)
The Scarab Murder Case (1936) (Wilfred Hyde-White)
The Garden Murder Case (1936) (Edmund Lowe)
Night of Mystery (1937) (Grant Richards)
The Gracie Allen Murder Case (1939) (William)
Calling Philo Vance (1940) (James Stephenson)
Philo Vance Returns (1947) (William Wright)
Philo Vance's Gamble (1947) (Alan Curtis)
Philo Vance's Secret Mission (1947) (Curtis)

Ventriloquists

The difficulties inherent in injecting a distinct personality into a wooden dummy have caused identity problems for a number of movie ventriloquists. In the most chilling story in the classic anthology *Dead of Night* (1945), ventriloquist Michael Redgrave went insane after becoming convinced that his foul-mouthed dummy Hugo was looking for a new partner. Anthony Hopkins gave a tour-de-force performance in 1978's *Magic* as another mentally unstable ventriloquist taking murderous advice from a dummy with an apparent mind of its own. Another dummy named Hugo (an obvious reference to *Dead of Night*) really did have a soul in the underrated 1964 fantasy *Devil Doll*. Bryant Halliday starred as Hugo's "partner," a ventriloquist who had transferred the soul of his assistant into his dummy. Aside from horror films, the most famous film ventriloquist remains Edgar Bergen. He enjoyed a prosperous career during the late 1930s accompanied by dummies Charlie McCarthy or Mortimer Snerd in comedies like *A Letter of Introduction* (1938), *Charlie McCarthy, Detective* (1939) and the W.C. Fields vehicle *You Can't Cheat an Honest Man* (1939). He earned a special Academy Award in 1937 for his creation of Charlie McCarthy. Major stars who have played ventriloquists include Erich von Stroheim in *The Great Gabbo* (1929), Danny Kaye in *Knock on Wood* (1954) and Lon Chaney in both the silent and talkie versions of *The Unholy Three* (1925 and 1930). In 1984's *Broadway Danny Rose*, theater agent Woody Allen had a hard time finding employment for a stuttering ventriloquist.

The Unholy Three (1925)	*Dead of Night* (1945)
The Great Gabbo (1929)	*Knock on Wood* (1954)
The Unholy Three (1930)	*Hypnosis* (aka *Dummy of Death*)
A Letter of Introduction (1938)	(1963)
You Can't Cheat an Honest Man	*Devil Doll* (1964)
(1939)	*Magic* (1978)
Charlie McCarthy, Detective (1939)	*Broadway Danny Rose* (1984)

Veterinarians

The cinema has typically portrayed veterinarians as gentle, charming animal lovers blessed with understated strength. James Stewart played a German vet who falls in love with Margaret Sullavan and plots to escape from the Nazis in 1940's *The Mortal Storm*. James Herriot's autobiographical novels about life as a Yorkshire veterinarian served as the basis for *All Creatures Great and Small* (1974) and *All Things Bright and Beautiful* (1979). In supporting roles, veterinarians provided the love interests in *Another Man, Another Place* (James Caan), *Baby Boom* (Sam Shepard) and *Turner and Hooch* (Mare Winningham). Vet William Shatner battled a host of hungry tarantulas in the 1977 science fiction thriller *Kingdom of the Spiders*. In contrast, *Billy: Portrait of a Street Kid* (1979) offered a realistic portrayal of a ghetto youth (LeVar Burton) given a chance to become a veterinarian's assistant. Patrick McGoohan played an atypical heartless veterinarian, unable to comprehend his daughter's love for her cat, in Disney's *The Three Lives of Thomasina* (1964). The most suspicious vet was probably Hal Holbrook in the 1972 murder mystery *They Only Kill Their Masters*.

The Mortal Storm (1940)	*Billy: Portrait of a Street Kid* (1979
In the Doghouse (1961)	TVM)
The Three Lives of Thomasina (1964)	*All Things Bright and Beautiful* (aka
Clarence, the Cross-Eyed Lion (1965)	*It Shouldn't Happen to a Vet*) (1979)
They Only Kill Their Masters (1972)	*Baby Boom* (1987)
All Creatures Great and Small (1974	*Turner and Hooch* (1989)
TVM)	*Bird on a Wire* (1990)
Another Man, Another Chance (1977)	*Beethoven* (1992)
Kingdom of the Spiders (1977)	
The Beasts Are on the Streets (1978	
TVM)	

Vice Academy

A successful film series—no matter how inept—will invariably spawn imitations. Nevertheless, it's hard to conceive that the *Police Academy* films (q.v.) could actually serve as a role model for another lowbrow comedy series such as *Vice Academy*. The first *Vice Academy* premiered in 1988, the same year as the fast-fading *Police Academy 5: Assignment Miami Beach*. It sparked the interest of B-movie viewers chiefly due to its two stars: former porn queen Ginger Lynn Allen and cult movie favorite Linnea Quigley. They played against type as two innocent undercover cops (Holly and Didi, respectively). Although by no means a good movie, *Vice Academy* was an improvement over an earlier *Police Academy* rip-off, the 1985 Linda Blair vehicle *Night Patrol*. In 1989, Allen and Quigley reprised their roles for a sequel costarring bodybuilder Teagan Clive as the cyborg Bimbocop. Its plot dealt with a villain named Spanish Fly who schemes to contaminate the city water supply with an aphrodisiac. Allen also headlined 1991's *Vice Academy III*, with Elizabeth Kaitan playing her new partner Candy.

Vice Academy (1988) *Vice Academy III* (1991)
Vice Academy II (1989)

Videotaped Films

American television movie producers, unlike their British counterparts, have long maintained that film's sharp, vibrant image compensates for its added expense when compared to videotape. As a result, very few U.S. made-for-TV movies have been shot on tape. The romantic ghost story *Sandcastles* (1972) was the first to employ a single videotape camera system, but even it was later transferred to film. *Special Bulletin* (1983) was shot on videotape to simulate the "look" of a television newscast. Oddly, there have also been a handful of theatrical features shot originally on videotape and then transferred to film. The 1965 videotape drama *Harlow*, starring Carol Lynley, was converted to film to compete theatrically with a rival biography of the blonde comedienne (confusingly, this second film was also called *Harlow* and starred Carroll Baker). Industrious producers dubbed this tape-to-film process "electronovision." The advent of high-definition videotape in the 1980s renewed interest in "filming" with videotape. However, *Julia and Julia* (1988), the first major movie shot on high-definition tape, turned into a box office disaster. Shortly after its U.S. theatrical release, it showed up — ironically — on videotape.

Harlow (1965) *Special Bulletin* (1983 TVM)
Two Hundred Motels (1971) *Desperate Intruder* (1983 TVM)
Sandcastles (1972 TVM) *Emergency Room* (1983 TVM)
The Catcher (1972 TVM) *The Invisible Woman* (1983 TVM)
Numero Deux (1975) *Rocket to the Moon* (1986 TVM)
Give 'Em Hell, Harry! (1975) *Julia and Julia* (1988)
Norman . . . Is That You? (1976) *The Little Victims* (1989 TVM)
Monty Python Live at the Hollywood Bowl (1982)

Vietnam

The "Forgotten War" was ignored in movies for most of its duration. The 1964 *A Yank in Vietnam*, a low-budget action picture, was the first to deal with U.S. involvement. In 1968, the propaganda adventure *The Green Berets* glorified the fighting, while the searing 1974 documentary *Hearts and Minds* criticized it. Surprisingly, TV movies dealt effectively with returning vets long before their theatrical counterparts. In 1969's *The Ballad of Andy Crocker*, Lee Majors returned home to find himself a stranger to those he loved. It seemed upbeat compared to the brutal frankness of Joseph Papp's production of the TV special *Sticks and Bones*, which several CBS affiliates refused to air. In the late 1970s, mainstream Hollywood finally addressed Vietnam in a roundabout fashion—*Coming Home* dealt with returning veterans, while Francis Coppola's *Apocalypse Now* portrayed the violence of war in a poetic manner. It was not until 1986's Academy Award winner *Platoon* and Stanley Kubrick's *Full Metal Jacket* that the major studios backed brutal, realistic portrayals of the Vietnam War. Those successes have been followed by low-budget clones (e.g., *Hamburger Hill* and *Platoon Leader*), big-budget clones (*Casualties of War*), and one or two films of genuine originality (*84 Charlie Mopic*).

A Yank in Vietnam (aka *Year of the Tiger*) (1964)	*P.O.W. The Escape* (1986)
The Anderson Platoon (1967)	*Full Metal Jacket* (1987) THE BEST!
The Green Berets (1968)	*Gardens of Stone* (1987)
The Ballad of Andy Crocker (1969 TVM)	*Good Morning, Vietnam* (1987)
Hearts and Minds (1974)	*Hamburger Hill* (1987)
Rolling Thunder (1977)	*The Hanoi Hilton* (1987)
The Boys in Company C (1978)	*Dear America* (1987 TVM)
Coming Home (1978)	*Bat 21* (1988)
The Deer Hunter (1978)	*The Iron Triangle* (1988)
Go Tell the Spartans (1978)	*84 Charlie Mopic* (1989)
Apocalypse Now (1979)	*Platoon Leader* (1989)
A Rumor of War (1980 TVM)	*Casualties of War* (1989)
The Children of An Lac (1980 TVM)	*Born on the Fourth of July* (1989)
Don't Cry, It's Only Thunder (1982)	*Air America* (1990)
Uncommon Valor (1983)	*Jacob's Ladder* (1990)
Missing in Action (1984)	*Fatal Mission* (1990)
Platoon (1986)	*Flight of the Intruder* (1991)
	Firehawk (1993)

Vigilantes

Although contemporary vigilante films appeared prior to 1974, the genre began officially with 1974's *Death Wish* (q.v.), a highly manipulative revenge tale in which an average guy turns cold vigilante after punks kill his wife and rape his daughter. Charles Bronson clicked in the lead role and the film scored big at the box office. In its wake, exploitative producers rushed out cheap imitations like *Vigilante* and *Vigilante Force*. The most financially successful of these rip-offs was 1980's *The Exterminator*, which starred Robert Ginty as a Vietnam vet who used a flamethrower to avenge a buddy's mugging. Abel Ferrera's feminist variation, 1981's *Ms. 45* (aka *Angel of Vengeance*), garnered some good reviews and has since earned minor cult status. *The Star Chamber*, *The Death Squad* and the Dirty Harry picture *Magnum Force* showed vigilantism used by law enforcers to "correct" loopholes in our legal system, a plotline derived loosely from 1942's *The Strange Case of Dr. Rx*. See also **Death Wish.**

The Mad Executioners (1963)	*Law and Disorder* (1974)
Magnum Force (1973)	*Vigilante* (aka *Street Gang*) (1976)
Death Wish (1974)	*Dirty Knight's Work* (aka *Trial by Combat*; *Choice of Weapons*) (1976)
The Death Squad (1974 TVM)	

Vigilante Force (1976)	Exterminator II (1984)
Siege (1978 TVM)	Sudden Death (1985)
The Exterminator (1980)	Streets of Justice (1985 TVM)
Ms. 45 (aka Angel of Vengeance) (1981)	Brotherhood of Justice (1986 TVM)
Fighting Back (1982)	Shadows Run Black (1986)
Young Warriors (1983)	Shoot First: A Cop's Vengeance (1991
The Star Chamber (1983)	TVM)
The Executioner, Part II (1984; there	Keeper of the City (1992 TVM)
was no Part I)	

Vikings

These Scandinavian pirates plundered the European coasts from the ninth to the eleventh century. They would appear to be ripe subjects for fact-based adventure films. Instead, filmmakers have shown an intense interest in fictionalizing Viking history. Producer-director Roger Corman proposed that there were statuesque Viking women who were just as tough as their men in the memorably titled *Saga of the Viking Women and Their Voyage to the Waters of the Great Sea Serpent* (1957). Hammer Films confirmed this hypothesis with its costume drama *The Viking Queen* (1967). It mixed time periods joyously with a plot in which a Roman soldier (Don Murray) falls in love with a Viking queen (Carita) battling the Druids. The Disney folks revealed that a Viking settlement survived into the twentieth century in the 1974 adventure-fantasy *The Island at the Top of the World*. And Terry Jones, of *Monty Python* fame, spoofed the Norsemen with 1989's *Erik the Viking*, in which the title character goes in search of a life more meaningful than killing and pillaging. Naturally, there have been some serious Viking films, such as 1958's *The Vikings*, a fine costume epic by any standard. Kirk Douglas and Tony Curtis starred as Norse brothers (although they didn't know it) vying for the affections of fetching Janet Leigh amid the rousing swordplay. *The Norseman* (1978) was intended as a serious film, but somehow Lee Majors as a Viking warrior struck a humorous chord. The expensive Norwegian epic *The White Viking* (1991) played only to arthouse audiences in the United States. Finally, there were no living Vikings in *Curse of the Viking Grave*, a 1991 Canadian TV-movie intended for youngsters.

Prince Valiant (1954)	The Viking Queen (1967)
The Saga of the Viking Women and	The Island at the Top of the World
Their Voyage to the Waters of the	(1974)
Great Sea Serpent (aka The Viking	The Norseman (1978)
Women and the Sea Serpent) (1957)	Berserker (1987)
The Vikings (1958)	Erik the Viking (1989)
The Last of the Vikings (1960)	Curse of the Viking Grave (1991 TVM)
Erik the Conqueror (1963)	The White Viking (aka Den Hvite
The Long Ships (1964)	Viking) (1991)

Violinists

Violinists (and other string musicians) have been faced with a variety of hard decisions. Young William Holden had to choose between a distinguished career as a violinist and a lucrative one as a prizefighter in *Golden Boy* (1939). That same year, Swedish violinist Leslie Howard had to decide whether to stay with his loyal wife (Edna Best) or run off with beautiful protegée Ingrid Bergman in *Intermezzo*. And in 1946's *Humoresque*, John Garfield played a moody musician torn briefly between wealthy patron Joan Crawford and his love of music. Real-life violin virtuoso Paganini was the subject of 1946's *The Magic Bow*. See also **Pianists; Trumpet Players.**

Golden Boy (1939)	*Jeremy* (1973)
Intermezzo (aka *Escape to Happiness*;	*Basileus Quartet* (1982)
Intermezzo, A Love Story) (1939)	*The Man With One Red Shoe* (1985)
My Love Came Back (1940)	*Duet for One* (1986)
The Phantom of the Opera (1944)	*The Living Daylights* (1987)
The Magic Bow (1946)	*Cello* (1990)
Humoresque (1946)	*Two Evil Eyes* (1990)
Rhapsody (1954)	
All These Women (aka *Now About All These Women*) (1964)	

Viral Epidemics

The threat of viral annihilation has been the subject of several movies. Quarantined scientists raced against the clock to combat an inexplicable, self-reproducing virus in *The Andromeda Strain* (1971). George Maharis tracked down a lunatic who stole a deadly experimental virus in 1965's *The Satan Bug*, a plot more or less borrowed from *Panic in the Streets* (1950) and *No Place to Hide* (1956). And Count Dracula revealed his plan to initiate viral warfare in the decidedly offbeat horror tale *The Satanic Rites of Dracula* (1973). In other horror films, Vincent Price met disease incarnate in 1964's *The Masque of the Red Death* and then battled a plague of vampirism in the underrated low-budget gem *The Last Man on Earth* (1964). A 1924 silent film also called *The Last Man on Earth* portrayed a world where a plague had wiped out most of the male population. A parasite, not a disease, was the culprit in David Cronenberg's 1975 cult thriller *They Came From Within*. In Lloyd C. Douglas's *Green Light* (1937), Errol Flynn discovered a cure for a more typical disease, Rocky Mountain spotted fever.

The Last Man on Earth (1924)	*What's So Bad About Feeling Good?* (1968)
Yellow Jack (1938)	
Isle of the Dead (1945)	*On Her Majesty's Secret Service* (1969)
Panic in the Streets (1950)	*Quarantined* (1970 TVM)
The Killer That Stalked New York (aka *Frightened City*) (1950)	*No Blade of Grass* (1970)
	The Andromeda Strain (1971)
The Command (1954)	*Killer By Night* (1971 TVM)
No Place to Hide (1956)	*The Satanic Rites of Dracula* (aka
80,000 Suspects (1963)	*Count Dracula and His Vampire*
The Last Man on Earth (1964)	*Bride; Dracula Is Alive and Well*
The Masque of the Red Death (1964)	*and Living in London*) (1973)
Spies a Go Go (aka *The Nasty Rabbit*) (1964)	*The Crazies* (aka *Code Name: Trixie*) (1973)
The Satan Bug (1965)	*Where Have All the People Gone?* (1974 TVM)
Project X (1968)	

The Specialists (1975 TVM)
The Missing Are Deadly (1975 TVM)
The Cassandra Crossing (1977)
Panic in Echo Park (1977 TVM)
Killer on Board (1977 TVM)
Plague (aka M3: The Gemini Strain)
  (1978)
Virus (1980)

The Plague Dogs (1982)
City Limits (1985)
Warning Sign (1985)
Wired to Kill (1986)
Quiet Killer (1992 TVM)
The Plague (1992)
Condition: Critical (1992 TVM)

Volcanoes

Mountainous rumbles and spurting lava have brought an end to numerous South Seas sagas, displaying a particular affection for Dorothy Lamour vehicles like *The Jungle Princess* (1936) and *Aloma of the South Seas* (1941). Historical pictures, such as *Krakatoa, East of Java* (1969) and *St. Helens* (1981), have tended to build plodding stories around their spectacular volcanic eruptions. *The Last Days of Pompeii* (1935) was an exception, thanks mostly to a fine performance by Basil Rathbone as Pontius Pilate. Yet, despite Rathbone and the thrilling Mount Vesuvius finale, the film lost almost $250,000 at the box office. James Mason and crew entered an extinct volcano at the beginning of their *Journey to the Center of the Earth* (1959) and then were blown out the top of Mount Etna at the film's climax (they managed to survive unharmed, though). The worldly Baron Munchausen and his followers duplicated the same feat in 1989's *The Adventures of Baron Munchausen*. Actually, the Baron and friends had been enjoying the hospitality of Vulcan inside his volcano home until Venus (aka Mrs. Vulcan) began displaying affection for the distinguished Baron. In *Superman IV: The Quest for Peace* (1987), the Man of Steel capped an erupting volcano with another mountain top and blow-dried the lava. Movie villains Fantomas and Ernst Blofeld used extinct volcanoes for elaborate hideouts in *Fantomas Strikes Back* (1965) and the James Bond picture *You Only Live Twice* (1967), respectively.

East of Borneo (1931)
The Last Days of Pompeii (1935)
The Jungle Princess (1936)
One Million B.C. (aka Man and His
  Mate; The Cave Dwellers) (1940)
Aloma of the South Seas (1941)
The Lost Volcano (1950)
Stromboli (1950)
Fair Wind to Java (1953)
Journey to the Center of the Earth
  (1959)
The Last Days of Pompeii (1960)
Atlantis, the Lost Continent (1961)
The Devil at Four O'Clock (1961)
Mysterious Island (1961)
Fantomas Strikes Back (1965)
One Million Years B.C. (1967)

You Only Live Twice (1967)
Krakatoa, East of Java (aka Volcano)
  (1969)
Creatures the World Forgot (1971)
Up Pompeii (1971)
Island at the Top of the World (1974)
The Land That Time Forgot (1974)
When Time Ran Out (1980)
St. Helens (1981)
Warrior Queen (1987)
Superman IV: The Quest for Peace
  (1987)
The Adventures of Baron Munchausen
  (1989)
Joe vs. the Volcano (1990)
Journey to the Center of the Earth (1993
  TVM)

Walking Tall

The real-life story of modern-day Tennessee sheriff Buford Pusser unexpectedly snowballed into a major hit in 1973. The film drew its biggest audiences in the Southeastern United States, the region where *Billy Jack* (q.v.), a similar man-against-corruption tale, encountered sleeper success in 1971. Screen heavy Joe Don Baker brought conviction — and a huge baseball bat — to the role of Pusser. Elizabeth Hartman played his quiet, supportive wife. When Baker showed no interest in a sequel, Bing Crosby Productions signed imposing Bo Svenson for the lead role. He played Pusser in two sequels and a very brief 1981 TV series. Brian Dennehy also played Pusser in the 1978 TV-movie *A Real American Hero*. The real Sheriff Pusser was supposed to play himself in another theatrical sequel, but he died in an automobile crash — under mysterious circumstances, according to some sources.

> *Walking Tall* (1973)
>
> *Part 2: Walking Tall* (aka *Legend of the Lawman*) (1976)
>
> *Walking Tall: The Final Chapter* (1977)
>
> *A Real American Hero* (1978 TVM)

The Waltons

Wholesome families have a way of lingering around — even when their TV series are cancelled. The Waltons, just like the Ingalls in *Little House on the Prairie* (q.v.), appeared in a series of telefilms after the demise of the long-running TV program. However, unlike the Ingalls, the Waltons originated in a theatrical film. *Spencer's Mountain* (1963), written by *Waltons* creator Earl Hamner, Jr., introduced the family that would evolve — with several changes — into the Waltons. Henry Fonda and Maureen O'Hara played the parents, with James McArthur in the eventual John-Boy role. Hamner first brought the Waltons to television in the 1971 telefilm *The Homecoming — A Christmas Story*, with Patricia Neal as Olivia Walton and future series regulars Richard Thomas (John-Boy), Ellen Corby (Grandma), Judy Norton (Mary Ellen), and David W. Harper (Jim-Bob). The series debuted in 1972 and enjoyed a successful nine-year run. Many changes occurred over the years, with even Olivia leaving Waltons Mountain after contracting tuberculosis. Shortly after CBS cancelled the series in 1981, the Waltons resurfaced in four made-for-TV movies on NBC. Erin (Mary Beth McDonough) married Paul Northridge (Morgan Stevens) in 1982's *A Wedding on Waltons Mountain*. That same year found Olivia (Michael Learned) returning from a sanitarium in *Mother's Day on Waltons Mountain* and the family reuniting for Thanksgiving in *A Day for Thanks on Waltons Mountain*. Richard Thomas did not appear in any of these post-series films. However, he returned as John-Boy over ten years later in *A Walton Thanksgiving Reunion*. See also **Television Series Reunion Films**.

> *Spencer's Mountain* (1963)
>
> *The Homecoming — A Christmas Story* (aka *The Homcoming*) (1971 TVM)
>
> *A Wedding on Waltons Mountain* (1982 TVM)
>
> *Mother's Day on Waltons Mountain* (1982 TVM)
>
> *A Day for Thanks on Waltons Mountain* (1982 TVM)
>
> *A Walton Thanksgiving Reunion* (1993 TVM)

Warsaw Trilogy
Andrzej Wajda's powerful trilogy of life in Poland during World War II made him a major force in Eastern European cinema. *A Generation* (1954), the first important post-World War II film to emerge from Poland, dealt with the "lost generation" of Warsaw youth who became involved with the Resistance. *Kanal* (1956) followed a group of resisters ordered to escape crumbling Warsaw through the city's intricate network of sewers. Quickly lost in the darkness, they become stalked by the Nazis above them. The 1958 *Ashes and Diamonds* shifted to the end of the war and focused on a youth forced to choose between love and carrying out an assassination. The title was derived from a gravestone inscription that appeared in the film and summarized Wajda's themes: "Here nothing but ashes will remain, the storm in an instant to oblivion will sweep them; from the ashes perhaps a diamond will emerge, shining victoriously for centuries, it will have blossomed for you."

A Generation (aka *Pokolenie*; *Generation*) (1954)
Kanal (aka *They Loved Life*; *Sewer*) (1956)
Ashes and Diamonds (aka *Popiol i Diament*) (1958)

Wax Museums
There are two basic types of wax museum movies. First, there's the one about the resident insane sculptor who molds figures by pouring hot wax over his murder victims. Lionel Atwill made this practice popular in 1933's *Mystery of the Wax Museum*, one of the first color horror films. Twenty years later, Vincent Price recreated the role in another technically historic horror film, the 3-D classic *House of Wax*. As the demented sculptors, Atwill and Price were splendid—no one has approached their level of depravity. Bad movie favorite Cameron Mitchell gave it a half-hearted shot in 1969's *Nightmare in Wax*, in which he injected folks with a drug that made them look (and act) like wax figures. The second type of wax museum film is the one where figures come to life. Although a popular television plot, it has been used sparingly on the big screen. In 1924's *Waxworks*, there was a nightmare sequence in which the wax figure of Jack the Ripper comes to life. Several decades later, another story called "Waxworks" was included in the anthology film *The House That Dripped Blood*. It starred Peter Cushing as a gentleman who becomes obsessed with an attractive, very lifelike figure.

Waxworks (1924)
Mystery of the Wax Museum (1933)
Charlie Chan at the Wax Museum (1940)
The Frozen Ghost (1945)
House of Wax (1953)
Samson in the Wax Museum (aka *Santo in the Wax Museum*) (1963)
Chamber of Horrors (1966)
Nightmare in Wax (aka *Crimes in the Wax Museum*) (1969)

The House That Dripped Blood (1970)
Terror in the Wax Museum (1973)
Lisa and the Devil (aka *The House of Exorcism*) (1975)
Waxwork (1988)
Seduction: Three Tales From the Inner Sanctum (1992 TVM) (the "Sacrifice" segment)

Welby, Marcus

Seven years after "retiring" from the long-running TV series *Father Knows Best*, Robert Young took up medical practice as the title character in the 1969 TV-movie *Marcus Welby, M.D.* The telefilm paired veteran general practitioner Welby with young, brash Dr. Steven Kiley (James Brolin). Naturally, the two doctors clashed initially before gaining respect for one another and becoming close friends. As intended, this shrewd drama appealed to a broad range of viewers and a *Marcus Welby, M.D.* TV series debuted on ABC the following fall. Young and Brolin repeated their roles in the TV series, as did Anne Baxter as Welby's love interest Myra Sherwood (she left the series after the first year). Penny Santon, who played Nurse Consuelo Lopez in the pilot film, was replaced by Elena Verdugo. The *Welby* series enjoyed a seven-year run on ABC, becoming the nation's highest-rated TV show in 1970-71. In 1984, Young reprised his role in *The Return of Marcus Welby, M.D.*, a novel attempt to revive the series (Elena Verdugo was back as Consuelo, but the Kiley character was not). The plot picked up several years after the original series with Welby working at a hospital where he's being forced into retirement. Although a new *Welby* series never materialized, this second TV-movie performed well enough to warrant another sequel four years later. *Marcus Welby, M.D.: A Holiday Affair* found the good doctor in France romancing divorcee Alexis Smith. It had little to do with the TV series, but even non-Welby fans had to admit that the hard-working physician deserved a vacation after all those years.

   Marcus Welby, M.D. (aka *A Matter of Humanities*) (1969 TVM)
   The Return of Marcus Welby, M.D. (1984 TVM)
   Marcus Welby, M.D.: A Holiday Affair (1988 TVM)

Werewolves

The subject of silent films like *The Werewolf* (1913) and *The White Wolf* (1914), the werewolf made little impact until Universal Studios introduced it at the end of its first horror movie cycle with 1935's *Werewolf of London*. Featuring not one but two lycanthropes, it abandoned familiar werewolf lore in favor of a more novel approach (dealing with a rare flower that cures lycanthropy). For Universal's next furry film, *The Wolf Man* (q.v.), it returned to the basics, integrating a gypsy fortune-teller and a silver-handled cane into a contemporary terror tale. The film made Lon Chaney, Jr. a horror star, and he repeated the role in four more movies. Hoping to capitalize on Universal's success, other studios also tried their hands at werewolf pictures. But things weren't always what they seemed. A plotting housekeeper convinced James Mason he was a werewolf in *The Night Has Eyes* — but he wasn't. June Lockhart suffered from the same delusion in *She-Wolf of London*. As the 1940s ended and science fiction films gained momentum, the popularity of the werewolf declined sharply. Fresh ideas were needed, and they came unexpectedly in the late 1950s in the form of two low-budget drive-in features. *The Werewolf* (1956) presented a creature created by a scientist, a theme aimed to please both science fiction and horror fans. Far more successful was the following year's *I Was a Teenage Werewolf*, a trend-setting mixture of teen problems, rock'n'roll, and an adolescent werewolf (Michael Landon). In 1961, Britain's Hammer Studios tried to revive the European legends with *Curse of the Werewolf*, a brooding, literary picture that was a box office disappointment. Except for a brief appearance in the anthology *Dr. Terror's House of Horrors*, the werewolf was silent through most of the 1960s. However, he rebounded strongly at the end of the decade in the guise of Spanish horror star Paul Naschy. His 1968 film *Mark of the Werewolf* (aka *Frankenstein's Bloody Terror*) was a European sensation and spawned eight sequels with colorful translated titles like *The Werewolf vs. the Vampire Woman* and *The Werewolf and the Yeti*. Still, the werewolf did not regain his popularity in the United States until the 1980s, when *The Howling* (q.v.) and *An American Werewolf in London* combined humor and horror for big box office bucks. The most original werewolf movie of recent years remains the spellbinding 1984 British fantasy *The Company of Wolves*, a fanciful adult reworking of Little Red Riding Hood. In addition to the werewolf, there have been a handful of "were-cat" movies, such as *The Cat People*, its 1982 remake, *Cat-Man of Paris*, and *The Cat Girl*. And in 1933's *Island of Lost Souls*, a panther is surgically transformed into a beautiful girl. But that's not really lycanthropy. See also **Daninsky, Waldemar; The Howling; Humanimals; The Wolf Man.**

The Werewolf (1913)	*The Maltese Bippy* (1969)
The White Wolf (1914)	*Werewolves on Wheels* (1971)
Werewolf of London (1935)	*Moon of the Wolf* (1972 TVM)
The Wolf Man (1941)	*Blood* (1973)
The Undying Monster (1942)	*The Boy Who Cried Werewolf* (1973)
The Night Has Eyes (aka *Terror House*) (1942)	*The Werewolf of Washington* (1973)
	The Beast Must Die (1974)
Return of the Vampire (1943)	*Legend of the Werewolf* (1975)
Cry of the Werewolf (1944)	*Wolfman!* (1979)
She-Wolf of London (1946)	*An American Werewolf in London*
The Werewolf (1956)	(1981)
I Was a Teenage Werewolf (1957)	*Full Moon High* (1981)
Daughter of Dr. Jekyll (a mixed-up	*The Howling* (1981)
movie claiming Jekyll was a	*The Company of Wolves* (1984)
werewolf) (1957)	*Silver Bullet* (1985)
How to Make a Monster (an actor in	*Teen Wolf* (1985)
makeup is the killer) (1958)	*The Monster Squad* (1987)
Curse of the Werewolf (1961)	*Teen Wolf Too* (1987)
Werewolf in a Girls' Dormitory (1961)	*My Mom's a Werewolf* (1989)
Dr. Terror's House of Horrors (1965)	

Whales

Whales on film have been portrayed as sympathetic creatures — with the notable exceptions of Herman Melville's immortal white whale *Moby Dick* and the people-eating Monstro in *Pinocchio*. Although Monstro was a true terror, it's hard to classify Moby as a villain, for Captain Ahab's crew perished solely because of its captain's obsession to kill the symbolic whale. The single-minded Ahab has been played by John Barrymore twice, in *The Sea Beast* (1926) and *Moby Dick* (1930), and by Gregory Peck in John Huston's 1956 adaptation. The killer whale *Orca* (1977) devoured quite a few humans, including Bo Derek, but his actions were in retaliation for the murder of his spouse (killer whales mate for life, we are told). Humans were also portrayed as thoughtless whale killers in *The White Dawn* (1974) and *A Whale for the Killing* (1981). Whales were glimpsed from a distance in the opening of *The Whales of August* (1987), but again, they played a symbolic part in the tender story of two elderly sisters. The crew of the *Enterprise* went back in time to save some important humpback whales in *Star Trek IV: The Voyage Home* (1986). The cartoon compilation *Make Mine Music* (1946) featured a segment on Willie, the Singing Whale. See also **Dolphins; Fish; Sharks.**

The Sea Beast (1926)	*Orca* (aka *Orca, the Killer Whale*)
Moby Dick (1930)	(1977)
Pinocchio (1940)	*A Whale for the Killing* (1981 TVM)
Make Mine Music (1946)	*Star Trek IV: The Voyage Home* (1986)
Moby Dick (1956)	*The Whales of August* (1987)
Namu, the Killer Whale (1966)	*When the Whales Came* (1989)
Island at the Top of the World (1974)	*Free Willy* (1993)
The White Dawn (1974)	

The Whistler

In the mid-1940s, when most detective series were coming to an end, Columbia launched this offbeat mystery anthology series. The films were inspired by a popular radio program, in which a mysterious narrator introduced each story with the ominous opening: "I am the Whistler—and I know many things." Only one film, 1948's *Return of the Whistler*, followed the radio format. The others were linked solely by their twisty plots and the presence of star Richard Dix. A former Oscar-nominated actor (for 1931's *Cimarron*), Dix was in the twilight of his career. The Whistler films allowed him to show his versatility, playing the hero in some pictures, the villain in others. In 1944's *The Whistler*, he played a husband so depressed over his wife's death that he hires a killer to murder him—only to discover his wife is alive. In 1945's *The Power of the Whistler*, Dix was a murderer suffering from amnesia. William Castle, best known for his gimmicky 1950s thrillers (e.g., *The Tingler*), produced and directed some of the entries. Following Dix's death in 1947, one more picture was made; then the series ended. Columbia revived it for television in 1954, producing thirty-nine half-hour episodes.

The Whistler (1944)	*Mysterious Intruder* (1947)
The Mark of the Whistler (1944)	*The Secret of the Whistler* (1947)
The Power of the Whistler (1945)	*The 13th Hour* (1947)
The Voice of the Whistler (1946)	*Return of the Whistler* (1948)

Whistling in the Dark

Edward Childs Carpenter and Laurence Cross's hit Broadway comedy *Whistling in the Dark* was about a mystery writer forced to devise the perfect murder. MGM first filmed it in 1932 with Ernest Truex as the hero and Edward Arnold the villain. That version made a nifty profit but was eclipsed by the 1941 remake starring Red Skelton as a radio sleuth called "The Fox," Ann Rutherford as his girlfriend, and Conrad Veidt as the heavy. The film's surprise success resulted in MGM's reuniting Skelton and Rutherford for two sequels. Their Southern honeymoon plans went astray when murder got in the way in *Whistling in Dixie* (1942). Baseball and mystery provided the mixture for the last film, *Whistling in Brooklyn*

(1943). George Haight produced and S. Sylvan Simon directed all three films.

Whistling in the Dark (1932)	*Whistling in Dixie* (1942)
Whistling in the Dark (1941)	*Whistling in Brooklyn* (1943)

Windmills

No movie has been able to top the splendid climax of 1960's *Brides of Dracula* for imaginative use of a windmill. In Terence Fisher's lively vampire film, an athletic Van Helsing (Peter Cushing) dives onto a revolving windmill, his weight pulling the arms into the shape of a cross. The light of a full moon behind him casts the shadow of the cross onto the ground—thus destroying a hissing vampire caught in its path. The Frankenstein Monster was burned in a windmill at the end of 1931's *Frankenstein*, only to escape from the flames in the beginning of 1935's *Bride of Frankenstein*. Windmills were used to signal enemy planes in Hitchcock's *Foreign Correspondent* (1940). In the underrated 1986 fantasy *Highlander*, Christopher Lambert and Clancy Brown staged an elaborate swordfight throughout Lambert's windmill home. Michael Caine played a spy whose kidnapped son was being held hostage in *The Black Windmill* (1974). No discussion of windmills would be complete without mentioning Don Quixote, the gallant Spanish gentleman who imagined them to be dragons. Of related interest, Joanne Woodward's river mill home provided an atmospheric setting for the 1964 mystery-thriller *Signpost to Murder*.

Frankenstein (1931)	*Highlander* (1986)
Bride of Frankenstein (1935)	*Army of Darkness* (aka *Evil Dead III:*
Foreign Correspondent (1940)	*Army of Darkness*) (1993)
Brides of Dracula (1960)	*Madame L'eau* (aka *Madam Water*)
Don Quixote (1972)	(1993)
The Black Windmill (1974)	

Witchcraft Series

The five *Witchcraft* films undermined a smart premise with weak plotting and poor thesping. The first film, 1989's *Witchcraft*, recalled *Rosemary's Baby* with its tale about a pregnant woman who discovers that her baby is a warlock—along with her husband and witch of a mother-in-law. Thematically, it functioned as a prologue, for the series' premise was introduced in 1990's *Witchcraft II: The Temptress*. The warlock baby grew into a seventeen-year-old named Will (Charles Solomon). However, instead of practicing black magic for his own ends, Will denied his dark side. He even dated a minister's daughter (Mia Ruiz), until a voluptuous witch (Delia Sheppard) almost lured him back into the fold of witchery (and a marriage of evil). Will fought off such temptations, however, and became a lawyer in *Witchcraft III: The Kiss of Death*. This third installment pitted the heroic warlock against a vampirelike creature that sucked the life out of its victims (shades of *Lifeforce*). In 1992's *Witchcraft IV: Virgin Heart*, Will got mixed up with a stripper/singer/witch, a warlock disk jockey, and a girl so suspiciously good that she had to be bad. The script borrowed shamelessly from David Lynch's *Blue Velvet* and Walter Hill's *Crossroads* (both 1986). Charles Solomon, who played Will in the middle three entries, lacked screen charisma and failed to bring out the potential complexities of his character's internal good/evil battle. Altogether, Elizabeth Montgomery did a much better job as a witch-passing-for-mortal in TV's *Bewitched*. See also **Witches.**

Witchcraft (1989)
Witchcraft II: The Temptress (aka *Witchcraft Part II: The Temptress*) (1990)
Witchcraft III: The Kiss of Death (1991)
Witchcraft IV: Virgin Heart (1992)
Witchcraft V: Dance With the Devil (1993)

Witches

Not surprisingly, witches show up in all kinds of movies: children's fantasies, comedies, horror flicks and literary adaptations. Margaret Hamilton played the most famous of them all—the Wicked Witch of the West in *The Wizard of Oz* (which also boasts Billie Burke as Glinda the Good Witch). Other children's films featuring notable witches include *Snow White and the Seven Dwarfs*, *Sleeping Beauty*, and *Bedknobs and Broomsticks*. Bewitching comedies have garnered laughs by casting against stereotype. Hence, instead of featuring witches with green skin and warts, both *I Married a Witch* and *Bell, Book, and Candle* offer curvaceous, blonde-haired witches (Veronica Lake and Kim Novak, respectively). The best horror film about witches is probably *Burn, Witch, Burn* (aka *Night of the Eagle*), in which Janet Blair resorts to witchcraft, first to further her husband's career and then to save his life. Barbara Steele was a revenge-minded witch in Mario Bava's eerie *Black Sunday*, and Mia Farrow discovered her neighbors belong to a witches' coven in *Rosemary's Baby*. On the literary side, prophesying witches open all film versions of *Macbeth*, and Arthur Miller's *The Crucible* remains a potent condemnation of the infamous Salem witch trials. Roald Dahl's charming children's book *The Witches* reached the screen in 1990, with Angela Huston making a marvelous Grand High Witch. See also **Witchcraft Series.**

Witchcraft Through the Ages (aka *Haxan*) (1922)
Maid of Salem (1937)
Snow White and the 7 Dwarfs (1938)
I Married a Witch (1942)
Day of Wrath (1943)
Weird Woman (1944)
The Woman Who Came Back (1945)
Macbeth (1948)
The Undead (1956)
The Crucible (*Witches of Salem*) (1957)
Bell, Book, and Candle (1958)
The Day the Earth Froze (1959)
Sleeping Beauty (1959)
Black Sunday (1960)
Horror Hotel (aka *City of the Dead*) (1960)
The Witches' Curse (1960)
The Witches' Mirror (1960)

Snow White and the Three Stooges (1961)
Burn, Witch, Burn (aka *Night of the Eagle*) (1962)
The Magic Sword (1962)
Terror in the Crypt (aka *Crypt of Horror*) (1963)
Witchcraft (1964)
The Devil's Own (aka *The Witches*) (1966)
The She-Beast (1966)
The Witch (1966)
A Witch Without a Broom (1966)
The Conqueror Worm (aka *Witchfinder General*) (1968)
Crowhaven Farm (1970 TVM)
Cry of the Banshee (1970)
Night of the Witches (1970)
Pufnstuf (1970)

The Witches' Mountain (1970)	*A Stranger in the House* (1978 TVM)
Bedknobs and Broomsticks (1971)	*Witches' Brew* (1980)
The Blood on Satan's Claw (aka	*Midnight Offerings* (1981 TVM)
Satan's Skin; Satan's Claw) (1971)	*Bay Coven* (1987 TVM)
Macbeth (1971)	*The Witches of Eastwick* (1987)
Night of Dark Shadows (1971)	*Spellbinder* (1988)
Simon, King of Witches (1971)	*Teen Witch* (1989)
Touch of Melissa (aka *Touch of Satan*;	*Witchery* (aka *Witchcraft*) (1989)
Night of the Demon) (1971)	*The Witches* (1990)
Daughters of Satan (1972)	*The Haunting of Morella* (1990)
Necromancy (aka *The Witching*)	*To Save a Child* (1991 TVM)
(1972)	*Warlock* (1991)
Race With the Devil (1975)	*Hocus Pocus* (1993)
Deathmoon (1978 TVM)	

(Note: Despite their titles, the Disney kiddie adventures *Escape to Witch Mountain* and *Return to Witch Mountain* have nothing to do with witches—only alien children.)

Withers, Hildegarde

Edna May Oliver first brought Stuart Palmer's umbrella-toting schoolteacher sleuth to the screen in 1932's *The Penguin Pool Murder*. It was a lively yarn, with a dramatic courtroom climax, but the film's highlight was the rapport between Oliver and costar James Gleason as Inspector Oscar Piper. The gruff, wisecracking Piper masked his respect for Hildegarde, calling her a "nosy old dame" but later conceding: "That old battleaxe is the best friend I have in the world." The pair teamed for two more RKO series entries, then Oliver bowed out due to poor health. Helen Broderick replaced her for one film, and then a miscast Zasu Pitts made the last two RKO Hildegarde Withers mysteries. James Gleason remained as Inspector Piper for all five films. In 1971, Eve Arden revived Hildegarde Withers for a TV pilot movie called *A Very Missing Person*, but a regular series never materialized.

> *The Penguin Pool Murder* (aka *The Penguin Pool Mystery*) (1932) (Edna May Oliver)
> *Murder on the Blackboard* (1934) (Oliver)
> *Murder on a Honeymoon* (1935) (Oliver)
> *Murder on a Bridle Path* (1936) (Helen Broderick)
> *The Plot Thickens* (aka *The Swinging Pearl Mystery*) (1936) (Zasu Pitts)
> *Forty Naughty Girls* (1937) (Pitts)
> *A Very Missing Person* (1971 TVM) (Eve Arden)

The Wizard of Oz

Published in 1900, L. Frank Baum's immortal children's novel was filmed twice in the silent era, first as a 1910 two-reeler starring Bebe Daniels (later a femme fatale) and then in 1925, with Dorothy Dwan as Dorothy and Oliver Hardy as the Tin Woodman. The screenplay for the latter version was written by L. Frank Baum, Jr. Of course, the most famous adaptation is MGM's classic 1939 musical *The Wizard of Oz*, which annually ranks among the most-watched films on television. Amazingly, it was not a commercial success when originally released. Budgeted at a hefty $2.8 million, it took *The Wizard of Oz* twenty years to recoup its cost. The cast, one of the finest ever assembled, was formed almost by accident. Shirley Temple, a huge box office star in 1938, was the first choice to play Dorothy. However, Twentieth Century-Fox, which owned her contract, refused to cooperate with MGM. (To atone for its poor decision, Fox cast Shirley in 1940's *The Blue Bird*, a similar fantasy—and a financial flop.) The rest of the original cast included Ray Bolger as the Tin Man, Buddy Ebsen (later Jed on *The Beverly Hillbillies*) as the Scarecrow, and Bert Lahr as the Cowardly Lion. However, Bolger, a Broadway dancer, lobbied for the role of the Scarecrow, and he and Ebsen switched parts. Then Ebsen developed an allergic reaction to the metallic paint used on his face and was replaced by Jack Haley, who gave his most memorable performance as the Tin Man. More liberal adaptations of Baum's book include 1976's *Oz*, an Australian rock musical, and *The Wiz* (1978), a film version of the hit Broadway play starring Diana Ross as an older Dorothy, Michael Jackson as the Scarecrow, and Richard Pryor as the Wiz. Although Baum wrote thirteen additional books (and many other writers have added to that total), few of those have made it to the screen. In 1914, he adapted his own novel *The Patchwork Girl of Oz* and then wrote and directed *His Majesty, the Scarecrow of Oz* (aka *The New Wizard of Oz*). An obscure musical version of *The Wonderful Land of Oz* appeared in 1969, and in 1971, Liza Minnelli (Judy Garland's daughter) and Margaret Hamilton provided voices for the animated *Journey Back to Oz*. In 1985, the Disney Studios released a costly, nonmusical called *Return to Oz*, which was based on Baum's novels *The Land of Oz* and *Ozma of Oz*. Despite impressive technical wizardry, it received scathing reviews and died quickly at the box office. John Ritter played Baum in the 1990 TV-movie biography *The Dreamer of Oz*. The same year, cult director David Lynch offered a warped Ozian analogy—complete with violence, sex and Elvis Presley songs—in *Wild at Heart*. Finally, Baum's original book played a major role in John Boorman's futuristic fantasy *Zardoz* (1974), which derived its title from The WiZARD of OZ.

The Wizard of Oz (1910)	*Journey Back to Oz* (1971)
The Patchwork Girl of Oz (1914)	*Oz* (aka *Twentieth Century Oz*) (1976)
His Majesty, the Scarecrow of Oz (aka	*The Wiz* (1978)
The New Wizard of Oz) (1914)	*Under the Rainbow* (1981)
The Wizard of Oz (1925)	*Return to Oz* (1985)
The Wizard of Oz (1939)	*The Dreamer of Oz* (1990 TVM)
The Wonderful Land of Oz (1969)	

The Wolf Man

The Wolf Man appeared in five Universal films in the 1940s, yet it's difficult to classify these movies as a series. That's because he was the featured monster only once—in his 1941 debut *The Wolf Man*. This simply plotted picture reaped benefits from a splendidly foggy atmosphere and a fine cast of Claude Rains, Ralph Bellamy, Warren William, Bela Lugosi, Maria Ouspenskaya, and Lon Chaney, Jr. as the sympathetic werewolf Larry Talbot. Despite a warm box office reception, Universal decided that Chaney needed some horrific support, so he was paired with the Frankenstein Monster (Lugosi) in 1943's *Frankenstein Meets the Wolf Man*. The two monsters' climactic confrontation lacked excitement and was cut short by a torrent of water released by the local villagers. But the film inspired Universal to package the Wolf Man, Dracula, the Frankenstein Monster, and a couple of mad scientists in *House of Frankenstein* (1944) and *House of Dracula* (1945). Thankfully, Chaney/Talbot/Wolf Man was cured in this last entry. He did, however, turn up in fur again in 1948's *Abbott and Costello Meet Frankenstein*. Lon Chaney, Jr. was the only actor to play Larry Talbot/the Wolf Man. North Carolina filmmaker Earl Owensby's *Wolfman!* had nothing to do with Talbot. See also **Werewolves**.

The Wolf Man (1941)	*House of Dracula* (1945)
Frankenstein Meets the Wolf Man (1943)	*Abbott and Costello Meet Frankenstein* (1948)
House of Frankenstein (1944)	

Wolfe, Nero

Rex Stout's heavyweight detective genius has been restricted to a handful of screen appearances. Edward Arnold made a delightfully self-indulgent Wolfe in 1936's *Meet Nero Wolfe*, an adaptation of Stout's classic mystery *Fer-de-Lance*. Arnold seemed well cast and the critics were kind, but a series failed to materialize. The following year, Walter Connolly took over the role in *League of Frightened Men* (aka *League of Missing Men*). Lionel Stander played Wolfe's legman Archie Goodwin in both films. Over forty years later, Stander was still playing in mysteries, as the Harts' chauffeur Max in the 1979-84 TV series *Hart to Hart*. Nero made his own television debut in the 1977 TV-movie *Nero Wolfe*, starring Thayer David and Tom Mason as Archie. The movie was a pilot for a series that was postponed when Thayer died unexpectedly. However, the hour-long TV series *Nero Wolfe* finally aired in 1981 with William Conrad in the lead and Lee (*Matt Houston*) Horsley as faithful Archie.

 Meet Nero Wolfe (1936)
 League of Frightened Men (aka *League of Missing Men*) (1937)
 Nero Wolfe (1977 TVM)

Wong, Mr. James Lee

Monogram initiated this low-budget film series in 1938, hoping to duplicate the success of the Charlie Chan and Mr. Moto mysteries. Hugh Wiley's Chinatown detective proved nowhere nearly as popular as either of his contemporaries, and the films are pretty obscure today. Boris Karloff, who was eager to break from horror movie typecasting, played Mr. Wong in all but the last entry. In 1940's *Phantom of Chinatown*, Keye Luke, Charlie Chan's former #1 son, played Wong, but he didn't prove to be right for the part.

Mr. Wong, Detective (1938)	*Doomed to Die* (1940)
Mr. Wong in Chinatown (1939)	*The Fatal Hour* (1940)
Mystery of Mr. Wong (1939)	*Phantom of Chinatown* (1940)

Worrell, Ernest P., *see* Ernest

Wrestling

Championship wrestling broadened its appeal—and its outrageousness—in the late 1970s and suddenly became a hot movie property. Subsequently, films tended to focus on the sport's sillier side. In contrast, John Ford's *Flesh* (1932) was a gloomy tale about a German immigrant wrestler (Wallace Beery) involved with shady characters. Richard Widmark was a loser trying to break into the London wrestling racket—and running afoul of kingpin Herbert Lom—in Jules Dassin's moody *Night and the City* (1950). Early wrestling comedies include *Swing Your Lady* (1937), with Humphrey Bogart as a promoter who sets up a male/female wrestling match, and 1945's *Here Come the Coeds*, which sent Lou Costello into the ring for one of his better vignettes. In Mexico in the 1960s, movie wrestlers turned into superheroes in highly popular series such as *Santo*, *Blue Demon* and *Neutron* (qq.v.). These films typically pitted the masked wrestlers against armies of vampires, werewolves and mummies. Probably, the most interesting films for American audiences were those starring the Wrestling Women. These rough-and-tumble señoritas never achieved the popularity of Santo, but they more than held their own against the baddies in wonderfully titled pictures like *The Wrestling Women vs. the Aztec Mummy* (1964). In the dubbed English version, the Wrestling Women were known as Loretta and Ruby. In the early 1980s, stateside lady wrestlers were the subject of *Below the Belt* (1980), *All the Marbles* (1981) and *Mugsy's Girls* (1985). Henry Winkler donned a blonde wig in the ring as a flamboyant wrestler trying to attract attention in 1978's *The One and Only*. Two 1985 movies, *Vision Quest* and *Hadley's Rebellion*, explored the world of high school wrestling. Sylvester Stallone took leave from the *Rocky* series (q.v.) long enough to make *Paradise Alley*, a nostalgic wrestling picture about three ambitious brothers. *Grunt! The Wrestling Movie* (1985) was a documentary-style satire (along the lines of *This Is Spinal Tap*) about an outrageous wrestler called Mad Dog Joe De Curso. Some real-life wrestlers made cameo appearances in the 1986 comedy *Bad Guys*, while wrestling superstar Hulk Hogan starred in his own feature, 1989's *No Holds Barred*. Paul Le Mat and Sylvester Stallone played arm wrestlers in, respectively, *P.K. and the Kid* (1982) and *Over the Top* (1987). See also **Blue Demon; Neutron; Santo.**

Flesh (1932)	*Blood and Guts* (1978)
Swing Your Lady (1937)	*Paradise Alley* (1978)
Here Come the Coeds (1945)	*Below the Belt* (1980)
Alias the Champ (1949)	*All the Marbles* (1981)
Bodyhold (1949)	*Tough Enough* (1983)
Night and the City (1950)	*Hadley's Rebellion* (1985)
Mr. Universe (1951)	*Mugsy's Girls* (aka *Delta Pi*) (1985)
Doctor of Doom (1962)	*Vision Quest* (1985)
The Wrestling Women vs. the Aztec Mummy (1964)	*Grunt! The Wrestling Movie* (1985)
Mad Bull (1977 TVM)	*Bad Guys* (1986)
The One and Only (1978)	*No Holds Barred* (1989)
Take Down (1978)	*The American Angels: Baptism of Blood* (1990)

Year in Title

Sweeping sagas with year-oriented titles include Bernardo Bertolucci's six-hour Italian epic *1900*, Horton Foote's nostalgic family drama *1918*, and Stanley Kubrick's science fiction classic *2001: A Space Odyssey*. George Orwell's bleak view of the future, *1984*, has been filmed twice, in 1956 and (appropriately enough) 1984.

One Million B.C. (1940)	*1900* (1977)
Terror From the Year 5000 (1958)	*September 30, 1955* (aka *9/30/55*; *24*
Panic in the Year Zero (1962)	*Hours of the Rebel*) (1978)
Daleks — Invasion Earth 2150 A.D.	*1941* (1979)
(aka *Invasion Earth — 2150 A.D.*)	*Class of 1984* (1982)
(1966)	*1990: The Bronx Warriors* (1983)
One Million Years B.C. (1966)	*1918* (1984)
2001: A Space Odyssey (1968)	*2010* (1984)
Summer of '42 (1971)	*1919* (1986)
Dracula A.D. 1972 (aka *Dracula*	*'68* (1988)
Today) (1972)	*Class of 1999* (1990)
Class of '44 (1973)	*1871* (1990)
Class of '63 (1973 TVM)	*The Spirit of '76* (1991)

Zombies

Commonly confused with ghouls, zombies are dead folks brought back to life, usually by means of voodoo. Ghouls (q.v.) are dead, too, but—unlike zombies—they must feed upon the flesh of the living for their sustenance. With their slow movements and blank stares (apparently indicating a lack of wit), zombies rank among the screen's duller, less menacing monsters. Still, there is something bothersome about being chased by a dead person. And zombies often display great strength, which comes in handy for murder. There have been only two zombie classics: The Halperin Brothers' *White Zombie* (1932) and Val Lewton's *I Walked With a Zombie* (1943). In the primitive but eerily effective *White Zombie*, Bela Lugosi played a zombie master named Murder Legendre. The film's most famous sequence shows a zombie falling silently to his "death" in a sugar mill, while his zombie coworkers continue to grind sugar emotionlessly. *I Walked With a Zombie* was a more literate movie, sort of a *Jane Eyre* set in the West Indies. Darby Jones's brief, powerful appearance during a climactic walk through the sugar fields is startling—one of the cinema's finest moments of quiet terror. In addition to *White Zombie*, Lugosi appeared in two other zombie movies: *Voodoo Man* (1944), a Monogram programmer costarring George Zucco and John Carradine, and the classically inept *Zombies on Broadway* (1945). In the latter film, gangsters import some real zombies (including Darby Jones again) as a novelty act for their night club. It was the only zombie foray into show business. A more common use of the undead was for soldiers, as in *Revolt of the Zombies* (1936), *King of the Zombies* (1941), and *Revenge of the Zombies* (1943). Cesare the somnambulist from the German classic *The Cabinet of Dr. Caligari* (1919) exhibited many zombie traits, although he was merely asleep, not dead. See also **Ghouls.**

White Zombie (1932)	*Voodoo Man* (1944)
Revolt of the Zombies (1936)	*Zombies on Broadway* (1945)
The Ghost Breakers (1940)	*Scared Stiff* (1953)
King of the Zombies (1941)	*Creature With the Atom Brain* (1955)
I Walked With a Zombie (1943)	*Voodoo Island* (1957)
Revenge of the Zombies (1943)	*Zombies of Mora Tau* (1957)

The Dead One (1961)
Plague of the Zombies (1964)
Zombies (aka *Zombie*; *I Eat Your Skin*;
  Voodoo Blood) (1964)
War of the Zombies (aka *Night Star —
  Goddess of Electra*) (1965)
Terror Creatures From the Grave
  (1965)
Sugar Hill (aka *The Zombies of Sugar
  Hill*) (1974)
The Dead Don't Die (1975 TVM)
Shock Waves (aka *Death Corps*) (1977)

Revenge of the Zombies (aka *Black
  Magic II*) (1981)
Zombie Island Massacre (1984)
I Was a Teenage Zombie (1987)
Zombie High (1987)
Dead Heat (1988)
Zombie Brigade (1988)
Hardrock Zombies (1988)
The Serpent and the Rainbow (1988)
Cast a Deadly Spell (1991 TVM)
My Boyfriend's Back (1993)
Weekend at Bernie's 2 (1993)

Zoos

While circuses (q.v.) have proven to be popular film settings, zoos have attracted the interest of few filmmakers. This favoritism toward circuses could be a result of the human-to-wild-animal ratio. In other words, circuses emphasize human performers over the animals, while zoos focus almost totally on the animals. At any rate, few films have been set principally in zoos. Loretta Young played a homeless girl who lived in one in the 1933 romantic-comedy *Zoo in Budapest*. Michael Gough ran a bizarre private zoo — he employed the lions to dispose of his enemies — in *The Black Zoo* (1963). And acclaimed documentary filmmaker Frederick Wiseman took his cameras inside Miami's MetroZoo for 1993's *Zoo*. Several films set primarily outside zoos have featured notable scenes behind the concrete walls. Both Simone Simon and Nastassia Kinski were attracted to the leopards in, respectively, the 1942 and 1982 versions of *The Cat People*. The ever-growing Venusian monster in Ray Harryhausen's *20 Million Miles to Earth* (1957) escaped from a Rome zoo and wreaked havoc before being destroyed. Ben Kingsley and Glenda Jackson "rescued" turtles from a zoo in 1985's *Turtle Diary*, while Clint Eastwood smuggled his orangutan into a zoo for a simian rendezvous in 1978's *Every Which Way But Loose*. The Mel Gibson-Goldie Hawn comedy *Bird on a Wire* (1990) and the offbeat French-Canadian *Night Zoo* (1987) featured climaxes in zoos. Although technically not zoos, the wildlife park in *The Beasts Are on the Streets* (1978 TVM) and the Sea World setting in *Jaws 3* (1983) deserve honorable mention. Likewise, *Jurassic Park* (1993) would have been a zoo for dinosaurs had it ever opened officially. See also **Circuses**.

Zoo in Budapest (1933)
Murders in the Zoo (1933)
The Cat People (1942)
20 Million Miles to Earth (1957)
The Black Zoo (1963)
Zebra in the Kitchen (1965)

Every Which Way But Loose (1978)
The Cat People (1982)
Turtle Diary (1985)
Night Zoo (1987)
Bird on a Wire (1990)
Zoo (1993)

More Books to Help You Get More Out of Life

Raising Happy Kids on a Reasonable Budget — As seen on Oprah Winfrey — this one-of-a-kind guide is packed with dollar stretching techniques and budgeting tips you need to raise happy and healthy kids — whether you have one child or ten! *#70184/$10.95/144 pages/paperback*

Clutter's Last Stand — You're in clutter denial. You think you're perfectly organized, yet closets and drawers bulge around you. You'll get rid of clutter, in every aspect of your life, with this delightful, humorous guide full of practical advice.
#01122/$10.95/280 pages/paperback

The Organization Map — You WILL defeat clutter and disorganization. This clear, effective, and encouraging guide is chock full of tips and advice for time-management, practical storage solutions, and more! *#70224/$12.95/208 pages/paperback*

Confessions of an Organized Homemaker — You'll find hundreds of tips and ideas for organizing your household in this totally revised and updated edition. Includes motivation builders, consumer product information, and more! *#70240/$10.95/224 pages/paperback*

Is There Life After Housework? — All you need to take the dread out of housework are some ingenious ideas, efficient methods, and a little inspiration — find it all in this bestselling guide. *#10292/$10.95/216 pages/paperback*

Slow Down and Get More Done — Discover precisely the right pace for your life by gaining control of worry, making possibilities instead of plans, and learning the value of doing "nothing." *#70183/$11.95/192 pages/paperback*

The Greatest Gift Guide Ever — At last, you'll buy the perfect gift for all those "hard to buy for" people . . . for any occasion. From buying electronic gadgets, to ordering from specialty catalogs, to shipping gifts long distances — this guide is a gift-giver's dream come true! *#70222/$8.95/192 pages/paperback*

How To Have a Great Retirement on a Limited Budget — Make your Golden Years truly golden. Here are dozens of practical, proven ways to enjoy a fun, full life when you retire. *#10288/$12.95/145 pages/paperback*

Use the order form below (photocopy acceptable) and save when you order two or more books!

- -